# International Explorations in Outdoor and Environmental Education

Volume 17

**Series Editors**
Annette Gough, RMIT University, Melbourne, Australia
Noel Gough, La Trobe University, Melbourne, Australia

**Editorial Board Members**
Niklas Gericke, Karlstad University, Karlstad, Sweden
Susanna Ho, Ministry of Education, Singapore, Singapore
Kathleen Kesson, Long Island University, Brooklyn, USA
John Chi-Kin Lee, The Education University of Hong Kong, Tai Po, Hong Kong
Justin Lupele, Academy for Education Development, Lusaka, Zambia
Greg Mannion, University of Stirling, Stirling, UK
Pat O'Riley, University of British Columbia, Vancouver, Canada
Chris Reddy, University of Stellenbosch, Stellenbosch, South Africa
Hilary Whitehouse, James Cook University, Cairns, Australia

This series focuses on contemporary trends and issues in outdoor and environmental education, two key fields that are strongly associated with education for sustainability and its associated environmental, social and economic dimensions. It also has an international focus to encourage dialogue across cultures and perspectives. The scope of the series includes formal, non-formal and informal education and the need for different approaches to educational policy and action in the twenty-first century. Research is a particular focus of the volumes, reflecting a diversity of approaches to outdoor and environmental education research and their underlying epistemological and ontological positions through leading edge scholarship. The scope is also both global and local, with various volumes exploring the issues arising in different cultural, geographical and political contexts. As such, the series aims to counter the predominantly "white" Western character of current research in both fields and enable cross-cultural and transnational comparisons of educational policy, practice, project development and research. The purpose of the series is to give voice to leading researchers (and emerging leaders) in these fields from different cultural contexts to stimulate discussion and further research and scholarship to advance the fields through influencing policy and practices in educational settings. The volumes in the series are directed at active and potential researchers and policy makers in the fields. Book proposals for this series may be submitted to the Publishing Editor: Claudia Acuna (Claudia.Acuna@springer.com).

Anne Marie Ross

# The Politics of Environmental Education Centres

## People, Power and Pedagogies

 Springer

Anne Marie Ross [iD]
School of Education
College of Human and Social Futures
University of Newcastle
Newcastle, NSW, Australia

ISSN 2214-4218　　　　　　　ISSN 2214-4226　(electronic)
International Explorations in Outdoor and Environmental Education
ISBN 978-3-031-82566-8　　　ISBN 978-3-031-82567-5　(eBook)
https://doi.org/10.1007/978-3-031-82567-5

© The Editor(s) (if applicable) and The Author(s), under exclusive license to Springer Nature Switzerland AG 2025

This work is subject to copyright. All rights are solely and exclusively licensed by the Publisher, whether the whole or part of the material is concerned, specifically the rights of translation, reprinting, reuse of illustrations, recitation, broadcasting, reproduction on microfilms or in any other physical way, and transmission or information storage and retrieval, electronic adaptation, computer software, or by similar or dissimilar methodology now known or hereafter developed.
The use of general descriptive names, registered names, trademarks, service marks, etc. in this publication does not imply, even in the absence of a specific statement, that such names are exempt from the relevant protective laws and regulations and therefore free for general use.
The publisher, the authors and the editors are safe to assume that the advice and information in this book are believed to be true and accurate at the date of publication. Neither the publisher nor the authors or the editors give a warranty, expressed or implied, with respect to the material contained herein or for any errors or omissions that may have been made. The publisher remains neutral with regard to jurisdictional claims in published maps and institutional affiliations.

This Springer imprint is published by the registered company Springer Nature Switzerland AG
The registered company address is: Gewerbestrasse 11, 6330 Cham, Switzerland

If disposing of this product, please recycle the paper.

*This book is dedicated to my family and friends—particularly Rémy Louise and children to follow, whom I hold in my heart, with love and hope.*

# Series Editors' Foreword

> It is really, really important that citizens learn to value their environment and to understand the science behind the great ecological dilemmas which face all of us. Never before has there been so much talk of education about sustainability, about biodiversity, and for citizenship.
>
> All these aspirations remain 'pie in the sky' unless every pupil has an entitlement to extend his or her study […] out of the classroom. It is in the field […] where acting locally becomes thinking globally.
>
> Professor Lord May of Oxford, Former President of the Royal Society (in Barker et al., 2002, p. 2)

Field study centres, or environmental education centres, have been a part of the provision and support for environmental education for decades, particularly in countries associated with the British Commonwealth, as Anne Marie Ross discusses in this volume. For example, the Field Studies Council in the United Kingdom, a registered charity, was founded in 1943, and it now operates a network of centres across England, Wales and Scotland which "aim to inspire everyone to be curious, knowledgeable, passionate and caring about the environment" (Field Studies Council, 2023, p. 4) by providing first-hand experiences in the real world to enable students to connect and engage with nature. These experiences are mainly residential and day field trips for those studying biology and geography, and more general outdoor and environmental experiences to get primary school students involved and engaged in the outdoors.

Providing students with opportunities for outdoor experiences was seen as important in 1943 and is probably becoming even more so with the growth of urbanisation in the past 80 years meaning that people can find it harder to encounter green spaces.

In a curriculum context, field study centres provide opportunities for students to engage in fieldwork associated with their biology and geography studies, in particular. However, the importance of such fieldwork has been questioned at times, as the UK centres found attendance falling away around the turn of the century. This led to studies arguing the value of fieldwork across the age range and across subjects by researchers such as Barker et al. (2002), Dillon et al. (2006) and Rickinson et al. (2004). For example, as Rickinson et al. (2004, p. 28) conclude from their review:

> Substantial evidence exists to indicate that fieldwork, properly conceived, adequately planned, well-taught and effectively followed up, offers learners opportunities to develop their knowledge and skills in ways that add value to their everyday experiences in the classroom.

Fortunately providing such opportunities, which was part of the justification for the creation of the field study centres in New South Wales that are discussed in this volume, has not been questioned, though at times in their history it has been a prime reason for their survival.

Together with the environment movement, the field study centres movement in the state of New South Wales (NSW) in Australia started to gather momentum in the 1960s. One of the first (Wirrimbirra) started out as a private venture, the Department of Education took over management from 1973, joining Muogamarra Field Study Centre which had been established in 1971. Today, the 24 NSW Environmental Education Centres describe their goals as being to

- provide authentic, curriculum-based fieldwork learning experiences that enable students to explore, investigate and understand the natural and made environments
- provide opportunities to understand concepts and systems and develop values that empower learners to become environmentally responsible citizens (NSW Department of Education, 2024)

The field study centres also have an important role in developing a sense of place. Each centre has its First Nations' history and provides opportunities for students to understand the Country from the local people's perspective as well as understand the area's biological and geographic characteristics from a Western settler perspective.

While there are research studies that focus on the activities of field study centre and arguments for their existence (see, for example, Morrison, 1974; Webb, 1980) to the best of our knowledge, no one before Anni Ross has researched the politics of the creation of the field study centres and the people caught up in those politics.

Environmental education is political. Environmental problems require political solutions, and environmental education has often been seen as a political priority more than an educational one. Getting Departments of Education to take environmental education seriously has long been a challenge, as we have written about separately, together, and with others (see for example, Gough, 1997, 2021, 2024; Gough & Gough, 2010; Gough et al., 2024). This has been a particular problem in Australia, and, in this volume, Anni Ross makes this very clear through her case study of the development of environmental education in NSW, seen through the lens of the development of field study centres. Each state in Australia has engaged with incorporating environmental education into the curriculum and practices of schools in different ways (Gough, 1997). NSW was the only state to go down a legislation pathway with an Environmental Education Bill (Parliament of New South Wales, 1992), but it was never enacted. While Australia now has a national curriculum with education for sustainability as a cross-curriculum priority, as discussed elsewhere (see, for example, Gough, 2021, 2024; Gough et al., 2024), this is no guarantee for it to actually be taught, and several states have gone with their own curriculum under an Australian Curriculum umbrella anyway.

No matter what has been going on with environmental education in the curriculum, field study centres, particularly in NSW (as discussed in this volume) and Queensland (see Renshaw & Tooth, 2018), have been there to support schools with their science, biology and geography fieldwork for both primary and secondary school students, and in some cases their social studies. They have also been places where the teachers have been able to enact active pedagogies such as enquiry and problem-based learning.

The stories of each of the centres are not sanitised as good news stories. Problems encountered with sites, staffing and working with schools are all discussed, as are the frustrations with the limited time centre staff often get to spend with a class of students on a day trip. While the goals noted above are definitely desired, reality can be different, but underneath each story is a teacher's passion to connect students with the centre's natural environment and to encourage their environmentally responsible behaviours.

The curriculum and centre practices were not the only things that were political. Even the change of name from field study centres to environmental education centres was political. Several principals were reluctant to change their centre's name as it was seen as potentially controversial in their communities, especially where there were natural resource conflicts, such as forestry.

All too often policy developments are written as if people were not involved. In contrast, the stories here enable the words of those involved to be heard, either directly or through secondary sources. Peopling the past is important as so often key players are made invisible.

This volume includes some discussions of a sample of field study centres elsewhere in the world, albeit limited by being desktop research. However, it does seem that the NSW experiences are in accord with those elsewhere. It would be good to see more research like this on centres in other countries.

## Acknowledgements

This foreword was written on the unceded lands of the Woi wurrung and Boon wurrung peoples of the Kulin Nations. We respectfully acknowledge their Elders, past and present, and what they have taught us about this land and sea.

| | |
|---|---:|
| La Trobe University | Noel Gough |
| Melbourne, Victoria, Australia | |
| RMIT University | Annette Gough |
| Melbourne, Victoria, Australia | |

# References

Barker, S., Slingsby, D., & Tilling, S. (2002). *Teaching biology outside the classroom: Is it heading for extinction? A report on biology fieldwork in the 14-19 curriculum* (FSC Occasional Publication 72). Field Studies Council.

Dillon, J., Rickinson, M., Teamey, K., Morris, M., Choi, M. Y., Sanders, D., & Benefield, P. (2006). The value of outdoor learning: Evidence from research in the UK and elsewhere. *School Science Review*, 87(320), 107–111.

Field Studies Council. (2023). *Trustees report and financial statements for the year ended 31 December 2023.* https://www.field-studies-council.org/about-us/annual-review-and-report/

Gough, A. (1997). *Education and the environment: Policy, trends and the problems of marginalisation* (Australian Education Review Series No. 39). Australian Council for Educational Research.

Gough, A. (2021). All STEM-ed up: Gaps and silences around ecological education in Australia. *Sustainability, 13,* 3801. https://doi.org/10.3390/su13073801

Gough, A. (2024). Changing politics for changing times: Re-thinking research stakeholders and strategies for environmental education. *Australian Journal of Environmental Education, 40*(3), 417–430. https://doi.org/10.1017/aee.2024.41

Gough, N., & Gough, A. (2010). Environmental education. In C. Kridel (Ed.), *Encyclopedia of curriculum studies* (Vol. 1, pp. 339–343). Sage.

Gough, A., Reid, A., & Stevenson, R. B. (2024). Environmental and sustainability education in Australia. In R. Thomas & M. Rieckmann (Eds.), *World review: Environmental and sustainability education in the context of the sustainable development goals* (pp. 297–317). CRC Press.

Morrison, R. G. (1974). Field studies in Australia. *The Australian Science Teachers' Journal, 20*(2), 47–60.

NSW Department of Education. (2024). *NSW Environmental Education Centres: About us.* Retrieved November 6, 2024, from, https://nsweec.schools.nsw.gov.au/about-us.html

Parliament of New South Wales. (1992). *Environmental education bill.* https://www.parliament.nsw.gov.au/Hansard/Pages/HansardResult.aspx#/docid/HANSARD-1323879322-1370

Renshaw, P., & Tooth, R. (Eds.). (2018). Diverse pedagogies of place: *Educating students in and for local and global environments.* Routledge.

Rickinson, M., Dillon, J., Teamey, K., Morris, M., Choi, M. Y., Sanders, D., & Benefield, P. (2004). *A review of research on outdoor learning.* Field Studies Council.

Webb, J. B. (1980). *A survey of field studies centres in Australia.* Australian National Parks and Wildlife Service.

# Preface

> New social concerns generate new intellectual and historical problems. Conversely, new interpretations of the past provide perspectives on the present and hence the power to change it. (Merchant, 1980, p. xvi)

The degree to which this story needed to be told was clear after working with several environmental education centres (EECs) in a research capacity with Associate Professor James Ladwig at the University of Newcastle. There was a desire to contribute to environmental education (EE) in some way, and also, like James and many others in the field, I did not want to see this history fade into obscurity, silenced by time. This book has its origins in idiosyncratic case studies of EECs within the New South Wales Department of Education in Australia and how these centres became established, and survived and thrived, given that the centres and the Department are, in many respects, antithetical to one another. The Department derived, as many bureaucracies are, from the clunky colonialist makeup of European Australia, set within a mechanistic, industrialising paradigm. In contrast, environmental and sustainability education (ESE) are action-oriented frameworks connecting us to our environment—both natural and built—and ourselves, through knowledge, understanding and empathy. Furthermore, ESE involves teaching humans to actively curb our actions and consumption in the pursuit of sustaining nature and ultimately ourselves. Given this dichotomy, I was interested in investigating how these centres functioned and changed over time and how they contributed to evolving ESE within their communities and the curriculum. What were the EEC educators' perspectives on best practice pedagogies and how have they changed over time? What were the external inhibiting and enabling factors to centre establishment, growth and impact and ESE development and progress, and what can we learn about working with a large bureaucracy?

I grew up in a patriarchal, protestant household, with Scottish Calvinist ancestry—classic sociological elements of the times for the farming family background and town in which I grew up. There was empathy for "other", particularly given my father was a 1955 ten-pound Scot (he once punched a man for calling him British so we will not go there). Yet, I felt a subliminal subconscious sense of hierarchy with racial and socio-economic undertones which is hard to distinguish as individual or collective. I imagine this was the hidden curriculum of the community in which I grew up—a stultifying paralyses of contrition simmered just under the surface. Much has changed, though I'm not sure how much. However, my family, community, education and the universities I attended were beholden to dominant northern knowledges and practices. I reveal this so that you have some insight into why this study may be filled with a very asymmetrical northern-centric knowledge balance— while I have attempted to go beyond these bounds I'm well aware that I'm blinded by my sociology—even with quite a few years of attempting to pull back the scales that blind me... I'm still blinded by my development.

Part of the solution, which is taking place, albeit on a small but increasing scale, is the decolonialisation of sociology (Connell, 2018). While I attempted to explore the places, or even edges, of other sociologies, the northern-centric hegemonic structures of knowledge, epistemology, methodology and language are strong and well ingrained (noted within the less stuck editing skills and insightful and knowledgeable nature of Annette Gough). Within this study, the northern conceptual frame with additions of southern (African, South American, Australian & New Zealand) content upholds the asymmetry of the global knowledge economy (Connell, 2018). While I may have caught some of the edges of the mosaic of other sociologies it is but a drop in the ocean and must be seen as such. Like the great biodiversity of natural environments, the diversity of other sociologies is many and varied, particularly when also considering the massive disruption and thus multiple forms of cultures over time and space (and the limited space with which to write about them). We know that a globalised combined sociology is epistemologically Eurocentric and violates other ways of being (Connell, 2018). Connell wrote about a third possibility for the decolonialisation of sociology (2015)—a solidarity epistemology where connections as well as differences are studied—known as "braiding the borders" (Bulbeck, 1998 cited in Connell, 2018, p. 404) or "connected sociologies" (Bhambra, 2014 cited in Connell, 2018, p. 404). "Ecologies of knowledges" (de Sousa Santos, 2014 cited in Connell, 2018, p. 404) is a valuable idea worth further development within ESE with the ideas of decolonising, de-parochialising the curriculum and teaching. The focus required of curriculum and teaching is the knowledge necessary given the major social questions facing humanity now (Connell, 2018). This question is first and foremost for decolonising sociology, and thus education generally ... and ESE is essential to this decolonising. In decolonising curriculum content, conceptual questions must be addressed. What we have at the moment is embedded and practised within a northern-centric knowledge structure. The way knowledge is developed, communicated, sustained—brought into being—the workforce of knowledge needs to be taken into consideration for change (Connell, 2018).

Understanding our history is essential to building effective and efficient pathways to the future without going over the same old ground. While the patchiness of ESE implementation, the dominance of education about the environment and technical approaches to change have been well documented, it is rare to have an extended historical account of a specific phenomenon that provides a clear view of the machinations. My focus on a specific structure reveals aspects often not included, or lost, in broader discussions of education and EE more specifically. It allowed the nuances of the machinations of power to be identified from the complexity that surrounds such a multidimensional convoluted subject matter. It highlighted shifts and changes in the field while also making the complexity of education as a socio-political endeavour explicit. There is an opportunity to lean forward, the possible provision of further understanding to support moving into a sustainable and connected future—or at least the provision of further evidence of what we are dealing with in a more implicit construct. Broadening my focus from a study of EECs within the education department in New South Wales to a global context provided an opportunity to delve further into this phenomenon on a universal scale through a comparison with some of the spaces that other EECs inhabit and where ESE originates and flows. Investigating other contexts opens up possibilities of other ways of knowing and being. Comparative analysis with other places and situations where EE/EfS emerged helps locate this story within a larger holistic frame and enables identification of blind and blank spots (Wagner, 1993) in our pursuit of a path to a future connected to the natural and built environment and sustainability.

One of the advantages of accommodating a history spanning over 50 years (1970–2024) is the chance to reveal the unconfined space of "what was", or a version of it, considering the multitude of historical narrations possible. Reflection is essential in understanding what worked, the changing times, and how affecting, or trying to affect, change has altered over time. The issues are immensely complex. Time and place assist in conceptualising what the variables might be.

> But regardless of whatever role we play in the stream of time, we are all embedded in it; we are a product of time to the present and are all part of the foundation for the future. (Fox, 2016, Ch. 1, para. 4)

This narrative highlights changes over time in the status and positioning of centres and the important influence of state, national and international governance, and departmental, political and economic factors. It reflects the historical connection of ESE to political cycles and ideologies not endemic to Australia, and their origins of influence. It exposes the interconnectedness and inseparability of educational change and political, economic and social change, in NSW, nationally and globally, with which ESE is intimately connected. No entities are isolated, and there are always contending and converging discourses. The birth and development of EE in the late 1960s to late 1980s, and the change to education for sustainability (EfS) in the early 1990s can be drawn somewhat in parallel with a comparatively affluent democratic society morphing to neoliberalism. The opportunity to compare and contrast this distinctive phenomenon of centres with representations around the globe permitted more attention to be given to the processes and politics of educational and EE policy formation—particularly given growth, or not, in parallel with globalisation, ESE and centres. The effect of international as well as national actors and institutions in education and environmental policies and the notion of policy formation culture reform (Rizvi & Lingard, 2009) cannot be ignored.

In this text, I aimed to navigate the intricate web of colonialist and hegemonic power structures, acknowledging the complexities that arise from their origins and manifestations. While colonialist practices originated primarily from European countries, it's essential to recognise the evolving nature of these power dynamics. For example, the influence of America, though geographically separate from Europe, has played a significant role in global colonialism. Traditional descriptors like 'Eurocentric' or directional terms such as 'Northern' and 'Southern' fail to capture the nuances of this phenomenon. Instead, we must grapple with the multifaceted nature of colonial legacies, which extend beyond geographical boundaries and defy simple categorization. Moreover, the globalisation of Western practices and the rise of multinational corporations further complicate our understanding of hegemonic power structures, underscoring the need for a nuanced and context-specific analysis.

Yet, how does one narrate a history without utilising simplistic labels or directional descriptors—or homogenising the frame? I have tried to emphasise context, be descriptive, include multiple perspectives, explore the ambiguity and highlight the contradictions, and complexity, to challenge the assumptions of the subject matter. Yet, this was difficult to contain. In some cases I have utilised the language of my sources. You will find the terms Northern, Southern, Eastern, Western, throughout this narrative where I have found them the best fit. However, the complexities and nuances of these terms needs acknowledgement.

The case study research was approved by the University of Newcastle Human Ethics Committee (H-2015-0014). Interview data was recorded between 2015 and 2017 with many key environmental educators from, and associated with, the NSW Department of Education EEC network—it includes some data from and about the Queensland network. Many of these people were instrumental in progressing the development of ESE and the work of the centres within their territories, and some had a greater influence on developments within Australia and beyond. Material used to compare with similar entities throughout the world was accessed through, to some extent, the interview data and conversations with various people who had insight into the phenomenon, but for the most part from desktop research. Some difficulties and constraints within this extended study include direct access to primary sources in English. Comprehensively understanding global representations of EECs through a desktop study proved challenging, with access and scope hindering inclusivity and critical analysis. Resources available online demonstrated a lack of critique (Griffiths, 2021; Huckle & Wals, 2015).

Throughout the case studies it was rare, particularly in early writing, to read material associated with Indigenous communities or the Global South—or anywhere where the language is not English (compounded by my monolingual nature and focus on the history of specific EECs). Some non-English-speaking researchers had articles within English language ESE-focused journals, but generally there was little available. The discourse around the United Nations Rio Summit (1992) and sustainability was one of the notable areas where equity for low socio-economic countries gained momentum—albeit hindered subsequently by neoliberalism. This expanded global edition of my study opened up an exploration of these other ESE entities. However, it is important to account for the lag between case studies of this history of a specific context and a desktop study in more recent times.

In the context of EE, it is important to understand that in addition to, and alongside globalisation, big changes in educational research and teaching started taking place about the time of its inception in the late 1960s. Changes to research and teaching impacted on the fledgling EE/EfS research that basically grew from the science disciplines (Disinger, 1993; Gough, 1997; Mrazek, 1993). Initially only the scientific method was regarded as a legitimate research approach. However, making sense of the world through understanding the cognitive structures that enable us to do so (the cognitive turn) and the role that language plays in our constructions of our world (the linguistic turn) became increasingly legitimate research methodologies in the social sciences and humanities (Stevenson & Robottom, 2013, p. 472).

> New research paradigms usually emerge in response to perceived limitations of and challenges to existing ones. (Stevenson & Robottom, 2013, p. 472)

When it comes to language, one could debate the value of words associated with the field of ecology being seconded to other disciplines and general vocabulary which seems to dilute and obscure original meaning. And there is confusion, reasoning and power around changing a concept such as "climate change" from "climate chaos" or "the Greenhouse effect" given that the climate does indeed change for various reasons but anthropogenic climate change is about the exacerbated greenhouse effect causing climate chaos. Additionally, this history navigates an initial male-centric, patriarchal and colonialist environment, which is discernible through the language of historical artefacts. At times, this perspective may have been overlooked due to my immersion in it. With the multitude of repertoires of unconscious, and conscious language practice, a focus on vernacular was an intention in this writing given dominant discourses are 'practices that systematically form the objects of which they speak' (Foucault, 1971/1972, p. 49)—what may or may not be said, and thought, are shaped by them (Spina et al., 2022).

One of my concerns in expanding the focus of this study to a more analytical global version was the possible loss of the "local". The people, the events, the topography, the environment that fills and interacts with the topography, the specific history, the serendipitous events—the importance of these place-based labyrinthine webs cannot be overstated. These elements made visible the intricacies of the system—the politics, the people, the power play (interplay of energy), the pedagogies that work in this space. The importance of place was illustrated in Renshaw and Tooth's (2018) in-depth case studies, *Diverse Pedagogies of Place: Educating Students in and for Local and Global Environments*. These studies detail EECs within the Queensland Department of Education system, theorising both the contexts of influence and the distinct pedagogical approaches to ESE. They included placed-based pedagogy focusing on advocacy, story, slow-time, walking, sacred place, shifting sands and "the edge"—that dynamic interplay within environments. Many of the themes have resonance with NSW EEC place, practice and pedagogies. This fundamental connection with the local allows a stable footing and repertoires of practice for expansion to view the encompassing global context, and to think deeply about the future. Yet, there was a concern that this global iteration could strip away descriptive elements to make way for contexts and analysis.

## Note on Environmental and Sustainability Terminology

In the last decade the term ESE has emerged as an inclusive expression for both "environmental" and "sustainability" education—ensuring the sustainability element is not excluded from environmental education and, importantly, that the environmental dimension is not precluded from sustainability. Researchers and practitioners (Lysgaard et al., 2016; Sund & Öhman, 2013; Sund & Gericke, 2021; Ontario Institute for Studies in Education: Sustainability & Climate Change Network, n.d.) have slowly started to use the ESE phrase as an alternate to the dominant education for sustainable development (ESD) terminology which many find problematic given its exclusion of the environment. I avoid using the term ESD where possible due to a desire not to give the term space, both literally and figuratively, and to avoid getting caught up in a terminology debate. Significantly, this view is also in concurrence with Dryzek (2005, 2022) and other scholars who view the natural environment and development as contrary terms. Nuances within the term "development" are investigated. This history makes use of ESE where it is convenient and appropriate while using environmental education (EE) and environmental education for sustainability (EfS[1]) for historical context.

Newcastle, NSW, Australia                                                                 Anne Marie Ross

## References

Connell, R. (2018). Decolonizing sociology. *Contemporary Sociology: A Journal of Reviews*, *47*(4), 399–407. https://doi.org/10.1177/0094306118779811
Disinger, J. (1993). The search for paradigms for research in environmental education. In R. Mrazek (Ed.), *Alternative paradigms in environmental education research: Monographs in environmental education and environmental studies* (Vol. VIII, 19–25). North American Association for Environmental Education.
Dryzek, J. (2005). *The politics of the earth: Environmental discourses* (2nd ed.). Oxford University Press.
Dryzek, J. (2022). *The politics of the earth: Environmental discourses*. Oxford University Press.
Foucault, M. (1972). *The archaeology of knowledge and the discourse on language*. (A. M. Sheridan-Smith, Trans.). Vintage Books (Original work published 1971).
Fox, A. (2016). *Chief guardian: The life and times of Allen Strom*. In N. Dufty, K. McDonald, S. Smith, D. Tribe, & K. Schaefer (Eds.). Australian Association for Environmental Education (NSW).
Gough, A. (1997). *Education and the environment: Policy, trends and the problems of marginalisation*. Australian Council for Educational Research.

---

[1] Note in Australia EfS is often used (Ferreira et al. 2019) rather than EEfS and often conflated with ESD (Gough et al. 2024).

Griffiths, T. G. (2021). Education to transform the world: Limits and possibilities in and against the SDGs and ESD. *International Studies in Sociology of Education*, *30*(1–2), 73–92. https://doi.org/10.1080/09620214.2020.1854829

Huckle, J., & Wals, A. E. J. (2015). The UN Decade of Education for Sustainable Development: Business as usual in the end. *Environmental Education Research*, 21(3), 491–505. https://doi.org/10.1080/13504622.2015.1011084

Lysgaard, J. A., Reid, A., & Van Poeck, K. (2016). The roots and routes of environmental and sustainability education policy research – An introduction to a virtual special issue. *Environmental Education Research*, *22*(3), 319–332. https://doi.org/10.1080/13504622.2015.1108392

Merchant, C. (1980). *The death of nature: Women, ecology and the scientific revolution*. Wildwood House.

Mrazek, R. (1993). Through which looking glass? Defining environmental education research. In R. Mrazek (Ed.), *Alternative paradigms in environmental education research: Monographs in environmental education and environmental studies* (Vol. VIII, pp. 9–17). The North American Association for Environmental Education.

Ontario Institute for Studies in Education: Sustainability & Climate Change Network. (n.d.). *Defining environmental & sustainability education (ESE)*. Retrieved May 20, 2024, from https://www.oise.utoronto.ca/scan/defining-environmental-sustainability-education-0

Renshaw, P., & Tooth, R. (2018). Diverse place-responsive pedagogies: Historical, professional and theoretical threads. In P. Renshaw & R. Tooth (Eds.), *Diverse pedagogies of place: Educating students in and for local and global environments* (pp. 1–21). Routledge.

Rizvi, F., & Lingard, B. (2009). *Globalizing education policy*. Routledge.

Spina, N., Smithers, K., Harris, J., & Mewburn, I. (2022). Back to zero? Precarious employment in academia amongst 'older' early career researchers, a life-course approach. *British Journal of Sociology of Education*, *43*(4), 534–549. https://doi.org/10.1080/01425692.2022.2057925

Stevenson, R., & Robottom, I. (2013). Critical action research and environmental education: Conceptual congruencies and imperatives in practice. In R. Stevenson, M. Brody, J. Dillon, & A. Wals (Eds.), *International handbook of research on environmental education* (pp. 469–479). Routledge for the American Educational Research Association.

Sund, P. J., & Gericke, N. (2021). More than two decades of research on selective traditions in environmental and sustainability education—Seven functions of the concept. *Sustainability (Basel, Switzerland)*, *13*(12), 6524. https://doi.org/10.3390/su13126524

Sund, L., & Öhman, J. (2013). On the need to repoliticise environmental and sustainability education: Rethinking the postpolitical consensus. *Environmental Education Research*, 20(5), 639–659. https://doi.org/10.1080/13504622.2013.833585

Wagner, J. (1993). Ignorance in educational research or, how can you not know that? *Educational Researcher*, *22*(5), 15–23.

**Competing Interests** The author has no competing interests to declare that are relevant to the content of this manuscript.

# Acknowledgements

I would like to thank Annette and Noel Gough for the opportunity to add to their book series and for their support along the publication path—from proposal to publication. My journey was nurtured and supported with steady guidance, helping me stay on course and gently redirecting me whenever I needed it. Annette's scholarship fed my PhD and this global edition. I am deeply indebted and thankful for Annette's guarding of an extensive environmental and sustainability education history so it is not silenced with time—and prolific research acumen in ensuring environmental and sustainability education is kept on the agenda. I'm forever grateful for Annette's generosity, calm, and academic prowess in nurturing environmental and sustainability scholarship in others.

I would also like to thank the editorial team at Springer/Springer Nature for their professionalism, encouragement, patience and kindness during the publication process.

I would like to thank James Ladwig, my PhD supervisor, for his boundless enthusiasm for learning, his encyclopaedic knowledge spanning education, sociology, philosophy—and seemingly everything else—and his grace, compassion and passion in facilitating the learning of others. I am profoundly grateful for his guidance and support throughout this journey.

I would sincerely like to express my heartfelt gratitude to all of my research participants, from those who filled in my initial online survey, or made contact via email, to those who gave up hours of their time or squeezed the time they could afford into their busy schedules. Your dedication and passion for your craft is exceptional. Thank you for your participation and patience.

Thanks goes to:

- Hannah Marie Byrne for the creation of the schematic maps
- Gabrielle Francesca Byrne for the wonderful koala photo in Chapter 2
- Fiona LaSpina for pinpointing locations regarding Nadgee Nature Reserve photos
- Gibberagong Environmental Education Centre for permission to print photos of Gibberagong (Muogamarra) Environmental Education Centre's and the EZEC Network's 50th anniversary celebrations

- Taronga Conservation Society for permission to print the photo of the Desert Immersive Classroom at Taronga Institute of Science and Learning
- Tyson Yunkaporta and Sydney University Press for permission to print an image of the Eight Ways of Learning Framework
- Craig Duncan for permission to print the emu egg and wattle in a coolamon photo from the Rising from the Embers Festival (a collaboration of the Wollotuka Institute, Local Land Services and the University of Newcastle—First Nations' and sustainability networking)
- Zach Schofield for permission to print a 2023 photo of Rising Tide's Blockade of the world's biggest coal port
- The New South Wales National Parks and Wildlife Service and University of Newcastle (Australia) Special Collections for permission to print Margaret Senior's illustrations; Parks Australia (permission to print Joan Webb's photos of the centres); and the Global Footprint Network, the World Environmental Education Congress, the Department of Climate Change, Energy, the Environment and Water, and Wikipedia Creative Commons for access and permission to print photos and illustrations
- The Australian Association for Environmental Education (AAEE) for all their support throughout this process
- My family and friends for all their support throughout the writing of my PhD and this global iteration. Michele, Michelle, and Anna—thank you for your invaluable encouragement and support.

Finally, I would like to thank and send enormous respect and gratitude to all the environmental and sustainability researchers and practitioners whose everyday praxis contributed and contributes to making shifts towards the ecocentric world we need. Absolutely, all the individuals and organisations working towards a more environmental, nature-centred and sustainable future. Your efforts in promoting ecojustice and meaningful change inspired this work.

This book was written on the unceded lands of the Awabakal and Worimi peoples. I respectfully acknowledge the traditional custodians, Elders past, present and emerging, and recognise the wisdom and knowledge held by First Nations' peoples—for land, sea and waterways.

I acknowledge the use of ChatGPT in exploring the initial global research pathway and supporting generative editorial tasks, including refining word choice, enhancing flow and improving sentence construction.

# Contents

**Part I  Introduction**

**1  Environmental Education Centres: Place and Purpose** .......... 5
    1.1  Introduction .......................................... 5
    1.2  Exploring the Complexity of ESE and EECs ................. 6
        1.2.1  Exploring EECs: The Value of School Relationships ..... 11
    1.3  Insights on Optimal ESE Practices: My Perspective ............ 11
    References................................................. 15

**2  Western Awakening: A Journey to Environmental Awareness** ...... 19
    2.1  Introduction ............................................. 19
    2.2  The Genesis of Environmental Awareness.................... 19
    2.3  Explorers, Scientists and Naturalists ........................ 20
    2.4  Acclimatisation Societies.................................. 22
    2.5  Collectors, Illustrators, Artists and Writers ................... 23
    2.6  Significant Changes Building Up to Federation ............... 26
    2.7  The Seeds of Environmental Awareness in Australia............ 27
    2.8  Advocacy and Legislation ................................. 28
        2.8.1  Scientific Activity................................. 28
        2.8.2  Bird and Animal Protection Legislation ............... 29
        2.8.3  The Rise of Wildlife Preservation Societies ............ 32
        2.8.4  Species Destruction ............................... 33
        2.8.5  Management in Flux .............................. 35
        2.8.6  Progressivism.................................... 36
        2.8.7  Protection of Native Flora .......................... 38
        2.8.8  The Rise of Ranger Leagues ........................ 38
        2.8.9  Bushwalkers and Urban Reformists.................... 39
        2.8.10  Parks and Playgrounds Movement.................... 43
        2.8.11  Another Catalyst for Change: The Role of Allen Strom ... 43
        2.8.12  The National Fitness Camps ........................ 44
        2.8.13  The Caloola Club................................. 45
        2.8.14  Education: Museum and Preservice Teacher Education ... 45

|   |   |   |
|---|---|---|
| | 2.9 Nature Study | 46 |
| |     2.9.1 Nature Study Practice and Contention | 47 |
| | 2.10 Progress and Conflict from the 1930s | 47 |
| |     2.10.1 Crosbie Morrison and His Conservation Critique | 49 |
| | 2.11 The Significance of Science | 50 |
| | 2.12 Green Awakening: The Rise of Environmental Awareness Post-WWII | 53 |
| | 2.13 Conclusion | 55 |
| | References | 55 |
| **3** | **Environmental Education Centres: A Philosophical Perspective** | **61** |
| | 3.1 Introduction | 61 |
| | 3.2 Education and Environmental and Sustainability Education | 62 |
| |     3.2.1 Education: History, Form, Function and Other Perspectives | 63 |
| |     3.2.2 Influences on the Development and Implementation of ESE | 64 |
| | 3.3 Social Reproduction and Social Reconstruction | 65 |
| | 3.4 Pro Environmental Behaviour | 65 |
| | 3.5 Religion | 66 |
| | 3.6 Development Variations | 67 |
| | 3.7 Governance, Capitalism: The Importance of Civics and Critical Thinking | 68 |
| | 3.8 Going Against the Dominant Grain | 69 |
| | 3.9 A Heuristic Frame | 69 |
| | 3.10 Decoding Colonial Histories | 70 |
| | 3.11 Indigenous Populations | 72 |
| | References | 73 |

**Part II New South Wales Case Study**

|   |   |   |
|---|---|---|
| **4** | **Silhouette and Source of Colonialisation: Australia's Struggles** | **79** |
| | 4.1 Introduction | 79 |
| | 4.2 First Nations' People of Australia: Connection to the Environment | 79 |
| | 4.3 The Beginning of Australia's Environmental Damage | 82 |
| |     4.3.1 The Effect of the Gold Rush | 83 |
| | 4.4 Conclusion | 83 |
| | References | 84 |
| **5** | **Seeding Change: Genesis of New South Wales Department of Education Environmental Education Centres** | **87** |
| | 5.1 Introduction | 87 |
| | 5.2 The Fauna Protection Panel | 87 |
| |     5.2.1 Progression Within the Fauna Protection Panel | 92 |
| |     5.2.2 The Development of Divide | 93 |
| |     5.2.3 Capacity and Resources | 93 |

|  |  | 5.2.4 | The Development of Conservation Societies............ | 95 |
|---|---|---|---|---|
|  |  | 5.2.5 | Publication Development............................ | 96 |
|  |  | 5.2.6 | Further Panel Progress.............................. | 97 |
|  |  | 5.2.7 | Education and the Fauna Protection Panel............. | 98 |
|  |  | 5.2.8 | The 1960s and Progressive Achievement ............. | 101 |
|  | 5.3 | NSW Education Reform and Reserve Development Collide ..... | | 103 |
|  | 5.4 | The Demise of the Fauna Protection Panel ................... | | 103 |
|  |  | 5.4.1 | Growing Rifts...................................... | 103 |
|  |  | 5.4.2 | Advocacy for National Park Legislation ................ | 104 |
|  |  | 5.4.3 | Waning of Political Favour ......................... | 105 |
|  |  | 5.4.4 | National Parks and Wildlife Bill and Political Machinations...................................... | 107 |
|  |  | 5.4.5 | The NSW NPWS and a Provocative Presentation: A Catalyst for Exodus ............................. | 108 |
|  | 5.5 | Reflection of this History................................... | | 109 |
|  | 5.6 | The Little Desert Dispute—Another Example ................. | | 110 |
|  | 5.7 | Conclusion................................................ | | 113 |
|  | References................................................... | | | 114 |
| 6 | **The Spectrum of Support: Personal to Global Structures** ......... | | | 117 |
|  | 6.1 | Introduction .............................................. | | 117 |
|  | 6.2 | Defining Environmental Education ......................... | | 119 |
|  | 6.3 | The Environmental Education Crisis Conference and Developments............................................. | | 120 |
|  | 6.4 | Global Support............................................ | | 123 |
|  | 6.5 | National Progress Through the Curriculum Development Centre.................................................... | | 123 |
|  | 6.6 | Australian Association for Environmental Education: Beginning................................................. | | 126 |
|  | 6.7 | Progress in NSW Environment and Education Bureaucracies .... | | 127 |
|  |  | 6.7.1 | Whole Child—Head, Heart, Hand: Progressive Education Sabotage........................................... | 128 |
|  | 6.8 | Advocating for Environmental Studies and Education Within FSCs.............................................. | | 129 |
|  | 6.9 | The Gould League of NSW and Gould League Advisory Service .................................................. | | 130 |
|  | 6.10 | The Association for Environmental Education (NSW).......... | | 132 |
|  | 6.11 | Conclusion............................................... | | 133 |
|  | References................................................... | | | 133 |
| 7 | **From Vision to Reality: Establishing EECs in New South Wales** ......................................................... | | | 137 |
|  | 7.1 | Introduction .............................................. | | 137 |
|  | 7.2 | FSC/EECs and the Gould League Advisory Service in NSW Education................................................. | | 141 |
|  |  | 7.2.1 | Wirrimbirra: Life Before FSCs Within the Department of Education........................................... | 141 |

|  |  | 7.2.2 | Muogamarra Field Studies Centre | 143 |
|  |  | 7.2.3 | Wirrimbirra Field Studies Centre | 146 |
|  |  | 7.2.4 | Growing Demand | 147 |
|  | 7.3 | Non-viable Primary Schools as Field Studies Centres | | 148 |
|  |  | 7.3.1 | Thalgarrah Field Studies Centre | 150 |
|  |  | 7.3.2 | Bournda Field Studies Centre | 151 |
|  |  | 7.3.3 | Awabakal Field Studies Centre | 153 |
|  |  | 7.3.4 | Wambangalang Field Studies Centre | 155 |
|  |  | 7.3.5 | Dorroughby Field Studies Centre | 157 |
|  | 7.4 | Developing Centres, Curriculum, Pedagogy and Networks | | 159 |
|  |  | 7.4.1 | Developing Confidence and Resilience in Risky Situations: Managing Risk | 159 |
|  |  | 7.4.2 | Centre Collaboration | 160 |
|  | 7.5 | A Snapshot of Developments Within Environmental Education | | 162 |
|  |  | 7.5.1 | Changes at Muogamarra Field Studies Centre | 163 |
|  |  | 7.5.2 | Royal National Park Field Studies Centre | 164 |
|  |  | 7.5.3 | Longneck Lagoon Field Studies Centre | 166 |
|  |  | 7.5.4 | Brewongle Field Studies Centre | 167 |
|  | 7.6 | Progressing Environmental Education Guidelines and Centre Policy | | 168 |
|  | 7.7 | One-Teacher Dilemma: Capping Capacity | | 171 |
|  | 7.8 | Early Field Studies Centre Critique | | 172 |
|  | 7.9 | Gaining Clerical and General Assistance | | 173 |
|  | 7.10 | The Importance of Good Relationships and Ecocentric Understanding | | 173 |
|  | 7.11 | Embargo, Threats of Closure and the Politicisation of EE | | 175 |
|  | 7.12 | A Shift in Oversight | | 176 |
|  | 7.13 | Field Studies Critiques in the Late 1970s | | 177 |
|  | 7.14 | A Snapshot of EE at the End of the 1970s | | 179 |
|  | 7.15 | Conclusion | | 180 |
|  | References | | | 181 |
| 8 | **Growth Amid Change: Institutionalisation and Rationalisation** | | | **185** |
|  | 8.1 | Introduction | | 185 |
|  | 8.2 | Economic and Political Change | | 186 |
|  | 8.3 | Pause and Momentum in Centre Establishment in NSW | | 187 |
|  |  | 8.3.1 | Downsizing of NSW FSCs Oversight | 188 |
|  |  | 8.3.2 | Conferences: Shaping Policy, Curriculum, and Working Conditions | 188 |
|  | 8.4 | Some EE Events in Australia in the 1980s | | 190 |
|  | 8.5 | Effecting Change on the South Coast | | 193 |
|  | 8.6 | Controversial Issues | | 197 |
|  | 8.7 | Political Advocacy and Action for More FSCs | | 198 |
|  |  | 8.7.1 | Shortland Wetlands [Now the Wetlands Campus of the Awabakal EEC] | 198 |

|  |  | 8.7.2 Breaking the Embargo: The Battle for Greater Teaching Capacity . . . . . . . . . . . . . . . . . . . . . . . . . . . . . . . . . . . . . . . . | 199 |
|---|---|---|---|
|  |  | 8.7.3 Field of Mars Field Studies Centre . . . . . . . . . . . . . . . . . . . | 200 |
| 8.8 |  | Change on a National Front in the Late 1980s . . . . . . . . . . . . . . . . | 201 |
|  |  | 8.8.1 Curriculum Clash: Struggle for Educational Influence . . . . | 202 |
| 8.9 |  | Webb Field Studies Review Revisited on the East Coast of Australia. . . . . . . . . . . . . . . . . . . . . . . . . . . . . . . . . . . . . . . . . . . . . . | 203 |
| 8.10 |  | Progression of EE in NSW and the Department of Education . . . . | 205 |
|  |  | 8.10.1 Environmental Education Curriculum Statement K-12 and FSC Policy . . . . . . . . . . . . . . . . . . . . . . . . . . . . . . . . . . | 208 |
| 8.11 |  | A Rush of Centres . . . . . . . . . . . . . . . . . . . . . . . . . . . . . . . . . . . . . . . | 209 |
|  |  | 8.11.1 Muogamarra Field Studies Centre Becomes Gibberagong FSC . . . . . . . . . . . . . . . . . . . . . . . . . . . . . . . . . . . . . . . . . . . | 210 |
|  |  | 8.11.2 Cascade Field Studies Centre. . . . . . . . . . . . . . . . . . . . . . . . | 211 |
|  |  | 8.11.3 Warrumbungles Field Studies Centre . . . . . . . . . . . . . . . . . | 211 |
|  |  | 8.11.4 Riverina Field Studies Centre . . . . . . . . . . . . . . . . . . . . . . . | 212 |
|  |  | 8.11.5 Observatory Hill Field Studies Centre. . . . . . . . . . . . . . . . . | 213 |
|  |  | 8.11.6 Rumbalara Field Studies Centre . . . . . . . . . . . . . . . . . . . . . | 213 |
|  |  | 8.11.7 Botany Bay Field Studies Centre [Now Kamay Botany bay EEC] . . . . . . . . . . . . . . . . . . . . . . . . . . . . . . . . . . . . . . . | 214 |
|  |  | 8.11.8 Mt. Kembla/Illawarra Field Studies Centre [Now Illawarra EEC]. . . . . . . . . . . . . . . . . . . . . . . . . . . . . . . . . . . . . . . . . . . | 215 |
| 8.12 |  | Significant State Educational Reform and Funding Opportunities . . . . . . . . . . . . . . . . . . . . . . . . . . . . . . . . . . . . . . . . . . | 216 |
|  |  | 8.12.1 Innovative Capacity Building . . . . . . . . . . . . . . . . . . . . . . . | 216 |
|  |  | 8.12.2 Visitation Cost to Public Schools. . . . . . . . . . . . . . . . . . . . . | 218 |
| 8.13 |  | Reform, Contraction and the Impact on Environmental Education . . . . . . . . . . . . . . . . . . . . . . . . . . . . . . . . . . . . . . . . . . . . . . | 220 |
|  |  | 8.13.1 Awareness and Growth of Environmental Education . . . . . | 221 |
|  |  | 8.13.2 Camden Park Education Centre [Now Camden Park EEC]. . . . . . . . . . . . . . . . . . . . . . . . . . . . . . . . . . . . . . . . . . . . | 222 |
|  |  | 8.13.3 Wedderburn Outdoor Resource Centre . . . . . . . . . . . . . . . . | 223 |
|  |  | 8.13.4 Georges River Education Centre [Now Georges River EEC]. . . . . . . . . . . . . . . . . . . . . . . . . . . . . . . . . . . . . . . . . . . . | 223 |
|  |  | 8.13.5 Red Hill Field Studies Centre . . . . . . . . . . . . . . . . . . . . . . . | 224 |
| 8.14 |  | Simultaneous State Educational Rationalisation with EE Support. . . . . . . . . . . . . . . . . . . . . . . . . . . . . . . . . . . . . . . . . . . . . . . . | 225 |
|  |  | 8.14.1 The Environmental Education Unit . . . . . . . . . . . . . . . . . . . | 226 |
| 8.15 |  | The Industrial Relations Commission Hearing (1994) . . . . . . . . . . | 227 |
| 8.16 |  | EE Programs and Professional Development . . . . . . . . . . . . . . . . . | 228 |
|  |  | 8.16.1 Earth Education . . . . . . . . . . . . . . . . . . . . . . . . . . . . . . . . . . | 228 |
|  |  | 8.16.2 Snapshot of Other EE Programs and Professional Development . . . . . . . . . . . . . . . . . . . . . . . . . . . . . . . . . . . . | 229 |
| 8.17 |  | A Weakening of a Positive Environment for EE Growth. . . . . . . . . | 230 |
| 8.18 |  | ESE Thought within the NSW FSC. . . . . . . . . . . . . . . . . . . . . . . . . | 231 |

|  |  |  |
|---|---|---|
| | 8.19 More Change and More Advocacy for Environmental Education | 231 |
| |     8.19.1 A Change in Environmental Education Centre Management | 233 |
| |     8.19.2 Taronga Park Zoo ǀ Western Plains Zoo | 234 |
| |     8.19.3 Penrith Lakes Environmental Education Centre | 235 |
| |     8.19.4 Rationalisation of the Metropolitan South Western Region FSCs | 238 |
| | 8.20 Diversification of ESE and the Demise of Founding Advocacy Groups | 239 |
| |     8.20.1 The End of the Gould League of NSW and the Association for EE (NSW) | 240 |
| | 8.21 Environmental Education within the Department | 242 |
| |     8.21.1 The Environmental Education Curriculum Statement Revisited | 242 |
| |     8.21.2 Official EEC Policy Statement and Name Change | 242 |
| | 8.22 Conclusion | 243 |
| | References | 245 |
| **9** | **Navigating Adversity: Thriving Through Highs and Lows** | **251** |
| | 9.1 Introduction | 251 |
| | 9.2 Expanding Horizons: NSW ESE's Global Contributions | 252 |
| | 9.3 National Environmental Education Council and Network | 252 |
| | 9.4 ESE Developments Within NSW | 253 |
| |     9.4.1 The NSW EE Council | 254 |
| |     9.4.2 Environmental Education Policy for Schools | 255 |
| | 9.5 Educating for Sustainability Initiatives | 257 |
| | 9.6 United Nations (UN) Decade & Australia's Environmental Education | 259 |
| | 9.7 Moves Toward a National Curriculum and Federal Funding Support | 260 |
| | 9.8 EECs and Technology | 262 |
| | 9.9 Assessing EEC Effectiveness in ESE Programs | 263 |
| | 9.10 EEC Networks: Consolidation and Growth | 263 |
| | 9.11 The Earth Citizen and Curriculum Framework | 264 |
| | 9.12 The Australian Curriculum | 267 |
| | 9.13 A Broadening of the National Approach | 269 |
| | 9.14 Declining Support | 269 |
| |     9.14.1 Change of Management Within the NSW EE Unit: Decrease in Authority | 270 |
| | 9.15 Waxing and Waning of ESE Favour | 271 |
| | 9.16 Rationalisation and Precarity in ESE/EECs | 273 |
| |     9.16.1 Reflection of This Repressive Period with a National and Queensland Focus | 274 |
| |     9.16.2 Communities of Practice: EECs Aligning with Departmental Priorities | 275 |
| | 9.17 UNESCO: Sustainable Development Goals | 276 |

|       | 9.18 | Who Cares About the Environment? | 277 |
|---|---|---|---|
|       | 9.19 | ESE: Initiatives | 278 |
|       | 9.20 | Australian Curriculum: Further Compromise | 280 |
|       | 9.21 | Chameleons: EEC Educators Keeping Ahead of the Game | 281 |
|       | 9.22 | Conclusion | 284 |
|       | References | | 284 |

## Part III  Changing Contexts

**10  Global Flourishing: Examples of EECs Manifestation** .......... 293
- 10.1 Introduction: A Global Context (1949–1968) .......... 293
- 10.2 National Parks .......... 294
- 10.3 Conservation Education .......... 295
- 10.4 Outward Bound: Embracing Adventure and Personal Growth .......... 296
  - 10.4.1 The Wegscheide Centre .......... 297
- 10.5 Charting ESE Global Governance .......... 297
  - 10.5.1 International Conferences .......... 298
  - 10.5.2 The Earth Charter .......... 300
  - 10.5.3 The United Nations Decade of Education for Sustainable Development .......... 301
  - 10.5.4 International Conferences Continued… .......... 301
  - 10.5.5 The Future We Want and the Education We Need for the World We Want .......... 302
  - 10.5.6 The UNESCO Roadmap for Implementing the Global Action Program (GAP) and Education for Sustainable Development .......... 302
  - 10.5.7 ESD: A Foundational Element of Education .......... 303
- 10.6 Reflection: Global Governance .......... 304
- 10.7 Emerging Field Study(ies)/Environmental/Outdoor Education Centres .......... 305
- 10.8 Global EEC Habitats: Diverse Environments Across Borders .......... 307
  - 10.8.1 Nordic Countries .......... 308
  - 10.8.2 EECs in Extreme Environments .......... 311
  - 10.8.3 Oases of Learning: Exploring Environmental Education in Desert Regions .......... 313
  - 10.8.4 Nature's Rights and Resistance .......... 315
  - 10.8.5 South America .......... 316
  - 10.8.6 EEC: Science/Conservation Foundation .......... 320
  - 10.8.7 Change Makers: People, Culture, and Environment in and Beyond EECs .......... 322
  - 10.8.8 Other Searches for EECs .......... 324
  - 10.8.9 EECS and Religion .......... 325
  - 10.8.10 Diversity in EECs .......... 327
  - 10.8.11 Africa .......... 328
  - 10.8.12 Some European Examples of EECs .......... 331
- 10.9 Conclusion .......... 336
- References .......... 338

**11 Global Echoes, NSW Reflections: A Study of EECs with NSW Insights** ........................................................... 347
    11.1 Introduction .................................................. 347
    11.2 Change Agents—Avant Garde ............................ 348
    11.3 Transforming Learning: Exploring Pedagogy, Curriculum, and Evaluation ........................................... 349
        11.3.1 Teaching Practice and Impact ....................... 349
        11.3.2 Assessment ............................................ 350
        11.3.3 The Lucas Framework ............................... 353
        11.3.4 Indigenous Knowledges/Education ................. 356
        11.3.5 First Nations' Knowledges/Education .............. 356
        11.3.6 STEM .................................................. 358
        11.3.7 Comradery and Larrikinism ......................... 360
    11.4 Enduring Tensions and Themes ........................... 361
        11.4.1 Preservice and Teacher ESE Education ............ 362
        11.4.2 Networking and Advocacy .......................... 363
        11.4.3 ESE Contestation—Bureaucracy and Politicking ... 364
        11.4.4 Waxing and Waning of Political and Curricula Favour ... 364
        11.4.5 Action Orientation .................................... 366
        11.4.6 Fractured Connections and Eroding Resilience—Reconnection ........................................... 367
    11.5 Ch-ch-ch-changes: Turn and Face the Strange ............ 368
    11.6 EECs and ESE Within the Normative Paradigm .......... 373
        11.6.1 The Silencing of EECs Within Established Bureaucracies ......................................... 374
        11.6.2 Conforming to Normative Society for Survival ... 375
    11.7 Inspiration from Movements Working Outside the Normative ... 377
    11.8 Effecting Change ........................................... 379
    11.9 Leadership .................................................. 379
        11.9.1 Shaping the Future: Environmental Educators—A Critical Role ........................................... 381
        11.9.2 Leadership for Transformational Change ......... 382
        11.9.3 Learning Leadership: School Strike for Climate (SS4C) ... 384
    11.10 Conclusion ................................................. 384
    References ....................................................... 386

**12 Conclusion: Challenging Times| Changing Tides—Meeting a Critical Juncture** ............................................. 391
    12.1 Conclusion ................................................. 391
    References ....................................................... 395

**Author Index** ..................................................... 397

**Subject Index** .................................................... 403

# About the Author

**Anne Marie (Anni) Ross** is an education researcher, project manager and educator with a focus on environmental and sustainability education. She works at the University of Newcastle, Australia, as a sessional academic and researcher (17 years), including teaching education for ecologically sustainable communities (2012-14) and managing the School Climate Change Initiative (2007-09) evaluation. Anni dreams of and, at times, contributes to a changing world paradigm.

# Abbreviations

| | |
|---|---|
| AAEE | Australian Association for Environmental Education |
| AEE (NSW) | Association for Environmental Education |
| AESA | Australian Education for Sustainability Alliance |
| AuSSI | Australian Sustainable Schools Initiative |
| ACARA | Australian Curriculum Assessment and Reporting Authority |
| CDC | Curriculum Development Centre |
| CEO | Chief Education Officer |
| CSIRO | Commonwealth Science and Industrial Research Organisation |
| DE-EEC | Department of Education Environmental Education Centre |
| EE | Environmental Education |
| EEC | Environmental Education Centre |
| EfS | Education for Sustainability |
| ESD | Education for Sustainable Development |
| ESE | Environmental and Sustainability Education |
| EZEC | Environmental and Zoo Education Centre Network |
| FPP | Fauna Protection Panel |
| FSC | Field Studies Centre |
| KLA | Key Learning Area |
| IUCN | International Union for the Conservation of Nature and Natural Resources |
| NGO | Non-government organisation |
| NPWS | National Parks and Wildlife Service |
| NSW | New South Wales |
| NSW EPA | NSW Environmental Protection Authority |
| RAREC | Rainforest Awareness Rescue Education Centre |
| SDGs | Sustainable Development Goals |
| UNEP | United Nations Environmental Program |
| UNESCO | United Nations Educational, Scientific and Cultural Organisation |
| WESSA | Wildlife and Environment Society of South Africa |
| WWF | World Wildlife Fund |

# List of Figures

| | | |
|---|---|---|
| Fig. 1.1 | Global distribution of anthropogenic stressors to marine species faced with extinction (2019). Attribution: Thomas Luypaert, James G. Hagan, Morgan L. McCarthy and Meenakshi Poti, CC BY 4.0 https://creativecommons.org/licenses/by/4.0, via Wikimedia Commons | 6 |
| Fig. 1.2 | The Sustainability Curriculum Framework Visual mnemonic. Sustainability Curriculum Framework: A guide for curriculum developers and policy makers (2010). Australian Department of the Environment Water Heritage & the Arts. Attribution: The Australian Department of the Environment Water Heritage & the Arts, now the Department of Climate Change, Energy, the Environment and Water. CC BY 4.0 https://creativecommons.org/licenses/by/4.0/ | 12 |
| Fig. 2.1 | Manna gum—Buckland Valley, Victoria, 2012 | 22 |
| Fig. 2.2 | Koala in a casuarina, North Stradbroke Island/Minjerribah, April 2022 | 34 |
| Fig. 2.3 | Anthropocentric vs ecocentric graphic. Attribution: IDA Projekt, CC BY-SA 4.0 https://creativecommons.org/licenses/by-sa/4.0, via Wikimedia Commons. The image of a woman is an addition to the original image | 37 |
| Fig. 5.1 | "Our endangered wildlife- The eastern native cat." Poster illustrated by Margaret Senior originally commissioned for the NSW Fauna Protection Panel (1948–1967). Printed with permission of NSW National Parks and Wildlife Service, and the Margaret Senior Archives, held by the University of Newcastle (Australia) Special Collections | 89 |
| Fig. 5.2 | Barrington Tops National Park, January 2022 | 91 |
| Fig. 5.3 | Track to Greenglades, Nadgee Nature Reserve, September 2022 | 92 |
| Fig. 5.4 | Wildlife Service I Fauna Protection Panel insignia, illustrated by Margaret Senior. Attribution: Printed with permission of NSW National Parks and Wildlife Service, and the Margaret Senior Archives, held by the University of Newcastle (Australia) Special Collections | 97 |

| | | |
|---|---|---|
| Fig. 5.5 | Poster illustrated by Margaret Senior originally commissioned for the NSW Fauna Protection Panel (1948–1967). Attribution: Printed with permission of NSW National Parks and Wildlife Service, and the Margaret Senior Archives, held by the University of Newcastle (Australia) Special Collections. | 100 |
| Fig. 5.6 | Poster illustrated by Margaret Senior originally commissioned for the NSW Fauna Protection Panel (1948–1967). Printed with permission of NSW National Parks and Wildlife Service, and the Margaret Senior Archives, held by the University of Newcastle (Australia) Special Collections | 102 |
| Fig. 5.7 | Emu chicks (*Dromaius novaehollandiae*), Little Desert NP, Victoria. Attribution: Patrick Kavanagh, CC BY 2.0 https://creativecommons.org/licenses/by/2.0, via Wikimedia Commons | 113 |
| Fig. 6.1 | The Gould Leaguer, (1969). NSW Department of Education 1(1), p.1 | 131 |
| Fig. 7.1 | Pied oyster catchers taking flight, Wonboyn Beach (Greenglades), Nadgee Nature Reserve, September, 2022. | 140 |
| Fig. 7.2 | Wirrimbirra, Gould Leaguer (1970), NSW Department of Education, 1(4), p. 6. | 143 |
| Fig. 7.3 | School children gather at the John D. Tipper Lookout, named after the Muogamarra Sanctuary founder. (Photo taken by Bill Payne for an article written by Patricia Morgan titled, 'This bush school is for city children'. Published in The Australian Woman's Weekly on August 16 1972 (pp. 24–26). Printed with permission from Gibberagong Environmental Education Centre and Hornsby Shire Council Recollect. https://sites.google.com/education.nsw.gov.au/muogamarra-through-time/muogamarra-view-from-j-d-tippers-look-out & https://hornsbyshire.recollect.net.au/nodes/view/5046) | 145 |
| Fig. 7.4 | "The field studies centre should provide areas for teacher inservice—Wirrimbirra, New South Wales" (Webb, 1980, p. 121). (Attribution: Joan Webb and the National Parks and Wildlife Service (now Parks Australia)) | 147 |
| Fig. 7.5 | Location map of the first two EECs within the NSW Department of Education (not to scale—schematic map) | 148 |
| Fig. 7.6 | "Diversity of habitats—the farm dam at Thalgarrah, New South Wales" (Webb, 1980, p. 112). (Attribution: Joan Webb and the National Parks and Wildlife Service (now Parks Australia)) | 151 |
| Fig. 7.7 | "The closed school at Jellat Jellat—the site of Bournda Field Studies Centre", New South Wales (Webb, 1980, p. 55). (Attribution: Joan Webb and the National Parks and Wildlife Service (now Parks Australia)) | 152 |
| Fig. 7.8 | Flannel flowers, Awabakal Nature Reserve 2021. | 153 |
| Fig. 7.9 | "Awabakal Field Studies Centre", (Webb, 1980, p. 132). (Attribution: Joan Webb and the National Parks and Wildlife Service (now Parks Australia)) | 154 |

| | | |
|---|---|---|
| Fig. 7.10 | "Wambangalang Field Studies Centre" (Webb, 1989, p. 13). (Attribution: Joan Webb and the National Parks and Wildlife Service (now Parks Australia)) | 156 |
| Fig. 7.11 | Sunset over the Hawkesbury, Muogamarra Field Studies Centre I 50 Year of Environmental Education Celebrations, August, 2022 | 165 |
| Fig. 7.12 | "The water habitat for study at Longneck Lagoon, NSW" (Webb, 1980, p. 55). (Attribution: Joan Webb and the National Parks and Wildlife Service (now Parks Australia)) | 167 |
| Fig. 7.13 | Location map of the 10 EECs within the NSW Department of Education (not to scale—schematic map) | 170 |
| Fig. 8.1 | The scenic viewpoint at Disaster Bay in Beowa National Park overlooking Disaster Bay and the Nadgee-Howe Wilderness Area. September 2022 | 194 |
| Fig. 8.2 | Location map of EECs within the NSW Department of Education, 1997 (not to scale—schematic map) | 237 |
| Fig. 8.3 | Location map of the EECs within the NSW Department of Education, 2024 (not to scale—schematic map) | 244 |
| Fig. 9.1 | View over valley, Muogamarra Field Studies Centre I 50 Years of Environmental Education Celebrations, August 2022 | 262 |
| Fig. 9.2 | The Sustainability Curriculum Framework Visual mnemonic. Sustainability Curriculum Framework: A guide for curriculum developers and policy makers (Australian Department of the Environment Water Heritage & the Arts, 2010). (Attribution: The Australian Department of the Environment Water Heritage & the Arts, now the Department of Climate Change, Energy, the Environment and Water. CC BY 4.0. https://creativecommons.org/licenses/by/4.0/) | 267 |
| Fig. 9.3 | SDG_wedding_cake. (Attribution: Azote for Stockholm Resilience Centre, Stockholm University, CC BY 4.0. https://creativecommons.org/licenses/by/4.0, via Wikimedia Commons) | 277 |
| Fig. 9.4 | Muogamarra Field Studies Centre I 50 Years of Environmental Education Celebrations, August 2022 | 283 |
| Fig. 10.1 | "Pullenvale Field Study Centre" (Webb, 1989, p. 19). (Attribution: Joan Webb and the National Parks and Wildlife Service (now Parks Australia)) | 307 |
| Fig. 10.2 | Bunyaville Environmental Education Centre. (Attribution: The State of Queensland (Department of Education), CC BY 4.0. https://creativecommons.org/licenses/by/4.0, via Wikimedia Commons) | 307 |
| Fig. 10.3 | Country Overshoot Days 2024. (Attribution: Global Footprint Network 2024, www.overshootday.org) | 310 |
| Fig. 10.4 | Bamfield Marine Sciences Centre from Bamfield Inlet. (Attribution: David Stanley, CC BY 2.0. https://creativecommons.org/licenses/by/2.0, via Wikimedia Commons) | 312 |

Fig. 10.5 *Melopsittacus undulatus* (Budgerigar) Bird-Alice Springs Desert Park. (Attribution: Richard. Fisher, CC BY 2.0. https://creativecommons.org/licenses/by/2.0, via Wikimedia Commons) .. 314

Fig. 10.6 Sitting Grey Crowned Crane (*Balearica regulorum*) at the Uganda Wildlife Education Centre, Entebbe. (Attribution: sarahemcc, CC BY 2.0. https://creativecommons.org/licenses/by/2.0, via Wikimedia Commons) .................................... 323

Fig. 10.7 Leopard, Okonjima, Namibia. (Attribution: Sonse, CC BY 2.0. https://creativecommons.org/licenses/by/2.0, via Wikimedia Commons) ............................................. 329

Fig. 10.8 Anthropocentric vs ecocentric graphic. (Attribution: IDA Projekt, CC BY-SA 4.0. https://creativecommons.org/licenses/by-sa/4.0, via Wikimedia Commons. The image of a woman is an addition to the original image)........................................... 337

Fig. 11.1 Desert immersive classroom, Taronga Institute of Science and Learning, Taronga Conservation Society. (Photo taken at the Environmental and Zoo Education Centre Conference July, 2022).. 352

Fig. 11.2 The Eight Ways of Learning Framework (Yunkaporta, 2010, p. 40). (Printed with permission from Sydney University Press) ......... 357

Fig. 11.3 Emu eggs and wattle in a coolamon. (Photo taken at Craig Duncan's display at the Rising from the Embers Festival at the Park on the Hill, Newcastle University, NSW, May 2022) ........ 359

Fig. 11.4 The Peoples' Blockade of the world's biggest coal port, Rising Tide, November, 2023. (Printed with permission from Rising Tide)................................................... 378

Fig. 11.5 2019-03_Fridays_For_Future_Dresden_(45). (Attribution: Ralf Lotys (Sicherlich), CC BY 4.0. https://creativecommons.org/licenses/by/4.0, via Wikimedia Commons) .................... 385

Fig. 12.1 What I interpret as existential angst! An artwork created with lolly wrappers.—artist unknown or difficult to identify. Displayed at the Waste as Art exhibition, The World Environmental Education Congress, Marrakech 2013 ............................... 393

# List of Table

Table 2.1 Initial development of bird and animal protection legislation in NSW (1879–1903).................................... 30

# Part I
# Introduction

Environmental and sustainability education (ESE) emanates from many disparate quarters these days. You find it increasingly in many bureaucratic, not-for-profit, and for-profit organisations. We find ESE concepts within science fiction and fantasy (Gough, 1998), and in visual and performative art such as in works by Andy Goldsworthy, The Theatre of the Oppressed or The Yes Men (Artnet, n.d.; ImaginAction, n.d.; McLeod, 2021). The environmental and sustainability landscape encompasses a broad spectrum of practices, ranging from capitalist-driven environmentalism, which sometimes involves greenwashing, to non-violent civil disobedience aimed at driving change. Within this spectrum, there exists a multitude of approaches to environmental and sustainability practices. However, in Australia, and seemingly in many other locations, efforts towards ESE appear to be ad hoc, lacking methical organisation, and predominantly occur on a small scale compared to subjects with measurable academic outcomes in formal educational systems—or the urgency with which it is required. Why isn't ESE systemic after over 50 years of development?

Many people have adopted environmentally friendly/sustainable practices, and many teachers and schools are advocates and practitioners—but many others have/are not. There are conflicting ideologies, and there is misleading information at play, including within the powers behind the media and social media. These entities seem intent on deliberately confusing the public through practices such as greenwashing (Parker, 2023; Yue & Li, 2023) and pseudo-science programs (Benjamin & McLean, 2022; Vijaykumar, 2019). Many people are ignorant, or downright dismissive and disbelieving of environmental science, and science generally (Otto, 2016)—and power and greed often win out over environmental considerations (Fox, 2014; Klein, 2014). Consumerism, an insatiable pursuit of more, has ensnared many individuals who, whether partially or wholly, consciously or unconsciously, resist letting go for the greater good (Dittmar, 2007; Henry, 1965; Weaver cited in Fox, 1979). Materialistic values are associated with less concern for the environment (Kasser, 2002). Consumerism is a system that perpetuates harm to the environment, perpetuates impoverishment and threatens humanity's future. Moreover, it seems that even those with limited resources aspire to materialistic ideals (Kasser, 2002).

While it is essential to recognise the complexity of individual motivations and the interplay of various, social, psychological and cultural factors, in the face of pressing needs for survival, billions of people find themselves with little mental capacity to consider factors beyond their immediate concerns (Bertrand et al., 2004; Mani et al., 2013; Mullainathan & Shafr, 2013). Further, multinational corporations wield significant influence, often overshadowing or undermining environmental and community efforts to foster connectedness and sustainability (Agyekum et al., 2022; Huckle, 2020; Menton et al., 2020).

The significance of ensuring that ESE is not drowned out amidst the noise, greenwashing and recalcitrance in policy formation and follow through cannot be overstated. The pervasive commodification of education, driven by broader trends of commercialisation, managerialism, and neoliberal ideology, underscores the urgent need to reclaim and prioritise educative, critical, and democratising approaches, as well as to recentre equity concerns. Both the environment and education are pivotal in advancing critical thinking, fostering democratic principles, and promoting equitable access to opportunities. Therefore, efforts to advance ESE must also encompass broader objectives of critical engagement, democratisation, and equity recalibration. Environmental Education Centres (EECs) have played and play a pivotal role in educating and supporting education for an ecocentric paradigm within an increasingly neoliberal environment.

Within this section, Chapter One develops an understanding of why EECs exist and Chapter Two explores environmental awareness, with New South Wales, Australia a specific focus. Chapter Three provides a philosophical lens for the development of this study.

## References

Agyekum, B., Siakwah, P., & Biney, I. K. (2022). Oil production, dispossession, and community development in Africa: A development education perspective. In O. Adwoa Tiwaah Frimpong Kwapong, D. Addae, & J. Kwame Boateng (Eds.), *Reimagining development education in Africa* (pp. 171–189). Springer. https://doi.org/10.1007/978-3-030-96001-8_10

Artnet (n.d.). *Andy Goldsworthy*. Retrieved May 2, 2024, from https://www.artnet.com/artists/andy-goldsworthy/

Benjamin, K. A., & McLean, S. (2022). Change the medium, change the message: creativity is key to battle misinformation. *Advances in Physiology Education, 46*(2), 259–267. https://doi.org/10.1152/advan.00021.2021

Bertrand, M., Mullainathan, S., & Shafir, E. (2004). A behavioral-economics view of poverty. *The American Economic Review, 94*(2), 419–423. http://www.jstor.org.ezproxy.newcastle.edu.au/stable/3592921

Dittmar, H. (2007). The costs of consumer culture and the "Cage within": The impact of the material "Good life" and "Body perfect" Ideals on individuals" identity and well-being. *Psychological Inquiry, 18*(1), 23–31. https://doi.org/10.1080/10478400701389045

Fox, A. (1979). Reflections. In W. Goldstein (Ed.), *Parks and wildlife: Australia's 100 years of national parks* (pp. 4–14). National Parks and Wildlife Service.

Fox, J. (2014) Gasland. *Kanopy Streaming*. Retrieved May 29, 2024, from https://www.kanopy.com/en/product/60541?vp=mdc

Gough, N. (1998). Playing with wor(l)ds: Science fiction as environmental literature. In P. Murphy (Ed.), *The literature of nature: An international sourcebook* (pp. 409–414). Dearborn.

Henry, J. (1963). *Culture against man.* Vintage Books.

Huckle, J. (2020). *Critical school geography, education for global citizenship.* ResearchGate. https://www.researchgate.net/publication/345849553_Critical_School_Geography_Education_for_Global_Citizenship

ImaginAction. (n.d.). *Theatre of the oppressed.* Retrieved May 2, 2024, from https://imaginaction.org/media/our-methods/theatre-of-the-oppressed-2

Kasser, T. (2002). *The high price of materialism.* Cambridge, MA: MIT Press.

Klein, N. (2014). *This changes everything: Capitalism vs. the climate.* Penguin Books.

Mani, A., Mullainathan, S., Shafir, E., & Zhao, J. (2013). Poverty Impedes Cognitive Function. *Science, 341*(6149), 976-980. http://www.jstor.org.ezproxy.newcastle.edu.au/stable/23491382

McLeod, K. (2021, January 26). Pranksters on a Mission: An Interview With the Yes Men. *The MIT Press Reader.* https://thereader.mitpress.mit.edu/an-interview-with-the-yes-men/

McLeod, K. (2021, January 26). Pranksters on a Mission: An Interview With the Yes Men. *The MIT Press Reader.* https://thereader.mitpress.mit.edu/an-interview-with-the-yes-men/

Menton, M., Larrea, C., Latorre, S., Martinez-Alier, J., Peck, M., Temper, L., & Walter, M. (2020). Environmental justice and the SDGs: From synergies to gaps and contradictions. *Sustainability Science, 15,* 1621–1636.

Mullainathan, S., & Shafr, E. (2013). *Scarcity: Why having too little means so much.* Macmillan.

Otto, S. L. (2016). *The war on science: Who's waging it, why it matters, and what we can do about it.* Milkweed Editions.

Parker, C. (2023, December 1). Social media ads are littered with 'green' claims. How are we supposed to know they're true? *The Conversation.* https://theconversation.com/social-media-ads-are-littered-with-green-claims-how-are-we-supposed-to-know-theyre-true-218922

Vijaykumar, S. (2019, August 13). Pseudoscience is taking over social media – and putting us all at risk. *World Economic Forum.* https://www.weforum.org/agenda/2019/08/pseudoscience-is-taking-over-social-media-and-putting-us-all-at-risk-07395f91a0/

Yue, J., & Li, Y. (2023). Media attention and corporate greenwashing behavior: Evidence from China. *Finance Research Letters, 55.* https://doi.org/10.1016/j.frl.2023.104016

# Chapter 1
# Environmental Education Centres: Place and Purpose

## 1.1 Introduction

Environmental education centres (EECs) exist at the nexus of human activity and environmental impacts—where people have seen a need for conservation/preservation, research and development, connections to nature, environmental and sustainability education (ESE), or action and advocacy. Centres are just one vehicle for ESE, however they were seen as an important element given their development, support and delivery of ESE for informal and importantly formal education set within a western consumerist paradigm (Gough et al., 2024).

Conservation, environmental awareness and ESE are very western concepts and must have seemed/seem bizarre in contexts where there was a closer connection to the environment and little connection to the consumerist lifestyle. From another perspective, for instance, the idea of wreaking havoc on your environment and needing to fight to safeguard it and educate your peoples in how to do so must seem/have seemed ludicrous to Indigenous people connected to sustainable ways of being. This, of course, for the moment is partly conjecture but an easy summation on reading many non-western and environmental perspectives given that many Indigenous communities were and are fighting against the western capitalist paradigm to retain their culture and land which includes an understanding of the environment that is alienated within this paradigm. The absurdity of disconnecting from the environment within capitalism/western culture is something to keep in mind as we move forward with this narrative—and something to revisit in the analysis of this story.

It was the global repercussions of environmental harm, from local/place that prompted the attention to environmental education (EE) on a global level (see Fig. 1.1 for an example of this destruction from 2019).

This frame could utilise factors of extinction/preservation of species, degradation/depletion of natural resources, social justice and Indigenous knowledges. NOTE: Many social justice issues take place in Indigenous, marginalised and poor

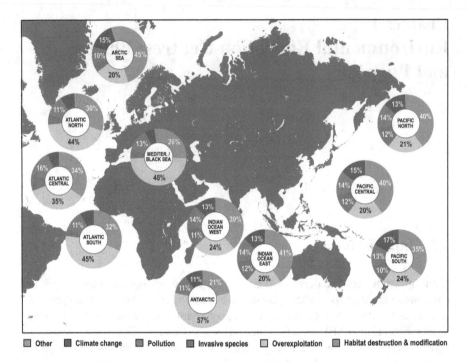

**Fig. 1.1** Global distribution of anthropogenic stressors to marine species faced with extinction (2019). Attribution: Thomas Luypaert, James G. Hagan, Morgan L. McCarthy and Meenakshi Poti, CC BY 4.0 https://creativecommons.org/licenses/by/4.0, via Wikimedia Commons

communities. Injustice within society tends to be associated with environmental damage (Bullard, 1993). A well-functioning environment is essential for well-functioning society.

## 1.2 Exploring the Complexity of ESE and EECs

Western study of the environment is multidisciplinary, encompassing ecology, geography, history, biology and chemistry to name a few. We have accumulating issues of land clearing, erosion, salinity, and eutrophication; population stress, excessive consumerism, and resource depletion; air, water, and land pollution; the damage caused by many exotic plants and animals; ozone depletion; and climate change (Withgott & Laposata, 2012). All of these issues are linked to multidisciplinary languages that are further shaped and intricately entwined with broader social issues.

> Ecosystems are complex, and our knowledge of them is limited, as the scientists who study them are the first to admit. Human social systems are complex too, which is why there is so much work for the ever-growing number of social scientists who study them. Environmental

problems by definition are found at the intersection of ecosystems and human social systems, thus doubly complex.

The more complex a situation, the larger the number of plausible perspectives upon it and the harder it is to prove any one of them wrong because the more necessary it becomes to be selective in choice of aspects of the complex situation to highlight. Thus, the proliferation of perspectives on environmental problems that has accompanied the development and diversification of environmental concern since the 1960s should come as no surprise. (Dryzek, 2022, p. 9)

Synergies in the "environment" can be linked to include the emergence of the global perspective, cybernetics and systems thinking, developments in ecology, increases in industrial powers to exploit and transform matter, increasing numbers of pollutants/disruptions to our environment, resource depletion linked to post war economic boom, and recognition of our finite resources (Berryman & Sauvé, 2013).

This can be extended into the neoliberal and decolonising present. Counterbalancing these detrimental environmental effects are a multitude of place-based and global communities of practice who work on ameliorating these issues in a plethora of ways (environmental, social, political—economic). The complexity of environmental issues is mirrored within EE given its counter-hegemonic nature which incorporates an intrinsically holistic, socio-political, character, particularly within the formal education system which is entrenched within our rationalist, scientific, capitalistic, consumerist society. The counter-hegemony of EE was recognised early in EE development.

> Environmental education is concerned with counter-hegemony or social reconstruction and it is argued that it has been subjected to incorporation within the existing hegemony in a neutralised form – the radical "action" component having been deleted and the less controversial cognitive and skill ones [retained] together with the name environmental education. (Greenall, 1981, p. 53)

Despite missing some of the distinguishing objectives of EE, programs were still categorised as EE. Whilst there were increases in environmental content within many subjects in the traditional curriculum of Australian schools, there was little evidence that such courses were considering "the more controversial political and moral aspects and collective responsibility inherent in environmental education" (Greenall, 1981b, p. 53). Annette Greenall saw future commitment to curricula wholly incorporating these changes as even less likely.

> As long as such action is countenanced, as it certainly is at present by the education authorities who, although professing a strong belief in environmental education, are loathe to stress its moral and political components, then the introduction of environmental education in its full meaning into schools will be negligible. (Greenall, 1981, p. 53)

Further,

> In addition to this confusion, incorporating environmental education into the curriculum in whatever form under whatever name will involve radical changes in the teaching methods, styles and organisation of most schools. (Greenall 1981, p. 53)

An example of the struggle for EE against the dominant hegemony is the growth of sustainable development in the 1980s (Berryman & Sauvé, 2013; Dryzek, 2005).

Now dominating EE with its triple bottom line of ecological, social and economic sustainability, although these were already encompassed within EE, sustainable development was orienting towards a broader outlook that did not necessarily cover all the distinctions of environmental issues (Berryman & Sauvé, 2013, p. 133). Ecological modernisation arose, with environmental protection seen as "essentially complementary" to economic growth (Dryzek, 2005), and EE was subsumed within education for sustainability (EfS) or, as is more often used internationally, education for sustainable development (ESD) (Berryman & Sauvé, 2013, p. 139).

Stevenson (2006) discusses the abstraction of ESD within policy discourse as "unpractised ESD" by the discussants with symptoms being:

- discourse reification tendencies—treating abstract concepts, ideas, or theoretical constructs as if they were concrete and tangible entities,
- a lack of focus on issues of pedagogy and politics in enacting local setting ESD, and
- a great divide between policy sloganism and implementation. (Stables and Scott 2002 cited in Stevenson, 2006, p. 287)

Stevenson goes on to say that the process of learning to live within ecological limits without human suffering, includes uncovering the power relationships and ideologies that underlie sustainable development discourse—negotiating and enacting change is tricky not just because change is hard but because it may also disturb vested interests (Stevenson, 2006).

Given the schooling system is thoroughly complicit, embedded and constrained within our consumerist western society, contrary to ESE, how do we educate for the anti-consumerism required to move our society, indeed the globe, to an ecocentric society—living within our means in a thriving ecosystem? This is the ultimate question. How do we gain the critical mass necessary to tip the scales away from 90 s till midnight on the doomsday clock? (Bulletin of the Atomic Scientists, n.d.). How quickly, and to what degree can our curriculum systems leverage the new, and not so new, ecocentric curriculum and pedagogies required?

When thinking of ESE I think of Landcare, Permaculture, Water/Stream Watch, Total Catchment Management, Learnscapes, Total Environment Centres, school kitchen gardens—practices that along with critical thinking are important in educating through doing. It really is what works within schooling systems that we are searching for given the great potential in engaging the most people. But I also think of organisations that have/are actively changing the neoliberal paradigm to an ecocentric one through education and mobilising action. I think of the people and organisations who have contributed to shifting a stuck and blinded paradigm within the silencing of action. People and organisations educating on First Nations' knowledges and practices are playing an important role. I think of people like Anne Poelina from the Martuwarra River community in Western Australia emphasising the need for a new epistemology among non-Indigenous people, urging a reset to address "overwhelm, confusion, and despair" (Dahr, 2023). Poelina stresses the importance of coming together and embracing Ancient Wisdom, highlighting a symbiotic relationship with the environment. I think of groups such as Guerreiras da

## 1.2 Exploring the Complexity of ESE and EECs

Floresta—Amazon Women Warriors, Brazil, The Chipko Movement in the Himalayan region of India, The Friends of Karura and the Green Belt Movement in Nairobi, Kenya—all acting and educating to stop deforestation (Bandyopadhy, 1999; Gaur, 2023; Loures & Sax, 2020; Nthuku, 2018; Schell, 2013; The Green Belt Movement, n.d.; Vilaysack, 2014). I also think of the Epop platform, based in New Caledonia, initially disseminating multimedia and discussion of the effects of climate change on their islands but opening up the dialogue to world-wide effects (ePOP Network, n.d.). There is the Long Now Foundation in the United States with its focal point on long-term intergenerational planning—prominent in Indigenous cultures but seemingly forgotten within the consumeristic neoliberal environment of the West (The Long Now Foundation, n.d.). Other organisations effecting change are Rising Tide, a grassroots climate action group based in Newcastle, New South Wales (NSW), where the biggest coal port in the world is situated (Rising Tide, n.d.). There is The Hunter Community Environment Centre undertaking citizen science projects and educating the community on the development of urban sprawl's devastating effects on threatened species habitats and ecosystems (amongst other things) (Hunter Community Environment Centre, n.d.). There is CERES an extensive community-based food security group who over many years have contributed to community and school ESE and beautified Melbourne in the process (CERES, n.d.; CERES School of Nature and Climate, n.d.). I'm highlighting the efforts of organisations driving cultural shifts towards necessary change and emphasising their role in normalising these changes to enable broader adoption. There are thousands of these groups that tend to be prominent in spaces, places and times where the nexus of environmental damage meets humanity. While these organisations are not the focus of this book, they are important in effecting the change we need and are indicative of what our EECs are and can be given the right leadership and support.

With, consumerism, economic growth at all costs and profit a priority antithetical to a healthy environment and communities, the state of environmental and sustainability practice depends on authentic policy and practice. Governance, whatever type, connection to these factors is important. With the weaving of profit, shareholder profit and development tightly woven into the fabric of our societies it is not an easy conundrum to navigate—yet one would consider nature and communities a priority as Adam Smith stated in his pioneering of capitalism in The Wealth of Nations (1776/1937). Thus, EECs within societies governed with a stronger societal rather than neoliberal concern were of interest to this study. It is the ethos within the system that is important. Active and local, place-based, whole-school education reap positive outcomes. Where are the systems that embed these practices? These are the representations looked for while being open to other promising forms along the way. Where are ESE practices within school articulated and championed? Where are students experiencing, living and learning ecocentrism? And are there EECs supporting these practices?

A cautionary tale for developing global representations of EEC comparisons can be elaborated from Dorothy Pearson's (1978) Master's thesis on "Fieldwork in environments out-of-doors", which included EE at the time. Pearson surmised that definitions for centres, fieldwork and field study were highly ambiguous. EE/

environmental education for sustainability (EfS) and ESD practice have been similar. The motives underlying ESE can be specific or broad, localised but with global impact in accumulation, with altruistic or vested interest—communal, philanthropic, or institutional. It was challenging to accurately portray the diverse genres within the fields of ESE. Locating representations of ESE to compare with the NSW Department of Education EECs proved a gargantuan conundrum by the ambiguity and enormity of the endeavour.

ESE has developed in many different guises over the years and emanates from many disparate quarters. Some have grown and then dissipated over time. For example, Goldfields EECs that were set up within some African national parks—at Pilanesberg, Table Mountain (Shongwe, 1996) and Kruger National Park (Ferreira, 2003)—no longer exist. Other ESE initiatives have undergone a hiatus before regaining strength—possibly by morphing into an entity that fits best with the current sociological, political and economic climate. For example, the Marine Education Society of Australasia is now united with the Australian Association for Environmental Education [AAEE] (Marine Education Society of Australasia, 2024). Other examples are all the ESE providers who have evolved through transformations from conservation to EE to EfS. We have ESE being offered by a diverse array of specific, and not so specific, not-for-profit, grassroots, national and international organisations. While iterations of ESE are a Western construct that do not always include the more than human, Indigenous ways of knowing and being have become a specific focus given their intrinsic connection to the environment and future generations. ESE within and outside of EECs have increasingly encompassed Indigenous knowledges and practices. You find conservative and radical ESE—education with a science focus and education that covers a wide range of socio-economic-political factors. Indeed, without a good understanding of the basic science behind environmental/ sustainability issues—energy, cycles, interrelationships, and change—it can be difficult to understand and comprehend the complexity and interrelatedness of the issues. This makes a local to global perspective a well-grounded, and not so overwhelming starting point.

Generally, ESE is set at a local, place-based level with technology facilitating networking over large areas—global connections linking and relating people, their programs and their organisations. There is the institutionalisation of sustainability, and to a certain extent ESE, within all levels of government—and importantly at a global level. Evidence for this can be found in government policies and legislation, funding and support, reports and publications, as well as international agreements and initiatives, and partnerships and collaborations between governments, Non government organisations (NGOs) educational institutions and other stakeholders. While this has provided ESE resourcing and thus a certain flourishing, it has also stifled and restricted ESE to comply with the will and wiles of governance.

## 1.2.1 Exploring EECs: The Value of School Relationships

While ESEs form, function and place within the curriculum is contested it is undeniable that the environment and sustainability are fundamental to life, and the continuation of life, and thus has a place in all formally taught disciplines—whether through content or context, as well as through cross-curricular and whole-school means given evidence supporting these pedagogical approaches. Its absence, or the absence of the critical analysis and action component of ESE, from many subjects within much mass schooling is a significant issue to be addressed. Integrating ESE within schooling systems can potentially educate student families and friends and importantly, prepares the next generation responsible for the Earth.

Ad hoc ESE programs and projects developed by those outside of education systems can provide invaluable expertise in informing the required ESE knowledges and practices. However, they are not part of the knowledge and power structure that is educational bureaucracy which generally has a history of seeing outside influence as "other" and additional to education as it is. Given the pressure on schools in many controlled, consumerist education systems, this is an important factor. EECs play an important role in providing support and education to schools, students and others, and those with a close relationship to schooling systems, or within these systems, have greater possibilities of effecting the necessary changes.

## 1.3 Insights on Optimal ESE Practices: My Perspective

ESD is a crucial part of the Sustainable Development Goals (SDGs), specifically Target 4.7, which aims to enhance the purpose and quality of education. This target, builds on the UN Decade of Education for Sustainable Development (2005–2014) and the Global Action Programme (2015–2019), and complemented by the United Nations Educational, Scientific and Cultural Organisation's [UNESCO's] (2020) ESD roadmap, seeks to ensure that by 2030, all learners acquire essential knowledge and skills to support sustainable development. This includes education on sustainable lifestyles, human rights, gender equality, peace, non-violence, global citizenship, and cultural diversity (UNESCO, 2020). A healthy environment is fundamental to the success of this directive.

Since the inception of EE and its transition into EfS/ESD… ESE, there have been numerous polices and frameworks developed. These provide a conceptual structure for consideration when developing and implementing ESE. From my perspective, as a starting point the *Sustainability curriculum framework: A guide for curriculum developers and policy makers* (Commonwealth [Australian] Department of the Environment, Water, Heritage, and the Arts, 2010) [see Fig. 1.2] provides good grounding, supported and guided by the conceptual *Earth Citizenship: Background paper for learning for sustainability—Draft working paper* (NSW

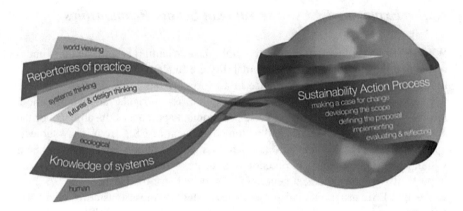

**Fig. 1.2** The Sustainability Curriculum Framework Visual mnemonic. Sustainability Curriculum Framework: A guide for curriculum developers and policy makers (2010). Australian Department of the Environment Water Heritage & the Arts. Attribution: The Australian Department of the Environment Water Heritage & the Arts, now the Department of Climate Change, Energy, the Environment and Water. CC BY 4.0 https://creativecommons.org/licenses/by/4.0/

Department of Education and Training, 2009). These are the documents I am most familiar with. The curriculum framework includes:

- the sustainability action process with the cyclic workflow of project> developing scope> defining the proposal> implementation> evaluation
- ecological and human knowledge systems, and
- Repertoires of practice in systems thinking, world viewing and futures thinking.

The Curriculum Framework informed the original Australian Curriculum cross-curriculum priority of Sustainability.

Yet it is important to go beyond this frame and look intently at power, politics and citizenship (implicit in the sustainability curriculum framework world viewing and future thinking), the effect of neoliberalism and alternate forms of social and environmental relations (Huckle & Wals, 2015). A critical and transformative approach to ESE is essential. In 2012 "The Education We Need for the World We Want" document produced by the People's Summit, which ran in parallel with the Rio + 20, the United Nations Conference on Sustainable Development spoke of the social, economic, and environmental impacts of financialisation within neoliberalism. It spoke of the global exhaustion caused by development and underdevelopment exacerbation (Huckle & Wals, 2015). These determinants have galvanised social movements, many seeking radical alternatives given the magnitude of the crisis/es. There was no alternate democratic collective international space within the global political order to enact multilateral cooperative decisions. The interests of some states, banks, and corporations under the guise of the interests of capital dominate and stifle present structures and are key to the crisis/es.

There is a demand for greater economic, political, and social democracy (Huckle & Wals, 2015). With the function of education pivoted towards producing

## 1.3 Insights on Optimal ESE Practices: My Perspective

consumerist, worker citizens who fit the neoliberal construct and education institutions themselves functioning within these neoliberal constraints, little was/is happening within formal education to develop understanding of, and thus emancipation from, these issues. Neoliberalism denies basic human rights and increases social and environmental injustice—respect for human and ecological rights comes from the urgently needed critical and transformative education.

Huckle and Wals (2015) provided a conceptual global education for sustainability citizenship (GESC) framework as a way of critiquing the UN Decade of Education for Sustainable Development and as a suggestion for corrective action. It is a combination of ecopedagogy, global citizenship education and sustainability/sustainable citizenship. In unpacking these concepts, we find ecopedagogy to be based on Paulo Freire's critical pedagogy with a focus on real life projects that opens discourse that allows critical analysis of sustainability issues. Global citizenry education needs further clarification given the variants. Huckle and Wals (2015) draw on Shultz's (2007) radical and transformative approach to global citizenry and Gaudelli and Heilman's (2009) topology of cosmopolitan, environmental, and critical justice, global democratic citizenship education. The sustainably citizenry component is someone who acts on sustainability both in public and private with consideration for intra and inter-generational equity (Dobson, 2011; Bullen & Whitehead, 2005; Huckle & Wals, 2015). There is a commitment to ecologism (Smith 1998 cited in Huckle & Wals, 2015). There is an awareness of the connections between social actions, economic practices, and environmental processes (Bullen & Whitehead, 2005 cited in Huckle & Wals, 2015). Further Van Poeck et al. (2009, 2013, cited in Huckle & Wals, 2015) strengthened Jickling and Wals' (2007) 'Enabling Thoughts and Action' version of ESD with the addition of contemporary accounts of sustainable citizenry that include:

- the use of ecological footprints —suggesting an ecological citizenry akin to post-cosmopolitanism (Dobson 2003 cited in Huckle & Wals, 2015),
- a (re)defining and (re)affirming of established rights within a site of struggle in an extended notion of liberal environmental citizenship (Gilbert and Phillips 2003 cited in Huckle & Wals, 2015), and
- resistance citizenship as sustainability citizenship—a corrective to unsustainable practices—a civic republican approach to citizenship (Barry 2005 cited in Huckle & Wals, 2015).

Van Poeck et al. (2013 cited in Huckle & Wals, 2015) sees this cultivated version of multidimensional sustainability citizenship as a channel for potential insights into the overlapping dimensions of scale, ethical, relational, and political dimensions (Van Poeck et al. 2013 cited in Huckle & Wals, 2015). These concepts too require definition or unravelling for us to be clear from the start as to what to be attentive to.

The scale dimension, like the 'world viewing' element of the curriculum framework, calls for students to investigate other ways and means of being. It introduces students to the ways, both personal and collective, that decisions impact on the human and more than human world of others. The ecological footprint as a starting point can draw out issues of justice and sustainable citizenry appeal. Structures of power, the capitalist world economy, the rise of neoliberalism and its social, environmental, and cultural implications and contemporary crises are educational topics for consideration. Revealed through this process is that while there is private/individual and public/collective action—if only the private/individual action is a focus we are complicit in the reproduction of the status quo. Private/individual action only privatises and depoliticises very political and public issues.

Students recognise sustainability as a normative notion within the ethical dimension. With principles such as those embedded within the Earth Charter (Earth Charter Commission, 2000), a sustainable world is indeed possible. The Earth Charter's overarching themes include:

- respect and care for the community of life,
- ecological integrity,
- social and economic justice, and
- democracy, nonviolence, and peace.

Through values education strategies students can consider the juxtaposition of right and wrong, justice and injustice, rights and obligations and sustainability versus unsustainability. Given the immersion of many students within the neoliberal paradigm, it is necessary to make the individualisation and financialisation elements of neoliberalism explicit, as this positioning can be difficult to comprehend. Case studies or narratives of ways and means of living with Earth Charter principles are beneficial in revealing these dichotomies.

As elsewhere, analysis, debate, agreements, and disagreements about the environment are based on assumptions, judgements, and contentions. Expression of people's apprehensions of the world is a shared language that enables interpretation and storytelling (Dryzek 1997 cited in Huckle & Wals, 2015). Yet around the world there are other ways and means, values, and interests that sustainability and citizenship can be based on. This understanding should be prominent when teaching or learning about the construction of concepts such as sustainability and citizenship. This is the relational dimension (Van Poeck et al. 2013 cited in Huckle & Wals, 2015). Within this dimension is media education for an understanding of the part that media plays in our understanding, misunderstanding or ignorance of global society and governance, globalisation, and sustainable development. Huckle and Wals even point to education sources for upper high school students including Held and McGrew (2002) on globalisation, Dryzek (1997… see 2022 for a more up-to-date rundown) for environmental discourse and Hopwood et al. (2005) for the politics of sustainable development and how Earth Charter principles may come to fruition. The use of social media can work as a conduit for revealing how movements such as the Earth Charter have changed ways of being in addition to the potential creation of global alliances (Huckle & Wals, 2015).

Lastly the political dimension calls for a focus on environmental and social justice. Through exploring issues students can uncover systemic causes and from there consider solutions. Real or simulated involvement in real sustainability issues can build knowledge, skills, and values contributing to sustainable citizenship—giving a good grounding in discourse involving the ideas and policies of governments, corporations, political parties, NGOs, and social movements (Huckle & Wals, 2015). This assists in completing the understanding of discourses as mentioned in the relational dimension.

In addition to the points outlined above, I was watchful for good education, inclusive of First Nations' knowledges, involving the essential science literacy of equilibrium, entropy, thermodynamics, nutrient cycles, artificial element lifecycles/non cycles, energy (as outlined), interrelationships and change. Broader disciplinary subjects such as civics, critical history and legal studies on a local, national, and global scale was also in my vision. Moreover, any discourse on multigenerational ethics was of interest.

## References

Bandyopadhy, J. (1999). Chipko movement: Of floated myths and realities. *Economic and Political Weekly, 34*(15), 880–882. https://www.jstor.org/stable/4407841

Berryman, T., & Sauvé, L. (2013). Languages and discourses of education, environment, and sustainable development. In R. Stevenson, M. Brody, J. Dillon, & A. Wals (Eds.), *International handbook of research on environmental education* (pp. 133–141). Routledge for the American Educational Research Association.

Bullard, R. D. (1993). Anatomy of environmental racism and the environmental justice movement. In R. Bullard (Ed.), *Confronting environmental racism: Voices from the grassroots* (pp. 15–39). South End Press.

Bullen, A., & Whitehead, M. (2005). Negotiating the networks of space, time and substance: A geographical perspective on the sustainable citizen. *Citizenship Studies, 9*(5), 499–516. https://doi.org/10.1080/13621020500301270

Bulletin of the Atomic Scientists. (n.d.). *A moment of historic danger: It is still 90 seconds to midnight*. Retrieved June 30, 2024, from https://thebulletin.org/doomsday-clock/

CERES. (n.d.). *Fall in love with the Earth again*. Retrieved June 9, 2023, from https://ceres.org.au/

CERES School of Nature and Climate. (n.d.). *Welcome to the CERES School of Nature and Climate*. Retrieved June 9, 2023, from https://school.ceres.org.au/

Commonwealth Department of the Environment, Water, Heritage, and the Arts. (2010). *Sustainability curriculum framework: A guide for curriculum developers and policy makers*. http://www.environment.gov.au/education/publications/curriculum-framework.html

Dahr, J. (2023, October 9). Holding the fire: Indigenous voices on the great unravelling ancient wisdom with Anne Poelina [Podcast]. *Resilience*. Post Carbon Institute Retrieved December 8, 2023 from https://www.resilience.org/stories/2023-10-09/holding-the-fire-episode-2-anne-poelina/

Dobson, A. (2011). *Sustainability citizenship*. Greenhouse. https://www.greenhousethinktank.org/static/2011/sustainability_citizenship.pdf

Dryzek, J. (2005). *The politics of the earth: Environmental discources* (2nd ed.). Oxford University Press.

Dryzek, J. (2022). *The politics of the earth: Environmental discources* (4th ed.). Oxford University Press.

Earth Charter Commission. (2000). *Earth Charter*. Retrieved May 29, 2023, from https://earthcharter.org/wp-content/assets/virtual-library2/images/uploads/Earth%20Charter%20-%20SGI%20brochure%20ENG.pdf

ePoP Network. (n.d.). *ePoP platform*. Retrieved July 12, 2023, from https://epop.network/en/

Ferreira, J. G. (2003). The assessment of an environmental education Center in Kruger National Park, South Africa. *Applied Environmental Education & Communication, 2*(2), 99–105. https://doi.org/10.1080/15330150390208316

Gaudelli, W., & Heilman, E. (2009). Reconceptualizing geography as democratic global citizenship education. *Teachers College Record, 111*(11), 2647–2677.

Gaur, M. (2023, August 10). *Chipko movement in India 1973, Leader, State, Comprehensive Study*. Retrieved November 2, 2023, from https://pwonlyias.com/chipko-movement/

Gough, A., Reid, A., & Stevenson, R. B. (2024). Environmental and sustainability education in Australia. In M. Rieckmann & R. T. Muñoz (Eds.), *World review: Environmental and sustainability education in the context of the sustainable development goals* (pp. 297–317). CRC Press.

Greenall, A. (1981). Environmental education: A case study of national curriculum action. In M. Lawson & R. Linke (Eds.), *Inquiry and action in education volume 1: Papers presented at the 1981 annual conference Adelaide, SA November 11–15* (pp. 7–14). Australian Association for Environmental Education.

Held, D., & McGrew, A. G. (2002). *Globalization/anti-globalization*. Polity.

Hopwood, B., Mellor, M., & O'Brien, G. (2005). Sustainable development: Mapping different approaches. *Sustainable Development, 13*(1), 38. https://doi.org/10.1002/sd.244

Huckle, J., & Wals, A. E. J. (2015). The UN decade of education for sustainable development: Business as usual in the end. *Environmental Education Research, 21*(3), 491–505. https://doi.org/10.1080/13504622.2015.1011084

Hunter Community Environment Centre. (n.d.). *A resource hub for environmentally conscious citizens since 2004: About the HCEC*. Retrieved October 8, 2023, from https://www.hcec.org.au/about

Jickling, B., & Wals, A. E. J. (2007). Globalization and environmental education: Looking beyond sustainable development. *Journal of Curriculum Studies, 40*(1), 1–21. https://doi.org/10.1080/00220270701684667

Loures, R., & Sax, S. (2024). Amazon 'women warriors' show gender equality, forest conservation go hand in hand. *Mongabay series: Global forests*. https://news.mongabay.com/2020/08/amazon-women-warriors-show-gender-equality-forestconservation-go-hand-in-hand

Marine Education Society of Australasia. (2024). *Welcome to MESA*. Retreived July 17, 2024, from http://www.mesa.edu.au/

NSW Department of Education and Training. (2009). *Earth citizenship: A conceptual framework for learning for sustainability—draft working paper*. NSW Department of Education and Training.

Nthuku, J. S. (2018). *An assessment of the role of community forest associations in the management of Karura Forest Kenya*. University of Nairobi.

Pearson, D. (1978). *Fieldwork in environments out-of-doors*. (Masters). University of New England, NSW

Rising Tide. (n.d.). *About Rising Tide*. Retrieved November 20, 2023, from https://www.risingtide.org.au/

Schell, E. (2013). Transnational environmental justice rhetorics and the Green Belt Movement: Wangari Muta Maathai's ecological rhetorics and literacies. *Journal of Advanced Composition*, 585–613.

Shongwe, B. (1996). *Environmental education offered by Delta environmental Centre: An evaluation case study of a programme in environmental education*. (PhD). University of Johannesburg, South Africa.

Shultz, L. (2007). Educating for global citizenship: Conflicting agendas and understandings. *Alberta Journal of Educational Research, 53*(3), 245–258.

Smith, A. (1937). *The wealth of nations*. W. Strahan and T. Cadell. (Original work published 1776).

Stevenson, R. (2006). Tensions and transitions in policy discourse: Recontextualizing a decontextualized EE/ESD debate. *Environmental Education Research, 12*(3), 277–290. http://www.informaworld.com/10.1080/13504620600799026

The Green Belt Movement. (n.d.). *Our history*. Retrieved November 10, 2023, from https://www.greenbeltmovement.org/who-we-are/our-history

The Long Now Foundation. (n.d.). *The Long Now Foundation*. Retrieved December 14, 2023, from https://longnow.org/

# References

UNESCO. (2020). *Education for sustainable development: A roadmap*. UNESCO. https://unesdoc.unesco.org/ark:/48223/pf0000374802

Vilaysack, K. (2014). Community based conservation in Kenya: A case study on Karura Forest. In S. Xiaogang & R. Murakima-Suzuki (Eds.), *Final report of the international internship in Kenya: August 26–September 7, 2013* (pp. 56–64). University of Tsukuba.

Withgott, J., & Laposata, M. (2012). *Essential environment: The science behind the stories* (4th ed.). Pearson.

# Chapter 2
# Western Awakening: A Journey to Environmental Awareness

## 2.1 Introduction

To understand the development of environmental education (EE) and environmental education centres (EECs) one needs to understand the genesis of environmental awareness. Historical factors and events laid the foundations, set the accumulating building blocks in place, built the momentum, and generally shaped ecological consciousness around the globe—each locality having a unique developmental blueprint which set the genotype of EECs. This chapter looks at the period from the mid 1800s when the concept of "environment" was invoked within western culture through the immense changes brought about by the industrial revolution (Wheeler, 1975). After escaping into the past and traversing events into the 1960s with a focus on the Australian scene, and specifically within the state of New South Wales (NSW), the chapter concludes in 1949 when the NSW Fauna Protection Panel (FPP) was created along with the position of the Chief Guardian of Fauna under the Fauna Protection Act, 1948 (NSW). This position is fundamental to the subsequent development of the field studies centres (FSCs) within the NSW Department of Education—later to be known as EECs.

## 2.2 The Genesis of Environmental Awareness

In the 1800s, western civilisation was increasingly disrupted with the advancement of the industrial revolution (Merchant, 1980; Wheeler, 1975) and many people were progressively absorbed into the industrialised workforce. This involved the movement of populations from agricultural areas into the bigger urbanised areas which the industrial revolution enabled. Many people were working long hours and living and working in poor conditions brought on by the deterioration of their environment. They were experiencing the first urban environmental problems of the modern era (Wheeler, 1975), with air and water pollution from factories, and crowded urban living conditions with poor sanitation (Dunlap & Jorgenson, 2012). This alienation of people from their natural environment gave rise to the modern Western conception of "environment" (Wheeler, 1975), and also Romanticism, a counter industrialisation movement where poets such as Wordsworth and artists such as John Constable lamented the loss of the countryside in words and paintings.

The importance of nature study in children's education started to be recognised through the work of Jean-Jacques Rousseau (1712–1778), and the study of ecology and sociology emerged out of the discipline of botany (Wheeler, 1975), with Ernst Haeckel coining the term "ecology" in 1866 (Mulligan & Hill, 2001). Significant for education, and EE in particular, Patrick Geddes (1853–1932), a Scottish Professor of Botany, had an interest in effecting change in both school and tertiary education. He believed that the quality of education and the environment were closely connected. Instead of the "three Rs" he wanted to see a psychological agenda of "three Hs: hand, heart and head" (Palmer, 1998; Wheeler, 1975). His avant-garde theory was that connection with the environment would produce better learning in addition to developing a creative attitude. Influenced by Le Play (1806–1882), a foundational sociologist, Geddes saw the environment as an interaction between place, work and people—a holistic approach (Wheeler, 1975), and he developed teaching processes for hands-on experience in the environment. While Geddes' FSC was in an urban environment, his work influenced the nature study movement that grew out of the Victorian era's fascination with nature (Palmer, 1998). These developments in western society highlight the increasing disconnect from traditional holistic education and nature, necessitating the creation, or re-creation of new terms, concepts, and practices in the fields of education and environmental awareness. "Ecology", nature play and holistic education entered the lexicon and discourse.

To further set the scene on a global scale, Darwin in *The Origin of Species* (1859) posited natural selection, broadcasting the connectedness of all living things (Wheeler, 1975). This inadvertently lent support to the existing notion of western superiority—and retrospectively, provided evidence of the sociological and subjective bias within scientific endeavour (Gould, 1996). However, for many years Darwin's theory was exploited as an ideological cover for abhorrent acts of violence against humanity and humanitarian principles (Barta cited in Pascoe, 2018).

## 2.3 Explorers, Scientists and Naturalists

According to Baker Proudfoot (1979), the re-shaping of colonial Australia was influenced by three major preconceptions brought by the British. First, a fear of the unknown; secondly, a pragmatic satisfaction in combating an alien environment; and, thirdly, the romantic view of nature as a delight for the scientific observer, or just an ability to recognise the innate beauty. It was the explorers, the scientists, the naturalists, the writers, the artists—including natural illustrators—and the journalists, who, over time, prised open the consciousness of the colonisers to the beauty of Australia as ancient land (Hutton & Connors, 1999; James, 2013; Mulligan & Hill, 2001).

Australia was new territory for the discovery of flora and fauna hitherto unknown in Europe, and many eminent scientists came to explore—and some made Australia home. Joseph Banks travelled with Captain Cook; Robert Brown and Ferdinand Bauer with Captain Flinders in 1801 (Baker Proudfoot, 1979). Allan Cunningham explored Australia from 1816 to 1828 being both an explorer and, importantly, a botanist. He was the first white man to explore Pandora's Pass, the Darling Downs and Cunningham's Gap. He returned in 1837 for a brief stint as Colonial Botanist but left dissatisfied with the unsuitability of his tasks which included supervising the Government cabbage garden and an expectation that he supply vegetables for the governor's table—tasks for a grocer rather than a botanist. Charles Darwin visited Australia in 1836 (Baker Proudfoot, 1979; Perry, 1966) and his observations of the colonialising population give some insight into how a society may have exacerbated environmental degradation beyond being in an ancient and arid land and within a colonising culture.

> The whole population, poor and rich, are bent on acquiring wealth; the subject of wool & sheep grazing amongst the higher orders is of preponderant interest. The very low ebb of literature is strongly marked by the emptiness of the booksellers' shops; for they are inferior even to those in the smaller country towns of England. (Charles Darwin 1839, p 529)

William Sharp Macleay, an eminent naturalist and entomologist, migrated to Sydney in 1839 where, in 1848, he inherited Elizabeth House from his father, also a keen naturalist. He took over his father's collection and encouraged others, including his cousins William John and George, in naturalistic pursuits. Using Elizabeth House as a meeting place for like-minded naturalists, he was largely responsible for outlining and introducing an Act in 1853 to incorporate and endow the Australian Museum (Baker Proudfoot, 1979; Mulligan & Hill, 2001). The Macleays hosted naturalists such as Joseph Dalton Hooker, a pioneer plant geographer who later worked at Kew Gardens and wrote on the plants of Tasmania in 1959, and Thomas Huxley, known as "Darwin's bulldog", an English biologist specialising in anatomy (Baker Proudfoot, 1979; Curtis, 1972; The University of California Museum of Paleontology Berkeley University, 1999). There seemed to be a lot of shooting by the original naturalists with native animals being caught off-guard having never experienced such weaponry as guns (Gammage, 2011).

Ludwig Leichhardt was another early explorer and naturalist. He explored Australia from 1842 until his disappearance in 1848 (Baker Proudfoot, 1979; Smout, 1966). Depicted as having reckless courage, his legend contributed to the spirit of high adventure that became a part of the Australian identity in the late 1800s and early 1900s.

Moritz Richard Schomburgk wrote widely on afforestation and spoke of the importance of forests for their effect on climate as well as their economic value while he was the botanist for the Adelaide Botanic Gardens from 1865 to 1891

**Fig. 2.1** Manna gum—Buckland Valley, Victoria, 2012

(Baker Proudfoot, 1979; Middelman, 1976). Ferdinand von Mueller, an explorer and botanist who emigrated from Germany in 1847, became the government botanist in 1853, based in Melbourne. He added new genera to the flora of Australia and sent double specimens to Kew Gardens stating that "the plants being so much more useful in Kew than in Australia" (von Mueller cited in Morris, 1974, para 2). A prolific writer, he was largely responsible for the international recognition given to the Australian scientific effort. He was one of the first to take a scientific interest in Victoria's forests (see Fig. 2.1 for a contemporary example of Victorian forest) and saw the utilitarian value predicting timber's commercial value. He also advocated for local forest management boards to protect against indiscriminate clearing (Baker Proudfoot, 1979; Morris, 1974).

## 2.4 Acclimatisation Societies

Acclimatisation societies were popular within western scientific/naturalist communities in the second half of the 1800s with their purpose being species exchange (Lever, 1992). In Australia, "acclimatisation" was synonymous with "naturalisation" and the movement was met with "covert hostility, or at best apathy, based on the not entirely misplaced belief that the societies were acting in the interest of the privileged minority" (Lever, 1992, p. 100). The NSW Acclimatisation Society was founded in 1861, chaired by the Governor and led by Dr. George Bennett of the Australian Museum, and Charles Moore, the director of Sydney's Botanic Garden (O'Connell, 2019). The importation of exotic animals and plants was due to settlers' perception of the Australian environment as impoverished, and a yearning for the environs of home in alien territory (Wilson, 2004). The title of a paper given by George Francis in 1862 to the South Australian Philosophical Society, in the hope of establishing an Acclimatisation Society in the colony of South Australia, gives their agenda as "The Acclimatisation of Harmless, Useful, Interesting and Ornamental Animals and Plants." Whilst many useful crops were introduced to support human habitation, the introduction of rabbits, blackberries, starlings, foxes and sparrows was destructive and provoked the ire of many farmers (O'Connell, 2019). These early acclimatisation societies, closely associated with the establishment of zoos, lost momentum in the 1870s or, when confronted by the error of their ways, changed tack to support the protection of native fauna and flora (Hutton & Connors, 1999; O'Connell, 2019).

It is unfortunate that little attention was, and within the conventional western psyche is, given to First Nations agricultural practices and food sources already accustomed to the Australian environment (Gammage, 2011; Pascoe, 2014, 2024; Gammage & Pascoe, 2021), though this situation is changing (Australian Council of Deans of Science, n.d.; Pascoe, 2024).

## 2.5 Collectors, Illustrators, Artists and Writers

The amateur scientists and nature-lovers who made an income as natural history collectors/illustrators due to the demand for Australian specimens acquired an appreciation of the unique Australian ecosystems (Hutton & Connors, 1999). The Goulds—Elizabeth, a talented natural illustrator, and John, a scientist—studied Van Diemen's Land and the Swan River, WA, in the 1830s. John Gould was one of the first scientists to warn of the possible extinction of Australian mammals. In his book, *Mammals in Australia* (1863), he pleaded for protection due to their decline as a result of hunting and habitat loss. He also called for a ban on exotic flora and fauna, due to the detrimental impact of species such as cats, foxes and rabbits (Baker Proudfoot, 1979; Gould, 1863; Hutton & Connors, 1999). The decline of native species and the replacement of primeval forests by exotics was documented by William Woolls in 1885 (Baker Proudfoot, 1979).

Collecting, illustrating and documenting native species was a popular pastime, particularly amongst women with means. Collectors dispatched their specimens to colonial museums and acclimatisation societies—sometimes to Kew Gardens and British societies (Hutton & Connors, 1999). Rarely do women get credit in their own right for the work they completed. Caroline Atkinson (1834–1872), based in NSW, an author, keen naturalist and illustrator, identified new plant species, and illustrated plants and animals, sending specimens to Woolls and Ferdinand Mueller (Chisholm, 1969). Harriet and Helena Scott in NSW were natural history illustrators and accomplished amateur naturalists and collectors in the 1800s with their studies of moths and butterflies, which they illustrated for their father's book *Australian Lepidoptera and Their Transformations, 1864* (Australian Museum, 2019). These accomplishments were in appreciation of the natural environment rather than preservation of it (Hutton & Connors, 1999) yet, in addition to the art and literature of the time, it brought the uniqueness of Australian ecosystems to the public's attention.

The influence of Romanticism, which had swept through Britain in the 1800s, took on a distinctive character in Australia. The environmentalist aspect of Romanticism, often associated with counterculture movements, seemed somewhat out of place in the Australian context (Hutton & Connors, 1999). The amiability or the simplicity and pleasure of the natural, or groomed natural, environment within Romanticism was lost in early colonial Australia (Baker Proudfoot, 1979). This peculiarity may have been influenced by the immense challenges posed by the new colonial frontier, the vastness of the country, and its unfamiliar and challenging environment.

Newcomers to Australia in the nineteenth and twentieth centuries exhibited mixed feelings toward the Australian landscape. Some found it alien and monotonous, while others were charmed by its uniqueness (Baker Proudfoot, 1979; Bonyhady, 2000). Some of the complaints about Australia were the reversal of the seasons, the heat at Christmas and the trees shedding bark rather than leaves with little variability in leaf colour (Marshall, 1966). This alienation, and delight, is illustrated with realistic representation of early Australian landscapes interspersed with paintings of Australian landscapes depicting European trees—evocative of a manicured and controlled Enlightened environment (Baker Proudfoot, 1979). Granted, many of these artists would have been trained in England making adaptive techniques an issue... as well as the pining for familiarity indicative of early colonialist populations. The artists who were likely to depict Australian scenes with European trees, or less authentic depictions, were most likely artists preparing for exhibitions or copying original work—often having left the colony. Genuine portrayals were more likely from field drawings or from artists trained in the topographical genre (McLoughlin, 1999).

Colonial art underwent significant change when John Glover from the 1830s painted eucalyptus trees as the centrepiece of some of his work. However, he was also an artist who contributed paintings of the coiffured English garden kind when he painted scenes from his landscaped farm in Tasmania (Bonyhady, 2000). Artists such as Eugene von Guerard, Nicholas Chevalier and W.C. Piguenit, in searching for romantic landscapes conveyed the great forest idea whilst the big forests were increasingly being unsustainably harvested for timber for building construction, furniture and the railways (Baker Proudfoot, 1979; Historical developments: Stage 6—Timber., n.d.). Some of the authentic Australian landscapes depicted were of lush landscapes reminiscent of English Parklands (Gammage, 2011). For instance, Joseph Lycett's *View of Lake George* (1825) or von Guerard's *View of Moroit* or *Tower Hill* (1855) or indeed John Lewin's or Augustus Earle's work. Robert Hoddle's *View of Melbourne* (1847ca.) belie the stark representation of Australia

(Gammage, 2011) pointing to some of the scenes being a reminiscence of the British landscape while others being authentic depictions of some of the lush landscapes under First Nations' people's management.

Von Guerard's *Tower Hill* and *Ferntree Gully in the Dandenong Ranges* (1857) influenced colonialists preservation ethic (Bonyhady, 2000). That being said, it took a century for *Tower Hill* (1855) to gain recognition. Louis Buvelot's work (from 1864), along with Glover's, shifted the earlier negative perception of eucalyptus to a positive portrayal (Bonyhady, 2000). Arthur Streeton's painting titled *Cremorne Pastorale* (1895) depicted an environment threatened by government drilling. Drawing the attention of a wide audience, the ensuing controversy encouraged the government to cease with this line of enquiry. Piguenit's *The Flood in the Darling* (1895) is also recognised as influencing an environmental clash (Bonyhady, 2000).

There are many examples of art and literature contributing to endearing the population to the Australian environment. Other artists to depict the Australian natural environment include Conrad Martens, and Australian impressionists Tom Roberts, Arthur Streeton and Charles Conder (Fox, 2016). For literature, Ellis Rowan was a natural illustrator and an author of adventure/exploration novels and Edmund Banfield was an author (Hutton & Connors, 1999). People gained a thirst for knowledge of the bush through the literature of Banjo Paterson, Charles Harpur and Henry Lawson (Fox, 2016).

Interestingly, leaving nature in its natural state was not in the forefront of artist and naturalists minds. Photographic artists were known to carry axes on their excursions, and many of their photos provide evidence of tree/shrub clearing for the perfect view. For examples, see Charles Walters work, or Bischoff's work from the late 1800s (Bonyhady, 2000; NSW State Archives, n.d.; State Library Victoria|National Library Australia, n.d.). One such artistic excursion in the pursuit of a good view was organised at Govett's Leap Falls in the Blue Mountains by Eccleston du Faur, a prominent campaigner for environmental protection, instrumental in the establishment of Ku-ring-ai Chase National Park. It involved photographer Joseph Biscoff, Piguenit the painter, and a party of Sydney Grammar and King's School senior schoolboys engaged in clearing trees for access and to create spectacular views (Bonyhady, 2000). Artists were not alone in being dismissive or oblivious to the environmental destruction caused in the pursuit of their craft. Naturalists use of the gun, or methods of trapping and killing their quarry back in the studio was normalised practice. Indeed, J.J. Audubon, namesake of the American National Audubon Society, had a huge appetite for hunting (Bonyhady, 2000). Photographic technology that enabled the imaging of birds and other animals occurred in the late 1800s and coincided with the shift in values and advocating for the creating, strengthening and enforcement of protection measures.

So, it took time for the colonial population to develop a deep affection for the Australian environment and the colonialist essence of occupying and appropriating is still strong. Nevertheless, an exploratory and progressive spirit emerged within segments of the population, including scientists, bird-watchers, naturalists, and bushwalking enthusiasts. This spirit found expression in the literature and art of the time, contributing to a growing appreciation of the Australian landscape (Hutton & Connors, 1999).

## 2.6 Significant Changes Building Up to Federation

Many factors facilitated cultural, social, and economic change from the mid 1800s up to Federation including, in addition to the gold rush, the abolition of convict transportation, self-government, wool production, political reforms, and infrastructure and urban development (Bessant et al., 1978). The repeal of convict transportation to NSW in the 1840s accelerated immigration to offset the impact of labour shortages. There was a freer and more democratic society with the building of communities and institutions reflecting free settler aspirations (Bessant et al., 1978).

The government instigated aspirations for social improvement in the 1880s (Hutton & Connors, 1999) with the reform of compulsory, secular schooling (Barcan, 1965; Hutton & Connors, 1999). For example, the Victorian Education Act of 1872 made Victoria the first Australian colony to offer free, secular, and compulsory education to children—and all children aged 6–15 years were required to attend school unless they had a reasonable excuse (Victorian Government, n.d.). The New South Wales Public Instruction Act of 1880 made school attendance compulsory for school-aged children (6–14 years of age) for a period of no less than 70 days every half-year (NSW Government: Education, n.d.). In NSW state school fees were lowered and in the early twentieth century cancelled (Hughes & Brock, 2008). With this increased education came increased literacy and a growing, technically educated middle class. Existing societies, such as the Royal Society of NSW became reenergised. The rejuvenation also triggered new nature organisations (Hutton & Connors, 1999). These organisations offered substantial networking opportunities for activists like David Stead, von Mueller and John Sulman among other newly politically active members. They facilitated regular interactions with journalists, scientists, and politicians.

Interest specific organisations were initially established within colonies. National bodies, such as the Australian Association for the Advancement of Science was established in 1888. It included the Preservation of Native Birds and Mammals Committee, formed toward the end of the nineteenth century (Hutton & Connors, 1999).

Advances in transport and communication saw passenger railway services start operations from 1855. Between 1870 and 1880 the number of passengers grew significantly, and the length of railway track increased nearly threefold (NSW Government: Transport of NSW, 2019). Bicycles also became affordable for the average worker with a bicycle craze in the 1890s (Hutton & Connors, 1999; Pettigrew & Lyons, 1979). People were able to get out of the city to enjoy the countryside. Telegraph communication started in 1858 with a line connecting Sydney, Melbourne and Adelaide. This wire communication connected Australia to the rest of the world from 1872 (Lewis et al., 2006; Museum Victoria Collections, n.d.).

Newspaper publication started in the early 1800s in NSW with the Sydney Gazette first published in 1803, the *Sydney Morning Herald* starting in 1831 and the weekly *Geelong Advertiser* was launched in 1840. Between the 1860s and the 1950s *The Argus*, a Victorian newspaper, was active in stimulating environmental debate. *The Victorian Review* (1879–1886), a monthly publication, was also important in publicising environmental issues (Bonyhady, 2000). Australia's first daily newspaper to distributed to all colonies, the *Daily Commercial News and Shipping List* went to print in 1891 (Womersley & Richmond, 2001; Wikipedia, n.d.). These advances in transportation and communication together with the event of an eight-hour working day, won in 1856, allowed the time and means for leisure activities such as outdoor recreation and interest group pursuits.

## 2.7 The Seeds of Environmental Awareness in Australia

It took considerable time for people to fully grasp that the world's resources were not limitless. The consequences of industrialisation, such as the loss of natural environments, wildlife, and the degradation of human habitats, were not immediately apparent to everyone (Hutton & Connors, 1999; James, 2013; Mulligan & Hill, 2001). Some individuals are still to reach this realisation.

The combination of abundant and rich resources, along with the harsh reality of survival, contributed to the prevailing cornucopian mindset in the new colonial frontier of Australia. Here, the boundaries of knowledge and western civilisation converged with the challenges of an expansive and unknown territory (Hutton & Connors, 1999). For First Nations' people there was contestation of ancient songlines.

> As there can be no law unless its jurisdiction is defined, to bring the bush under the rule of British law lines needed to be drawn on it marking what was what and who owned it. The Aboriginal lines—the songlines, and the lines separating one clan's land from another's—were invisible to Europeans and did not show up on their maps, any more than Aboriginal laws showed up in their legal system or their worldview. The new maps performed the essential legal—and probably psychological—function of filling in the savage emptiness. (Watson, 2014, p. 278)

There was limited awareness that European farming methods were ill-suited for the Australian climate and soils (Perroni, 2018). Many settlers did not foresee that the initially favourable farming conditions they encountered when acquiring land would eventually deteriorate (Fox, 2016). Furthermore, as the Crown Land Act of 1884 (NSW) came into effect, some farmers resorted to overstocking smaller areas in an attempt to offset rising costs, further straining the land's resources. The proliferation of rabbits compounded the environmental challenges (Fox, 2016). The 1890s saw a decade-long depression (Bessant et al., 1978), and the turn of the century brought a severe drought (Fox, 2016). These events, alongside ecological and human disasters highlighted in the Royal Commission on Western Lands in 1901, including sandstorms and the growth of non-edible scrub, shed light on the fragility of the environment (Skilbeck, 2021). All these changes contributed to the conception and growth of environmental awareness in Australia.

## 2.8 Advocacy and Legislation

### 2.8.1 Scientific Activity

The first colonialist calls for protection of species and specific environments came from the scientists who had seen firsthand the uniqueness of the Australian environment and its susceptibility to degradation given its ancient and arid fragility (Hutton & Connors, 1999). Scientific activity and interest were strong from 1850s onward. Hardworking amateurs were able to have an impact although professional biologists were making the distinction between theoretical and experimental biology and populist natural history [the beginning of discipline compartmentalisation and academic characterisation] (Hutton & Connors, 1999). Natural history associations, both in cities and regionally, grew from the mid 1800s and had both scientific and keen amateur members. From this diverse grounding, the first preservation/conservation activists emerged. By the 1880s, concern for environmental preservation among scientists and naturalists was increasing with urbanisation and industrial/pastoral expansion (Hutton & Connors, 1999). The populist nature of field naturalist clubs and societies was instrumental in advocating for the preservation of flora, fauna, and land reservation (Hutton & Connors, 1999). The rise in conservation sentiment and the increasing popularity of naturalist clubs were driven by enhanced public transportation access and the widespread availability of bicycles to the general public.

Colonial presses were keen to report on the activity of scientific societies and many societies, with talented writers, published articles in their local newspapers. Indeed, *The Argus's* proprietor and editor, Edward Wilson, was a founding member of the Acclimatisation Society (1861), an offshoot of the Zoological Society of Victoria (1857–1861). There was a string of natural history writers at *The Argus* with Donald McDonald contributing nature articles from 1881. He influenced Charles Barrett, an ornithologist and a Thoreau enthusiast, who wrote nature articles. Barrett and two other friends called themselves "*The Woodlanders*" after Thomas Hardy's 1887 novel, and their weekender "Walden Hut" after Thoreau's novel of 1854. The Woodlanders influenced Alec Chisholm who became a journalist, an ornithologist like Barrett, and one of the first conservation activists. Chisholm contributed feature articles in Sydney and Brisbane (Hutton & Connors, 1999). In NSW Caroline Atkinson, natural history illustrator and author, and Stead, one of the first conservationists in NSW, often contributed to the *Sydney Morning Herald* (Hutton & Connors, 1999; XA). Stead also wrote a "Nature Notes" column for the *St George Call* which contributed to the popularity of bushland (James, 2013).

## 2.8.2 Bird and Animal Protection Legislation

The Animals Protection Act 1879 (NSW) was "to encourage the importation and breeding of Game not indigenous to the Colony of NSW and also to prevent the destruction of Native Game during the breeding season" (para. 1). It was specifically for the protection of deer, antelopes, five exotic and over 25 native bird species in a closed season with provision for the gazettal of areas for bird and animal reserves. Scheduling changes were announced through the Government Gazette with the Colonial Secretary authorised to include or remove species from the schedule. This legislation seems to have been enacted in conjunction with the dedication of the National Park, later the Royal National Park, which was established specifically for recreation and use by acclimatisation societies in 1879 (National Parks, Australia: New South Wales, 1979). The Act ensured the sustainability of hunting (Boom et al., 2012).

In the 1870s there had been an enquiry into the health of living conditions in Sydney, specifically the inadequacy of its sewage disposal (Pettigrew & Lyons, 1979). There was a very high child mortality rate and extreme overcrowding. Urban reformers were troubled not only by the lack of space and fresh air in the tenement housing but by the lack of public recreation space provided in the planning process. While John Lucas, a member of the Legislative Assembly, was advocating for public space in 1879, the NSW Zoological Society formed with an agenda of introducing and acclimatising songbirds and game animals (Pettigrew & Lyons, 1979). It was in this climate that the National Park was established under Trust management for recreation purposes. The trust was authorised to "establish ornamental plantations, lawns, gardens, zoological gardens, a racecourse, facilities for cricket and other lawful games, a rifle and artillery range, other amusements and accommodation houses" (National Parks, Australia: New South Wales, 1979, p. 94). So, when the National Park was set up there were two views of conservation that were not easily differentiated: the utilitarian focus on future exploitation as per the acclimatisers; and conservation for perpetuity. While the Park was an expression of conservation for perpetuity, it was easily compromised and initially there were many grand plans and ventures that did not fit with the agenda for national parks as we know them today (Pettigrew & Lyons, 1979).

Issues raised by individuals led to the earliest animal protection campaigns within organisations such as the Royal Society of NSW, which was established in 1866 after earlier scientific associations had become defunct (Hutton & Connors, 1999). It was the Zoological Society of NSW (1879), closely associated with acclimatisation, which convinced the NSW government to pass the Birds Protection Act in 1881 (Hutton & Connors, 1999; Royal Zoological Society of New South Wales, 2016). Deer and antelope were no longer protected. Table 2.1 outlines initial successive bird and animal legislation in NSW (1879–1903) which saw a decrease in exotic animal protection and successive increases in native bird and animal protection. During this time the progression of preservation, protection, conservation and recreation continued with Ku-ring-gai Chase National Park dedicated in 1894

**Table 2.1** Initial development of bird and animal protection legislation in NSW (1879–1903)

| Year | Act | Protection | Reason/ Mechanism for protection/ significant changes |
|---|---|---|---|
| 1879 | The Animals Protection Act 1879 (NSW) | In a closed season: Protection for: Deer, antelopes Five exotic bird species Over 25 native bird species | Breeding of exotic game. Prevent destruction of native game in the breeding season. The gazettal of areas for bird and animal reserves. Colonial secretary authorised to include or remove species from the schedule. |
| 1881 | Birds Protection Act (NSW) | For 5 years: Protection for: Imported birds (six species), and Songbirds (25 native and exotic species) After 5 years: Protection in the closed season for: Scheduled Imported Native (over 13 species) Songbirds. | Preserves where birds were completely protected. No protection for deer and antelope. |
| 1893 | Bird Protection Act (NSW) | For 5 years: Protection for: Imported birds (13 species), and Native birds (>12 species) After 5 years: Protection in the closed season for: Imported birds (13 species), and Native birds (>35 species) | Repealed the 1881 legislation. Maintained the practice of superior protection for exotic species. |

(continued)

## 2.8 Advocacy and Legislation

**Table 2.1** (continued)

| Year | Act | Protection | Reason/ Mechanism for protection/ significant changes |
|---|---|---|---|
| 1901 | Birds Protection Act (NSW) | All birds protected in the closed season: Imported birds (13 species), and Native birds (>47 species) | Repealed the 1893 legislation. No superior protection for exotic species. |
| 1903 | Native Animals Protection Act (NSW) | Protection until Jan 31, 1905 then in the closed season: Red kangaroo Wallaroo Native bear (koala) Wombats Platypus Echidna or native porcupine Sugar gliders Flying opossums | Amended the Birds Protection Act, 1901 allowing the Colonial Secretary to enact, alter, or annul periods of absolute protection for all scheduled or specific species, and if annulled decree the closed season. |

Boom et al. (2012), Hutton and Connors (1999), National Parks, Australia: New South Wales (1979), Royal Zoological Society of New South Wales (2016)

(National Parks, Australia: New South Wales, 1979). Establishment was encouraged by du Faur, the colonial surveyor and geographer, who enjoyed exploring this area (Hutton & Connors, 1999). Other colonies followed suit—in South Australia Belair National Park was declared in 1891, and Victoria's Wilson's Promontory National Park and Western Australia's John Forrest National Park were declared in 1898.

Early conservation efforts aimed to address the deficiencies and poor enforcement of state laws governing the feathers and bird skin industry often went unheeded. These endeavours marked some of the earliest conservation campaigns (Hutton & Connors, 1999). While the campaign initially emphasised the value of birds as pest insect predators to garner support from an anthropocentric perspective, it also highlighted the impending threat of native species loss.

International pressure mounted when the International Ornithologists Conference convened in London in 1905, urged the Federal Government[1] to protect Australian birds. Of particular concern was the international oil trade that involved boiling

---

[1] Under the *Commonwealth* of Australia Constitution Act 1900 only limited and specific powers were delegated to the Federal Government. These powers were generally where uniform national laws were deemed beneficial such as those for trade, immigration, communication and national transport (Hutton & Connors, 1999). Powers for all other considerations remained with the states. However, over the years the Federation has gained substantial financial and legal leverage over the states. For example in 1942 where the Federation took control of income tax (Hollander, 2009). This two levels, three when you consider local government, have provided checks and balances for

penguins and mutton birds for oil production (Hutton & Connors, 1999). Various organisations began collaborating across state boundaries.

In 1908, both the Linnaean Society of NSW and the Australian Ornithologist Union independently decided to coordinate efforts. They advocated for Commonwealth legislation to complement existing state protection laws, an end to the introduction of exotic birds, and the establishment of a 'bird day' in schools (Hutton & Connors, 1999). In a significant move, representatives from all ornithological societies met with Prime Minister Deakin in 1908. Deakin suggested that it would be more effective to encourage women not to wear bird feathers and recommended new laws for regulating exports, a matter he pledged to discuss with the customs minister (Hutton & Connors, 1999).

### 2.8.3 The Rise of Wildlife Preservation Societies

Due to the failure of the initial deputation, there was a renewed push for protection at a state level and the agenda was expanded to include native mammals. The campaign was doubled in 1909 and public education strategies were improved (Hutton & Connors, 1999). Additionally, two groups that had an important impact on future outcomes were formed: The Gould League of Bird Lovers, with a motto of "education is more potent than legislation in furthering the cause of conservation," was established in Victoria in 1909 and then spread to NSW and Queensland and later WA, and the Wildlife Preservation Society of Australia was established in Sydney.

David Stead joined The Field Naturalists' Society of NSW (which replaced the Natural History Association of NSW [1887]) in the 1890s (Hutton & Connors, 1999; National Library of Australia, n.d.), with a self-developed interest in natural history sparking his concern for preservation (Hutton & Connors, 1999). He tried to educate others through articles published in the *Sydney Morning Herald* and through advertising, to establish an organisation for the purpose of wildlife preservation (XA). He knew he needed to gain support, to "get the general rank and file" within the community on side to effect change (XA). He had little success in motivating the Society to participate in advocacy until 1909. In protest over an affair that had become public, the Swedish Consul-General, Count Birger Mörner, resigned from the Royal Zoological Society and transferred his support to Stead. They called a public meeting to form the Wildlife Preservation Society of Australia (now the Australian Wildlife Society [2013]) with over 50 people joining up, many professionals from the Zoological Society (Hutton & Connors, 1999; James, 2013).

Members of the Society's first council included some naturalists, some politicians, one of the Warragamba Walkers, the secretary of the Royal Zoological Society, a founding member of the Royal Australasian Ornithologist's Union in

---

the complicated area of environmental protection from time to time (Hollander, 2009). Additionally, Federal funding over the years has been fundamental to ESE.

Melbourne and the Chairperson of the Fisheries Board and the National Park Trust (James, 2013). They looked at how they could get a better wildlife administration process. They submitted proposals for legislation for a service responsible for the administration of legislation pertaining to the protection of plants and animals that provided an effective law enforcement team (Strom, 2017). They wanted free ranging guardians with one of their functions being to educate people (XA). They also wanted a list of pest species and the protection of all unlisted native species (James, 2013).

Educating the public was an important function of the Australian Wildlife Preservation Society. Education strategies included lantern lectures and pamphlet distribution. Their advocacy was far reaching. They contacted famous actresses to persuade them to stop wearing osprey plumes and organised lectures by prominent explorers. They educated on the economic and scientific value of wildlife (James, 2013).

In support of bird protection, in 1910 another deputation met with the Customs Minister, Frank Tudor, who promised to do what he could including amendment of the Tariff Bill to prohibit certain exports (Hutton & Connors, 1999). In the war years of 1914–1918, protection of birds and conservation of native forests were among the commissioner's concerns when new protectionism and tariff policy was reviewed by the Commonwealth.

In 1918 the Birds and Animals Protection Act (NSW) replaced the Bird Act of 1901 and Native Animals Act 1903. Birds and mammals, not all animals, were protected unless scheduled. There was provision for open seasons on protected species and closed seasons on scheduled species. Additionally, sanctuaries could be declared. (Fox, 2016; National Parks, Australia: New South Wales, 1979). Police, and honorary rangers conferred by the minister, were tasked with the responsibility of regulating the legislation (James, 2013; Strom, 2017). The number of unprotected animals fell severely while only ten bird species lost their protected status (National Parks, Australia: New South Wales, 1979).

### 2.8.4 Species Destruction

To give an idea of the destruction of species, under the Pasture and Stock Protection Act 1880 (NSW), kangaroos and wallabies were declared noxious. Approximately three million bettongs and potoroos (rat-kangaroos) were shot for bounties from 1883 to 1920. Three of these species are now extinct though some of this demise may be due to the introduction of the red fox (Boom et al., 2012; Short, 1998). From 1884 to 1914 there were at least 460,000 bounties paid for the heads of the brush-tailed rock-wallaby which is now listed as vulnerable and is not found in most of its former range (Boom et al., 2012; Croft, 2005; Short, 1998; Short & Milkovits, 1990). More than four million possum and 60,000 wallaby skins were up for sale in New York and London in 1906 (Troughton cited in Boom et al., 2012). In NSW, marsupials were taken off the list of noxious animals in 1932 yet:

While the kangaroo industry's current focus is upon the "sustainable use of wildlife," the history of attitudes towards kangaroos as "pests" is so deeply and widely entrenched that it is impossible for the industry to meet welfare standards (Boom et al., 2012, p. 17)

Other animal losses include over 2.5 million mutton birds sold through Launceston markets from 1904 to 1908 according to the Tasmanian Commissioner of Police (Hutton and Connor 1999), and 5.8 million Australian furs traded from the period 1919–1921 according to the American Museum of Natural History (Hutton & Connors, 1999). In 1921–1922 there were many scientific and commercial collecting expeditions and there was great fear of species extinctions (Hutton & Connors, 1999). During the Depression, some governments rescinded protection policy amidst great protest from wildlife groups. Queensland rescinded the protection of koalas and possums in 1927, resulting in the deaths of over one million possums and half a million koalas in 1 month (see Fig. 2.2 for a contemporary photo of a koala in the bush). In 1930, NSW, after much protest, restricted licences to the unemployed but the result was more than 800,000 possum deaths in 2 months (Hutton & Connors, 1999). Victoria at this time outlawed the selling of skins from interstate.

The thylacine, also known as the Tasmanian tiger, met its demise on September 7, 1936. While it was not our first extinction and certainly not our last, its extinction

**Fig. 2.2** Koala in a casuarina, North Stradbroke Island/ Minjerribah, April 2022

is well-documented. There were instances of deliberate misinformation about the nature and numbers of this unique species (Paddle, 2000), all in the pursuit of short-term economic gain. Furthermore, science struggled, and failed, to capture and counteract the fearmongering in time to save the species (Paddle, 2000).

Robert Paddle's (2000) comprehensive study, focusing on the social construction of scientific knowledge and an exploration of accurate observations versus scientific perceptions influenced by popular mythology surrounding the Tasmanian Tiger, revealed significant insights. He raised important questions about the intellectual, historical, and moral education of scientists, particularly regarding their ability to stay informed and respond effectively to such situations. He also questioned our society's intellectual, historical, and moral education, highlighting our vulnerability in believing untruths rather than adhering to the facts (Paddle, 2000).

Paddle's thesis underscores the repercussions of neglecting our intrinsic connection to the broader natural world, resulting in detrimental consequences such as self-deception and a diminished sense of empathy for others (Paddle, 2000). However, the issue of resource allocation within the ecological realm has also posed challenges. It often fluctuates in response to economic conditions and is seldom accorded a central role within the framework of economic rationalism.

### 2.8.5 Management in Flux

Due to weak governmental regulation in the late 1800s, public management within state structures needed to be strengthened (Hutton & Connors, 1999). In particular, positions in science and conservation were insecure. For example, in 1873 Ferdinand von Mueller, lost his directorship of the Melbourne Botanic Gardens due to management wanting an ornamental rather than scientific focus, but remained the government botanist until his death in 1896 (Morris, 1974). In Brisbane, in 1893, after a public outcry, F.M. Bailey was reinstated with 60% of his former wage as the colonial's botanist and director of Brisbane Botanic Gardens. He had been retrenched in a wave of government cutbacks. In 1893, NSW director-general of forests, after being enticed 3 years earlier from South Australia with a higher salary, had his position abolished as part of economic savings (Hutton & Connors, 1999). Charles Lane-Poole, an experienced forester, who was proceeding to train forestry staff and had drafted a forest bill for WA that was regarded as an exemplar by his peers, was forced to resign in 1921 because of disagreements over vested interest leases and concessions. He became Forest Advisor and Inspector-General of Forests for the Commonwealth Government, but he continued to criticise state governments for land settlement practices that resulted in clear felling of native forests and their lack of support for sustainable forestry (Hutton & Connors, 1999).

## 2.8.6 Progressivism

Progressivism emanating from the United States started to influence Australia in the mid to late 1800s. George Perkins Marsh's (1864), *Man and Nature; or, Physical Geography as Modified by Human Action*, a book about the destructive effects of human domination of nature from the earth's crust to the atmosphere, was disseminated in the Australian press in the 1860s (Hutton & Connors, 1999). Progressivism is a political and social reform movement (Milkis, 2019) that has had an ambiguous definition. However, in progressing human beings need to be connected to the land and their history on and in it (Dewey, 1916). Progressivist reform introduced planned use and renewal of native forests for the benefit of humanity (Hutton & Connors, 1999). Yellowstone, the world's first national park, was declared in 1872, the same year that the word "conservation" was initially applied with its contemporary meaning of "conserving scarce natural resources." It was also the year of the inaugural Arbor Day (Wheeler, 1975, p. 6). Ferdinand von Mueller in Victoria, using the arguments of utility, ethics, aesthetics and public health, advocated for practical measures such as the establishment of local forest boards for preservation (Hutton & Connors, 1999). von Mueller's arguments were put before the Royal Society in NSW in 1876 by Reverends Clark and Woolls. Several colonies conducted or promised numerous royal commissions to investigate timber conservation, yet these efforts yielded no tangible results (Hutton & Connors, 1999).

With British demand for Australian hardwoods increasing, given the arrival of the railway age, colonies had to address the issue. South Australia, with few forest resources, led the way. Progressivism nourished the notion that a country's greatness could be gleaned from its resources, thus supporting wise use and sound scientific management (Hutton & Connors, 1999). It gave backing to the establishment of national parks and it saw the establishment of forestry departments within states. Yet, even when systematic management with rational assessment of forest resources was set up, bureaucrats were fighting the embedded interests of various forest users (Hutton & Connors, 1999).

For example, in 1894, the conservator of forests in South Australia complained to the Australian Association for the Advancement of Science that he had a "lack of power to defend the forests against parochial interests" (Hutton & Connors, 1999, pp. 51–52). Institutional arrangements within Australia's political structures were influenced at the start of the 1900s by a combination of the new Federation, advocacy groups and the rise of Labor Parties (Hutton & Connors, 1999). Yet, new state-level structures started to be influenced by the resources industries they set out to control, and some groups, particularly utilitarian foresters, found themselves continuing their calls for effective management practices. There was a Forestry Royal Commission in NSW in 1908 (Our forests, 1908), subsequently followed by the Forestry Act 1909 (NSW). In 1915 the NSW branch of the Australian Forest League was established (Hutton & Connors, 1999) and in 1916 NSW established the Forestry Commission of NSW through the enactment of the Forestry Act 1916

[NSW] (Forestry Corporation, 2016), which replaced the Forestry Act 1909 [NSW] (Carron, 1985).

Mastery of resources was also part of progressivism and encompassed engineering projects such as dams and irrigation that contributed to environmental degradation (Hutton & Connors, 1999). Yet, the social base of this movement involved more than technocratic utilitarianism; it encompassed moral benefit, commitment to nature protection and anti-materialist values as well—it incorporated Romanticism's love of the land (Hutton & Connors, 1999, p. 20): "Progressivism produced the rational and aesthetic enjoyment of nature that united and inspired Australia's first-wave environmentalists."

Moves to protect the environment were couched in anthropocentric rather than ecocentric terms, a situation that continues to today, (see Fig. 2.3 for a graphic depiction of anthropocentrism versus ecocentrism).

Economic usefulness, national efficiency goals, recreational value and public health benefits of sanitation were the arguments put forth by first-wave conservationists in an effort to protect birds, preserve native ecosystems, and enact pollution controls in the late 1800s and early 1900s (Hutton & Connors, 1999). Yet, while utilitarianism was a substantial part of the early environmental movement support, groups contended for the preservation of native forests on ecological grounds and for intergenerational equity, but governments often gave into vested interest for short-term gain. When institutional arrangements are made, their intent is vulnerable to redirection under the influence of powerful resource industries (Hutton & Connors, 1999).

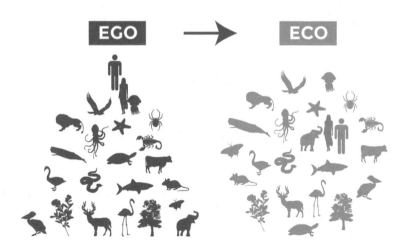

**Fig. 2.3** Anthropocentric vs ecocentric graphic. Attribution: IDA Projekt, CC BY-SA 4.0 https://creativecommons.org/licenses/by-sa/4.0, via Wikimedia Commons. The image of a woman is an addition to the original image

## 2.8.7 Protection of Native Flora

Protection for birds and animals tracked a long, arduous and convoluted path, but safeguarding of native plants took a lot longer. It was 1927 before the Wild Flowers and Native Plants Act (NSW) came into effect. It repealed some of the sections of the Local Government Act 1919 (NSW) and the Railway Act 1912 (NSW), and certain other Acts, to sanction wildflower and native plant protection (National Parks, Australia: New South Wales, 1979). Native plants were able to be proclaimed as protected, via gazettal notification, throughout the state or in specific regions, for a limited or unlimited period. Native plants and wildflowers within the jurisdiction of the Forestry Commission were also protected, ensuring protection on all Crown land. Protection was also covered for species taken on private property if unauthorised by the landowner. The minister had the authority to issue licences, with conditions, to pick protected wildflowers or native plants for scientific purposes. Significantly, in addition to police and honorary rangers being given regulatory responsibilities, the Act provided for authorised public servants associated with land administration, and landowners and lessees, to also enact regulatory consequences (Mulligan & Hill, 2001).

The segregation/segmentation of species for protection, separated from the total ecology of the landforms—the habitat, the niche, exemplified in the legislation—was also embodied in the administration, with the Wild Flowers and Native Plants Protection Act, 1927 (NSW) managed by local government rather than the Chief Secretary's Department,[2] as with the Birds and Animals Protection Act, 1918 (NSW). Additionally, the legislative history illustrates which species were viewed as important. First, concern concentrated on exotic birds and animals, and native birds; followed by some native mammals; followed in 1918 by most animals, other than those listed in the schedules; followed by protected plant species. Unfortunately for reptiles and native rodents, they were excluded from the legislation.

## 2.8.8 The Rise of Ranger Leagues

In response to the 1927 legislation regarding rangers, Walter Trinick, the Sydney branch manager of *The Argus* newspaper (Melbourne) and an early conservationist, formed a Ranger League and encouraged public servants to join. He had his

---

[2] The Chief Secretary's Department was a vestige from colonial days that was abolished in 1975 (it was revived on two occasions of no consequence to this story). Some of the responsibilities of the Department included: (1) the protection and welfare of the Aboriginal population; (2) Lord Howe Island; (3) gaming, racing, betting and poker machines; (4) theatre regulation and licensing; (5) censorship and regulation of literature, art, films and plays; (6) custody of the great seal; (7) electoral matters; and finally, and significantly for this story, (8) environmental protection and fisheries. According to Strom (2017), this Department had a history steeped in early colonialism. It had retained characteristics of parsimony and conservatism.

assistant, Dot Butler, an avid bushwalker and conservationist, write to all the editors of house journals in the public service departments to promote the League—they consequently attracted 700 members (Mulligan & Hill, 2001). In 1928, John Tipper became the organisation's founding president (Gowers, 2002). The Ranger League's objective was to provide protection, including bushfire protection, and preservation of bushland around Sydney as per the Wild Flowers and Native Plant Protection Act 1927 [NSW] (Gowers, 2002; James, 2013), and foster an interest in nature (Mulligan & Hill, 2001). Some of the achievements of the Ranger League were an annual exhibition of wildflowers from the Sydney region, having the cabbage tree palm, common in the Illawarra, declared a protected native species, and to have the term "wild flowers" replaced by "native flowers" within the official nomenclature (Mulligan & Hill, 2001).

Unhappy with the response of government to protect animals, the Wildlife Protection Society of Australia stepped up political pressure by establishing a militant auxiliary (James, 2013). David Stead and John Tipper, as part of an organising committee, called Sydney's honorary rangers to a conference in 1929. Additionally, society councillors talked on radio, answered inquiries via phone, and wrote articles to publicise the plight of native animals.

In 1930 an amendment to the Birds and Animals Protection Act, 1918 (NSW), the Birds and Animals Protection (Amendment) Act, 1930 (NSW), extended the remit of legislative enforcement for animal protection. In addition to police and honorary rangers, public school teachers, conditional purchase inspectors, people associated with state forests through connection or employment with the Forestry Commission of NSW, stock inspectors, Department of Agriculture field officers, Fisheries inspectors, and Metropolitan Water Sewerage, and Drainage Act 1924 (NSW) rangers were included as rangers due to their vocation (Strom, 2017).

The ranger system was problematic. Administration of both the native plant and animal legislation was severely understaffed with each having a part-time administrator within their respective offices (Strom, 2017). Proposed rangers had three challenges: they had to know they were eligible, take it upon themselves to become informed about the legislation, and be prepared to take on the difficult, tricky, and brave—given the lack of support—task of enforcing the legislation. According to Strom (2017), rangers were treated like they were a burden and were often criticised. However, with assiduous police officers and enthusiastic rangers there was an effect on protection with many rangers doing great work in educating the public, and by the interwar period, with greater movement around the country, people were starting to regulate their own habits (Strom, 2017).

### 2.8.9 Bushwalkers and Urban Reformists

From the mid to late 1800s onwards, there were four distinct groups trying to effect change in conditions for preservation, conservation and recreation of and in the natural environment—each with distinct areas of interest. They had similarities, which assisted their causes, and differences that set them apart. These groups were the scientists, the naturalists, the bushwalkers and the urban reformists (Hutton & Connors, 1999).

Bushwalkers wanted natural environments for adventure, solace and sanctuary, and the urban reformists wanted to improve their urban environment and wellbeing (Hutton & Connors, 1999). These various agendas, responding to both natural and urban environmental loss, tended to be anthropocentric. Both these groups had an urban membership base, a distinction from the scientist, naturalist and acclimatisation groups which radiated out into the countryside. These distinguishing factors are important in understanding the disunity within advocate groups which shaped the events within this history. Bushwalkers focused on the national park campaigns while the urban parks and playground groups, and related organisations, focused on the public health of cities, generally through the reserve of urban parkland and heritage. Despite these differences, however, there was considerable cross-over (Hutton & Connors, 1999).

While exploring the natural environment had its roots in colonial adventure, the extent to which explorers were assisted, through well-worn First Nations' paths and guidance, must be acknowledged (Hutton & Connors, 1999).

> The idea of the colonial adventure—of expanding the boundaries of western knowledge and accomplishment through great feats of human endurance—galvanized the entire community in the three decades preceding World War I. One did not have to be an imperialist to be affected by the romance and bravery of the genre of adventure tales, fictional and non-fictional, which flooded the Australian markets in these years. (Hutton & Connors, 1999, p. 63)

### 2.8.9.1 Bushwalkers

The thirst for adventure, exploring new environs yet to be surveyed, and testing one's mettle in the great outdoors, inspired many bushwalkers and bushwalking groups (Hutton & Connors, 1999). By the 1890s, Sydney had a population of half a million people and a direct rail link to the (Royal) National Park. The national parks were popular places. The Warragamba Walking Club, open to both sexes, was founded in 1895 (XA). It conducted walking tours utilising roads and tourist lodging for long excursions (Hutton & Connors, 1999).

There were many others inspired to explore off the beaten track. Myles Dunphy was one of the most proactive supporters of national parks in the 1900s (Hutton & Connors, 1999; James, 2013). Dunphy established the (men only) Mountain Trails Club in 1914 to explore the countryside. Club members tested their self-reliance and resourcefulness, developing bushcraft and designing specialist bushwalking/camping equipment along the way (Hutton & Connors, 1999). The club's membership was by invitation only and they embraced mateship and democratic values. Many of the small membership (no more than 20 in the first 14 years) had architectural, engineering, artistic and business skills. Dunphy, an excellent draftsman, produced many detailed maps thoroughly covering the topography of the countryside, naming features with First Nation place names, poetic and standard terms (Hutton & Connors, 1999).

The Mountain Trails Club was instrumental in organising popular recreational walking groups. By 1922 there were three new bushwalking clubs. With the increased popularity of bushwalking, the Mountain Trails Club established the Sydney Bush Walkers in 1927. Open to the general public, its goals were to encourage an appreciation, and preservation tendencies, of the natural environment (Hutton & Connors, 1999). Bushwalking and hiking became even more popular during the Depression years of the 1930s (Strom, 1979). There were so many bushwalking clubs by 1932 that a NSW Federation of Bush Walking Clubs was formed to work together for conservation of "primitive" areas (Strom, 1979). Additionally, in 1933, The National Parks and Primitive Areas Council (1933–1962), a conglomeration of bushwalking clubs including the Mountain Trails Club, Sydney Bush Walkers, Bush Tracks Club and Coast and Mountain Walkers, (National Parks, Australia: New South Wales, 1979) were exploring and documenting sites to be set aside as parks and primitive areas (Strom, 1979).

Paddy Pallin, an original member of the Sydney Bush Walkers Club (Hutton & Connors, 1999), at a loss during the Depression, started making lightweight camping equipment (James, 2013). The manufacture of gear such as tents made out of airship fabric—japara silk tents, framed rucksacks, purpose-designed camping cook ware, lightweight, easily packed sleeping bags and the famous Paddy Pallin blanket roll and gunnysack (Strom, 1979)—made hiking much more practicable.

### 2.8.9.2 Networking—Shifting the Conservation Agenda

Of course, a plethora of people and events contributed to the immense and wideranging tapestry of changes that evolved into the initial manifestation of EE, action, legislation and regulation. My purpose here is to pick up enough threads to outline the foundation of EECs in NSW.

Community groups such as the Gould League of Bird Lovers, and general protectionist groups generated by the first preservationists and conservationists, were partially institutionalised due to their associations with government and industry (Hutton & Connors, 1999). These groups shifted Australian consciousness and taught the value of the forests and fauna. Success within the political system was slow and sometimes retrograde but resulted in the progress of new institutional arrangements—national parks, forestry departments, nature study in schools, and governance within urban public health, parklands and town planning (Hutton & Connors, 1999). Political strategies employed by people trying to effect change were public meetings, lobbying, and educating the general public. Debating and focus on conservation issues were opened up within the imperialist hegemony (Hutton & Connors, 1999). Once the initial bureaucratic regulatory structures had been set up, scientist involvement in the movement waned (Hutton & Connors, 1999).

The networking within the preservation, conservation, recreation groups in Sydney and beyond was complex and wide-ranging and very important in shifting the conservation agenda. For instance, David Stead was also an active councillor in the Naturalists' Society of NSW and authored many books about fish, crustaceans, trees and rabbits. He was the general editor of the Shakespeare Head Press Australian Native Books (Walsh, 1990; Webb, 1998). Constance Le Plastrier, an educationalist and author, joined the Council of the Naturalists' Society of NSW. She had an interest in botany and in 1933 wrote *The story of our plants: First Steps in Australian Botany* (Webb, 1998). She introduced one of her students, Thistle Harris, to the Naturalists' meetings. Harris became a member of the Club and a teacher, educationalist and naturalist teaching biology and nature study (Kass, 2018) at Sydney Teachers College from 1938 to 1961. She wrote many books on Australian native plants and nature study and was an active conservationist, who formed a partnership and later marriage with Stead (James, 2013). Harris also became an active member of the Wildlife Preservation Society of Australia. She joined the Australian Forest League and took an interest in the Junior Tree Wardens, the League's younger membership. She compiled and edited *The Junior Tree Warden* first published in May 1937, was the Honorary Secretary of the Illawarra-Bankstown Federation of Junior Tree Lovers in 1935 and the Honorary Editor of the *New Horizons in Education* from 1940 to 1944 (Webb, 1998).

Stead had made a living working/consulting in the fish industry, so these networks were also strong. He, with others advocating for wise fisheries, influenced a voluntary decrease in the number of trawling vessels and the Fisheries and Oyster Farms Act 1935 [NSW] (James, 2013). Stead was on the Town Planning Committee, which had delegates from affiliated community groups such as the Australian Forest League and the Parks and Playground Movement (James, 2013). He was the president of the reformed state branch of the Australian Forest League in 1930 and he was also on the committees of many other groups such as the NSW Geographical Society (James, 2013), the Aquarium Naturalists, the Gould League of Bird Lovers, and the Royal Zoological Society of NSW. Additionally, he was an Honorary member of the American Fisheries Society and a Fellow of the Linnaean Society of London (Walsh, 1990).

### 2.8.9.3 Urban Reformists

There was a big cross-over of town planners and architects into conservation, including Arthur Small and Walter Burley Griffin. Burley Griffin, within a breakaway Town and Country Planning Institute, maintained links with the Town Planning Committee, through Small and Stead. Similarly, Stead and Small were involved with the Parks and Playgrounds Movement that had been set up by Charles Bean in 1930 and included affiliated delegates such as suburban progress associations and local Tree Lovers' Leagues (James, 2013). Bean was the well-known Australian official historian and war correspondent in the First World War but before this, he had worked on the *Sydney Morning Herald* and often wrote on the topic of progress in town planning. He had experienced what was happening in America, Canada and England while travelling in his position as London Correspondent for the *Sydney*

*Morning* Herald (James, 2013). In 1939 Bean was also a member of the NSW National Fitness Council which conducted camps that included nature study. The NSW State director of Physical Education became the Fitness Council's Executive Officer. Marie Blyes and Paddy Pallin were on the Council's Youth Hostel Committee. Pallin was also involved in the Scouts and the Federation of Bushwalkers (James, 2013). Blyes belonged to several bushwalking clubs and was a Federation of Bushwalking Clubs Secretary and editor of its annual journal (James, 2013). These are just a sample of the extensive network of urban reformists.

### 2.8.10 Parks and Playgrounds Movement

The Parks and Playgrounds Movement, established in 1930, followed an earlier Playgrounds Association that had some prominent women members (a journalist and a Premier's wife, for example) and some members of the Town Planning Association which had been established in 1913 and included a Parks and Playground Committee (James, 2013). According to Bean, the little free space that was available in urban areas was there by chance, and, unfortunately, many children were playing in dust or damp because of poor drainage and sewage (James, 2013). Park advocates wanted play spaces near children's homes and schools with sandpits, trees shelter and space. The planners wanted greener suburbs and Sydney to be encircled in a green belt. Promotion of their cause included articles and presentations on child welfare. They met with governing bodies to acquire land and sometimes furnished the land with play equipment. The Parks and Playground Movement represented men's, women's and children's sport and recreation, town planning, health bodies, biological, conservation and historical societies, progress associations, private and co-opted members. There were more than 80 groups by 1937 (James, 2013).

### 2.8.11 Another Catalyst for Change: The Role of Allen Strom

Integral to this story is another significant figure, Allen Strom, whose knowledge, skills and networks had been developed over many years. Strom, a member of the Wildlife Preservation Society of Australia assisted the FPP, the Caloola Club and conservation in general, particularly with education, in achieving wins throughout this history.

Strom had a rich history threaded through the fabric of the education institutions within NSW. He had won a Sydney Teachers College Scholarship and majored in Arts and Crafts/Industrial Arts for primary and junior high school teaching (1932–1933). In 1934 he taught at Newtown Demonstration School (Strom, 2017) where he met Ern Hodgkins, a member of Dunphy's Mountain Trails Club (Strom, 1979). He then taught at Yanco Agricultural High School and Narrandera High School (1934–1936) where he was challenged to keep up with students who had a keen interest in biology, geology and the outdoors. In 1937 he returned to Sydney to teach at Enmore Activity School with the intention of furthering his learning in nature study (Fox, 2016). Enmore had been set up as a pilot school for "slow-learning adolescent" boys after Dr. Harold Wyndham, the Department of Education's first research officer, and the Director General, Ross Thomas, became concerned for both intellectually advantaged and disadvantaged students. The school was an experiment in practical education, with a program of three-years' duration encompassing a cross-curricular ethos.

At Enmore, Strom met Jim Thompson, a physical education teacher who later became an area director able to give Strom access to the Western Sydney Area for EE purposes. He then became reacquainted with Ern Hodgkins who introduced him to Dunphy and other members of the Sydney Bushwalkers Club. Dunphy and Moutrie Cullen, a teacher and shores studies specialist, encouraged Strom to study mineralogy/geology and general science at Sydney Technical College (now the University of Technology, Sydney). He completed the course in 1943 (Fox, 2016), graduating with a distinction, before being transferred to Canterbury Boys High School the following year (Strom, 2017). Subsequently Strom spent a lot of time exploring the bushland in the Sydney region (Strom, 1979). In 1946 Strom was a field officer with the National Fitness Program and the first education officer at the Australian Museum. From 1947 until he took up his position as the Chief of the FPP, Strom was a lecturer in arts and crafts at Balmain Teachers College (Strom, 2017).

### 2.8.12 The National Fitness Camps

In 1939 two hundred Enmore Activity School students were the first to participate in the National Fitness camping movement at Broken Bay. Gordon Young, a Canadian expert, was brought to Australia by the NSW Education Director General to set up a progressive program in physical education in line with the national fitness agenda (Fox, 2016) which emerged from concern for the health of the urban child. Jim Thompson, a Gordon Young convert, suggested Enmore students would be a perfect cohort for the fitness camp. About the same time, Strom had met Keith Ingram on a Forest League field trip. He was a teacher from Parramatta with a nature study focus. Strom organised for Ingram to participate at Broken Bay. While the students participated in physical activity pursuits they also had the opportunity to connect with nature at a deeper level as a tent had been set up with activities to stimulate curiosity in nature study. "Looking back on it now, what impressed me was that here was an opportunity in this wonderful place to relate these kids, who had been so starved of nature, directly to the natural systems" (Strom cited in Fox, 2016, Ch. 4, para. 15).

Strom became the Honorary Field Studies Officer for the National Fitness Council in 1940. This involved setting up trails for activities, providing resources and instructions for staff and searching for new camping sites for the growing camping scheme (Fox, 2016). Together with Jeanne Golding, Strom produced six fieldwork handbooks in 1942 with the approval of the Minister of Education, Clive Evatt. The Physical Education Branch of the NSW Department of Education began Fitness Camps, providing public secondary school camps and holiday camps. Without specialist teachers such as Strom, the nature study curriculum within the school and holiday camps would have relied on a visiting teacher's interest in nature study.

### 2.8.13 The Caloola Club

A Walkers Club was established with the Principal of Enmore Activity School, Syd Lenehan, and Strom selected keen students who had previously experienced the Fitness Camps as participants. Initially supported by the National Fitness Council (Fox, 2016), the new club engaged in exploration trips and conservation education programs (Strom, 1979). Activities included camping, bushwalking, canoeing, cycling and courses in naturecraft as well as coaching in geology, botany and ecology (Fox, 2016). Other young people subsequently became involved and, in 1945, the Walkers Club became the independent Caloola Club (to climb high), an expeditionary society (Strom, 1979). They explored, studied, surveyed and documented many terrains around the state. The father of one of the Enmore students who had been involved in one of the fitness camps, Bill Dingeldei, offered his motor garage office as a meeting place (Fox, 2016) and reconditioned a truck into a bus for club transportation (Fox, 2016; XA). The Undersecretary of the Chief Secretary's Department, Cec Buttsworth, assisted in securing vehicle registration, with tight restrictions, for the Caloola Club. (Fox, 2016).

### 2.8.14 Education: Museum and Preservice Teacher Education

It was through his work in the National Fitness Camping Program that Strom became an Education Officer at the Australian Museum and established the Museum Education Service in NSW (Strom, 1979)—taking education to the students. With Harris, a biology and nature study lecturer (Kass, 2018) at Sydney Teachers College, Strom organised joint camps for students from Balmain and Sydney Teachers College.

These 2-week camps were held at Sydney Teachers College's residential property on the Nepean River at Castlereagh late in the summer holidays. In the first week approximately 13 students were taught primary school nature study including programming, preparation, activities, follow up and revision. Study included:

> … geology from the surrounding country to the river pebbles; what makes the soil; the typical plant; plant adaptations and where they live; the plant ladder of life; an ant colony; bird beaks and what they catch and eat; the Brushtail Possum; Aborigines' food supply; resource

use of the floodplain farmers; soil erosion; the cycle of erosion; making "fossils;" story of the river; river life zones; life about a river pebble; an insect collection; an aquarium of river life or pond life and what the rules are for keeping it alive and more topics. (Fox, 2016, Ch. 5, para. 23).

The sixth day involved a student presentation of work and a collective reflection on values. In the second week of the camp a group of 30 primary school students participated in the camp, taught by the training teachers (Fox, 2016). These camps ran from 1956 to 1958 when Strom became the Chief Guardian of Fauna for the FPP.

Education was seen as a pre-requisite to effective legislation, given that without public opinion laws seemed to carry no gravitas. This was noted to be the case for conservation legislation, particularly about fauna and flora protection (Morrison cited in Pizzey, 1992). Education was also seen as necessary for effective action to counteract some of the detrimental effects of human habitation on the natural environment (Morrison cited in Pizzey, 1992). Furthermore, environmental protection legislation did not happen without electoral advocacy (Strom, 2017), yet the government's priority was the economy.

## 2.9 Nature Study

While environmental awareness, action, and legislation progressed slowly, nature study and science, through object lessons, were incorporated into the curriculum in the second half of the 1800s (Barcan, 1965). The NSW Public Instruction Act 1880 changes saw an introduction of history but a new emphasis on "the three Rs". Changes in 1905 saw literature and history become more prominent in the curriculum. Object lessons were largely replaced by nature study in the primary school curriculum after 1905 when the curriculum liberalised further.

According to Dorothy Kass (2018), nature study was supposed to encompass connection to and understanding of the environment. Kass, from her historical studies, found that nature study was integral to the New Education ideas of the late 1800s and early 1990s which incorporated, "learning by doing" and "self-activity"—new ideas at the time. This new nature study was to involve the handling and observation of nature—immersion in nature through investigation with the teacher as a fellow investigator and guide. It involved experiments and class discussion, the utilisation of the local environment and the establishment and utilisation of school gardens. Furthermore, it involved "correlation" with other subjects, which were also to be reformed within the ideas of New Education (Kass, 2018). Yet, according to Kass, many educational historians found New Education to be "pluralistic and sometimes contradictory" (2018).

## 2.9.1 Nature Study Practice and Contention

In Australia, about the late 1800s, nature study was used to challenge the rote learning approach to teaching elementary science. Teachers were intended to encourage curiosity and delight (Kohlstedt, 1997). Views on the relationship of science to nature study were questioned as it was difficult to stimulate learner interest without affecting the objectivity of the subject matter (Kohlstedt, 1997). There was far less argument about the validity of nature study as science in Australia compared with the United States where there had been accusations of sentimentality and fear of feminisation of the education system (Kohlstedt, 1997). There was also resistance from overburdened teachers, social scientists concerned about a lack of systemisation and science educators wanting to boost their work and status. Notably, Kohlstedt (2010) states that there was a backlash of positivist, masculine insistence on disciplinary science training that contrasted with nature study. However, in NSW, Peter Board, Director and Under-secretary of the NSW Department of Public Instruction from 1905 to 1922 (Wyndham, 1979), found nature study appropriate for young people and suitable in forming the foundations needed for later scientific study (Kass, 2018). Nature study persisted in Australia and had a resurgence after the Second World War (Kohlstedt, 1997).

Nature study was still practised in Australia and New Zealand well after it was out of favour in most United States schools (Kohlstedt, 2010). A School Nature Study Union was established in England in 1903 and persisted until 1994, even though nature study had faded in Britain (Kohlstedt, 1997). In later years this Union recruited from many countries including Australia (Jenkins & Swinnerton, 1996).

## 2.10 Progress and Conflict from the 1930s

The 1930s saw:

- the gathering of support for a Greater Blue Mountains national park and a snow country national park within NSW and Victoria via the promotion and development of proposals by Dunphy and the National Parks and Primitive Areas Council,
- support for the conservation of wildlife via the Wildlife Preservation Society, with Stead at the helm,
- support through private funding to publish material about conservation affairs,
- calls for a national parks service based on the United States Service established in 1916,
- calls for effective planning by people such as Burley Griffin and groups such as the Parks and Playground Movement, and
- concern for the issue of soil erosion. (Strom, 1979, p. 66)

There was conflict between those who understood the aridity and carrying capacity of Australia and those who aspired to prosperity and unlimited growth, a debate that continues. In 1921, Griffith Taylor, a member of Scott's Antarctic expedition of 1909, had his textbook banned by the Western Australian education department due to his assessment of the limitations to growth given the ancient aridity of the land (Hutton & Connors, 1999). National and imperial rivals, with Commonwealth funding, organised a tour by Vilhjalmur Stefansson, who had advocated human settlement of the Arctic lands. Stefansson discredited Griffith, pronouncing Australian deserts capable of sustaining large human and animal populations (Hutton & Connors, 1999; Stefansson, 1924).

In the 1930s, as a result of catastrophic soil erosion in the Victorian Mallee, there were constantly blocked roads, railways and stock water channels. Sand sheets buried fences and croplands (Pratley & Rowell, 1980). Major agricultural policy was developed in response to man-made disasters rather than as a proactive process (Pratley & Rowell, 1980). In a report to the House of Representatives Standing Committee for Long Term Strategies, titled *Australia's Population "Carrying Capacity": Two Ecologies* (1994), Professor Jonathan Stone's presentation emphasised the central issues of Australia's arid geology and anomalous fertile area. He argued persuasively, with strong scientific community support, for a "sophisticated neo-Malthusian schema, far more compassionate than the original." (p. 17).

In 1938, the Soil Conservation Act (NSW) led to the establishment of the Soil Conservation Service. An initial survey of NSW found that 48.3% of the 48 million hectares in the Central and Eastern Divisions were affected to a considerable degree by soil erosion (Strom, 1979). The urgent need to combat erosion benefited the fight to conserve forests as vegetation stabilises the water catchments, particularly in the upper, steeper regions (Strom, 1979). Yet disagreement still existed and in the late 1970s destruction of forests on steep slopes, including clear-felling, and overstocking on cleared peripheral lands continued.

After a bushwalker campaign, Garrawarra Primitive Reserve, now the southern extension of the Royal National Park, was reserved in the 1930s. This was the first dedication since Ku-ring-gai Chase in 1894. Bouddi Natural Park, New England National Park and Morton Primitive Reserve were also declared in the 1930s (Strom, 1979).

In 1944, the Kosciuszko State Park Act (NSW) was legislated. It was the first park to be permanently reserved and could only be revoked by a special Act of Parliament. There was no security for other parks until the enactment of the National Parks and Wildlife Service Act 1967 [NSW] (National Parks—Australia: New South Wales, 1979; Strom, 2017). Previously, national parks, state parks and historic sites were managed by individual Trusts. These Trusts were under the authority of the Parks and Reserves Division of the Department of Lands. They could be revoked at any time and were subject to the Mining Act 1906 [NSW] (National Parks, Australia: New South Wales 1979).

## 2.10.1  Crosbie Morrison and His Conservation Critique

Crosbie Morrison's address to the Australian Institute of Political Science in Canberra in 1950, titled "Education for Conservation," provides some understanding of where along the nature study—conservation education spectrum Australia was situated. Morrison was a Victorian naturalist with a background in zoology who became an influential spokesperson for conservation (Pizzey, 2000). Morrison's address spoke of the importance of narrative and interrelationships of disciplines when it comes to educating about our environment. As an example, Morrison talked of the direct and indirect ways that humans have detrimentally affected Australia since European settlement. The two direct effects he named were the destruction of native flora and fauna and the introduction of exotic species. The indirect effects were seen as numerous, but an example was given of erosion caused by a species imbalance due to the disruption of natural limits caused by human impact—for example, birds relocating due to cars near their habitat, causing their insect diet to increase in number and thus dieback of tea-tree and, consequentially, erosion (Morrison cited in Pizzey, 1992).

Morrison argued that formal education was essential to give conservation its proper emphasis, and press and radio could then have a stronger impact. Morrison considered nature study a necessity as one needs to know it to understand it. He found that children were naturally curious but that this could be lost in the focus on "the three Rs". Morrison, had observed nature study in schools in all states and found that while all asserted they were in favour of natural history, it was not to interfere with the academic curriculum (Morrison cited in Pizzey, 1992).

Morrison noted the effectiveness of the Gould League and, in NSW, the Junior Tree Wardens. The Forest League's Schools Branch worked closely with the NSW Department of Education and in the 1920s, through the Horticultural and Nature Study Bulletin, they distributed information on nature study, wildflowers and forests (James, 2013). They developed forest songs for children and ran school literacy, art and photographic competitions. Practically, school nurseries were developed for plant propagation, and the Forestry Commission's Gosford State Forest Nursery ran forest camp schools. The League, with Harris, revived Arbor Day, advocating for a School Forest Bill and school forest plantations (James, 2013; Webb, 1998). They also supported school wildflower gardens. During the Second World War years, the number of Junior Tree Wardens exceeded 200,000 (James, 2013) and following the 1936 School Forest Areas Act (NSW), 17 schools had their own school forest. From the mid to late 1930s, members of the Schools Branch of the Forest League, including Harris, advocated for revision of the nature study syllabus. They wanted a participatory, field-based program that tapped into students' need for "intellectual adventure" (James, 2013, p. 117).

Effective nature study teachers were those who were involved with conservation—it was part of their life. The majority of teachers did not have the necessary knowledge as they did not have a personal interest in the subject. As Morrison argued, teachers do not like to teach what they do not know (cited in Pizzey, 1992).

Biology was introduced as a school subject in the 1920s (Fawns, 1988). While biology was included within general science for the lower secondary years, and some schools provided biology, botany, or agricultural science beyond the intermediate standard, this was limited by the number of facilities and available qualified staff. Soil erosion was taught within social studies (Morrison cited in Pizzey, 1992).

In the past, tertiary education and teacher education were seen as the core of the problem with a lack of natural history content within the curriculum. Due to the huge influx of biological knowledge, specific disciplines such as zoology and botany emerged in the mid 1920s—much of the old natural history material was omitted to make way for genetics and cytology within the three-year university Bachelor's degree. The nature study side of zoology was not taught, with the systematics handed over to the museums (Morrison cited in Pizzey, 1992). Field zoology was rare. Field research generally picked up pace in 1957 when the Commonwealth Science and Industrial Research Organisation's (CSIRO) Wildlife Research Division, established in 1949, started concentrating on native animals after initially focusing on the rabbit epidemic (Morrison cited in Pizzey, 1992; Strom, 2017). Nevertheless, study of living organisms in the environment in the 1950s was deficient. Morrison pointed out the importance of studying animals in their natural habitat, particularly in Australia, where there is so much to learn given the uniqueness of the environment. Nature study was included in teacher education courses but these courses were only designed to teach how to teach. Students were learning the nature study content and how to teach it at the same time, and thus were not as confident as when the knowledge was already in place (Morrison cited in Pizzey, 1992).

Morrison saw recreational education as effective but largely teaching to the converted (Morrison cited in Pizzey, 1992). There were many publications associated with bushwalking clubs and naturalist societies—newsletters/bulletins and journals. Morrison was the editor of *Wild Life* from 1934 to 1954, a popular natural history magazine. On a Sunday evening, he hosted a 15 min radio show of the same name that entertained a national audience (Pizzey, 1992). This show lasted nearly 28 unbroken years (1938–1966). This was in addition to the presentation of a children's radio club on 3DB broadcast through the 1940s–1960s (National Film & Sound Archive: Australia, 1988).

## 2.11 The Significance of Science

Science within Western culture, the education system, and within environmental and sustainability education (ESE) and EECs plays a major role. EE extends beyond conventional disciplinary borders. It encompasses fundamental values and perspectives that may differ from or challenge broader scientific concepts linked to societal continuity (Hart, 2002). In 1983, the strong connections between EE and science education were stated by the United Nations Educational, Scientific and Cultural Organisation (UNESCO) who drew on the synergies of critical thinking and skills such as observing, analysing, and hypothesising (Dennis & Knapp, 1997).

## 2.11 The Significance of Science

Environmental educators shared Dewey's aspiration for nature study to be interdisciplinary and to permeate the curriculum (Dennis & Knapp, 1997).

> The real remedy is to make nature study a study of nature, not of fragments made meaningless through complete removal from the situations in which they are produced and in which they operate. When nature is treated as a whole, like the earth in its relations, its phenomena fall into their natural relations of sympathy and association with human life, and artificial substitutes are not needed. (Dewey, 1916, p. 277)

Dewey found nature study (the antecedent of ESE) to appeal to students' natural curiosity about the world around them. He found nature an appropriate context for learning about science (Dennis & Knapp, 1997; Dewey, 1916). While ESE covers a holistic range of subjects, the utilisation of FSCs to learn about science was one of the reasons field studies were enabled through the bureaucracy of the NSW Department of Education. Nevertheless, Western science has a history marked by both achievements and controversies and is thoroughly embedded within the Western industrial complex.

Building upon the scientific and philosophical revolution of the seventeenth century, the Enlightenment era from the late 1600s through the 1700s witnessed remarkable advancements in reasoning and the continued evolution of "science" from its foundations in natural philosophy (Edelstein, 2010). Nourishing the Enlightenment from a western perspective was René Descartes' mind-body dualism (Skirry, n.d.) and Francis Bacon's theory that nature should be studied methodically and harnessed for human benefit (Bacon, 1620; Descartes, 1641; Edelstein, 2010). This period of intellectual transformation was nurtured by pivotal elements, notably the groundbreaking invention of the printing press and the gradual establishment of an expansive distribution network and the proliferation of literacy aligned with a gradual reduction in its prohibitive cost (Helmers et al., 2021; Munck, 2000). There was a significant rediscovery and translation of enduring philosophical masterpieces authored by luminaries such as Plato and Socrates (Edelstein, 2010; Machlup, 2014) and a disconnect from Aristotelian influenced abandonment of philosophical study (Edelstein, 2010). The Enlightenment encompassed, individualism, human progress through education and empiricism, and a skepticism of traditional authority (Edelstein, 2010; Bristow, 2017).

Locke's theory of natural rights and social contract further underscored the Enlightenment's significance for human relationships with nature. It suggested an individual's entitlement to benefit from natural resources (Locke, 1689; Munck, 2000). The Enlightenment era's profound shift in thinking set the stage for intense societal and intellectual transformation, shaping the course of modern thought and scientific inquiry that feeds technological advancement—which in turn contributes to advancing scientific inquiry.

It is important to acknowledge that the idea that science is value-neutral and objective that is conveyed within formal science teaching as part of the hidden curriculum (Apple, 1990) is unhelpful in moving toward an ecocentric paradigm. The limitations of the hypothetico-deductive reasoning methodology need further critique within school science, so the students understand that instances of assumptions and simplifications, limited scope, incomplete knowledge, confirmation bias, limited causality, practical limitations and struggles to accommodate new knowledge do occur. Science does not take place in a vacuum and has its own sociology. The history, nature, and practice of science is bound up in the complexity of purposes, practices and processes of economic, expansionist practices (Guardiola-Rivera, 2010). Power structures within the science fraternity, and society in general, and the history of these power struggles are important in understanding the nature and practice of science.

For science education, a subject much maligned, the addition of these factors can bring an authenticity, connection and deep understanding. In today's world there is even greater disconnect given the technological world we live in (Robinson, 2010). There is importance in bringing the excitement of discovery that science has to offer back to the teaching of science. Indeed, industry connected STEM (science, technology, engineering, and mathematics) education, has been developed to invigorate teaching and learning in these disciplines and increase student numbers due to a lagging uptake of vocations related to these disciplines (Anderson, 2020; Idin, 2018).

Further, the commercialisation of scientific research, indeed all research, plays a part in the disenchantment of science (research)—the power play within these structures that silences and amplifies different scientific fields depending on economic value. For instance, there is a lot of energy and resources directed at reverse genetically engineering animals such as the thylacine, woolly mammoths, the bucardo goat and other extinct animals while invasive species, land clearing, and hydrology changes are causing extinctions and putting living species existence at jeopardy (Invasive Species Council, 2023; Lean, 2023a, b). Australia has, for some time, had one of the highest rates of animal extinction in the world—the highest for mammals (Invasive Species Council, 2023). Philosophical questions related to reverse genetic engineering such as those relating to identity and authenticity and what we owe or do not owe to vanishing species are in addition to the complicated environmental debates (Lean, 2023a). I think factors like these lead to a certain disenchantment of science.

Why are these factors important to an understanding of our environment? Because our environment, or our western understanding of our environment, is essentially based on science whether the environment is natural or built or anywhere along that binary spectrum. The environment is incredibly complex and multifaceted while at the same time highly political from a human perspective. The impacts on nature, and justice within humanity given the environment's integrate connection to the wellbeing of human society, both intra and inter-generationally, and visa versa, are significant.

The history of science underscores the intersection of power, money, and the development of scientific knowledge, often hindering avant-garde discoveries for financial gain. This fracture, to some extent, can be attributed to scientific illiteracy, which, if addressed, could empower individuals to navigate the world with a deeper understanding (Simard, 2021).

Efforts to reform science education, making it more engaging and accessible, have been ongoing, with initiatives such as Bill Bryson's (2003) book *A Short*

*History of Nearly Everything* and Bryan Cox's interactive television experience *Stargazing Live*. However, the focus on science education can be dated back to at least the 1950s and the explosion of school science education programs in the wake of the Russian Sputnik program and the competition that entailed (Steeves et al., 2009). While STEM education has aimed to enhance science teaching, environmental perspectives sometimes receive inadequate attention (Gough, 2021). ESE, and EECs, can serve as conduits for systems thinking, breaking down disciplinary barriers and fostering a profound connection with our world.

The human tendency for quick fixes often impedes sustainable progress. For instance, experiments on fungi's impact on plant shoot growth, yielding inconsistent results, led to the continued widespread use of fertilisers, showcasing the allure of immediate solutions (Simard, 2021). In Suzanne Simard's *Finding the Mother Tree* (2021), the intricate relationships within nature challenge the limitations of the scientific method. Simard's experiences in forestry reveal the slow acknowledgment of symbiotic tree relationships through Mycorrhiza due to competition, profit-driven motives, and a reductionist scientific approach. This struggle to comprehend nature's complexities echoes in works like Peter Wohlleben's *The Hidden Life of Trees* (2015), Collin Tudge's *The Secret Life of Trees* (2005), and Peter Tompkins and Christopher Bird's *The Secret Life of Plants* (1973). The difficulty in disseminating such knowledge and fostering change raises questions about societal aversion to change—and the power structures and intrinsic nature within science itself.

Simard's insights from the "Mother Tree Project" highlight the transformative potential of recognising trees, plants, fungi and all non-human agency—much learnt with grateful acknowledgement from First Nations' knowledge and understanding. Her call to turn to the intelligence of nature itself and the philosophy of treating all living creatures and the world's gifts as of equal importance underscores the need for a paradigm shift (Simard, 2021).

This exploration of the history, nature, and practice of science is highly important in the context of EECs. It forms part of the fabric within which Western education, ESE, and EECs are woven. Conscientisation of the history, nature, and practice of science within ESE and EECs is crucial in discovering, and enabling others to discover, new ways of being, and ESE and EECs are an appropriate learning ground for science with all its complexities.

## 2.12 Green Awakening: The Rise of Environmental Awareness Post-WWII

Science forms part of the narrative in the rise of environmental awareness. But it is to the changes from the end of World War II and continuing into the 1960s that are the focus in this section. During this period, society began to recognise the profound impact of human activities on the environment, leading to a burgeoning movement that sought to address and mitigate these effects. There were concerns about air, water, and land pollution, land clearing, erosion and salinity. The direct and indirect environmental impacts of war such as flooding as a direct cause of the destruction of river and drainage systems was a major problem (Hamblin, 2012).

According to Strom (1987), the development of a major community drive in environmentalism began in the 1950s and 1960s. People were seeking a better world after the First and Second World Wars. Car ownership was more common so people were able to leave the stresses of the urban environment and access the great outdoors without relying on public transport. Television joined radio and the print media in broadcasting conservation topics, and conversely promoting consumerism. The environmental coverage started to make an impact with stories of environmental vandalism. People wanted something done about resource management and the "horrors of the urban living" (Strom, 1987). There was a global upsurge in awareness and interest in environmental issues and growing membership of the significant number of conservation groups nationally and in NSW, many formed with the support of the FPP, which also expanded before becoming part of the NSW National Parks and Wildlife Service.

On a global scale Rachel Carson (1962) and those in the Club of Rome were prominent in raising the alarm about environmental degradation and limitation (Meadows et al., 1972) and contributing to the individual and collective recognition of developing and cumulative problems regarding some of the effects of overpopulation and industrialisation on a not so cornucopian world. The publication of Carson's *Silent Spring* in 1962 brought environmental issues to the forefront of public attention. It highlighted the dangers of pesticides, particularly DDT, to the environment and wildlife and played a pivotal role in the environmental movement leading to increased awareness and regulation of pesticides. Carson was the beginning of our understanding that conservation is not entirely compatible with the foundational values underpinning scientific and technological knowledge (Robin, 1998).

However, it is back to the years after the Second World War with its greater political possibilities that this narrative needs to focus. While the war held the conservation movement back through loss of workforce and resources, there was greater conservation advocacy dynamism, possibly to compensate for the losses of war (Strom, 1979; XA). Before the war's end, in 1944, the "fur trade" was putting pressure on the NSW Chief Secretary's Department for a regular open season for some species, particularly possums. This put pressure on the Department because, while possums were a nuisance, they also attracted public sentiment. They had higher emotive significance than kangaroos (Kingsmill pers. comm. quoted in Strom, 2017). It became known that there was a practice of fur-trade royalties funding wildlife authorities in Victoria and Tasmania. Gerald Kingsmill, from within the Chief Secretaries Department, visited Victoria and consequently an interdepartmental committee was setup to investigate fauna protection administration for NSW. This exploration into conservation of wildlife included high level representation from the Chief Secretary's Department, the Department of Agriculture and the Australian Museum. The consequential legislation, the Fauna Protection Act, 1948 (NSW) was, in hindsight, seen as progressive and received praise both nationally and internationally, according to Strom (2017). The consequences of the Fauna Protection Act, 1948 (NSW) will be a thread to be picked up in Sect. II where we explore the early context and development of EECs within the NSW Department of Education.

## 2.13 Conclusion

This detailed context specific to Australia and particularly NSW is outlined in order to set the scene and understanding of environmental awareness and the environment in which EECs were able to be established and developed in NSW. Developments and characteristics within other states, territories, counties and countries will be dependent on their geographies, topographies, histories, cultures, and setting within the colonialist development of the globe. Accordingly, these contexts craft the backdrop for unique ESE representation. It is impossible to set the intricate and multidimensional scene for each depiction. Yet, given the shared colonialisation experience of many sites of EECs there may be lessons to learn from this developing close analysis of the NSW system.

From this portrait of the settlement and development of early Australia, it is evident that the conception and development of environment awareness in NSW had a long and rocky road. Throughout, there was a basic tension between the exploration and understanding of a new and exciting land with novel and unknown species and terrains on the one hand, and the rapid destruction of this unique environment (evident in the loss of cultures, species, deforestation, massive erosion issues and the introduction of invasive animals and plants), on the other. All of this occurred at a time of enormous change in society as technology gained momentum. In this period, four distinct advocacy groups emerged, generally working in unison—the naturalists, scientists, bushwalkers and urban renewalists. The underlying tension between economic developers and environmental sympathisers often treats these different groups as a monolith, as if all those concerned with the environment are the same. But even from these early days, the differences among "environmentalists" and the emergence of these distinct groups lay the groundwork for debates that shaped the formation of the EECs in important ways. These commonalities and tensions crystallised in the creation of the Act that enabled the immediate precursor to the EEC, the Fauna Protection Act, 1948 (NSW).

## References

*Animal Protection Act* 1879 (NSW). Retrieveed June 30, 2017, from https://www.legislation.nsw.gov.au/acts/1879-6a.pdf

Anderson, J. (2020). The STEM education phenomenon and its impact on school curriculum. *Curriculum Perspectives, 40*(2), 217–223. https://doi.org/10.1007/s41297-020-00107-3

Apple, M. (1990). *Ideology and curriculum* (2nd ed.). Taylor & Francis.
Australian Council of Deans of Science. (n.d.). *Indigenous science*. Retrieved July 26, 2024, from https://www.acds.edu.au/teaching-learning/indigenous-science/
Australian Museum. (2019). *The Scott sister's collection*. Retrieved January 7, 2019, from https://australianmuseum.net.au/learn/collections/archives/scott-sisters/
Bacon, F. 2014). *Novum organum: Or, true suggestions for the interpretation of nature* (J. Devey Ed.): Project Gutenberg. (Original work published 1620).
Baker Proudfoot, H. (1979). Strange new world. In W. Goldstein (Ed.), *Parks and wildlife: Australia's 100 years of national parks* (pp. 36–45). National Parks and Wildlife Service.
Barcan, A. (1965). *A short history of education in New South Wales*. Martindale Press.
Bessant, B., Blackmore, W., Cave, P., Cotter, R., Mellor, S., & Waterson, D. (1978). *Australian history: The occupation of a continent*. Eureka Publishing.
*Birds and Animals Protection (Amendment) Act* 1930 (NSW). Retrieved June 30, 2017, from https://www.legislation.nsw.gov.au/acts/1930-12.pdf
*Birds and Animals Protection Act* 1918 (NSW). Retrieved June 30, 2017, from https://www.legislation.nsw.gov.au/acts/1918-21.pdf
*Birds Protection Act* 1881 (NSW) No. 41a. Retrieved June 30, 2017, from https://www.legislation.nsw.gov.au/acts/1881-41a.pdf
*Birds Protection Act* 1893 (NSW). Retrieved June 30, 2017, from http://classic.austlii.edu.au/au/legis/nsw/num_act/bpao1893n16239/
*Birds Protection Act* 1901 (NSW). Retrieved June 30, 2017, from http://classic.austlii.edu.au/au/legis/nsw/num_act/bpa1901n26220/
Bonyhady, T. (2000). *The colonial earth*. Melbourne University Press.
Boom, K., Ben-Ami, D., Croft, D. B., Cushing, N., Ramp, D., & Boronyak, L. (2012). 'Pest' and resource: A legal history of Australia's kangaroos. *Animal Studies Journal, 1*(1), 17–40.
Bristow, W. (2017). Enlightenment. In E. N. Zalta (Ed.), *The Stanford encyclopedia of philosophy*. Retrieved, https://plato.stanford.edu/entries/enlightenment/
Carron, L. T. (1985). *A history of forestry in Australia*. Australian National University Press.
Carson, R. (1962). *Silent spring*. Fawcett.
Chisholm, A. (1969). Atkinson, Caroline Louisa (1834–1872). In *Australian Dictionary of Biography* (Vol. 3), (online 2006). http://adb.anu.edu.au/biography/atkinson-caroline-louisa-2910/text4183
Croft, D. (2005). Kangaroos maligned: 16 million years of evolution and two centuries of persecution. In M. Wilson & D. Croft (Eds.), *Kangaroos myths and realities* (3rd ed., pp. 17–31). The Australian Wildlife Protection Council.
Curtis, W. (1972). Hooker, Sir Joseph Dalton (1817–1911). In *Australian dictionary of biography* (Vol. 4). Retrieved July 12, 2018, from http://adb.anu.edu.au/biography/hooker-sir-joseph-dalton-3789
Darwin, C. (1839). Narrative of the surveying voyages of his majesty's ships Adventure and beagle, between the years 1826 and 1836, describing their examination of the Southern Shores of South America, and The beagle's circumnavigation of the globe (V 3). In J. van Wyhe (Ed.), *The complete work of Charles Darwin online* (2002). Retrieved February 25, 2025, from https://darwin-online.org.uk/content/frameset?itemID=F10.3&viewtype=side&pageseq=548
Dennis, L. J., & Knapp, D. (1997). John Dewey as environmental educator (Editorial). *Journal of Environmental Education, 28*(2), 5. https://doi.org/10.1080/00958964.1997.9942817
Descartes, R. ([1641] 2013). *Meditations on first philosophy: With selections from the objections and replies*. Cambridge University Press.
Dewey, J. (1916/2009). *Democracy and education: An introduction to the philosophy of education*. MobileReference.com. https://ebookcentral.proquest.com/lib/newcastle/detail.action?docID=543077
Dunlap, R., & Jorgenson, A. (2012). Environmental problems. In G. Ritzer (Ed.), *The Wiley-Blackwell encyclopedia of globalization* (pp. 1–8). Blackwell Publishing Ltd.
Edelstein, D. (2010). *The enlightenment: A genealogy*. University of Chicago Press.

# References

*Fauna Protection Act* 1948 (NSW). Retrieved June 15, 2017, from https://www.legislation.nsw.gov.au/acts/1948-47.pdf

Fawns, R. (1988). The cultural roots of school biology in Australia—From vitalism and mechanism to dialectic materialism. *Research in Science Education, 18*(1), 268–275.

Forestry Corporation. (2016). *History: Marking a centenary of forestry in NSW.* Retrieved October 14, 2018, from https://www.forestrycorporation.com.au/about/history

Fox, A. (author) N. Dufty, K. McDonald, S. Smith, D. Tribe, & K. Schaefer (Eds.). (2016). *Chief Guardian: The life and times of Allen Strom.* https://www.amazon.com.au/Chief-Guardian-Times-Allen-Strom-ebook/dp/B01H8IEORQ

Francis, G. (1862). *The acclimatisation of harmless, useful, interesting, and ornamental animals and plants.* Paper presented before the *Philosophical Society, Adelaide South Australia, May 13, 1862.* Adelaide, SA: Philosophical Society of South Australia.

From Wikipedia. (n.d.). *Daily commercial news and shipping list (Sydney, NSW: 1891–1954).* TROVE. Retreived July 26, 2024, from https://trove.nla.gov.au/newspaper/title/641

Gammage, B. (2011). *The biggest estate on earth: How aborigines made Australia.* Allen & Unwin.

Gammage, B., & Pascoe, B. (2021). Country: Future fire, future farming. In M. Neale (Ed.), *First knowledges series.* Thames & Hudson | National Museum Australia.

Gough, A. (2021). All STEM-Ed up: Gaps and silences around ecological education in Australia. *Sustainability, 13*(7). https://doi.org/10.3390/su13073801

Gould, J. (1863). *Mammals in Australia.* John Gould.

Gould, S. J. (1996). *Mismeasure of man.* WW Norton & Company.

Gowers, R. (2002). Tipper, John Duncan (1886–1970). In *Australian dictionary of biography* (Vol. 16). Retrieved July 12, 2018, from http://adb.anu.edu.au/biography/tipper-john-duncan-11867/text21247

Guardiola-Rivera, O. (2010). *What if Latin America ruled the world? How the South will take the North through the 21st century.* Bloomsbury Publishing.

Hamblin, J. D. (2012). Environmental dimensions of world war II. In T. Zeiler & D. DuBois (Eds.), *A companion to world war II* (pp. 698–716). Wiley-Blackwell.

Hart, P. (2002). Environment in the science curriculum: The politics of change in the Pan-Canadian science curriculum development process. *International Journal of Science Education, 24*(11), 1239–1254. https://doi.org/10.1080/09500690210137728

Helmers, H., Lamal, N., & Cumby, J. (2021). Introduction: The printing press as an agent of power. In *Print and power in early modern Europe (1500–1800)* (pp. 1–17). Brill.

Historical Developments: Stage 6—Timber. (n.d.). *Dean Maddock & Vaughn Littlejohns.* Retrieved July 26, from https://sites.google.com/education.nsw.gov.au/ittstage6/home/industry-report/historical-developments

Hollander, R. (2009). Rethinking overlap and duplication: Federalism and environmental assessment in Australia. *Publius: The Journal of Federalism, 40*(1), 136–170. https://doi.org/10.1093/publius/pjp028

Hughes, J., & Brock, P. (2008). *Reform and resistance in NSW public education: Six attempts at major reform, 1905–1995.* NSW Department of Education and Training.

Hutton, D., & Connors, L. (1999). *A history of the Australian environment movement.* Cambridge University Press.

Idin, S. (2018). An overview of STEM education and industry 4.0. *Research Highlights in STEM Education, 194.*

Invasive Species Council. (2023, May 22). *Australia's extinction rate likely worse than thought.* [Press release]. Retrieved July 20, 2023, from https://invasives.org.au/media-releases/australias-extinction-rate-likely-worse-than-thought/#:~:text=In%20the%20lead%2Dup%20to,every%20decade%20since%20the%201960s

James, P. (2013). *Cosmopolitan conservationists: Greening modern Sydney.* Australian Scholarly Publishing.

Jenkins, E., & Swinnerton, B. (1996). The school nature study union 1903–94. *History of Education, 25*(2), 181–189.

Kass, D. (2018). *Educational reform and environmental concern: A history of school nature study in Australia*. Routledge.

Kohlstedt, S. (1997). Nature study in North America and Australasia, 1890-1945: International connections and local implementations. *Historical Records of Australian Science, 11*(3), 439.

Kohlstedt, S. (2010). *Teaching children science: Hands-on nature study in North America, 1890–1930*. The University of Chicago Press.

Lean, C. (Narrator), K. Lynch & D. Rutledge (Producers). (2023a, April 6). De-extinction, pt 1 *The Philosopher Zone* [Radio broadcast] https://www.abc.net.au/radionational/programs/philosopherszone/de-extinction-pt-1/102149400

Lean, C. (Narrator), K. Lynch & D. Rutledge (Producers). (2023b, April 13). De-extinction, pt 2 *The Philosopher Zone* [Radio broadcast] https://www.abc.net.au/radionational/programs/philosopherszone/de-extinction-pt-2/102173886

Lever, C. (1992). *They dined on eland: The story of the acclimatisation societies*. Quiller Press.

Lewis, W., Balderstone, S., & Bowan, J. (2006). *Events that shaped Australia*. New Holland.

Locke, J. (2013). Two treatises of government, 1689. *The anthropology of citizenship: A reader*, pp. 43–46 (Original work published in 1689).

Machlup, F. (2014). *Knowledge: Its creation, distribution and economic significance, Volume III: The economics of information and human capital (Vol. 781)*. Princeton University Press.

Marsh, G. P. (1864). *Man and nature, or physical geography as modified by human action*. Sampson Low, Son and Marston.

Marshall, A. J. (Ed.). (1966). *The great extermination*. Heinemann.

McLoughlin, L. C. (1999). Vegetation in the early landscape art of the Sydney region, Australia: Accurate record or artistic licence? *Landscape Research, 24*(1), 25–47.

Meadows, D., Meadows, D., Randers, J., & Behrens, W. (1972). *The limits to growth: A report for the Club of Rome's project on the predicament of Mankind*. Retrieved January 6, 2017, from http://www.donellameadows.org/wp-content/userfiles/Limits-to-Growth-digital-scan-version.pdf

Merchant, C. (1980). *The death of nature: Women, ecology and the scientific revolution*. Wildwood House.

Middelman, R. (1976). Schomburgk, Moritz Richard (1811–1891). In *Australian dictionary of biography* (Vol. 6). Retrieved July 12, 2018, from http://adb.anu.edu.au/biography/schomburgk-moritz-richard-4543/text7445

Milkis, S. (2019). Progressivism: Political and social-reform movement. In *Britannica*. Retrieved July 12, 2018, from https://www.britannica.com/topic/progressivism

Morris, D. (1974). Mueller, Sir Ferdinand Jakob Heinrich von (1825–1896). In *Australian dictionary of biography* (Vol. 5). Retrieved July 1, 2018, from http://adb.anu.edu.au/biography/mueller-sir-ferdinand-jakob-heinrich-von-4266

Mulligan, M., & Hill, S. (2001). *Ecological pioneers: A social history of Australian ecological thought and action*. Cambridge University Press.

Munck, T. (2000). *The enlightenment: A comparative social history 1721–1794*. Bloomsbury Academic.

Museum Victoria Collections. (n.d.). *The Australian telegraph network 1854–1877*. Retrieved June 12, 2018, from https://collections.museumvictoria.com.au/articles/2625

National Film & Sound Archive: Australia. (1988). *Australian Radio Series (1930s–1970s): A Guide to Holdings in the National Film and Sound Archive of Australia*, p.215. https://www.nfsa.gov.au/sites/default/files/11-2016/nfsa_radio_series_collection_amended.pdf

National Library of Australia. (n.d.). *Field Naturalists' Society of N.S.W*. Retrieved June 16, 2018, from https://trove.nla.gov.au/work/34738805?q&versionId=43036987

National Parks—Australia: New South Wales. (1979). In W. Goldstein (Ed.), *Parks and wildlife: Australia's 100 years of national parks* (pp. 93–107). National Parks and Wildlife Service.

*Native Animal Protection Act* 1903 (NSW). Retrieved June 30, 2017 from http://classic.austlii.edu.au/au/legis/nsw/num_act/napa1903n18300/

# References

NSW Government: Education. (n.d.). *Public Instruction Act 1880*. Retreived July 26, 2024, from https://education.nsw.gov.au/about-us/history-of-nsw-government-schools/government-schools/public-instruction-act-1880#:~:text=Compulsory%20attendance%20under%20the%201880,seventy%20days%20every%20half%2Dyear

NSW Government: Transport of NSW. (2019). *History of the NSW railways*. Retrieved August 23, 2023, from https://www.transport.nsw.gov.au/projects/community-engagement/sydney-trains-community/culture-and-heritage/history-of-nsw-railways

NSW State Archives. (n.d.). *Joseph Bischoff—The man behind the camera*. Retrieved February 22, 2024, from https://archivesoutside.records.nsw.gov.au/joseph-bischoff-the-man-behind-the-camera/

O'Connell, J. (2019). *1861 First acclimatisation society*. Australian food timeline. Retrieved July 12, 2018, from https://australianfoodtimeline.com.au/1861-first-acclimatisation-society/

Our Forests. (1908, October 30). *Australian Star*. http://nla.gov.au/nla.news-article229101171

Paddle, R. (2000). *The last Tasmanian tiger: The history and extinction of the Thylacine*. Cambridge University Press.

Palmer, J. A. (1998). *Environmental education in the 21st century: Theory, practice, progress and promise*. Routledge.

Pascoe, B. (2014). *Dark Emu: Aboriginal Australia and the birth of agriculture*. Magabala Books.

Pascoe, B. (2018). *Salt*. Black Ink Books.

Pascoe, B. with Harwood, L. (2024). *Black duck*. Thames & Hudson Australia.

*Pastures and Stock Protection Act 1880* (NSW). Retrieved Auguest 17, 2017, from http://classic.austlii.edu.au/au/legis/nsw/num_act/paspa1880n32363/

Perroni, E. (2018 October 19). *Protecting Australia's diverse soils and landscapes*. Sustainable Food Trust. https://sustainablefoodtrust.org/news-views/protecting-australias-soils/

Perry, T. (1966). Cunningham, Allan (1791–1839) *Australian dictionary of biography*. National Centre of Biography. Retrieved January 26, 2019, from http://adb.anu.edu.au/biography/cunningham-allan-1941

Pettigrew, C., & Lyons, M. (1979). Royal National Park—A history. In W. Goldstein (Ed.), *Parks and wildlife: Australia's 100 years of national parks* (pp. 15–30). National Parks and Wildlife Service.

Pizzey, G. (1992). *Crosbie Morrison, voice of nature*. Law Printer.

Pizzey, G. 15 (2000). Morrison, Philip Crosbie (1900–1958). *Australian Dictionary of Biography*. National Centre of Biography, Australian National University. Retrevied July 12, 2018, from http://adb.anu.edu.au/biography/morrison-philip-crosbie-11177

Pratley, J., & Rowell, L. (1980). Evolution of Australian agriculture. In *Principles of field crop production* (5th ed., pp. 1–25) Retrieved March 16, 2018, from https://www.csu.edu.au/__data/assets/pdf_file/0005/2805521/Chapter1_PratleyRowell.pdf

Robin, L. (1998). *Defending the Little Desert: The rise of ecological consciousness in Australia*. Melbourne University Publishing.

Robinson, K. (2010, October 14). *Changing education paradigms*. RSA ANIMATE. [YouTube]. Retrieved July 6, 2023, from https://www.youtube.com/watch?v=zDZFcDGpL4U

Royal Zoological Society of New South Wales. (2016). *History of RZS NSW*. Retrieved October 8, 2017, from https://www.rzsnsw.org.au/about-us/history-of-rzs-nsw

Short, J. (1998). The extinction of rat-kangaroos (Marsupialia: Potoroidae) in New South Wales, Australia. *Biological Conservation, 86*(3), 365–377. https://doi.org/10.1016/S0006-3207(98)00026-3

Short, J., & Milkovits, G. (1990). Distribution and status of the brush-tailed rock-wallaby in South-Eastern Australia. *Australian Wildlife Research, 17*(2), 169–179. https://doi.org/10.1071/WR9900169

Simard, S. (2021). *Finding the mother tree: Uncovering the wisdom and intelligence of the forest*. Penguin.

Skilbeck, M. (2021). *Loving and studying nature: Celebrating the earth through history, culture and education*. Springer.

Skirry, J. (n.d.). 'René Descartes: The mind-body distinction' *Internet encyclopedia of philosophy: A peer reviewed academic resource*. Retreived August 14, 2023, from https://iep.utm.edu/rene-descartes-mindbody-distinction-dualism/

Smout, R. (1966). Leichhardt: The secrets of the sandhills: A legend and an enigma. *Journal of the Royal Historical Society of Queensland, 8*(1), 55–80. https://plato.stanford.edu/entries/enlightenment/

State Library Victoria| National Library Australia. (n.d.). *Photographer Charles Walter*. Retreived May 29, 2024, from https://www.esplash.me/pdf/fs_410_photographer_charles_walter.pdf

Steeves, K. A., Bernhardt, P. E., Burns, J. P., & Lombard, M. K. (2009). Transforming American educational identity after Sputnik. *American Educational History Journal, 36*(1/2), 71–87. https://www.proquest.com/openview/c753f6122f164390cb935070519f98a9/1?pq-origsite=gscholar&cbl=29702

Stefansson, V. (1924, July 18). Views on desert lands: What history teaches. *The Sydney Morning Herald*. http://nla.gov.au/nla.news-article16134699

Strom, A. (1979). Some events in nature conservation over the last forty years. *Parks and Wildlife, 2*(3–4), 65–73.

Strom, A. (1987). *A background to environmental education: Some memoirs of Allen A. Strom, A.M. Occasional Publication*. Association for Environmental Education (NSW).

Strom, A.(author) N. Dufty, K. McDonald, D. Tribe, S. Smith, & K. Schaefer (Eds.). (2017). *Some aspects of nature conservation in New South Wales during the 1950s and 1960s*. https://www.amazon.com.au/dp/B071RNRK8H/ref=rdr_kindle_ext_tmb

The Parliament of the Commonwealth of Australia. (1994). *Australia's population 'carrying capacity': Two ecologies*. Australian Government Publishing Service. Retrieved December 12, 2017, from http://www.aphref.aph.gov.au_house_committee_reports_1994_1994_pp457.pdf

The University of California Museum of Paleontology Berkeley University. (1999). *Thomas Henry Huxley (1825–1895)*. Retrieved August 22, 2023, from http://www.ucmp.berkeley.edu/history/thuxley.html

Tompkins, P., & Bird, C. (1973). *The secret life of plants*. Harper and Row.

Tudge, C. (2005). *The secret life of trees*. Penguin.

Victorian Government. (n.d.). *Education week: 150 years of facts—Learn how Victoria's public education system has been shaped over the past 150 years*. Retrieved July 26, 2024, from https://www.vic.gov.au/education-week-150-years-facts

Walsh, G. (1990). Stead, David George (1877–1957). In *Australian dictionary of biography* (Vol. 12). Retrieved July 12, 2018, from http://adb.anu.edu.au/biography/stead-david-george-8634

Watson, D. (2014). *The bush: Travels in the heart of Australia*. Hamish Hamilton.

Webb, J. (1998). *Thistle Y. Harris: A biography of Thistle Yolette Stead*. Surrey Beatty & Sons.

Wheeler, K. (1975). The genesis of environmental education. In G. Martin & K. Wheeler (Eds.), *Insights into environmental education* (pp. 2–19). Oliver & Boyd.

*Wild Flowers and Native Plants Protection Act* 1927 (NSW). Retrieved June 30, 2017, from https://www.legislation.nsw.gov.au/acts/1927-2.pdf

Wilson, K. (2004). *The flight of the huia*. Canterbury University Press.

Wohlleben, P. (2015). *The hidden life of trees*. Black Inc Books.

Womersley, J., & Richmond, M. (2001). *AussieData: From prehistory to the present*. Wakefield.

Wyndham, H. (1979). Board, Peter (1858–1945) *Australian dictionary of biography*. Australian National University. Retrieved August 11, 2016, from http://adb.anu.edu.au/biography/board-peter-5275

# Chapter 3
# Environmental Education Centres: A Philosophical Perspective

## 3.1 Introduction

> Freire consistently reminds us that the education process is never a neutral one: it either functions to maintain the status quo or to challenge it (Sinwell, 2022).

Over time, globalisation has seen the diversification of race and ethnicity within many nations. This phenomenon effects educational policy given its ties to the imagined national identity. Additionally, the age of terrorism (given a starting point of September 11, 2001) has also seen the strengthening of borders and a fear of difference which has affected national policies including educational policy (Rizvi, 2007; Gilroy 2004 cited in Rizvi & Lingard, 2009, p. 17).

Distinct country characteristics, given specific cultures, previous policies and national and local histories are apparent in the phenomenon of globalised policy formation, process and enactment (Rizvi & Lingard, 2009). However, key for the development of environmental and sustainability education (ESE) is its discursive policy formation with international agency given it was amongst the first to blur the boundaries of the nation/state (Rizvi & Lingard, 2009). International organisations and intergovernmental conferences played, and continue to play, a major role in local ESE policy development (Stevenson, 2013), though influence waxes and wanes over time and space. There was international influence, provision and development of ESE policy given the global imperative. In the 1970s environmental education (EE) was a new concept that had a global, top-down approach in addition to crucial grass-roots input. Many education systems were pulled into the concept kicking and screaming or alternatively embraced it with a perfunctory approach—uptake and understanding was/is slow and fitting in with established education systems difficult.

In relation to globalisation, it is argued that there has been an attenuation of the relationship between nation and politics with each being the project of the other now (Appadurai 1996, cited in Rizvi & Lingard, 2009). Another phenomena relating to policy is the shift to using policy portfolio assemblages to address cohesion of social issues (Rizvi & Lingard, 2009). Education policy can be aligned and inclusive with/of other portfolios and, conversely, other policy areas have increasingly included educational/pedagogical elements—for example, health, cultural and welfare policies and practices. Another ongoing circumstance is the general use of palimpsest policy formation practice (Rizvi & Lingard, 2009) which, while understandable through the distrust in risk taking issues and possibly the precautionary principle, may hinder the development of the avant-garde practices necessary to enact the radical changes necessary.

ESE is implicitly and explicitly influenced by other policies and thus a brief focus on the complex processes and politics of educational, and specifically ESE, policy formation will highlight the value of adopting the theoretical concept of "assemblage" (Deleuze & Guattari, 1987; Rizvi & Lingard, 2011). The "assemblage" concept evokes a systems thinking approach to consider complex configurations of policy inputs and their implications. This study sought a descriptive exposure of some of the competing discourses and the setting in which they were enacted. To be cognisant of the effect the assemblage has on our psyche, we need to re-conceptualise reflexively and thus make visible the balance of contrary forces.

## 3.2 Education and Environmental and Sustainability Education

> responsible social democratic action is the goal of all education (Dennis and Knapp [relating Dewey's writing to EE] 1997)

Conceptions of the purposes of education have changed markedly over the years. While education for all is still a global priority, in many Western countries it is often highly individualistic, competitive and market driven. New public managerialism has seen the discursive development of self-responsibility (Rose 1999, cited in Rizvi & Lingard, 2009) and a shift from government to governance (Rhodes 1997 cited in Rizvi & Lingard, 2009). Multiple private and public participants have changed the field of the old binary hierarchies. The dichotomy between education being geared to education for critical, global, sustainable, future thinking citizens and education being purely for competitive national economic gain is problematic. Many of the means for educating for the economy often disregard the essential factors of education for the whole person—inclusive of a healthy environment in which to live and an understanding of the necessity for the inclusion of the non-human environment. One example is the testing required for comparative educational outcomes within economised educational policy that generally has a significant detrimental effect on a wholistic education. Global education comparison indicators include PISA (Programme for International Student Assessment) [initiated in 2000], and some OECD World Education Indicators (OECD, 2022), including Education at a Glance, an annual publication. Many countries in the Global South are included in OECD comparisons and participation in PISA testing has been known to be a requirement for World Bank funding (Rizvi & Lingard, 2009).

The importance of education in understanding and acting on environmental issues has been stated by many. It was integral in publicising environmental problems, mobilising people into action, and advocating for change within the legal and parliamentary systems in the late 1800s to early 1900s. In the early days of EE Stapp (1970), Strom (Fox, 2016; Strom, 2017) and Morrison (Pizzey, 1992) talked of its importance given democratic citizenry obligations. Before EE was conceived Carson (1962) spoke of education's gravity in informing about environmental degradation given the public being forced to live with it and ultimately being responsible for it (Linke, 1980). It was the reason for the Education and the Environmental Crisis conference run by the Australian Academy of Science in 1970 and was a significant strategic approach in addressing environmental dilemmas starting at the UN Conference on the Human Environment (1972) and continuing through all its global iterations.

### 3.2.1 Education: History, Form, Function and Other Perspectives

In searching for other ways and means of ESE it seems important to acknowledge other forms of education. To start with, before the western institutionalisation of education in the late 1800s, education was much more a family, community experiential endeavour. Privileged students learned Latin, history and the sciences either at universities (boys) or through a tutor (generally girls where the education was more creativity based). There were also charity schools set up for various reasons including, social welfare, philanthropy, religious missions, social control and stability, and economic productivity. But these schools were not for all. Farming communities often needed their children to work on farms. There was also a prevalence of child labour in many societies. Education in Indigenous communities tended to remain an everyday experiential happening. There have been schools since the Egyptian era, but mass education began from the nineteenth century with industrialisation and mechanisation.

The past close interrelationship between humans and their environment is another point to consider. People surrounded by nature and interacting with nature was much more an everyday experience before the industrial revolution. For example, through harvest thanksgivings and sacrificial offerings (Linke, 1980, p. 14). In many Indigenous populations this intricate inseparability is still evident, for example, in First Nations' totemic relationships. Australian First Nations' cultural economy was based on subsistence as many Indigenous cultures are—the idea of a Cornucopian environment was a western concept.

## 3.2.2 Influences on the Development and Implementation of ESE

There is a distinct difference in the inherent ethos of traditional and modern, western cultures that needs to be addressed up front. An awareness of these differences will be beneficial in understanding how we humans find ourselves with the dilemmas we face. More traditional cultures generally only produced timely fundamental needs. There is a difference in a fixed number of wants and the infinite number of wants demonstrated within modern consumerist culture—individual and collective desires for the present and the future. The infinite number of wants, within our consumerist society, produces a restlessness within culture (Henry, 1963).

Some similarities of traditional and western cultures include the disposition to provide or at least attempt to provide fixes for conflict and suffering (Henry, 1963). Added to this is a human lack of genetically determined governance of interpersonal relations and you have a culture that is perpetually searching for interpersonal satisfaction—away from disappointment and inner conflict with a rudimentary skill set focused on survival (Henry, 1963). Modern culture makes for an individualist society—with encouragement and inculcation by consumeristic interests (Henry, 1963) contributing to fragmentation and loss of community. However, ancient civilisations tended to have greater individual knowledge and skill while within modern culture there tends to be individual specialisation with a reliance on the collective. Harari says this has left space for imbeciles to survive where they once would not have survived as the fittest (2014).

Norms and values can stifle creativity and potential (Nietzsche, 1878). This suppression can impact on critical thinking and produce a conformity within society that is not well reasoned. This herd mentality is relevant to ESE as sometimes we have spurts of sustainable practice that is based on herd mentality rather than a fundamental understanding of the issue. This can impact on the long-term viability of the sustainability practice as practitioners can easily break the practice given it was a superficial learning in the first place. The use of reusable coffee cups after Craig Reucassel's *War on Waste* television series (ABC, 2017) is an example: Many people got into using "keep cups" for coffee instead of the one off takeaway version… for a while (complicated by them not being allowed to be used by coffee shops during the COVID pandemic). The cups issue is much more complex than stated given that many of the takeaway cups now have a biodegradable lining—yet it is unnecessary waste where convenience and desire trumps sustainability (speaking from experience). It may also just be that often, sadly, convenience and desire do trump sustainability. However, the three series of *War on Waste* have effectively highlighted many waste streams and had an enormous positive impact (for example, soft plastic collection at Woolworths and Coles supermarkets… for a time, and the sale of irregular fruit and vegetables) and there is a greater percentage of people using keep cups than before the show aired in 2017. Furthermore, Reucassel went on to delve into the money behind politics that influences environmental factors in *The Big Deal* (Jungle Entertainment/ABC, 2021). *The Big Deal* in turn may have influenced communities of political practice and democratisation with the growth and representation of the Teal independents in Australian federal politics for example. Many Teal politicians are concerned about environmental issues, with climate change featuring prominently on their political agenda. Thus, people were motivated to be involved in democracy which impacts environmental decision making.

## 3.3 Social Reproduction and Social Reconstruction

The War on Waste and The Big Deal are instances of contributions to social reconstruction within Australian society. Education and society are intricately linked in a co-evolutionary relationship with social learning crucial to social, cultural and material reproduction (Kaukko et al., 2021). Western mass education has long been an instrument of social reproduction and maintenance (Sterling, 2003). However, together, education and society can change by mutually reenforcing each other's altered perspective—a relationship of mutual transformation (Sterling, 2003). In this way education is involved in social reconstruction rather than social reproduction.

Postcapitalist politics seeks to take control of the economy and develop new social forms of production and social reproduction more in line with ecocentric and equitable behaviour. These involve such innovations as barter markets; co-operatives; local currencies; universal basic income; community enterprises; participatory economics; and co-operative schools. Supporters include anti-globalisation; anti- growth; deep green; eco-socialist; and eco-feminist campaigners (Huckle, 2020).

## 3.4 Pro Environmental Behaviour

Pro-environmental behaviour is shaped by a myriad of personal and social factors, which can be categorised into 18 distinct influences according to Gifford and Nilsson (2014). These encompass personal aspects such as childhood experiences, education, personality traits, and one's sense of control and values. Additionally, political ideologies, worldviews, and a sense of responsibility play significant roles. Cognitive biases, attachment to places, age, gender, and chosen activities further contribute to shaping environmental attitudes and actions.

On the social front, factors like religious beliefs, urban-rural disparities, social norms, socioeconomic status, and proximity to environmental hazards exert considerable influence. Cultural and ethnic backgrounds also impact environmental behaviours. Importantly, pro-environmental actions may not always stem directly from these influences; individuals may be motivated by non-environmental goals that they have prioritised (Gifford & Nilsson, 2014).

It's crucial to recognise that the interplay of these diverse influences can lead to a variety of environmental outcomes. The complex interactions among the 18 categories ultimately determine individual and collective behaviours towards environmental stewardship (Gifford & Nilsson, 2014).

## 3.5 Religion

With religion being so influential in the governance of our supposedly secular society, it is worth reflecting on religion in relation to power, capitalism, science and development. Religion, and specifically monotheistic religion as the historically dominant religion within the power structure in many western countries, can influence dangerous behaviours and attitudes. While it is challenging to authoritatively reference these ideas, having lived through Scott Morrison's prime ministership in Australia and Donald Trump's presidency in the United States, I am confident in stating that these periods resulted in some dangerous outcomes for climate change and environmental progress. For a wide variety of evidence, readers are encouraged to review media coverage and policy changes during Scott Morrison's prime ministership in Australia and Donald Trump's presidency in the United States.

Religious piety[1] can lead to the perception of being divinely favoured, rather than privileged, and this can impact on a sense of responsibility, accountability, and empathy to environmental issues. Religious fatalism, the belief that outcomes are preordained by a higher power is an example. While there are positive elements for environmental stewardship and sustainability (Schliesser, 2024) there are elements of environmental/sustainability apathy or ignorance. These negative aspects do not by any means represent the views or actions of all religious individuals or communities but there are tropes of domination over nature and favoured divinity within that can impact on action and responsibility for environmental problems and solutions.

It seems fitting to consider Weber's theory of the protestant work ethic and capitalism given the use of Weber's (1864–1920) archetype of rationalism in the case studies—the New South Wales (NSW) Department of Education serving as an archetype of Weber's analysis of bureaucratic reasoning. According to Weber, the protestant work ethic heightened feelings of an individual's anxiety due to the inability to unload burdens and thus holding lifelong guilty desires until the judgement day. This, according to Weber, fed into a selfless energy to work—all work being holy rather than that which stemmed from the Church. There was a focus on community rather than family. Furthermore, there was a displacement of

---

[1] Reflecting on my views of piety, I have found my thoughts infinitely in the negative, having experienced elements and people of religion as judgmental, intolerant, hypocritical, narrow-minded, self-righteous, or oppressive, and in some cases seeing demonstrations of the promotion of exclusionary ideologies or discriminatory practices. I have perceived religion and piety as rigid, dogmatic, and restrictive. This is not to say that I haven't experienced compassionate, inclusive, or morally uplifting elements of religion in abundance. However, my perception of piety's potential benefits or positive aspects is influenced by the negative. Perhaps Moliere's classic comedy satirising religious hypocrisy, and blind piety had a lasting effect!

miracles—prosperity came from methodical thinking, honesty, and hard work over an extended period. People turned to science which fed the positive feedback loop of science and technology. Weber saw Protestant characteristics, particularly Calvinism, as the catalysts for capitalism (Weber, 1905).

## 3.6 Development Variations

Religion is a substantial influence on humanitarian and sustainability-oriented approaches ubiquitous in international development agencies and non government organisations (Schliesser, 2024). An example is included in the history of the Talitha Kumi School Campus EEC, Beit Jala, Palestine, one of the EECs chosen to include within this study. Initially, Anglicans and Lutherans worked together until 1886, when Prussian Lutherans separated due to political and theological differences with England. The German Lutherans focused on social work and education, while British Anglicans prioritised conversion efforts. Today, the Evangelical Lutheran Church in Jordan and the Holy Land (ELCJHL) continues its mission by offering education and healthcare to Palestinians, regardless of faith, while also meeting the spiritual needs of the Arab Lutheran community. The original Protestant mission aimed to support the poor and provide education for Christians, not to establish a new church. It was later that graduates of the Lutheran schools helped found the local Evangelical Lutheran Church, with many members becoming refugees when the State of Israel was created (Evangelical Lutheran Church in Jordan and the Holy Land (n.d.). The EEC is part of this Church's mission.

However, religion is just one of many contending perspectives of development. In addition to the humanitarian viewpoint there are capitalist, anthropocentric sustainability, ecocentric development, cultural development, feminist development and post-development interpretations. Capitalist development, along with education for sustainable development (ESD), which tends to be anthropocentric sustainability embedded within capitalism, dominates much of the western world and many global institutions. In contrast, we have post-development perspectives challenging dominant mainstream development practices, as are cultural and feminist perspectives which have gained ground advocating for inclusive and equitable policies and practices.

These movements emphasise cultural geography, delving into meanings, identities, and representations. Post-structuralism rejects the modernist notion of universal knowledge, reason, and values, as well as the Marxist structuralist claim that historical events and social phenomena (such as schooling) could be explained solely within overarching systems like modes of production or ideologies. Instead, it asserted that knowledge, rationality, and morality are socially constructed, shaped by historical and geographical contexts, and intertwined with power dynamics, reflecting and influencing social relations (Huckle, 2020). Implementing the Sustainable Development Goals (SDGs) involves questioning the dominance of economic growth-oriented models, such as the integration of environmental concerns into capitalist systems, in discussions about development (Georgeson & Maslin, 2018; Huckle, 2020).

## 3.7 Governance, Capitalism: The Importance of Civics and Critical Thinking

One criticism levelled at the documentation associated with the UN Decade of Education for Sustainable Development (2005–2014) was its failure to address the effect of neoliberalism—its prioritising of economic growth and profit, and general attributes of privatisation, deregulation, free markets, and individualisation—on the environment (Huckle & Wals, 2015). While the impact of neoliberalism is complex and depends on policies, practices and the socio-political environment at a localised level, the detrimental effect of neoliberalism and its hegemony on the environment, and society, is well documented (Dryzek, 2022), and in relation to ESE started around the time of the Rio conference (United Nations, 1992).

The Decade had on a reformist agenda, whereas a clear movement away from current economic polices is necessary—we cannot move forward as a critical mass without truth telling and depolarisation of viewpoints. We need more than shifts in values, lifestyles, and policy, or, at least, we cannot have these changes without some serious truth telling, understanding and depolarisation of views, and change in how our governance operates.

Missing from the Decade was critical questioning of the factors that have made sustainability so difficult to achieve. Why were alternate liberal and radical views, other possible forms of political economy to complement the necessary ecocentric knowledge, values, behaviours and lifestyles not addressed (Huckle & Wals, 2015)? The United Nations Educational, Scientific and Cultural Organisation (UNESCO), like many of our governance systems operates within the neoliberal paradigm. Power, politics, and citizenship have rarely been addressed within the analysis of the Decade.

Neoliberal effect on specific locations depends on policies and practices. However, the cultural influence of neoliberalism often shapes the development of these policies and practices—within hyper consumerism, individualisation, privatisation, and profit as the main driver. Big business influences and curtails governance. The neoliberal effect on government policies effects the environment, and industry and citizen's attitudes and behaviours. These factors can be barriers to the implementation of ESE (Lawn & Prentice, 2015).

## 3.8 Going Against the Dominant Grain

In opposition to the neoliberal turn is the World Social Forum where one of their convictions is that growth at all costs is environmentally unsustainable. Other convictions include that such a growth focus imprints a democratic deficit and is destructive to long-standing cultural traditions (Rizvi & Lingard, 2009). There are lessons to be learned from the Global South and Indigenous communities who, while constrained by globalisation, also innately and covertly resist.

## 3.9 A Heuristic Frame

Lucas' typology of "about", "in" and "for" the environment is a frame frequently utilised within the history of EE given the necessity of a schema for working with an ambiguously defined concept. Still, even Lucas bemoaned the eventual sloganism of his frame (1991 as cited in Gough, 1997) that has been, over time, overly and often inappropriately used. Paul Vare and Bill Scott's (2007) addition of "why" to Lucas' frame has been utilised within this text to explain the past, essentially in terms of how political influences and economic priorities rather than environmental advocacy are evident in global, national and local education policies. The addition of "why" to Lucas' topology as an initial heuristic frame provides a deeper analysis of critical learning and theorising about curriculum and pedagogy—about what the EECs represent and where they could be heading. What's more, with a focus on language, this heuristic allows a deeper investigation of how power, control and discrimination structures within society are mediated through language given language's role in constructing our world (the linguistic turn) [Stevenson & Robottom, 2013, p. 472].

Vare and Scott (2007) concluded that in order to address the "why," the complementary approaches of ESD1 (informed, skilled behaviours and ways of thinking, useful in the short-term) and ESD2 (building critical thinking capacity and developing enquiring minds inherent in sustainable living) need to be addressed. Strategies for doing so include:

- promoting learning as an outcome, as well as a means to an end,
- balancing the employment of information and communication on one hand with facilitation of learning through mediation,
- trusting the unplanned direction learners may take, and
- evaluations that go beyond the "what has been learned?" outcomes to the "how do we know" as an additional source of learning. (Vare & Scott, 2007).

In moving forward, Stevenson's advice for educator practitioners is to stay/be involved in constructing the discourse, to have input in its historical, pedagogical and political positioning, and to be involved in the research process as part of the transformation. In addition, "learning forward" is advised in order to stay nimble in our unpredictable future (Stevenson, 2006).

Without supporting structures for learners to build new contexts they can feel "confused, insecure, frightened" they may retreat to normalised contexts or try and build from scratch unnecessarily (Jackson, 2011, p. 30). M.G. Jackson interprets Stephen Sterling's (2001) second order learning as involving elaboration and rearranging of existing concepts or making visible previous interconnections that were not visible. Best educational practice seeks to develop learner's second-order learning ability (Jackson, 2011) presumably to alleviate disconnection from culture which could have perceived negative personal and communal consequences. Jackson equates Sterling's third-order learning as transformative learning—where no amount of rearrangement will close the gap of cognitive dissonance. Jackson states that unless educators have gone through a transformative learning experience, they are in no position to develop and deliver ESD/education for cultural transformation (ECT) programs.

## 3.10 Decoding Colonial Histories

Enlightenment ideas and technological advancements played a part in the justification and facilitation of colonial activities (Mignolo 2011 cited in Connell, 2018). This, of course, is a simplification as the causes of colonial expansion are multifaceted and rooted in a complex interplay of economic, political, and social factors. However, the discovery and subsequent colonialisation of the global south—those regions not considered a part of the civilised world— was an obvious advantage for any nation or business. Richs flowed, and still flow from one to the other (Guardiola-Rivera, 2010).

The competition of western civilisations for energy and trade utilising the south's natural resources and human capital had its beginning in the late 1400s. Parts of Africa and Asia were initially colonised in the 1400s (Brown Mitchell, 2023) and colonialisation of the Americas began in the Caribbean and South America in the late 1400s and early 1500s—starting with the Spanish and Portuguese (Guardiola-Rivera, 2010). Generally, the conquistadors used the system the Spanish had used to regain territory from the Muslims from the 700–1400s where the Spanish Crown granted Muslim and Jewish gold, labour, and agricultural production to those that assisted in forced conversion to Christianity (Lockhart & Schwartz, 1983). While the Spanish Crown attempted to abolish this system in 1512–1514 and again in 1542 the frontier was lawless with the tyranny of distance. Religious authorities prohibited slavery within Christian teachings and the debate against slavery started early but without effective resolve. So, the tussle for power between European governance and settlers who became wealthy and politically influential with their southern spoils led to ineffectual laws (Encyclopedia Britannica, n.d.; Guardiola-Rivera, 2010).

As the colonies grew and settlers amassed wealth and influence, the empires reaped substantial economic benefits, consolidating their global dominance amid much contestation. The British Empire, in particular, accumulated vast fortunes through its extensive colonisation efforts. Brazilian gold, attained through trade and commerce, enabled Britain to concentrate on investments in the manufacturing sector, significantly contributing to the Industrial Revolution (Guardiola-Rivera, 2010). This influx of wealth shifted the financial centre of Europe from Amsterdam to London in the 1800s (Coispeau, 2016).

So, the beginning of trade in the Americas was the beginning, or an escalation, in clandestine trade given the tyranny of distance with the inability of enforceable governance (Guardiola-Rivera, 2010). Laws for the development of capitalist markets, property rights, democratic institutions and small-scale agricultural production (Smith, 1776) were progressively setup by the English and French. These gradually replaced forced labour. Massive industries have been set up off the back of colonialisation. Little of the spoils have gone or go to the colonised countries. Inequitable power dynamics persist both among and within developed and developing nations. These dynamics, for example, play defining roles in the origins and outcomes of climate change, as seen in instances like deforestation in the Amazon (McQuade, 2019).

Of course, history saw a growing global cultural dynamism and cross-border/global interaction—this is a very westerncentric outline of colonialisation (Conrad, 2012) that suits the purposes of this narrative. Harari's imperial cycle framework provides an understanding of the diverse values, beliefs, and discourses within empires. It outlines the initial formation of an imperial culture, followed by its adoption by the colonised inhabitants. Later in the process, there is a demand for equal status by the inhabitants, yet the imperial culture has already taken root. Finally, the founding empire loses its dominance, but the imperial culture continues to flourish (Harari, 2014). This framework offers an appreciation of the spectrum from Indigenous to Empire binaries and the diversity of experiences within it. Absolutely, colonial experiences and impact are diverse with variable amplitude. They are only one of the factors influencing place, however, they are a dominant theme (Ziltener & Künzler, 2013). To be fair one would need to balance the detrimental effects of colonialisation with the argued good which includes the benefits of economic development and infrastructure, education and modernisation, healthcare and medicine, cultural exchange and globalisation and technological innovations. Yet there are distinct disadvantages for the colonised people and nature—and the benefits tend to be rooted in a colonial mindset of paternalistic, racial superiority and cultural ignorance of other ways of being (Mills, 2007; Sullivan & Tuana, 2007).

## 3.11 Indigenous Populations

Mistreatment of Indigenous populations had occurred for centuries preceding Darwin's theory and well before the British colonialisation of Australia. There was convenience from an economic and power perspective, for western civilisations to view colonised land as untouched and pristine and Indigenous populations' culture as inferior. Yet, traditional cultures of foragers around the world, including in the harshest and inaccessible environments—for example, the Siberian Tundra, the Amazon, and the desert of Australia—had altered their environments. The foragers that had been there for millennia had brought about dramatic changes—the environment was not pristine having had its ecology completely reshaped by the foragers (Harari, 2014; Pascoe, 2014; Steffensen, 2020). For instance, fire has been used to manipulate food sources for millennia in Australia (Steffensen, 2020). Not only that, but evidence of populations being more than nomads has finally been brought to the public's attention. For example, Oscar Guardiola-Rivera (2010) writes of intricate irrigation systems in the Amazon and Bruce Pascoe (2018) discusses evidence of elaborate structures for collecting food in the form of fish traps, extensive areas of agriculture, and human settlements within the colonial explorer documentation.

Yet, sustainability was a key principle for indigenous populations (Magni, 2017)—there was a harmony between humanity and the world (Guardiola-Rivera, 2010). For Indigenous cultures nature resists private appropriation which is short-term and unsustainable. This contrasts with the private parallel universes, and it involves intra and intergenerational equity (Guardiola-Rivera, 2010).

Amerindians altered their landscapes and humanised them, yet in western terms indigenous people were seen to have no agency, to be at risk or vulnerable and in a state of dependence (Guardiola-Rivera, 2010). The fictional and scholarly image of Indigenous people of Latin America the world over was set as sleepy tropical places run by overlords—foreign bosses running farming enterprises with uprooted and passive workers. There was rubber in Brazil, cocoa in Venezuela, cotton in Guatemala, Nicaragua and Peru, sugar in the Dominican Republic and Haiti, and bananas in Caribbean Colombia (Guardiola-Rivera, 2010). The second Industrial Revolution (late 1800s-early 1900s) saw a rise in national and regional elites. There was push back from elites on ex-slaves and those who had been free who had been demanding land, freedom and citizenship. For them the bananas and coffee in Colombia, Costa Rica, Panama and Brazil and the rubber in Brazil and the meat and cereal of Argentina and Uruguay and once more sugar in the Caribbean and oil in Mexica and Venezuela was intended everlasting punishment given the damage to ecosystems and living conditions (Guardiola-Rivera, 2010). In Argentina, Chile, Costa Rica, Cuba, Uruguay and Puerto Rio the riches exchanged for products moved the power to the export-based elites undermining the racial harmony based nationalist ideologies. The progress of western science and technologies concealed a scientific racism and social Darwinism. A deficit discourse of underdeveloped and backward—to be saved by the supposedly civilised Europe and United States model of nationhood (Guardiola-Rivera, 2010). The story of inferiority as an obstacle in the path of progress. Landholdings were expanded by sacrificing commoner peasants who were generally Indian or black. For example, the enclosure and privatisation of state-owned lands in Mexico which preceded the Mexican Revolution of 1910. There had been rebellion beforehand in 1810 and guerrilla warfare continued from the forested surrounds after 1821 Mexican Independence was achieved.

There were many uprisings in the late 1700s, including those in Latin America, North America, Haiti, and Bolivia. The latter inspiring the Karateist movement of the late 1900s in Bolivia to fight for long term sustainability rather than short term gain (Guardiola-Rivera, 2010). Like the Zapatista in south-eastern Mexico the focus is on equalising the unfair economic and political system in line with the Amerindians and Afro-Latin Americans of the 1500–1800s.

This focus on America, and specifically Latin America, is set as an example of Indigenous retaliation for loss of land and livelihood, and the portrait of Indigenous peoples that has proliferated within western society since colonialisation. For while there are differences within each colonised region across America, Africa, Asia and Australia, there is a thread of similarity throughout. Importantly, while Australia was being colonised there was significant resistance to colonialisation happening throughout the world while the industrial revolution was collecting momentum—and there was war within Australia too, though you would not have known it by the history that had been perpetuated (Perkins, 2022).

# References

Brown Mitchell, J. (2023). European exploration. *Britannica*. Retrieved August 13, 2023, from https://www.britannica.com/topic/European-exploration

Carson, R. (1962). *Silent spring*. Fawcett.

Coispeau, O. (2016). *Finance masters: A brief history of international financial centers in the last millennium*. World Scientific.

Connell, R. (2018). Decolonizing sociology. *Contemporary Sociology: A Journal of Reviews, 47*(4), 399–407. https://doi.org/10.1177/0094306118779811

Conrad, S. (2012). Enlightenment in global history: A historiographical critique. *The American Historical Review, 117*(4), 999–1027.

Deleuze, G., & Guattari, F. (1987). *A thousand plateaus* (trans. B. Massumi). University of Minneapolis Press (Original work published 1980).

Dennis, L. J., & Knapp, D. (1997). John Dewey as environmental educator (Editorial). *Journal of Environmental Education, 28*(2), 5. https://doi.org/10.1080/00958964.1997.9942817

Dryzek, J. (2022). *The politics of the earth: Environmental discourses* (4th ed.). Oxford University Press.

Encyclopedia Britannica. (n.d.) Encomienda: Spanish policy *Britannica*. Retrieved August 15, 2023, from https://www.britannica.com/topic/encomienda

Evangelical Lutheran Church in Jordan & the Holy Land. (n.d.). *Environmental Education Centre*. Retrieved July 26, 2024, from https://elcjhl.org/eec

Fox, A. (author) N. Dufty, K. McDonald, S. Smith, D. Tribe, & K. Schaefer (Eds.). (2016). *Chief Guardian: The life and times of Allen Strom*. https://www.amazon.com.au/Chief-Guardian-Times-Allen-Strom-ebook/dp/B01H8IEORQ

Georgeson, L., & Maslin, M. (2018). Putting the United Nations Sustainable Development Goals into practice: A review of implementation monitoring and finance. *Geo: Geography and Environment, 5*(1). https://doi.org/10.1002/geo2.v5.1, https://doi.org/10.1002/geo2.49

Gifford, R., & Nilsson, A. (2014). Personal and social factors that influence pro-environmental concern and behaviour: A review. *International Journal of Psychology, 49*(3), 141–157. https://doi.org/10.1002/ijop.12034

Gough, A. (1997). *Education and the environment: Policy, trends and the problems of marginalisation*. Australian Council for Educational Research.

Guardiola-Rivera, O. (2010). *What if Latin America ruled the world? How the south will take the north through the 21st century*. Bloomsbury Press.

Harari, Y. (2014). *Sapiens: A brief history of humankind* (trans. Y. Harari, J. Purcell, & H. Watzman). Vintage. (Original work published 2011).

Henry, J. (1963). *Culture against man*. Vintage Books.

Huckle, J. (2020). *Critical school geography, Education for Global Citizenship*. ResearchGate. https://www.researchgate.net/publication/345849553_Critical_School_Geography_Education_for_Global_Citizenship.

Huckle, J., & Wals, A. E. J. (2015). The UN decade of education for sustainable development: Business as usual in the end. *Environmental Education Research, 21*(3), 491–505. https://doi.org/10.1080/13504622.2015.1011084

Jackson, M. G. (2011). The real challenge of ESD. *Journal of Education for Sustainable Development, 5*(1), 27–37. https://doi.org/10.1177/097340821000500108

Kaukko, M., Kemmis, S., Heikkinen, H. L. T., Kiilakoski, T., & Haswell, N. (2021). Learning to survive amidst nested crises: Can the coronavirus pandemic help us change educational practices to prepare for the impending eco-crisis? *Environmental Education Research, 27*(11), 1559–1573. https://doi.org/10.1080/13504622.2021.1962809

Lawn, J., & Prentice, C. (2015). Introduction: Neoliberal culture/the cultures of neoliberalism. *Sites: A Journal of Social Anthropology and Cultural Studies, 12*(1), 1–29. https://doi.org/10.11157/sites-vol12iss1id312

Linke, R. (1980). *Environmental education in Australia*. George Allen & Unwin Australia.

Lockhart, J., & Schwartz, S. B. (1983). *Early Latin America: A history of colonial Spanish America and Brazil*. Cambridge University Press.

Magni, G. (2017). Indigenous knowledge and implications for the sustainable development agenda. *European Journal of Education, 52*(4), 437–447. https://doi.org/10.1111/ejed.12238

McQuade, J. (2019, April 19). Earth Day: Colonialism's role in the overexploitation of natural resources. *The Conversation*. https://theconversation.com/earth-day-colonialisms-role-in-the-overexploitation-of-natural-resources-113995.

Mills, C. (2007). White ignorance. In *Race and epistemologies of ignorance* (Vol. 247, pp. 26–31). State University of New York Press.

Nietzsche, F. (1908). *Human, all too human: A book for free spirits*. Newcomb Livraria Press. (Original work published in 1878).

OECD. (2022). *Education at a Glance 2021 OECD Indicators*. Retrieved April 21, 2023, from https://www-oecd-org.ezproxy.newcastle.edu.au/education/education-at-a-glance/

Pascoe, B. (2014). *Dark emu: Aboriginal Australia and the birth of agriculture*. Magabala Books.

Pascoe, B. (2018). *Salt*. Black Ink Books.

Perkins, R. (2022). *The Australian Wars* [Documentary]. Retrieved August 14, 2023, from https://www.sbs.com.au/ondemand/tv-series/the-australian-wars?cid=od:search:gg:con:alwayson:dsa-tvseries:prog&gclid=EAIaIQobChMI0euAstnbgAMVMBCDAx1oUggkEAAYASAAEgJ3CvD_BwE&gclsrc=aw.ds

Pizzey, G. (1992). *Crosbie Morrison, voice of nature*. Law Printer.

Reucassel, C. (Presenter, Director), & Welkerling, S. (Producer). (2017, May 16). *The War on Waste*. [documentary]. ABC. https://iview.abc.net.au/show/war-on-waste/series/1

# References

Reucassel, C. (Director), Van Vuuren, C. (Presenter) & Jacques, A. (Producer). (2021, September 12). *The Big Deal*. [documentary]. Jungle Entertainment/ABC. https://makeitabigdeal.org/#about

Rizvi, F. (2007). Postcolonialism and Globalization in Education. *Cultural Studies: Critical Methodologies, 7*(3), 256–263. https://doi.org/10.1177/1532708607303606

Rizvi, F., & Lingard, B. (2009). *Globalizing education policy*. Routledge.

Rizvi, F., & Lingard, B.(2011). Social equity and the assemblage of values in Australian higher education *Cambridge Journal of Education, 41*(1), 5–22. https://doi.org/10.1080/0305764X.2010.549459

Schliesser, C. (2024). Religion matters: Religion and the sustainable development goals (SDGs). *Religions, 15*(3). https://doi.org/10.3390/rel15030337

Sinwell, L. (2022). Teaching and learning Paulo Freire: South Africa's communities of struggle. *Education as Change, 26*(1), 1–19.

Smith, A. (1937). *The wealth of nations* W. Strahan and T. Cadell (Original work published in 1776).

Stapp, B. (1970). A strategy for curriculum development and implementation in environmental education at the elementary and secondary levels. In J. Evans & S. Boylan (Eds.), *Education and the environmental crisis. 24–26th April. Canberra* (pp. 23–37).

Steffensen, V. (2020). *Fire country: How indigenous fire management could help save Australia*. CSIRO Publishing.

Sterling, S. (2001). *Sustainable education: Re-visioning learning and change*. Green Books.

Sterling, S. (2003). *Whole systems thinking as a basis for paradigm change in education: Explorations in the context of sustainability*. (PhD). University of Bath, UK. http://www.bath.ac.uk/cree/sterling/sterlingthesis.pdf

Stevenson, R. (2006). Tensions and transitions in policy discourse: Recontextualizing a decontextualized EE/ESD debate. *Environmental Education Research, 12*(3), 277–290. http://www.informaworld.com/10.1080/13504620600799026

Stevenson, R. (2013). Researching tensions and pretensions in environmental/sustainability education policies. In R. Stevenson, M. Brody, J. Dillon, & A. Wals (Eds.), *International handbook of research on environmental education* (pp. 147–155). Routledge for the American Educational Research Association.

Stevenson, R., & Robottom, I. (2013). Critical action research and environmental education: Conceptual congruencies and imperatives in practice. In R. Stevenson, M. Brody, J. Dillon, & A. Wals (Eds.), *International handbook of research on environmental education* (pp. 469–479). Routledge for the American Educational Research Association.

Strom, A.(author) N. Dufty, K. McDonald, D. Tribe, S. Smith, & K. Schaefer (Eds.). (2017). *Some aspects of nature conservation in New South Wales during the 1950s and 1960s*. https://www.amazon.com.au/dp/B071RNRK8H/ref=rdr_kindle_ext_tmb

Sullivan, S., & Tuana, N. (2007). *Race and epistemologies of ignorance*. Suny Press.

United Nations. (1992). Agenda 21. *United Nations Conference on Environment and Development*. Retrieved July 26, 2023, from https://sustainabledevelopment.un.org/content/documents/Agenda21.pdf

United Nations. (n.d.). *United Nations Conference on the Human Environment, 5–16 June 1972, Stockholm*. Retrieved May 6, 2023, from https://www.un.org/en/conferences/environment/stockholm1972

Vare, P., & Scott, W. (2007). Learning for a change: Exploring the relationship between education and sustainable development. *Journal of Education for Sustainable Development, 1*(2), 191–198. https://doi.org/10.1177/097340820700100209

Weber, M. (2012). *The Protestant ethic and the spirit of capitalism* (trans. S. Kalberg). Routledge. (Original work published 1905).

Ziltener, P., & Künzler, D. (2013). Impacts of colonialism–A research survey. *Journal of World-Systems Research, 19*(2), 290–311.

# Part II
# New South Wales Case Study

# Chapter 4
# Silhouette and Source of Colonialisation: Australia's Struggles

## 4.1 Introduction

The events of colonialisation are important in understanding the historical development of each country and thus the backdrop to environmental damage and hence environmental and sustainability education (ESE) development. Colonialisation has had a lasting, and continuing, impact on the world. The traumatic exploitation of natural resources degrades the land and pollutes water and the atmosphere with serious consequences on biodiversity, human health and culture. Whether it be rubber and then later palm oil and lumber from the Malay peninsula or timber, minerals and opium from Myanmar or diamonds, ivory, bauxite, oil, timber, minerals, precious metals and gemstones from Africa—colonised cultures are at a deficit. Thus, we need to understand colonialisation in order to understand the world we inhabit and the crises we are in the midst of, and into the future. The extent and thus generational equity impact of colonialisation on culture and the natural environment is paramount to this story (McQuade, 2019). While much colonial destruction has been discussed in relation to environmental awareness given their cause-and-effect relationship, this chapter outlines some of the effects of colonialisation on First Nations' populations and the environment, specifically in an Australian context.

## 4.2 First Nations' People of Australia: Connection to the Environment

The uniqueness and diversity of the southern continents, their flora and fauna, their similarities and differences can be partially explained by the cleaving of Laurasia (North America, Europe and Asia) and Gondwanaland (Australia, South America,

Africa, India and Antarctica) from Pangaea 160 million years ago and the subsequent separation of Australia from Gondwanaland over 40 million years ago. As a result, Australia as we know it was shaped by biological isolation—in addition to the characteristics of situational geological stability and an erratic climate. The presence of a unique, ancient rock landmass has resulted in nutrient-deficient soil due to the limited geological activity for soil profile renewal (Flannery, 1997; Rolls, 2000; White, 1994). Another distinction of the Australian environment are the seasons. Australian seasons are subtle and diverse—distinct from the northern four seasons (Smith, 2013). There is an array of season categorisation indicative of the diversity of climatic conditions (Australian Bureau of Meteorology, n.d.; Smith, 2013). For instance, in the Gariwerd (Grampians) of southwestern Victoria there are six seasons in the Brambruk people's calendar, whereas, the Yanyuwa people of the Gulf of Carpentaria recognise five seasons (Smith, 2013). As discussed, land management practices of First Nations' people have had a significant impact from at least 65,000 years ago (Gammage & Pascoe, 2021). Some argue First Nations' impact could extend to some 120,000 years ago (Paddle, 2000). Land stewardship ensured the flourishing of life, made food sources abundant, predictable and convenient, and it was actioned at a local level with intra and inter-generational consideration (Gammage, 2011).

Given the extensive duration of First Nations' people's occupation of Australia, it comes as no surprise that there were an estimated 200–600 tribes, further divided into clans, living in the country when European colonialisation began. The estimated population at that time ranges from 300,000 to 700,000 people, with each tribe having its unique language, customs, norms, and religion (Harari, 2014). Characteristics within First Nations' cultures, distinct from those of western culture, include an obligation to renew the land, to find an equilibrium with environments and to renew where possible. First Nations' culture also encompasses lateral, non-linear thinking, consensus, reciprocity, harmonious justice rather than adversarial punishment, relationships rather than the binary. Eternal time encompassing past and future generations (Watson, 2014) with people connected spiritually to Country (Dingle, 1988).

Within an Australian context, Rachel Perkin's documentary on the *Australian Wars* (2022) discusses the colonial frontier violence, and colonial frontier massacres from 1788 to 1930 have been mapped by The Centre for twenty-first Century Humanities at the University of Newcastle, New South Wales (NSW) (https://c21ch.newcastle.edu.au/colonialmassacres/map.php). Clashes between First Nations' people and settlers were reported within the first 10 years of colonial occupation. Similar to other Indigenous populations, some of the events that have contributed to the systemic inequality faced by First Nations' people in Australia today include the loss of land, removal from family and culture, the introduction of western diseases and culture, and attempts at assimilation (Australian Human Rights Commission, n.d.; Pascoe, 2014). There was much turmoil in the nineteenth century as First Nations' people attempted to protect their lands from colonisers claiming it as farmland (Pascoe, 2014).

## 4.2 First Nations' People of Australia: Connection to the Environment

Australian First Nations people stand in stark contrast to the technocratic, mechanistic, anthropocentric coloniser culture. The devastation of the natural environment is intertwined with the enormous suffering of First Nations' communities—the consequence of the path of 'progress' brought about by colonialisation (Bonyhady, 2000; Flannery, 1997; Lines, 1991/1999; Marshall, 1966). As examples, Eric Rolls documented the transformation of grasslands in the Hunter-Pillaga region due to sheep grazing, which led to the dispossession of First Nations' people, the destruction of their villages, and the rapid onset of soil degradation (Pascoe, 2014). Early farmers observed a swift change from soft, spongy soil to compacted soil, which accelerated water runoff and supported the dominance of different grass species (Gammage, 2011; cited in Pascoe, 2014). Evidence of prior agriculture and its architects was destroyed as depopulation by disease and the arrival of sheep advanced (Pascoe, 2014).

The first immigrant nature-lovers and field naturalists provided contrary characteristics to colonialism. They socialised with First Nations' people in garnering information about the ecology of their environment. For instance, Georgina Molloy, a field collector at Swan River (Western Australia) was assisted in the bush by Battap while the rest of the colonists were at war with the Nyungar. And Count Strzelecki, an explorer and scientist, argued for First Nations people's rights in 1845 (Hutton & Connors, 1999). He had avoided starvation for 3 weeks in the Victorian bush with the assistance of First Nations' guides Charlie Tarra and Jackey (Australian Museum, 2021a). Generally, however, any contributions First Nations people made in acting as guides and field assistants to early naturalists were as part of imperial science and thus "unwittingly lead [sic] to further economic expansion and degradation of the very landscapes that both Aborigines and nature-lovers cherished" (Hutton & Connors, 1999, p. 27). There was no collective challenge to colonialisation from European society (Hutton & Connors, 1999). Sympathy from explorers and naturalists did not stop Europeans from exploring or taking land—superiority and entitlement were not questioned (Pascoe, 2014). For these people the land was terra nullius—land belonging to nobody—and so there for the taking.

In 1967 Australians voted to remove references in the Australian Constitution that discriminated against Aboriginal and Torres Strait Islander people (Jeffes, 2020). The Mabo decision in 1992 overturned the *terra nullius* declaration and the 1993 Native Title Act recognised Aboriginal and Torres Strait Islander continuing connection and rights to land (Australian Museum, 2021b). With much of Australia's First Nations' history hidden within colonialised historical accounts of the last 240 years, it is only relatively recently that the general public is hearing about Indigenous innovations, agriculture and science and what the country looked like before British colonialisation. For instance, the yams growing within the spongy soil that disappeared for the arrival of hooved livestock (Pascoe, 2014). There is still much truth telling to be told, or more to the point, listened to, about First Nations' suffering from discriminatory policies and practices that were rooted in a colonial mindset of racial superiority and cultural ignorance. The act of truth-telling holds the power to reveal and heal the ancestral ghosts embedded within our colonial history. In Australia's colonial past there were massacres (Perkins, 2022), dispossession of land, forced removal of children (known as the Stolen Generations) and social and economic marginalisation (Australian Museum, 2021b). There was a consistent paternalistic policy framing of First Nations peoples as in need of salvation, support and protection. Through this enormous adversity many First Nations' communities have survived and held onto and revived or are reviving their cultures. While there are huge improvements to be made, many First Nations' communities are inviting all Australians to move forward in reconciliation and to learn from the Ancient Wisdom they have accumulated over 65,000 odd years of inhabiting this beautiful unique and arid continent. There is much to learn about how to live with the Australian environment in a sustainable way—as an integral part of it.

## 4.3 The Beginning of Australia's Environmental Damage

After 1788, newcomers to Australia struggled for survival in an unfamiliar land while subjugating resources for the benefit of the monarchy and nation, leading to the exploitation of Australia's abundant resources. Merchants played a significant role in this exploitation, actively seeking goods for European markets in addition to filling gaps in their supply. This led to extensive environmental degradation and the mistreatment of First Nations people. Industries such as timber extraction, whaling, sealing, and the rapid growth of the sheep trade thrived without much consideration for sustainability (Bonyhady, 2000; Lines, 1991/1999).

The first autocratic officials were unable to enforce environmental laws—or just simply failed to create them if these laws clashed with the want or the ways of the people or the economy. For example, Governor Hunter had trouble protecting the initial water supply. He attempted to legislate protection mechanisms in 1795 with a reiteration necessary in 1796—much to Hunter's displeasure. Governor King reconsidered his initial enthusiastic stance for the sealing industry after advocacy against the carnage, yet failed to enact laws (Bonyhady, 2000). The slaughter was excessive, brutal and brutalising (Lines, 1991/1999). Short-term gain was valued more highly than restraint—or the power to enact laws against the overwhelming proactive annihilation of seals was perceived as just too impotent (Bonyhady, 2000; Lines, 1991/1999). King had also recognised the increased damage caused by flooding after deforestation along the Hawkesbury and did prohibit the clearing of cedars while also encouraging replanting. However, this regulation and suggestion was not enforced and was thus ineffectual (Bonyhady, 2000). Bligh's attempt to protect the urban environment, through regulating development and preserving open space, contributed, along with the rum rebellion, to his downfall (Bonyhady, 2000). These are early examples of concerns about sustainability losing out to short-term economic gain. By the end of the 1800s, electoral pressure often rendered the government unwilling to enact environmental protection legislation (Bonyhady, 2000). Sound familiar?

Early colonialisation had significant environmental impacts: Between 1880 and 1910, more than half of the four million hectares of the 'big scrub' rainforest straddling the New South Wales-Queensland border was cleared for dairy farming, sugar cultivation, and timber harvesting. Similarly, in the Strzelecki and Otway Ranges of Victoria, a similar area was cleared for dairy farming, leaving no standing vegetation. The felled vegetation was burnt given the means for profiting from these resources had yet to be established (Williams, 1997).

The accounts provided by A. J. 'Jock' Marshall (1966) and William Lines (1991/1999) depict the harrowing deforestation and mass slaughter of iconic Australian wildlife, including kangaroos, seals, whales, birds, and various other species. Reading about these events is quite confronting. While we must consider the challenges of survival in a foreign land, the sheer cruelty and wastefulness of these actions are staggering. However, recognising this history, including, unequivocally, the history of our First Nations, is an essential step toward constructing a more sustainable and humane world.

### 4.3.1 The Effect of the Gold Rush

During the 1850s, the gold rush in both NSW and Victoria marked a transformative era in Australian history. European colonialisation of Australia accelerated, and the appropriation of Australian resources such as timber, whales, seals, and the growth of the sheep trade was overshadowed when six ships, carrying a total of eight tons of gold, arrived in Britain in 1852, greatly increasing trade (Annear, 1999; Bessant et al., 1978). The rushes triggered a massive influx of immigrants from around the globe, including from China, the United Kingdom and Europe, including Scandinavia, and the United States (Annear, 1999; Bessant et al., 1978; Griffiths, 1983). This influx impacted population growth and the economies of both colonies in addition to ushered in new political ideas and progressive thought such as the eight-hour day (National Museum Australia, n.d.). The gold rush also accelerated the environmental destruction—denuding, eroding, and polluting large areas of land and waterways without any forethought (Bessant et al., 1978).

## 4.4 Conclusion

Colonialisation has had devastating impact on Indigenous populations and the environment. However, First Nations' Peoples habitation of Australia has left an indelible footprint. This imprint tends to be in keeping with reverence and connection to the environment and sustainability practices, including intra and intergenerational equity. Colonialisation in Australia, on the other hand, with its fast and furious social, cultural, political and economic changes over little more than 250 years has wrought extreme destruction on a fragile and ancient land as well as on First Nations' people. The environmental impact, accompanied by local and global concern gradually cultivated the growing awareness outlined in Chap. 2. The following chapters focus on the events that led to the establishment and development of the EECs within the NSW Department of Education and the structures that supported this process.

# References

Annear, R. (1999). *Nothing but gold: The diggers of 1852*. Text Publishing.
Australian Bureau of Meteorology. (n.d.). *Indigenous weather knowledges*. Retrieved June 30, 2024, from http://www.bom.gov.au/iwk/
Australian Human Rights Commission. (n.d.). *Track the history timeline: The stolen generations*. Retrieved September 3, 2023, from https://humanrights.gov.au/our-work/education/track-history-timeline-stolen-generations
Australian Museum. (2021a). *Paul Edmund de Strzelecki*. Retrieved September 15, 2023, from https://australian.museum/about/history/exhibitions/trailblazers/paul-edmund-de-strzelecki/
Australian Museum. (2021b). *Terra nullius*. Retrieved October 14, 2023, from https://australian.museum/learn/first-nations/unsettled/recognising-invasions/terra-nullius/
Bessant, B., Blackmore, W., Cave, P., Cotter, R., Mellor, S., & Waterson, D. (1978). *Australian history: The occupation of a continent*. Eureka Publishing.
Bonyhady, T. (2000). *The colonial earth*. Melbourne University Press.
Dingle, T. (1988). *Aboriginal economy: Patterns of experience*. McPhee Gribble| Penguin.
Flannery, T. F. (1997). *The future eaters: An ecological history of the Australasian lands and people*. New Holland Publishers.
Gammage, B. (2011). *The biggest estate on earth: How aborigines made Australia*. Allen & Unwin.
Gammage, B., & Pascoe, B. (Eds.). (2021). *Country: Future fire, future farming*. Thames & Hudson| National Museum Australia.
Griffiths, A. (1983). Australian immigration. In O. Koivukangas (Ed.), *Scandinavian emigration to Australia and New Zealand project: Proceedings of a Symposium, February 17–19, 1982, Turku, Finland* (pp. 24–29). Institute of Migration.
Harari, Y. (2014). *Sapiens: A brief history of humankind* (trans. Y. Harari, J. Purcell, & H. Watzman). Vintage. (Original work published 2011).
Hutton, D., & Connors, L. (1999). *A history of the Australian environment movement*. Cambridge University Press.
Jeffes, E. (2020). Who knows best? Paternalism in aboriginal policy. *NEW: Emerging scholars in Australian Indigenous Studies, 5*(1). https://doi.org/10.5130/nesais.v5i1.1554
Lines, W. (1991/1999). *Taming the great southern land: A history of the conquest of nature in Australia* (Reprint ed.). The University of Georgia Press.
Marshall, A. J. (Ed.). (1966). *The great extermination*. Heinemann.
McQuade, J. (2019, April 19). Earth Day: Colonialism's role in the overexploitation of natural resources. *The Conversation*. https://theconversation.com/earth-day-colonialisms-role-in-the-overexploitation-of-natural-resources-113995.
National Museum Australia. (n.d.). *Gold rushes*. Retrieved May 29, 2024, from https://www.nma.gov.au/defining-moments/resources/gold-rushes#:~:text=Between%201851%20and%201871%20the,the%20government%20and%20fellow%20diggers
Paddle, R. (2000). *The last Tasmanian tiger: The history and extinction of the Thylacine*. Cambridge University Press.
Pascoe, B. (2014). *Dark Emu: Aboriginal Australia and the birth of agriculture*. Magabala Books.
Perkins, R. (2022). *The Australian Wars* [Documentary]. Retrieved August 14, 2023, from https://www.sbs.com.au/ondemand/tv-series/the-australian-wars?cid=od:search:gg:con:alwayson:dsa-tvseries:prog&gclid=EAIaIQobChMI0euAstnbgAMVMBCDAx1oUggkEAAYASAAEgJ3CvD_BwE&gclsrc=aw.ds

# References

Rolls, E. (2000). *Australia: A biography, the beginnings from the cosmos to the genesis of Gondwana, and its rivers, forests, flora, fauna, and fecundity*. University of Queensland Press.
Smith, C. (2013). Four seasons in Australia: Time to rethink? *EarthSong Journal: Perspectives in Ecology, Spirituality and Education, 2*(5), 9–10.
Watson, I. (2014). *Aboriginal peoples, colonialism and international law: Raw law*. Routledge.
White, M. (1994). *After the greening: The browning of Australia*. Kangaroo Press.
Williams, M. (1997). Ecology, imperialism and deforestation. In T. Griffiths & L. Robin (Eds.), *Ecology and empire* (pp. 169–184). Edinburgh University Press.

# Chapter 5
# Seeding Change: Genesis of New South Wales Department of Education Environmental Education Centres

## 5.1 Introduction

This chapter explores the bureaucratic life and times of the New South Wales (NSW) Fauna Protection Panel (FPP), which was considered cutting-edge for its time. This panel was inaugurated through the 1948 Fauna Protection Act, an event introduced at the end of Chap. 2's exploration of the development of environmental awareness. The differences in the social, political, economic and environmental setting for the Panel from its inauguration to its demise are striking. Throughout this time the groundwork was laid for an environment where field studies centres (FSCs) were possible within the NSW Department of Education.

## 5.2 The Fauna Protection Panel

> Here was a very large advisory group, considerably larger than recent research is showing to be the most effective number of a group, seven, to reach a consensus. But in many ways, the group of individuals assembled as representatives, while dominated in the early days by the bureaucrats on the Panel who tried to stifle an imaginative approach to wildlife conservation, soon became absorbed in imaginative possibilities. In moving in this direction, their enthusiasm began to educate those who may have had a different vision. So "by the end of the fifties something of a revolution in thinking had occurred not only in the Panel but also within the community… it is now clear that the wildlife service went into the 60s with a clear cut program and a capacity of considerable effectiveness." (Strom cited in Fox, 2016, Ch. 7, para. 30)

In many ways, the Fauna Protection Act (NSW) was a leap forward, shifting the agenda in favour of environmental management and protection, largely through the creation of the FPP. Additionally, the creation of the FPP led to an overt official broadening of environmental concerns, with fauna protection later formally linked with flora protection and the protection of ecosystems. Each aspect of the environment that gained public attention carried with it political and government struggles—epitomised in the career of a central figure in the establishment of the environmental education centres (EECs): Allen Strom.

Neither the Birds and Animal Protection Act 1918 (NSW), nor its 1930 amendment, nor the Wild Flowers and Native Plant Protection Act 1927 (NSW), provided adequate resourcing for the protection of flora and fauna. The Fauna Protection Act (NSW) was legislated in 1948, nearly 40 years and two world wars after the Wildlife Preservation Society instigated advocacy for managed wildlife reserves and guardians/educators (Hutton & Connors, 1999, XA). The legislation established the FPP and a Chief Guardian of Fauna to administer the Act which replaced the Birds and Animals Protection Act 1918 (NSW) and its 1930 amendment (National Parks, Australia: New South Wales, 1979). The Panel was tasked with:

- establishing and managing faunal reserves (later to become nature reserves),
- engaging in educational activities (see Fig. 5.1 for an illustrative example of an environmental awareness poster distributed by the FPP),
- encouraging the establishment of faunal societies (later flora and fauna protection societies/conservation societies),
- the authority for the protection and care of fauna,
- conducting or cooperating in research for the protection and care of fauna, and
- advising the Minister on protection matters (Fox, 2016; Strom, 2017).

Under the Fauna Protection Act, fauna was defined as birds and mammals, native, introduced and imported. Rats and mice were excluded, with the water rat being the only exception. Reptiles, fish and amphibians were unprotected. While the FPP considered extending protection to reptiles, it was not until the draft Conservation Act (NSW) in the 1960s that the protection of reptiles and some insects was recommended. It took the National Parks and Wildlife Act 1974 (NSW) to enact this protection (Fox, 2016; National Parks and Wildlife Act 1974 (NSW); Strom, 2017).

The Panel was responsible to the Chief Secretary (late to be termed Minister) of the Chief Secretary's Department and had representation from the Departments of the Chief Secretary, Agriculture, Lands, Tourist Activities, Water, Soil and Forestry Commission, and Education. The Forestry Commission had a separate seat at the table. Four of these departments had their senior civil servant, the Under Secretary, as their FPP representative—the Department of Lands, Agriculture, the Chief Secretary's Department and Tourist Activities (Strom, 2017). There was a representative of the agriculture and grazing sector who was also from the Government benches. The Australian Museum and the University of Sydney each had a representative (Fox, 2016). The final three Panel members comprised a well-known philanthropist with protection tendencies (animal enclosures—sanctuaries/zoos), Ted Hallstrom; a mammologist at the Australian Museum nominated by the Linnaean Society, Ellis Troughton; and Strom, nominated by the Wildlife Preservation Society of Australia and supported by the Sydney Bushwalkers Club. These Panel members were to represent "preservation, conservation, protection or scientific investigation

## 5.2 The Fauna Protection Panel

**Fig. 5.1** "Our endangered wildlife- The eastern native cat." Poster illustrated by Margaret Senior originally commissioned for the NSW Fauna Protection Panel (1948–1967). Printed with permission of NSW National Parks and Wildlife Service, and the Margaret Senior Archives, held by the University of Newcastle (Australia) Special Collections

of fauna" (Strom, 2017, Ch. 1, para. 30). The first Chief Guardian was Frank Griffiths, previously a senior clerical officer in the Chief Secretary's Department.

According to Strom, the Panel was a tool of political and bureaucratic administration with no burning desire to see conservation succeed (Strom, 2017). It operated in a context of compromise between personalities and policies (Fox, 2016), and members knew that change would come from the electorate (Strom, 2017). Strom observed departmental heads assuming the function of "super-politician"—filtering out recommendations that were seen to be too contentious. Strom found this practice an injustice in the organisation of the NSW public service—making a "cipher" of the Minister and proving counterproductive to innovation (Strom, 2017, Ch. 4, para. 14). There were, of course, conflicts for Panel members who were unlikely to go against the demands of their job (Fox, 2016). Most Panel members saw themselves not as planners but as a reference group. Only one of these early members of the Panel made a systematic effort to visit established faunal reserves to understand potential management problems and that was Harold Messer from the Department of Conservation who also understood the necessity of badgering the bureaucracy, according to Strom (2017).

The networking instigated by the Panel was beneficial for the progress of conservation. Examples of this networking are peppered throughout this history. However, as an example, the panel member with a particular interest in grazing and agriculture and from the Government benches, Roger Nott, became the Minister for Mines in the late 1950s. Strom, with Nott's assistance, was able to secure protections for some sections of Bungonia limestone, a unique environment in the Southern Highlands, by extending the area of reserve—for a short time only, however, as the protection was later relaxed.

There was an initial lack of understanding of ecosystems with many Panel members focused on "single species" protection with no understanding of the need for habitat protection. Generally, an anthropocentric mentality loomed large. Over the years many Panel members came to understand conservation matters through their involvement with the Panel, and it was Cec Buttsworth, the Chief Secretary's Department representative, who persuaded Strom, a strong advocate for conservation, to take on the position of Chief Guardian of the FPP after the death of Frank Griffiths in 1958 (Fox, 2016).

In the early days, the Panel had to work exceedingly hard to win a minimum of nature reserves. One difficulty was that the Ministry for Lands had to approve land being dedicated as faunal reserve. According to Strom, this Department was archaic in its thinking and still in "unlocking the land" mode. Conservation was not a priority. Strom also alleged that to make matters worse, many within the Lands Department assumed they were more knowledgeable than the experts. Competing interests in the 1950s included soldier settlements, wheat expansion out west, and the breakup of many estates (Fox, 2016). Only land that was perceived as not valuable for other purposes was seen as appropriate for conservation.

The first four extensive reserve proposals included areas of rainforest and snow gum environments (within Barrington/Gloucester Tops) (see Fig. 5.2 for a contemporary photo of Barrington Tops National Park), open forest and sandstone flora

## 5.2 The Fauna Protection Panel

**Fig. 5.2** Barrington Tops National Park, January 2022

habitat (country from feeder catchments into the Shoalhaven River), aquatic birds and associated ecosystems (the Macquarie Marshes), and a sampling of mallee and mulga inland (the Western Plains). These proposals had been developed by Griffiths and Strom.

They were carefully pursued by Griffiths as the Chief Guardian in the early days. Strom had the mapping and surveying skills, and networks (including scientific networks), to see through the misinformation/sleight of hand that was delivered by the bureaucracies generally—there were times where they tried to bamboozle with terminology. For instance, the Department of Mines' response to the proposed Tinderry Range Reserve was described by a government geologist friend of Strom's as "disconnected geological phrases from a geological dictionary" (Fox, 2016, Ch. 8, para. 13). Strom often travelled to study potential faunal/nature reserve ecosystems—he had direct understanding of the geography, geomorphology and biodiversity of the entire State of NSW (Fox, 2016; Strom, 2017). Strom also had the skills to get things done (Fox, 2016).

These proposals however, in the early days of the Panel, got nowhere—they were simply purposefully ignored. There was no response to the submission for a nature reserve from the Western Lands Commission. Similarly, the long-awaited response from the Department of Lands for the other three proposals was negative as the Department of Lands were unwilling to assist in defining the boundaries given the descriptions made. This was a "Catch-22" given that there was no resourcing of field survey staff or cartographers. Making the approval process more arduous and time consuming, the Lands Department interpreted the Fauna Protection Act 1948 (NSW) to mean that approval was necessary from all departments and authorities that might have had an interest in the lands in question. Mines Department approval proved especially difficult. These issues took a long time to overcome but the agenda slowly shifted forward with the collaborative effort and growth of reserve advocates and the expansion of the capacity of the Panel (Fox, 2016; Strom, 2017).

### 5.2.1 Progression Within the Fauna Protection Panel

It took 5 years to secure the first reserve, John Gould Faunal Reserve on Cabbage Tree Island, in the now Port Stephens Shire, in 1954. Several more followed across NSW—Boorgana, Barron Grounds, Lion Island, Gurumbi and Nadgee (see Fig. 5.3

**Fig. 5.3** Track to Greenglades, Nadgee Nature Reserve, September 2022

for a contemporary photo of Nadgee Nature Reserve). While some of the acquisitions were handed over by the Department of Land apparently for convenience or as a demonstration of benevolence, others were due to recommendations by conservation groups (Strom, 2017). For example, it was Strom with his survey and mapping skills and the Caloola Club who promoted Nadgee Faunal (Nature) Reserve. Other preservation-minded organisations such as the Illawarra Field Naturalists' Society, along with other local groups, advocated for Barren Grounds Faunal (Nature) Reserve (Strom, 2017; Fox, 2016).

### 5.2.2 The Development of Divide

Emotional protection of animals as opposed to management of animals is a theme throughout the life of the FPP and beyond. Enmeshed within this is the enormous divide between the discourse in rural areas and that in the much more populated cities (Strom, 2017). Additionally, there was very little scientific data on pest native species which initially made it difficult to make informed decisions. At one stage, the Panel was looking for evidence that wedge-tail eagles and wombats were causing rural damage. This was taking time given staffing issues. Clive Evatt, the Chief Secretary (1950–52), decided to protect both species which caused farmer outrage. The Cabinet reversed the protection quickly but not before the FPP bore the blame and were labelled disparagingly as "protectionists." At one stage Evatt changed the open season on kangaroos to an individual licence system without education and evidence calling the open season "fauna destruction" not "fauna protection." Fortunately, the matter was taken out of his hands. Evatt's decisions contributed to making change in wildlife management difficult into the future (Strom, 2017).

### 5.2.3 Capacity and Resources

The capacity and credibility of the FPP grew from the late 1950s. Noteworthy was the methodical mapping work carried out gratis by Gordon McKern, a retired mining engineer, who from 1958 undertook to map all established sanctuaries and vacant Crown land found on Parish Maps (Fox, 2016) onto county maps of the Central and Eastern Divisions of NSW. This enabled the assessment of the sanctuaries and the systematic processing of ecosystem selection for proposed nature reserves (Strom, 2017). Additionally, and significantly, once the FPP staff grew in the late 1950s and 1960s, detailed field studies of proposed nature reserves were possible.

Wildlife Service development required fieldwork, yet the Fauna Protection Act 1948 (NSW) made no provision for appropriate staff and government administrators were reluctant to seek staff from the Public Service Board. Originally, Panel discussion revolved around the Chief Guardian of Fauna Protection carrying out fieldwork—totally unrealistic given his already considerable workload. Suggestions to second staff from other agencies or recruit Honorary Rangers came to naught. According to Strom, "It was an atmosphere of apology, an aversion to 'empire building'" (Strom, 2017, Ch. 6, para. 4).

Initially, when the FPP asked for two field officers, Clive Evatt, Chief Secretary (1950–52), changed the request to five which was not well-received by Treasury. It took 4 years for the request to be granted (Strom, 2017). The Panel was chagrined when their request was refused due to lack of finances, so they made a deputation to the new Chief Secretary, Gus Kelly (1952–1959). Eventually Treasury agreed to fund a field officer and a vehicle in the 1953/1954 budget.

The field officer position attracted little remuneration, but Strom saw this as advantageous as only the truly dedicated would apply (Strom, 2017). It was a trailblazing job with tasks including:

- making detailed studies of potential reserve areas,
- policing the offence provisions,
- establishing/encouraging fauna societies, and
- studying the management of kangaroo populations.

Fred Hersey was appointed to the position in 1954. After 4 years of wrangling they had the Chief, a field officer and a shorthand writer/typist. Hersey was the first permanent ranger appointed for field work for the whole state in wildlife conservation. He had been a member of the Caloola Club so was familiar with many of the landscapes. He understood the needs and problems and had a background in citizen-based nature conservation. He could win support for nature conservation. While he had no tertiary qualifications for the job, he had a thirst for knowledge and was very approachable (Strom, 2017).

In 1955 the FPP was also given approval for a biologist to work out of the Museum of Australia on a scant salary offered by the administration. The position was advertised twice with no applications forthcoming. As the protocol was only to advertise Departmental vacancies twice, the position was abolished but the Chief Guardian of the FPP was not advised of this. It was 2 years between the initial approval and the discovery during a FPP inquiry that the position had been abolished (Strom, 2017).

Strom had a good network within the Department of Education stemming from his teaching years. He had negotiated Allan Fox's secondment as Education Officer in 1965 with the Inspector of Schools. Fox, an excellent community conservation educator, had been one of Strom's students at Balmain, was involved in the National Fitness Camps, and had been a member of both the Caloola Club and the National Parks Association of NSW. The Inspector was happy to support conservation education and the Department of Education paid for Fox's salary for the 2-year secondment (Strom, 2017).

### 5.2.4 The Development of Conservation Societies

In 1950 the FPP minutes noted that Crosbie Morrison, editor of *Wild Life* magazine, had been making enquiries. He had been urging the establishment of nature clubs and had been informed that assistance would be given in the formation of such clubs. He was interested in publishing the information in his magazine. This inquiry prompted the panel to develop some form and function around the issue and it was thought that "natural history clubs" should be encouraged and assisted. Strom was interested in developing community fieldwork as it could increase interest and capacity in natural history, assist in the understanding of the influence of ecology in wildlife management, and grow familiarity with concerns for conservation (Strom, 2017).

In 1951 Clive Evatt, the Chief Secretary, attended a Panel meeting inquiring about advancement of faunal societies. It was clear he wanted them developed. The subject was brought up once more at the next meeting by Frank Griffiths, with the Panel requesting he write up a statement of aims and functions for the societies, which he did and presented to the next meeting. The statement read:

> That Faunal Societies could assist in the protection and preservation of fauna in the following ways: (a) Educating the local public by distributing literature regarding protection, and by arranging film shows, lectures, etc. (b) Obtaining local press publicity for the work of the Panel and of the Society. (c) Collecting information locally about fauna, their habitats and movements, and in assisting the Panel in any surveys it might undertake. (d) Advising the Panel on local matters in connection with the protection of fauna. (e) Co-operating with trustees of parks and reserves established for the preservation of fauna and flora, or for recreation purposes. (f) Assisting in ensuring that the laws relating to sanctuaries, are observed. (g) Working for the establishment of local reserves and sanctuaries. (h) Preventing the destruction of natural habitats and encouraging the planting of trees. (Strom, 2017, Ch. 7, para. 33)

Strom saw this as "surprisingly activist-oriented" for its time, particularly given that "they were prepared and presented to the FPP by Frank Griffiths, a product of the establishment; finally, they were approved by the FPP, a bastion of the establishment, without alteration" (Strom, 2017, Ch. 7, para. 34).

Faunal societies must have been viewed as a way through the impasse of being under-resourced with an enormous task at hand and an extremely parsimonious Public Service Board. Fauna protection societies became flora and fauna protection societies—later some became nature conservation societies. While the societies were to be independent, the Panel agreed to "supply assistance and co-operate closely in their activities" (Strom, 2017, Ch. 7, para. 37). The Panel found through experience that it was best to motivate but not direct these groups. They were very localised groups, interested in local issues, working on local issues (Strom, 2017). These groups became extremely popular and successful. In 1955, an inaugural annual conference saw the beginnings of the Nature Conservation Council of NSW established to act as an umbrella organisation for all conservation groups in NSW (Fox, 2016; James, 2013; Strom, 2017). The Chief Guardian chaired the original meetings (1955), organised the venue, arranged for minute keeping and supplied the venue for the endorsed conference committee (executive committee) to follow-up actions (Strom, 2017). Strom started to chair these executive meetings once he became Chief Guardian. It was not until the mid 1960s that the organisation became officially known as the Nature Conservation Council of NSW with a comprehensive constitution. The close relationship between the FPP and the Council, which included the Executive meeting in the FPP rooms, lasted until the FPP ceased operations. The section of the Fauna Protection Act 1948 (NSW) relating to the establishment and support of conservation groups was not repeated in the National Parks and Wildlife Act 1974 [NSW] (Strom, 2017; Fox, 2016).

Another group that was supported by the FPP was the National Parks Association of NSW. At its first conference in 1955, the nature conservation societies had agreed to strive for a national parks service. Two years later the National Parks Association of NSW was established as the main driver for a national park service in NSW (Strom, 2017).

The NSW Ranger Patrol was another self-organised conservation protection group (Strom, 2017). It seems to have been active in the early 1950s according to newspaper articles such as "Florists' shops raided for Christmas bells" (The Sun, 1952) and "Rangers' Patrol at work" (The Gosford Times and Wyong District Advocate, 1954). The FPP encouraged ex-officio and honorary rangers (Strom, 2017). The Rangers' League of NSW established a special Field Unit to assist with education and enforcement. Recruiting, informing and educating ex-officio and honorary rangers was essential given that until 1960 only one ranger was employed. Information appeared in the [Department of] *Education Gazette* and the Teachers Handbook, a guide for teachers produced by the NSW Department of Education. However, the duties of an honorary ranger were not published until 1962. Few field officers or lands inspectors became rangers. In addition, Strom noted, "There is no doubt that there were many very helpful honorary rangers, exceeded unfortunately, by many who were quite incompetent" (Strom, 2017, Ch. 7, para. 17). There was a great need for ranger education. The *Rangers' Bulletin* was first produced in 1952. Initially the Bulletin consisted of three or four pages with a print run of 2500 (Strom, 2017). In 1955, 7000 copies of the *Rangers' Bulletin* went to teachers and wildlife conservation societies (Fox, 2016). In addition to education, the FPP started to carefully vet potential rangers and inform them about legislation, available literature and what was expected before they took on the role. Strom noted that together with close permanent staff liaison, these tactics proved effective in ensuring effective honorary and ex-officio rangers (2017).

### 5.2.5 Publication Development

The *Rangers' Bulletin* was replaced by the *Wildlife Service*, a quarterly journal, in 1959 which had an agenda to maintain ranger interest, garner support from community members, give a voice to the work of the FPP, and inform about fauna protection. A journal had been mooted by the publications subcommittee of the Panel in 1953 but it took a long time to come to fruition (Strom, 2017). The Government Printing Service provided 20,000 copies per quarter with the FPP insignia and posted copies to the supplied mailing list at no cost (see Fig. 5.4 for an image of the FPP Wildlife Service insignia.). They also gave great assistance in the printing of various coloured posters and publications over the life of the FPP. One such publication was the Fauna Protection Panel Annual Report, which proved an.

effective education document. Some printing was paid for, but the significant amount of free printing assisted greatly in education and freeing up monies for other Panel ventures. In the final year (1967), up to 60,000 copies of *Wildlife Service* were printed with some issues up to 64 pages. It had a broad distribution, from schools to rangers and other relevant societies.

### 5.2.6 Further Panel Progress

When Strom became the Chief Guardian in 1958 his budget was minuscule. He requested £8000 but the parliamentary budget provided just £200 (Strom, 2017). However, further support and balance on the Panel had come with the replacement of Hallstrom in 1957 by a quick succession of Commonwealth Science and Industrial Research Organisation (CSIRO) Wildlife Division personnel—Dr Robert Carrick

**Fig. 5.4** Wildlife Service | Fauna Protection Panel insignia, illustrated by Margaret Senior. Attribution: Printed with permission of NSW National Parks and Wildlife Service, and the Margaret Senior Archives, held by the University of Newcastle (Australia) Special Collections

who was replaced by Francis Ratcliffe, who was replaced by Dr. Harry Frith who remained on the Panel until the end. The CSIRO personnel provided much needed practical scientific, professional support and guidance. Dr. John Evans replaced Roy Kinghorn, as the Australian Museum FPP representative, continuing to provide great reference and advice (Strom, 2017). In 1958 Tom Moppett, a conservationist, filled Strom's Panel position. Roy Lucas took the Department of Conservation position and provided wide administration knowledge. Another Panel replacement was a grazier who was an effective conduit with the Western District. Simultaneously, the Panel temporarily halted requests for scientific staff and instead called for much needed field officers and wardens/rangers. They wanted to get on with inspections and plans for faunal reserves and education (Fox, 2016). Wardens/rangers were situated and worked on their reserves and field officers dealt with other matters regarding fauna (Strom, 2017). In 1962, there were three field officers and eight inspection districts in addition to the metropolitan district. When Tom Moppett became Deputy Chair in 1964 there were still two vacancies, one being the Linnaean Society nominated Panel position originally held by Troughton, and the other the grazier position. While the grazier position was filled in September 1964, the Linnaean Society nominated position remained vacant until March 1966.

In 1964 an amendment to the Fauna Protection Act 1948 (NSW) enabled the establishment of wildlife and game refugees on land "other" than that owned by the Crown. This allowed for the encouragement of landowners to retain valuable natural bushland or wetland. The amendment also increased the Panel membership, allowing a member from the Western Lands Commission, a member of the police force, nominated by the Premier, and a member of the CSIRO (Strom, 2017). The two conservation positions (Linnaean and Frith's) were filled in March 1966 by Professor Brereton from the University of New England and Dr. Carolin, a botanist, both committed academic conservationists. There were other changes of departmental personnel on the Panel but the most significant was Howard Stanley as the new representative of the Department of Lands in July 1965.

### 5.2.7  *Education and the Fauna Protection Panel*

> It was going to take many years of hard talking to lift the dead hand of bureaucratic indifference to "public education" motivated by an enlightened understanding of wildlife conservation. What was not realized was that without sympathy in the electorate, the purpose of the Fauna Protection Panel would be forgotten by Government. (Strom, 2017, Ch. 3, para. 34)

In order to educate school students about the FPP and their work, the FPP tried to get conservation education resources disseminated throughout the NSW public school system, but without success. The Department of Education's attitude was that they had nature study in the primary curriculum and geography in secondary and that was sufficient (Fox, 2016).

I was well aware that the administration of education did not approve of teachers encouraging those moral values in pupils likely to be somewhat at odds with the establishment. (Strom, 2017, Ch. 7, para. 10)

The first FPP formal education efforts involved targeting school children with art and essay prizes for conservation themed work. This was disbanded after dismal results in 1956 (Fox, 2016; Strom, 2017).

No one on the Panel was brave enough at that time, to suggest the provision of resource material and practical guidance for teachers, which might stimulate interest and develop skills leading to the production of teaching programmes based on existing curriculums and aimed at establishing an awareness of the conservation and management of resources. Most members of the Panel would not have thought in such terms and those that did, soon realized it was far beyond the resources of the one-man wildlife service. (Strom, 2017, Ch. 7, para. 6)

Strom saw a double standard with schooling: "It has seen fit to expect children to accept the preservation ethic whilst they are children but to reject the childhood concepts with the advent of 'maturity'" (Strom, 2017, Ch. 7, para. 6). He saw all formal education as dominated by the basics and public examinations. "My experience with formal education is that it is beset with a continuing stress on the acquisition of 'basics' and the ability to score well in public examinations" (Strom, 2017, Ch. 4, para. 6). Strom went so far as to say that the "Education Department for years used the Gould League of Bird Lovers and later, the Junior Tree Wardens as a smokescreen for the lack of purposeful programs in conservation education" (Strom, 2017, Ch. 7, para. 7).

Strom's memoirs in 1987 state that he found that the methodology used in the conventional teaching of history and geography destroys any relevance the subjects have to student's lives, yet history and geography spell out real life situations and are fundamental to environmental education (EE) programs (Strom 1987). Harris thought along the same lines and had been advocating for change. In an edition of *New Horizons* in 1943, in relation to the 1941 Social Studies curriculum, Harris had asked, "Are we really teaching history when we tell them pleasant little stories about noble men and leave them to figure out why such noble creatures have left the world in such a mess?" She talks of exploitation and colonialism and goes on to say,

It seems fairly clear that with such an unreal attitude the details of the social studies will hardly be such as will give the child that clear picture of his environment, past and present, essential to his development as a good citizen. (Harris quoted in Webb, 1998, p. 72)

Strom stressed environmental encounters and the welfare of the environment (Strom 1987; Webb, 1998).

In regard to education, the FPP gave up trying to gain access to schools as without teacher interest it was difficult to gain any traction. The Panel requested the Department of Education give "greater emphasis" to fauna protection but was informed that they had already included fauna protection and nothing more would be possible (Strom, 2017). Following further pressure on the Department of Education Panel representative regarding the possibility of conservation advisors within the school system, it was suggested Strom was wasting his time (Fox, 2016).

The education of teachers was viewed as showing more promise than trying to educate students directly. Strom believed that an understanding of the natural sciences and an opportunity to experience nature in the field would instil a conviction for wildlife conservation (Strom, 2017). Strom's philosophy was one of conservation and sustainable human habitat—through understanding, valuing and thus encouraging care (Fox, 2016).

Educational conservation material was published to educate the public about conservation (see Fig. 5.5 for an example of the FPP's conservation awareness posters).

A Caloola Club journal entitled *Yarrawonda*, covered nature conservation issues with an emphasis on knowledge building during field trips/work. Some of the tutorials were subsequently included in a book on Australian ecology used by first year biology students at the University of NSW. These were also published by the FPP as *A Background to Nature Conservation: Some Processes Which Help to Build and Destroy Natural Habitats* (Fox, 2016, Ch 5, para. 53), over 40,000 copies of which were distributed (Fox, 2016). The seven chapters were "Ecology as an Introduction", "From the Rocks Came the Soils", "Plants, Like Humans, Live in Communities", "Plants Invade and Colonise", The Interdependence of Plant and Animals", "When the Plant Communities are Upset", and "Some Conclusions and Actions for Future Guidance". These chapter titles suggest that, through understanding ecosystems, there would be a desire to act to preserve them—the defining element of EE, an

**Fig. 5.5** Poster illustrated by Margaret Senior originally commissioned for the NSW Fauna Protection Panel (1948–1967). Attribution: Printed with permission of NSW National Parks and Wildlife Service, and the Margaret Senior Archives, held by the University of Newcastle (Australia) Special Collections

action component. It must be remembered that the emphasis was on the issues of the times, and these became broader and more complex from the 1960s onward.

## 5.2.8 The 1960s and Progressive Achievement

In the mid 1960s conservation issues were often part of the everyday discourse. Some of the concerns of the day in Australia included pollution/damage from rutile and beach sand mining, pine plantations replacing native forest, kangaroo numbers decreasing while still damaging farming land, draining of coastal wetlands for flood mitigation, loss of mangroves, toxins starting to enter the human environment (polluted waterways and air pollution), declining koala numbers, hazard reduction burning and bird smuggling (Fox, 2016).

After years of complex and often frustrating negotiations with various NSW government departments the FPP had accomplished a great deal by 1966. They had achieved increased education within the community at a local level. Fifty-two nature reserves had been established with nearly 150 more proposed. Approximately 146 wildlife refuges were proclaimed covering 2,167,321 acres. The FPP assisted in the establishment and support of over 50 local faunal protection societies, flora and fauna protection societies, and conservation societies. They helped galvanise the conservation movement with the Nature Conservation Council of NSW and the National Parks Association of NSW set up as umbrella organisations. They produced an abundance of educational publications with the assistance of the government printer (see Fig. 5.6 for another example of a FPP educational poster). They made inroads into the management of fauna, particularly kangaroos, and faunal research. There were 16 officers taking wildlife conservation into the community and eight administration staff backing them up.

With Fox as Education Officer, Wildlife Service staff were reorganised in 1965 into Education and Publicity, Reserves, Wildlife Management, and Law Enforcement rather than by districts. There were information centres at Barron Grounds and Hallstrom Nature Reserves, and warden/rangers with a priority to educate the public at other reserves (Strom, 2017). The FPP contributed to a climate for the establishment of the NSW National Parks and Wildlife Service (NPWS) in 1967. They contributed to a biennial Interstate Fauna Authorities Conference between 1948 and 1968 which assisted in educating and coordinating across the states and territories regarding conservation (Strom, 2017). So, over the years, the FPP had become an effective, formidable body with a strong people and media powerbase fuelled by the wise conduct of Strom (Fox, 2016). Respect was gained from the environment movement, the rural community, the scientific community and some political quarters, primarily in the Country Party. "Allen Strom was an effective and inspiring 'conductor' of harmonious achievement played frequently under extreme interdepartmental antagonism" (Fox, 2016, Ch. 11, para. 99).

The Fauna Protection Act 1948 (NSW) provided for control of the destruction of native animals, but practices morphed into management to ensure the "preservation

**Fig. 5.6** Poster illustrated by Margaret Senior originally commissioned for the NSW Fauna Protection Panel (1948–1967). Printed with permission of NSW National Parks and Wildlife Service, and the Margaret Senior Archives, held by the University of Newcastle (Australia) Special Collections

of species." By the mid 1960s the term "conservation" was being used in newspaper reports (Strom, 2017), signalling the growing understanding and discourse moving from the separation of specific species to a more holistic view of ecosystems. This had been a change well accepted in the FPP—in its program, publicity and dealings with the public. Such was the success of the FPP that the administration of the Wild Flowers and Native Plants Protection Act 1927 (NSW) was moved to the jurisdiction of the Panel in September 1966. The draft Wildlife Conservation Bill (NSW) which the FPP had instigated in the 1960s defined wildlife as "biotic communities and the environments that produce these communities" (Strom, 2017, Ch. 1, para. 26)—a leap forward.

As an example of the FPP's success, the 1966 Annual Report demonstrated substantial achievement in the establishment and management of nature and wildlife reserves, education and publicity programs, and wildlife management within a budget of $40,000. Support for this success was achieved through the network which included the NSW government printing service, the NSW Education Department, the National Herbarium of NSW, the Royal Botanic Garden and the CSIRO Wildlife Research Division (Fox, 2016).

## 5.3 NSW Education Reform and Reserve Development Collide

Decentralisation and ensuing curriculum diversification (Barcan, 1965, 1988) saw an emerging increase in field studies activities which coincided with regulated education practices evolving within the NSW nature reserves. The wildlife service within the FPP had found the need to consider limits to the types of usage within their reserve areas (Strom, 2017). The public was welcome because of the necessity to educate and endear the public to the reserves, but it was also necessary to set up guidelines to protect these sanctuaries. Plans were developed for maximum numbers, appropriate activities and areas of restriction, advertised and regulated by staff. Specific reserves and areas within reserves were set as "educational nature reserves" under strict support, taking the pressure off other reserves whilst still fulfilling an educative role. Strom stressed the objective of nature reserves as "reserves of biotic diversity" as opposed to national parks that were overwhelmingly seen, by the public, politicians and bureaucrats, as recreational areas. The FPP was keen to encourage research within the nature reserves, as was the trend overseas. The need for clear educational programs had been set.

## 5.4 The Demise of the Fauna Protection Panel

### 5.4.1 Growing Rifts

As time went on, rifts between the Department of Lands and the FPP became more pronounced. For example, in 1958, Strom, as Chief Guardian of Fauna, was invited by the Australian Academy of Science, to sit on a NSW Sub-Committee to advise on several aspects of parks and reserves. Charles Elphinstone, at the time the Panel member for the Department of Lands, strongly objected as he felt the position should go to the Lands "Parks and Miscellaneous" Branch where "Park Trust" management resided along with racecourses, cemeteries, and showgrounds as a minor operation. The Panel stood by the Chief Guardian of Fauna (Strom, 2017).

Another issue the Panel, and Strom via his membership on the Bouddi National Park Trust, engaged with was rutile and sand mining (Fox, 2016). The Panel requested the establishment of an Inter-Departmental Committee to examine the impact of mining. While the Department of Mines ignored the request, public awareness and political pressure eventually translated into a change in government policy. Accordingly, the Sims Committee was set up in 1965 to resolve conflict between sand miners and conservationists on the North Coast—and it brought down its report in 1968 (Hutton & Connors, 1999). The Committee had been called for by Tom Lewis, the Minister for Lands, and was within the State Planning Authority. It was chaired by Sims, a junior officer and urban planner who had at the time completed a detailed study of urban development on the North Coast (Fox, 2016). In progressing the study, Sims was assisted by two field officers, one from the NSW Herbarium and one from the Panel. The process was restricted in that it could not recommend suitable areas for national parks or reserves.

The power wielded by the mining companies was great. The Minister for the Departments of Lands and Mines decided which lands would be available for reserve and he chose only those lands not affected by mining leases. Only 96 of the proposed 640 square kilometres were set aside for national parks and only 19 of these were exempt from sandmining (Hutton & Connors, 1999). This finding galvanised the conservation movement into action. Whilst the tussle between the Mines and Lands Departments and conservationists continued, this line of narrative will not be continued here. It does, however, demonstrate how Strom and the Panel finally faced serious adversaries.

## 5.4.2 Advocacy for National Park Legislation

While nature reserves had some security as an Act of Parliament was required to repeal them, the national parks, sanctuaries and other reserves administered by the Parks and Reserves Division of the Department of Lands did not, with the exception of the Royal National Park, Kosciuszko State Park and Ku-ring-gai Chase National Park, which had been legislated in 1879, 1944 and 1961 (dedication 1894) respectively. The Parks and Reserves Division of the Department of Lands was also seriously under-resourced. Yet support for the protection of species increased as a result of the promotion of national parks for recreational purposes (Hutton & Connors, 1999).

The National Parks and Primitive Areas Council had proposed a national park authority to the McKell government in the 1940s (National Parks, Australia: New South Wales 1979). Along with the Wildlife Preservation Society of Australia, the NSW Federation of Bushwalkers Clubs and the Parks and Playgrounds Movement of NSW, the Council had been continually petitioning the Government to establish a national parks service since the Second World War. Some of the members were enthusiastic in wishing to emulate the parks set up in North America. These ideas coalesced and gained traction in 1955 when a detailed statement for a national parks service, separate from the Department of Lands, was prepared and widely distributed (Fox, 2016). The establishment of a national parks service and the training of rangers was recommended to Parliament in a private members bill by Lewis, who in 1960 was a relatively new member of the opposition. This got the topic onto the agenda and into the media. While the bill failed, continual agitation by Lewis and other national parks advocates, particularly the National Parks Association of NSW, kept national parks on the government and bureaucratic agenda.

A consequence of the national park discourse was that the Department of Lands appointed Howard Stanley to the position of Administrator of a Parks and Reserves Division in the Department of Lands. Indeed, he had been sent to gain knowledge of the American national parks, and other systems, and attend the first World

Conference on National Parks in Seattle in 1962, a conference organised by the International Union for Conservation of Nature and Natural Resources (Adams, 1962; Fox, 2016). Additionally, then Labor Premier, Robert Heffron, agreed to a national park authority in the run up to the 1962 election.

A Special Executive Committee was established within the NSW Labor Party to investigate the issue of national parks. They had consulted Strom who was encouraged to draft a national parks bill to establish an appropriate authority (Fox, 2016). A detailed report from the Special Executive Committee, which relied heavily on Strom's input, outlined six reserve types ranging from high-density recreation areas to primitive wilderness. The report also sought to ensure there were clear protections from mining and development. The report encouraged an alliance with the FPP and indeed included a note of thanks to Strom from the Assistant General Secretary of the Labor Party thanking him for the material that would educate Labor delegates. These events would not have been seen as apolitical. However, no progress was made before the next election in 1965 when the Labor Party lost power and Lewis became the new Government's Minister for the Departments of Lands and Mines.

### 5.4.3 Waning of Political Favour

In 1966 Strom and his team had been working on kangaroo management and were at the stage where a statement could be made regarding kangaroo meat and skin as a renewable resource related to wildlife conservation (Strom, 2017). Strom and his team asserted that there were alternative or adjunct farming possibilities. Whilst also having the established Parks Branch within his Department, the Minister for Lands and Mines, who had been made responsible for the staff of the FPP from 1 August 1966, showed interest in the well supported (scientifically and socially) initial process for a controlled kangaroo meat market. However, Stanley, Administrator of the Parks and Reserves Branch, enticed Strom's main kangaroo project staff member into his service with a higher salary. It is clear from Strom's account of the events that took place around the kangaroo management submission that he was being sidelined. For example, his submission was handled by someone with no experience, and Lewis went on to state that any further work would need to be completed with Strom's remaining staff. When Strom got Panel permission to request another officer, Lewis was too busy to discuss the issue (Strom, 2017).

In the research for his biography of Strom, Fox accessed Strom's correspondence and Ministerial briefings and found them annotated derogatorily, "with destructive and mostly erroneous criticism" by Stanley, at the time, the Department of Lands representative. Stanley was a supporter of the American national park system and a contender for the position of Director of any potential NSW national park system (Fox, 2016). The under-mining that occurred may well have played a part in the deteriorating relationship between Strom and Lewis, a relationship which had started out quite amicably with Strom educating an enthusiastic, newly elected

Lewis in the early 1960s as to what was needed in an Australian reserve system. Later, Lewis began to regard Strom as a fanatic (Hutton & Connors, 1999). Further, Lewis did not allow the final "Fauna Protection Panel Annual Report" for 1966–67, an indication of its growth and success, to be printed and tabled before Parliament as previous reports had been (Fox, 2016; Strom, 2017).

Bureaucrats and Minister Lewis subsequently requested that the Chief Guardian keep his briefing notes to a page in length. However, Eric Willis, the Chief Secretary and Strom's old superior who had a background in geography, understood their value and urged Strom to continue with his detailed briefing notes. Lewis and Willis were political rivals (Fox, 2016). Indeed, Willis had been surprised when the FPP was taken away from his portfolio.

It became known that the National Parks Bill was to be redrafted as the National Parks and Wildlife Bill. Three assistant directors—one each for administration, parks, and wildlife—were to report to an overall director. The Chief Guardian of Fauna was to become a public servant—a downgrade from a statutory position. There was no consultation with the FPP personnel in the preparation of the new bill (Fox, 2016).

The movement of the FPP out of the Chief Secretary's Department and into the Department of Lands was seen to explain the absence of nature reserve approvals from the Department. The number of proposals had been increasing due to a more streamlined ecosystem identification & submission processing method and more staff to effect change. There were nearly 150 reserve proposals at the time of the takeover—many with proposed management plans (Fox, 2016).

Thus, there was no opportunity for the Panel to discuss the integration of the old Wildlife Act and its accumulated scientific and democratic input with successful programs in animal management that had been developed over time. This was all to be placed in the hands of administrators with less knowledge and experience. Strom baulked at changes to the kangaroo management plan but was told his unwillingness to cooperate would be reported to the Under Secretary and Minister if he continued. When the FPP background briefing notes on the Bill garnered no response from the Department of Lands, Strom made inquiries and was informed by the Undersecretary that the Department was being lumbered with a portfolio it had no interest in. The papers were sitting on junior clerks' desks awaiting responses which the Undersecretary suggested Strom's staff should do—public staff doing political work (Fox, 2016).

It was believed Strom was kept uninformed due to his statutory position status. Politically and bureaucratically he could have been seen as a threat, especially given his influence within many networks. Fox suggested numerous reasons for Strom's sidelining by the conservation bureaucracy:

- the inertia of the Department of Lands in conservation matters,
- the contrasting needs of conservation that were being advanced by Strom,
- personal and political egos competing for dominance within the emerging environmental bureaucracies,
- fear of Strom's well-developed profile,

- personal and political conflict within the leading governance,
- an incorrect notion that Strom was a Labor man,
- Lewis' desire to bring a national parks service to fruition,
- the smouldering of endemic conservation thought by an American system brought to bear not by the United States but by Australian bureaucrats lacking local understanding but with great faith in the American system, and
- the appointment of a director from the American system without the appropriate indigenous knowledge and skill required (Fox, 2016).

### 5.4.4 National Parks and Wildlife Bill and Political Machinations

The National Parks and Wildlife Bill was put to Parliament in December 1966 but collapsed in the upper house which had an opposition majority.

> If it had not been for the caprice of a few Labor Members in the Legislative Council, the whole structure built up by the Fauna Protection Panel over the previous, almost twenty years, would have been thrown into the melting pot to be stirred up by the gathering of bureaucrats and an unsympathetic Minister of the Crown, with an unknown national parks service. (Strom, 2017, Ch. 16, para. 89)

The acceptance of the need for national parks and nature conservation worldwide played a substantial part in support for new legislation, as did the need for a unified coordination of personnel in ensuring that established and future proposals for national parks worked in harmony in sampling all possible ecosystems (National Parks, Australia: New South Wales 1979). Between December 1966 and the following October, when the Bill was passed, various conservation organisations including the National Parks Association of NSW, the National Trust, and the Nature Conservation Council of NSW provided comment encouraging amendments.

The December edition of *Wildlife Service* was partly motivated by the growing antagonism between those who wanted reserves for conservation and those who wanted them for recreation. The journal set out to illustrate that both conservation and recreation could be served as it was in the Warrumbungles National Park which included a Wildlife Refuge. Strom, who was on the Management Trust Committee, had guided this venture (Fox, 2016).

Having access to both public and government information in his position as the Panel Education Field Officer and as a state councillor on the National Parks Association of NSW, Fox was alarmed at the lack of plans for some of the proposed national parks and thus the possibility of boundary disputes with vested interests. The National Parks Association of NSW produced a journal in January 1967 outlining the weaknesses of the Bill which necessitated redrafting. A National Parks Association of NSW meeting was also called to discuss the issue (Fox, 2016).

Forty proposed amendments were received after the bill was rejected in December 1966. The most important for conservationists was that the new authority was to be independent of the Department of Lands (Strom, 2017). This was the only amendment that was accepted. The proposed changes caused acrimony within the conservation movement. Some did not want to put at risk the opportunity for national parks legislation. Some considered parks for recreation was the goal. Others fought for amendments such as for a Nature Conservation Commission with a deputy commissioner in charge of wildlife conservation administration, another in charge of national parks administration, and both positions overseen by a chief commissioner (Fox, 2016; Strom, 2017).

Legislation finally passed in October 1967. The NSW NPWS had 40 members from the FPP and Parks and Reserves Branch of the Department of Lands together with the 160 people employed through the Trusts who had oversight of the existing national parks. At the time of establishment there were 52 nature reserves, 12 national parks, seven state parks, and six historic sites with an area of 860,760 ha (National Parks, Australia: New South Wales 1979). The 1967 Act repealed the FPP and office of the Chief Guardian of Fauna and amended the Fauna Protection Act 1948 (NSW) and the Wild Flowers and Native Plants Protection Act 1927 (NSW). It vested all the powers, duties and responsibilities contained within these Acts to the Director, NSW NPWS[1] (NSW Government: State Archives and Records, n.d.).

### 5.4.5 The NSW NPWS and a Provocative Presentation: A Catalyst for Exodus

The overall Director of the NSW NPWS was to be Sam Weems, an American with a long history in one United States national park. According to Fox, he was, however, inexperienced in the NSW park/reserve system and the overall United States ecosystems and unable to identify parks by their ecological, landscape and historical context. Weems did not understand nor support the reserve system that Strom and the FPP had set up—a system that had been hailed by scientific and land administrators in Australia and worldwide (Fox, 2016).

Strom had asked to be returned to the Department of Education on a number of occasions but learned from confidantes within the Department of Public Service and the Education Department that his request had not been passed on (Strom, 2017), so he had a conference with the Public Service Board in late 1967. "I had no intention of being party to the annihilation of the wildlife service, once the National Parks and Wildlife Act became law." (Strom, 2017, Ch. 16, para. 17).

Then, in a conference with Weems and a Public Service Board Inspector in February 1968, Strom found that the Director-General of Education, Harold Wyndham, was happy for him to return to the Department of Education as the

---

[1] The National Parks and Wildlife Act 1974 (NSW) altered the 1967 Act by consolidating and amending the law relating to the establishment, preservation and management of national parks, historic sites and Aboriginal Sites (NSW Government: State Archives & Records, n.d.).

Advisor in Conservation (Strom, 2017). Strom commented, "Well, I know [sic] Wyndham because I'd been in the Teachers College and I'd met him on a number of occasions. He'd actually been, as a matter of fact, to a couple of functions at the Caloola Club." (XA). Processing this move, however, took time.

Fox had been requested to speak at the Annual Meeting of the Wildlife Preservation Society of Australia on 27 February 1968, but due to illness Strom was an enthusiastic proxy. While there was an embargo on public statements which were not vetted by the Minister for Lands, this talk had been booked well in advance, allowing Strom to bypass protocol—his speech was not vetted (Fox, 2016). Strom had given a copy to a *Daily Telegraph* newspaper reporter as earlier requested. The next day his most controversial views about the NSW NPWS were revealed in print. They included:

- that the NSW NPWS favoured national parks over nature conservation,
- that nature conservation would be setback catastrophically,
- that it was not too late to save the wildlife program via a restructure of the Service,
- that the Service needed independence from Ministerial dominance, and
- that the Service had the potential to become, "another public service agency handing down agreeable picnic-style usage of parks and law-interpreted protection of wildlife." (Strom, 2017, Ch. 12, para. 26).

Strom had inverted the advice of Kingsmill, who had once been the Under Secretary for the Chief Secretary, who said, "be expressive as you wish but never get it into print and avoid being cited." Strom got press coverage knowing that it would most likely hasten the desired-for end to his association with the NSW NPWS (Fox, 2016, Ch.7, para. 46).

On February 28 Strom was instructed to take immediate leave before commencing work at the Department of Education as Advisor in Conservation (Fox, 2016).

> We must be ever grateful for pioneers like Allen Strom who did, indeed, "rock the boat!" In fact he rocked it too hard, and was overlooked as the founding Director of the fledgling National Parks & Wildlife Service. But, fortunately, the somewhat embarrassed Government of the day sought to "reward" him in some way, and offered him the unique position of Advisor in Conservation within the Dept of Education. Little did they realise that Allen would then beaver away over the following decade to get things moving regarding getting kids and teachers out of the classroom into the REAL environment (which is ever outside the classroom window!). And that started the ball rolling, because what Allen was doing became contagious. (K. McDonald, email December 19, 2016)

## 5.5 Reflection of this History

Themes that are peppered through the history of the conservation movement extend into the establishment and development of the FPP, to a lesser or greater degree. These themes are illustrated in the *The Life and Times of Allen Strom: Chief Guardian* written by Allan Fox and edited by McDonald, Dufty, Tribe and Schaefer

(2016) after Fox's death, and reinforced in *Some Aspects of Nature Conservation in NSW During the 1950s and 1960s*, written by Strom but published posthumously with the editing expertise of Dufty, McDonald, Tribe, Smith and Schaefer (2017). All of these people have had a significant influence promoting the EE agenda within NSW, nationally and internationally.

Emerging themes throughout this chapter include:

- the dichotomy of the dominant anthropocentric as opposed to ecocentric nature looming large,
- a bottom-up/top-down effect on governance and bureaucracy—the dominant hegemony. This is illustrated in the effect of lobby groups within the electorate on the upper levels of government and the bureaucracy and, additionally, the impact of global governance that started to intensify at this time,
- the effect of collegiality, networking and collaboration, and political interconnectedness—exemplified throughout,
- examples of the placating of egos within bureaucracy and the waxing and waning of political favour—threads that run through this rich history, and
- significantly, an attempted silencing that weaves its way through the fabric of this story.

Within the history of the FPP, the internal events and political shenanigans and circumstances of the day illustrate the difficulties faced by the Panel. Despite the difficulties, and with clear successes, the evolution of the Panel sets the scene for the establishment of the NSW NPWS and also the FSCs within the NSW Department of Education which became the EECs we know today.

## 5.6 The Little Desert Dispute—Another Example

This story of the FPP is one perspective of the story which has many synergies in other contexts within NSW, other states and other countries. Another is the Little Desert dispute in Victoria. The parallels with what was happening with the development of conservation, resource management, the dawning of an understanding of finite resources within bureaucracies, and the environmental revolution of the 1960s–1970s in NSW, Victoria and elsewhere are many and I do not wish to repeat them. But the Little Desert saga is significant. This dispute was a marker of the transition from conservation to environmentalism. It saw an example of the dawning of a finite world, urban environmental activism for nature. As with the FPP, it was/saw the creation of a public and scientific consultation mechanism for land management issues due to public demands—and their deterioration or collapse amidst an economic squeeze and de-democratisation.

Similar to the FPP narrative, the Little Desert dispute demonstrates the interconnectedness of government, science and the community with bureaucrats influenced by science, scientists influenced by community concerns and their own concerns as community members, and community influenced by bureaucrats—each influencing

## 5.6 The Little Desert Dispute—Another Example

the others (Robin, 1998). Both these histories reflect the variety of perspectives on the natural world that can be traced back to utilitarian, scientific, romantic, and aesthetic traditions (Robin, 1998).

The Little Desert on Wotjabaluk people's country is rich in First Nations' history and ongoing habitation and utility. It is on the border of Victoria and South Australia and like many harsh environments the low-resource base has resulted in greater ecological specialisation, thus diversity—it is rich in species but not agriculturally productive. The area had attracted field naturalists and ornithologists since early European settlement (Robin, 1998).

The Commonwealth Government, through the Rural Reconstruction Commission reports (1944–46) set the states land management objectives to avoid the debacle of solider settlement land being marginal and too small to be viable as had happened after World War I. In Victoria, the Land Utilisation Advisory Council 1950–1970 was set up to gather multiple forms of expertise including mapping and surveying, forestry, catchment and soil knowledge. Victoria's extradepartmental authority was more flexible than the Federal prescription of senior bureaucrat members and allowed for a wide range of expertise.

As with NSW, conservation bureaucracies had developed in the early 1900s. They were associated with science but focused on resource conservation rather than nature conservation (Robin, 1998). The conservation philosophy within bureaucracy set the parameters for the Little Desert dispute. They were crucial. Whether Little Desert should be conserved was only part of the concern, the others were power and economics.

The Little Desert protest was a major environmental campaign in Australia in 1969. The dispute was sparked by a proposal by the Victorian government to turn a large part of the Little Desert into farmland. The lead up to the public fight for the Little Desert saw the involved scientists and bureaucrats being shrewd and strategic enough to collect evidence, address the most powerful people and channels to support their cause in advocating for the Little Desert. The battle for the Little Desert was fought in the city where the strongest power structures existed though the local structures were indeed an important and integral part.

The Save Our Bushland Action Committee was inaugurated in 1969 to oppose the Victorian Minister for Lands, also Conservation, Sir William McDonald's proposal for the Little Desert Development Scheme, which was originally for 44 wheat farms but was scaled down to 12 sheep farms. The Safe Our Bushland Action Committee was a united front of eight conservation groups, including the Field Naturalists'Club of Victoria and the National Parks Association, who advocated for people's rights to undeveloped bushland and the right to participate in the decisions about future land use.

The Little Desert Dispute had already garnered media through conservation reports but the Save our Bushland Action Committee organised two well attended meetings in Melbourne in 1969 which were supported by pro-conservation media coverage. A deputation to the Premier was also supported. Most of the media and opinions surrounding the Little Desert dispute was against the settlement proposal. The majority held Labor and Country Party opposition within the Legislative

Council discredited the government's stance on the Little Desert settlement. An inquiry into the Little Desert Settlement Scheme in October 1969 heard official and unofficial evidence from bureaucrats frustrated at their department's dismissal of their advice. With a barrage of negative media the Legislative Council blocked the scheme's funding before the publication of the inquiry report. The inquiry uncovered evidence that the settlement scheme was set to reduce the tax burden for wealthy satellite farmers and not the rural battlers (Robin, 1998).

The Little Desert National Park of 945-hectares had been declared in 1968 but the area was increased in 1969 to 35,300 hectares to protect mallee fowl. This park extension however did not include the Little Desert's unique ecosystems that included mallee scrub, grasslands and wetlands and therefore did not appease the people. The protest to protect the area continued.

In 1969, during the Galbally inquiry on opening the Little Desert for settlement, ecologist Malcolm Calder proposed the establishment of a national park with an associated FSC, similar to those in operation in Britain. The testimony from ecologists at the Galbally inquiry contained scientific argument, but additionally non-scientific argument. This debate relating to social responsibility nurtured in the School of Botany at the University of Melbourne, which had a history of participating in public scientific matters.

For populations surrounding the Little Desert, the economy influenced local council's interest in conserving the Little Desert. Tourism increases attributed to the publicity whipped up by the controversy filled the gap for business after the 1967–1968 drought. The country people did not understand the city folk where the want of nature in its unaltered state stemmed from—it was tourism that swayed the local people of the Little Desert region to see conservation's potential. First Nations people were some of the first to advocate for eco-tourism given the double benefits of conservation while providing a livelihood. Barriers between city and country people were broken down through the tourism/dispute connection (Robin, 1998).

Sensing the electoral pressure the Liberal state government started addressing, or at least giving lip service to conservation. There were promises of a Land Resources Council and more national and forest parks and wildlife reserves. The Little Desert Dispute had economists and conservations on the same side and there was a concern about due process. However, the clash saw the beginning of a group concerned about the cost of development to the land itself—the natural environment became an entity.

The public called for public consultation and greater accountability within process. Riding the tide of victory jubilation, the Conservation Council of Victoria replaced the Save Our Bushland Action Group acting as a contact point for government regarding conservation issues. It had a good understanding of bureaucratic process but not necessarily the interests of the groups it represents.

The promised Land Resources Council became the Land Conservation Council an independent, yet government approved authoritative body responsibly for public land management matter inquiries. So, the Little Desert advocacy produced a permanent public consultation mechanism on land management. This was the beginning of the end for the Lands portfolio within the Victorian Government which was

**Fig. 5.7** Emu chicks (*Dromaius novaehollandiae*), Little Desert NP, Victoria. Attribution: Patrick Kavanagh, CC BY 2.0 https://creativecommons.org/licenses/by/2.0, via Wikimedia Commons

supplanted with conservation and finally disbanded in 1983. It was the end of frontier development which was replaced with an understanding of the finiteness and fragility of remaining lands. Urban support for the conservation of the Little Desert area in the 1970–80 s saw the Land Conservation Council's recommendation to gazette most of the Little Desert as a national park—its last recommendation before it was disbanded. Little Desert was designated a national park in 1988 (see Fig. 5.7).

This history is an example of people power effecting environmental decisions and the shift from conservation to environmentalism. It also demonstrates, through the prism of time, the power to effect the creation of democratic and environmental protection mechanisms—and years later the power of capitalist forces in dismantling these mechanisms. In 1997 the Environmental Conservation Council Act took away the mechanism for public representation and scientific justification.

## 5.7 Conclusion

This chapter has chronicled the establishment and expiration of the FPP, and the significant progress in conservation instigated and supported by it. Furthermore, this chapter foregrounds the importance of education for both Panel members, and the general public, in progressing conservation and the evident groundswell of support for conservation. Moreover, some of the intransigence, vested interests, and egos of bureaucracy and politics have been recounted. The extensive networks within and beyond the environmental movement have continued developing in yet more intrinsic ways and examples of developments within other contexts have been presented. The chapter closes with a fracture between the ecocentrism of conserving the unique diversity of NSW's ecosystems and a more anthropocentric conserving of land for general recreational purposes, and some silencing of many years of knowledge and endemic expertise in the area of conservation within the state of NSW. The chapter ends with Strom hastily facing a change in trajectory into the NSW Department of Education—the seeds sown for the establishment and funding of the first FSC, and the initiation of plans for many of the others.

There is evidence of a move from loss of species and environment—the disconnect, to a systems approach towards conservation. In addition, a distinction between ecocentric and anthropocentric viewpoints can be drawn. Some of the themes running through this history include the bottom-up/top-down effect on governance and bureaucracy, the effect of collegiality/networking/collaboration, the political interconnectedness, the placating of egos within bureaucracy, and the waxing and waning of political favour. Yet there are also familiar themes that echo through the pages regarding education. Nature study, conservation education, environmental and sustainability education have never been perceived as important in education—at least not in relation to the rest of the curriculum. Additionally, only teachers who had/have an interest in the area who were/are competent or willing to teach these topics taught/teach it. Many teachers did not learn/have not learnt the subject within their education/teacher education and so do not feel confident to teach it.

This chapter has established the context for the development of the NSW FSCs within the NSW Department of Education. These NSW FSCs later became the NSW EECs. The following chapters encompass the golden era of the development of environmentalism, indeed democratic governance for and by the people, which preceded neoliberalism or flourished despite the emergence of a fledgling neoliberalism.

## References

Adams, A. (Ed.). (1962). *First world conference on national parks*. United States Department of the Interior.
Barcan, A. (1965). *A short history of education in New South Wales*. Martindale Press.
Barcan, A. (1988). *Two centuries of education in New South Wales*. NSW University Press.
Fox, A. (author) N. Dufty, K. McDonald, S. Smith, D. Tribe, & K. Schaefer (Eds.). (2016). *Chief Guardian: The life and times of Allen Strom*. https://www.amazon.com.au/Chief-Guardian-Times-Allen-Strom-ebook/dp/B01H8IEORQ
Hutton, D., & Connors, L. (1999). *A history of the Australian environment movement*. Cambridge University Press.
James, P. (2013). *Cosmopolitan conservationists: Greening modern Sydney*. Australian Scholarly Publishing.
National Parks—Australia: New South Wales. (1979). In W. Goldstein (Ed.), *Parks and wildlife: Australia's 100 years of national parks* (pp. 93–107). National Parks and Wildlife Service.
NSW Government: State Archives & Records. (n.d.). *National Parks and Wildlife Service*. Retrieved January 8, 2016, from https://www.records.nsw.gov.au/agency/17
Robin, L. (1998). *Defending the Little Desert: The rise of ecological consciousness in Australia*. Melbourne University Publishing.

# References

Strom, A.(author) N. Dufty, K. McDonald, D. Tribe, S. Smith, & K. Schaefer (Eds.). (2017). *Some aspects of nature conservation in New South Wales during the 1950s and 1960s*. https://www.amazon.com.au/dp/B071RNRK8H/ref=rdr_kindle_ext_tmb

The Gosford Times and Wyong District Advocate. (1954, September 14). *Rangers' Patrol at work*. Trove. Retrieved May 30, 2024, from https://trove.nla.gov.au/newspaper/article/167381116?

The Sun (1952, November 27). *Florists' shops raided for Christmas bells*. Trove. Retrieved May 30, 2024, from https://webarchive.nla.gov.au/awa/20190513025905/https://trove.nla.gov.au/list?id=114451

Webb, J. (1998). *Thistle Y. Harris: A biography of Thistle Yolette Stead*. Surrey Beatty & Sons.

# Chapter 6
# The Spectrum of Support: Personal to Global Structures

## 6.1 Introduction

During the late 1960s, questioning the prevailing perspective that regarded nature as subservient to the domains of science and economics, and as a passive entity, increased (Robin 1998). Additionally, texts such as *The Great Extermination* by A. J. Marshall in 1966 startled many as it vividly depicted the extinctions that had occurred and were currently in progress. It also provided insights into the causes of these extinctions and the urgent need to halt them.

However, in Australia, there was a somewhat derogatory perception of environmentalism within non-urban communities, viewing it as an urban, middle-class and intellectual pursuit (Fox, 2016; Strom, 2017). The working class often accepted environmental impacts associated with industry or development simply because industry provided necessary jobs or, in the case of development, particularly in the early history, land (Bonyhady, 2000).

Economic growth had been expansive in the post war era with Australia's period of economic growth continuing through to the 1970s. However, the 1973–1974 oil crisis led to a loss of confidence in the welfare state's ability to address social inequalities, due to the ensuing recession and unemployment (Hughes & Brock, 2008). From 1968 to 1973 Australia experienced a petroleum shortage and thus crisis. Still, while development was seen as essential, conservation was not marginalised. Development powers embraced a defensive stance in response to environmentalism while confrontational environmentalism characteristics emerged with the confidence of political power (Robin, 1998).

Education, like the economy, was expansive into the 1970s. The transformation of society through the welfare state, with education as a major vehicle for change, continued through the late 1960s and early 1970s (Hughes & Brock, 2008). Significant federal initiatives in education after the 1972 election of the Whitlam Government were:

- the Karmel Report (1973) which backed an educational devolution and community participation agenda,
- the Australian Commonwealth Schools Commission (1974 [subsumed into the Department of Employment Education and Training in 1987]) which established financial support and a climate of acceptance for devolution of schooling and curriculum development to school communities along with Piagetian cognitive principles,
- the Curriculum Development Centre [CDC] (1973) which researched and resourced major curriculum development initiatives, and
- the abolition of fees for university degrees.

The School Commission saw 2000 grants under the Innovations Program between 1974 and 1977 although the amount allocated for curriculum development was modest (Hughes & Brock, 2008). Resource dissemination monies were not available for CDC projects (Greenall, 1987). However, there were 343 grants with some aspect of EE (CDC, 1978a), and the State Development Committee and Regional In-service Committees utilised significant Commonwealth funding in their mission: $2,660,000 from 1974 to 1975 in New South Wales (NSW) alone (Hughes & Brock, 2008).

In the mid-1970s, a pivotal shift occurred in Australia's perspective on heritage, as both built and natural heritage were integrated under the framework of the National Estate within the Australian Heritage Commission (Robin, 1998). Simultaneously and influentially, the environmental landscape witnessed the emergence of green activists, particularly in the 1970s, forming a unionist collective with a strong focus on urban environmentalism and the overall quality of life. Their organisational ethos prioritised egalitarianism and participation, setting them apart from established norms (Robin, 1998).

It took some time for conservation to be embraced as a responsibility of the Australian Government. The Whitlam government, elected in 1972, saw the establishment of the first Minister and Department for Environment and Conservation addressing environmental concerns. In this period, Linke's exploration of EE highlighted the ongoing preparation of federal initiatives (Linke, 1980). A significant catalyst for global environmental governance was the 1972 UN Conference on the Human Environment, which prompted nations to address environmental legislation, management, monitoring, research, finance, information exchange, education, and training (Linke, 1980). Linke emphasised that subsequent actions were crucial to translating these statements of intent into tangible results. Internationally, environmental awareness led to substantial legislative developments. Environmental Impact Assessments became a standard practice for major development projects, providing a framework to assess and mitigate potential environmental harm. These shifts mark a transformative period in environmental consciousness and governance. Social, political and economic conditions were conducive to the developing concept of EE.

## 6.2 Defining Environmental Education

Multiple definitions of EE developed essentially simultaneously around the western world in the late 1960s and early 1970s. One of the early definitions came from the first issue of the *Journal of Environmental Education* in 1969. Professor Bill Stapp and his colleagues at the University of Michigan (Stapp et al., 1969, p. 31) defined EE as that which is aimed at producing a citizenry that is knowledgeable about the biophysical environment and its associated problems, aware of how to assist in solving environmental problems, and motivated to work toward solutions. Incidentally, the Stapps, both Bill and Gloria, came to play a significant role in developing EE in Australia and around the world (Fox, 2016; Gough, 2001). He was appointed to direct the International Environmental Education Project for the United Nations Educational, Scientific and Cultural Organisation (UNESCO)/United Nations Environmental Program (UNEP) in 1974 (Fensham, 1987, 1990) and as part of the process visited Australia where he inspired people to join the EE movement and advocated for hands-on experience of environmental issues and problems (McDonald, 2015).

A widely disseminated definition of EE emanated from the International Union for the Conservation of Nature and Natural Resources (IUCN) at an international workshop relating to EE in the school curriculum in the United States (1970).

> Environmental education is the process of recognising values and clarifying concepts in order to develop skills and attitudes necessary to understand and appreciate the interrelatedness among man, his culture and his biophysical surroundings. Environmental education also entails practice in decision-making and self-formulating of a code of behaviour about issues concerning environmental quality. (IUCN quoted in Gough, 1997, p. 45)

This definition was utilised by the CDC in their Interim Report in 1975, Martin in his review of the objectives of EE in 1975, and Linke in his analysis of EE in Australia in 1980 (Gough, 1997). This is by no means an exhaustive list of definitions but rather a glimpse to attain an understanding of the shifts in agenda.

In an effort to clarify some of the ambiguity that surrounded the emerging field of EE, Lucas's 1972 doctoral thesis, titled "Environment and EE: Conceptual Issues and Curriculum Implications", set up a useful model, identifying three independent, primary classes of EE—"about," "in," and "for" the environment. This conceptualisation of EE was presented at the 1975 Australian National Commission for UNESCO Seminar on "Education and the Human Environment" (Greenall, 1980; Fensham, 2015). This terminology has proved enduring over the decades and has been embedded into a great deal of the literature at a state, national and international level.

Wheeler wrote in 1975 that EE could be mistaken for "ecological conservation education" and that a mass of overlapping approaches could dissipate its effect. He stated that this "gives rise to a dilemma of identity … that EE was being taught partially and incoherently, with virtually no overall thought or organisation" (Wheeler, 1975, p. 18). He elaborates…

> The objectives for environmental education vary according to the values and interests held by those advocating the necessity to teach about the environment. Those who advocate holding conservationists' ideals want a form of environmental education that sets its objectives firmly on the promulgation of the wise use of natural resources. The educationists who urge the implementation of environmental education curricula in schools and colleges vary in their objectives according to their respective emphasis upon environment as a concept; or on education as a process stimulated or hindered by environmental experiences. Much discussion has also taken place on the definition of "environment". Is the "natural environment," or the "built environment" the one to be considered? Does the term "human environment" cover the total environmental setting for human beings including natural and social phenomena?(Wheeler, 1975, p. 19)

These concerns, written with Great Britain in mind, echo much of the confusion about the establishment and development of EE as documented in conference presentations and journal articles both in NSW, Australia and globally. At the Australian UNESCO seminar in 1975, Linke said that EE would have no academic currency or place in the curriculum until defined in a practical way that is accepted by teachers and education administrators (Linke, 1977). EE is concerned with values, attitudes and social action in resolving environmental problems (Greenall, 1987). The degree of EE dissemination clear about the problem solving and critical thinking aspect of EE has varied throughout its history (Gough, 1997).

## 6.3 The Environmental Education Crisis Conference and Developments

At the 1970 Australian Academy of Science conference Strom was appalled by the suggestions put forward concerning what might be adopted to educate the community, from cradle to grave. From Strom's reflection, it is assumed that most of the suggestions involved the same old existing approaches—nature study and conservation education. His 1987 deliberation elaborated,

> Environmental education is not synonymous with nature study or natural history or ecology or even knowing what pollution is or does. Environmental education must first and foremost, make everyone of us aware that the human animal is but part of the great ecosystem which govern all ecosystems. (Strom, 1987, p. 7)

There were some interesting papers given, however. For example, Beverley O'Neill outlined the state of EE in Australia and reported that there seemed little in the curriculum about the impact humans were having on the environment (O'Neill, 1970). O'Neill's concluding remarks may be seen as prophetic,[1] and increasing in relevance given the rise in accountability:

---

[1] See Education for Sustainability and the Australian Curriculum Project: Final Report for Research Phases 1 to 3 by the Australian Education for Sustainability Alliance (2014) for evidence of the slow progress of the teaching population paying more than lip service to ESE.

## 6.3 The Environmental Education Crisis Conference and Developments

> Nevertheless, it is apparent that, at present, most of the environmental education in our schools is being given at the discretion of individual teachers. There are many teachers who are deeply concerned and aware of their responsibilities in this area, but, equally, there must be many who, for various reasons, do not feel this concern. They are not likely to notice that the syllabuses on which they base their lessons are deficient, let alone try to impart to their students the basis of environmental ethics. Even those teachers who are convinced of the need for environmental education must be affected by the pressure of examinations and the necessity to fulfill the prescribed syllabus requirements. (O'Neill, 1970, p. 46)

Bill Stapp also presented at the 1970 conference. Stapp had a similar ethos to Strom. Both were believers in dissonance (Fox, 2016),

> The motivation for environmentalism must arise from encounters with environmental issues. The aim is to shock and disturb those who experience the encounters so that they are motivated to learn the answers, and then, come hell and high water, to have them to work to correct stupidity, ignorance and plain greed. Environmental education must enshrine that procedure if it is to be meaningful, and it must provide a continuing drive for that process to go on and on, long after the schoolroom is left behind. (Strom, 1987, p. 7)

Strom also became acquainted with Richard Piesse, the Director of the Australian Conservation Foundation, through his reaction to the conference. Together they wrote a special publication for the Foundation (Piesse & Strom, 1970) investigating the possibility of Field Studies Centres (FSCs) for Australia and recommending a system similar to that in the United Kingdom (Fox, 2016). These centres, run by the British Field Studies Council, were well established and were funded by fees and public subscription with indirect support from local education authorities (Morrison, 1974). The Piesse and Strom document outlines the United Kingdom situation, with a focus on England where the organisation was most extensive, but also covering centres in Canada and the United States. It additionally outlined a couple of floor plans of established centres, sample budgets and staffing arrangements; summarised developments in Australia, drew on conservation initiatives and outlined possible criteria and responsibility. They recommended a Field Studies Council impelling state and federal funding and lands for a system of centres (Piesse & Strom, 1970).

The scientific and community push for FSCs and other environmental initiatives was successful. It gained political recognition when the pre-federal election Labor Party platform included, "the establishment of field study centres in consultation with the Commonwealth and State Departments of Education and Australian Universities Commission" (Australian Labor Party, 1971, p. 14). Other relevant proposals outlined in the platform, under the title "Conservation and Environment," included a central body to control and coordinate nature conservation activities and increased research funding for conservation studies across various programs. Additionally, under the heading "International Science", the Platform supported overseas exchanges for scientists and technologists through a scheme of post-doctoral and senior fellowships. To achieve these outcomes, they needed adequate science education, more science teachers with improved training, more graduates, both undergraduate and postgraduate, and the upholding of traditional freedoms for scientists. After Labor won the 1972 Federal election, the FSC platform was endorsed at the first National Conservation Study Conference, run by the Australian Conservation Foundation in 1973 (Morrison, 1974).

In a 1974 critique of field studies in Australia, Rob Morrison stated that it was too late to advocate a "common pattern of development" for FSCs, with some autonomous and some Department of Education centres already existing and "considerable development in some individual schools" (Morrison, 1974, p. 59). While there were many different types of FSCs, Morrison focused on places where school students participated in curricular, recreational and social activities. He also concentrated on the field studies aspect of EE or outdoor education not because it is the most important aspect, or to draw boundaries, but because the topic of EE was too vast to develop for a research paper (Morrison, 1974, p. 49).

While Morrison's study explored field studies in Australia, the circumstances of EE in Australia were investigated through a national survey conducted during 1973–74 by Russell Linke. Funded by the Australian Research and Development Committee, the survey was based on an earlier developmental study sponsored by the Australian Conservation Foundation (Linke, 1980). Linke outlines the Australian Conservation Foundation's comprehensive conservation directory (1973) which included organisations establishing formal relations with various state departments of education to facilitate EE within primary and secondary schools (Linke, 1980, pp. 42–43). These community resources were wide ranging and included botanical and zoological gardens, museums and various wildlife sanctuaries. They did not, however, have the resources to coordinate a substantial and steady educational impact.

With the popularity of outdoor education, schools and community groups faced excessive waiting times in accessing available sites. Other issues Linke noted were:

- a lack of time to make arrangements,
- a lack of confidence in knowledge about outdoor studies (in-service courses had been conducted on plant and animal identification and basic ecology),
- a lack of background localised knowledge of many of the popular field study areas, and
- a lack of interest on the part of teachers (surmised from the number of teachers conducting EE) (Linke, 1980, pp. 113–114).

In some states, metropolitan schools, or a cluster of schools, were acquiring their own rural outdoor study areas as a result of the closure of some remote single teacher schools. Conversion of these schools to FSCs was viewed as a remedy for the short supply of sites being experienced at the time. Linke's study noted the lack of coordination with individual schools and teachers initiating their own experimental programs. A more systematic and organised approach was needed to achieve a substantial and consistent educational impact (Linke, 1980).

## 6.4 Global Support

The United Nations Conference on the Human Environment in 1972 saw education and training as vital for environmental policies (Gough, 1997). EE, both formal and informal, became one of the major vehicles for remedying environmental problems at both the UNESCO—UNEP Belgrade International Workshop on Environmental Education, 1975 and the 1977 Tbilisi UNESCO-UNEP Intergovernmental Conference on Environmental Education. The goal of the International Workshop was to develop a framework and direction to further EE via the UNESCO-UNEP international program. The Belgrade Charter stressed action, "working individually and collectively toward solutions of current problems and prevention of new ones" with abilities of "awareness, knowledge, attitudes, skills, evaluation ability and participation" expanded in the Charter objectives (Gough, 1997, p. 19).

The objective of the Intergovernmental Conference (1977) was to obtain commitment from various countries, through administrative and government decision makers at a very high level, and to establish EE as a priority area of national policy (Fensham quoted in Gough, 1997, p. 18). The Belgrade Charter was modified at Tbilisi. For example, the objectives concerning evaluation ability and participation were deleted, there were minor changes to the wording of the attitudes and skills objective statements, and a significant change was made in the knowledge objective with the removal of humanity's responsibility for the crisis (Gough, 1997, p. 44). Peter Fensham recalled the omission of the evaluation objective as being political. Apparently, "it was unlikely that the participants at such a meeting would endorse an objective that had as its aim a potential critique of government programs" (Fensham cited in Greenall, 1981a, p. 80).

## 6.5 National Progress Through the Curriculum Development Centre

Linke's study gained further purpose when he became the CDC Environmental Education Committee Chairperson in 1974. The Federal Government established the CDC in 1973 to work closely with state and territory school systems, teacher educators, researchers and other groups associated with education, such as professional bodies. They researched curriculum needs and developed priorities for action, school curriculum and associated educational resources (Austlit, 2012). EE was one of the five priority areas the CDC was directed to address by the government in 1974 when it was an Interim Council, and then again in 1977 when it became a legitimate Council [the Centre was legislated in 1975] (CDC, 1978c; Greenall, 1981a).

The original CDC EE Committee, established by interim Council in 1974, had assessed the needs of EE and submitted a proposal for development and support. (Greenall & Womersley, 1977). Teacher education proved the greatest need; awareness and understanding of EE, change in attitude toward EE, and development of skills and increased communication and exchange of ideas relating to EE, all needed significant input (Greenall, 1987). Findings were that Australia was very much in the vanguard of EE activity on the world stage but, as Linke had found, "despite this multifarious activity, much of the Australian endeavour is uncoordinated, isolated and of uncertain effectiveness" (CDC, 1978c, p. 10).

The resulting action plan included support structures in the form of a national information centre, local information resources, FSCs, regional EE consultants, and an evaluation and materials development team to focus on teachers, which would ultimately benefit students (Greenall, 1981b; Greenall & Womersley, 1977; Spring & Greenall, 1975). The Australian UNESCO seminar on "Education and the Human Environment," in Melbourne in 1975, along with submissions from other interested parties, strengthened the report without causing major structural change to it (Greenall & Womersley, 1977). The report gave little thought to scaffolding the change from teaching of content to "attitude and behaviour change" (Greenall, 1987), nor was EE defined clearly. This was possibly politically expedient, although it must be said that EE definition was still evolving at the time. The expected expansionist budget for 1975 did not eventuate, leading to the deferral of this approximately two-million-dollar proposal as the CDC had its budget cut (Greenall, 1987). With the change of federal government in 1975, EE lost its broad political support and priority. However, an EE Study Group established by the CDC Council in 1976 and chaired by Peter Fensham, had an essentialist brief of making recommendations for school-based curriculum development in collaboration with the states and territories (Greenall, 1987; Greenall & Womersley, 1977). The EE Study Group was inclusive of related government bodies such as departments of environment, education, housing and community, as well as industry and environmental organisations, in calling for the enactment of necessary actions (Greenall & Womersley, 1977).

Recommendations included:

- the acceptance of EE and its significance with emphasis on recognition and awareness of the diverse teaching workforce,
- EE curriculum resources for a diversity of disciplines,
- open communication channels for the effective and efficient flow of EE both nationally and globally,
- the forging and maintenance of global links, particularly regional, and
- the establishment of a national EE council (CDC, 1978c).

One of the dot points within the CDC 1978 report was to make senior administrators concerned with education and environmental management and aware of, amongst other things, the international status of EE. While this report recognised that the EE found within formal education did not meet EE expectations and that EE was evolving, it recommended case studies of existing work rather than new exemplars of practice (Greenall, 1987). It did, however, acknowledge and prioritise the need for increasing teacher awareness of EE. Unfortunately, prioritisation was lost when other supporting agencies, including state departments of education, supported case studies, papers and evaluation reports for teachers, and in-service activities with little spotlight on increasing awareness. Once more, there were no details of aims and definitions for EE and guidance on teacher assistance was absent.

The CDC created a program which produced statements, frameworks and educational resources. Three initiatives were coordinated by the CDC, two of which stemmed from the CDC's Study Group on EE. These initiatives were:

- the EE Project funded over 2 years to support the resource development necessary for teachers and schools to develop EE policy and programs and its implementation into schools (Greenall, 1979),
- a multi-media, interdisciplinary, kit of materials *Investigating the National Estate*, and
- an EE Resources Project funded by the Commonwealth Department of Environment, Housing and Community Development which began in 1975. It supported the development of four facets of the national estate: the built environment; the fragile environment; First Nations people and the environment; and, decision making and the environment. These units targeted lower and middle secondary students (Greenall, 1979).

Submissions for the EE project did not meet expectations of education "for" the environment with most teachers and education department personnel missing the affective or action-oriented objectives (Greenall, 1987). Additionally, few involved more than one or two disciplines, so the interdisciplinary nature of EE was absent. A few resources were commissioned to add substance to the production of the resource books (CDC, 1981a, b; Greenall, 1987).

The Centre produced the first national statement on EE in 1980, mostly funded by the Commonwealth Department of Environment, Housing and Community Development (Greenall, 1987)—*Environmental Education for Schools: Or How to Catch Environmental Education* (Greenall, 1980). Distributed to all schools, it provided policy guidelines (Greenall, 1987). Greenall described the modified set of the Belgrade and Tbilisi objectives within this statement as compromised due to the watering-down of the environmental problem emphasis (Greenall, 1981a).

Within project dissemination there was a lack of systemic support. The state and territory liaison officers that were part of the CDC EE project support network and the production of materials were out of synchronisation—the network existed from 1978 to 1979 while materials were not available for dissemination until late 1980. Additionally, these CDC network commitments tended to be an add-on to the workload of already overstretched liaison officers, rather than resourced 1 day per week as intended (Greenall, 1987). Furthermore, CDC support shifted to other foci in 1980.

In working on establishing the national EE agenda within the CDC, it was found that rather than explicit opposition, protest was expressed in "structural and constitutional ignorance and apathy" (Greenall, 1981a, p. 251). Additionally, there were difficulties for teachers practicing EE.

Counter-hegemony in Australian education is probably as rare as elsewhere. It is more likely that Australian schools will "swim with the tide" rather than "anticipate future developments." Attempts to teach publicly critical social problems can meet powerful opposition. (Greenall, 1981a, p. 61)

The CDC was absorbed into the Federal Department of Education in 1981 (Austlit, 2012), dissolving a developing environmental studies core EE curriculum for Australian schools with a design for environmentalism to pervade the core (Greenall, 1987). The Australian Employment, Education and Training Act 1988 disbanded the Curriculum Development Council that oversaw the Centre (Australian Government: Federal Register of Legislation, n.d.).

At the end of the 1970s, the defining character of EE was still ambiguous and contested—seen as "field studies in Science or Geography, or just more educational jargon." (Smith, 1978, p. 5). So, while Greenall and Womersley (1977) and Greenall (1980) had defined terms and provided aims for EE, there was a lack of systemic support and funding, contributing to the slow and confusing development of EE—as did the "to-ing and fro-ing" of political favour.

## 6.6 Australian Association for Environmental Education: Beginning

The experiences and evidence of the CDC EE committee/study group revealed a need for greater EE coordination, better lines of communication, and a desire for a supportive, collaborative network, in addition to a need for a push for coordinated EE curriculum. CDC associates involved in the Environmental Education Project, including John Smith, Jim Wilson and Brian Foreman, had been investigating and progressing the formation of an Association (CDC, 1978a, b, 1978/79, 1979a, b, c, d, e; Fensham, 2015). The Project's national newsletter assisted in disseminating information and coordinating activities.

The Australian Association for Environmental Education (AAEE) took shape and was launched in 1980, using the *AAEE Newsletter*, (renamed *OzEEnews* in 1989) as the vehicle for supporting a growing network of environmental educators (AAEE, 2015). In 1980, the AAEE held its first conference where a draft constitution was developed. The *Australian Journal of Environmental Education* had its inaugural edition in 1984, paving the way for the development, support and progression of environmental and sustainability education (ESE) research and theory, and thus furthering praxis, within the Australian context.

## 6.7 Progress in NSW Environment and Education Bureaucracies

In the second half of the 1900s, the "environment" was becoming more of a feature in state bureaucratic entities. The NSW State Planning Authority was established in 1963 tasked with the difficulties of administering non-Crown land usage (Strom, 1987). While the NSW State Pollution Control Commission was enacted in 1970, it took until 1992 for it to evolve into the NSW Environmental Protection Authority [NSW EPA] (ARDC: Research Data Australia, n.d.). The Department of Conservation also underwent great change depending on which political party was in government.[2] Specialisation importance within governance can be gleaned from department groupings and their nomenclature.

In the NSW Department of Education, economic prosperity brought substantial educational reform at various times during the period under consideration (Hughes & Brock, 2008). Harold Wyndham was appointed Director-General of Education in NSW in 1952 (Barcan, 1965). He was the first Director-General not to have had a trajectory from primary school teaching, through the ranks of inspector and administration within the Department. Wyndham had university experience including post-graduate work overseas, and as Secretary to the Department of Education from 1948 to 1951. He was regarded as cultured and thus better suited for the position given Australia's more sophisticated character in the context of the 1950s boom and globalisation. Wyndham took on the task of reorganising secondary education at a time when there was a shortage of teachers, buildings and funds. He chaired the Committee to Survey Secondary Education in NSW in 1953, which tabled its report in 1957.

The aim of the Committee was to examine the objectives, organisation and course content of public school education provided to adolescents. The findings were to enable a way forward for a good general education that would deliver a diversity of curriculum to meet the varying abilities and skills of all pupils (Barcan, 1965). Wyndham believed that the academic tendency of secondary courses had "sanctioned the omission of elements necessary for ordinary citizenship" and created "wastage of ability" (Yelland cited in Hughes & Brock, 2008, p. 56) given the academic stronghold of an elite curriculum directed to university entrance. Recommendations included a transition from primary education at about the age of 12, to four compulsory years of comprehensive high school education with no entry examination. Curriculum was to include initial compulsory core subjects with guided electives introduced in consecutive years. This compulsory 4 years of

---

[2] Constant alteration of groupings for government departments is dependent on political power. The Department of Environment has been particularly changeable at a national and state level. For instance, the NSW Office of Environment and Heritage was established in 2011 and abolished in 2019 after the election—subsumed within the NSW Department of Planning, Industry and Environment (NSW Government 2019). Since the 2022 change in government this department has been split into the NSW Department of Climate Change, Energy, the Environment and Water, and the NSW Department of Planning, Housing and Infrastructure.

schooling was to end with the School Certificate examination. A final non-compulsory 2 years culminating in a Higher School Certificate was to provide an avenue to university.

The Wyndham Report coincided with the mid twentieth century identification of adolescence as a developmental stage, made possible by the affluence of the times (Barcan, 1965). Comprehensive, co-educational schooling began and changed schooling culture, as it was known. The outcome of comprehensive education was large schools with students organised into groups generally called "houses." Core subjects included English, social studies, science, mathematics, music, art, crafts, physical and health education and religious education (taught by visiting clergy).

There had been growing discipline problems from the mid 1950s, particularly for low achieving students (Barcan, 1965). Learning through hands-on outdoor activities and being immersed in the natural environment has been proven over the years to increase learning engagement for low achieving students (Lieberman & Hoody, 1998) with the first evidence of this in NSW possibly emanating from the experience of Enmore Activity School at the Broken Bay National Fitness Centre camps. Wyndham would have been aware of this, given that he was one of the creators of the Enmore experiment.

Despite some apprehension, the Wyndham recommendations were put to NSW Parliament, and were accepted in 1961. Two education boards were established: The Secondary Schools Board and the Board of Senior School Studies. The required practicality of the planned Wyndham proposals necessitated greater freedom of decision making for individual school principals. This was due to varying conditions of the buildings and equipment, and staffing (subject knowledge and numbers) of secondary schools (Barcan, 1965).

### 6.7.1 Whole Child—Head, Heart, Hand: Progressive Education Sabotage

Progressive education developed in the late 1960s and throughout the 1970s. The child development theories of Piaget stimulated the acceptance of child-centred education. The importance of first-hand experience was stressed. Progressive methods of teaching and alternative forms of schooling were gaining momentum. Ivan Illich's (1971) ideas that education should be de-schooled were popular, as was the work of Neil Postman and Charles Weingartner (1969) who were attempting to turn education on its head (Hughes & Brock, 2008). Dr. John Vaughan, an advocate of child-centred learning and devolving of curriculum to the school /teacher level, was well placed to effect change. He was the Director of the Studies Directorate in the NSW Department of Education and the Executive Officer for the Secondary Schools Board and the Board of Senior School Studies as well as being a member of these Boards. Vaughan ultimately inspired curriculum development change—a turning point from teacher to student-centred learning—reflexivity of teaching practice.

The three Vaughan reports from 1974 to 1978 (*Aims of Secondary Education, Base Paper on the Total Curriculum, and Aims of Primary Education*, 1974, 1975, 1978 respectively) called for the curriculum development process to include greater teacher and school participation (Hughes & Brock, 2008). Distinct subject areas were questioned, and a more cross-curricular approach favoured. This complemented the purposes and pedagogies of EE. However, the initiatives failed due to lack of resourcing and the highly centralised structures controlling schools. The Directorate of Studies was set up in 1973 to coordinate curriculum policy yet there were other head office directorates and an intricate web of departmental and interdepartmental committees which had input into the school curriculum. Many of these statutory boards and committees were dominated by academics insisting on academic "depth and merit" (Hughes & Brock, 2008, p. 95). It has been very difficult for NSW to move toward whole school, whole child education.[3] Devolution and child-centred learning concessions were made but central control was maintained with head office structures strengthened.

However, in 1975, there was a need to broaden the curriculum prescriptions from the Wyndham Scheme for senior secondary students given an increase in low ability pupils continuing on to senior studies (Hughes & Brock, 2008). Courses under the banner of "other approved studies" were introduced. They did not contribute to the HSC aggregate mark and were generally one-unit Year 11 courses for students who did not intend to continue to tertiary education. An additional purpose of these courses was for teachers to develop curriculum to meet local needs. In some cases, the Year 11 course supplemented the need for 12 units in Year 11 when a student intended to undertake a three-unit course through to the HSC. Some of the courses developed were "environmental studies" courses.

Thus changes to education, curriculum diversification to cater for a wide range of abilities (including those not likely to go to university [Barcan, 1965]), and an increase in field work (AA; GA; Linke, 1980; Morrison, 1974) were conducive to the establishment of FSCs and the programs they developed.

## 6.8 Advocating for Environmental Studies and Education Within FSCs

On an educational front, Rex Meyer, the Director for the Advancement of Teaching within the School of Education, Macquarie University, was on a mission to channel the resources of the diverse plethora of FSCs in NSW for the environmental studies cause (Meyer, 1972; Pearson, 1978). In an April 1972 address at the David G. Stead Memorial Wildlife Research Foundation of Australia, Meyer drew on the aims of

---

[3] The domination of university academics discipline-based curriculum on the school curriculum and attempts to gain some control over it are evident from the early twentieth century (Hughes & Brock, 2008).

the National Park Service in the United States to outline the type of centres he envisaged for EE in Australia. These aims talked about citizens being introduced to their total cultural and natural environment, both past and present, to develop a more ecocentric citizen, able to take responsibility and action in environmental problem solving. Meyer proposed that the various centres established in Australia could easily be inclusive of environmental studies. These centres included FSCs for biological and earth science research, national parks and conservation society centres, those concentrating on specific environmental foci such as ornithology or botanical art, and those interested in fitness, adventure, bushwalking, sporting or recreation camps.[4]

> This planet is the only place we can call home. It is small, over-crowded and littered with our refuse. Our survival depends on understanding our relationship with this environment; we must look closely at every aspect, not just that part that appeals to our particular sectional interest.(Meyer, 1972, p. 4)

## 6.9 The Gould League of NSW and Gould League Advisory Service

The Gould League of Bird Lovers NSW, established by two teachers in Wellington NSW in 1910, quickly grew to having branches in most schools (Johnston & Tribe, 1982). In the late 1960s one of Strom's strategic positions was as a member of the Gould League Council of NSW (Fox, 2016). About the time that Strom moved to the Department of Education, the organisation underwent radical change to widen their educational gaze and effectiveness by encompassing EE—they became The Gould League of NSW (Strom, 1987).

Strom was attempting to reinvigorate the Gould League into EE action. In 1969, the *Gould Leaguer* (NSW Department of Education 1969a) produced by Strom, was amalgamated with the *Junior Tree Warden Journal* (see Fig. 6.1). Strom had instigated this merger when he started out as Advisor of Conservation at the Department (Fox, 2016). This publication was an effective vehicle for disseminating information regarding conservation/EE, the development of FSCs and their progress and, when necessary, galvanising support (NSW Department of Education, 1969, 1970, 1971a, b, 1972a, b, 1973a, b, 1974, 1975). The reason for surveying field studies sites was provided in the inaugural edition:

> To demonstrate or initiate studies arising from the science and geography syllabuses of schools and to provide a means of bringing learners into close contact with natural resources and natural resource management so that vital attitudes towards conservation may be developed. (NSW Department of Education, 1969, p. 7)

---

[4] Some of the content of Meyer's talk had been previously published in The Living Earth Journal in 1971.

Fig. 6.1 The Gould Leaguer, (1969). NSW Department of Education 1(1), p.1

In 1971 David Tribe, a teacher at Wakehurst Primary School, along with teachers Henry Bingham and John Kelly, set up the Gould League Advisory Service—advising teachers about EE. They had been encouraged to join the League by Strom in his role as Advisor in Conservation. Tribe had met Strom at an in-service event where Strom took participants to Muogamarra. The Gould League Advisory Service contacted schools and let them know they were available for support.

One teacher professional development event worth mentioning, due to its regional support and hands-on, experiential, and productive nature, took place in

North-West NSW in the 1970s. David Maher, the Regional Director of Education for North-West NSW, released 30 teachers so that they could participate in a 3-week travelling EE seminar/workshop. According to Fox, this highly productive in-service produced resources and enabled EE. Treating the working groups as one would a class of students minimised/eliminated any perceived difficulty participants had felt with regard to programming and presenting EE. Additionally, a plant identikit was developed (Fox, 2016).

## 6.10 The Association for Environmental Education (NSW)

In September 1972, Piesse and the Australian Conservation Foundation sponsored a public meeting at Macquarie University organised and chaired by Meyer and convened by Strom (Fox, 2016). Attendees included Beryl Strom, Kevin McDonald, Joan Webb, lecturers at Newcastle College of Advanced Education (CAE) and the Ku-ring-gai CAE respectively, and Tribe. All these people either had or went on to have a significant impact on EE.

The seminar, titled Environmental Studies in NSW, garnered significant support from government agencies and tertiary education organisations to establish a working group for future action (Fox, 2016; Strom, 2017). Morrison (1974) observed that the Association for Environmental Studies in NSW had run its first activity in the field in December 1972. The Field Studies or Environmental Studies Association became the Association for EE NSW [AEE (NSW)] (McDonald, 1999; NSW Department of Education 1973a). EE advocates in the Hunter Region including Kevin McDonald, Arthur Munro and Brian Gilligan, formed the Awabakal Association for EE in 1975. Throughout the state, other regional networks were developed. For example, Dufty set up the AEE NSW Country Region (McDonald, 1999). The Associations worked closely together and were a strong force in pursuing FSCs in NSW, lobbying governments for EE (both formal and non-formal), a formal EE curriculum, and a Council of EE (Fox, 2016).

> So one of the very strong roles of the Association for Environmental Education, and also of these field studies centre conferences, was to actually lobby for, not just an inspector that had environmental education as part of his or her portfolio, but to have a specialist position in the Department of Education that could coordinate environment education within the state, including environmental education centres. FA

The AEE (NSW) was instrumental in building EE capacity and networks, and conferences were initiated in 1976. These conferences took place over several days in various locations across the state. Papers, roundtables and poster presentations were presented on current environmental and EE issues, and site tours of EE interest were undertaken. In addition to important networking and professional development initiatives, a crucial aspect of conferences was the planning and refining of strategies to further EE and environmental improvements. The AEE (NSW) was influential in lobbying politicians and ministers for more FSC/EECs and the conferences were a space to coordinate strong and sustained influence. Conference plenary sessions included resolutions for action and adoption, forwarded to various influential agencies, including the state government.

An annual award for outstanding contributions to EE in NSW commenced in 1981 (McDonald, 1999; Fox, 2016). A list of award recipients for the 1981 to 2015 period reveals that four FSC/EEC principals, Gilligan, Dufty, Chris Prietto and Stuart DeLandre, and three FSC/EEC managers, Tribe, Geoff Young, and Syd Smith, were beneficiaries. There is evidence throughout the research data that there was a very close connection between the AEE (NSW) and the centres/centre staff with many of the staff participating and taking on roles within the organisation. Conversely, many did not experience the influence of the AEE (NSW). Distance from the Association (both space and time) and the distraction of local events were factors.

## 6.11 Conclusion

This chapter has outlined progressive reform and support for ESE during affluent times. It covers various efforts from local advocacy and organisational formations and reconfiguration to changes in form and function at both state and national levels. Additionally, it discusses international efforts regarding EE frameworks, commitment, and policy. Despite this progress, there has been some pushback.

Some of these organisations, such as the Gould League of NSW and the AEE (NSW), were explicitly involved in the establishment and development of ESE and EECs in NSW. Others such as the CDC were implicit supports to the early EECs, being integral to the understanding, support, and progress of ESE within Australia. Additionally, changes within the education system and the development of departments specific to environmental protection served as incidental yet fortuitous and possibly unwitting supports. All of these organisations and changes were happening and active in the early days of the establishment and development of EECs within the NSW Department of Education.

## References

ARDC: Research Data Australia. (n.d.). *AGY-1145 | State Pollution Control Commission NSW State Archives collection.* Retrieved July 26, 2024, from https://researchdata.edu.au/agy-1145-state-control-commission/164986

Austlit. (2012). *Curriculum Development Centre: History.* The University of Queensland. Retrieved March 10, 2016, from https://www.austlit.edu.au/austlit/page/A55120

Australian Association for Environmental Education (AAEE). (2015). *35 years of OzEEnews.* Australian Association for Environmental Education.

Australian Government: Federal Register of Legislation. (n.d.). *Employment, education and training Act 1988*. Retrieved Accessed January 18, 2016, from https://www.legislation.gov.au/Details/C2004A03673
Australian Labor Party. (1971). *Platform, constitution and rules as approved by the 29 commonwealth conference 1971*. Australian Labor Party, Federal Secretaiat.
Barcan, A. (1965). *A short history of education in New South Wales*. Martindale Press.
Bonyhady, T. (2000). *The colonial earth*. Melbourne University Press.
Curriculum Development Centre (CDC). (1978a). *Environmental Education Project Newsletter 1* (June).
Curriculum Development Centre (CDC). (1978b). *Environmental Education Project Newsletter 4* (December).
Curriculum Development Centre (CDC). (1978c). *Report of the Curriculum Development Centre Study Group on Environmental Education*. Curriculum Development Centre.
Curriculum Development Centre (CDC). (1979a). *Environmental Education Project Newsletter 9* (October).
Curriculum Development Centre (CDC). (1979b). *Environmental Education Project Newsletter 8* (August).
Curriculum Development Centre (CDC). (1979c). *Environmental Education Project Newsletter 5* (February).
Curriculum Development Centre (CDC). (1979d). *Environmental Education Project Newsletter 6* (April).
Curriculum Development Centre (CDC). (1979e). *Environmental Education Project Newsletter 7* (June).
Curriculum Development Centre (CDC). (1981a). *Environmental education: A sourcebook for primary education*. Curriculum Development Centre.
Curriculum Development Centre (CDC). (1981b). *Environmental education: A sourcebook for secondary education*. Curriculum Development Centre.
Fensham, P. (1987) Environmental education in 1977: A Tbilisi benchmark. Environmental education: Past, present and future. *Third National Environmental Education Seminar and workshops. 11–13 February. Ursula College, Australian National University, Canberra, ACT* (pp. 19–26), Commonwealth Department of Arts Heritage and Environment.
Fensham, P. (1990). Bill Stapp Down Under again. *OzEEnews, 42*, 2.
Fensham, P. (2015). Environmental education: A personal retrospective from our first president. *OzEEnews, 132*, 3–4.
Fox, A. (author) N. Dufty, K. McDonald, S. Smith, D. Tribe, & K. Schaefer (Eds.). (2016). *Chief Guardian: The life and times of Allen Strom*. https://www.amazon.com.au/Chief-Guardian-Times-Allen-Strom-ebook/dp/B01H8IEORQ
Gough, A. (1997). *Education and the environment: Policy, trends and the problems of marginalisation*. Australian Council for Educational Research.
Gough, A. (2001). For the total environment: Bill Stapp's contribution to environmental education. *Australian Journal of Environmental Education, 17*, 19–24.
Greenall, A. (1979). The Environmental Education project. *Newsletter, 5*(February), 13–14.
Greenall, A. (1980). *Environmental education for schools or how to catch environmental education*. Curriculum Development Centre.
Greenall, A. (1981a). *Environmental education in Australia: Phenomenon of the seventies: A case study in National Curriculum Development*. Curriculum Development Centre.
Greenall, A. (1981b). Environmental education: A case study of National Curriculum Action. In M. Lawson & R. Linke (Eds.), *Australian Association for Research in education conference: Inquiry and action in education volume 1, Adelaide, S.A., November 11–15, 1981* (pp. 7–14). National Library of Australia.
Greenall, A. (1987). A political history of environmental education in Australia: Snakes and ladders. In I. Robottom (Ed.), *Environmental education: Practice and possibility* (pp. 3–21). Deakin University Press.

# References

Greenall, A., & Womersley, J. (Eds.). (1977). *Development of environmental education in Australia: Key issues*. Curriculum Development Centre.

Hughes, J., & Brock, P. (2008). *Reform and resistance in NSW public education: Six attempts at major reform, 1905–1995*. NSW Department of Education and Training.

Johnston, C., & Tribe, D. (1982). The role of the Gould league of New South Wales in environmental education in Australia. In M. Cowan & W. Stapp (Eds.), *International case studies in environmental education: Environmental education in action* (pp. 146–150). National Institute of Education.

Lieberman, G., & Hoody, L. (1998). *Closing the achievement gap: Using the environment as an integrating context*. State Education and Environment Roundtable. Retrieved January 10, 2010, from http://www.seer.org/extras/execsum.pdf

Linke, R. (1977). Preface. In R. Linke (Ed.), *Education and the human environment* (p. 12). Curriculum Development Centre.

Linke, R. (1980). *Environmental education in Australia*. George Allen & Unwin Australia.

Marshall, A. J. (Ed.). (1966). *The great extermination*. Heinemann.

McDonald, K. (1999). A brief history of the association: The history of the Association for environmental education (NSW). In *22 annual seminar: Education for catchments. 25–26 September. Wyong, NSW*. Association for Environmental Education (NSW).

McDonald, K. (2015). The legacy: The EE movement in the hunter region. *OzEENews, 135*, 18.

Meyer, R. (1972). *Planning an environmental studies Centre* (Reprint series: No. 17). School of Education, Centre for Advancement of Teaching Macquarie University.

Morrison, R. G. (1974). Field studies in Australia. *The Australian Science Teachers' Journal, 20*(2), 47–60.

NSW Department of Education. (1969). *The Gould Leaguer 1* (1).
NSW Department of Education. (1970). *The Gould Leaguer 1* (4).
NSW Department of Education. (1971a). *The Gould Leaguer 1* (6).
NSW Department of Education. (1971b). *The Gould Leaguer 1* (5).
NSW Department of Education. (1972a). *The Gould Leaguer 1* (7).
NSW Department of Education. (1972b). *The Gould Leaguer 1* (9).
NSW Department of Education. (1973a). *The Gould Leaguer 1* (10).
NSW Department of Education. (1973b). *The Gould Leaguer 2* (1).
NSW Department of Education. (1974). *The Gould Leaguer 2* (2).
NSW Department of Education. (1975). *The Gould Leaguer 2* (4).

O'Neill, B. (1970). Environmental education in Australian schools. In J. Evans & S. Boylan (Eds.), *Education and the environmental crisis conference. 24–26th April. Canberra, ACT* (pp. 38–48). Australian Academy of Science.

Pearson, D. (1978). *Fieldwork in environments out-of-doors*. (Masters). University of New England.

Piesse, R., & Strom, A. (1970). *Establishing field studies centres in Australia*. Australian Conservation Foundation.

Robin, L. (1998). *Defending the Little Desert: The rise of ecological consciousness in Australia*. Melbourne University Publishing.

Smith, J. (1978). What else is happening? *Environmental Education Project Newsletter, 1*(June), 5.

Spring, G., & Greenall, A. (Eds.). (1975). *A proposal for the support of environmental education in Australia: An interim report of the CDC environmental education committee*. Curriculum Development Centre.

Stapp, W., Bennett, D., Bryan, W., Fulton, J., MacGregor, J., Nowak, P., et al. (1969). The concept of environmental education. *The Journal of Environmental Education, 1*(1), 30–31.

Strom, A. (1987). *A background to environmental education: Some memoirs of Allen A. Strom, A.M. Occasional Publication*. Association for Environmental Education (NSW).

Strom, A.(author) N. Dufty, K. McDonald, D. Tribe, S. Smith, & K. Schaefer (Eds.). (2017). *Some aspects of nature conservation in New South Wales during the 1950s and 1960s*. https://www.amazon.com.au/dp/B071RNRK8H/ref=rdr_kindle_ext_tmb

Wheeler, K. (1975). The genesis of environmental education. In G. Martin & K. Wheeler (Eds.), *Insights into environmental education* (pp. 2–19). Oliver & Boyd.

# Chapter 7
# From Vision to Reality: Establishing EECs in New South Wales

## 7.1 Introduction

When Strom abruptly found himself working back at the New South Wales (NSW) Department of Education in 1968, he was given a desk in the corner of the typing pool in the Bridge Street engine of the Department. Fox states that Strom's new position was political with the Public Service Board wanting to look after an extremely dedicated senior public servant—the position of "Advisor in Conservation" was not a strategic Departmental decision. Rather than feeling demoralised by demotion to a typing pool, Strom got onto his mission and found a great amount of support within the Education Department (Fox, 2016).

Strom noted in his developing ideas about the justification, substance and purpose of EE in and for discussion with the Director General and five of the regional Directors of Education:

> Environmental Education is not a media for propagating a cause. It aims to alert the community so that responsible administration can take action. Maybe causes are wanted, but using Environmental Education programmes [sic] propagate a particular attitude is dangerous. I.e. mining and miners. The value judgements should be made by the citizens, not for him... But how many are capable of making the decision? We will always be dependent upon the informed fraction of the community. (Fox, 2016, Ch. 12, Para. 43 & 44)

Strom's notes go on to say that EE programs need to make people aware of administrative decisions and actions and assess them for their effect on the environment, and assess the impact of newspapers and mass media. Programs need to provide environmental encounters. Program outcomes include knowledge about resources, their use and management and being able to make value judgements. Programs should aim to explain the student's world around them—its history, value and problems, and plans for the future. Strom advocated utilising students' environments in doing this (Fox, 2016; Strom, 2017) and stressed that environmental education (EE) was not a new subject but one that utilises the existing curricula to benefit the students and the community (Fox, 2016).

Strom provided a project plan to the Assistant Director-General (Services) Charles Ebert, instigating a policy meeting with five regional directors of Education (Fox, 2016). Ebert was a contemporary of Wyndham's who had attended the same primary and high schools—Kensington Public and Fort Street High School—a few years after Wyndham (Hughes, 2002). After this meeting, the Deputy Director General of Education (Chairperson), Mr. Hedley Yelland (Hughes, 2002) noted in relation to Strom's statement of duties that:

> Mr Strom's statement of duties is related entirely to conservation and his work hitherto has been concentrated on assisting teachers and pupils to appreciate more fully the need for conservation, and the bringing to the attention of the Department and other government agencies the urgency of the conservation problem…. If he is to assist in the field work required at both primary and secondary levels, he will need somewhat wider terms of reference, with the emphasis of science observation in the field. It is recognised that the ultimate benefit of such observation will transcend the requirements of the Science, Geography and Nature Science Syllabuses, and will lead to a heightened understanding among school pupils and teachers of the principles of conservation.[1] (Yelland quoted in Fox, 2016, Ch. 12, paragraphs. 47 and 48)

Yelland goes on to state that, "agreement was therefore reached" that Strom would provide an advisory service in field excursion work with the immediate purpose of fulfilling the aims of the science, geography and natural science syllabuses. He elaborated:

> Assistance of this kind presupposes:
> - Surveys of suitable natural reserves
> - Production of notes on these areas with material suitable for both primary and secondary teachers
> - Conduct of in-service courses for teachers
> - The setting up, in selected schools on a pilot-scheme basis, of external or field laboratories capable of meeting the needs of some of the scientific observations required. If owing to the lack of staff, the work is hindered, priority should be given to the Science area.

---

[1] In Strom's 1969 memos, he talks about EE but says the term "environmental education" was new to him at the 1970 "Education and the Environmental Crisis" conference. There could be a multitude of reasons for this anomaly. There is no doubt Strom did indeed teach beyond "conservation education." However, it is clear from the Director's correspondence about the initial policy meeting with the five Education Directors that they were talking about "conservation education." This is understandable, particularly given that the nascent stage of EE in 1969 was little known in Australia at the time. While EE replaced conservation education it seems over a transition period these terms were at times conflated and used interchangeably. It is difficult to be definitive about which is being discussed within the literature without definition. However, as discussed (Bonyhady, 2000), as the industrial revolution progressed, "professionalised" conservation became less about a continual supply of natural resources and more a "form of intensive resource exploitation predicated on radical interference with the environment" (2000, p. 9). Conservation became a disparaging word for those advocating for protection and proper management or preservation of ecosystems. Additionally, it is important to keep the defining feature of 'action' within EE at the forefront.

To carry out this work Mr Strom will require:

- An additional field officer
- A regular clerical service for the production and distribution of material
- Field equipment and an annual financial appropriation
- The cooperation of the In-service Training Division. (Yelland quoted in Fox, 2016, Ch. 12, para. 49)

According to (Fox, 2016), Ebert directed Yelland's expanded directive to a sympathetic Education bureaucracy via the regional directors of the Metropolitan, Newcastle and South Coast Regional Directorates.

The primary and secondary education directors found Strom's proposals ambitious and unrealistic given the Department's finances (Fox, 2016), however, they were probably not aware of the background preparation work Strom and Fox had already done while working within the Fauna Protection Panel (FPP). Strom and Fox had been interested in field studies centres (FSCs) from 1966 onwards. They had conducted a literature search on the subject and contacted Dr. Eric Bird, a geography academic at the Australian National University who was knowledgeable about the English FSC system (Fox, 2016). In 1966 Fox, as Field Officer at the FPP, presented a paper at the University of New England's "Education in Conservation" seminar where he emphasised the value of nature reserves in formal and informal education. FSCs, in conjunction with nature reserves, had been suggested as a way forward. Strom and Fox, both with experience in outdoors education, had already discussed this potential and had been planning centres at Barron Grounds, Hallstrom and Nadgee Reserves (see Fig. 7.1 for a contemporary photo of Nadgee Nature Reserve).

The education services set up in reserves by the FPP received popular support. A FPP request for funds for a centre at Barron Grounds was not successful at the 1966/67 budget estimates. However, money was set aside the following year for a FSC—at a time when the FPP was in limbo because of the announcement of the Government's proposal to abolish it (Strom, 2017). Panel funds were frozen and rolled into the NSW National Parks and Wildlife Service (NPWS) which was established on July 4, 1967.

Once in place as the advisor for conservation, Strom started canvassing suitable "conservation education" areas in reserves and on Crown land in the Sydney region. With school groups, he carried out mapping and investigating the geology, landscapes, history and ecology. Fox points out that many within Education across the hierarchy, from regional directors and school inspectors to principals and teachers, were enthused by Strom's sense of purpose and commitment. Strom, Harris and Webb had also influenced many of them as teacher educators (Fox, 2016).[2]

The ten areas that he listed in his proposed program as District Field Centres, were already well-studied by him and had been involved in earlier work, some even with pre-prepared notes used on Club [Caloola] studies. They were also unaware of the work both Strom and I had been engaged in relating to the operations of field studies centres that Strom had ideas

---

[2] For instance, both Webb and Tribe had been taught by Thistle Harris. Some of the environmental educators within FSCs had been taught by Webb.

**Fig. 7.1** Pied oyster catchers taking flight, Wonboyn Beach (Greenglades), Nadgee Nature Reserve, September, 2022

of developing in some of the nature reserves and national parks for which he was [sic] member of NPWS management committees. … Three areas had been studied for such development and we had the ear of Mr Bruce Loder, the Service's architect to design a suitable building. The areas were, Barren Grounds and Muogamarra Nature Reserves and the Bouddi and Warrumbungle National Parks. (Fox, 2016, Ch. 12, para. 55)

As noted, prototypes for conservation education, which aimed to motivate people into actively caring about their environment, were evident at places like Barron Ground.

The concept of FSCs, in a NSW conservation sense, was originally aimed at providing education for all within the national park/nature reserve environment. Strom stated, "They would provide a wide opportunity for education over the whole spectrum of the environment and hopefully sensitise participants to see the environment as the integration of natural and man-made systems" (Strom, 1987, p. 6).

Strom's move to the Department of Education was significant as centres were within the Education jurisdiction and thus only available to service government schools. Indeed, Strom later lamented, "One can imagine the educative potential of even ten field studies centres if these were an active campaign to encourage use by all schools and the community" (2017, Ch 15, para. 19).

## 7.2 FSC/EECs and the Gould League Advisory Service in NSW Education

The establishment of Muogamarra and Wirrimbirra FSCs, the first two FSCs within the NSW Department of Education were the culmination of an enormous amount of politicking and clever manoeuvring within and outside the Department of Education. Serendipitous and advantageous circumstances also provided the appropriate environment and resources for their foundation. The first two centres made visible how field studies could function within the Department. Importantly, these centres were immensely popular and highlighted the benefit centres provide to education. This was particularly important at a time when schools were adapting to administering and teaching a much larger and more diverse academic cohort, and the changing curriculum and pedagogy this necessitates.

The next section of this chapter and the following chapter provide descriptive vignettes of the establishment and functioning of each of the centres.[3] These descriptions outline important events, examples of pedagogy and curriculum, and, inhibiting and enabling factors in the development of FSC/EECs. These chapters are interspersed with snapshots of events that took place on an international, national, statewide, community and departmental level that impacted the development and functioning of the centres. These factors in addition to what is learnt from this history regarding effecting change in large bureaucracies is discussed in the final chapters.

### 7.2.1 Wirrimbirra: Life Before FSCs Within the Department of Education

Years before Strom found himself back in the Department of Education, an education facility with a focus on the environment had been developing at Bargo, southwest of Sydney. In 1962, Carmen Coleman from the Wildlife Preservation Society of Australia, had purchased a property called Wirrimbirra, the Wiradjuri word meaning "to preserve" (David G. Stead Wildlife Memorial Research Foundation of Australia, n.d.; NSW Government: Public Service Commission, n.d.). The purpose of the property was to establish a conservation centre for meetings and activities in memory of Stead who had passed away in 1957 (Webb, 1998). Wirrimbirra was handed over to the Association for the David G. Stead Memorial Wildlife Research Foundation of Australia (Incorporated) in 1964. Monies from the David G. Stead Memorial fund, set up in 1958 after Stead's death, were diverted into the cause, and Thistle Harris, Stead's widow, enthusiastically came on board, paying the remainder of the mortgage (Webb, 1998).

---

[3] The variability of data genre and availability for each Centre has provided for chronological and political evolution within an inconsistent structure.

The aims set out by the Association for the David G. Stead Memorial Wildlife Research Foundation of Australia (Incorporated) owning Wirrimbirra were:

- to initiate, promote and further research, scientific, technical or other, into all aspects of the conservation of wildlife of the Commonwealth,
- to maintain sanctuaries, reserves, and to carry on experimental work,
- to co-operate with organisations, universities and institutions in experiments or research into the use of national parks, playgrounds and similar areas, in the proper management, cultivation and preservation of Australian indigenous fauna and flora,
- to publish information related to these aims and objects and to arrange lectures and carry on educational courses for the furtherance of these objects, and to establish fellowships and scholarships for work in conservation, and
- to establish and maintain museums, arboretums and collections related to its objects (Webb, 1998, pp. 145–146).

These aims suggest an intention to be a private wildlife service or a not-for-profit wildlife service, noting the distinction between private and public.

The Wirrimbirra property was on the Hume Highway, between Tahmoor and Bargo, and had the southern railway line running through it (which was to cause problems and add to the argument for the withdrawal of the Department of Education's support in 1996). The property included 12 acres between the railway line and the Hume Highway and 90 acres to the east of the rail after additional parish land was purchased and Crown land sought. Wirrimbirra Gardens, and buildings associated with the enterprise, were allocated 12 acres of the property. The enterprise was very much a community collaboration: The wooden gates to Wirrimbirra were a retirement present from Harris' Sydney Teachers College colleagues; Carmen Coleman, an accountant and driver of the initial project, worked on a plan for an education and research centre; and Milo Dunphy and landscape gardeners perfected the plan for Wirrimbirra Gardens (Webb, 1998).

The first Board included Harris, Strom and Ivor Wyatt of the National Trust of Australia (NSW). Wyatt's mother had been a great friend of David Stead and was the founder of the National Trust of Australia in 1945. David G. Stead's son, Robert L. Stead was the Honorary Treasurer. To secure Wirrimbirra into perpetuity, the Foundation, lobbied by Harris, relinquished the freehold of Wirrimbirra to the National Trust of Australia (NSW) in 1965, but established a leasing arrangement, costing a pound per year, which enabled taxation concessions on gifts and exemption from local government rates (Webb, 1998).

The *Wildlife Research News*, the newsletter of the Foundation, kept the community informed and educated about the environment and the wide range of activities taking place. Residential facilities were built from 1972 to 1974 with companies contributing some funding. For example, the Persoonia Cabin was funded with the support of the Colonial Sugar Refining Company (Webb, 1998).

Bill Hicks, the first President of the Foundation, credited Strom as having "guided the Environmental Field Studies Centre into being" (quoted in Webb, 1998, p. 226). Yet there were many involved. Mel Fackender, a well-known conservationist from the Illawarra, became the on-site ranger for Wirrimbirra from 1965; there was the Strom Demonstration Natural Area and pool, intended as a demonstration site for teachers and schools; Harris prepared a secondary school assignment; and volunteers acted as educational officers.

Strom and Fox observed that the ranger, Mel Fackender, engaged the public with his engrossing naturalist narratives and that Wirrimbirra had become a popular destination for local schools who had recognised this great field resource (Fox, 2016) [see Fig. 7.2 for an early promotion of Wirrimbirra Field Studies].

### 7.2.2 Muogamarra Field Studies Centre

Muogamarra Nature Reserve was an amalgamation of the Hallstrom Nature Reserve and John Tipper's Muogamarra Sanctuary (Strom, 2017). Tipper was an avid conservationist. He belonged to the Wildlife Preservation Society of Australia, was founding president of the Rangers' League of NSW (1929) and assisted in establishing the Australian Bushland Conservation Association in 1932. To protect part of the Hawkesbury region north of Sydney Tipper took out a lease for 2000 acres of land from the Department of Lands. The land overlooked the Hawkesbury River and was around the Muogamarra Ridge, Awabakal for "Preserve for the future" (Gowers, 2002).

The Sanctuary opened in 1935 with limited access during the wildflower season, from mid-August to late September. To preserve the vegetation, Tipper set up a volunteer fire brigade and ultimately a study centre and museum. In 1953, Tipper

**Fig. 7.2** Wirrimbirra, Gould Leaguer (1970), NSW Department of Education, 1(4), p. 6

relinquished the sanctuary to trustee administration supported by the State Government. He held the position of president and resident curator but grew increasingly unhappy with management practices once the NSW NPWS administered the Sanctuary in 1967. He ended his association with the Sanctuary in 1968 due to a combination of ill health and dissatisfaction over the level of protection afforded First Nations relics on site (Gowers, 2002).

Muogamarra FSC[4] opened in 1971 after an agreement between the NSW NPWS and the NSW Department of Education. NSW NPWS supplied the building and the NSW Education Department supplied the teacher and the necessary education equipment (Fox, 2016). Strom was able to persuade the second Director of the NSW NPWS, Don McMichael (1969–1973), of the value of a FSC on Muogamarra Nature Reserve utilising the previously allocated funds (Strom, 2017). The Wyndham Scheme gave validity to the argument for establishing FSCs within the Department, given the emphasis on a diversity of subjects in addition to field work in Year 11 and 12 subjects (Strom, 2017; XA).

Fox, Senior Education Officer at NSW NPWS; Bruce Loder, the NSW NPWS architect; and Strom worked on the design of the building, which was to be a template for others. The design specifications included being suitable for up to 40 students and two teachers, low maintenance with natural lighting provided by wooden shutters to bench height, and a 2000 litre water tank. A generator was to supply energy when necessary. The building was to be easily transportable so it could be used as a research station. Classroom facilities were to include a lockable storeroom and teacher preparation area. Opposite walls were to have workbenches with lockers underneath. There was to be a chalkboard and projector area at one end and a reception area with hooks for bush and wet weather gear at the other (Fox, 2016). There were already septic toilets and basins on site. Apparently, the building was made with pine logs treated with arsenic and in later years the building could not be used in case students licked the white powder off the walls.

The site chosen was a hundred metres from the Hawkesbury sandstone escarpment and overlooked Peats Bight. There was access to temperate rainforest, and woodlands and heaths typical of Sydney sandstone vegetation. It was at the end of a track a few kilometres off the Pacific Highway (Fox, 2016). Strom had suggested the building be erected in a position close to the railway and ranger's quarters for access and supervision but it was built some distance from these facilities (Strom, 2017). There was also no connection to the electricity supply.

There was a teacher shortage in NSW around 1970. A reluctant NSW Department of Education staffed the complex, built by the NSW NPWS, when it was pointed out that if they did not they would be letting another agency do their job (Strom, 2017). Barbara Hamilton was the first teacher-in-charge at Muogamarra (Fox, 2016). A practicing educator who had come from the Sydney Church of England Grammar School in Moss Vale (Morgan, 1972), Hamilton had a B.A. in Town and Country Planning, a Diploma in Education and an interest in Botany (Woolley, 2016). She

---

[4] Later to become Gibberagong Field Studies Centre.

had previous experience taking her students on field excursions around the Southern Highlands, the Murray Valley, and Central Australia (Morgan, 1972). In 1971 Hamilton went to the NSW Department of Education and applied for the position at Muogamarra on the spot after seeing an advertisement for a teacher to establish a program at the new FSC (Woolley, 2016). She had 6 months to set up the program[s] (Morgan, 1972; Woolley, 2016).

Muogamarra had its official opening and opened on a full-time basis in 1972 (Hamilton, 1973; Morgan, 1972).[5] An article in the *Australian Woman's Weekly* (1972; see Fig. 7.3) described the purpose of Muogamarra as educating for change in attitudes and behaviour in relation to the Australian environment and the preservation of reserves. In an article Hamilton wrote for *Education, the Journal of the NSW Public School Teachers Federation* (1973), she noted that the Centre was a pilot that was being monitored by Meyer from Macquarie University, and Strom, amongst others (Hamilton, 1973). She also noted that time in the classroom was kept to a minimum with fieldwork and hands-on experience being the intention. Hamilton went on to say that,

**Fig. 7.3** School children gather at the John D. Tipper Lookout, named after the Muogamarra Sanctuary founder. (Photo taken by Bill Payne for an article written by Patricia Morgan titled, 'This bush school is for city children'. Published in The Australian Woman's Weekly on August 16 1972 (pp. 24–26). Printed with permission from Gibberagong Environmental Education Centre and Hornsby Shire Council Recollect. https://sites.google.com/education.nsw.gov.au/muogamarra-through-time/muogamarra-view-from-j-d-tippers-look-out & https://hornsbyshire.recollect.net.au/nodes/view/5046)

---

[5] It should be noted that Willis was the Minister for Education from 1972 and Tom Lewis Minister for the NSW NPWS before he became Premier from 1975 to 1976 before the fall of the Liberal Government. Willis ousted Lewis as Premier in the last few months of the Liberal Government's reign. Strom had worked under both of these politicians in the FPP. Rivalry between these two ministers has been previously noted and continued with Lewis hosting a grand opening with only the Inspector of Schools in charge of the Gould League, Colin MacDonald, invited.

> The centre offers a basic preliminary introduction to fieldwork. Various courses are available but they are not prescriptive. Any student or teacher wishing to use the reserve and its many possibilities in a different way is encouraged to devise his own program of study. Nor is the use of the reserve restricted to science subjects; in particular I would like to see art classes using the wide variety of natural forms as inspiration as well as the more conventional use by natural science, senior science, geography, biology and related subjects. (Hamilton, 1973, p. 17)

The article stated that students showed a need for experience in observation and the recording of data. The article stressed that fieldtrips contributed to learning about the natural environment and how to conserve it, rather than just being a day out. The limitations of a one-day outing were discussed along with the desire expressed by students and teachers for a residential experience, including night viewing of nocturnal animals. The article goes on to mention the well-established nature of English centres, the already developed plans for more centres in NSW, and the need for adult learning centres in both natural and built environments. In detailing the protocols for booking Muogamarra, a month's notice was requested with the maximum number of students set at 40. Available resources and supports were discussed, along with the intention of pre and post work, integrated into a larger study focus. The article concluded with an invitation to teachers to visit and observe the centre during school hours in order to gauge its potential for themselves.

Other projects were happening, and other groups were utilising Muogamarra. For example, marsupial research was being undertaken to the south of the site by the University of NSW's Marsupial Research Centre (Morgan, 1972). Meyer was also taking science students to the FSC in the early to mid 1970s.

Muogamarra FSC was very popular for school activities in conservation education (Fox, 2016). Hamilton had the support of Strom (Woolley, 2016) and in years to come she supported new FSC teachers such as Keith Armstrong at Wirrimbirra (1973) and Simon Leslie at Wambangalang (1975) by teaching them about managing and teaching in these new found centres. EE gained so much traction that the NSW Department of Education dedicated a school inspector to the growing field which was announced in the January 1973 edition of the *Gould Leaguer* (NSW Department of Education, 1973).

### 7.2.3 Wirrimbirra Field Studies Centre

The Gould League of NSW contributed to the development of Wirrimbirra by building a lecture, display and laboratory room in remembrance of one of their pioneers, Mr. J. E. Roberts, Secretary from 1938 to 1962 (Webb, 1998). Once the facilities were established, the Department of Education was encouraged to contribute to the development of a FSC. They came on board in 1973 designating Wirrimbirra FSC[6]

---

[6] Later to become Wooglemai Field Studies Centre.

as a School for Specific Purpose (gazetted)[7] and staffing it with Mr. Keith Armstrong who transferred from Sylvania High School. The Department also supplied the furniture and equipment. Wirrimbirra FSC was available to public schools from Monday to Friday during school terms (see Fig. 7.4 for a photo of the Allen Strom school demonstration nature area). Mr. Colin MacDonald, the Inspector of Schools in charge of EE, was enthusiastic about the centre being a prototype for future FSCs (Webb, 1998). Harris was on the interview panel for Keith Armstrong's position. They had different ideas about teaching with Armstrong very much focused on experiential, hands-on explorations while Harris favoured old school identification and classification. Armstrong's pedagogy suited the circumstances given that his classes were up to 40 students in size.

### 7.2.4 Growing Demand

The activities of the Gould League Advisory Service proved to be in such demand that a dedicated full-time position was requested from the Inspector of Schools in charge of the Gould League at the NSW Department of Education, Colin MacDonald.

**Fig. 7.4** "The field studies centre should provide areas for teacher inservice—Wirrimbirra, New South Wales" (Webb, 1980, p. 121). (Attribution: Joan Webb and the National Parks and Wildlife Service (now Parks Australia))

---

[7]The New South Wales Government Gazette is the permanent public record of official NSW Government notices.

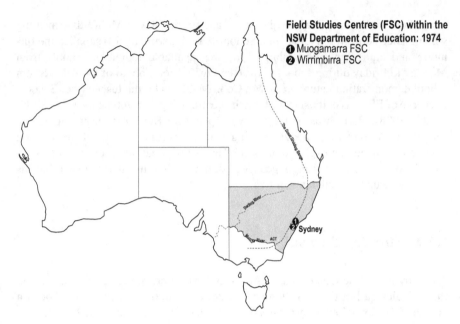

**Fig. 7.5** Location map of the first two EECs within the NSW Department of Education (not to scale—schematic map)

Frank Haddon was seconded from the Central Coast. He had been very involved in EE and became the first senior education officer of the Gould League of NSW in 1974 (Johnston & Tribe, 1982). There was great collaboration with the NSW NPWS. Strom and Haddon carried out many one-day in-service EE courses at Royal National Park, Bouddi, Kurnell/Towra and the Blue Mountains with Fox and Wendy Goldstein of the NSW NPWS Education Unit (Fox, 2016).

For FSCs, once Wirrimbirra and Muogamarra (see Fig. 7.5) were up and running and proving to be very popular, every NSW education region wanted a FSC. There was a great flurry of centres being set up—pushed by local communities advocating for them through their local political members and/or the NSW Department of Education. It is worth noting that the first two centres were joint ventures. The Gould League of NSW, other community organisations and the NSW NPWS had significant input while the NSW Department of Education supplied a teacher and some equipment.

## 7.3 Non-viable Primary Schools as Field Studies Centres

In 1974, Arthur Frost, Staff Inspector (Manual Arts background), and Colin MacDonald, Inspector of Schools (Science background), were the head office inspectors who played a crucial role (DA; MacPherson, 2015; NSW Department of

## 7.3 Non-viable Primary Schools as Field Studies Centres

Education, 1973, 1977) in the development of FSC in alliance with Strom and Haddon (Johnston & Tribe, 1982; Fox, 1979). Inspectors held positions of power and influence. Frost's position, in particular, seemed to have been significant and powerful enough to effect change and get FSCs established and functioning within the NSW Education system—a staff inspector was a step up from the initial inspector ranks (MacPherson, 2015).

> Yes, there's a whole lot of politics with Arthur Frost too. He was a great one for working the system to help FSCs. He knew how the bureaucracy worked.... He used to drive a V8 Holden Statesman to conferences, which used to make us all laugh.... Arthur used to go to bat in the Department for us. He used to speak for us. If anything were going to happen he'd tell us… we were where he got his credibility from, through coordinating FSCs. So he was very instrumental in keeping us on stream. AA

It is also likely that Frost, like Strom, had informal connections to others higher up in the chain of command and that some of these people had quite an interest in the progression of EE, as has been highlighted with the Wyndham link previously. The next centres opened in closed primary schools while Frost and Strom were in head office (NSW Department of Education, 1977).

In the 1880s, according to Welch (2018), there were over 100 small provisional schools across rural NSW. Provisional schools were in remote locations in private buildings built by local effort and staffed by itinerant, often unqualified teachers. Provisional schools were unable to maintain the minimum attendance of 25 students. Additionally, Bridger (1997) found that between 1889 and 1903 provisional schools were subsidised. Communities however, had to supply the building and the teacher. Thus, from the 1970s, when the NSW Department of Education started to make these schools redundant, rural communities appealed for their continual benefit to the community in some way. The closing of non-viable small primary schools coincided with extra money from the Federal (Whitlam) Government for state schools. With environmentalism in a diverse array of forms, and thus EE, popular at the time, many closed schools were utilised as FSCs or EE professional development sites. It was common for high schools to advocate to have these small schools set up for school excursions. Redundant Cascade Primary School, for instance, became an annex for Dorrigo High School (Bridger, 1997). Another example was a principal in the Illawarra having the keys for an abandoned school in the Southern Highlands. In exchange for site maintenance, this deserted school could be used for excursions. In addition to small redundant schools transforming into FSCs, there was pressure on the NSW Department of Education for others.

The *Education Gazette*[8] advertised positions for a "teacher-in-charge" at Bournda and Thalgarrah FSCs in late 1975. Jack Miller and David Kennelly were successful in gaining these positions respectively, beginning at the start of 1976.

---

[8] The Education Gazette: Inside Education series was first published by the Department of Education to comply with the requirements of the Teaching Services Act 1970 (NSW). It publishes personal and general notices in addition to amendments (NSW Government: State Archives & Records, n.d.).

A few of the old guard teachers-in-charge remember being interviewed by MacDonald and Frost, or Frost at least—in some cases the other interviewer was the regional director. Their understanding of environmental issues was queried, and it was impressed upon them that their mission was to have the centres cater for K-12 students, particularly those undertaking HSC subjects.

> So it was a fairly forward thinking, radical proposition. Radical in that sense of ahead of current practices of the times and so on. And because it didn't exist in the education consciousness in New South Wales, in Australia I suppose… to have proposed establishing these special schools for environmental education probably would not have been successful in its own right. KA

The centres were to cater for a broad range of subjects. Although Kennelly recounts being told by Frost not to consider classes below Year 4, he did include younger ages in his endeavour (DK). Miller remembers these inspectors and someone from Wirrimbirra interviewing him in 1975 and felt that Strom was very close to what was happening. Strom and Fox were instrumental in setting up Nadgee Nature Reserve and had a keen interest in the area (Fox, 2016; Strom, 2017). There was concern about the woodchip industry on the South Coast at the time that Bournda was established. Both Strom and Fox knew Miller, an avid bushwalker and active member of the National Parks Association of NSW. The inspectors and Strom took Miller out to lunch in Sydney after he was successful in gaining the position of Bournda teacher-in-charge and told him that they thought he could survive the woodchipping situation.

While Thalgarrah and Bournda were the first FSC positions advertised, those for Awabakal, Wambangalang and Dorroughby followed within a year or two. It is not the intention of this study to delve too deeply into what was happening at most of the centres before Departmental personnel took up their positions. However, from the information obtained it appears that there was significant, specific, place-based community activity occurring.

### 7.3.1 Thalgarrah Field Studies Centre

Armidale College of Advanced Education lobbied the NSW Department of Education to open Thalgarrah as a FSC. Thalgarrah was a small, closed one-teacher school that had been vacant for some time. It was on seven acres surrounded by a grazing enterprise (see Fig. 7.6).

The school was gazetted on the 26 March 1976. The Liberal Minister for Education, Neil Pickard, signing off on it (NSW Department of Education, 1976c). It comprised a wooden classroom with a veranda, a small office with a storeroom attached, a weather shed, bubblers/wash shed, and two small toilet blocks, one for each sex.

When Kennelly arrived as teacher-in-charge, the place was empty of chairs, paper and many other school essentials. The district inspector advised him to visit

**Fig. 7.6** "Diversity of habitats—the farm dam at Thalgarrah, New South Wales" (Webb, 1980, p. 112). (Attribution: Joan Webb and the National Parks and Wildlife Service (now Parks Australia))

other closed schools in the district to gather supplies in addition to visiting the Dumaresq store, an old closed school where excess school furniture was stored. Functioning schools in the area supplied their surplus chalk, paper and cleaning equipment. Kennelly's wife Julie, also an environmental educator, reflected on David's experience.

> Dave saw the educational function of the FSC as engaging students in the natural environment in a manner consistent with the objectives of the curriculum. Dave had a strong interest in matters of the natural environment, the manner in which the environment was used and a strong ethic of resource conservation. His approach was "cross curricular" with activities delivered being derived from all "subject" areas. He also had a keen awareness of the isolation of many schools in the region and worked consistently to attract remote and small schools to TFSC. This outlook towards EE appeared to be commonly held at the time, but of course it evolved over time and the role of the FSC/EEC altered accordingly. JK

### 7.3.2 Bournda Field Studies Centre

In March 1973, the Bega High School Inspect Group brought the need for a local study area to the attention of the Bega-Tathra Conservation Society (DA). The area of focus had been utilised by Jim Collins, the science master, for many years (DA). The Conservation Society requested the NSW Department of Education take an interest in the site becoming a FSC. Establishment was difficult with major issues such as land tenure (1973). The Bournda site was partly reserve for public recreation and partly Crown land. Its recommended inclusion in the Bournda Nature Reserve had been rejected; nevertheless, it was the NSW NPWS who controlled this unused space (DA).

The former Jellat Jellat Public School reopened as Bournda FSC in February 1976 (DA) (see Fig. 7.7). A Regional Employment Development and Australian Schools Commission Innovation Project grant funded improvements to the facilities, such as the High Ridge Hut, toilet facilities, Sandy Beach Creek Suspension Bridge, and track upgrades. Community voluntary work kept costs at a minimum. Gazettal of Bournda FSC took place on the 7 May 1976, approved by the newly appointed Labor Education Minister, Eric Bedford (NSW Department of Education, 1976b).

Early documentation from Bournda set out the objectives and pedagogy for the centre:

1. To foster an awareness of the inter-relationship between humans and their environment, and the consequences of their activities in the environment,
2. To promote a feeling of concern about the quality of human environment,
3. To develop a commitment to the principle of conservation of the environment, and
4. To develop abilities and attitudes which will assist in the solution of human environmental problems.

Once the objectives were settled, it seemed that the most likely theme to follow in order to achieve them was a discovery one—hence "discovering the Bournda environment." A

**Fig. 7.7** "The closed school at Jellat Jellat—the site of Bournda Field Studies Centre", New South Wales (Webb, 1980, p. 55). (Attribution: Joan Webb and the National Parks and Wildlife Service (now Parks Australia))

program of "discovering ••• " units was designed on topics such as rocks, landforms, streams, coasts, plants, trees and animals.

Additional to the Bournda area program, and in response to local area demand, extra material is being prepared on similar lines for units on farms, industries, towns, national parks and nature reserves, land use and maps. These latter units are designed for use, not at Bournda, but within a few kilometres from the Centre. DA

Kennelly and Miller formed a great friendship, supporting each other by phone. They were both experiencing the management of these new innovative experiences in remote locations, and their experiences differed markedly from those in metropolitan centres.

Opening of centres happened in quick succession. Awabakal and Wambangalang opened later in 1976. Once more, the events that led to their establishment were unique.

### 7.3.3 *Awabakal Field Studies Centre*

There was a major local community political push to get the Awabakal FSC and Nature Reserve founded in the mid 1970s (see Fig. 7.8 for a contemporary photo of flannel flowers and the heath community at Awabakal Nature Reserve—overlooking the Pacific Ocean).

The Awabakal Association for EE, established for this purpose, had an initial meeting in 1975 instigated by Mrs. Betty Roberts, Inspector of Schools (McDonald, 2015; Webb, 1980). The Awabakal Nature Reserve is another example of

**Fig. 7.8** Flannel flowers, Awabakal Nature Reserve 2021

community activism winning natural environment preservation over development given at the time, the Awabakal Association for EE was in a conflict with the proponents of sand mining at Dudley Bluff. The mine was subsequently approved with stringent conditions (Webb, 1980).

Awabakal Association for EE field days progressed a detailed documentation of the natural history with many teachers supporting these events (Webb, 1980). A temporary adviser in EE, teacher Mr. Boris Sokoloff, was seconded by the NSW Department of Education at the end of 1975, and prepared resources and encouraged site usage as a field study area. The Association was particularly active and in-service education sessions for teachers, working bees and trail days occurred on the site. In March 1976, the opportunity was taken to repurpose a temporary demountable building, associated with renovations at Dudley Public School, as a FSC. The demountable was moved to a block owned by the NSW Department of Education between the school and the proposed nature reserve (see Fig. 7.9).

A teacher-in-charge position was advertised in the Education Gazette on 3 August 1976, and Brian Gilligan, a qualified science teacher with majors in geography and geology, commenced in the role in October. The Centre gazettal took place on 13 August 1976 (NSW Department of Education, 1976a).[9] In November, the government dedicated approximately 121 hectares of land encompassing intertidal rock platforms, coastal cliffs, clifftop sand dunes and a permanent fresh water

**Fig. 7.9** "Awabakal Field Studies Centre", (Webb, 1980, p. 132). (Attribution: Joan Webb and the National Parks and Wildlife Service (now Parks Australia))

---

[9]These events indicate a significant amount of activity taking place within the Hunter Region, NSW Department of Education for these developments to take place.

lagoon as a nature reserve (NSW Legislative Assembly, 1976; Webb, 1980). Richard Face, the local Labor member, had pressed Parliament for these resources. The Reserve and FSC were officially opened in 1978 (ZA). Gillian wrote many resources, and others such as McDonald and Munro drafted material for the site. Barbecue facilities were built by Gilligan's brother to provide a welcoming experience, with the local butcher and shop assisting with supplies so that a not-for-profit lunch could be provided.

A broader view of EE, including studies of the effect of human activity on the environment, was being advanced at Awabakal from as early as 1976 (Webb, 1980). In time, Gilligan found that while the site was biogeographically significant, the range of study sites was somewhat limiting and isolated. He increasingly found the need to organise visits to other locations such as Blackbutt Reserve, Kooragang Island, Seaham Swamp and areas closer to the visiting schools.

### 7.3.4 Wambangalang Field Studies Centre

This centre was setup as a residential FSC in the Central West, about half an hour's drive from Dubbo. It is on a piece of the old stock reserve around wheat and sheep farming land with pine and eucalyptus woodland (Fox, 2016). The old, closed school site developed into a FSC and other old school buildings from local closed schools were added to the complex (see Fig. 7.10). Once more, local interest in utilising redundant schools was decisive. Simon Leslie was the first teacher-in-charge at Wambangalang. Neil Dufty, a teacher with an earth science degree and 2 years' experience as a seasonal part-time ranger with the NSW NPWS, was employed as the assistant teacher from 1976 to 1980. While at Wambangalang, Dufty started the Association for Environmental Education Country Region (Association for Environmental Education [AEE] NSW), using the basic forms of communication available at the time.

> Well before fax or… and certainly miles before email. So, I did this all by…sending out just a little newsletter. When I say sending out—snail mail…phoning people, having little meetings. And a lot of the people that came on board were farmers. So that was a major move, I think, in the right direction. But this is a long, long time before we had Landcare and probably well before a sustainable farming approach. ND

Importantly, a "Friends of Wambangalang" group was set up to inform and grow acceptance in the local farming community. Community/centre relationships were critical in progressing the centre, with the locals providing much needed support. The travelling stock reserve across the road was used for field studies and the local farming community expanded the diversity of learning experiences by allowing fieldwork on their properties. They also contributed their time and expertise in farming practices. An environment developed which nurtured the exchange of ideas and work. The word "environment" had negative connotations in pre-Landcare days, and both Leslie and Dufty initially talked of the centre as an outdoor education

**Fig. 7.10** "Wambangalang Field Studies Centre" (Webb, 1989, p. 13). (Attribution: Joan Webb and the National Parks and Wildlife Service (now Parks Australia))

facility—teaching EE under the guise of outdoor education until, over time, the community saw merit in its work and the centre gained its trust and support. Other staff cheekily dubbed Wambangalang the "kangaroo shooting company" as they were in locations where "environment" was more acceptable, if not in vogue. Wambangalang FSC developed what became known as the Wambangalang Scheme, an environmental program that was completed at the centre but involved both pre and post schoolwork. FSC staff would visit the schools to inform staff and their classes about their pending FSC experience and deliver the pre-visit activities/curriculum. Learning started off with being "in" the environment to learn "about" the environment with education "for" the environment integrated when understanding and trust developed—it was always the aim. Many of the school groups stayed for 5 days. Often students were from isolated areas and learning the skills of socialising was arguably as important to them as the formal elements of education. For School of the Air students, a visit was their first introduction to many normalised school activities such as forming a line. Conversely, inner city students, many from culturally and linguistically diverse backgrounds, were often astonished by the vastness of the rural environment. This experiential learning was extremely valuable.

In addition to the natural woodland, educational resources included First Nations people's heritage, farms, soil conservation projects, and wildlife (Fox, 2016). Bob Newton, the next teacher-in-charge, developed the site extensively, adding aviaries and ponds. The centre had a special NSW NPWS licence to hold endangered species so that visitors could learn to identify the species and thus assist in their protection. Providing accommodation enabled Wambangalang to be a role model for sustainable living including gardening and recycling. The informative newsletter provided environmental news of state, national and global interest, regional school networking, interesting activities, nature games for students, and resource guides.

### 7.3.5 Dorroughby Field Studies Centre

Dorroughby was a small, closed primary school on nearly a hectare of land about half an hour from Lismore, a socioeconomically depressed region at the time. It became the site for a FSC application as efforts to put the site to good use were limited and needed support. Ken Hoy, an inspector of schools in the region, was keen to see redundant schools put to good use (ZA). Ian Clements, a social science teacher with a strong interest in educating and participating in rainforest regeneration, became the first teacher-in-charge at Dorroughby. His background included coordinating field studies within his high school and he had also participated in an EE in-service workshop at Cascade Public School. The gazettal of Dorroughby FSC took place on 21 January 1977.

There was a 6-month timeframe to get Dorroughby FSC setup. The site was overgrown with lantana and other weeds and Clements brought his tractor up from his farm four kilometres away to clear the site, (eventually the centre could afford to buy its own equipment). Inadvertently, observing their new long-haired neighbour working diligently to establish the centre, earned respect from the generally friendly yet conservative farming community. Clements' action in caring for and working the land went a long way to breaking down the barriers and developing good relationships for the centre, particularly with one farming family whose property surrounded the centre—access to property was essential.

There was an old chamferboard (a form of weatherboarding/cladding) classroom divided into two, and a toilet block some distance from a weather shed. Additionally, a cooking facility installation made the classic Federation-style formal residence functional for large groups. Regional funding provided for a shower building and parent/teacher accommodation. The student dormitory housed 40 bunks, similar to backpacker accommodation. One of the first Public Works pole constructions saw a simple outdoor eating area but the process of sourcing supplies from the NSW Department of Education stores via a catalogue and ordering system was laborious. Once the site was up and running, Clements insisted on manageable groups of 35 (30–32 students plus accompanying teachers and parents). The location was quite isolated. Rainforest regeneration and some fruit trees eventually beautified the site.

Many field excursions were developed to areas that were accessible via foot. For instance, there was a walk up to Rocky Creek Dam and into the Gibbergunyah Reserve and return—a day trip. Other experiences included visiting local macadamia, tropical fruit and dairy farms. Importantly, in an effort to branch out, Clements gained a bus licence and did a deal with the local bus company—creating business for them and securing a low hire rate for the centre. In addition to enabling excursions to places such as Mount Warning, the bus transported students to and from Dorroughby when costs would otherwise have been prohibitive. There were numerous accounts of the residential component providing a positive environment for student development and relationship building.

During Clements' first year or two at Dorroughby, a logging dispute developed at Terania Creek, less than half an hour's drive from Dorroughby FSC. Forestry logging plans had became public knowledge in 1975 and direct action began about 1979 (Bible, 2009). This significant regional event had national consequences. The end of the confrontation came with the remaining forest being gazetted as national park by the Wran Labor Government, and becoming the "Nightcap National Park" in 1983 under the Forestry Revocation and National Park Reservation Act 1983 [NSW] (Adams, 2016).

Isolated on the far North Coast, a network of like-minded professionals developed between Clements, a few foresters, and NSW NPWS rangers. Len Webb, a rainforest ecologist at Griffith University, Queensland, who had played a role in influencing Neville Wran's Terania Creek decision, mentored Clements and Rob Coinman, a forestry ranger, who is now a rainforest ecologist himself. Clements said of Len Webb:

> And he grabbed Rob and I and he said, "I understand you can't be at the coalface over there in Terania but you've got a bigger role to play. Come along and walk with me in the rainforest." IC

Len Webb understood the importance of an informed citizenry and opened a large and influential circle to both Clements and Coinman.

> He was just really a subversive underneath it all and his subversive message to us is (was) that we should expand the awareness and the importance of rainforest and all ecosystems and that we should be unrelenting in promulgating that from whatever vantage point. IC

There were examples of the mingling of social classes generally in the 1970s. Academics, working class, for example construction and industry group workers, and foresters, all interacted in the public sphere—the pub. There was an understanding that entailed a certain larrikinism that radiated empathy… an understanding of the environment within and across the class structures.

## 7.4 Developing Centres, Curriculum, Pedagogy and Networks

### *7.4.1 Developing Confidence and Resilience in Risky Situations: Managing Risk*

Taking risks is important in the development of confidence and resilience, and an important element of learning (Hartley-Brewer, 2001; Koole, 2020; Zittoun, 2014). Given the risk aversion and stringent compliance regulations in today's society and thus education system, it is interesting to illustrate how risk and trust historically developed in isolated situations where they are paramount. Teachers-in-charge had a great responsibility in taking students unknown to them into the environment—sometimes camping (Fox, 2016). Teachers-in-charge were ingenious and innovative in developing strategies to minimise risk in these situations, often in remote places, without limiting the experience for students. It was important to know the students in a potentially life-threatening situation with minimal staff. Following are some examples of this gleaned from interviews.

Teachers-in-charge had autonomy in developing strategies that were fit for purpose—and they worked. Further, they were trusted to be responsible with their charges. Systems were in place to ensure that everyone was accounted for and that everyone understood the risks. The ability to take risks and build confidence and resilience, and to achieve by doing, was highly valued.

> I didn't ever behave like I was shackled by insurance companies and in the whole 20-year period, whatever it is, under my management there was never a serious accident. There was never even… there was hardly a minor accident. … but I wouldn't compromise. … And I'd give them a system of pairing. And a buddy system. Where I could call out at any time … I showed them where they could jump off and take a risk. But, they had a protocol to follow to make it safe. … And so, that aspect, I think was significant. Because there was going to be nothing that would destroy the ability to do it. GA

Strategies were developed to ensure the most effective learning, and seamless bushwalks took place with students given the opportunity to be the teacher and impart knowledge to their peers. Students became the expert in certain aspects of the bushwalk, learning the role of an element(s) of the environment, utilising all their senses to understand it, and then reinforcing that knowledge by teaching it to their peers. Meanwhile, the walk progressed without the stop/start and bottleneck congestion of attempting to teach too many students in a confined narrow space.

> When you're on a long trail, where I was very often, with a bunch of people in a long strung out line, so to speak, then you can't stop and take advantage of the features that are going to direct the group to the focus of their study. Because you've got to wait and constantly gather them together and sometimes there isn't a big enough space. So I developed a technique where I would use three of the participants. And I would get them to point out—physically point out—touch, smell, a feature and then down the track, I'd leave another three and they would add information to that feature, and then another three down the track that would kick that into the overall system that we were walking through. And that was not only a great disciplinary technique; it was a great teaching technique because even though

> they're getting the snippets of knowledge from me, they're playing a role in explaining that feature, or putting that feature into a context of understanding of the overall system that you're wandering around in. And so you learn to observe key things in an actual theme that are going to illustrate a concept and so then you've got to get the individual to immerse themselves in that feature or have some sort of interaction with it. And at the time … your concern is not that they're content tested at the end of it, is can they remember a Flindersia australius, but are they aware of the role that fungi are playing, or how the soil is being [affected] or whatever…. cycles. GA

Teachers-in-charge had free rein and often produced innovative programs (Fox, 2016). The following excerpt illustrates the importance of building trust and confidence in risky, unfamiliar spaces and one technique used to build trust and connection with fellow students.

> I used to do these activities when you go in the bush you've got to have a buddy and you've got to have… "It's not about just you. It's about us all getting out of the bush. And here's the dangers we could confront and so we're all going to work together. And that is going to save us." And so as part of that introduction, I would do some more or less personal development activities. But I would do one activity… because you had to develop trust right. So everybody would line up and they would put their hand on the shoulders of the person in front and I'd show them how to do this massage right. Loosen up the shoulders, … bang, bang, bang, down the spine, a bit of a rub above the backside… like a proper massage. And then they'd all be doing it to each other and then they'd turn around and reciprocate, do it to the person who'd done them. The kids would all have fun, it was an icebreaker but it also got the message across, "Hey you know. We're in this together." GA

## 7.4.2 Centre Collaboration

Collaboration between the centres was intense in the early days of establishment. Centre staff wanted to learn and share their learning and practice in an effort to further FSC/EE.

> We were encouraged to work together in those early times and in the first two years I made visits to Wirrimbirra, Muogamarra, Bournda and Wambangalang, all by public transport—usually a rail warrant. I even visited in my holidays the site of the soon to be opened Dorroughby FSC. DK

### 7.4.2.1 Field Studies Centre Educator Conferences

The FSC educator conferences, initiated in 1976 at Wirrimbirra, were extremely important in providing support and professional development to centre staff. This was the first group of environmentalists coming together on behalf of the state government. This looks somewhat radical these days, or in days of conservative and repressive governance, which is ironic given that development would have had a significantly greater detrimental impact were it not for environmental and sustainability education (ESE) and environmentalism.

## 7.4 Developing Centres, Curriculum, Pedagogy and Networks

Education was not the focus of the NSW NPWS who had an emphasis on "interpretation." Nor was it the focus of the Forestry Commission, who also had an interest in EE. There was no Environmental Protection Authority until 1991. It was a new frontier on the periphery and those involved were "outcasts" in many ways, both within the NSW Department of Education, and the communities in which they worked and lived. There was no template for how to setup and run these centres with the new teachers-in-charge largely given the keys and left to their own devices. The professional and social connection, and collaboration were crucial in developing the centres.

> The teachers-in-charge got together at Wirrimbirra and basically just compared notes… I was just soaking up all that I could to try and get some clues about how to go… So when we came back after that and got into the start of the 1977 school year then basically I was sort of operational and had a bit more confidence about how to go about things. EA

The conferences significantly impacted EE discourse by shaping perspectives on EE theory, pedagogy, curriculum development, and implementation. Additionally, they fostered collaborative sharing of insights, facilitating the establishment, maintenance, and effective administration of environmental education centres (EECs). Exchange of ideas and practice with the FSCs in Queensland started from the early days. One Queensland environmental educator remembers the hospitality of David Tribe and Allen Strom when he travelled to NSW to investigate "How does one do this thing called environmental ed?" in the early 1980s. This exchange continues to this day and includes conference attendance.

The second conference at Wambangalang saw the first world FSC volleyball championship take place. Only male teachers-in-charge attended, and a female education consultant who was present noted the gender bias and started to assist in neutralising gendered language. The bias was possibly more a sign of the times than a characteristic of the teacher-in-charge community. However, the conditions they found themselves in and the camaraderie of their like-minded missions did go a long way to developing strong bonds between the early FSC staff. The consultant saw them as knockabouts—hippies, with one a lone "rugger bugger" (a rugby union fanatic).

> So it was challenging but very exciting times, and certainly, I think for all that we actually bonded well, and also appreciated the different techniques that we had to use tailored for the different situations that we were in. FA

Kennelly noted that many of the issues raised at the early conferences continued to resonate into the future—promotion and publicity, policy issues for the operation of the centres, and EE as a subject and its placement within the curriculum (DK).

## 7.5 A Snapshot of Developments Within Environmental Education

Strom provided a large amount of field support—guidance, open communication and personal demonstrations. Strom retired in 1977 (NSW Department of Education, 1977; Fox, 2016) and Haddon became the new Curriculum Consultant for EE, continuing some of the functions of Strom's Advisor in Conservation position (Curriculum Development Centre [CDC], 1978), working in the curriculum development section of head office. In addition to liaising with teachers-in-charge of FSCs, Haddon's position description included working with teachers and other consultants in progressing environmental programs specific to schools and their districts. In 1978–1979, Haddon was seconded on a one-fifth time basis to be the State Liaison Officer for the CDC EE project.[10] Tribe took on Haddon's position as Education Officer, Gould League of NSW (1977). There was much provision of inservice education for teachers and a Gould League of NSW weekly television segment on the *Super Flying Fun Show* that aired for seven and a half years (Johnston & Tribe, 1982),[11] along with lectures, demonstrations and assistance in developing EE programs and resource materials within schools.

Noteworthy were the development and use of school grounds for EE, and the sensory environmental awareness activities that Tribe had adopted from the United States after a Teachers Service Fellowship to the United States to investigate their system in 1976. Lectures and workshops based on these adopted programs and activities influenced many teachers-in-charge of the EECs and their professional development and teaching activities.

> Advocated by two people who are influential here, partly through the movement … through the activity of David Tribe, were Bill Stapp and Joseph Cornell. And Bill Stapp was more… he didn't call his stuff outdoor education, he may have been one of the first people to call it environmental education, I'm not sure. But Joseph Cornell did the outdoor education learning. Learning by sensory interactions, so tree hugging and all that sort of stuff which David Tribe basically taught me about. And he, David Tribe, was very instrumental in promoting all of that through the Gould League he was involved with at the time. KA

The Gould League of NSW coordinator network was established due to the demand to organise EE activities (Johnston & Tribe, 1982). Coordinators were college/university lecturers, FSC teachers, other school staff and the general public, and some of the participants went on to become FSC teachers-in-charge.

The Gould League had convened an annual national conference for those interested in EE by the mid 1970s. Its purpose was to coordinate activities, networks and communication and to discuss problems and needs in an effort to progress EE. In 1977, the conference focus was FSCs with topics covering the worth of FSC,

---

[10] In addition to Haddon being the NSW CDC network representative, Frost and Meyer had input into the CDC study and recommendations.

[11] This practice was started by David Tribe before he took on the position of Gould League Education Officer and then extended to further television coverage by Haddon.

## 7.5 A Snapshot of Developments Within Environmental Education

objectives and strategies, teaching strategies, the scope and development of programs, factors to consider in centre establishment, evaluation of FSCs in relation to EE, alternatives to FSCs, and in-service training for FSC staff. A host of EE mentors attended including Joan Webb, Haddon, Tribe and Henry Bingham. Frost attended for the NSW Department of Education (Gould League, 1977). Noted at the conference was:

> That teachers are sick to the teeth of being told both in written and verbal form, what they should or might do. Many have said, "Don't tell us what to do—show us." While field study centres continue to demonstrate practical approaches and strategies performed by people who are actually working in the real situation confronted by similar problems, they will not lack for customers. (Williams, 1977, p. 2)

Additionally, and interestingly, considering the dearth of research and evaluations within these centres over the years, it was noted that effective evaluation of the centres was lacking:

> On the surface it seems that the enthusiasm which generates itself in the activities of developing Field Study Centres comes from teachers who have an eagerness for the task of enthusing students in the outdoors. These people seem to experience a temporal pressure that does not allow them to engage in the seemingly complicated task of evaluating what they are doing. The task of evaluation is therefore largely left to various members of the academia who are in a lesser position to reflect in their evaluation the affinity for the process which is shared by the practitioners. Either the teachers are going to have to take themselves apart from their commitment to working with students in order to review their activities with some perspective and feeling for the subject area, or else those people concerned in producing research papers which feature the evaluative process in relation to outdoor studies are going to have to devote more time to developing better first-hand knowledge of the subject they set out to research. The situation at present is that piecemeal attempts are made by the researchers through collaboration with the practitioners to develop a "precis concept" of the operation they intend to evaluate. (Foreman, 1977, p. 15)

Illustrated in this text is the broad and illusive categorisation of education within the centres. Additionally, it is highly unlikely that NSW teachers-in-charge had the time to undertake evaluative practice given their staffing circumstances, as will become apparent throughout this narrative. This text does, however, demonstrate consideration of the nature of evaluation from the inception of FSCs.

### 7.5.1 Changes at Muogamarra Field Studies Centre

In 1977 Barbara Hamilton was disappointed to be informed that she was to be replaced in the position of teacher-in-charge at Muogamarra (Woolley, 2016). Several factors may have led to this outcome, and these have been inferred from the evidence at hand. Strom retired in 1977 and the NSW Department of Education desired the centres to develop fieldwork in line with the state curriculum, particularly for the senior years. This aspiration may have become more pressing without Strom there to champion the EE cause. Although K-12 were targeted, visitation at Muogamarra was mostly upper primary classes. Further, teachers were invited to develop their own program if the programs on hand did not suit (Morgan, 1972). Perhaps after a few years of the Muogamarra pilot, they found that teachers did not have the knowledge base or capacity to develop their own fieldwork and there may have been a perceived need for further development in this area. The NSW Department of Education may have wanted someone who was more familiar with the state curriculum and the functioning of the state system. Hamilton's replacement, Bruce Foott had been teaching an environmental studies elective at Galston High School—a rarity in the 1970s. In recognition and appreciation of Hamilton's work in teaching at Muogamarra, an insect, *Peripsocus hamiltonae*, was named after her (Psocodea Species File, n.d.; Smithers, 1977).

When Foott took over, he concentrated on targeting K-12 through providing fieldwork opportunities that aligned with the syllabi, particularly with high school geography and science where the main fieldwork focus lay. This had been one of the directives in his job interview with Frost and MacDonald. Additionally, history resources, including pre and post-activities, were developed to align Muogamarra's rich First Nations and early European settlement past with the history syllabus. With the first convict road going through Muogamarra, unfortunately straight over one of the First Nations engravings, there were many contact sites to explore. Historical excursions were developed where students, given clues, and through observation, had to build a picture of what had occurred on the site—enquiry, hands-on learning (see Fig. 7.11 for a contemporary photo of a view from the Muogamarra site).

### 7.5.2 Royal National Park Field Studies Centre

Royal National Park FSC opened in 1978 as a shared facility. Wendy Goldstein, an environmental educator with the NSW NPWS, lobbied strongly for its establishment. Gary Schoer, a science teacher from Jannali Boys High School, was the first teacher-in-charge operating out of a small office in the NSW NPWS main office. The Superintendent made him feel unwelcome. Apparently, the centre establishment was a higher-level decision made without much consultation or consensus. There were no clerical or general staff support for a short time.

To coincide with the 1979 Royal National Park Centenary, historical documentation was showcased in a history professional development seminar. Staff used the Centenary as a stimulus to get schools involved. Publicity, resource development and in-service education for teachers were Schoer's initial priorities.

> All of us I think at the time used the mantra doing education "in the environment," about the environment," but to be true environmental education, of which there was no real policy at the time, it was education "for the environment." And sometimes we added, well I added the extra one, education "from the environment" like if you wanted to estimate the height of a tall thing, using trigonometry or whatever, we would use a tree rather than a roof. GS

Before long, the centre moved to the old dancehall next to the Hacking River where there was space for equipment, but this resulted in diminished collegiality and

## 7.5 A Snapshot of Developments Within Environmental Education

**Fig. 7.11** Sunset over the Hawkesbury, Muogamarra Field Studies Centre | 50 Year of Environmental Education Celebrations, August, 2022

professional development with the NSW NPWS staff and Schoer missed it. Nevertheless, he tapped into those interested in EE and the NSW NPWS resources. Harold Senior, one of the first rangers at the Park, gave talks to students. Initially, work was concentrated on the park. Schoer conducted many major staff development activities and developed resources. The government printer was well utilised. Schoer describes some of his teaching memories as follows:

> So, where we could we pushed the "for" but I think the best thing we did was sensitising students to the environment. And even making teachers feel relaxed. I really did hone the skills of being a quality teacher in those days. I remember being on a bus with kids who were about six heading to Wattamolla or somewhere to the beach. And anyway, the fog had come down and it was a bit drizzly and a bit cold and terribly misty up on the plateau down there. And the teachers are starting to grumble saying, "Oh, this is going to be a great day." And so just before the bus stopped… I used to occasionally go on the buses with them… I said, "Look, we're really lucky. We're going to go to a lookout. But," I said, "You're not going to see many things from the lookout but guess what. The thing you are going to see is real cloud… You're going to be in the middle of real cloud." And as the kids were getting off, they were looking around. Holding each other's little hands and they're shaking their heads and they're saying, "Oh, real cloud!" I thought it was absolutely fantastic. So the idea of… Yeah, teachable moments is another common phrase that we all used to use. An eagle flies overhead. Right oh, what do you do? "Down on your backs. Look up. We're so lucky. We haven't seen an eagle for two weeks. Oh look at this eagle." GS

Over the years Schoer extended his work into teaching "on-school"—utilising the school grounds.

Webb's (1989) study noted that there was open communication between rangers and FSC staff and that the centre was restricted to 4 days a week during school terms. Due to high demand, it was only available for public schools. Technical and Further Education (TAFE), Guides and church groups used the centre, but generally there was a policy to exclude weekend and school holiday use (Webb, 1989). Webb observed the programs having an ecological emphasis with the promotion of awareness, responsibility, and management of the national park.

### 7.5.3 Longneck Lagoon Field Studies Centre

Longneck Lagoon, a popular bird-watching haunt on the road between Pitt Town and Cattai, near Windsor on the Hawkesbury floodplain, opened as a FSC in 1977 (NSW Department of Education, 1978). The Lagoon and surrounds encompassing approximately 150 acres was a Gould League of NSW project and by 1972 had been reserved for fauna and flora. The Long Neck Lagoon Trust had been set up to steer the management of the project with the intention of opening a FSC (NSW Department of Education, 1972).

Kevin Rozzoli, the Local Member for Hawkesbury, was on the Trust. In 1974, the League were in the process of fencing the site when they learnt the project was under threat from the proposed Sydney to Newcastle natural gas pipeline which was due to run through the centre and across the Lagoon (NSW Department of Education, 1974). The League pressed ahead, completing the fencing, building a teaching facility, revegetating, and building an access road. It provided environmental lessons and activities at the facility and staffed the centre with a Gould League of NSW senior education officer, Haddon, and latter, Tribe. They taught 2 days a week at Longneck Lagoon FSC until the NSW Department of Education provided a teacher-in-charge and assisting teacher in April 1978 (see Fig. 7.12).

Setup of the facility was a little more extensive and laborious with mud deposited from the Easter 1978 floods having to be scraped off the walls. Only the building existed so sourcing and setting up the centre with essential equipment was the initial priority along with developing resources. As with all the centres, publicity was important. Warwick Giblin, teacher-in-charge, and David Bowden, assisting teacher, spent a lot of time publicising the centre and its services which included talking to various organisations. There was also a lot of in-service teacher education.

One early debacle was the felling of nearly all the trees along a 24 metre strip, rather than the agreed 20 metre width for the gas pipeline easement. The National Trust claimed that none of the necessary guidelines were followed ("Pipeline cuts swathe through Longneck", 1980). Advocacy from the centre, the NSW Department of Education, and the NSW Minister for Planning and Environment (IA), Eric

7.5 A Snapshot of Developments Within Environmental Education

**Fig. 7.12** "The water habitat for study at Longneck Lagoon, NSW" (Webb, 1980, p. 55). (Attribution: Joan Webb and the National Parks and Wildlife Service (now Parks Australia))

Bedford, and a great deal of publicity, saw erosion control measures put into place and rehabilitation of the site (IA).[12]

Due to its wetland bird habitat status, Longneck Lagoon had strong links with the Australian Museum, the Royal Botanic Gardens, and a range of other organisations and researchers. Dufty continued the ties with the birding community when he became teacher-in-charge in 1987.

### 7.5.4 Brewongle Field Studies Centre

In 1978, Warwick Giblin became the administrator of the Brewongle[13] FSC, another redundant school some 26 kilometres away from Longneck lagoon. The centre was a venue for students to conduct field work associated with the school curriculum and was the only centre developed to cater for students with disabilities, featuring accessible paths, buildings and shower/toilet facilities (Webb, 1980). Originally the closed Sackville North School, a heritage sandstone building on the Hawkesbury River, the school had been upgraded with a kitchen, showers and accommodation and rebadged a camp. Both the Metropolitan West Region and the St George Region

---

[12] Note Bedford had just moved into this ministerial role after being Education Minister.
[13] Dharug for "camping place" (Giblin, 1978).

of the NSW Department of Education had input into the centre with the St George Region taking up 50% of the patronage. A report had advised against the addition of Brewongle as a FSC due to its close proximity to Longneck but it was a very different style of student experience, had strong community backing and was reportedly favoured by one of the local directors. There was a strong outdoor education element to the Brewongle camp with some EE needed to get those involved on the EE agenda. The school was renamed Brewongle FSC in 1978 but was not gazetted until 1979. In 1978, there was little time for Longneck staff to do anything other than facilitate the Brewongle experience with teachers resourced to undertake the encounter and students oriented to the site. However, in 1979, Bowden transferred to Brewongle 4 days a week and in 1980, he became the teacher-in-charge of the Brewongle facility. Upgrading of Brewongle included A-framed sleeping shelters. During the upgrade Bowden and his clerical assistant worked out of Longneck, moving to Brewongle in late 1979, early 1980 (IA).

In the late 1900s-early 2000s, sustainability was integrated into the Brewongle programs.

> Around this time at the Environmental Education Centre I developed a sustainable agricultural program which included excursions to farms that implemented sustainable management practices. So that sustainability thread started being embedded into the programs at Brewongle. I also established a renewable energy program. Now that's another… the renewable energy program was the first one in Australia. So that was very exciting. We had a solar tracker put in the grounds of the Centre. JD

## 7.6 Progressing Environmental Education Guidelines and Centre Policy

It took some time for policies to be developed for the establishment and functioning of EE and FSCs, and the centres played an essential role in this. The Education Department's centralised Human Resources unit determined regional staffing levels, while staffing allocation was at the discretion of the regional director. Professional direction was from the central curriculum branch while administration was regional (Wilson, 1979). The *ad hoc* establishment of the centres (Webb, 1980) resulted in a lack of guidelines on how FSCs should operate. To this end centre staff started to document centre structure and function at the Longneck Lagoon/ Brewongle FSC staff get-together in September 1979 (IA; Webb, 1980). It included a rationale, role description, structure of the centres, training of personnel, mode of operation and administration.

> RATIONALE
> Environmental education is that education which develops an awareness of the environment, emphasising both the human and natural elements, and of the relationships between these phenomena. Environmental education is concerned with the development of knowledge, skills and attitudes so that an awareness and an understanding can be reached concerning the finite, nature of resources and the role played by society in the use of these resources.

## 7.6 Progressing Environmental Education Guidelines and Centre Policy

> The ultimate goal of environmental education is for people to develop an awareness of their environment that will lead to a personal sense of involvement and eventually to the shaping of an environmental ethic to guide each person's behaviour.
> 
> Directly concerned with the quality of life, environmental education cannot be considered as a single subject, but rather as a synthesis of all school disciplines, understandings and skills.
> 
> The Department of Education Field Studies Centres in N.S.W. act as agents of reference for schools on environmental education. These regionally based Centres have been established in response to a desire by various groups within the community for children to be better equipped with the knowledge, skills and attitudes necessary to make decisions on issues concerning environmental quality. (IA; Webb, 1980, p.22)

The role of the staff was to:

1. provide support for the implementation of EE whether at the centre, school, or another field location,
2. assist schools in embedding EE in their programs and practice,
3. provide in-service professional development to schools/teachers—to guide teachers to confidently teach EE independently,
4. produce resources, and
5. "promote an active, pupil orientated approach to EE, emphasising processes at work within the environment" (IA; Webb, 1980).

The structure of FSC highlighted the similarities and differences within centres. The varying locations, accommodation facilities (residential/day visit), staffing levels, degree of community involvement and regional support constituted the diverse nature of the centres. In clarifying the unique teaching role, the document states:

> By its very nature, this occupation requires, to varying degrees, that staff fulfil a number of roles. These include education (to communicate to most age groups in many disciplines), administration and organisation. Such abilities should reflect in a positive way, commitment to sound environmental practices. Staff may produce documents to support the objectives of environmental education.
> 
> Invariably, the Centres interact with a wide range of community interest e.g. local landholders, government agencies and private enterprise. Thus, public relations is an important consideration.
> 
> In light of this rather unique occupation, personnel are specially selected from interested teachers throughout the state. IA

The mode of operation emphasised the importance of pre- and post-visit development and ensured the active engagement of the visiting teacher, with the centre teacher "complementing" the visiting teacher in an effort to facilitate and encourage confidence in the teaching of EE (IA).

By the end of 1977, the first edition of the NSW Department of Education *Environmental Education Journal* had promoted FSCs at Wirrimbirra, Muogamarra, Bournda, Wambangalang, Thalgarrah, Awabakal, and Dorroughby. Jindabyne and Bunberry Sidings (within a school) were also on the list. The journal stated that the Department hoped for one centre per region (NSW Department of Education, 1977). Showcasing Wirrimbirra, the article classified three centres as residential. In addition to Wirrimbirra it is assumed the others were Wambangalang and Jindabyne with Thalgarrah and Dorroughby still in development.[14] Listed in the 1979 *Statement on Departmental Field Studies Centres* were 10 centres (see Fig. 7.13) of which six provided residential facilities: Wirrimbirra, Dorroughby, Bournda, Wambangalang, Thalgarrah and Brewongle (IA).

Confronted by the anomaly of an entity within the school system that taught but did not have a stable body of students, nor responsibility for the assessment and the day-to-day continuum of school life, FSCs were categorised as "schools for a specific purpose—class four" (IA). As many of the centres were old one-teacher primary schools, it must have seemed logical to class centres similarly. "Teacher-in-charge" was the classification given to the specialised teachers within

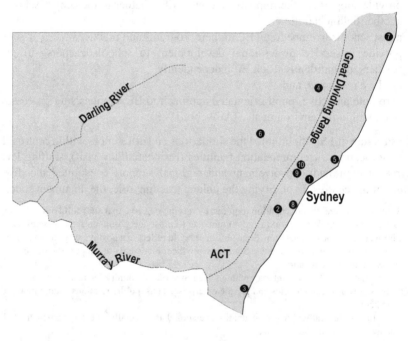

**Field Studies Centres (FSCs) within the NSW Department of Education: 1980**
❶ Gibberagong FSC  ❻ Wambangalang FSC
❷ Wooglemai FSC  ❼ Dorroughby FSC
❸ Bournda FSC  ❽ Royal National Park FSC
❹ Thalgarrah FSC  ❾ Longneck Lagoon FSC
❺ Awabakal FSC  ❿ Brewongle FSC

**Fig. 7.13** Location map of the 10 EECs within the NSW Department of Education (not to scale—schematic map)

---

[14] Jindabyne and Bunberry Sidings, via Parkes, were no longer within the FSC listing in 1983 (AEE [NSW]). While they had been mentioned by one or two interviewees, the story behind their inclusion and exclusion is elusive.

these centres—a small step up from being a teacher but not close to a principal category. Centre staff were responsible to their district inspector and the regional director.

## 7.7 One-Teacher Dilemma: Capping Capacity

Having only a single teacher-in-charge at most of the centres (only Wambangalang had two[15]) made growing the capacity of FSCs difficult. There was no lack of potential given that these centres were extremely popular for school excursions. In addition, it was sensible and economical for a school to fill a whole bus, generally about 60 students. Teachers-in-charge at the centres were reliant on the assistance of visiting schoolteachers. In many cases, this was used as a way of initiating teachers into the knowledge and skills necessary to enable confident EE teaching. Each centre handled the situation differently. For example, Bournda often found it necessary to facilitate a few school visits rather than concentrate on one school group at a time so that expected student numbers could be attained; Dorroughby capped student numbers at 35, some just handled the numbers but often noted the difficulty.

> Some days I'd take up 60 students that was not only dangerous but very hard to give the students a really good experience. AA

It was also problematic for teachers-in-charge to be sick or to attend professional development days.

Without a student population there was no precedent for extra staffing at the centres. In the late 1970s, the centres started advocating for an assisting teacher. Later, when it was possible, teachers-in-charge had to create a teaching role and somehow pay for it to justify the cost. Nevertheless, initially, the ceiling of one teaching staff member per FSC was a problem.

> So, if two people wanted to come down on the one bus, the standard thing I would do would be to arrange to meet a person who wasn't going to be with me. And it usually was the person who was the most capable if you like, to come down with me in the bush where we were going to run the excursion and we'd walk it through and show them the exact sites that they could use and tweak any worksheets that we might have been working on, whatever. But then the person I would have with me would be the one who needed my support more than the other. So that's the way I tended to do it. HA

---

[15] It is presumed that this is because accommodation allowed for two staff members, but another factor could be that it was the result of successful lobbying from the region.

## 7.8 Early Field Studies Centre Critique

One of the early teachers-in-charge talked about mounting frustration at the seemingly superficial nature of some of the field studies lessons.

> The other frustration I was feeling by about then was a frustration with the fact that we were only managing to achieve what I regarded as a fairly superficial level of awareness raising. And yes, you gave people an experience of using their senses and learning something about the natural world or the Aboriginal world or history, but it was pretty superficial rather than really engaging them with their interaction with the environment in a more sort of comprehensive and in-depth analysis. Now I tried to deal with that a bit by preparing materials for teachers to do things in their local school… what we struggled to do was to translate that into something that had more depth. EA

The difficulty in recruiting visiting teachers to take EE into their schools was a source of disappointment.

> Whilst I think we can give ourselves a couple of ticks for awareness raising and experiential memorable experiences for students, the extent to which we were able to empower teachers so that you got a multiplier effect on that stuff was pretty limited in my experience. Now maybe some of the other field studies centres had more success. EA

Nevertheless, awareness and skills development were an important part of the EE process (Webb, 1980). From early on, teachers-in-charge were encouraging school teachers to be involved and were increasingly exasperated by the difficulty in getting classroom teachers to participate. Teachers-in-charge conducted pre- and post-activities to ensure learning connected to substantial intellectual quality—so the experience included both understanding and engaging with the environment and connecting with the curriculum on a deeper level.

There is evidence of visits to schools to prepare teachers and students for their impending experience. This assisted the FSC educator in connecting with the class—getting an understanding of class and individual student requirements and dispositions. Some school visit tactics had novel hooks.

> And so if you were with a group and you needed to distract their teacher from them [given the teacher-centred teaching of the times], I think Bruce taught me this, I'd carry a few things and the one that stands out, you've seen it a dozen times, was the box with the mirror in it and the big label on the box, "The world's most dangerous animal." So you'd use that to initiate some animation in the kid's room. You said, "Look… if you sit there quiet while I talk to… I'll show you what this animal is."… And of course they'd wet themselves till it happened but then when you showed them that would immediately—they'd burst into comments, which would reinforce the idea mainly that yeah, we're wreaking the place. And so you had a bit of an opportunity to see what level of animation your group was going to have, what your management issues were going to be in the field. GA

There is also evidence of excellent progress in covering the Department of Education's field studies outcomes. While the following extract is from a teacher-in-charge and thus is a public representation of success from within, it also demonstrates that personnel are clearly comfortable in proactively supporting the agenda.

There is no doubt in my mind that Longneck Lagoon FSC is meeting these aims by enabling children to gain first-hand experience in a natural environment developing field skills in investigating and problem solving. WG

## 7.9 Gaining Clerical and General Assistance

Interview data (IA) indicates that all centres had clerical and general assistance—a move that must have taken place between 1978 and 1979 given that there was no assistance for most centres when they began. It was Ian Clements, teacher-in-charge at Dorroughby, who achieved part-time clerical and general assistants for the centres. This was something the North Coast region was proud of even though it did not succeed in gaining funding for a car for the centre. This was an issue, given the large amount of travel the teacher-in-charge was required to do, particularly in a rural location. Teachers-in-charge were doing everything for a while until Clements was motivated to make a submission for a clerical and general assistant. There was already some allocation for a cleaner, but the funding was based on the requirements of non-residential rather than residential facilities—a different battle to the one for assistant.

> So I was doing the cleaning, conducting the teaching program, designing the teaching program and I was also doing the grounds work, our mowing and disposing of the waste… But no I thought, "Well no, I haven't got the hours to possibly cover all bases and am I going to allow my resource to be reduced to a servicing function when I'm trained to be an educator." IC

After the proposal for assistance for the centres was submitted to the NSW Department of Education, a senior inspector flew up from Sydney to assess Clements' situation and ensure it was legitimate. "Because they've got (had) no idea that there are such institutions operating, let alone how they operate" (IC).

The visit enabled "the hierarchy" to get an understanding of centre operation and led to recognition and, importantly, an allocation of ancillary and clerical assistance for the centres. Over the intervening years, their hours were extended a little beyond the original agreement.

## 7.10 The Importance of Good Relationships and Ecocentric Understanding

Individuals within the bureaucracy could make or break EE and the work within the centres. Significant in the treatment of the centres and their staff was the relationship between FSCs and their regional director, in addition to the general understanding of EE and its importance in the development of society within the Departmental structure. Often support would wax and wane depending on those within the regional hierarchy. The link with regional office could be a gateway to support and funding or an obstacle to FSC progress depending on the personalities involved. At times the issues were due to a clash of culture or personality.

> Yeah, the Regional Director at the time would not let me leave the centre to visit schools as other teachers–in-charge did as he thought I was not an appropriate person to represent the region. I was also sent a transfer form after three years because he didn't like the length of my hair. He confirmed this personally when I finally met him. AA

In other situations, the problems were associated more with the rigidity of the system and less with understanding regional supervision of the centres. The theme of doing "battle" with the system and some of the personnel looms large within the data.

> Here was the impediment of just… a difficult bureaucracy to handle, and in some cases I also found my supervisor, which would be a cluster director or inspector of schools, not highly sympathetic to what we were doing, and quite rigid in his or her views. So… I certainly had some battles, strong battles with directors and schools because we were not classed as principals, but were expected to carry out the role of principals. FA

Some of the supervising personnel within the NSW Department of Education had no idea how to access such a holistic, cross-curricular area not constrained to a single discipline. Often supervisors were narrowly focused on their speciality with little understanding of the bigger picture.

> I mean he just had no idea how to assess what I was doing. No clue whatsoever. I mean, he assessed that in the field I was an effective educator but as to achievements on syllabus or curriculum he was flat out getting his head around what I was doing and I'd take him into a room where I had all these worksheets, not that I used them a lot. But I must have had… I don't know… 100 different worksheets that covered various areas and various subject areas various physical areas… any inspector's got a very narrow focus. If they were secondary, they were either English, or History or… and if they were primary well they basically didn't do outdoor education or environmental education in primary schools so what's his yardstick or her yardstick? So, from my point of view in the educational practice, there was a sham accountability but really, there was bugger all. GA

Yet, there were also Departmental personnel who supported the centres and worked with them in developing EE and navigating a complicated bureaucracy, exemplified in the following two quotes.

> He was fantastic. They just treated you like you are a professional and that you were an equal. And that they had experience that they could share with you and help you, and so long as you kept the lines of communication open. GA
>
> The Regional Director in the North Western region in the 70s was very supportive and a variety of inspectors visited Wambangalang due to it being within their portfolio as a "special school." FA

## 7.11 Embargo, Threats of Closure and the Politicisation of EE

By the end of the 1970s, it was clear to the NSW Department of Education that these centres were going to require more resourcing than was initially envisaged.

> So I suppose another major hurdle was that the Department had to fund these things, and some of the costs were actually much greater I think then what they thought. FA

Accordingly, an embargo was placed on centre establishment and development.

> Growth of existing Centres and the establishment of new ones has been very much restricted this year due to a directive issued by the Policy and Planning Group in the Department. Apparently they are uncertain and, sadly, yet to be convinced of the educational merit of field studies centres. IA

Threat of closure or subsumption within the Department of Sport and Recreation is a theme that runs throughout this history. Sport and Recreation Centres—the National Fitness Camps rebadged—have a very different purpose, distanced from the educational roots of EE.

Any politicisation of the EE staff, both on a professional and personal level, was purely for the advancement of EE. While staff were and are a cross-section of the political spectrum, one unifying element was their desire to progress EE. Yet, the bureaucracy, many of those acting for the bureaucracy, and the politicians, were generally unable to distinguish this defining character.

> From a political view, we weren't highly linked into the political world. Having said that, quite a few of us certainly in the 70s, were members of the Australian Conservation Foundation, Wilderness Society et cetera and we were seen as, certainly in the local communities, but also by the Education Department and politicians, as being greenies. And that certainly polarised us, and I think as I explained before, a few of us had some issues politically because of particular stances that we took in our broader life on environmental issues, which polarised the community back in those days in particular… I've worked for left-wing Labor politicians, and I've linked with the Greens, and also conservative parties as well, wherever I've been. So, one of the inspectors got wind of those linkages and felt that I was running a political agenda at the Environment Education Centre and I said "Which political party am I aligned with? There's this one and this one—I've links with all of them. Politicians are part of the community, and they will help support what we do, and maybe even better, they are a conduit to funding, and it's important that they are on side whoever they are. Both sides – all sides of politics." So, there was maybe some pressure there to possibly close the Centre in that case because they saw that I was politically motivated but they didn't… I tried to explain that environmentalism is multi politics, you can't take politics away from anything we do and in fact, the whole school system is politically driven and politically persuaded. So what's the difference—I don't think he particularly got that point, I think he saw me once again, as a bit of a green freak show and also the fact that I… I think had so much linkage into the community, such strong links. Far more than… you would have in an internal school community. He saw me, I think, as a threat, and I think probably that's a good way of summarising how we were seen in terms of the education system. FA

An interesting observation in the quote above is the perceived threat centres posed to some politicians and the NSW Department of Education because of their extensive community links. This is a theme that carries through from Strom and his experiences with the FPP.

Woven throughout the data is the importance of politics in shifting EE and the centres forward, and warding off the threat of closure at times. Politicians used the centres to gain favour with the community who were backing the centres:

> If there was some political mileage in it for the politicians, we got a jersey… It was on from day one. We had to play politics all the way. And David Tribe, he was playing politics for us at one stage too… but we were always—well, whoever had the ear of whoever was in power… Whoever knew someone would do the deed. We were always playing around with that. And of course, the Department didn't really want us. They wanted to give us to Sport and Rec at one stage… We were always under threat of being closed. So political in those days, still are. AA

The vested interests within the well-established learning areas of science, history and geography were battling the new upstart environmental educators. So the centres were fighting three or more entrenched curriculum areas. The theme of the power play between and within the curriculum was touched on in previous discussion relating to the attempts to shift schooling in NSW to a more "whole child—head-heart-hand," student-centred pedagogy. This theme is entwined with the battles that centre staff, and EE in general, have had in changing what we learn and/or how we learn it, given that ESE is so antithetical to traditional ways of learning.

While the gazettal process was important in securing the centres, and indeed, at times staved off their closure, it is difficult to ascertain the exact details of the process and who was involved. When a centre is gazetted it has the same status as a school. The process provides a school number and establishment funding and staffing. It is difficult to close a school. Gazettal was immensely important for the centres. It appears that the process started in 1976 with the first of the old schools being established as FSCs and it seems that some teachers-in-charge were involved or instigated the process.

> I mean it's fantastic the environmental ed centres are still going but we made sure through a lot of lobbying that these centres were schools. That was critical. That was… because you can't close down a school, pretty much. Only through numbers. We made sure that that happened. So they could get rid of the environmental ed coordinator… central coordinator, they can do whatever else they want to, but they've actually got to close a school politically. But even based on legislation they've got to carry out certain activities, and the main one is to say that no one is turning up—and that's not going to happen. So the bottom line was that we made sure that… and we fought to become a principal of a school. And they're listed and gazetted as schools. And that was the win. It's game set and match. FA

## 7.12 A Shift in Oversight

About the time of Arthur Frost's retirement, greater regional independence saw the employment of teachers-in-charge being managed by the regions. One of the old guard thought the political and environmental nature of many of the first few intakes of teachers-in-charge was intentional and conceivably due to Frost's authority. It was possible that regional selection was influenced by consideration of potential negative consequences from more senior ranks, particularly after the embargo. Increasing politicisation of education could also have had an effect.

Centre educators remember Frank Haddon overseeing the centres but his oversight was not the same as that of Frost who was from within the system at a more strategic level. Frost was able to keep FSC staff informed of any matters pertinent to their cause such as annual budget allocations and it was Frost who organised the centre conferences. Teachers-in-charge would write annual reports and present them at the conferences (not too arduous when there was fewer than 10 attendees). Post-presentation submission of reports to Frost and the regional directors kept all authoritatively informed. These reports would outline numbers through the centres and their Year groups—K-12. It was many years before the practice of annual reporting became mandatory for all schools. After Frost retired the teachers-in-charge of FSCs were answerable to a regional director, and the powerful positions that had influenced the establishment and development of the centres were no longer accessible. The Curriculum Consultant for EE did not have this power. Haddon took over the organising of the conferences, but centre staff led the content.

> And Frank loosely oversaw us but not like Arthur Frost. Arthur used to go to bat in the Department for us. He used to speak for us. If anything was going to happen he'd tell us.... I was saying that Arthur was more like our principal and we were his staff. And he had control over, not what we actually taught but how the centres ran. He organised the conferences and told us what was going on and how much funding we were going to get next year... after him the people that took over his role didn't have as much power within the Department. They were under regional directors themselves and they were answerable to them. I don't know who Arthur was answerable to, he seemed like he was answerable to himself ... When Frank Haddon took over he used to organise the conferences but it was more led by us. But he would tell us what was going on. AA

## 7.13 Field Studies Critiques in the Late 1970s

Joan Webb published the findings of her survey of FSC in Australia, funded by the Australian NPWS, in 1980. It noted that the term "EEC" was more appropriate than the outdated "FSC" (Piesse quoted in Webb, 1980). The literature review concluded that EE research was an emerging field, and there was limited evidence on the effectiveness of field studies and community nature centres. Webb also highlighted a trend of resources being primarily directed at primary students, with relatively less attention given to decision-making adults and teenagers in these centres. Webb called for further research to investigate how young children handle environmental responsibility and their readiness to make the necessary decisions related to environmental issues (Webb, 1980).

Unravelling the difference between outdoor or conservation education using Swan's 1969 description, Webb points to EE being about citizens developing concern for environmental quality and thus being involved in environmental problem solving, with an interest in nature being a by-product of the learning rather than an aim (Webb, 1980). The study noted that centres had moved significantly towards approaches studying the human impact on the total environment rather than studies of ecology. Interestingly, for evaluative purposes, with some environmental educators seeing attitudinal change as the main objective, it was thought that the effect of EE could not be measured until tested via the undertaking, or not, of environmental action later in the affected student's life (Webb, 1980).

One major issue addressed in Webb's report was the FSCs not being available to private schools and the general public—a frustration for many within the environmental groups and some within the NPWS who would like to have seen the centres open to all 7 days a week (Webb, 1980). At this stage, the NSW NPWS was the only NPWS to have an EE policy—they were keen for centres to be utilised by all. Webb, noting the Education Department/governmental monopoly of FSCs in Australia, derided the sporadic, uncoordinated community involvement (few individuals carrying much of the load) compared with that of the United States "Let it be said that lack of awareness, which stems from lack of education, is creating a vicious cycle, and where commitment does exist, often this is stifled by a lack of funds" (Webb, 1980, p. 108).

At the time of Webb's study, there were a variety of FSCs in NSW. There were 48 centres in all: ten FSCs within the NSW Department of Education FSC network, 13 closed schools utilised by schools for studies, 10 sport and recreation centres, seven tertiary FSC, two managed exclusively by a school (one private and one public) and six private centres which accepted the general public but most of their clientele were school students. In analysing the number of students through centres within Queensland and NSW, Webb concluded that Queensland's network was providing services more efficiently with more centres per head of population and with plans for more, whereas NSW had no future plans, having "closed the doors to expansion" and looking for a more efficient use of centres (Webb, 1980, p. 135).[16] However, both states were only catering for a fraction of the school population (6.1% and 2.2% respectively). Webb established that the cognitive and skills components were being taught well while the personal relevance and problem solving/decision-making aspects of EE were neglected.[17] Webb considered that sports and recreation facilities had great potential for EE given their extended residential capacity, and their greater overall capacity in having more staff and bigger facilities, yet the EE within their programs was minimal. The Gould League of NSW had over the late 1970s and early 1980s conducted professional development at these centres

---

[16] Furthermore, Queensland had a policy of two teachers per centre from their establishment with the number of staff growing over the years (Stevenson, examiners report, December 17, 2019; Webb, 1980; in addition to one of the study interviews).

[17] It should be noted that development within the FSCs under investigation is difficult to tease out given the plethora of NSW centres, let alone to study nationally. Additionally, from many interview accounts, while Queensland does have EECs, there are also many Outdoor Education Centres (EECs are primary education whereas the outdoor education centres are secondary oriented—but practices within are variable), whereas the Centres in NSW are clearly defined EE or Outdoor Education (Fitness Centres). All centres are considered in Webb's analysis.

but their focus on fitness and outdoor education took and takes precedence—changing ethos is not easy. Webb's study questioned the reasoning behind the placement of NSW FSCs and their efficiency in being in locations that could provide for a sufficient number of schools, with a diversity of experiences unavailable to schools themselves (Webb, 1980). The study suggested other EE possibilities such as wide-ranging EE consultants for the Riverina, which was a large region without a centre. This was something the FSC staff themselves had suggested from the early days—more staff taking EE to schools. Webb's study outlined a pressing need for a demand for FSC services but suggested no further expansion until policy and rationale development—something the centres were in the process of formulating, albeit within their structure, part of which Webb references (Webb, 1980).

While a broader base and a greater shift to EE was advocated, as outlined in the 1975 Belgrade Charter (more progressive problem solving/action based/connected education) (UNESCO| UNEP, 1975), it was noted that some centres—Arbury Park in South Australia, many in Queensland, and, within NSW, Awabakal, Bournda, Wambangalang, and Muogamarra—were working towards achieving this effectiveness (Webb, 1980). To answer the question, "Are the field studies centres staffed by NSW education officers achieving their objectives as they relate to visiting school children?" a case study of Awabakal FSC was undertaken. It established there was significant achievement of centre objectives with the embedding of the centre visit in an overall program of study developed by centre staff in consultation with the visiting classroom teacher (Webb, 1980).

Like AEE (NSW), Webb called for:

- Clear policy,
- EE coordination by a permanent body of people in each state—representative of departments,
- a regional consultancy network,
- key coordinators within schools,
- resource dissemination capacity for schools, and
- once clear criteria, objectives and functions of FSCs are set, the expansion of FSCs. (Webb, 1980, p. 120).

## 7.14 A Snapshot of EE at the End of the 1970s

Environmental issues were very much in the media at the end of the 1970s. Government departments were involved in the push for change. For example, the NSW Minister for Education, Eric Bedford, in 1978 stated,

> There is increasing concern over such issues as wood chipping, uranium mining, sand mining, preservation of whales and seals, preservation of trees, containerization, oil transportation, recyclable products and disposal and reclamation of useful items from domestic and industrial garbage waste.

> Children in school today will be the adults of the next generation who have to utilize and identify the issues which lie behind these complex challenges. (Education Minister, Eric Bedford cited in the NSW Public School Teachers Federation, 1973, p. 17)

There had been at least seven major national conferences and many state conferences providing the space for cross-pollination and opportunities for divergent thinking within the field. For instance, Lee Williams, organiser from Queensland's Department of Education, had presented aims for FSC through his 1977 presentation to the second AEE (NSW) Conference at Newcastle (Sokoloff, 1977). The CDC EE priority was also inputting into the education system from the second half of the 1970s.

The core of EE within NSW at the end of the 1970s was:

- the museum EE group (The Australian Museum 1978–79)—open to FSCs,
- FSCs which were generally hubs of activity acting as regional advisory centres for teachers (IA),
- the Gould League of NSW and the 70 Gould League of NSW coordinators being set up around the state, and
- the curriculum projects that were supported by the CDC (Haddon, 1979).

By the end of the 1970s, there had been substantial growth within EE but it was still ambiguous with the predominance of education "about" and "in" the environment but not great progress in education "for" the environment (Robottom, 1983a). The difficulty in changing the paradigm of education within a schooling structure embedded within a dominant capitalist structure was continuing. There was a state priority given to internal, local developments with dissonance between the understanding on a national level (CDC) and the state representatives of the national projects. CDC initiatives involved political negotiation with state departments. It was Haddon who was the NSW representative who interacted significantly with FSCs and the schoolteachers who had to deal with principals and curriculum committees embedded in a disciplinary, academic orientation (Robottom, 1983a). National thought, through the CDC, was that orientation towards environmental action was not produced from knowledge and skill development alone (Robottom, 1983b). It seems that the elements conducive to action were most likely to be developed/developing through the types of programs, pedagogy, practices and role modelling growing and emanating from the FSCs. Yet the apathy in the NSW Department of Education in the late 1970s emerged with unsuccessful attempts to establish an advisory board in EE to guide teachers (Strom, 2017).

## 7.15 Conclusion

This chapter has provided a brief history of the establishment of the first wave of FSCs. Muogamarra, Wirrimbirra, Thalgarrah, Bournda, Awabakal, Wambangalang, Dorroughby, Royal National Park, Long Neck Lagoon and Brewongle FSCs were all set up from 1972 to 1980, many in old school buildings. All centres had strong advocacy and support from local communities, the Gould League of NSW, the AEE (NSW) and many had strong individual advocates with political connections.

Teachers-in-charge had to be innovative by necessity given the unconventional, experimental, avant-garde nature of their newfound vocation and the isolated, unprepared and ill-equipped work environments they found themselves in. The teaching and management autonomy that came with the job was highly valued. Teachers-in-charge pioneered strategies for constructivist EE teaching while developing student confidence and resilience.

Most centres had only one staff member inducing even greater innovation in the art of risk-management given a busload of students in isolated natural environments where the potential for injury in unfamiliar territory was very real. The one teacher cap was problematic and debilitating for centres. It restricted professional development opportunities, and importantly, centre capacity to build their EE reach.

Collaboration between the centres was intense given a keen and crucial thirst for learning and an innate desire to share their practice. Given the isolated nature, both physically and mentally due to EE/FSC novelty, the FSC educator conferences were integral to supporting the professional development of centre staff. Conferences engendered a learning community of practice and an understanding of the importance of the individuality of places and spaces and the diversity within place and community. There was empathy for each other's unique situation and the differences within their practice.

This chapter has charted early moves by centre staff to document the form and function, implementation and processes of EE and FSCs through the commencement of EE and FSC policy development. This helped establish a process for the operation of the centres and importantly EE's place within the school curriculum. Plans and initiatives to progress EE and the FSCs and improve their working conditions, and security, were activated in an era where the education establishment and the Teachers Federation were often oblivious to EE/FSC existence and predicament. Good relationships, networking and being politically pragmatic were key.

The receding of the prosperous economy was mirrored in the social and political spheres with the neoliberal turn (Harvey, 2007). While the groundswell for FSCs continued with many supporting conferences within and outside the centres and the input of innovative professional development, the pushback from the NSW Department of Education's rationalisation impacted EE and the centres, and restrictions were placed on the *ad hoc* and opportunistic development of FSC.

# References

Adams, C. (2016, March 28). The Battle to Save Terania Creek Rainforest. *The Northern Star.* https://www.northernstar.com.au/news/the-battle-to-save-terania-creek-rainforest/2977253/#/0

Bible, G. (2009, August 15). Direct action saved Terania. *The Northern Star.* https://www.northernstar.com.au/news/direct-action-saved-terania/296606/

Bonyhady, T. (2000). *The colonial earth.* Melbourne University Press.
Bridger, G. (Ed.). (1997). *Timber town histories Dorrigo Plateau New South Wales.* Cascade Field Studies Centre, NSW Department of School Education.
Curriculum Development Centre (CDC). (1978). *Environmental Education Project Newsletter, 1*(June).
David G. Stead Wild Life Memorial Research Foundation of Australia. (n.d.). *Wirrimbirra Sanctuary.* Retrieved March 15, 2018, from http://www.wirrimbirra.com.au/
Foreman, B. (1977). Evaluation of field study centres in relation to environmental education. In *Field study centres: Gould League National Environmental Education Conference 1977 Brisbane, Queensland* (pp. 15–18). The Gould League.
Fox, A. (1979). Reflections. In W. Goldstein (Ed.), *Parks and wildlife: Australia's 100 years of national parks* (pp. 4–14). National Parks and Wildlife Service.
Fox, A. (Author), Dufty, N., McDonald, K., Smith, S., Tribe, D., & Schaefer, K. (Eds.). (2016). *Chief Guardian: The life and times of Allen Strom.* https://www.amazon.com.au/Chief-Guardian-Times-Allen-Strom-ebook/dp/B01H8IEORQ
Giblin, W. (1978, October 12). Letter to the editor. *Macquarie Towers Review.*
Gould League. (1977). Field study centres. In *Gould League National Environmental Education Conference 1977, Brisbane, QLD.* Gould League.
Gowers, R. (2002). Tipper, John Duncan (1886–1970) *Australian Dictionary of Biography* (Vol. 16). National Centre of Biography, Australian National University. Retrieved July 12, 2018, from, http://adb.anu.edu.au/biography/tipper-john-duncan-11867/text21247
Haddon, F. (1979). NSW. *Newsletter, 7*(June), 9.
Hamilton, B. (1973). Muogamarra Field Study Centre. *Education: Journal of the NSW Public School Teachers Federation., 54*(11), 173.
Hartley-Brewer, E. (2001). *Learning to trust and trusting to learn.* Institute for Public Policy Research. https://citeseerx.ist.psu.edu/document?repid=rep1&type=pdf&doi=4e4e8198a810898a373c6ff8ffcb9e79d23020b5
Harvey, D. (2007). *A brief history of neoliberalism.* Oxford University Press.
Hughes, J. (2002). Harold Wyndham and educational reform in Australia 1925-1968. *Education Research and Perspectives, 29*(1), 1–268.
Johnston, C., & Tribe, D. (1982). The role of the Gould League of New South Wales in environmental education in Australia. In M. Cowan & W. Stapp (Eds.), *International case studies in environmental education: Environmental education in action* (pp. 146–150). National Institute of Education.
Koole, B. (2020). Trusting to learn and learning to trust. A framework for analyzing the interactions of trust and learning in arrangements dedicated to instigating social change. *Technological Forecasting and Social Change, 161*, 120260.
MacPherson, R. (2015). *The institute: A centennial history of the Institute of Senior Educational Administrators, formerly known as the Institute of Inspectors of Schools and Senior Educational Administrators, and before that as the Institute of Inspectors of Schools NSW.* Strategic Book Publishing and Rights Co.
McDonald, K. (2015). The legacy: The EE movement in the hunter region. *OzEENews, 135*, 18.
Morgan, P. (1972, August 16). This bush school is for city children. *The Australian Woman's Weekly*, pp. 24–26.
NSW Department of Education. (1972). *The Gould Leaguer, 1*(7).
NSW Department of Education. (1973). *The Gould Leaguer, 1*(10).
NSW Department of Education. (1974). *The Gould Leaguer, 2*(2).
NSW Department of Education. (1976a, August 13). Awabakal Field Studies Centre. *Government Gazette of the State of New South Wales,* (103), 3421.
NSW Department of Education. (1976b, July 16). Bournda Field Studies Centre (480). *Government Gazette of the State of New South Wales,* (92), 2994.
NSW Department of Education. (1976c, March 26). Thalgarrah Field Studies Centre (7331). *Government Gazette of the State of New South Wales,* (41), 1352.

# References

NSW Department of Education. (1977). *Environmental Education, 1*(1).
NSW Department of Education. (1978). Longneck Lagoon Field Studies Centre. *Government Gazette of the State of New South Wales,* (154), 4566.
NSW Government: Public Service Commission. (n.d.). *Dedicated staff at Wirrimbirra transform the lives of Aboriginal families and children in Western NSW.* Retrieved November 1, 2023, from https://www.psc.nsw.gov.au/reports-and-data/state-of-the-nsw-public-sector/state-of-the-nsw-public-sector-report-2021/case-studies/dedicated-staff-at-wirrimbirra-transform-the-lives-of-aboriginal-families-and-children-in-western-nsw
NSW Petitions. (1976, November 9). *Questions without notice.* Legislative Assembly, p. 2517. Retrieved January 18, 2018, from https://www.parliament.nsw.gov.au/search/Pages/results.aspx?k=awabakal%20november%209%201976
NSW Public School Teachers' Federation. (1973). Three new field centres for environment studies. *Education: Journal of the NSW Public School Teachers Federation, 59*(9), 17.
Pipeline cuts swathe through Longneck. (1980, June 25). *Windsor and Richmond Gazette, 91*(49).
Psocodea Species File. (n.d.). *Peripsocus hamiltonae Smithers, 1977.* Retrieved July 26, 2024, from https://psocodea.speciesfile.org/otus/874853/overview
Robottom, I. (1983a). *The environmental education project evaluation report.* Curriculum Development Centre.
Robottom, I. (1983b). Science: A limited vehicle for environmental education. *The Australian Science Teachers' Journal, 29*(1), 27–31.
Smithers, C. (1977). Psocoptera of Muogamarra Nature Reserve. *Records of the Australian Museum, 31*(7), 251–306. https://doi.org/10.3853/j.0067-1975.31.1977.215
Sokoloff, S. (1977). Report on conference on environmental education. *Hunter Natural History,* (August), 176–178.
Strom, A. (1987). *A background to environmental education: Some memoirs of Allen A. Strom, A.M. Occasional Publication.* Association for Environmental Education (NSW).
Strom, A. (Author), Dufty, N., McDonald, K., Tribe, D., Smith, S., & Schaefer, K. (Eds.). (2017). *Some aspects of nature conservation in New South Wales during the 1950s and 1960s.* https://www.amazon.com.au/dp/B071RNRK8H/ref=rdr_kindle_ext_tmb
UNESCO, & UNEP. (1975). *The Belgrade Charter: A framework for environmental education.* https://unesdoc.unesco.org/ark:/48223/pf0000017772?posInSet=1&queryId=2b333c3f-050c-4850-a7f5-fe68d1561211
Weber, M. (2012). *The Protestant ethic and the spirit of capitalism* (trans. S. Kalberg). Routledge. (Original work published 1905).
Webb, J. (1980). *A survey of field studies centres in Australia.* Australian National Parks and Wildlife Service.
Webb, J. (1989). *A review of field studies in Eastern Australia.* Australian National Parks and Wildlife Service.
Webb, J. (1998). *Thistle Y. Harris: A biography of Thistle Yolette Stead.* Surrey Beatty & Sons.
Welch, A. (2018). The city and the bush. In A. Welch, R. Connell, N. Mockler, A. Sriprakash, H. Proctor, D. Hayes, et al. (Eds.), *Education, change and society* (pp. 74–111). Oxford University Press.
Williams, L. (1977). Why field study centres? What can they achieve? In *Field Study Centres Gould League National Environmental Education Conference, 1977, Brisbane, QLD.* Gould League.
Wilson, J. (1979). Field study centres in Queensland and New South Wales: Impressions by a Victorian. *Environmental Education Project Newsletter, 9*(October), 4.
Woolley, D. (2016). *Hill View Bushwalkers.* Retrieved January 15, 2017, from http://www.hvb.org.au/images/HVBHistory/hvb-history-v5_feb-19-Awith-cover-NXPowerLite-Copy.pdf
Zittoun, T. (2014). Trusting for learning. In P. Linell & I. Markova (Eds.), *Dialogical approaches to trust in communication* (pp. 125–151). Information Age Publishing.

# Chapter 8
# Growth Amid Change: Institutionalisation and Rationalisation

## 8.1 Introduction

The 1980s saw personnel in the established centres, the Association for Environmental Education [NSW] (AEE [NSW]) and the Gould League of New South Wales (NSW), working hard to gain traction for Environmental Education (EE) and the flourishing of the centres. This work would come together toward the end of the decade with the release of the 1989 *EE Curriculum Statement* and the development of the *Field Studies Centre (FSC) Policy Statement* (1989b). Additionally, an understanding and thus relationship with the Teachers Federation was developed. The mid to latter half of the 1980s saw the removal of the embargo on field studies centres (FSCs), followed by the most progressive time in the history of EE in NSW. However, these events were eclipsed and affected by the biggest changes within the NSW Department of Education since the Wyndham era—changes aligned with a shift from a welfare economy to one of economic rationalism (Pusey, 1991).

This chapter covers the next sequence of FSC establishment, the initial push for more, including:

- Shortland Wetlands [now known as The Wetlands Campus of Awabakal EEC] and the Field of Mars,
- the big rush—Cascade, Warambungles, Riverina, Observatory Hill, Rumbalara, Botany Bay [now known as Kamay Botany Bay] and Mt. Kembla/Illawarra [now Illawarra] EECs,
- and the thrust for the final centres—Red Hill and Penrith Lakes.

The rationalisation of the Metropolitan South Western Region FSC resources gained centre status for Camden Park and Georges River FSCs and triggered the inclusion of the Zoo Education Centres into the network. These developments are nestled within their place, and spheres or immediate influence.

## 8.2 Economic and Political Change

Fundamental changes within the economic and political structure of Australia were occurring on a national level during the 1970s and 1980s. According to former Prime Minister Paul Keating, despite the lowest economic growth rate in 27 years from 1974 to 1983, the Whitlam years (1972–1975) saw Australia become a country that was "fairer, more decent, more open, more confident, more exciting" (7:30 Report, 2014, 2:57). Foreign policy was re-oriented to a post-imperial outpost—shifts in social programs saw Medicare, support for secondary and tertiary education, and rights for women. This, however, blew out the budget. Keating noted in his reflection on the Whitlam era, in comparison to the Hawke/Keating era the difference in "Cabinet craft, the specialisation, and the common ownership by each Cabinet Minister in the whole program, or of each stage Cabinet discussion, or of each issue" was profound. This suggests that proprietorship has gone. In addition, Keating argues that goodwill disappeared from federal government given the Coalition's gracelessness in opposition—and a schism ensued (7:30 Report, 2014). This fundamental fissure within the fabric of the Australian political system has had a detrimental effect on planning and decision making within Australian governance, and for controversial topics such as the environment this effect is particularly exacerbated.

In writing about the effect of economic growth in *Australia's 100 years of National Parks*, Fox (1979) draws on the economist James Weaver (1971) who argues that the economic premise of "more is better" is false on the grounds that it ignores both what happens when a purchaser realises expectations have been met, and what happens to society and the environment in the production of additional goods. Expectations increase and there are dehumanising effects from the massive "undemocratic, bureaucratic and hierarchical organisation" required to feed economic growth (Weaver cited in Fox, 1979, p. 7).

Fox talks about a revolt against a move toward a newer, liberal education in an education system with an economic growth mindset. He argues of this new education, particularly those areas emphasising environmental sensitivity, being under attack by industry and technology interests (Fox, 1979). Education, he says, is supporting economic growth, teaching students extrinsic rather than intrinsic value as this is needed to feed the economy. The environment is commodified and there is a lack of time to slow down and value it (Fox, 1979).

Industrial interests, most likely having learnt from the combined efforts of conservation groups, can unite in trying to contest terrain from the conservation movement. An example given by Fox (1979) was an overseas expert who argued, with press giving his views great support, that multi-purpose parks with such activities as forestry, grazing, mining and conservation were an efficient model, yet this was not the case. Instead, he argues, the future will only see further pressure given resource squeeze and profit motive (Fox, 1979). Whilst Fox is talking specifically about national parks and reserves, this is relevant for environmental and sustainability education (ESE) given that he positions education within this economic paradigm but also sees education as the potential liberator. Fox goes on to say that,

> National parks are somewhat like a straw which biosphere people might clutch in an attempt to steady their decline as humans. But in so doing they should remember that the parks will survive only as long as the user can learn from ecological people and sense themselves as part of nature not apart from nature. (Fox, 1979, p. 11)

Further, Fox outlines critical thinking and action as a way forward:

> Environmental education programmes if they are effective, must be more than natural history lessons; they must provide environmental encounters and show people how to become involved in the decision making process itself. This is probably the only way to break the "tragedy of the commons," to give those who have no economic gain a say in the future of the commons. Without the consciousness of people to the decisions which lay ahead, I see little hope. The programmes must deal with living people, systems, and processes of life, and investigate the human intervention in ecosystems and the driving forces of economics and politics. (Fox, 1979, p. 13)

As early as the late 1970s, Fox was talking about the rhetoric of public involvement in decision making, written into planning processes, being only lip service (Fox, 1979)—a sign of the movement away from community involvement.

## 8.3 Pause and Momentum in Centre Establishment in NSW

No centres were set up within the NSW Department of Education in the early 1980s. Max Delaney carried out an inquiry into the growth of FSCs while there was an embargo on centre establishment. There were dozens of requests for support for various developments to become a FSC within the NSW Department of Education (IA).

> There was no policy of where they should be established, how many per region or per school enrolments or in relations to population centres and travel times from schools to FSCs or their location in a variety of environments. AA

The inquiry resulted in a rationale for where centres should be. One centre in each region was favoured by the inquiry, but the regional directors pushed for equality—they wanted the same number of centres in each region. While regional directors pushed for equivalent resourcing, some of the criteria developed were directly related to the educational vision of the centres.

> One criteria for choosing a new site was the likelihood of it introducing a new ecosystem or natural physical study site. For example, there was no wetland environment to begin with, so the Wetland Centre at Shortland was seen as a worthwhile proposition. XB

## 8.3.1 Downsizing of NSW FSCs Oversight

In 1981, owing to government cutbacks, the Curriculum Consultant for EE and Gould League of NSW Education Officer positions amalgamated with Haddon continuing in this role (Johnston & Tribe, 1982). It is assumed this loss may have contributed to the NSW Department of Education's encouragement of the establishment of regional EE committees, which gained sparse response (AAEE, 1982). Tribe returned to schools for a time, becoming the principal of Manly Vale Public School, which he set up as a "centre for excellence in environmental education" (NSW Department of School Education, 1993; DT).

## 8.3.2 Conferences: Shaping Policy, Curriculum, and Working Conditions

Many changes within the NSW centres are captured in glimpses specific to the Departmental FSC/EECs through the reminiscence of the foundational teachers-in-charge. For instance, the importance of the biennial conferences in planning direction was expressed:

> Well the field studies centre conferences were also important events. Obviously, they dealt very much with the conditions in field studies centres; and when I say conditions, not only the physical conditions but also the conditions of employment with the Department of Education. ... So one of the very strong roles of the Association for Environmental Education, and also of these field studies centre conferences, was to actually lobby for, not just an inspector that had environmental education as part of his or her portfolio, but to have a specialist position in the Department of Education that could coordinate environment education within the state, including environmental education centres. FA

In addition to planning time, there was great value in teachers-in-charge learning from each other's diverse experiences, skills and situations.

> It served the best purpose imaginable. Walk a mile in my shoes.... And you got to see each of their environments and you got to see how they interfaced with their community, which is always different. And you got to understand that a range of approaches is valid. And that, especially if the approach taken is geared towards either the clientele or the opportunities available. Everyone had different opportunities. Everybody could invent that role in whatever way they wished. And that is unbelievable professional freedom. GA

The conferences attracted others interested in the field because the attendees were among the few experts in EE at the time, and the emerging field and its developing pedagogies were gaining popularity. Additionally, there were teachers who were actively pursuing EE in their schools. There were also some politically expedient conference attendees who either had been, were, or could be beneficial to the cause.

> In those days, it was a broad spectrum. In those days we had lots of advisors... curriculum advisors. And they were based regionally. So you'd get a few of them. But also the centres would have links to the community and so sometimes it was politic to invite those people

## 8.3 Pause and Momentum in Centre Establishment in NSW

*along because they were in some way or another backing the centre. But you'd get head office consultants. You'd get regional consultants. And then you'd get people outside education...they would in some of the sessions outnumber the field studies centre crew.... I think that perhaps there wasn't much happening in environmental education and these people would see probably, "Ah, here's this elite that have been chosen and so we want to do it too so let's go along." But you'd also get teachers who were doing their thing... they'd get an invite. And that was always really good. Or even at times, you'd be taken out to a school, taken out to areas. GA*

At one stage, people working on the "Do the Right Thing/Keep Australia Beautiful" campaign attended centre conferences. They were writing resource material for schools. This was a big issue for some of the centre staff given that the campaign was paid for by a levy on the packaging industry, ostensibly avoiding deposit legislation. Years later one of the teachers-in-charge consulting for the Keep Australia Beautiful Council was disassociated from the project after suggesting container deposit refunds and refusing to compromise.

The advantage of the FSCs was the freedom to innovate. The disadvantage was no rules were set which made consistent management difficult. Staffing was also an issue. Newly appointed FSC teachers-in-charge had a blank canvas, as there was no existing EE policy or EE/FSC process or procedures within the NSW Department of Education. There was no direction on how to run a FSC, nor what and how to teach—no position description. Fieldwork compatible with the classroom/curriculum was the brief.

The conference held in 1980 at Thalgarrah was significant in initiating the notion of the development of EE policy. There was always a senior official with EE in their portfolio at the conferences, generally an inspector. At Thalgarrah, Foott had invited a staff inspector to assist in progressing centre form and function. He suggested two distinct matters—one industrial regarding the administration and management of the centres, the other revolving around curriculum. This initiated the focus on a FSC policy and an *EE Curriculum Statement*, both of which took nine years to come to fruition.

There was an acrimonious meeting with the NSW Department of Education about working conditions in the late 1970s. The topic stayed shelved for a while until the old guard gave way to newer personnel and the acrimony subsided from the corporate memory. As it was a new concept, there were no Teachers Federation or Departmental policies for FSC working conditions, and as can be read from the description of the setup of the centres, things could be less than ready, to say the least.

Foott had been a Federation Representative when teaching in high school and thus had taken up the task of representing FSCs in their bid for better conditions. It took some time for the Federation to start supporting FSCs but after much discussion, they helped establish links with Head Office within the NSW Department of Education. Nevertheless, the Department refused to talk to the FSCs without the Federation, or unless the situation met the criterion of "in dispute with NSW Department of Education." This position motivated the FSC staff to develop their own policy and working conditions. Foott, Clements and Chris Koettig formulated a draft during a conference at the Royal National Park. With a bit of tweaking, this became the centres' policy about 10 years later. From then on, the FSC had standing with the NSW Department of Education—the relationship changed.

## 8.4 Some EE Events in Australia in the 1980s

Bill and Gloria Stapp visited Australia once more in 1982, with Bill presenting at both the AEE (NSW) conference at Mitchell College of Advanced Education, Bathurst, and the Australian Association for Environmental Education (AAEE) conference in Brisbane (AAEE, 1982). Funded by a Senior Fulbright Fellowship, the Stapps toured Australia and reported on the state of EE sponsored by the Australian—American Education Foundation, the AAEE, the Frank Daniel Butt Memorial Foundation, and Griffith and Monash Universities. The Stapps visited Awabakal, Wambangalang, Dorroughby and Brewongle and while findings and recommendations are too broad to attribute to the NSW FSC specifically, it is possible, and can also be surmised from the data collected for this history, that Stapp's finding: "While in Australia we were exposed to some environmental education strategies, approaches, and activities that we considered to be outstanding and/or exemplary efforts in environmental education" and the advice, "That staff in environmental field study centres [sic.] direct attention to ways to prevent staff burn-out" (Stapp & Stapp, 1982, p. 9) would have been, in some part, directed to the NSW FSCs staff.

> So, probably the most influential was Bill Stapp, and he certainly gave a lot of guidance for environmental education pedagogies, and also a range of interesting activities... into the field. He was a leading educator in the United States and he had a lot of clout. And he got on this bandwagon and there was some fantastic stuff that came out for teachers to use, and obviously we picked up and learnt greatly from these people. Mainly at environmental education conferences, not at field studies centre conferences. But David Tribe did bring around a range of other educators that... for example sensory awareness I think was one of the activities or range of activities so... feel a tree and a whole range of... all these lovely little games and activities, which I did by the way well into the 1990s. Probably still being done now. FA

In addition to practice, the Stapps influenced the fledgling field of EE theory and research.

> So people like Duane Toomsen and Professor William Stapp from the United States provided a lot of academic guidance in terms of teaching and learning and also theoretical theory and also research. FA

The inaugural AAEE Conference was held at Arbury Park Outdoor School in South Australia in 1980. Haddon, listed as Consultant, EE at the Directorate of Studies, the NSW Department of Education, presented at this conference on how EE was progressing in NSW.

- There were 12 FSC located throughout the state. This must have included Jindabyne and Bunberry, which had been included in the first edition of

## 8.4 Some EE Events in Australia in the 1980s

*Environmental Education*, a NSW Department of Education publication in 1978. Royal National Park, Longneck Lagoon and Brewongle had been added to the growing number of FSC by 1980. (In Webb's study Jindabyne and Bunberry were no longer listed as within the FSC network but rather within the Department of Sport and Recreation and attached to Dulwich Hill High School respectively [1980]).

- Teaching environmental awareness was a new component in the new primary science syllabus.
- Broad based environmental programs were being developed utilising the "Man and the Environment" component of the secondary geography syllabus.
- *The Gould Leaguer* (with additional collaboration from The Energy Authority of NSW, The Public Works and Schools Building Research and Development Unit) was expecting to exceed demand with their 50,000-print run by the end of the year.
- The NSW Department of Education was expecting at least three new regional EE consultant appointments by 1981. They would supplement the FSCs who also acted as advisors.
- There was an environmental resource officer paid by the State Pollution Control Commission in the NSW Department of Education producing State Litter Reduction Campaign curriculum material (Haddon, 1980).
- The Premier, Neville Wran, was backing a NSW EE Council through requesting the State Pollution Control Commission set up a forum for its creation. It was to represent the Gould League of NSW, the State Pollution Control Commission, the NSW Department of Education, NSW National Parks and Wildlife Service (NPWS), the NSW Planning and Environment Commission, the Australian Museum, Taronga Park Zoo Board, the AEE (NSW), the Nature Conservation Council of NSW, and the National Trust of NSW (Haddon, 1980).

The AEE (NSW), through a few regions, had been trying to educate the NSW Department of Education about the cross-curricular nature of EE that should "permeate the total curriculum." It was trying to rectify the assumption that EE belonged to the science discipline and was the focus of primary school only (AAEE, 1982). Within the compartmentalisation of the high school disciplines, EE was problematic—but still achievable.

In 1982, the Minister for Planning and Environment proposed an EE Advisory Committee within the Environmental Planning and Assessment Act 1979 (NSW). This was not the Council, a statutory body, advocated for, but still it represented progress in enabling promotion and coordination of EE across NSW (AAEE, 1982). By 1985, however, the EE Advisory Committee had been abolished (ZA). A series of EE in-service workshops was hosted by the Gould League in early 1980 and 1981, and conducted by Duane Toomsen and Joseph Cornell with his *Sharing Nature with Children* (Johnston & Tribe, 1982). While there were some teachers-in-charge who were not overly influenced by these visiting environmental educators, there were many who were. The workshops greatly assisted teachers in developing their EE practice. It was the FSC teaching staff who adopted many of these practices and ensured their enduring further dissemination within the state. The following excerpts illustrate both views of the impact of these educators.

> They were interesting people to meet and you might have picked up a couple of little thoughts and activities or perspectives here and there but they didn't totally, dramatically change the way we did anything in my view. EA

> It had a huge effect with many educators using it… Duane Toomsen utilised Piaget's theory of child development. In-service participants experienced having to design lessons—including the investigation, invention and implementation stage. There were some excellent outcomes with the creation of inventive lessons, such as "Chocolate Chip Mining" and "For the Future," where the concept of sustainability, and empathy for future generations, was revealed through wise use of resources—chocolate chips, and the mining of the chips with as little, or no, damage to the cookie; and smarties… These activities could be given in a classroom… The activity does the teaching and the students do the learning by actually investigating then inventing, and lastly, which hardly ever happens in education, implementing what you have learnt and seeing the outcome. AA

A book titled *Outlook Australia*, containing EE activities developed by the collaboration of American and Australian environmental educators, including Clements and Foott, and edited by Tribe, was published in 1989. While there was criticism on a national level (AAEE, 1990), of the lack of critical pedagogy within this publication, some of these activities did have an element of education "for" the environment when practised by environmental educators with clear intentions. Additionally, the necessity for sensitisation to the environment for many students who were already showing signs of disconnect from their environment, both natural and built, and the value of this education in a system unwilling to be open to controversial issues, needed to be accounted for. There was frustration in trying to move EE toward educating "for" the environment a bit quicker, but many EE educators on the ground were dealing with the intransigence of a hegemonic system difficult to shift. In the right hands, the connection between cognisance and action is revealed and enlightenment ensues. The educator involved in the EE is of the utmost importance (Pearson, 1978; Webb, 1979, 1980) and many of the educators within the centres were very good pedagogues with an excellent knowledge of their content and craft while acting as role models for teachers, students and the community alike. Consideration of specific time and place is important in valuing these activities (Renshaw & Tooth, 2018). In saying that, these activities became very popular and are still utilised within the formal ESE system and further. Some of these activities still have a place given the need for an effective element in ESE and the increasing disconnect that is being experienced within society.

> Perhaps a little bit less to do with learning but to do with the whole student and this relates to a range of things including the rapidly growing disconnect young people have with their natural environment. And as time goes by an increasing number of kids will not have experiences in the natural world. Now that could be a physical separation, our cities are getting larger, transport is getting more difficult, all that stuff. Or that could be a social separation where things like their parents may not have seen or don't see the value in taking the kids for a bushwalk, taking the kids to the national park, allowing kids to do that unstructured nature play, those sorts of things. So when you do have kids in the EECs you can allow them to experience I suppose that rawness, that unfiltered, that unsanitised closeness to nature.

*There's of course a few policy related things there. Safety issues and all that kind of stuff. But it does allow.... It removes those barriers, it removes those filters. VB*

## 8.5 Effecting Change on the South Coast

Before continuing, it is worth pausing to elaborate on some of the events that began evolving in the 1970s and were enacted throughout the 1980s. They have had a significant impact on the centres and how they operate. In attempting to flesh out the theme of "controversial issues," a case study of "Bournda Field Studies Centre" and the experiences of Miller has been developed.

The significant environmental conflicts of the 1970s, such as logging at Terania Creek, provoked a strong response from the environmental movement and influenced FSCs topics taught in EE and the issues that were addressed. Some of the earlier teachers-in-charge were involved, outside of their work, in environmental groups trying to change logging and mining practices. Most FSC personnel stayed out of it but some were in centres that were in the thick of it. What does one do when teaching EE and the antithesis of it is on your doorstep? Many principals were conscious of conforming within the NSW Department of Education, with good reason considering that actions could, and at times did attract the ire of the Department and Ministers. Public perception was important given the newness and unfamiliarity of the EE concept. Another point to take into consideration was the strong conservative science ethos held by some centre staff.

At Bournda, Miller was close to the destruction of the South East forests radiating out from a woodchipping mill (see Fig. 8.1 for a contemporary photo encompassing Nadgee Reserve which Strom and Fox were instrumental in setting up). There was scant environmental protection legislation at the time. After work hours, Miller was active in the movement against woodchipping in the area. In his teaching he was always balanced—giving both the forestry and conservation sides of the story. He was an active community member; people requested he represent them on many occasions, to further the conservation cause. Miller was, at different times, on the local district National Parks Advisory Committee, on a local State Park Trust,[1] in the local Bushfire Brigade and politically active as a local shire councillor.

Through Miller's involvement in the forestry debate he was seconded for three months by the Wran Government to the Ashton Committee enquiry into woodchipping which tabled its findings in 1978 (NSW Government: Office of Environment and Heritage, n.d.-a; Department of Environment Climate Change and Water [NSW], 2011; Milton, 2022). The result was the transfer of Nelsons Lake and several other coastal catchments from State Forest to National Park as well as additional environmental restrictions placed on the Forestry Commission's operations.

---

[1] Miller, elected as the chairperson of the Park Trust, was able to smooth the path for the movement of Bournda to the National Park, a move that was to take a few months originally but ended up taking years.

**Fig. 8.1** The scenic viewpoint at Disaster Bay in Beowa National Park overlooking Disaster Bay and the Nadgee-Howe Wilderness Area. September 2022

Shortly after this there was the first Departmental enquiry into Miller's operations. A team of inspectors found everything above board—"'smelling like roses' was, I think, the comment they used." Miller's actions provoked the ire of the Forestry Commission on more than one occasion. "But it was all a bit worrying at the time because what I thought I was doing, and still think that I was doing, was in the ambit of what citizens should be able to do in a democracy" (JM). Furthermore, but not to take away from the significance of Miller's statement, a FSC principal stated that, "there are some people that can distinguish between Jack's role as a conservationist and his role as a principal but his enemies properly didn't" (DB).

Miller was subject to death threats in the middle of the night, and had his phone disconnected for an 18-month period. He experienced having his feet spat on in the street. It was difficult for his family, with his children attending a very small school, feeling the effects of a polarised community. "It was pretty unpleasant." However, through Miller's community work, respect and community standing was built over a dozen or so years.

Another battle occurred after Miller and Chris Grounds were involved in the writing of a resource for Year 12 Geography (Bournda Field Studies Centre, 1989). It can be assumed that the content of this material would have differed from a traditional geography curriculum resource; it would have touched on some controversial issues given the forestry activity occurring in the Bega/Tathra region. About this time, Miller was elected to Bega Council. Bournda EEC was threatened with relocation—effectively closure, given that the new location was about six hours away. While Hansard indicates lack of numbers as the reason (Brown, 1991a), it was strongly felt by many research informants, and Hon. Richard Jones in NSW Parliament, that this was a cover up for the real reason which was Miller's involvement in politics. Indeed, their experiences point to some truth in the matter. Miller and the woodchip industry clashed on a number of occasions and the impact of this was acute for those in the NSW Department of Education bureaucracy who, because of their position, had to get involved in protecting the centres.

> *He became politically involved while he was still an employee of a government department, which is not really allowed. So that's why the Minister was involved and I had to keep that centre open and help keep the peace with the politicians to ensure things were okay and that it didn't wash over to the other environmental ed centres who were doing a pretty good job really, and were politically independent of local politics... even though they may not have wanted to... Yeah, it was a challenge to ensure they remained schools. SS*

There were moves afoot by politicians to change the status of the centres from specific purpose schools, as gazetted, to places where education occurred. Although a justification was given for classification change, it was strongly felt by many in the EE community that the proposed change was being pursued to allow for easy closure of these centres.

> *But we'd had it gazetted and that so it takes two years to close a school down. And so we were a school so they tried to change our status from a school for specific purposes to something else, to places where education took place, that's right. Yeah, that was a big one. AA*

Miller was busy in his own territory,

> *I seemed to be flat out keeping my head above water in an area where there was a very strong anti-conservation ethos... I was just flat out keeping the doors open against a lot of pretty powerful forces that wanted to close them... I was flat out trying to keep my head above water with the bloody woodchip industry. I just kept coming up against that. Every time we'd try and do something a bit more interesting they'd try and close us down or belt us over the head. JM*

Miller was instructed to stay out of trouble and thought that Council would be a good way to effect change.

> *I'd been hammered by these enquiries and basically told, "although everything is okay at the moment, for goodness sake keep your nose clean from now on, Jack." That was basically the story, and I was on the Council so I was doing what I could during the Council. JM*

However, Council proved to be a battle ground too. Miller served on the Bega Council from October 1987 to September 1999 when an administrator was appointed to the Council (personal communication, Bega Valley Shire Council, March 3, 2019). It seems the majority and minority factions on Council were at loggerheads, making functioning as a council untenable. The relationships between staff, particularly senior staff and Council members, was central to the problem.

> *The issues have ranged over a variety of planning matters, some issues of policy and some specific major items including the Merimbula Tip and the General Manager's second dwelling. (Office of the Commissioner, 1999, p. 402)*

These sagas have grown into battle legend within the centre network. Viewpoints about political advocacy are both positive and negative regarding events that took place at Bournda. The events seem to have contributed to centre staff being wary of participating in environmental politics.

Well before this incident, a very strong and vocal Friends of Bournda FSC support group was established. Influential local people set it up including a lieutenant colonel in the Australian infantry in the Vietnam War, an ex-Australian Law Reform Commission solicitor, an academic lawyer who had relocated to Bega, an accountant, and the editor of the local newspaper. This group was instrumental in ensuring that Bournda remained where it was. The Minister was bombarded with letters of support for Bournda.

In the early years, 1977 or 78, a World Environment Day Dinner was planned. It started off as 40 people to enjoy a pig spit at the centre with a speaker for entertainment. It morphed into a sell-out dinner at Bega Town Hall with over 340 guests with such speaking luminaries as the chair of the Australian Heritage Commission, David Yencken; the executive director of the Australian Conservation Foundation, Rick Farley; the chairperson of the National Farmers Federation, John Coombs; and the Secretary of the Maritime Union of Australia. Well-established organisations such as the NSW Farmers Association and the Chamber of Commerce booked a table. Money raised supported the centre. Thus, the Friends of Bournda FSC provided much needed political and financial support. That Bournda was in a marginal seat might also have played a part.

> But I think if you've got a lot of community support it translates into the political system and leads to infrastructure and money and facilities and all that sort of stuff flowing your way. Personally it suited me pretty well.... Well I think I mentioned the fact that there was a conservation society down there.... I don't think they operated through the Department of Education. They just went straight to the politicians and... when you have them by the balls their hearts and minds will follow. JM

Miller credited Kennelly and Foott as being excellent EE pedagogues while underselling his own effect. Yet, some of Miller's education stories tell of some wonderfully effective education, particularly community education. Additionally, he was a great environmental/sustainability role model... "So, it's not do as I say as much as do as I do."

> I mean the sorts of things that I used to admire from people like Bruce and David were the initiatives that they came up with to make learning in this so good, where I guess with me it was more a broad brush experiential thing. JM

Many parents were involved in their children's EE at Bournda. "Once parents saw that you didn't have horns growing out of your head, and a tail growing out, and you weren't a devilish sort of character you got on alright with them" (JM).

In an attempt to educate the public to live environmentally responsible lives, Bounda marked out the FSC carpark to advantage those with the least vehicle size/capacity.

> They were all formalised parking areas, parking spots for cars. On the first one we put, "Reserved for vehicles of less than 1500cc capacity," and the second spot, "Reserved for

> *vehicles with 2 or more persons," things like that. And parents would come in with kids and they'd look at these things and they'd be driving large cars, and hopefully I made them think. JM*

Miller conducted effective sustained immersions in the natural environment. For example, he used to take First Nations students who were in a suspension cycle at school out camping for a few days. Organisation and agreements took place between Miller and the students over a few meetings. Students connected, learnt to look after themselves in the bush—they built resilience.

One project was a Farm Tree Management Competition. Miller, along with the chairperson of the local Pastoral Protection Board (Rural Lands Protection Board), the Dairy Farmers Association in the Bega Valley, and the Livestock and Grain Produces Association (NSW Farmers) travelled to each competing farm judging the entrants. Strong bonds formed and these relationships came into their own when Bournda FSC was threatened with closure.

> *Each of those blokes through their organisations were active in their own political spheres on the right of politics. But there was enough in it there, as a result of those sort of contacts to save the Field Studies Centre from being relocated. JM*

Miller tells a story about meeting one of his students years later when planting native trees and shrubs with a group on a badly eroded creek on a farm in Central Tilba.

> *she and her husband are successful farmers, business people, and have really tried very hard to integrate dairying into a sustainable production system and this planting was part of it. And when I went there, she came up to me… and she's a woman of I suppose 50, and publicly said to the dozen of us there, she said I had made her a conservationist. And the story she told was that I'd gone with a group of kids, she went to Narooma High School, to the top of… almost the top of the catchment of Tantawangalo Creek, which is the catchment of a weir, Tantawangalo Weir that supplies the town of Merimbula and other small villages with water. And we walked down this steep granite, coarse granite, forested slope to the creek and I spoke to them after they walked down, and it was probably a quarter of an hour walk down. Very steep and very hard, and they were kids of Year 8 or 9, or 10 or 11… I don't know what they were. And then we walked down to the weir, I hadn't told them there was a weir at the bottom. And that was an area that was proposed to be woodchip logged. And that was all it was. There was no written work associated with it. And anyway, apparently that was what did it. And she described it all to the dozen or so and then came and gave me a hug. JM*

## 8.6 Controversial Issues

The *Controversial Issues in Schools* policy statement was released in 1983 (NSW Department of Education, 1983). The policy is indicative of the times given the community action of the 1960s and 1970s and the rise of the necessity for an understanding of problems, and empowerment and action within EE (without taking away from the necessity for a policy for addressing controversial issues *per se*). According to the policy, parental consent is required to discuss controversial issues encountered on excursions (NSW Department of Education, 1983).[2] Additionally, material of an "overtly political nature" needs to be published historical material, or required for teaching the official curriculum, in order to be distributed to students. This could make teaching "for" the environment difficult.

> *But I don't go in and say we should stop logging...that's loaded in terms of the community and the principals trust us to not antagonise sectors of the community. We base our activities on understanding those connections and saying that we need to care for the environment. There's just no value in us attacking any particular groups or activities at a school. It just puts you on a back foot if you're offside with the community and my feeling is that we've managed to walk that line... I mean there's probably people that might criticise us ... but our job is to work within the policy framework of the Department of Education and that includes teaching controversial issues in schools. And as far as I'm concerned if we stick to what the syllabuses say... it doesn't mean we have to not highlight issues or ignore things. We have pretty frank discussions with kids but if you set it up so that the educational activity gets them talking about it that's different from going in there and launching into things.* DB

Another principal elaborated on some of the techniques used in dealing successfully with controversial issues:

> *I was trained in a lot of those techniques... values dilemmas, values clarification,....the idea of role-playing, putting kids into roles. Debriefing them and taking them out of role, getting them to do things like problem solve like that kind of thing in a role, then taking them out of it. So you're broadening their thought processes about these things, making them think about these issues. And on controversial issues like, "What would you do if?" That's the way to do it. "What would you do if?" Without exposing your position. I don't think as environment educators we've got the right to be hammering our own point of view and trying to... You don't teach dogma in environmental ed.* TA

The *Wetland* special edition of the *Australian Journal of Environmental Education*, included a paper written by Awabakal teacher-in-charge, Brian Gilligan, who argued for the necessity of educator impartiality, a middle of the road stance, in order for acceptance by the majority, to effect change (Gilligan, 1986). This was possibly an attempt to solve the polarisation of controversial environmental issues that Gilligan was experiencing within his activism.

## 8.7 Political Advocacy and Action for More FSCs

### 8.7.1 Shortland Wetlands [Now the Wetlands Campus of the Awabakal EEC]

With the Hunter Region abounding with significant water/wader bird sites, particularly migratory birds, there was significant interest within various community groups including the Hunter Bird Observers. In the early 1980s, the Hunter Wetlands Group formed within the Newcastle Flora and Fauna Protection Society (KMc).

---

[2] This policy has been updated on a number of occasions.

8.7 Political Advocacy and Action for More FSCs

There was concern about increased development on nearby Kooragang Island where large areas of wetlands and plant communities had been destroyed. Max Maddock, a keen bird watcher, particularly egrets, and an Associate Professor in Education at the University of Newcastle, approached Gilligan and McDonald about the possibility of buying some old Marist Brother football playing fields and the derelict Hamilton Rugby Club building next to them at Shortland, the purpose being to develop educational wetlands as egrets nested in paperbark forest in close proximity to the area (KMc).

Over several years, funds were sought from businesses and Council, and a Bicentenary grant was secured to develop the site. The Hunter Wetlands Trust was set up to manage the funds. Gilligan was able to persuade Alan Beard, the regional director of the NSW Department of Education, Hunter Region, to allow Shortland to be an annex of Awabakal. Staff were able to reside at Shortland as it was much more centrally located for school visits. Beard's commitment contributed to the Wetlands eventuality. Many within the community were involved in Shortland's establishment. Businesses assisted with the necessary work of constructing the wetlands. Gilligan, in addition to being the teacher-in-charge, became the director of the Wetlands Centre Incorporated. The centre was managed by a Board elected by a Council, elected by the Hunter Wetlands Trust (KMc). The Shortland Wetlands was opened by Neville Wran in 1985. There was a lot of publicity about these proceedings within the local news and enormous school patronage followed for many years.

## 8.7.2 *Breaking the Embargo: The Battle for Greater Teaching Capacity*

There was considerable quarrelling and wrangling within the bureaucracy and government of the day before new NSW FSCs could flourish. The hiatus in FSC establishment ended around 1985/1987 with Education Minister Rod Cavalier's (1984–1988) push for the establishment of the Field of Mars in his electorate. There was also strong support for a centre from the Ryde-Hunters Hill Flora and Fauna Preservation Society. Invited to visit FSCs, he visited Muogamarra and Shortland Wetlands to observe their operation. Teachers-in-charge were advocating for more teachers and better conditions. They wanted to ensure the centres were given the presence and resourcing to ensure their facilities had security from the threat of closure and could operate at capacity—ensuring that EE was effectively implemented and reaching as many people as possible.

In 1986, only Wirrimbirra and Wambangalang had assisting teachers (ZA). But in 1987 Cavalier found a provision which enabled him to allocate teachers at his discretion, so he appointed seven: an extra teacher to most of the centres. He had to fight within Cabinet to have Treasury increase the budget to support the extra staff and to establish the Field of Mars. He had been impressed with what Gilligan was doing with the Wetlands so one teacher went to Awabakal, operating out of the Wetlands.

Muogamarra missed out on an assistant teacher, much to Foott's dismay given his advocacy. Two teachers went to the Field of Mars FSC, also located in the North Sydney region. On the North Coast, Dorroughby also effectively missed out on acquiring an extra teacher as the regional director on the North Coast was keen to get Cascade FSC within the centre network and so he allocated Dorroughby's extra teacher to Cascade. Clements, teacher-in-charge at Dorroughby, over 250 kilometres away, was responsible for them and the centre—further staff funding was not forthcoming.

Centre politicking suited Rod Cavalier's political agenda.

> But that was because we were politicking and it happened to suit his politics. The Department of Education did increase the number of centres but I would suggest it was because of local pressure both from within and outside the Department rather than any bureaucratic policy... but certainly, at the time when Rod Cavalier was in we were really under the pump. I think he was the reason the Department got told to pull its head in because that was when they were trying to get rid of FSCs as that is when I sighted that memo about the department divesting itself of FSCs to Sport and Recreation. AA

### 8.7.3 Field of Mars Field Studies Centre

Community activism stopped the Field of Mars area, off Pittwater Road, East Ryde, becoming a landfill site. The Ryde-Hunters Hill Flora and Fauna Preservation Society had formed in 1966 specifically to preserve, conserve and manage the site. With a rich history of First Nations and European occupation, the area supports at least six endemic plant communities, several of them critically threatened and vulnerable, including the vegetation of a small area of Wianamatta shale surrounded by Hawkesbury sandstone (NSW Government: Office of Environment and Heritage, n.d.-a, n.d.-b; Pearson, 1978). In 1978 the Field of Mars was a "natural, multi-disciplinary field studies centre" (Pearson, 1978, p. 124) with the potential to be an Urban FSC. Managed by the Ryde Council with community support, it had an honorary ranger, Mr. Wally Doyle. Time and effort made the Reserve an educational resource. The Council had established a visitor's centre and walking trails. Parts of the area, including an old rubbish tip site, had been revegetated/regenerated (Pearson, 1978). There was advocacy to have the Field of Mars join the NSW Department of Education network and, with the Reserve in his electorate, Rod Cavalier wanted that too.

The Field of Mars FSC opened in 1987 with Howard Barker as the first teacher-in-charge. Chris Koettig, became the assistant teacher in April 1987. The Field of Mars is the only purpose-built facility on land owned by the NSW Department of Education. Because it was on Crown Land vested in the Minister for Lands, it, and a metre around its perimeter, became the property of the NSW Department of Education.

Barker only stayed for a few years and Koettig then became the teacher-in-charge with Steve Papp becoming the assisting teacher. Some centres had started employing casual teachers. Koettig had done so while at Longneck Lagoon FSC and continued this practice of increasing capacity at the Field of Mars. The input of enthusiasm and additional expertise in various areas of EE embellished centre activity in addition to building capacity.

## 8.8 Change on a National Front in the Late 1980s

On a national level, the Commonwealth Department of Arts, Heritage and Environment seminar in Canberra in 1987 gave some space for EE practitioners, academics and bureaucrats to reflect on the path EE was taking. Workshops outlined the inhibitors and enablers of past, present, and possible future practice for FSCs; primary and secondary education; and, teacher and community education. For NSW, the National Parks and Wildlife Service (NPWS), the Department of Environment and Planning, Technical and Further Education (TAFE), and some tertiary education and colleges of advanced education had delegates present. McDonald represented the AEE (NSW) and Tribe attended (no organisation or allegiance specified). Barker was there representing the Royal Botanic Gardens. The NSW Department of Education had a few representatives in attendance including Young. For FSCs, Foott and Miller were in attendance while Rob Newton and Richard Jones represented Wambangalang.[3] Peter Hardy from the curriculum policy division of the Department was there, appropriate given the *EE Curriculum Statement* was due out in 1987 (Commonwealth Department of Arts Heritage and Environment, 1987).

Brian Foreman from Arbury Park Outdoor School in South Australia led the FSC workshop. Many FSC workshop attendees favoured a name change to embrace the concept of EE rather than the confining connotations of "field studies." The centres were becoming more diverse and holistic with recreation merging with education programs.[4] Centre visitation numbers as a criterion for centre success was recognised as problematic. Envisaging a more expansive, holistic practice for the future, the involvement of community and diversification were elements touched on. There was a diversity of funding and management from government, community and private sources. It was noted that recognition attracted funds. There was apprehension that the active element of EE might lead to a reduction in government support. Looking ahead, there was anticipation of heightened politicising of government FSCs role being in conflict with contemporary government. Further, there were considerations for adopting strategies aimed at aligning EE centres more closely with

---

[3] Was this the same Richard Jones who was an advocate for environmental concerns as a NSW Legislative Council Parliamentarian from 1988 to 2003? He was well informed about EEC matters.

[4] Note this is in relation to FSCs in Australia so very broad.

the broader environmental movement (Commonwealth Department of Arts, Heritage and Environment, 1987).

There were several national influences of significance in the 1980s. *Our Country, Our Future*, a statement on the environment released by Prime Minister Bob Hawke, overlooked EE (AAEE pers. comm., January 22, 2018). However, there was sufficient interest in EE in the late 1980s for a national EE strategy titled *Learning for Our Environment* to be launched in 1989 and, $400,000 in grants made available for EE activities (Gough, 1997). Furthermore, for ESE The *Hobart Declaration on Schooling*, the 1989 agreed-upon national goals for schooling, provided top-down guidance to states and territories, for students to develop "understanding of, and concern for, balanced development and the global environment" (Ministerial Council on Education Employment Training and Youth Affairs, 1989, p. 1).

### 8.8.1 Curriculum Clash: Struggle for Educational Influence

The history of Federal and state education in Australian has always seen the states guarding their curriculum from Federal intervention via resistance, both explicitly and implicitly (Reid, 2005). This involves dynamic strategic manoeuvring, where education ministers, bureaucrats, organisations, and teachers all play significant roles in safeguarding their values and beliefs of curriculum integrity within their field of influence. However, Section 96 of the Australian Constitution allows the Federal Government to provide funding and thus potentially exert some control over the curriculum and pedagogy (Mockler, 2018).

In the late 1980s, in an effort to control the open-ended spectrum of school-based curriculum design, John Dawkins, Minister for Employment, Education and Training in the Hawke government, attempted a top-down approach of control and accountability by starting a dialogue about designing a national curriculum (Mockler, 2018). Contention of consistency, non-duplicity, and the need to develop contemporary skills for improved economic performance started to challenge concerns about addressing the diversity of student needs, contexts, places and spaces, and equal opportunities for all children. Dawkins' approach to a national curriculum as outlined in the *Strengthening Australia's Schools: A Consideration of the Focus and Content of Schooling* (1988), sketched a possible curriculum framework for major areas of knowledge in addition to what was considered appropriate skills and experiences for the schooling years (Mockler, 2018). Progression to, and substance of, a national curriculum has been an ongoing power struggle. Advancement has been generally dependent on state and federal political allegiance being in accord (Mockler, 2018).[5] Top-down pressure, from Dawkins as Federal Education Minister, to state and territory ministers, to education directors, saw curriculum mapping

---

[5] A state election in 1988 disrupted the Labor state/federal alliance with the Liberal party taking power in NSW.

exercises undertaken in the late 1980s. Fraught attempts to write a common framework followed (Yates & Collins, 2008) with learning areas identified and statements and profiles developed (Mockler, 2018).

Given the mooted national curriculum, there was lobbying for EE to be included as a curriculum focus (AAEE pers. comm., January 22, 2018). The 1989 audit of EE curriculum materials and then a map of the cross-curriculum study of "environment" were set in train after the Australian Education Council widened its scope of the national collaborative curriculum activities. These activities came into being in 1994 with the release of *A Statement on Science for Australian Schools* and *A Statement on Studies of Society and Environment for Australian Schools*. There was advocacy for EE content with a social critical stance, called for through papers from academics such as John Fien, Noel Gough, Annette Greenall Gough, Greg Hunt and Steve Malcolm through the 1991 Australian Curriculum Studies Association Conference titled "National Curriculum for Environmental Education? Politics, Problems and Possibilities." Unfortunately, rejection followed; the socially critical stance was viewed as too critical (Gilbert et al., 1992; Gough, 1997) by bureaucrats and politicians through the Curriculum and Assessment Committee. It became, "about" the environment. However, elements of the Tbilisi Declaration and other United Nations Educational, Scientific and Cultural Organisation (UNESCO) statements on EE are within these national statements (Gough, 1997).

## 8.9 Webb Field Studies Review Revisited on the East Coast of Australia

Meanwhile, another review of centres and EE was undertaken in the late 1980s. Webb was once more contracted by the NPWS to review FSCs as an educational resource. This time funding restrictions limited the survey to the eastern states and caused author concern relating to research robustness (Webb, 1989, vi). Some changes noted were:

- an increase in centres,
- an increase in the provision of integrated programs that were issue-oriented,
- increased use by school and community groups,
- greater delegation of responsibility to educational regions,
- greater EE interest in other government departments and community organisations,
- a shift in centre staff philosophy, and
- greater emphasis on concept and skills development and use of simulation activities.

Additionally: "Staff continue to be capable, dedicated and experienced, and have to display a flexibility that fits them for any task; generalists syndrome" (Webb, 1989, p. vii).[6]

Limitations included that some educators had not processed the difference between EE and natural history or ecology—the "taking action" component, and the efforts within non-formal EE were still problematic (Webb, 1989). Once more, Webb's study included all types of FSCs. The Webb study indicates that in both NSW and Queensland the Departmental networked centres provided EE in-service training, resources and advice to schools and that the close association of EE to FSCs in NSW prompted a renaming of the centres to environmental education centres [EEC] (Webb, 1989). There is, however, documentation that contains both the FSC and EEC nomenclature for the centres within this study from about 1987 until 1999 when they were officially renamed EECs. This indicates that the name change may have been a little problematic and some of the arguments are documented in study interviews. Some of the earlier teachers wanted to stay with field studies because they were driven by it and its connection to the curriculum—getting students out of the classroom into the natural environment. Some felt they had worked hard to build up a strong following as FSCs and that it may be difficult to operate with a title that could have emotive connotations. Since the change, there have been periods where the political landscape is particularly unfriendly to the term "environmental."

> And there were some people who were not overly keen on that, they felt that we were better off sticking very closely to the curriculum and supporting curriculum with fieldwork. But with the environmental education policy for schools it gave us that imperative to start to provide something to support schools as they try to develop environmental management plans and try to integrate environmental education with their other curriculum areas. *QA*

Webb's other recommendations included:

- a shift in focus from primary to secondary education with the compartmentalisation of disciplines within high school being problematic,
- a call for each state to have top level joint policy between NPWS and education departments for effective community EE,
- greater involvement of NPWS in EE rather than interpretation,
- a computer network for centres and EE coordinating bodies, and
- greater preservice and in-service teacher education and greater research in specified areas.

Once more, there was a call for greater education across the non-formal sector. The study noted that most centres had high levels of regional support from within both Queensland and NSW education departments. Significantly, FSCs were supplying much of the expertise to support teachers to develop their school-based EE programs. It was noted that support was shifting from the NSW Department of Education with NSW NPWS backing, to support dominated by other government

---

[6] Webb noted that private enterprise was starting to fill a gap but essentially for adult education.

agencies. It was recognised that in NSW the demand for EE and for new centres had increased with support for an urban and marine centre growing and greater community interest in EEC usage. Shortland Wetlands was given as an example of the change. The study juxtaposed EE development in NSW with FSC support, and Victoria, where EE was school based with supports from Education and other agencies. Webb questioned the ability of teachers to incorporate EE into their programs successfully, particularly at times of EE in-service course and consultant cutbacks—where FSCs come into their own (Webb, 1989, pp. 28, 30).

The study notes greater restraints on centres with restrictions placed on centres. Permission for overnight stays was needed from the regional directors in NSW, and other unspecified restrictions were hampering effective use of FSCs in some regions. Additionally, the cost of transportation to and from FSCs was often prohibitive (Webb, 1989). Webb's research indicates little opportunity for professional development of centre staff for FSCs within the NSW Department of Education yet professional development was well attended by NSW Sport and Recreation facilities and Queensland centre staff even though training in business management was essential for the effective running of FSCs. The study went on to suggest ways of staffing the centres to encompass informal education, including, but not exclusive to, other departments staffing centres on weekends. In a book chapter written about the same time as this review, "Off-School Field Centres for Environmental Education," Webb's characterisation of the existing situation for EE is still poignant and relevant today considering the crucial nature of ESE and the massive task of teacher ESE professional development required.

> *There is no way that any state system could move directly to school based environmental education without the in-servicing of teachers in the field, and that would operate best through the field studies centre network where teachers can see the way in which their pupils are changed by the field experience, and learn from the teaching methods of personnel operating the centre. Second, even if classroom teachers reached the point where they could effectively conduct their own school-based environmental programmes, there would still be a place for the experience of visiting a particular centre or facility. (Webb, 1990, p. 120)*

## 8.10 Progression of EE in NSW and the Department of Education

Over the period of the 1970s–1980s, the Museum Education Group, a formidable group, grew with the placement of officers within various organisations.

> *So… there were people in environment, in the Environmental Protection Agency, National Parks, all of the museums, the Zoo. And then later, very briefly, but their incarnation as education officers didn't last very long, at the Wetlands at Homebush Bay. They were in, all sort of… disparate organisations, but they were all environmental education officers in their various institutions… It lasted for quite a few years. They did reports, we had meetings and what have you. They were very, very important in advancing the interests of environmental education as well. KA*

In 1985, the EE Officers Group (ZA) had been established after a recommendation in *The Scope of Environmental Education in NSW* (1984) report by the short-lived NSW EE Advisory Committee.[7] It was a joint venture between the NSW Departments of Planning, Environment, and the NSW Department of Education. Other interested governmental organisations were encouraged to join. The core group was the State Pollution Control Commission, The Department of Environment and Planning, NSW NPWS, Higher Education Board, Department of Technical and Further Education (TAFE), and the NSW Department of Education. While the group understood it had no power or formal advisory function, the opportunity for networking and coordinating initiatives was perceived as valuable (ZA). The museums and Taronga Park Zoo were represented at meetings. While no FSC teachers-in-charge were contacts for the EE Officers Group, Young, then a representative for the NSW Department of Education, was the contact person.[8]

As previously discussed, the idea of an EE policy for NSW Department of Education was first mooted at the Thalgarrah FSC conference in 1980 where the pressing need for formal documentation on the operation of FSCs and EE more generally was discussed. Over the years, there were committees to write and re-write the EE policy for schools with heavy representation of FSCs.

> *we always thought environmental education policy but we weren't quite sure whether there was a real willingness to see one through. And so it wasn't just us pushing the government and the bureaucrats, it was the Association for Environmental Education as well. But eventually we learnt that yes, there would be one definitely being developed. HA*

Haddon stepped down as EE consultant sometime in the mid 1980s. Schoer took on the role during 1985 and had a part to play in pushing the policy forward. Young, a teacher from inner Sydney, who had experience in EE and First Nations education, then took up the EE consultant position.

> *He was right into Aboriginal scenes and inner-city education pushes and whatever… he'd been doing some good values type clarification activities… values spectrums and all this sort of thing, which we got into increasingly as we started to see our role beyond just field studies. HA*

Young had significant input into the *EE Curriculum Statement*—developing it to completion.

> *We wanted a policy to hang our teaching on and we wrote it actually with the help of Geoff Young…. The first one was commenced with a conference of about 30 or 40 people up in the Blue Mountains made up of teachers, consultants and FSC staff. Geoff Young who was the Environmental Education Consultant in Head Office was the main one who pulled it all together. But I think everybody from an EEC, or field studies centres as they were called at that stage, plus consultants from the Department. I don't know if there were independent schools there or not. I think it was an internal thing so it was all Departmental people.*

---

[7] Other recommendations by this Committee were the expansion of FSCs, the development of EE policies, curriculum development by education systems, and training and professional development opportunities (ZA).

[8] Barker was the contact person representing the Royal Botanic Gardens at the early Environmental Education Officers Group meetings. McDonald represented the Higher Education Board.

## 8.10 Progression of EE in NSW and the Department of Education

> *Because the Environmental Education Policy was going to be integrated into all subject areas, science, agriculture, geography consultants, etc from Head Office were there.... And the field studies centres were involved right from the start—all of us. Geoff invited other people to come from different curriculum areas for their input and then it was developed over a number of conferences and a few heated moments. AA*

Foott wanted the inclusion of the issue of population but Young did not. Population is an emotive topic within the Australian discourse and is often silenced—puzzling given that it has such huge implications for a hot, arid country with a small carrying capacity (The Parliament of the Commonwealth of Australia, 1994). In addition to the population debate, a few of those involved in the development of the curriculum statement found that it was rather busy with developers wanting it to be all things to all people—detracting from the main focus of EE.

> *I said that when we were writing the environmental education policy. "Don't blur it with all this other stuff." We used to have quite long discussions with Geoff Young about it saying, "Look, it's not a policy for everybody. It's an environmental education policy"… I can remember it took a while to swing Geoff around on some issues. Geoff Young [said]… this policy had to be mandatory, which was a huge stumbling block. And eventually after some debate and lobbying, those essential elements were accepted into it. It ended up being quite a good statement I thought. GA*

Syd Smith supervised Young during his time developing the curriculum statement and assisted with pushing it "up the rungs" within the NSW Department of Education. Smith had started in the Curriculum Directorate in 1978 as a geography consultant sitting across from Haddon—thus, he had a good insight into the EE area.

Interestingly, the North Coast Region had developed an EE policy. Stan Gilchrist, Clements' boss, had supported Clements and his network of like-minded professionals in this venture by supported monthly development meetings and costs, in addition to the necessary Departmental advocacy. The policy was being implemented but was awaiting formal recognition while the state-based education statement was developed.

The 1988 state election saw a change in Government with Cavalier replaced by Terry Metherell as Education Minister. They both were responsible for unpopular changes in education which decentralised the power structure further away from the bureaucracy of the centre (MacPherson, 2015). Given the temper of the times and thus downturn in policy, both Cavalier and Metherell had a poor reputation within the education community generally.

> *He caused a lot of trouble, Terry. We all went on strike and I said, "Bring back Rodney." AA*

However, both had a positive effect on EE and the development of FSCs. While there was an advocacy connection with Rod Cavalier, when Metherell was elected, the baton was passed to Tribe who had been lobbying Metherell for some time. Metherell, together with Tim Moore, the Environment Minister, pushed to further the environmental cause and proved very effective with the EE statement, new centres and the EE committee set up on their watch.

## 8.10.1 Environmental Education Curriculum Statement K-12 and FSC Policy

The *Environmental Education Curriculum Statement K-12* (1989a) was released in 1990 after a long period of gestation and birth. To assist in its implementation, a launch support package included an introduction kit, a reproducible explanatory pamphlet, a poster, and a video which broadcast on SBS television in June 1990 (NSW Department of School Education, 1990). The Statement declared that, "It is mandatory for schools to ensure that EE is incorporated in the whole school curriculum." (NSW Department of School Education, 1989a, p. 10). EE was identified as a cross-curricular component of education.

> Environmental education need not be seen as a totally new and separate subject but rather as an orientation or emphasis within the existing total curriculum. It is best approached as an across-curriculum initiative. By integrating environmental education within broad learning areas students can develop understandings, skills and attitudes which enable them to participate in the care and conservation of the environment. *(NSW Department of School Education, 1989a, p. 5)*

Significantly, and possibly ironically, the Statement calls for the consideration of investigating controversial issues within the guidelines of the 1983 "Controversial Issues in Schools memorandum." The Curriculum Statement was substantial with 90 pages introducing EE, curriculum implementation, program integration, a K-12 framework, assessment and evaluation, learning processes including problem solving and sensing the environment, learning strands and resource support suggestions (NSW Department of School Education, 1989a).

Other developments in 1989 included a FSC guide for teachers sponsored by Comalco (promoting recycling), and a FSC guide for teachers, schools and the general public (not sponsored by Comalco) with an introduction by Minister Metherell. Importantly, a policy statement for field studies eventuated, produced with significant input from a report by a field studies working party titled *Working Party on Environmental Education Centres [Field Studies Centres]* (NSW Department of School Education, 1989b, c, d; ZA). The *EE Curriculum Statement* and FSC policy were two documents that centre staff had been working on for close to 10 years. The FSC policy working party report acknowledged and thanked the staff of EECs, and the regions, for the compilation of the material within the report. The 1989 FSC policy statement preamble recognised EE as a curriculum priority in addition to acknowledging its intrinsic cross-curricular nature. It recognised the diversity of centres and the central and regional initiatives that responded to local community needs in developing them. EE was defined as students acquiring appropriate knowledge, skills and attitudes to help them form their own judgements about socially and environmentally responsible lifestyles so they can participate in environmental decision-making.

> Field Studies Centres are part of the Department's formal provision for environmental education throughout the state. They act as resource centres by offering learning experiences to visiting groups of students at all levels from Kindergarten to Year 12, in-service training

> *for teachers and an advisory function for schools. They also provide opportunities for cooperation with community groups. It should be noted that the classroom, the school and the local environment will provide the primary setting for environmental—learning and for developing field study skills. Visits to Field Studies Centres should complement and augment the school's environmental education program across the curriculum. (NSW Department of School Education, 1989b, p. 1)*

The purpose of the FSC policy statement was to clarify the role of centres and to provide working guidelines. Staffing, duties of staff; conditions of employment; guidelines for selection, induction, and professional development of staff; and travel and safety guidelines were included. Options for a diverse range of funding sources were outlined including the option for not-for-profit charging of fees.

There was a new rush on centres. This was part of a suite of EE reform that the newly elected Liberal Greiner Government planned, heavily supported by Metherell. This included the "Greening of Schools Program" launched in June 1989 (NSW Department of School Education, 1989a).

The *EE Curriculum Statement* influenced the future development of the centres and there was discussion about changing the name of the FSCs to EECs. This robust statement acknowledged the National Conservation Strategy Australia listing of EE as a national priority area for improving capacity to manage the environment wisely (NSW Department of School Education, 1989a, p. 2). It also reflected ESE characteristics similar to those within the UNESCO documents, the Curriculum Development Committee (CDC) policy statement, and other states' policies (Gough, 1997). The centres were heavily involved in the Statement launch and rollout into schools through in-service education for teachers, presenting at staff meetings, and the delivery of centre teaching programs and special events—they lead implementation. The *EE Curriculum Statement* listed FSCs as an EE resource.

> *But one of my key roles was rolling it out in schools when I first started… There was a lot of momentum at the time. And that is probably one of the reasons why the Environmental Education Curriculum Statement got a look in and went forward. A lot of other things were happening and schools were picking up the baton already. So the hardest thing was going into schools that didn't have anything going, but I really can't remember going into any school that wasn't…. didn't have a positive leaning. EB*

## 8.11 A Rush of Centres

The number of established centres started to increase in the late 1980s/early 1990s. The Riverina FSC was founded in collaboration with the Soil Conservation Service in Wagga Wagga, the first in this region. Cascade, Warrumbungles, Rumbalara, Botany Bay, Observatory Hill and Mt. Kembla/Illawarra FSC were all set up in 1989–1990 with Terry Metherell as Education Minister pushing the EE agenda as he promised when in opposition.

## 8.11.1 Muogamarra Field Studies Centre Becomes Gibberagong FSC

Some major changes took place at Muogamarra/Gibberagong in the second half of the 1980s. After much advocacy for another teacher, Steve Wright came on board in 1989. Wright was involved with a few of the EE support groups including the NSW Gould League Council and the Manly-Warringah Region branch of the AEE (NSW) where he held the position of publicity officer in the early 1980s (McDonald, 1983). He had been involved in a committee that was creating posters advertising the location of FSCs and their function. By the time Wright started at Muogamarra it had been moved to the old NSW NPWS training centre at Bobbin Head, Ku-ring-gai Chase National Park (NSW National Parks and Wildlife Service, 2002). There was a teaching facility with a science laboratory, library and overnight accommodation for 30 students. It had been shifted in 1984 from Muogamarra Nature Reserve due to the perceived fire risk given that there was only one track in and out (Fox, 2016; NSW National Parks and Wildlife Service, 1998, 2002). An interim move was made to Kalkari in Ku-ring-gai Chase National Park when it was gazetted in 1985 as Kalkari FSC, a specific purpose school (1985). Foott had requested a shopfront site in Hornsby at the time of the move, so they could have an environmental presence with the community as well as teachers and students.[9]

In 1987, there was a name change from Kalkari to Gibberagong meaning "plenty of rocks," the First Nations name for the local creek (Geographical Names Act 1966, NSW Government, 1987; Pocket Oz Travel and Information Guide Sydney, 2015). Incidentally, on the back of producing a First Nations Teachers Resource Kit (1983), Foott at Muogamarra/Gibberagong received a grant to employ a First Nations person for 12 months for program support. Muogamarra was a site for in-service education and the running of associated programs for the First Nations' Education Unit, set up within the NSW Department of Education head office in the early 1980s. There were First Nations student camps and Teachers Aides courses with up to 40 participants—new in the mid 1980s. All these activities assisted in raising the profile of First Nations Education in NSW.

> Owen Dennison and David Ella are two people who have had a significant input to the teaching programs particularly traditional cultural perspectives at some centres—particularly Gibberagong and Rumbalara EECs—and through them and the individuals there at the time perhaps had influence to some degree on other centres. PA

There was something of a battle to induce the NSW Department of Education and NSW NPWS [Lands] to allow camping within the Park/Reserve. The Muogamarra field site was used for classes between April–September with sites in Ku-ring-gai Chase National Park used alternatively (Webb, 1989).

---

[9] Another ESE dissemination strategy was having more staff within centres to travel to sites within or near schools to teach, as opposed to more centres. This was advocated by centre staff within the Department of Education from the very start.

## 8.11.2 Cascade Field Studies Centre

In 1976, the Cascade Public School was closed due to declining numbers but given it held important EE workshops for teachers, a FSC was proposed for the site (Bridger, 1997). Weekend camps were held and under the guidance of Geoff Tomlin, later a casual teacher at Cascade FSC, the Mobong, Showerbath, and Cascade walking tracks were developed. The centre was used by Dorrigo High School in the early 1980s and the old library from Dorrigo Public School was moved onto the Cascade site and became the dining hall. Cascade FSC's office was a state forest worker's hut moved to the site with the help of the Rotary Club. A few locals looked after the site until it became an annexe of Dorroughby FSC in 1987 with Geoff Bridger working at Cascade through the teacher-in-charge of Dorroughby FSC, Clements. In 1989, Bridger became the teacher-in-charge of Cascade FSC, a residential centre within a rich history of timber getting in NSW (Bridger, 1997). One of the arguments for its development was for students to learn about these areas in an immersive way.

## 8.11.3 Warrumbungles Field Studies Centre

Jack Renshaw (Labor Premier from 1964 to 1965) helped develop the Warrumbungles National Park, which was in his electorate. Incidentally, Strom had taught Renshaw's child at Broken Bay so they had a connection (Fox, 2016). Strom was on the Trust for the National Park and closely guided the Warrumbungles development.

Many interests came together to form the Warrumbungles FSC. It had been proposed by the head of Siding Spring Observatory, run by the Australian National University, in collaboration with the NSW Department of Education, working out of Tamworth, on the edge of the Warrumbungles. Don Goodsir was instrumental in the Warrumbungles FSC establishment. He was on the National Park Advisory Committee. Goodsir was a teacher, keen on the environment and active within the NSW Gould League Council (XA). Jane Judd, a science teacher who was working in a local Catholic school a few days a week, was offered two days a week to set up the centre in 1989. According to an interviewee, the extra staff member that was supposed to go to Thalgarrah through the Rod Cavalier staffing increases ended up at the Warrumbungles FSC. Initially there was no building and Judd attracted centre visitation while working out of the Coonabarabran cluster office. Staffing consisted of Judd and a part time clerical assistant. A portable building, an old library from one of the Tamworth schools, was delivered to the proposed FSC area in 1992, an old staff room arrived for an office a year or so later, a general assistant arrived about the same time, a sitting area was landscaped between the buildings, and a toilet arrived a year later.

Schoolwork took place in bushland or at the Observatory given that students came in busloads and these numbers could not fit in the classroom. Visiting schoolteachers took responsibility for camping with students at the National Park facilities. Departmental policy changed continually while Judd continued to develop programs, with input from visiting schools. Initially the Observatory was a main focus, but visitation by the Warrumbungles FSC was phased out when centre visitation became a money-making venture for the Observatory.

## 8.11.4  Riverina Field Studies Centre

The Soil Conservation Service built an education centre on their property at Wagga Wagga with funding from a Bicentenary grant in 1988 (NA). This was at the time that the NSW Department of Education was looking for a place to operate a FSC. The Department thought it only right that the Riverina should have a centre given that all the other regions did—peer pressure at the regional director level. The driving force behind the move was a number of Soil Conservation Service scientists and soil conservationists. The Soil Conservation Service scientists were keen to pass on their knowledge of natural resource management but wanted professional educators to handle the students while they continued their work—teaching not being their forte. Operationally, the NSW Department of Education supplied the furniture while the Soil Conservation Service paid for the utilities. Both the Soil Conservation Service and the NSW Department of Education supplied an education officer, Garry Faulkner for Soil Conservation Services and Keith Collin for the NSW Department of Education (NA). Collin had worked at Jindabyne Sports and Recreation Camp, giving him the incentive to try for the Riverina position. He had to work out of the regional office for the first six months until staffing allocation approval by Education head office came through. There was a Departmental agreement to provide EE services for both public and private schools. Centre gazettal occurred on 2 May 1989, along with Warrumbungles and Cascade, signed off by Terry Metherell (NA).

There was a collaborative working environment for many years. The centre developed excellent working relationships with schools in the region through their clerical assistant who was well connected to other school administration staff, and through the Primary Principals' meetings. This was a connection other departments and organisations, including other EE centres/bodies, did not have. Tragically, Faulkner passed away and not long after the Soil Conservation Service amalgamated with other organisations—a series of organisational name changes and downsizing occurred. The original Soil Conservation Service interest in education dissipated.

Charles Sturt University and other organisations were and are important collaborators in numerous projects. Program examples include: Saltwatch; an Endangered Native Fish Breeding Program; Catchment EE Package K-6 CEEP Kit; the Murrumbidgee Water Quality Kit; and the Geographic Information Systems resource to name a few. A group of critical friends, the Riverina Environmental Education Centre Program Working Group, has replaced the original management group and spend time ensuring all centre programs are relevant and current (NA).

## 8.11.5 Observatory Hill Field Studies Centre

The Gould League of NSW and the AEE (NSW) had planned an urban FSC for some time (ZA). There was a perceived need for students to engage with urban issues—to understand the environment that most of the population is immersed in and its significant history. There had been an Urban Studies Centre Subcommittee within the abolished EE Advisory Committee (ZA). The AEE (NSW) had made a deputation to the Minister for Education, Rodney Cavalier, and consequently the Minister had requested an appropriate building from the Premier, Bob Carr, with the proposition well supported. Some departments/organisations did not want government bureaucracies involved and others offered their support—though some offers seemed like self-interest veiled in insubstantial backing. Generously however, the Gould League of NSW offered $20,000 for the proposal. The EE Advisory Committee had been disbanded due to the Government wanting fewer committees; however, so much work had already taken place in progressing the centre proposal that the NSW Department of Environment and Planning invited members of the dispersed sub-committee to regroup as a working party. *A Report on an Urban Studies Centre for New South Wales* was finalised in June 1986.

Observatory Hill FSC is located in an old Fort Street Girls High School building that had been utilised as offices by the NSW Department of Education, next to Fort Street Public School. It is a prime historical location within The Rocks overlooking the Sydney Harbour Bridge (Dowd, 1993). In addition to the centre's focused programs, they offer urban trails and resources for teachers who prefer independent work. Paulene Dowd was the first principal of the centre which started in 1990 and Glen Halliday started as a teaching assistant about the time of the rebadging to EEC (1999). Due to the nature of the centre, there are many partnerships with various departments in addition to partners in the various programs that the centre undertakes.

## 8.11.6 Rumbalara Field Studies Centre

Barry Cohen, a former Labor Federal environment minister (1983–1987), supported the use of an established rainforest centre as Rumbalara FSC. There was also support from Chris Hartcher, the local Liberal state minister and then Minister for the Environment. Cohen had been heavily involved in the original rainforest information centre that was built with a Commonwealth Bicentenary grant when there was a drive to save Australia's remaining rainforest. When the original community group ran into difficulty with the centre as a commercial venture, the Gosford City Council approached the NSW Department of Education to take over the centre as a FSC. So, the NSW Department of Education took on a centre that was unable to handle the resourcing, both in financial and voluntary labour terms.

Strom and the AEE (NSW) were influential in the establishment and progress of Rumbalara FSC, which was designed as a one-day centre (Brown, 1991b). The building was sited on the west-facing slope of the steep Rumbalara Mountain, close to Gosford for accessibility, rather than near the rainforest on the other side. In 1991, the centre was opened by Virginia Chadwick, Minister for Education. Dufty became the principal, and Ross Wellington became the assisting teacher. Both Dufty and Wellington became involved with many of the local environmental committees and they included knowledgeable and experienced community members in resourcing their activities.

Rumbalara had many community links along with links with councils and the NSW NPWS, and had student and teacher representatives on its committee. There were over 50 teaching sites involved at Rumbalara, ranging from urban to coastal to agricultural. Amongst other activities, Rumbalara provided rainforest experiences where students became familiar with leeches—changing preconceived ideas about the unknown.

There was a positive and productive relationship between environmental educators at Rumbalara, Wellington and Dufty, and Maddock, the teacher educator, environmental educator and egret researcher/enthusiast from the University of Newcastle.

### 8.11.7 Botany Bay Field Studies Centre [Now Kamay Botany bay EEC]

Don Goodsir, the Cluster Director for Miranda and responsible for EE in the Metropolitan East Region, was instrumental in establishing the Botany Bay FSC and Observatory Hill FSC in 1990 (XA). The moment was right given the 1988 Bicentenary. Apparently, this was another instance of two teachers intended for one centre spread across two centres—meaning greater range but diminished impact. The principal of the Royal National Park FSC initiated some of the first programs and organised the opening ceremony in 1990 before John Atkins became the Principal in 1991 (QA). For the first four years the centre worked out of the NSW NPWS offices in Botany Bay National Park. Metropolitan East Region Properties funds saw the refurbishment and thus relocation to the "old Kiosk" building. As with some of the other centres, there was no formal agreement negotiated for the building—a headache that Sid Smith tried to unravel and settle while in a position to do so.

The core of centre programs revolved around the history of Botany Bay, the wetlands and the marine ecosystems while there was increasing provision for sustainability education programs, often in collaboratively with their Regional counterparts, Royal National Park and Observatory Hill (QA).

## 8.11.8 Mt. Kembla/Illawarra Field Studies Centre [Now Illawarra EEC]

In the beginning, Mt. Kembla FSC was an old closed Broken Hill Propriety (BHP) colliery on 260 hectares on Farmbrough Road, West Wollongong. The site included four heritage-listed houses, with gardens designed by Edna Walling, a well-known landscape gardener. Mt. Kembla FSC was established by an enthusiastic consortium comprising amongst others NSW NPWS, NSW Department of Education, and the Department of Tourism, Sport and Recreation, who wanted to develop the site as the gateway to the Illawarra Escarpment. Laurie Kelly, the local Labor Member for the Illawarra, had pushed for a commitment before Labor lost government in 1988 and a $25,000 grant was secured for the setup. Stuart DeLandre, who had an extensive history of teaching EE and a graduate diploma in EE in addition to further study in ecology and curriculum development, was seconded to set up the centre and refurbish it as a suitable educational centre. He was active within the AEE (NSW), had written for the Science Teachers' Association, and had been a part of a regional team contributing to the draft EE statement about the early 1980s. DeLandre become the principal of the centre. There was great regional support from the regional director, Dr. Terry Burke, and Allan Cobbin, the Director who had taken charge of EE within the South Coast Region. The appointment of a second teacher was a regional decision. The aim of the centre was to teach EE to students—not to be a consultant. A significant development at the centre instigated by Cobbin, was the securing of $3000p.a. seeding grants for EE action projects within schools. These grants had a big impact in the area and continued until BHP was struggling in the early second decade of the millennium.

The Mt. Kembla FSC became the Illawarra FSC when they were forced to relocate after the floods of 1998 caused major slippage and the site was declared unsafe. DeLandre and his assisting teacher worked from the boot of their car with Illawarra Senior Campus as a base—a sense of place, which was a feature of the experience for many of the students as well as the staff, was lost. In 2003, with the NSW Department of Education and Training experiencing difficult times and the venture seeming too difficult, one of DeLandre's directors, Alan Thomas, secured a site at Killalea State Park, administered by the NSW NPWS. A demountable classroom was transported to the site to accommodate the centre. The site was in close proximity to many schools and could take advantage of two beaches, an estuarine environment, and rainforest ecosystems for EE purposes.

## 8.12 Significant State Educational Reform and Funding Opportunities

Amidst the noteworthy and progressive changes initiated by Education Minister Metherell in collaboration with Tim Moore, Minister for the Environment, there were simultaneous shifts in general governance and education that significantly transformed opportunities in both overt and subtle ways. The 1980s witnessed a return to fundamental principles with a management review in 1988 (Harris, 2001) and the endorsement of a corporate planning process, as highlighted in the Scott Report of 1989 (Frew, 1990). These changes marked a pivotal moment in education, comparable to the impact of the Wyndham Scheme, disrupting the traditional academic control over the curriculum and facilitating the decentralisation of education to regional and local levels (Hughes & Brock, 2008). The Education Reform Act of 1990 (NSW), influenced by the recommendations of the Scott (1989) and Carrick Reports (1989), alongside the 1988 White Paper introducing the NSW Board of Studies (BOS [1990–2013]) as the curriculum development authority, ushered in elements such as "competition, choice, diversity, efficiency, standards, accountability, performance indicators, deregulation, and privatisation" — reflective of a shift towards public managerialism (Hughes & Brock, 2008, p. 142).

### 8.12.1 Innovative Capacity Building

In addition to the small school funding allocation there were sometimes extra Departmental or other department monies available to the FSCs, such as from the NSW Office of Environment and Heritage program. The extra NSW Education Department funding was very dependent on the advocacy skills and relative power of the person in charge of the centre. There may also have been money associated with professional development or First Nations' education that could be justified as a centre expense within the Departmental budget.

Commonwealth Government funding also played a significant role in the establishment and development of the centres. Many of the FSC staff were skilled grant writers and grant recipients. Federal grant success allowed the centres to build their facilities and capabilities in various ways and it was during this time that they gained some potency within the NSW Department of Education. An example of this funding was a Commonwealth program from the Keating era (1991–1996) that gave unemployed people experience in a chosen field. For FSCs, this funding provided much in the way of trail and signage construction and revegetation work, in addition to money for staff and, at times, vehicles. At Dorroughby, for instance, Clements' experience of losing a highly sought-after assistant teacher to Cascade FSC motivated him to fund additional staff. Through Federal and state grants, Clements was able to extend Dorroughby's potential. At one stage there were 14 people on a labour program, two and a half teachers, sometimes three, as well as extra hours for

## 8.12 Significant State Educational Reform and Funding Opportunities

the school and general assistant. Clements always had someone trained for the many occasions that he was called on to participate in in-services, principal days or new curriculum initiatives. Clements was accountable for four grants at one point.

> *I didn't start it with that in mind initially but I was looking for a way in which I could find the funds to employ my own assistant teacher. And what happened is that as I went through the process of applying for these grants to establish rainforest, et cetera, et cetera, I figured that I could run them in a manner that required me to manage that undertaking. So therefore I could justify and it was accepted, that I could use funds to employ someone to replace me. So through the back door I ended up with... well I ended up with more than two teachers. But even today right, at Dorroughby Field Studies Centre they still only have one point something teachers allocated. So, it hasn't been solved. Because these things stick. IC*

The misfit phenomenon the centres experienced extended to the Departmental understanding of their unique funding sources. Clements recalls an interview with a Departmental representative:

> *Without having any comprehension of what I was doing, what I was up to, the programs that were being run, he launched into this critique. Everything I showed him he criticised. And he pointed out that there were these formats that had been introduced that the principals had to fill out at the end of every day and compile at the end of every week and it was reporting all these different aspects that were in different fields and blahblahblah, he went on with this. And I tried to gently say, "Well look, I don't have a fixed client school-base, I don't have parents and citizens association, dadadadada." And this guy kept... I tolerated it... he's the boss... I had to listen to what he had to say, and I did try and argue my point of view a couple of times but I found it was pointless. And as he left he said, "Look, I'm going to be putting in a negative report." I said, "Oh, alright then. But who are you going to put in the negative report to?" He said, "Well, what do you mean?" I said, "Well the funding that I'm receiving from the Department of Education, that amounts to, apart from wages for my two auxilliaries, which I partly pay, is $25,000." "Oh."*

> *"And then I'm on this other budget here from a state organisation which is $60,000. And then I'm on this other budget from the Commonwealth and that's approaching half a million." ... "So, which one?" I said, "If you criticise me and all these programs that we've set up with all this funding that we've got, well the system's going to miss out on all this money." Anyhow, he got the message and he got all red faced. He never backed down but he took off with his tail between his legs. IC*

During the 1990s, Rumbalara had acquired a vehicle through Australian Government funding yet it was difficult to get permission to use it for school and site visits. Even though the vehicle was acquired by Rumbalara, the NSW Department of Education and Training were the managers of it and at one stage wanted the vehicle returned. Dorroughby had the same issue with a vehicle acquired through Federal Government grants:

> *I ran these programs to have surpluses. And under one surplus I could justify, and it took me about three or four years to accumulate these side funds to buy a car... And I went ahead and I bought, through the government, a little Subaru Forester sort of thing. IC*

Apparently, the NSW Department of Education and Training had to refund Dorroughby $25,000 after it confiscated the vehicle. At an earlier stage, after a long wait, and a favourable supervisor, Dorroughby did acquire a Departmental car—yet it was not appropriate for the conditions.

> And he tried everything he could and he got me a car in the end. They got me a Mitsubishi Colt... Can you imagine that out on this four-wheel-drive mud and slush? And it was shredded by the time I'd had it a couple of years. And then they took it back and they wouldn't give me another one. So that's why I had to turn around and buy one. IC

Creative fund raising through various grants and sponsorships assisted centres to build capacity and when the Education Act 1990 (NSW) brought in reforms, the centres were viewed as cost recovery centres. The 1990 Education reform was to provide for centre global budgets, increasing accountability and administration requirements. It did, however, streamline the process of employing casuals.

> I think initially all/most centres had one teacher. The first to have two teachers were the overnight centres. It became an issue with the day centres as many had the opportunity to book in more schools but didn't have enough teachers to support the visiting schools. It also coincided with the emphasis on numbers of students/schools using the centres. Administration and accountability requirements also increased the need for a second teacher. It was more difficult to hire a casual teacher before EECs had their own "global budget" (which gave them more autonomy). Prior to this a teacher-in-charge had to do a lot of paperwork via the regional office, which had control of all the funds, to get a casual teacher. JA

### 8.12.2 Visitation Cost to Public Schools

Costs for students has always been a fraught issue. While being able to employ casuals increased capacity and provided a rich source of positive, divergent and diverse human resource, it also brought equity issues to the fore. Many centre staff had philosophical issues with charging state schools money to visit a state facility.

> And because we were a one-teacher centre we had to charge poor kids more than wealthy kids were being charged... If they went to Gibberagong there were two teachers. So their day visit fee might have been $3 and ours was $6. It was that kind of thing because we only had one teacher so I had to hire extra teachers. So, who had to pay for that? The kids who were coming. And they were coming from the poorest part of Sydney. TA

Many teachers-in-charge kept student fees at a minimum. There were battles with the NSW NPWS to stop park fees being imposed on students. For many years the only cost for students at some centres was a resource recovery fee so that centres could replenish their resources, for example, water testing material. Other than this, the centres were largely free for public students for the first 20–25 years.

> Something I believe we agreed on is that it was public schools first and that the cost to public schools should be at least kept to a minimum although we needed to recover costs for the resources that we used... The material recovery cost was a point of contention for centre staff... we had different ways of doing this, different views of the world. FA

Gibberagong charged approximately a dollar a head for many years as a resource recovery measure. Yet some centres had been practicing cost recovery and building a security nest egg for some time—Field of Mars being the lead example of this.

## 8.12 Significant State Educational Reform and Funding Opportunities

Their capacity building has been advantageous in these times of economic rationalism.

Costs remain an issue with factors being equity and consistency.

> *In New South Wales that is a big issue, that everyone charges all these different sort of rates and it becomes... In the metropolitan area it becomes a bit of an issue when a principal sees one particular EEC charging... $18 and another one charges $5. AB*

Cost to students, and keeping the centres for public students, were strong values played out within the interview data. It says an enormous amount about the altruistic nature and collegiality of centre staff that they considered collectively sponsoring the staffing of each of the remaining one-teacher centres (seven) for a 0.2 teacher from a pooling of a portion of their funding from their Resource Allocation Model. This funding would have enabled the employment of a temporary teacher and possible leveraging of another one or two days—enabling capacity building. Unfortunately, the NSW Department of Education and Training did not want to take on the burden of the other associated costs this venture would have entailed.

Generally centre staff had the view that public schools took booking priority with private schools allocated any remaining timeslots. According to one of the study interviewees, there was pressure to allow private schools to attend the centres at no cost when Chris Hartcher was Minister for the Environment (1992–1995). This was a problem for many centre staff given that private schools were already being funded by the federal public purse. Gibberagong's EEC Council supported staff in standing up for a recovery cost fee and thus private schools paid the public school fee plus a cost for the casual teaching staff that were necessary for the visit. Foott was always battling to ensure public schools held their priority placing given there were so many private schools in the area. They were always trying to visit given they had heard about the centre's success. From the interview data, many of the centres ensured that private schools paid for the experience while the cost for public schools was kept at a minimum.

> *I personally did not feel comfortable with taking private schools.... I didn't think it was proper to use the resources that were publicly paid for for a private purpose. I know that other centres resolved that issue for themselves. It was not something I ever agreed with. What I did agree with was the location, the venue, is a public place, both of them are public parks and I was willing to make available the information and the private schools could run excursions themselves by negotiation that their 30 kids and my 60 kids were not in the same place at the same time... What I would do sometimes later on ... I employed casual teachers to work... if it was mutually acceptable to the casual teacher on a day when they were not working for me, if the private school wanted to pay that person in their own right to run an excursion then that was their choice. So they would pay at least for the staff member. I mean I know other centres did it, particularly in the country where some of the overnight places like Wambangalang and so on, you haven't got as big population of kids to draw from... there were obviously days available so whatever arrangement you would come to. And that created an opportunity for the public school kids because it paid for certain things. Everybody had to make their own choice about that. As a day centre I didn't feel right about renting us out to private schools. Certainly not ever ahead of a public school. KA*

## 8.13 Reform, Contraction and the Impact on Environmental Education

The 1990 reforms had an intrinsic impact on the NSW education system. Greater powers were vested in the Education Minister. They selected Board of Studies members in addition to approving syllabi (Hughes & Brock, 2008). The Education Act 1990 (NSW) heralded a change from a NSW education system with a "government for society" focus to public administration as per private managerialism (Riordan & Weller, 2000). The neoliberal agenda was embraced by the NSW government. The Carrick Report (1989) encouraged school registration and implied criticism of cross-curricular priority practice, and it named among others, EE. The report stated that some schools were not integrating cross-curricular areas within KLAs (Key Learning Areas—terminology used to identify and group subjects in Australia) but rather teaching them as stand-alone subjects. Critics thought there was sectional interests susceptible to political bias within some of these cross-curricular areas (Riordan & Weller, 2000). Furthermore, the role of inspectors was renounced and chief education officers (CEOs) became the main membership of a greatly reduced Institute of Senior Educational Administrators (MacPherson, 2015). The reformed NSW Department of School Education offered one third of the existing positions.

The downsizing severely affected EE with many EE consultants—consultants in general, at a regional and state level disappearing (Brown, 1991b). And it occurred at a crucial time given the need for support in the roll out of the *EE Curriculum Statement*. It was left to the EEC/FSCs to support its implementation. Within this climate, the EE consultant position was stranded, with no immediate replacement when Young moved to the State Pollution Control Commission in 1990 (AAEE, 1990). There is mention of "Mary Clark" and "Hettie" being responsible for EE in the early 1990s but only once each within the interview data. Perhaps the ownership of the role was in name only, or tenuous at least—this was a politically difficult time with major changes and cutbacks. The teachers-in-charge ran their own show, reporting to their regions, while the coordinator position was vacant. Throughout the history of the coordination of the centres within the Curriculum Studies Area/Curriculum Directorate, there have been times where there was nobody supporting the centres or EE, and other times where there were numerous consultants working on ESE projects. For instance, Koettig spent a few months in 1986/1987 assisting Geoff Young in the Curriculum Directorate—progressing the *EE Curriculum Statement*. Later Dibley spent time working with Smith in putting together the policy package. Much of the money funding these positions seems to have come from the state and Federal environment departments.

The Education Act 1990 (NSW) changed centres' funding and administration and the consequences for the rollout of the *EE Curriculum Statement* were minimal rollout resources with no direct funds to assist with implementation. "But its implementation is always questionable because there's no direct funds allocated to it" (GA).

Furthermore, it was found that the mandating of the *EE Curriculum Statement* was ineffective. It was easy for schools to tick curriculum boxes that were "about" the environment rather than being authentic EE, that is if held accountable at all—which they were not. Few study informants remembered the *EE Curriculum Statement* as mandatory, indicating that the result was not effective. With the hindsight of time and experience, accountability for practice is a crucial missing policy reform factor.

> You've got to remember the 1989 document was actually a statement. It wasn't necessarily a policy so it didn't have that kind of level. It was actually in the early 2000s that there is actually an environmentally policy as there is for schools... as there is today. You've also got to remember that... environmental education is a perspective; even though there are requirements I believe still in the new Australian National Curriculum to teach it if you like... it's a perspective and many schools kind of avoided environmental ed as a perspective over the years. And when there was a statement in the 1980s it wasn't in any way mandated on schools as far as I remember. The environmental ed policy in the 2000s certainly was mandated but, a school could just tick off that they had done some curriculum based work. FA

### 8.13.1 Awareness and Growth of Environmental Education

There was a general increase in community awareness regarding the environment about the time of the release of the *EE Curriculum Statement* with environmental issues at the forefront of public attention (Greenall Gough, 1989) and EE advancing in tandem with support structures such as the Hobart Declaration (1989). There was growth in membership of the AEE (NSW) in 1990. The Manly Warringah AEE (NSW) branch was revitalised and the Illawarra chapter established under the guidance of DeLandre (Brown, 1991a, b). There was advocacy to regain support for EE and to get the Board of Studies involved in the EE curriculum given the Board's recent establishment and control of the NSW curriculum. The Manly-Warringah AEE (NSW) branch, with Tribe, was particularly active, as attested to in NSW Government Hansard (Brown, 1991b).

> The Association feels that at present, in spite of a well-developed and released environmental education policy, implementation at a school level is faltering. This is partly due to the current uncertainty surrounding curriculum development and partly due to the rapid and comprehensive changes affecting the NSW education system. The scope and speed of the change has meant that in some educational regions, support for the implementation of the Environmental Education Curriculum Statement has not been forthcoming as we would have hoped. (Brown, 1991a, p. 7)

One positive move at a state government level was the establishment of the Environmental Trust Grants. Millions of dollars from trade waste revenue was set aside for environmental restoration and rehabilitation, research and education. The Minister for Education and Youth Affairs, along with a representative from the AEE (NSW) and other conservation organisations, were to be on the selection panel. Tribe became one of the representatives (AAEE, 1990; Brown, 1991a; Young,

1990). Over the years these grants have supported the growth of EE within the centres and the state generally.

There was growth of EE resources in the South Western Metropolitan Region in the early 1990s as well. Annexes were established at Wirrimbirra FSC to get around the limited resourcing of FSCs. The district inspector/inspector of schools, Richard Booth, a keen bushwalker, and Alan Laughlin, the regional director, were both keen supporters of EE. Given the demand for EE, Camden Park and Georges River were opened, each with a teacher under the auspices of the teacher-in-charge of Wirrimbirra. Camden Park Education Centre was set up as an annex in 1991 and Georges River Education Centre was added in 1994. Wedderburn Resource Centre was also managed as an annex through Wirrimbirra.

### 8.13.2 Camden Park Education Centre [Now Camden Park EEC]

Camden Park FSC at the Elizabeth Macarthur Agricultural Institute, Menangle, was opened in 1991 in partnership with the Department of Agriculture, with a food and fibre, and natural systems focus (NSW Department of Education and Training, 1998). The 1600-hectare site between Camden and Menangle had been managed by the Department of Agriculture since the mid 1980s. Peter Nicoll was the teacher deployed to setup Camden Park Centre and he worked out of Wirrimbirra and a small office building at the Belgenny Farm site.

The inaugural teaching year at Camden Park was difficult and lonely with a small classroom and office and only portable toilet facilities. Nicoll initiated booking and routine practices and pro-formas such as statements of duty, protocols for cooperative roles with Agricultural staff, and facility use agreements. Teaching programs were also developed in addition to a business model for centre cooperation into the future. Promised teaching resources and support from the Department of Agriculture were minimal and disappointing. Nicoll did not apply for the teacher-in-charge position and returned to school teaching after three terms. Brian Trench took on the role of teacher-in-charge at the end of 1991. The relationship between the Department of Agriculture and Education, imperfect initially given the differing agendas and disciplinary understandings and practices, has improved over the years with increases in physical, financial, and intellectual support.

### 8.13.3 Wedderburn Outdoor Resource Centre

Wedderburn Outdoor Resource Centre was listed in *A Survey of Field Studies Centres in Australia* (Webb, 1980)[10] as being established in 1979 as a Departmental Outdoor Resources Centre catering for day visits and staffed by a permanent part-time staff member. It focused on Year 3 and 4 curriculum topics. Programs and activities encompassed knowledge of, and awareness and concern for the environment, according to the classification criteria established for the survey. It was situated on the old Wedderburn Public School site with creek and dry forest habitat where the focus was koala conservation in a small area of bushland under threat from urban expansion to the south of Campbelltown (Webb, 1980).

Unfortunately, there were site maintenance issues with the building being in a poor state with extensive termite damage to buildings. Furthermore, the numbers of school students visiting the centre were poor.

### 8.13.4 Georges River Education Centre [Now Georges River EEC]

About the time consultancy positions within the NSW Department of Education and Training were contracting in the 1990s Sharyn Cullis was appointed teacher-in-charge of Georges River FSC. Cullis had returned to schools after being a social and First Nations education consultant in curriculum development within the Department. Initially a careers advisor, Cullis later became head teacher in social science at Moorebank High School where a pivotal event in bringing the Georges River FSC to fruition took place. Cullis started teaching about the Georges River because she had developed related resources and the students were displaying an extreme disconnect to the river—a dislike for the river environment. She was a secondary teacher with a strong connection to the Georges River having grown up on its banks—playing extensively in and on it. Cullis had watched the developing human impact and became a strong advocate for protecting and rehabilitating the river.

Margaret Simpson, an ex-consultant and the principal of Sylvania Primary School, organised "A day in the Life of the Georges River" in which many schools, including Moorebank, participated—a program that connected students to their river for the day in November 1992 (pers. comm. Georges River Libraries; Liverpool City Council). It was a huge event and the Georges River FSC became a reality due to it, along with lobbying from community, the Oatley Flora and Fauna Conservation

---

[10]There was a date discrepancy with interview data and the Environmental Education Centre Policy Statement (1998) listing Wedderburn as being established in 1991. Perhaps this was the year the Centre started being managed through Wirrimbirra if it was not initially, or perhaps there were some changes that instigated a rebirth of the Centre.

Society and the Georges River Catchment Management Committee, both of which Cullis was a member. At the time, Mark Latham and Craig Knowles were Liverpool Council Lord Mayor and Deputy Lord Mayor respectively, with Knowles also being the NSW member for Moorebank and later moving into the position of NSW Minister for Water and Minister for Urban Affairs. A collaboration between the Council and the Department of School Education developed and Cullis was invited to set up the FSC given her involvement in lobbying for its establishment. At first the centre occupied a condemned building on the Milperra Moorebank floodplain that stank of possum urine. The building could not accommodate the students because, as with other centres, they came by the busload. The centre ran like a mobile centre teaching from various sites on the river. The Council eventually built a new facility next to the Chipping Norton Community Centre.

Georges River EEC's demographics were different from many of the other centres—it was urban with a high proportion of its student population from low socio-economic backgrounds. The centre used many sites in their programs, having high quality bush land and many human impacts to consider. Many students had low expectations about environmental quality having grown up amid environmental degradation. Their lives lacked opportunities to experience the natural environment—they really appreciated what the FSC had to offer. It is all relative.

### 8.13.5 Red Hill Field Studies Centre

In 1993, 18 centres were open, with Red Hill approaching establishment (NSW Department of School Education, 1993). Around this time, it became important that the centres contributed a unique ecosystem or situation and developed inspiring programs suited to their location (space and place). Red Hill fitted the criteria, being at Gulgong, a historic gold mining town with a rich history and many heritage buildings. Once again, it was a strong push from sections of the local community that actively supported the establishment of Red Hill FSC. The centre was named after the central school in which it was established. At one stage the site was going to be bulldozed and the local community worked hard with their local state parliamentary representative to save the site. A local teacher, David Warner, had researched historical, urban FSCs in England. The project was a collaboration between the NSW Department of Education and Training and Mudgee Shire Council. The Council converted one of the big rooms into a basic kitchen and one of the buildings into dormitories. The Department supplied an administration office. In 1994, the positions were advertised for a teacher-in-charge and an assisting teacher for an urban FSC focused on history. The positions were taken up by Sue Fuller and John Holscher respectively. They were allocated a budget and given the first term of 1995 to set up the empty spaces and develop the programs.

Initially, the centre was all about preserving the local history and bringing it alive for visiting students. Red Hill was renowned for role-playing historical situations with their visiting students, taking them back in time to be involved in old farming/

living practices. It used the town environment to investigate history. One of the first resources developed was on how to use the environment to investigate history and to that end they paid teachers to attend an in-service to explore the matter. There was heavy involvement with Gulgong's 125th anniversary at the same time as the centre's establishment. The local community was greatly involved in the centre, feeling they had ownership. The FSC was there for the community and many in the community contributed their expertise to the programs. The FSC conferences introduced EE to the centre and programs diversified into areas such as "Learnscapes," permaculture and "Earth Education" in which Fuller became heavily involved.

## 8.14 Simultaneous State Educational Rationalisation with EE Support

In 1993 there was another restructure of the NSW Department of School Education, further reducing the 150 cluster directors (formerly inspectors) to 88 directors of schools (MacPherson, 2015). Also, the 1993 *New Focus on Environmental Education* document, produced by the NSW Department of School Education NSW, outlined plans for EE. It specifically promotes the EE achievements of the Liberal Government that took power in 1989. Admittedly, the *EE Curriculum Statement* and the Greening of Schools Program, both launched in 1989, were important steps in progressing EE. The document affirmed both the incorporation of EE into the schools' total curriculum, and the *EE Curriculum Statement's* aims of assisting students to make informed judgements about maintaining and improving the environment through the development of appropriate skills, understanding, attitudes and values. No doubt there was some excellent progress made in many schools but retrospectively, it would appear to be a call made too soon.

One of the key observations in the 1993 Report was that approximately 95,000 students visited the centres annually and that specialist teachers supported by regional offices provided unique first-hand study experiences in a range of environments. Importantly, the Report announced that an Environmental Education Unit was to be created within the Department of School Education's Specific Focus Programs Directorate, with Tribe to be the CEO.

"The Greening Schools Program," a beautification program, was broadened to include recycling programs, waste minimisation, energy conservation, seed propagation, and bush regeneration. Community groups and government agencies were providing funds for these activities which environmentalists had lobbied for resolutely. Programs such as "Streamwatch," "Frog Watch," "Salt Watch" and "SCRAP (School Communities Recycling All Paper)" were happening in many schools and eight schools were designated as Centres of Excellence in EE (NSW Department of School Education, 1993).

A Ministerial Advisory Council of Environmental Education, chaired by the Director-General of School Education, Dr. Ken Boston, had been set up by the

Education Minister, Chadwick (NSW Department of School Education, 1993). It was to supply high-level policy advice to the Minister. Others on the Council included the Director-General of the NSW Environmental Protection Agency, the Managing Director of NSW TAFE Commission, and representatives from the Teacher Education Council of NSW and government and non-government schools. The Council was also to have three Members of Parliament from all sides, including independents, available to offer advice. Community representatives with relevant experience were to be selected by the Minister in consultation with key environmental interest groups. Terms of reference included: state-wide strategic planning in liaison with all conservation/environmental groups; local education resource centres; public authorities and youth associations; co-ordination, monitoring and reporting on government initiative implementation; and the creation of EE priorities for government schools and colleges—including supporting resources and curriculum advice. The *New Focus on Environmental Education* document (1993) discusses the intention of the recently formed Quality Assurance Directorate, under the commission of Minister Chadwick, to carry out a study on the status of environmental studies in schools and the extent of student and staff awareness of EE issues. The document also sets up liaison between the Council and the Ministerial Advisory Council on Teacher Education with the latter tasked with an inquiry into the pre-service and in-service requirements for EE (Godfrey, 1994; NSW Department of School Education, 1993).

## 8.14.1 The Environmental Education Unit

David Tribe became the Acting and then CEO within the NSW Department of School Education, Curriculum Directorate's EE Unit in 1994. Tribe had been a strong advocate for an EE Act of Parliament, which had been passed by the Legislative Assembly but faltered in the Legislative Council (Smith, 1993, 1994). The trade-off was implementation of some aspects of the Bill including the establishment of the EE Unit, a ministerial EE advisory council, a quality assurance review of EE within the NSW Department of School Education, and a review of EE teacher education requirements as outlined in the government's *A New Focus* report. Tribe's duties included informing policy and overseeing EE within schools and FSCs.

While the EE Unit was up and running, it was by no means well resourced. The Nature Conservation Council NSW in 1994 resolved to advocate for its better resourcing. (Godfrey, 1994). Additionally, they wanted community EECs within the newly-established NSW EPA (NSW Environmental Protection Authority, 2018), EE officers in local councils, and better pre-service and in-service of EE within the teaching profession.[11]

---

[11] Note that there was an election looming in March 1995.

Throughout this history discovering funding sources has proven quite elusive. However, one instance of funding success was when Tribe, as CEO, was offered $30,000 to spend on EE. This funded the ropes course at Wambangalang ($15,000) and a camp for disadvantaged students administered by the teacher-in-charge of Wirrimbirra, Steve Benoit.

## 8.15 The Industrial Relations Commission Hearing (1994)

Within the FSCs there were staff who found lingering animosity within the bureaucracy towards them and their centre. It lasted for many years, only dissipating when certain individuals within the system retired. Many in the NSW Department of Education bureaucracy could not understand the Department spending on schools which had no pupils and thought Sport and Recreation was a more fitting portfolio. This illustrates a lack of understanding of the work within education that these centres provide—the specialised ESE support for teachers and students within schools as well as fieldwork.

There were long memories within the NSW Department of Education and Foott found the Department unsympathetic to the FSCs' cause when they found themselves before the Industrial Relations Commission in 1994. This came about after the Education Act 1990 (NSW) added further to the teacher-in-charge accountability in regard to writing annual reports (already happening in centres but protocols were tightened), financial management, raising money—basically making teachers-in-charge responsible for everything a principal was responsible for without the recognition or understanding of the centres having no permanent student population.

In 1993, the Teachers Federation, with Foott as their representative, lobbied for the centre educators, taking the salary and status matter to the Industrial Relations Commission of NSW. The Department of School Education made a counter claim. With inspections of the centres and data gathered in 1993, the case was heard in March 1994 (Australasian Legal Information Institute, 1994). At that stage, most of the 18 centres senior educators were employed on their substantive salary with the addition of a "teacher-in-charge" allowance. However, five were employed as primary principals [PP6] (or in payment only). Additionally, one was on a primary principalship with the addition of the "teacher-in-charge" allowance. The Federation wanted the teachers-in-charge to have principal status, to be achieved by altering the FSC status to that of "school." The Federation also sought an allowance for overnight stays for those residential centres. The addition of pupil free days was sought but it was conceded that this relief was already within the teacher-in-charge provision. The Commission concluded that, "We are of the view that the dedicated teachers who run 'Field Studies Centres' are providing an appropriate and important function in the education teaching service of New South Wales" ("Australasian Legal Information Institute", 1994, conclusion, para. 1). The Commission did not find equivalence to principals necessary and set the title as "Teacher-in-Charge." They set two global salaries, dependent on staffing which took into consideration allowances claims. The salary set for "teachers-in-charge" of centres with less than two fulltime teachers was equivalent to the PP5 (primary school with 1–25 students) level while those with more staff was set at an equivalent PP6 (primary school with 26–159 students). Relief was defined as a management issue (Australasian Legal Information Institute, 1994). Therefore, FSCs received the money but not the status.

The Commission outcome prompted Foott to crusade for principalship, which was achieved just before his retirement around 2010. In accomplishing this, Foott had the Primary Principals' Council, where he had been an observer for several years, onside. With their support, and that of Federation and other environmental educators, principal status was achieved. Foott felt that a significant factor in gaining recognition was that the old guard within the bureaucracy had departed the establishment and the corporate memory had changed. It should be noted that there are discrepancies within the data regarding the teacher-in-charge/principalship positions. It can be surmised that principalship was at the discretion of division superiors. Principalship was granted with the change from FSC to EEC at the turn of the millennium for some teachers-in-charge. There was discussion about the loss of principal status for principals in the PP5 and PP6 school category (this was across the NSW Department of Education) but the outcome was unclear within the data. Only the term "principal" seems to be associated with EECs in the NSW Industrial Relations Commission (Industrial Gazette), Crown Employees (Teachers in Schools and Related Employees) Salaries and Conditions Award 2017 (Industrial Relations Commission of New South Wales, 2017). Nevertheless, the fight for status did not seem settled and secure.

## 8.16 EE Programs and Professional Development

### 8.16.1 *Earth Education*

Refocusing on centre EE practice, there was inspirational EE professional development around the country in the early 1990s. "Earth Education," a different approach to EE, had been developed by Steve Van Matre in the United States and workshops were conducted throughout Australia in 1991, having a significant impact on FSC/EECs. The educators at Muogamarra/Gibberagong, both Foott and Wright, took the opportunity to attend a five-day "Earth Education" course in Canberra. The workshop confirmed what they were doing but also opened their eyes to a better way to teach EE.

> We both came back totally convinced that it was on the right track. Well, it reinforced what we were doing but it made us think that there was a better way to teach environmental education. BF

An example of education for, in and about the environment, Van Matre's "Earth Education" movement was developed in the 1970s in the United States and some of their programs were workshopped and developed further in Australia and elsewhere around the world. Incensed by the inconsistent development of EE and seeing an essential need for a connection between people and the natural environment, Van Matre established the Institute of Earth Education in 1990 (Van Matre, 1990) to provide an alternative to EE programs. Set up to "acclimatise" participants to the natural environment, these programs are designed as a magical immersion into nature with the fundamental concepts of energy, cycles, interrelations; and change revealed to students. Many EE researchers argue that one needs to experience connection with the natural environment in order to develop attitudes and favourable behaviours towards the environment (Lengieza et al., 2023; Tilbury et al., 2005).

Foott and Wright were inspired to develop a program similar to the "Earth Education" programs. They wrote *Spaceship Earth* in 1995 (Foott & Wright, 1995), a teaching program for the primary school classroom which included a field trip in the natural world. *Spaceship Earth* included 32 classroom lessons and seven fieldwork activities—all experiential learning that complemented the science, mathematics and English KLAs. All the necessary resources for the program arrived at the school in a space capsule made out of a 100 mm drainage pipe covered with a sticker of the earth and containing a mythical creature. The whole experience convinced Foott that science, geography and history should be replaced by EE in primary school and the lower years of secondary school.

Foott and Wright took their *Spaceship Earth* program to a centre conference with the aim of encouraging each centre to develop a program within one of the primary school years, this being the least discipline-disconnected schooling sector and thus the easiest target group. The idea was to share the programs across centres so that there was coverage across all year levels, for primary school at least. One was produced at Bournda and the Illawarra but only the *Spaceship Earth* was generic and thus applicable across the board. At one stage, *Spaceship Earth* sold 32 copies at a conference in Queensland. Cam McKenzie was one of the Queensland EE educators who embraced the program, taking *Spaceship Earth* to Bunyaville FSC/EEC.

## 8.16.2 Snapshot of Other EE Programs and Professional Development

An example of the various state programs that were supporting EE is "Streamwatch", an action research water quality monitoring program that was launched by the Ministers for Environment and Education in 1990. The Water Board's Environment Management Unit managed the program.[12] In 1992 Bill Stapp was back in Australia. He presented in Sydney on action research in EE and water quality monitoring in streams on a global level. Many teachers involved in "Streamwatch" attended the

---

[12] Streamwatch is now managed by the Greater Sydney Landcare Network (In 2000 Streamwatch was renamed Waterwatch in areas outside Sydney Water's jurisdiction). The Australian Museum managed Steamwatch from 2012 to 2018 (Australian Museum 2019).

workshop (Tribe, 1992). Stapp had consulted with Carolyn Pettigrew at the Water Board in 1990 regarding the development of the "Streamwatch" program (Fensham, 1990). Another example of collaborative EE programs later in the decade was "Envirothon," a competition in which Year 11 students investigate an environmental issue and present ideas for management. It was conducted through the EE Unit, FSCs and the NSW NPWS (Tribe, 1999a).

The NSW EPA had significant input in EE in the 1990s with 12 environmental educators. It had an EE Committee making great inroads with community EE (Godfrey, 1994). Some of the initiatives included the "Who cares about the environment" report surveying people's thoughts on environmental topics in addition to an EE kit for secondary schools. They were also facilitating discussion about EE policy needs so that all environmental educators had the tools to plan, design, implement and evaluate their programs.

The early 1990s saw the FSCs, called EECs in some circles, continue to support EE within schools.

> *The work of NSW Department of School Education Field Studies Centres continues to be of an innovative and high standard and AEE members benefit greatly from their liaison with AEE. Innovative programs such as Earth Education, support for recycling programs and the production of practical resources for teachers are invaluable to teachers who continue to seek ways of developing or enhancing their EE programs. (Brown, 1992, p. 10)*

A document written by Allan Watterson and Barker titled *Schools Environmental Audit: A Guide to Best Practice Environmental Management* was published by the Keep Australia Beautiful Council in 1994. It was one of the signs of the start of wise resource use within schools.

> *The advantages of adopting environmentally sound Best Management Practices are two-fold: there will be significant savings in ongoing maintenance costs, and the school will have the opportunity to model easy-to-implement energy, water and waste minimisation strategies to the local community. (Godfrey, 1994, p. 14)*

## 8.17 A Weakening of a Positive Environment for EE Growth

Relating to curriculum, at a national level, EE had been a discrete learning area for national collaborative curriculum activity. In 1991, it was combined with "Study of Society" and "Aboriginal Studies" to create "Studies of Society and Environment" (Gough, 1997, p. xvi).

*The Eltis Report*, 1995, was in response to complaints from NSW teachers about the new syllabi developed to align the state syllabi with the developed national statements and profile maps. Teachers complained that the resulting syllabi had too many outcomes, leading to an overloaded curriculum (Hughes, 2018). The Eltis Report found that the state KLAs defined in the Education Reform Act 1990 (NSW) had lost identity and integrity and as a result, NSW decoupled from the Federal agenda, as did all the other states.

## 8.18 ESE Thought within the NSW FSC

The controversy about "sustainability" is complex and has been drawn out in the ESE literature over the years. Within the centres there was a lot of controversy over the change of terminology with many arguing that "sustainability" and "development" are the antithesis of each other and that without the "environment" named within the terminology there was the potential for "environment" to lose its importance. While documents pertaining to education for sustainable development (ESD) talked about EE being within, many in the EE camp conversely talked about "sustainability" being a subset of EE.

> *I don't have a problem with teaching sustainability but it isn't environmental education it is just a concept within it. AA*

However, the FSC/EECs, keen to fit with the paradigm that would sustain them, moved with the times. The Rio Summit was closely monitored with guidelines and findings incorporated within centre practices.

> *There were two fields of thought back in the mid 90s between those that were now wanting to move into sustainability education and those that wanted to stay environmental ed and really probably wanted to stay in field studies centres... do more the outdoor ed. So, there were kind of three different schools of thought and...there were some strong characters back in those days. FA*

Therefore, there were centres with a greater emphasis on sustainability, some with an EE focus, and yet others that found an outdoor education component beneficial. Years later, with the development of the Earth Citizen and Sustainability Curriculum Framework, there were still issues with "sustainability."

> *I had a problem with that too because nobody could define sustainability for me. Arguing about, were we talking about economics sustainability or environmental sustainability. I always find these things have a very anthropocentric rather than an ecocentric view. So they lose me when they're not holistic and [are] people-centred. AA*

While there were great transitions and yet flux and ambiguity within ESE praxis there were great shifts within EE research that had been influencing, driving and grounding ESE practice within the FSCs since their inception.

## 8.19 More Change and More Advocacy for Environmental Education

In 1995, the NSW State Government changed from Liberal to Labor. After the election, the Ministerial Advisory Council of Environmental Education was disbanded (Gough, 1997), once more throwing the EE movement into disarray and spurring action. By 1996, there were moves by the newly elected Labor Government to utilise the NSW Environmental Trust monies to reorganise the State Forests and NSW

NPWS. State politician lobbying saw the retention of environmental restoration and rehabilitation, greening of schools, and EE Environmental Trust grants (Tribe, 1996a).

Concerned about the stagnation and in some cases retrograde developments within EE, a deputation of the AEE (NSW) presented to the Minster for Education in 1996 to discuss the present state and future direction of EE.[13] Apparently at this particular meeting in 1996, the long-awaited *Quality Assurance Review of EE in NSW Government Schools* was released,[14] discussions for a ministerial council to advise the Ministers for Education and Environment on EE matters were underway; a survey into teacher in-service EE was being undertaken, and a submission for the provision of a Year 11 and 12 environmental studies syllabus was requested from the AEE [NSW] (Tribe, 1996a).

After the election, regional education clusters within the NSW Education Department's structure were abandoned (Hughes & Brock, 2008). Forty small district offices with district superintendents (MacPherson, 2015) were set up near schools while there was a central state-wide administration (Hughes & Brock, 2008). A 1996 restructure saw the Quality Assurance Directorate removed and the Curriculum Directorate downsized while developing district-based consultation supported curriculum implementation (MacPherson, 2015). Later, a 1998 restructure of the NSW Department of Education and Training, combined school education with TAFE with the loss of 600 jobs.

It took until 1996 for the Board of Studies to have a set of guidelines that required syllabus and related material to incorporate the ethos of EE (Tribe, 1996a).

> The Board of Studies now has a set of guidelines requiring syllabuses and other materials to incorporate aims, objectives, outcomes, content, teaching, learning and assessment strategies which are environmentally sensitive and appreciate the complexity and fragility of the Australian and global biophysical environment and which encourage **rational, informed and sensitive consideration of its use.** (Tribe, 1996a, p. 5)

The changes in educational administration and process, seemingly more frequent since the 1990 educational reforms due to the politicisation of education, created instability. With power and responsibility shifting within regions once more, there was difficulty in coordinating EE programs across the state. This instability of direction within Departmental policy had also made the administration of schooling difficult and educational activity prescriptive (Hughes & Brock, 2008).

> So I always felt it was easier to apologise than to get permission so I sort of sailed ahead and did what I felt like doing... The Department of Education changed policies regularly but I was doing what the staff wanted, the schools wanted, that were visiting, and setting up programs that suited what they wanted when they were visiting. MA

The continuing changes must have been difficult for those progressing EE and one can see why a quality of flexibility would be beneficial. Centre staff, along with others in the field, have become pragmatic, perhaps with a tendency for chameleon-like

---

[13] Deputations were common practice within the AEE (NSW).

[14] The promised review of EE teacher education requirements is more elusive.

characteristics—adapting and adopting to changing circumstances as seen fit for survival.

A new document—a green paper titled *A New Approach to Environmental Education in NSW*, was released in 1996 (NSW Environmental Protection Authority, 1996). It proposed the establishment of a Council on Environmental Education to serve in an advisory capacity for the Ministers for Environment and Education.[15] This council would replace the previous individual departmental advisory bodies aiming to save money, avoid duplication and develop a cooperative framework. This new document introduced the term "sustainability." The consultation document that followed, *A New Approach to EE in NSW: Consultation and the Next Steps* (NSW Environmental Protection Authority, 1998), called for clearer definitions of EE, ESD and the objectives of EE, and refreshingly identified challenges including[16]:

- a history of a lack of leadership from federal and state government,
- ESD as a foundation for EE, and
- the clash between EE programs and economic issues.

## 8.19.1 A Change in Environmental Education Centre Management

Due to the severe restructure in 1996, Tribe retired and Syd Smith took on the role of CEO within the Department of School Education (Tribe, 1996b). Tribe continued in his role as the AAEE state delegate for NSW among other pursuits. For ESE it was another fortuitous and serendipitous event given Smith held significantly more power. He was a high-ranking education official with a passion for the environment who needed to be integrated into the system. One of the last batch of inspectors appointed just prior to the Inspectorate being abolished in April 1990, Smith was the Cluster Director on the Central Coast from 1989 to 1993. When his contract finished in 1993, Smith was seconded by Boston to evaluate the educational resources of the Australian Broadcasting Commission before moving to the Quality Assurance Directorate in 1996. When this Directorate closed, Smith became CEO of the EE Unit (MacPherson, 2015).

> When I started we had Syd Smith who was the guru and the CEO of environmental education and he was up there with all the other CEOs in the Department. *OA*

Smith was given the responsibility of running the EECs by Burke, the assistant director at the time. It was the first time this had been done at a central level. Smith was accountable for how the centres operated state-wide—previously officers oversaw management or curriculum but not both. Indeed, directors were happy for Smith to take on this role. Directors often knew nothing about EE—there was still a

---

[15] As discussed in the AEE (NSW) deputation.
[16] Note this document emanated from the relatively new EPA.

great ignorance within the NSW Department of Education and Training about the centres. It was not a priority, with centres left to manage on their own. Due to the *ad hoc* and serendipitous nature of the development of FSCs, and the severe rationalisation within the NSW Department of Education and governance generally, Smith went about formalising the informal—ensuring the centres and EE were secure.

One of the issues Smith attempted to rectify while in the EE Unit was the agreements with the NSW NPWS. Many of these agreements were peppercorn arrangements, handshake agreements, made at an earlier time when departments worked together in governance for the public good. These agreements, which benefited the community they served, do not translate into economic rationalism with departments trying to work with minimal funding and indeed generate money where possible. While an agreement was made, it does not seem likely that it has been upheld. The agreements seem to be made on a case-by-case basis taking up valuable EEC principal time and effort. Another issue had been changes within NSW NPWS management where without understanding previous agreements, new management has attempted to evict the FSC/EECs. Further, having two bosses was an issue for many EEC teachers-in-charge/principals working in national parks.

### 8.19.2 Taronga Park Zoo | Western Plains Zoo

In 1996 Taronga Park and Western Plain Zoos, who also manage a mobile zoo that visits sites that do not have access to zoo facilities, joined the FSC network. The zoos' aims differed from those of the FSC in that they work with animal species on a global scale and have a much larger visitation catchment. Their priority focused on the zoo rather than the NSW Department of Education and Training objectives. Nevertheless, they have the same curriculum outcomes to meet. The NSW Department of Education had been requested to support the resourcing of staff for the Zoo centres though they also had Catholic/private schools support, being facilities for the whole population. From 1996, the Zoos joined the FSC network in a professional capacity.[17] This coincided with the change from regions to clusters with Burke instigating the merger.

> Terry Burke who said to me, "And we've got two other little appendages here that don't have a correct line of authority as well and they are the zoos. Taronga Zoo and Western Plains Zoo. I want you to include them with the environmental ed centres because they're doing a similar task. They're really promoting the teaching and learning of environmental ed." So when we ran the conferences after that the zoos came along as well and they shared their acumen and ideas with the environmental ed centres. So it enriched both groups. SS

*The Quality Assurance Review of EE in NSW Government Schools,* undertaken by the Quality Assurance Unit within the NSW Department of School Education with

---

[17] Gradually the NSW Environmental Education Centre Network became the Environmental and Zoo Education Centre Network (EZEC).

Tribe's involvement, took a long time to be made public (Smith, 1994). For some reason it was not released until 1996 under a new state Government.[18] One of the overall findings was that many within the NSW Department of School Education did not know what EE was. Additionally, a high proportion were not active in the field. Findings included:

- it was often only dedicated teachers who supported EE in schools,
- teachers within science, human society and its environment (HSIE) and technological and applied studies (TAS) were more likely to support EE than those in maths, and personal development, health and physical education (PDHPE),
- mandatory requirements were not clear to the teaching profession, and
- integration of EE was difficult for teachers and it was often seen as an add-on to the official curriculum (S. Smith, 1999b).

Recommendations included:

1. the development of resources to support the cross-curricular nature of the *EE Curriculum Statement*,
2. the development of a statement of student EE learning outcomes,
3. EE professional development be available and accessible to school staff, and
4. flexibility within FSCs to ensure maximum capacity in supporting EE (Tribe, 1996a, p. 5).

The Quality Assurance report gave Smith a starting point—a framework for developing ESE further.

As discussed, the EE Unit was severely understaffed from time to time. Tribe was the only staff member in the Unit when it was first set up (Smith, 1994). In 1997, there was only Smith within the EE Unit carrying out the work of overseeing the FSCs and EE in NSW (Tribe, 1998). Furthermore, the EE networks within schools must have fallen into disarray from time to time with the changes in education governance, changes in regional jurisdictions, and teacher attrition and movement—change management was/is always an issue given that often it is one teacher carrying the EE load within a school. In 1997, the EE Unit was once more setting up an EE network of teachers in the 40 school districts within the state with the purpose of communicating sound EE practice (Tribe, 1997).

### 8.19.3 Penrith Lakes Environmental Education Centre

Penrith Lakes Environmental Education Centre at Cranebrook joined the other 19 FSCs in 1997 (NSW Department of School Education, 1997). It was officially opened the following year (NSW Department of Education and Training, 1998).

---

[18] I could not find a copy of this document available. Richard Jones, a staunch environmentalist politician in the Legislative Assembly asked questions as to why the Review had not been released in 1994.

Penrith Lakes was an old quarrying site. Reclamation resulted in the creation of seven connected artificial lakes (Penrith Lakes) specifically to be used for the Olympics rowing site. There was 2000 hectares of recreational area (NSW Department of Education and Training, 1998).

Initially, the Social Science Teachers' Association had developed a resource about the Penrith Lakes Scheme. They saw great potential in the scheme's application to the geography curriculum. A steering committee explored the potential for a centre. The partnership included the NSW Department of Education and Training, the Catholic Education Office at Parramatta, the University of Western Sydney, the Western Sydney Institute of TAFE, the NSW Minerals Council and Penrith Lakes Development Corporation. The centre was to provide for all students, both private and public, primary, secondary and tertiary (NSW Department of Education and Training, 1998).[19] Politicians such as John Aqualina were also on the steering committee. Contributing to the push for the centre was interest in the Lakes area from the AEE (NSW).

The site had significant appeal to schools wanting to visit and the consortium wanted resources to deal with the educational side of their business, the restoration work and the Olympic site. Some thought the setup of the centre was to placate the local community who were unhappy with mining developments in the area. The centre was somewhat controversial, thought by some to be "window dressing" for the Olympics.

Eventually there was a commitment for funding by the Education Minister, Chadwick, but with the loss of the election in 1995, the commitment floundered. Funding, through John Aquilina, the new Labor Education Minister, took some time to eventuate. Steve Etheridge's position as principal of the centre and the change in the Education Department from regions to clusters happened about the same time. Instead of regions holding the funds, funds devolved to schools within clusters. For some time, Etheridge's new position seemed precarious with no ownership within the education bureaucracy. Additionally, if there had not been someone so involved with the project, the threads of commitment may have been lost in the ensuing bureaucratic and political changes. The whole situation went some way in destabilising the commitment of the project consortium and they did not want to be called a FSC. Etheridge came up with the "environmental education centre" (EEC) nomenclature that satisfied all parties. It fit with the popularity of environmental matters at the time. Finally, funding came through and Penrith Lakes was the first EEC established (see Fig. 8.2 for a centre locality map updated to 1997).

Etheridge, the first principal at Penrith Lakes, had been a geography/social science teacher actively involved with the Western Sydney Social Science Teachers' Association and later the social science/HISE consultant for the Western Sydney region. In this position, he had been on the steering committees for both Longneck Lagoon and Brewongle, and for the development of Penrith Lakes EEC.

---

[19] Contrary information says that a second teacher was provided with Catholic Education partnership funds but also from the sale of the geography resource, negating expense for visiting schools. Perhaps it was a mixture of both.

8.19 More Change and More Advocacy for Environmental Education

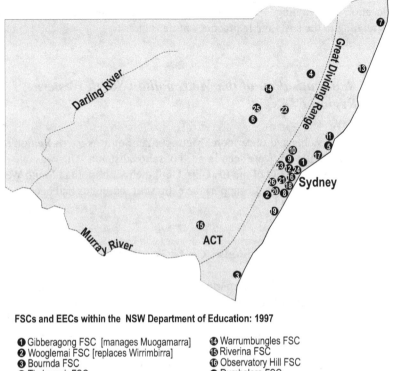

**FSCs and EECs within the NSW Department of Education: 1997**

- ❶ Gibberagong FSC [manages Muogamarra]
- ❷ Wooglemai FSC [replaces Wirrimbirra]
- ❸ Bournda FSC
- ❹ Thalgarrah FSC
- ❺ Awabakal FSC
- ❻ Wambangalang FSC
- ❼ Dorroughby FSC
- ❽ Royal National Park FSC
- ❾ Longneck Lagoon FSC
- ❿ Brewongle FSC
- ⓫ Shortland Wetlands FSC [annex of Awabakal FSC]
- ⓬ Field of Mars FSC
- ⓭ Cascade FSC
- ⓮ Warrumbungles FSC
- ⓯ Riverina FSC
- ⓰ Observatory Hill FSC
- ⓱ Rumbalara FSC
- ⓲ Botany Bay FSC
- ⓳ Illawarra (Mt Kembla) FSC
- ⓴ Camden Park Education Centre (EC) [annex of Wirrimbirra]
- ㉑ Georges River EC [annex of Wirrimbirra]
- ㉒ Redhill FSC
- ㉓ Penrith Lakes EEC
- ㉔ Taronga Zoo Education Centre
- ㉕ Western Plain Zoo Education Centre
- ㉖ Wedderburn Outdoor Resource Centre [annex of Wirrimbirra]

**Fig. 8.2** Location map of EECs within the NSW Department of Education, 1997 (not to scale—schematic map)

Etheridge updated the Penrith Lakes Scheme geography curriculum resource once he was principal of the EEC. Schools bought the resource that proved popular. It contributed to the popularity of the centre for school visitation and adding to the funding to employ additional staff. The centre went on to develop other resources, units of work connected to curriculum where the centre experience was just one part of a much larger study.

Program areas included studies of the Penrith Lakes scheme, heritage studies, the Olympic site, First Nations archaeology, geology, water quality, and rehabilitation of the environment, particularly mining restoration/sustainability (NSW Department of Education and Training, 1998). The Minerals Council funded some of these programs relating to the sustainable practices of their industry.

### 8.19.4 Rationalisation of the Metropolitan South Western Region FSCs

When the clusters changed once more, Metropolitan South Western Region's four FSCs and additional staff, were seen in need of rationalisation. This was one of the first tasks for Smith as CEO of the EE Unit. Until then Metropolitan South Western Region had found the money to support the extra staff, but funds had become much tighter and dispersed.

#### 8.19.4.1 Wirrimbirra Field Studies Centre Becomes Wooglemai FSC

As discussed earlier, the NSW Department of Education leased Wirrimbirra in the 1970s as a FSC. In the early to mid 1990s, due to the David Stead Foundation being under financial stress and there being conflict within the voluntary Foundation Board, the Department of School Education was asked to increase their lease payments significantly. Rejecting this request, the Department settled on Wooglemai as an alternative site. Another explanation proffered in both the literature and the interview data, is that the railway line that transects Wirrimbirra proved too dangerous. There had been attempts to have an overhead bridge built but while there were great efforts to progress the bridge, it never eventuated (Webb, 1998). Furthermore, the Wirrimbirra site was limited in the types of study sites it provided. It seems a range of issues—escalating costs, Occupational Health and Safety concerns becoming increasingly restrictive due to accountability functions exacerbating, and limited study opportunities—contributed to other site options being canvased. About this time, Steve Benoit was the teacher-in-charge with Nicoll the assisting teacher. In 1994, Wirrimbirra's Departmental FSC operations began to operate day trips to Wooglemai, at Oakdale which proved successful, and the relocation and name change to Wooglemai occurred in 1995.

The Wooglemai FSC site had reasonable facilities and lease arrangements and offered access to the adjacent Nattai National Park with its great walking trails. It was the best option at a crucial time. The name change was officially recorded in accordance with Departmental policy in the Education Gazette, as detailed in the 1997 Annual Report. Wooglemai was declared, coinciding with the closure of Wirrimbirra FSC (NSW Department of School Education, 1997). Wirrimbirra continued to operate as a sanctuary until the late 2010s when the Stead Foundation was forced to return the site to the National Trust.

### 8.19.4.2 Rationalisation

While the trajectory of Wirrimbirra represents a sombre decline for community initiatives, the emergence of Wooglemai as an FSC was marked by its own set of initial difficulties. Benoit, teacher-in-charge at Wooglemai, had the extra burden of managing and administering the South Western Region annexes with no extra resourcing and the difficulty of them being a considerable distance from Wooglemai. He was apparently keen for a solution to this untenable situation. The resolution chosen was to gazette two of the centres and close the other, Wedderburn. Gazettal was significant; it gave the centre a school number which provided a certain amount of security—it is a difficult process to close a school. Significantly, gazettal came with an establishment grant which was approximately $20,000.[20] Nicoll, who had taught at the centre since 1994, became the Principal of Wooglemai in 2005.

Both Camden Park and Georges River Education Centres were opened as EECs in late 1999 (Tribe, 1999b) and were gazetted within the NSW Department of Education and Training in January 2000 (NSW Department of Education and Training, 2000).[21] Trench and Cullis were successful in reapplying for their positions and their title changed from teacher-in-charge to principal. Due to the nomenclature change in 1999, these centres became EECs rather than FSCs. Wedderburn's staff allocation supplemented centres in other regions rather than Georges River and Camden Park as expected.[22]

## 8.20 Diversification of ESE and the Demise of Founding Advocacy Groups

Various environmental departments, both state and Federal, had become dominant participants in what had become the holistic state-wide endeavour of ESE, with the overarching umbrella of Federal support. Within NSW in the 1990s there were many other participants within the EE field. By the late 1990s, there were several national programs running that had been advocated for by a variety of environmentalists. Programs such as "Waterwatch", "Saltwatch", "Airwatch", the globe project

---

[20] Note that there was no evidence in data accessed that funding occurred for this rationalization. Centres were already up and running and money was tight. Additionally, there is evidence of regions attempting to utilise this funding for expenses other than EECs, although not in this specific instance.

[21] Shortland Wetlands was also gazetted in August, 2000. Also note that Shortland Wetlands EEC became The Wetlands EEC at some stage in line with the Wetlands Centre which changed its name in 2005 to the Hunter Wetlands Centre Australia (Birdforum, n.d.). Additionally in 2022 The Wetlands and Awabakal EECs became known as the Awabakal EEC with two campuses—Dudley and The Wetlands (NSW Department of Education, n.d.).

[22] Apparently .2 went to The Wetlands and Dorroughby while .1 was allocated to Thalgarrah but please note that information about staff allocation within the data set was relatively elusive.

"Communicating Over the Catchment" and Landcare Australia were all projects supported by NSW schools (NSW Legislative Assembly, 1998).

So, much of what the AEE (NSW) and the FSCs had set out to achieve was accomplished.

> What it used to carry out single-handedly is now being carried out by a growing number of various environmental education organisations throughout the state. (Tribe, 1999b, p. 13)

FSC educators were not the only environmental educators. There were environmental educators within other departments in addition to private EE consultants.

> The things that were actually driving it have now moved away. So, that's also why I think it's a more difficult gig... the pinnacle of what we were trying to do came about in about, ...the mid 1990s...all those battles that started back in the early 70s had been pretty much won. I'm talking about not just in the EECs but also in the environment movement. And there were numerous people in it and there were industries... People could go and earn a living in private enterprise... So, there was tons of work...it was a burgeoning industry. So, it became something else. And I think the environmental ed centres started to lose there because other people were doing it. The world had kind of moved on and they started to pretty much dismantle a lot of the things that we fought for in environmental ed centres and within schools. FA

This quote suggests that once institutionalised, and once the popularity or political power of the environmental/sustainability movement waned, there was the progressive dismantling of achievements within the new economic structure.

### 8.20.1 The End of the Gould League of NSW and the Association for EE (NSW)

In 1998, the Gould League of NSW was looking for members for its Council, seeking rejuvenation—support from students, teachers and schools (Tribe, 1999a)—but without success, and soon they succumbed to the downturn in community interest.

> So the emphasis in environmental education began to wane quite a bit and there was less and less money to the Gould League which became less and less effective and that's where nobody turned up to support it—we were getting a bit old.... We joined in with the Gould League Victoria. They [NSW] went into liquidation.[23] DT

The downturn also affected the AEE (NSW) and the AAEE. Within the AEE (NSW) in 1998, motions passed unanimously at the AEE (NSW) conference were to:

- press the Government for EE to be accounted for in school annual management plans,

---

[23] While the Gould Leagues in NSW, Queensland, Tasmania and South Australia have closed, the Victorian Gould League acts as a de facto national body. There is one other active state Gould League at Herdsmans Lake Wildlife Centre, Western Australia. (Gould League, n.d.).

## 8.20 Diversification of ESE and the Demise of Founding Advocacy Groups 241

- have the NSW Department of Education and Training monitor the implementation of the mandatory requirements of the *EE Curriculum Statement* via the annual school report, and
- to increase the staffing levels of the one-person EE Unit (Tribe, 1998).

The last initiative of the AEE (NSW) was a pamphlet outlining how to make environmental policy and plan submissions titled "Public Participation in the Decision-Making Process" (Tribe, 1999a). At the end of 1999, the AEE (NSW) announced that it would be folding. The AEE (NSW) intentions, as outlined at their conference in 1998, did not come to fruition.[24] At that stage, there were only three branches remaining—Central Coast, Hunter and Western Sydney (Tribe, 1999b; Heck, 1999)—and these received an even distribution of the remaining monies.

The last project of the AEE (NSW) was a biography of Strom's life by his friend and long-time colleague, Fox (2016). Strom died in 1997. The AEE (NSW) became a Chapter within the AAEE. There was a definite downturn in interest within the EE associations toward the end of the millennium with the Australian Capital Territory Chapter within AAEE struggling at the time that the AEE (NSW) folded. The AAEE was also going through a renewal process (Heck, 1999).

In the early new millennium, with the original AEE (NSW) changed significantly, according to one informant, it became increasingly important for EECs to solidify their network.

> *So, when I first started there was a regular AEE meeting every year or every other year so you were always going to something and meeting your peers but all these other people as well. But, when that sort of started to die down it really became more important for the EECs to build a communication network on their own. EB*

While the AAEE was an obvious support, there was a need for a local, state-wide focus relating to the various, specific rules of NSW governance. The centres had lost a significant support base—the AEE (NSW) and the Gould League of NSW. By 1998 there were more than 45 teachers and 21 clerical staff within Departmental FSC/EECs.

---

[24] Although the call for EE accountability lived on in the School Environmental Management Plans (SEMPs) initiated with the publication of the NSW Environmental Education Policy (2001) which was supposed to be mandatory.

## 8.21 Environmental Education within the Department

### 8.21.1 The Environmental Education Curriculum Statement Revisited

In light of the changes happening on a global, national, and state level, particularly Agenda 21 originating from the Rio de Janeiro Conference in 1992, and the curriculum and structural changes of the 1990 Reform Act (NSW), the EE Unit started to revisit the *EE Curriculum Statement* (NSW Legislative Assembly, 1998; Smith, 1998, 1999b; Tribe, 1995). Issues had become much more complex than at the beginning of EE.

> And what has happened since then is it's become more social, it's become more global, it's become more ... talking about urban areas, talking about climate change, talking about big issues, talking about poverty, talking about equality. All those things have slipped in now to become part of the sustainable agenda whereas then it was much more simple.... But it's become more embracing, more complex now, and much more integrated. XB

The findings and recommendations of the Quality Assurance Review (circa 1996) gave plenty of scope as to where the policy needed change. In addition, it had been observed that approaching EE within the school curriculum in a holistic way was difficult due to schooling's formalised subject structure (S. Smith, 1999b). This was unfortunate given the interdisciplinary nature of ESE and is indicative of the institutionalisation of the traditional disciplines and schooling structure.

> Unfortunately, the curriculum is so... put into silos that you don't see the cross-references XB

Smith believed that while centrally developed curriculum intended to influence what was taught, it is the teachers who are the important factor in how and if the curriculum is enacted in the classroom (Smith, 1998, 1999a, b). Learning from the first attempt, the policy was to provide clear guidelines for the minimum responsibilities of schools and how learning outcomes could be achieved in the KLAs. Addressing the reluctance of some teachers to attend to EE, Smith held workshops. At the 1999 AAEE International Conference, Smith attempted to address the problems curriculum writers have in transforming curriculum intent into practice by educating educators about the changes.

### 8.21.2 Official EEC Policy Statement and Name Change

The EEC policy statement became available in 1998, outlining the role of EECs. The document covered staffing, administration and funding of the centres, in addition to the duties of centre teachers and issues of safety management. Importantly, it provided the locations and contact details of the centres (NSW Department of Education and Training, 1998). It was essentially a tailored schools version of the statement produced in 1989—it outlined what centres had to offer. The mid to late

1990s saw changes in credentialing of people working with school children and changes in insurance—there was much greater accountability. "And so doing things informally, unofficially became extremely difficult," (KA)—there was a lot more paperwork, for example, about excursions. FSC/EEC staff produced templates to streamline the process to make it as palatable as possible for teachers and schools in a climate where teacher/school workload was already high.

> *The Environmental Education Centres Policy.... that was almost like a service level agreement. If schools were going to go to an environmental education centre they were guaranteed of getting the sort of service that those policies and those documents described. And so it was the Department's way of saying, "These EECs, field studies centres as they were called then, are staffed by Department of Education teachers. They will provide curriculum-based learning experiences. You can be guaranteed a certain quality of educational program if you bring your kids here." So that was a way of ensuring that there was a consistent approach to what the field studies centres did. VB*

According to the Environmental Education Policy (2001), it was 1999 before the title of the centres was officially changed from "Field Studies" to "Environmental Education" to reflect the wider role of EE within schools and the centres' role within it (see Fig. 8.3 for a location map of the centres as of 2024). The implications of the name change provoked a great amount of discussion amongst centre staff. The early centres were very fieldwork driven within their environmental imperative and were worried that the name change might impact people undertaking fieldwork. The hands-on outdoor experience was paramount for the survival of the centres with field work connected to the curriculum their lifeline.

## 8.22 Conclusion

This chapter described the changes that took place, specifically for the NSW FSCs/EECs within the NSW Department of Education from the 1980s into the 1990s. It documents the emerging shift from EE to education for sustainability (EfS) within the centres and the nascent shift to educational economic rationalism within NSW. It discusses some of the persistent challenge of solidifying EE's position in both education and society amidst the evolving constraints of social and political dynamics. This is especially noteworthy in the context of the transition from a welfare economy to economic rationalism, which has resulted in consequential downsizing. While the *EE Curriculum Statement* and *FSC policy* were achieved after a 10-year labour, their dissemination coincided with the severe rationalisation associated with the Education Reform Act 1990 (NSW), affecting the resourcing of effective implementation. Reform brought teachers-in-charge greater responsibility and freedom for managing the centres in a financial and accountability capacity.

A FSC renaissance, due to an enormous amount of politicking on the part of local community, the AEE (NSW), the Gould League of NSW and other EE advocates, including education ministers who supported the centres, saw great advancement within ESE and FSCs. Greater teaching capacity was achieved for some of the

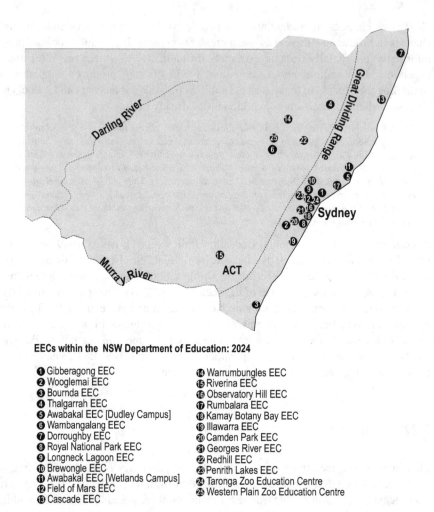

**Fig. 8.3** Location map of the EECs within the NSW Department of Education, 2024 (not to scale—schematic map)

centres yet some regions decided to utilise their second teacher to open another one-teacher FSC. Shortland Wetlands, the Field of Mars, Cascade, Warrumbungles, Riverina, Observatory Hill, Rumbalara, Botany Bay, Mt. Kembla/Illawarra and Red Hill FSCs were established, as was Penrith Lakes EEC. Importantly, although the proposed Environmental Education Act was not passed, some of its key provisions—such as the establishment of an Environmental Education Unit and an audit of departmental schools—were implemented. There was the rationalisation of the Metropolitan South Western Regions FSC resources with Wooglemai replacing Wirrimbirra and Camden Park and Georges River Education Centres becoming FSC/EECs while the Wedderburn resource facility was closed. Zoo Education

Centres were integrated into the FSC/EEC network. Finally, there was a name change from FSCs to EECs.

The focal point of this chapter, delves into the complexities of the NSW Department of Education FSCs/EECs and ESE initiatives. It unveils the dynamic interaction among communities, their place/surroundings and governance. This discussion, along with the chapter on environmental awareness, reveal the interconnecting threads that weave these entities and happenings into the broader national and global context. On an international,[25] national and state level there was a lot of EE resourcing with many planning documents and programs developed. There were also various Federal funding grants available to entrepreneurial teachers-in-charge/principals. In contrast to the 1970s and early 1980s, the 1990s saw competition within the field which was becoming increasingly privatised. There was power play too between Commonwealth and state and territory governments over school curriculum and discipline contestation ensued. Significantly, there was the ending of the Gould League of NSW and the AEE (NSW) in its original form. Both were instrumental in growing EE within the NSW education system and generally, within NSW, and they contributed to national and global change with a bottom-up approach.

While this chapter and the previous three chapters' focus is necessarily an idiosyncratic, descriptive reveal, in order to utilise a Weberian analysis of bureaucratic reasoning, it pays tribute to the people, communities, and places that shaped ESE and EECs creation and evolution in NSW and, in part, Australia. While this narrative is specific to NSW, synchronistically ESE and EECs were finding form in their own habitats around the world. The following chapter continues the development within the EECs of the NSW Department of Education while Sect. 8.4 broadens the narrative scope to showcase diverse examples of EECs from around the world, offering a comparative perspective for analysis.

# References

7:30 Report. (2014, October 21). Gough Whitlam 'changed the country's idea of itself' says Paul Keating. *ABC News*. Retrieved May 1, 2024, from https://www.abc.net.au/news/2014-10-21/gough-whitlam-changed-the-countrys-idea-of-itself/5831476

Australasian Legal Information Institute. (1994). *Application by the New South Wales Teachers' Federation for a new award and application by Department of School Education for an award*. AustLII. Retrieved July 26, 2017, from https://www.austlii.edu.au/cgi-bin/viewdoc/au/cases/nsw/NSWIRComm/1994/22.html?context=1;query=%22field%20studies%20centre%22%20;%E2%80%A6

Australian Association for Environmental Education (AAEE) (1982). *Newsletter No. 11*, (November).

Australian Association for Environmental Education (AAEE). (1990). NSW Environmental Education Trust. *OzEEnews*, 43.

Birdforum. (n.d.). *Hunter Wetlands Centre Australia - BirdForum Opus*. Retrieved June 1, 2024, from https://www.birdforum.net/opus/Hunter_Wetlands_Centre_Australia

---

[25] Detailed in Chap. 10.

Bournda Field Studies Centre (Ed.). (1989). *The biophysical environment and contemporary issues of Bega Valley Shire*. Bournda Field Studies Centre.
Bridger, G. (1997). Cascade Public School 1926–1976. In G. Bridger (Ed.), *Timber town histories Dorrigo Plateau New South Wales* (p. 1, 92–93). Cascade Field Studies Centre, NSW Department of School Education.
Brown, M. (1991a). Delegate's reports: NSW. *OzEEnews, 45*, 7.
Brown, M. (1991b). Delegate's reports: NSW. *OzEEnews, 46*, 8.
Brown, M. (1992). Delegate's reports: NSW. *OzEEnews, 52*, 10.
Commonwealth Department of Arts Heritage and Environment. (1987, February 11–13). *Environmental education: Past, present and future: Third national environmental education seminar and workshops*. Commonwealth Department of Arts Heritage and Environment.
Department of Environment Climate Change and Water (NSW). (2011). *Mimosa rocks National Park plan of management*. NSW National Parks and Wildlife Service. Available at: https://www.environment.nsw.gov.au/-/media/OEH/Corporate-Site/Documents/Parks-reserves-and-protected-areas/Parks-plans-of-management/mimosa-rocks-national-park-plan-of-management-110246.pdf
Dowd, P. (1993). Profiling field studies centres. *InforMER, 2*(4), 4–5.
Fensham, P. (1990). Bill Stapp down under again. *OzEEnews, 42*, 2.
Foott, B., & Wright, S. (1995). *Spaceship earth: An environmental science program for primary schools – Teachers manual*. The Good Passenger Company.
Fox, A. (1979). Reflections. In W. Goldstein (Ed.), *Parks and wildlife: Australia's 100 years of national parks* (pp. 4–14). National Parks and Wildlife Service.
Fox, A. (author), Dufty, N., McDonald, K., Smith, S., Tribe, D., & Schaefer, K. (Eds.). (2016). *Chief Guardian: The life and times of Allen Strom*. https://www.amazon.com.au/Chief-Guardian-Times-Allen-Strom-ebook/dp/B01H8IEORQ
Frew, B. (1990). The effects of the Scott Report on the administration of the NSW Department of Technical and Further Education. *Journal of Tertiary Education Administration, 12*(2), 405–418. https://doi.org/10.1080/0157603900120207
Gilbert, R., Gordon, K., Heopper, B., & Ray, L. (1992). Love's labours lost: Writing a national statement. *Curriculum Perspectives, 12*(4), 25–27.
Gilligan, B. (1986). Politics of protection—Wetlands. *Australian Journal of Environmental Education, 2*, 25–28. https://doi.org/10.1017/s0814062600004377
Godfrey, K. (1994). StatEEments: NSW. *OzEEnews, 60*(7), 14.
Gough, A. (1997). *Education and the environment: Policy, trends and the problems of marginalisation*. Australian Council for Educational Research.
Gould League (n.d.). *History*. Retrieved October 30, 2024, from https://gould.org.au/about-us/history/
Greenall Gough, A. (1989). A parvovirus-like agent associated with Psittacine beak and feather disease. *OzEENews, 41*, 1.
Haddon, F. (1980). Recent events and developments of interest in NSW. In *Australian trends in environmental education: 1st Australian Association for Environmental Education Conference, Arbury Park, SA* (pp. 52–54). Australian Association for Environmental Education.
Harris, C. (2001). History curriculum development in New South Wales: Issues of control and its impact on teachers. Education. In *Futures and new citizenships proceedings of the 10th national biennial conference of the Australian curriculum studies association*. http://www.acsa.edu.au/pages/images/2001_history_curriculum_development_in_new_south_wales.pdf
Heck, D. (1999). President's report. *OzEEnews, 79*, 3.
Hughes, J. (2018). *A background paper on the history of the New South Wales curriculum since 1989: Context, cases and commentary on curriculum change*. NSW Government: Education Standards Authority.
Hughes, J., & Brock, P. (2008). *Reform and resistance in NSW public education: Six attempts at major reform, 1905–1995*. NSW Department of Education and Training.

Industrial Relations Commission of New South Wales. (2017). Crown employees (teachers and schools and related employees) salaries and conditions award 2017. *Industrial Gazette*, May 5, 237–205.

Johnston, C., & Tribe, D. (1982). The role of the Gould League of New South Wales in environmental education in Australia. In M. Cowan & W. Stapp (Eds.), *International case studies in environmental education: Environmental education in action* (pp. 146–150). National Institute of Education.

Lengieza, M. L., Aviste, R., & Swim, J. K. (2023). Connectedness to nature through outdoor environmental education: Insights from psychology. In J. ČinČera, B. Johnson, D. Goldman, I. Alkaher, & M. Medek (Eds.), *Outdoor environmental education in the contemporary world* (pp. 49–82). Springer.

MacPherson, R. (2015). *The institute: A centennial history of the Institute of Senior Educational Administrators, formerly known as the Institute of Inspectors of Schools and Senior Educational Administrators, and before that as the Institute of Inspectors of Schools NSW*. Strategic Book Publishing and Rights Co.

McDonald, K. (Ed.). (1983). *Environmental education in NSW: 1983 handbook*. Association for Environmental Education (NSW).

Milton, V. (2022). Sacred sites battle on Biamanga mountain captured in rare book by Yuin tribal elder, photographer. *ABC News*. Retrieved from https://www.abc.net.au/news/2022-05-15/rare-photo-book-paved-way-for-aboriginal-land-rights-in-nsw/101059944

Ministerial Council on Education Employment Training and Youth Affairs (MCEETYA). (1989). *The Hobart declaration on schooling*. MCEETYA.

Mockler, N. (2018). Curriculum. In A. Welch, R. Connell, N. Mockler, A. Sriprakash, H. Proctor, D. Hayes, et al. (Eds.), *Education, change and society* (4th ed., pp. 333–360). Oxford University Press.

NSW. *Hansard. Legislative Assembly*. (October 15, 1998). Retrieved July 26, 2017, from https://www.parliament.nsw.gov.au/Hansard/Pages/HansardResult.aspx#/docid/HANSARD-1323879322-18634

NSW Department of Education. (1983). *Controversial issues in schools: Policy statement*. Retrieved December 12, 2017, from https://education.nsw.gov.au/policy-library/policies/controversial-issues-in-schools

NSW Department of Education. (1985). Kalkari Field Studies Centre (S.S.P.). *Government Gazette of the State of New South Wales* (88), May 31, 2443.

NSW Department of Education and Training. (1998). *Environmental Education Centres: Policy statement*. NSW Department of Education and Training.

NSW Department of Education and Training. (2000). *Department of Education and Training Annual Report*. NSW Department of Education and Training.

NSW Department of School Education. (1989a). *Environmental education curriculum statement K-12*. Macquarie Press.

NSW Department of School Education. (1989b). *Field studies centre policy statement: Developed from the report of the working party on Field Studies Centres*. Edited by Schools Directorate. NSW Department of Education.

NSW Department of School Education. (1989c). *Field studies centres*. Edited by Schools Directorate. NSW Department of Education.

NSW Department of School Education. (1989d). *Field studies centres: A guide for teachers*. Edited by NSW Department of Education. NSW Department of Education.

NSW Department of Education. (n.d.). *Awabakal Environmental Education Centre*. Retrieved June 1, 2024, from https://awabakal-e.schools.nsw.gov.au/about-our-school.html

NSW Department of School Education. (1990). *A kit to introduce the environmental education curriculum statement K-12. Curriculum Support Branch Directorate of Curriculum and Educational Programs*. Macquarie Press.

NSW Department of School Education. (1993). *A new focus on environmental education*. NSW Department of Education and Training.

NSW Department of School Education. (1997). *Department of School Education's annual report*. NSW Department of School Education.

NSW Environmental Protection Agency (EPA). (2018). *About the NSW EPA: Our organisation*. Retrieved July 26, 2023, from https://www.epa.nsw.gov.au/about-us/our-organisation/about-nsw-epa

NSW Environmental Protection Authority. (1996). *A new approach to environmental education in NSW: A NSW Government green paper*. NSW Environmental Protection Authority.

NSW Environmental Protection Authority. (1998). *A new approach to environmental education in NSW: Consultation and the next steps*. NSW Environmental Protection Authority.

NSW Government: Office of Environment & Heritage. (n.d.-a). "*Baronda*." Retrieved April 22, 2018, from https://www.environment.nsw.gov.au/heritageapp/ViewHeritageItemDetails.aspx?ID=5061816

NSW Government: Office of Environment & Heritage. (n.d.-b). *Field of mars reserve*. Retrieved October 23, 2018, from https://www.environment.nsw.gov.au/heritageapp/ViewHeritageItemDetails.aspx?ID=2340198

NSW National Parks and Wildlife Service. (1998). *Marramarra National Park, Muogamarra Nature Reserve and Maroota historic site plan of management*. NSW National Parks and Wildlife Service.

NSW National Parks and Wildlife Service. (2002). *Ku-ring-gai chase National Park and Lion Island, Long Island and Spectacle Island nature reserves: Plan of management*. Office of Environment and Heritage. https://www.environment.nsw.gov.au/resources/parks/pomfinalkuringgaiislands.pdf

Office of the Commissioner. (1999). *Bega Valley Shire Council Public Inquiry*. Office of the Commissioner.

Pearson, D. (1978). *Fieldwork in environments out-of-doors*. Masters thesis, University of New England.

Pocket Oz Tavel and Information Guide Sydney. (2015). *Waterways: North and north west*. Retrieved February 22, 2019, from http://www.visitsydneyaustralia.com.au/waterways-north.html

Pusey, M. (1991). *Economic rationalism in Canberra: A nation-building state changes its mind*. Cambridge University Press.

Reid, A. (2005). *Rethinking national curriculum collaboration: Towards an Australian curriculum*. Australian Government, Department of Education, Science and Training.

Renshaw, P., & Tooth, R. (2018). Diverse place-responsive pedagogies: Historical, professional and theoretical threads. In P. Renshaw & R. Tooth (Eds.), *Diverse pedagogies of place: Educating students in and for local and global environments*. Routledge.

Riordan, G., & Weller, S. (2000). The reformation of education in NSW: The 1990 Education Reform Act, a decade later. Paper presented at the *AARE Conference, December 4–7, 2000*. Australian Association for Research in Education.

Smith, K. (1993). StatEEments: NSW. *OzEEnews, 56*, 18.

Smith, K. (1994). StatEEments: NSW. *OzEEnews, 57*, 16.

Smith, S. (1998). Rewriting the environmental education curriculum statement. In *Book of proceedings for the environmental education through community projects, 21st annual seminar, 19–20 September 1998* (pp. 109–113). The University of New England/Australian Association for Environmental Education.

Smith, S. (1999a). Designing a new NSW environmental curriculum statement for the 21st century (Abstract). In *Southern Crossings – Pointers for change, international conference on environmental education (Program), University of NSW, Sydney, Australia., 14–18 January* (p. 67). Australian Association for Environmental Education.

Smith, S. (1999b). The new NSW environmental Education curriculum statement: Preparing students for life and citizenship in the 21st century. In *Southern crossings – Pointers for change, international conference on environmental Education, University of NSW, Sydney, Australia, 14–18 January*. Australian Association for Environmental Education.

Stapp, W., & Stapp, G. (1982). *Summary of Senior Fulbright Fellowship on environmental education in Australia*. Australian American Education Foundation, Australian Association of Environmental Education, Frank Daniel Butt Memorial Foundation, Griffith University School of Australian Environmental Studies, Monash University Graduate School of Environmental Science, and Graduate School of Education.

The Parliament of the Commonwealth of Australia. (1994). Australia's population 'carrying capacity': Two ecologies. In report by the *House of Representatives Standing Committee for long term strategies*. Australian Government Publishing Service.

Tilbury, D., Coleman, V., & Garlick, D. (2005). *A national review of environmental education and its contribution to sustainability in Australia: School education*. Australian Government Department of the Environment and Heritage and Australian Research Institute in Education for Sustainability (ARIES).

Tribe, D. (1992). Delegate's report: NSW. *OzEEnews, 51*, 4.

Tribe, D. (1995). School Education Initiatives. *OzEEnews, 61*, 8.

Tribe, D. (1996a). State and Territory Reports: NSW. *OzEEnews, 65*, 5.

Tribe, D. (1996b). State and Territory Reports: NSW. *OzEEnews, 64*, 6.

Tribe, D. (1997). State delegate report: NSW. *OzEEnews, 68*(July), 9.

Tribe, D. (1998). State and Territory reports: NSW. *OzEEnews, 75*, 10.

Tribe, D. (1999a). State and territory reports: New South Wales report. *OzEEnews, 77*, 12.

Tribe, D. (1999b). State and territory reports: New South Wales Report. *OzEEnews, 79*, 13.

Van Matre, S. (1990). *Earth education: A new beginning*. The Institute for Earth Education.

Webb, J. (1979). An Australian in Iowa. *Environmental Education Project: Newsletter, 5*(February), 7.

Webb, J. (1980). *A survey of field studies centres in Australia*. Australian National Parks and Wildlife Service.

Webb, J. (1989). *A review of field studies in Eastern Australia*. Australian National Parks and Wildlife Service.

Webb, J. (1990). Off-school field centres for environmental education. In K. McRae (Ed.), *Outdoor and environmental education: Diverse purposes and practice* (pp. 107–124). The MacMillan Company of Australia.

Webb, J. (1998). *Thistle Y. Harris: A biography of Thistle Yolette Stead*. Surrey Beatty & Sons.

Yates, L., & Collins, C. (2008). *Australian curriculum 1975–2005: What has been happening to knowledge?* Retrieved February 22, 2019, from https://www.aare.edu.au/data/publications/2008/yat081051.pdf

Young, G. (1990). Delegate's reports: NSW. *OzEEnews, 44*, 18.

# Chapter 9
# Navigating Adversity: Thriving Through Highs and Lows

## 9.1 Introduction

This chapter briefly outlined some of the developments in Australia that have influenced the trajectory of environmental and sustainability education (ESE) and environmental education centres (EECs). While practices, pedagogies and curriculum, in addition to enabling and inhibiting factors are touched on within this descriptive reveal, it is the final section that will draw these themes into analysis.

The narrative unfolds against the backdrop of significant moments, including the Sustainable Schools Initiative, the Australian Curriculum, and the contextualisation of global initiatives within the New South Wales (NSW) framework. The unfolding story captures the trajectory of EECs within the NSW Department of Education, navigating political cycles, ideologies, and global influences. Emphasis is placed on the intricate interplay of educational change with political, economic, and social shifts, revealing the inseparable nature of these entities.

Environmental matters became increasingly formalised within departments and government positions over the latter half of the 1900s. In this sense they became more "institutionalised." This history recounts significant sustainability funding opportunities; the eventual dismantling of support and ESE structures, including the Environmental Education (EE) Unit; the continuing rhetoric of ESD; and the Australian Association for Environmental Education (AAEE) undertaking a considerable ESE workload given government recalcitrance. Within the precarity of today, this story finishes with centre educators, after years of adopting and adapting to insecurity and change, refining their collective skills as chameleons—able to fit with the times and shift ESE in a positive direction as best they can without succumbing to the continuing neoliberal agenda of our times. There is also another resurgence in ESE supports, albeit under austerity, driven by the crescendo of climate change impacts, other environmental challenges and increasing calls for action amidst the tightening grip of neoliberalism.

© The Author(s), under exclusive license to Springer Nature Switzerland AG 2025
A. M. Ross, *The Politics of Environmental Education Centres*, International Explorations in Outdoor and Environmental Education 17, https://doi.org/10.1007/978-3-031-82567-5_9

## 9.2 Expanding Horizons: NSW ESE's Global Contributions

Australia was participating in international ESE initiatives at the turn of the new millennium. Generally, Australia has a penchant for importing ideas, at times without discretion, from countries deemed antecedents of our colonialism (Rizvi, 2007). While this habit has brought some valuable contributions to EE in the form of divergent research and pedagogical perspectives—"Earth Education" for instance—it can also be to the detriment of embracing endemic ideas or possibly beneficial ideas that may originate from a broader worldview (Woolmington, 1972). Australia has developed unique, place-based initiatives. For example, the Fauna Protection Act 1948 (NSW) was unique legislation—a forerunner of conservation legislation. Further, Australia was/is well known for advocating for socially critical approaches to pedagogies for EE (Greenall Gough & Robottom, 1993). As this and the subsequent chapters discuss many Australian ESE academics and practitioners engaged in collaborations globally furthering the international agenda for ESE praxis. In the late 1990s, the NSW Department of Education and Training took some responsibility for representing Australia in the Organisation for Economic Cooperation and Development (OECD) EE projects with Syd Smith as a representative (NSW Department of Education and Training, 1999). The Environment and Schools Initiative (ENSI) network of experts, initially founded by the OECD in 1986, involved teachers and researchers in action research to gather evidence-based ESE data. Over 30 years ENSI extended its reach from classroom projects to school development, grounds, teacher education, school networks, networking schools with research institutes, and linking schools to communities (Affolter, 2018; Posch, 2018).

## 9.3 National Environmental Education Council and Network

On a national level, the National Action Plan discussion paper, *Today Shapes Tomorrow: Environmental Education for a Sustainable Future,* was produced in 1999. It provided an understanding of what interested Australian citizens thought was necessary to build EE into the future. The paper noted that implementation of EE to that point had not been systemic, and holistic approaches were rare (Environment Australia, 1999). It outlined that the environment was seen as a political rather than an educational priority with little input from education or industry. Furthermore, the EE research built over previous decades was essentially ignored, as were the coordinating efforts of a previous EE committee within the Australian Environmental Council in the 1980s (Gough, 1999, 2011).

The result, *Environmental Education for a Sustainable Future: National Action Plan* (Environment Australia, 2000) recommended the establishment of a national EE council and an EE network to transform environmental awareness into informed action. The national framework implementation plan recommended:

- raising the profile of EE. This included an independent Australian EE Foundation in an Australian university. The Australian Research Institute in Education for Sustainability [ARIES] at Macquarie University was federally funded in 2003 to undertake applied EE research (but it no longer exists),
- improving the coordination of EE activities,
- improving EE resource materials,
- more professional development opportunities for teachers in the formal education sector,
- more integration of EE principles in all formal education settings. This focus references *The Adelaide Declaration on National Goals for Schooling in the Twenty-first Century* (1999) which calls for all students to "have an understanding of, and concern for, stewardship of the natural environment, and the knowledge and skills to contribute to ecologically sustainable development" (Ministerial Council on Education Employment Training and Youth Affairs [MCEETYA], 1999, goal 1.7),
- increased resourcing for community organisations in their pursuit of EE, and lastly,
- longer term priorities.

The plan gave very little for schools to work with and little connection to anything to do with nature (Gough & Cutter Mackenzie, cited in Karena, 2010).

The AAEE was represented on the National EE Council, established in 2000, and the National EE Network, established in 2001 through members membership of the Association. For example, Smith was one of the Network members (AAEE, 2002). The National EE Network scrutinised where each state and territory was in relation to EE policy, programs, teacher professional learning—and progress, structure and implementation of their sustainable school programs.

## 9.4 ESE Developments Within NSW

Within education at a state level, there was a move back to the primacy of literacy and numeracy in the early 2000s (Hughes, 2018). Mandatory outcomes were culled further with the favouring of literacy and numeracy after a revisit of the *Eltis Review* (Eltis & Crump, 2003 cited in Hughes, 2018). This meant another detrimental effect for the progress of ESE within NSW.

## 9.4.1 The NSW EE Council

In November 1999, under an amended Protection of the Environment Administration Act 1991 (NSW), Labor's holistic version of an EE body took effect when the EE Council of NSW convened for the first time (Tribe, 1999).[1] As with the Federal body, the environment portfolio was moving the agenda (also noted by Gough, cited in Karena, 2010). Membership of the Council was wide reaching within the state entities. Representing education and EECs was Smith, head of the EE Unit within the NSW Department of Education and Training Curriculum Directorate. Additionally, Young, ex-head EE consultant within the Department, was manager of the Community Education Unit within the NSW Environmental Protection Authority (EPA).

One of the first objectives was to set up a holistic 3-year EE plan. The process of developing the plan was comprehensive, collaborative and inclusive. In 2001, a discussion paper and working paper were developed (NSW Council on Environmental Education, 2001a, b). The first NSW EE 3-year plan was released in 2002, *Learning for Sustainability: NSW Environmental Education Plan 2002–2005*. This comprehensive plan counted on collaboration between government state agencies, non-Government organisations, industry and the community to continue and further ESE (NSW Council on Environmental Education, 2002). The plan outlined strategies, actions, responsibilities and performance indicators. Specifically, for the NSW Department of Education and Training, it called for promoting ecologically sustainable ways of decision-making and living. This included the continued implementation of the "Our Environment—It's a living Thing campaign," programs such as "Living Waters, Living Communities," (p. 29) and curriculum and school management initiatives about specified resources which had been developed to support specific stages and key learning areas (KLAs) (p. 36). Examples include "Stormwater—Everyone's Responsibility Every Day," "Journey with a Purpose," and components of the "Sustainable Schools Program" including School Environmental Management Plans and an accreditation program. The Department also had responsibility in developing understandings of global environmental issues and social equity issues in addition to understanding of the connection between the environment, the social, the personal and the political. Through the *EE Policy for Schools*, the 3-year plan called for continuing the syllabi and, in cooperation with the established Environmental Education Coordination Network (a network of lead government agencies implementing and developing major EE programs and reporting to the Council), to implement a coordinated approach to developing and utilising resources. Lastly, the Plan called on the Department to work with NSW NPWS to develop consistent protocols to facilitate joint program development for EECs in national parks.

The category "Environmental Education providers" did not include EECs. This list included: pre-schools, schools, tertiary/vocational education, industry training,

---

[1] The previous body had been disbanded after the election in 1995.

government agencies, community-based adult education providers, unions, environmental interest groups, and other community organisations (NSW Council on Environmental Education, 2002, p. 52). EECs were listed, however, to take action in calls for the expansion of experiential learning in "recreational, ecotourism and community information activities" (p. 37). A noteworthy exclusion for formal environmental educators with substantial professional experience.

### 9.4.2  Environmental Education Policy for Schools

The NSW Environmental Education Policy and associated documentation was rolled out from 2001 (NSW Department of Education and Training, 2001a).[2] This important revised EE document was released along with resources to assist with its implementation—a substantial 165-page document titled *Implementing the Environmental Education Policy in Your School* (NSW Department of Education and Training, 2001b). A sign of the changing times was that additional copies were made available for sale through the NSW Department of Education and Training. There is a presumption that previous resources were complimentary. Evidence such as the past generosity of the government printing service supports this supposition. The policy focused on curriculum, management of resources and management of school grounds (electricity, water, waste and biodiversity). Many resources supported it. There were documents for each KLA introducing the policy, outlining the objectives, and identifying where and how strategies for each specific KLA could be applied. There were also support documents for the management of resources such as *Energy Management in NSW Schools* (DET, 2001). The EECs once more had significant input into the policy and were integral in its rollout and associated teacher professional development.

> Well… there was a strong relationship [between the FSC/EEC staff and the central office of the DET] because first of all they were in-puts in helping us write the policy and also they were a major player in implementing the policy. And it was a two-way thing they were really the foot soldiers if you like in getting things off the ground and teaching teachers how to do things. It wasn't just teaching kids. XB

The policy, implementation plan and resources supported the integration of ESE into the KLAs as well as through major holistic curriculum activities. The policy and plan involved extensive professional development for teachers, school staff and communities. Workshops outlined the policy and demonstrated how to incorporate

---

[2] While within the data there is evidence of the EE Policy being unstable, it now appears that the EE Policy retains its importance. An updated version (2020) with the same 2001 references to EECs is still available from the NSW Department of Education's policy library. An observation over the course of this study is that access to documentation within the Department can be variable. Interestingly the policy is now only available to NSW Department of Education employees while the implementation document remains available for the public.

resource management within learning and generally how to incorporate holistic learning within a school (personal experience).

The EECs and zoos were supporting, and supported within, the documentation. They played (and play) an important role in supporting teachers and principals to meet policy requirements. They were listed in the section on learning opportunities outside school, and the document Foreword acknowledged their role.

> In 1999, field studies centres were renamed environmental education centres (EECs) to reflect the broader role that environmental education is now playing in schools. Zoo education centres and environmental education centres in NSW are effective in demonstrating ecologically sustainable development to students. This is vital to the development of environmentally aware and responsible citizens who will advocate for the environment in the future. (NSW Department of Education and Training, 2001a)

With the rollout of the *EE policy* including a substantial sustainability component, EEC educators had become more actively involved in delivering ESE in their local schools.

> They went into the school and said, "Okay, well this is what you can do here. Have you thought about doing that?" and so on. So, it was a practical exercise—rather than just saying, "Here's a policy. Go for it."—And in the early days in curriculum that's what they did. XB

There was recognition of EEC staff as leaders in their field.[3] Their advice and services were sought when the NSW Department of Education and Training and the Australian Government were implementing ESE initiatives. EECs supported global/national environmental movements that were reflected in their programs. EEC personnel working within schools on ESE was a significant shift. There was diversification.

> But with the environmental education policy for schools it gave us that imperative to start to provide something to support schools as they try to develop environmental management plans and try to integrate environmental education with their other curriculum areas.... The best way for people to learn these things—well I actually think engaging kids in doing... and that was part of the environmental education policy that kids were actually acting in some way for sustainability for the environment.... But we rode the coattails of the environmental education policy and... that was very strong in the early part of this century. QA

Initially, EEC personnel were worried that the EE component would be lost within the new sustainability focus on schools, but this did not occur. "And I think there was probably a little core of people that... were getting a bit edgy that, 'Hang on. Yes, this is all important but let's not forget the main game.'" EB

Rather, the EECs became more important in providing all aspects of ESE to schools.

> When the Environment Education Policy came out there was a lot of discussion with the EECs prior to that coming out in the sense that some perceived that it excluded the EECs

---

[3] This had happened on numerous occasions before but seemed broader and more wide-ranging with the extensive policy rollout, the increase in the number of centres, and the greater exposure within school grounds—student and teacher place-based education.

from part of the delivery or support of the Environmentally Education Policy to schools and teachers. Over time it's been shown that that isn't the case and in fact the EECs provide for schools possibly the most important professional learning base and services and environmental education programs to schools. So whilst the EE Policy 2001 focused [on] work that was going on within the school, the EECs have maintained a critical role in supporting schools and teachers in implementing that policy. VB

The NSW Department of Education and Training, through its regional operations, was supportive of ESE in a holistic context.

We had a period there through the late 90s and the early 21st century when in each of the regions, one of the school education directors had an environmental education responsibility as part of their portfolio. So, they would have meetings and they would… well often it wouldn't be them but they'd put together a team of teachers and us, who would be producing something for the region… and there would be regional events and regional efforts to try and do something around the area… the education for sustainability concepts. So, that was the high-water mark. QA

In addition to the national and state councils and networks, Smith and his contemporaries had formed a NSW Department of Education and Training Environmental Management Committee at a Head Office level. It was designed to coordinate operations across directorates. People who managed infrastructure, school sites, maintenance, buildings and equipment, asset management and accounts, in addition to people from the Curriculum Directorate and the Officer for Environment Management, all were involved. All were crucial in sustainability initiatives—systems thinking was an essential element.[4]

## 9.5 Educating for Sustainability Initiatives

Dovetailing with the *NSW EE policy* implementation was the Australian Sustainable Schools Initiative (AuSSI) and Sustainable Schools NSW, evidence of what is achievable when the necessary support structures are in place.

There was a network of professionals across different government departments. Department of Environment, Sydney Water, Land and Water, whatever, and they formed a fantastic team who met regularly… So the Sustainable Schools Program came out of a team of people such as that… Geoff Young was at the Department of Environment, Syd was at DET, they developed the idea for the Sustainable Schools Pilot Program. They wrote the submission, got the funding, got national funding for it. Those people were part of the National Environmental Ed Network—NEEN. So we had the state government level network, and then they fed into a national network with similar people from all over the country. XC

AuSSI began in 2003 as a pilot in NSW and Victoria funded by the Australian Government. The initiative was a holistic learning program revolving around the

---

[4] Apparently, this inspirational structure of a committee was later to be seen by the Director of Curriculum as being overreach, going beyond the role of educators, and getting involved in the actual physical and financial management of the Department of Education and Training.

implementation of efficiency strategies in relation to the management of school resources including water, electricity, waste materials and biodiversity. Measureable environmental, economic, social and curriculum outcomes were intrinsic to the program as was the involvement of the whole school community (ARTD Consultants, 2010; Funnell & Larri, 2005). Launched nationally in 2004, this integrated approach was a partnership between the Australian Government, State and Territory governments, and the Catholic and Independent Schools sectors (ARTD Consultants, 2010). In 2005, the Federal Government committed $2 million over 4 years to the AuSSI program with over 600 schools involved (Campbell & Nelson, 2005).[5]

The Sustainable Schools NSW Program was developed in 2002 (NSW Department of Environment & Heritage, 2014) and the NSW AuSSI pilot program was implemented in 2003. It involved 200 primary and secondary schools supported by 20 casual teachers (NSW Department of Education and Training, 2003). It was a joint venture between the NSW Departments of Environment and Conservation, and Education and Training and the Commonwealth Department of the Environment and Heritage. Developed to lead to more environmentally sustainable behaviour among students, teachers and community while enhancing the school environment and reducing resource use, the program involved developing School Environmental Management Plans through student-led auditing of resources.

Sustainable Schools Support Teams, generally supported by EECs, were at the centre of the program support structure. Over 1500 schools (2000 people) from both the public and private sector have been involved in some way. They had either registered on the Sustainable Schools NSW website, participated in professional development, or developed a School Environmental Management Plan (Australian Education for Sustainability Alliance, 2014, p. 52).

Another example of ESE programs and professional development offered throughout the 1990s and 2000s was the "Learnscapes" initiative where learning programs are planned around the school landscapes and designed to maximise student interaction and learning within the environment—meeting syllabi and EE outcomes (Skamp & Bergmann, 2001). The same concept was developed in England by Eileen Adams in the early 1990s (Learning Through Landscapes, n.d.). In NSW professional development courses were set up by Smith in 1997 (Tribe, 1997). Helen Tyas Tungaal, the teacher who developed "Learnscapes," with a team of environmental educators in NSW (Tyas Tungaal, 1999), also produced a "Hands On Learnscapes" package in 1996. The organisation "Hands On Learnscapes" Incorporated was established, and upon successfully securing Environmental Trust Grants, it established the School Learnscapes Trust. The Trust provided consultancy services for pilot projects funded by the NSW Department of Education and Training. Other schools could access consultancy on a fee-for-service basis (Tyas Tungaal, 1999). There was a long relationship between "Learnscapes" and the NSW

---

[5] Note, this reference is text from a letter to the school community signed by Campbell and Nelson, Federal Minsters for the Environment and Heritage, and Education, Science and Technology, respectively. It was released with Educating for a Sustainable Future: A National Environmental Education Statement for Australian Schools in 2005.

Department of Education and Training with "Learnscapes" being included in Departmental documentation such as the *EE policy* and implementation document, and the Sustainable Schools NSW program.

While the NSW Department of Education and Training was initially happy to support such an innovative EE initiative, later on it had to dissociate from "Learnscapes" as it could not be seen to be supporting a private company. In 2005, the NSW Department of Education and Training produced a document titled *Landscape Management in NSW Schools* (2005) which relates to management strategies to reduce the cost of landscape maintenance and to improve school grounds. Nevertheless, it is linked to the *EE policy* and contains case studies of landscaping linked to learning.

> So that was another really big thing. And there was a lot of funding went out and we went out to some schools on the Central Coast and try to help them implement this Learnscapes which is basically developing your grounds for sustainability education, but getting the kids to really think holistically… like the whole school community not just the kids, the school community… all the teachers. So that was a big thing and I remember spending a lot of time doing that and working with three schools on the Central Coast to implement those. PB

"Learnscapes" was a significant program in the life of ESE within NSW and some of the FSC/EECs. It is also indicative of the shift from a welfare state to private managerialism, where people supplying resources and services are reliant on charging a fee for services within an environment of diminished public funds.[6]

## 9.6 United Nations (UN) Decade & Australia's Environmental Education

The 2005 statement, *Educating for a Sustainable Future*: *A National Environmental Education Statement for Australian Schools* gave a national focus to ecological sustainability in schools (Australian Government Department of Environment and Heritage, 2005). Developed in collaboration with all sectors, it added support for developing a systematic approach. Significantly, it was the first national document promoting a national approach to EE to be endorsed by the Ministerial Council on Education, Employment, Training and Youth Affairs (Campbell & Nelson, 2005).[7] The statement references both "ecological sustainability" and "environmental education for sustainability"—putting the environment back into sustainability. The contribution of EE is acknowledged within this document as are the components of critical, holistic, creative thinking, action, and the interconnectedness of the

---

[6] Is this due to lack of funds or waning of popularity or favour with funding bodies?

[7] It should be noted that the Commonwealth Department of Education was apprehensive about being involved "They would not come to NEEC. They would not be part of that. They would be pulled kicking and screaming." It was the partnership of Peter Woods and Greg Manning in these Federal departments that got the Statement established. "But again, led by the Environment Department." (ZZ)

ecological, social, political and economic systems. Written by Annette Gough and Brian Sharpley, this document gives a framework for EE for sustainability from K-12 to be utilised in conjunction with existing state and territory documentation. This systemic intent connects the United Nations Educational, Scientific and Cultural Organisation (UNESCO) Decade of Education for Sustainable Development [2005–2014] (UNESCO, 2005) to those on the ground working on ESE within schools.[8] A whole-school approach, including resource management and the AuSSI, is elaborated upon. Experiential, inquiry-based learning, values clarification and analysis pedagogies are among the important strategies outlined (Australian Government Department of Environment and Heritage, 2005). Smith was on the Statement Project Steering Committee representing NSW.

There was Federal funding available for ESE through provision for professional learning and environmental science-related innovations in schools. Grants were available through both the Australian Government Quality Teaching Program, and the Australian School Innovation in Science Technology and Mathematics Project (Campbell & Nelson, 2005). The funding for the former was not specific to ESE but was available to it.

## 9.7 Moves Toward a National Curriculum and Federal Funding Support

After the Federal election in 2007, The Labor Party formed the majority of Federal and state governments and there was a concerted push for a national alignment within education (Mockler, 2018). In 2008, the Australian Curriculum Assessment and Reporting Authority (ACARA), an independent statutory authority, was established through an Act of Parliament after agreement between the Federal, state and territory governments (Hughes, 2018).

---

[8] Other outcomes influenced by the UN Decade of Sustainable Development include: Caring for our future: The Australian Government Strategy for the United Nations Decade of Education for Sustainable Development, 2005–2014—released in 2007. There was also the Business Roundtable for Sustainable Development and the Australian Research Institute in Education for Sustainability (ARIES). ARIES have produced significant sustainability documentation such as A National Review of Environmental Education and its Contribution to Sustainability in Australia (Tilbury et al., 2005), Whole School Approaches to Sustainability: A Review of Models for Professional Development in Pre-service Teacher Education (Ferreira et al., 2006), Mainstreaming Sustainability into Pre-service Teacher Education in Australia (Ferreira et al., 2009), and Mainstreaming Education for Sustainability in Pre-service Teacher Education in Australia: Enablers and Constraints (Steele, 2010). The 2007 Strategy for the UN Decade of Education of Sustainable Development outlined the National Environmental Education Statement for Australian Schools, the Australian Sustainable Schools Initiative, and the National Goals for Schooling and National Statements of Learning as drivers for Ecological Sustainable Development in formal schooling (Australian Government: Department of the Environment and Heritage, 2007).

## 9.7 Moves Toward a National Curriculum and Federal Funding Support

In 2008 the national overarching education statement, the *Melbourne Declaration for Educational Goals for Young People*,[9] expanded the reference to ESE, calling for active and informed citizens who "work for the common good, in particular sustaining and improving natural and social environments" (MCEETYA, 2008, p. 9). It directed environmental sustainability to be integrated across the curriculum—"a focus on environmental sustainability will be integrated across the curriculum and all students will have the opportunity to access Indigenous content where relevant" (MCEETYA, 2008, p. 14).[10]

At the same time that support within the NSW Department of Education and Training was waning, grants were still available through the Australian School Innovation in Science Technology and Mathematics Project. In 2007 the Federal Government gave EECs $50,000 to support Sustainable Schools NSW AuSSI activities, specifically to support the Sustainable Schools NSW website. In 2008 professional development supporting 440 teachers was funded by the NSW Department of Climate Change. In 2009 similar funds sustained the training of 280 teachers. This support structure, and these programs and funding, kept EECs busy given they were generally the nexus on which these programs were built.

> And also, at the time, as well, it lined up with other things that were happening in other sectors of state government. I think we had two successive three-year plans. Strategic state government plans for sustainability education… So schools were one player, and that for businesses, industry and government sectors—there were benchmarks being set. But, not only was it a plan, there was money being put to it. So this policy came out of a time when there was significant momentum for sustainability education, there were strategic plans across all government, at all levels of government, for implementation across society. And money to back it up. RA

With significant funding from other sources, the EE Unit was in a position to employ staff to assist with various projects. Butler employed Caddey as the Senior Education Officer/Coordinator in charge of Sustainable Schools in 2005. Caddey became the acting EE coordinator, and then took on the sustainability policy advisor role (2005–2014). Caddey provided policy and implementation resources, support and advice. He played a fundamental role in coordinating EEC conferences and communication. Along with the many principals who were very active, politically astute and excellent pedagogues, there was work on enhancing the centres' role and function within the NSW education system. The EEC conference, held earlier in the year with guest speakers and the principals' conference or meetings where strategic planning was central, were important forums for ESE and centre development. The Commonwealth Government funded these for many years through the EE Unit.

---

[9] Note the Melbourne Declaration for Education Goals for Young People was succeeded by the Alice Springs (Mparntwe) Education Declaration in December 2019.

[10] The "access Indigenous content where relevant" wording in this quote is included as within the Australian Curriculum First Nations content is a cross-curricular priority alongside ESE and there are strong synergistic links between these subjects.

## 9.8 EECs and Technology

Each centre has found its own equilibrium when it comes to the use of technology. While experiencing the environment is paramount—the "in" the environment being important, EECs utilise technology in many diverse and innovative ways. Generally, technology is put to good use in managing, communicating and networking. Used for promotion, booking and coordination, it also effectively supports the teaching programs providing the facilities for pre and post visit work and resources. Technological support has changed significantly over the years. One of the earlier teachers-in-charge remembers. "In the 70 s we used to sit out and do... little fact sheets using a Gestetner and a typewriter and then mail those out to the schools that were coming, or just ring them" (FA).

Many centre staff, although acknowledging the possibilities of technology enhancing the outdoor experience if used smartly, are wary of technology compromising the experience of connecting to the environment, outdoors. However, there are some great uses of technology in centres.

For example, at Gibberagong (see Fig. 9.1 for a contemporary photo of Gibberagong's Muogamarra site). they were intending to put cameras on a native beehive with a counter and sensors for temperature, rain and humidity. In the past

**Fig. 9.1** View over valley, Muogamarra Field Studies Centre I 50 Years of Environmental Education Celebrations, August 2022

they would have been reliant on a few snapshots of data. This was an opportunity to take the centre to schools—another way of reaching a larger audience with engaging learning. Another idea was the use of remote sensors in different habitats for real time long-term experiments, adding greatly to the learning experience. The equipment needed weatherproofing and to be cost effective before it could be used extensively by centres, but this no doubt will happen or has happened. Wise technology use can increase the audience and enhance student engagement and learning. The Field of Mars EEC was frequently mentioned as leading the way in utilising technology to great advantage.

## 9.9 Assessing EEC Effectiveness in ESE Programs

Some of the ESE funded programs of the 2000s, were evaluated throughout the decade. A review of the NSW Sustainable Schools Program (Funnell & Larri, 2005) indicated that the EECs played an integral role in the program.

> Environmental Education Centres were a source of support to SSSTs [sustainable schools support teams] during the pilot of the SSP and given appropriate roles and professional development may well become an ongoing source of support to schools in relation to the types of activities that have been undertaken thus far by SSSTs. (Funnell & Larri, 2005, p. 30)

Most of the Sustainable Schools Support Teams were based in EECs. Similarly, the School Climate Change Initiative (2007–2009) was based on learning communities where the EEC input was integral to the success of the individual initiatives (Ladwig et al., 2010). Of interest is the reluctance of the NSW Department of Education to utilise these evaluations to their full potential. Neither the NSW Sustainable School Initiative Evaluation nor the full evaluation for the School Climate Change Initiative have been made public by the NSW Department of Education.

## 9.10 EEC Networks: Consolidation and Growth

Within the centres, the Primary Principals' Association State Council was used by the Environmental and Zoo Education Centre (EZEC) Network to promote themselves. "You've still got to promote that good work because if it goes unnoticed by those that make big decisions it is all for nothing" (SA).

Principals like Foott and Miller had kept the centres in the forefront for many years but things were waning in the mid to late 2000s. Foott had applied for observer status within the Association—it had supported him in his quest for principal status. Foott was apparently a hard act to follow.

In addition to ESE promotion, the State Council enabled EEC consideration in Council policies. It was/is a good platform to keep cognisant of educational issues in NSW. A platform to keep informed about issues that are making it more difficult for principals to consider ESE.

The mission to look at improving the effectiveness of the EECs to deliver high-quality learning programs aligned to the *EE Policy* for the students and teachers that visited the centres continued. Additionally, high quality professional development for teachers needing support in the implementation of the *EE Policy* in their schools and classroom programs was scrutinised. There was an exploration of ways to support pre-service teaching with resulting relationships formed with Macquarie, New England and Sydney Universities. With in-service teaching, the Melbourne Declaration, and with the Australian Curriculum on the horizon, there was an opportunity to embed the service and the programs that the EECs provide to teachers individually and to schools more broadly.

## 9.11 The Earth Citizen and Curriculum Framework

The next iteration of the NSW learning for sustainability plan, *The NSW Environmental Education Plan Learning for Sustainability 2007–2010*, created an action that gave rise to the development of a conceptual framework—*Earth Citizenship: A Conceptual Framework for Learning for Sustainability* (NSW Department of Education and Training, 2009). Simultaneously, NSW managed one of the projects that emerged from the National Environmental Education Network which looked at where the different states and territories were in terms of EE policy, programs, teacher professional learning, and where they were in terms of the progress, structure and implementation of their sustainable school programs. NSW reviewed EE approaches and frameworks nationally and globally (Skamp, 2009). This led to the NSW Department of Education and Training developing a draft Earth Citizen document. At that point in time, NSW was the only jurisdiction to have an EE policy that specifically mentioned sustainability in the broad sense. Other jurisdictions talked about EE as an integrated part of their learning but often just related to science and geography. "So New South Wales and to a certain extent Victoria… led the way with their Sustainable Schools programs as a way of introducing sustainability to teachers" (VB).

Butler, with a background in curriculum development, saw a place for developing a curriculum framework to support ESE in what had been a piecemeal, silo curriculum arrangement that made integration across the syllabi difficult. The Board of Studies was ostensibly developing an integrated holistic approach to ESE, but in fact were not actively producing anything substantial as required by the Department of Environment *Learning for Sustainability* plan (Environment Australia, 2000; NSW Council on Environmental Education, 2002). A few people had attempted to set ESE curriculum standards, Kim Walker and Helen Sharp (n.d.), for instance. Yet nothing had gained traction or been set as a foundation by the mid to late 2000s although the national statement (2005) provided guidance. Furthermore, development of a framework was supported by the national and state plans, the *Adelaide*

## 9.11 The Earth Citizen and Curriculum Framework

*Declaration*, and later the *Melbourne Declaration* and the Sustainability Statement—all backed by the overarching UN Decade for Education for Sustainable Development. For EECs, the development of an ESE curriculum is important given they are constrained by the syllabus in some respects.

> While it's really, really valuable to have that discipline base, you've got to have opportunities for students to integrate across, otherwise they never join the dots… now if we wanted to truly support environmental ed centres to perform the function they should be performing, we would have to reform the bigger picture in which they exist. XC

While it was the Board of Studies responsibility to develop curriculum and the Curriculum Directorate's position to implement it, the EE Unit went about developing a framework by leveraging the involvement of one of the architects of the Quality Teaching Framework, Associate Professor James Ladwig. The Quality Teaching Framework, incorporated into Departmental practice, was very favourable at the time. The Directorate supported and contributed to the funding of the Earth Citizen project. While this document remained a draft in October 2009, it was an instrumental document. Other funders included the NSW Environmental Trust, the NSW Department of Environment, Climate Change and Water, and the Australian Government Department of Environment, Water, Heritage and the Arts. The document placed the necessary components of being a citizen for the earth and learning for sustainability within four encompassing circles: wellbeing, citizenship, practice and knowledge. Wellbeing nested within being a change agent, biosphere custodian and global citizen. This then nested within systems seeking and testing, world viewing and valuing, and futures thinking and designing. This in turn nested within ecological systems and processes, and social systems and technologies (NSW Department of Education and Training, 2009). An essential aspect of the framework was the "repertoires of practice" necessary within the "systems seeking" and "world and futures thinking" in order for them to be adopted and adapted and become a reality in people's lives.

The development of this document was a broad collaboration with a host of academic advisors, including Ladwig, Nicole Mockler, and curriculum consultants. Once more, the EEC/Zoo personnel played a significant role in development. They were involved in workshopping the framework—devoting a whole conference to working on the concept. Butler wrote the document with other Project team members from the NSW Department of Education and Training's EE Unit.

With a diversity of views about ESE within the centres, the development of the Earth Citizen document was seen from different perspectives. In addition to the problems of defining sustainability, some found the development overly anthropocentric. However, for some it fitted into its time and space and was seen as the way to shift or move ESE into the future. "They were talking about a very anthropocentric view, sustainability, not an ecocentric view. The view on sustainability really wasn't what I'd call sustainability. It was just about sustaining people on the planet, not all living things" (AA).

> But the thing that I still use now, that I'm trying to keep alive, is that curriculum document that talks to Earth Citizens and talks to understanding exactly what we need to have as far

as our students' journeys are concerned from K-12. And that was a real privilege to be involved in that thinking… And I still use that now most weeks… to inspire and to encourage and to show how we package up learning journey from kindergarten kids and how it is different, right up to our Year 12 cohorts and we're doing stuff with universities now as well and that fits in…. I guess the perspective I hold onto from that significant event is just to understand what "future thinking" means, what "systems thinking," means and "world viewers," means… from a perspective of custodians of conservation. VA

The Earth Citizen document was important because, even though it did not make it to a final version, it was a significant input into the national framework published the following year.

This eventually developed into a project to write the Sustainability Curriculum Framework for the Australian Government. So in the lead up to the publication of that framework there was extensive consultation within the National Environmental Education Network; a review of the NSW policy, the policy settings in various states and territories… and the situation that was happening with pre and in-service teaching. VB

The Australian Government Department of Environment, Water, Heritage and the Arts published *The Sustainability Curriculum Framework: A guide for Curriculum Developers and Policy Makers* in 2010. Its frame is similar to that of the Earth Citizen document. Certainly, Butler, Ladwig and Mockler developed the *Earth Citizen* and the *Sustainability Curriculum Framework,* together with an unpublished assessment document, to address sustainability pedagogy, curriculum and assessment needs (J.G. Ladwig, pers. comm., July 26, 2019). The published curriculum framework is depicted by an image of the world globe wrapped in a flowing cloth of sustainability action process, trailing off into a two-pronged tail, similar to a Siamese fighting fish tail. It captures the essence of the framework. The centrality of the globe expresses the significance of the action process. One section of the tail contains the ecological and human knowledge systems while the other comprises the systems thinking, world viewing and future and design thinking with the all-important "repertoires of practice" (see Fig. 9.2).

Incidentally, Skamp (2009) stated in his detailed critical review of international best practice and research evidence regarding the implementation of ESE within primary and secondary education which nourished the Earth Citizen document:

Learning outside the classroom is an imperative in an EfS curriculum framework. It also reinforces the role of EE Centres provided their focus moves with the changing emphases in EfS, for example, to ecological foot printing and links with communities in addressing local environmental issues. Curriculum developers must ensure learning outside the classroom is integral to a curriculum framework. (Skamp, 2009, p. 61)

The *Sustainability Curriculum Framework* (Commonwealth Department of the Environment, Water, Heritage & Arts, 2010) was timely for the development of the Australian Curriculum. It outlines sustainability outcomes for students at the end of Year 2, 6 and 10 within the three organisers; sustainability action process, knowledge of ecological and human systems, repertoires of practice with systems thinking, and world and futures thinking. The Sustainability Curriculum priority organising ideas within the Australian Curriculum are based upon the Sustainability Curriculum Framework organisers, and these organising ideas filter through the

**Fig. 9.2** The Sustainability Curriculum Framework Visual mnemonic. Sustainability Curriculum Framework: A guide for curriculum developers and policy makers (Australian Department of the Environment Water Heritage & the Arts, 2010). (Attribution: The Australian Department of the Environment Water Heritage & the Arts, now the Department of Climate Change, Energy, the Environment and Water. CC BY 4.0. https://creativecommons.org/licenses/by/4.0/)

content descriptions and elaborations of the Australian Curriculum into the NSW syllabuses' outcomes and content (or they are supposed to).

> So the Sustainability Curriculum Framework in the lead up to the development of the Australian Curriculum with sustainability as cross-curriculum area… We have actually reset I suppose some of the language of teachers and I suppose set a higher level of expectation of what students should be learning about and thinking about in relation to sustainability at those milestones, early primary, end of primary and end of secondary. VB

## 9.12 The Australian Curriculum

Unfortunately, and disappointingly, the desired holistic national curriculum was not to be. There is little evidence of consideration of the Framework in the development of the Australian Curriculum (Gough, 2011) with the stronghold of the major curriculum disciplines maintained. Even though sustainability was to be one of the three cross-curricular priorities, the science, mathematics, English and history curricula were developed before thought went into the concept of a holistic curriculum, which disadvantaged ESE from the genesis.

> The structure that existed when the Board of Studies was formed in the early 90s or the late 80s, that structure has won. It's kept its influence because the syllabus committees were formed around the subject disciplines. The CEOs, the heads of teams in the Board of Studies were heads of teams of disciplines. It was all set up so there could be no other outcome. Like there was not a team of curriculum hand grenade throwers that had influence in the meetings. So the idea of having a multidisciplinary approach was made impossible by the institutional setup of the Board of Studies and by the institutional set up of the national body, made even worse by the fact that Gillard took four subjects alone and had them

written up, which prevented a holistic or integrated approach. So the outcome is what you'd expect. You can't develop curriculum that way if you want something… So when they talk about skills for the 21st century, we developed documents based on skills of the 19th century. XC

The rationale for the Australian Curriculum for Science K-10 shifted from a focus on contemporary science, including climate change, adaptation, biodiversity and ecological sustainability, to a focus on a scientific literacy that does not include these elements (Gough, 2011). Environmental science was not listed within the science understanding strand in the *Curriculum Statement* while the traditional science subjects were—even though Earth and Environmental Science is a Year 11 and 12 Australian Curriculum course. There were also questionable associations foreseen as being difficult for the necessary cross-curricular connection in the "Science Understanding" and "Science as Human Endeavour" components of the traditional sciences. There was little connection within the mathematics curriculum, and minimal reference in history to how humans use the environment—and no broadening to human impact and shaping on the environment and vice versa (Gough, 2011). Furthermore, it is argued that without the content descriptors, elaborators, and assessment standards of the established learning areas, it is difficult for sustainability to be a priority (Hill & Dyment, 2016). Indeed, the content and skills within the sustainability cross-curricular priority were viewed as implicit and lacking (Prescott, 2016).

> So what we find is because of the holistic nature of the biosphere almost any environmental education topic or project is going to be radical, it's going to annoy vested interests massively, and it's going to be seen as a wound in the side of some developer, some industrialist, or whatever, okay. And that is the nature of it. So it's inherently problematic for education and yet it has to be done. So it means that until this way of thinking somehow becomes some part of the hegemony it's going to be fighting to get a foot in the door. And yet kids do understand it. So it's inherently political and it is going to annoy the shit out of vested interests. It is part of the problematic of the whole thing. We know there are people who play the game for the environment very, very well, they're diplomats, they're marketers, they're optimists. They can take people along with them. There's a whole bunch of skills there that we want everyone to develop so they don't feel that every issue has to be dealt with by marching with a placard down the street… If you can't see it, you can't counter it. You've got to be aware that it's happening. XC

The effectiveness of the Australian Curriculum's cross-curricular priority of "sustainability" is reminiscent of the effectiveness of the *EE Curriculum Statement* and Policy. While sustainability is now, often implicitly, within the curriculum there is still no accountability of outcomes.

> Now we've got accountabilities for teachers to implement the Australian curriculum and yet I think I'm seeing the same pattern emerge where the sustainability cross-curriculum priority, because it isn't a feature of every learning area and there would be some teachers who are not doing it well and so now there are some schools who aren't implementing the Environment Education Policy or the sustainability cross-curriculum priority. VB

## 9.13 A Broadening of the National Approach

In 2009 a new National Action Plan had been developed in conjunction with the non-statutory National Council on Education for Sustainability [ex-National EE Council] (Commonwealth Department of the Environment Water Heritage and the Arts, 2009). This plan was much broader in focus with the following strategies: demonstrating Australian Government leadership, reorienting education systems to sustainability, fostering sustainability in business and industry, and harnessing community spirit to act. Sustainability within university courses and through a whole of university approach had a strong focus within this document, which was another Australian support for the UN Decade of Education for Sustainable Development—at the halfway point. Once more, educating for ecological sustainability or ESE are not touched on. The environment takes its place with "social," "political," and "economic" imperatives. However, biodiversity and ecological integrity is conserved with appropriate valuing, appreciating and restoring within this documentation.

There were significant developments in early childhood education with the production of the National Quality Framework for Early Childhood Education, *Belonging, Being and Becoming: The Early Years Learning Framework for Australia* in 2009 (Council of Australian Governments & the Department of Education, Employment & Workplace Relations, 2009 cited in Gough, 2011). The learning framework included communicated connecting and contributing to the world in addition to being socially responsible and respectful of the environment. Implementation has foundational significance for ESE.

## 9.14 Declining Support

Sustainable Schools NSW received funding from the NSW Office of Environment and Heritage until 2017, and the program was managed by the AAEE NSW Chapter when it lost its funding (AAEE, 2019).[11] An evaluation of the AuSSI published in 2010 found that overall there had been substantial progress made toward the achievement of AuSSI goals. One of the findings was that resources, such as EECs, provided a focus and resource for ESE professional development and school activities. One third of schools had registered with the program (3000). Even though recommendations included the continuation of the program, by 2011 AuSSI had ended and the National Government was failing to provide adequate support (Garg, 2017). AuSSI program documentation shows that funding bodies expected the program to be self-sustaining after a certain time and resource allocation.

---

[11] The program had received a small amount of funding to caretake the program but it is not known if this is continuing.

## 9.14.1 Change of Management Within the NSW EE Unit: Decrease in Authority

Smith, Chief Education Officer (CEO), retired in 2004 and Kevin Butler became the EE Manager. It was a significantly less authoritative position than that of CEO. His job description was to provide strategic advice and leadership, and to manage operational support for schools and regions in developing, implementing and evaluating projects in the support and implementation of EE within schools. In addition to the downgrading of the position, contract positions replaced ongoing positions.

> I think when Syd Smith retired, that was a significant event.... He was exceptionally senior and as a consequence of that he was able to do things and get money for centres. He had a lot of influence... The thing about Syd Smith's position is that it was a full-time position. After that they became contract positions. So that meant that then Kevin's position went and then it was left to the other two education officer roles which were Vicki and Mark and that became just one position and then eventually that became no positions. VC
>
> And it was very clear that a number of feathers had been ruffled by the wonderful Syd Smith. XC

When Butler took over the management of the EE Unit there was a lot of money in projects but none to spare for the centres. However, Butler did take Syd's place in representing the NSW Department of Education and Training on the state and national level networks.

Within schools, unfortunately, the *EE Policy for Schools* lost its incentive and was no longer a strong document as there was a pullback in terms of Departmental and school commitment. School Environmental Management Plans were generally included in the school management plans of schools that were successful in implementing ESE, yet this was rare (Ladwig et al., 2010). There was a broad range of schools completing School Environmental Management Plans; some successfully integrating whole school or cross-curricular ESE, some just ticking the boxes, and many not completing this work at all. In hindsight, as with the *EE Curriculum Statement*, there was disappointment at the eventual loss of effectiveness of the *EE Policy*. The lack of accountability for the implementation of the policy was seen as the issue.

> a couple of years after it was implemented, I kind of looked at it and thought well there is no reporting function and nobody is actually identified as having responsibility for checking that this is being done. If anything I think that that is one of the downfalls of that policy. And that's a critical point, it's just in hindsight that would be one of the things that should have been addressed. VB

## 9.15 Waxing and Waning of ESE Favour

At a state level, the NSW EE Council was disbanded about the time that Frank Sartor became Minister for the Department of Environment, Climate Change and Water, (circa 2008). Apparently, it was not a high priority. The Government had no clear ESE agenda (EA).

> From a New South Wales perspective, about 10 years ago a Labor Environment Minister, Frank Sartor, really did a disservice to the environment. He didn't reinstate or establish or re-establish the NSW Council on Environmental Education and so a whole policy area that had high level, whole of NSW government commitment, fell away completely and so the shift in that priority from the government position had a knock-on effect essentially. It is difficult to even try to estimate what impact that really had but I believe it has been far-reaching. VB

Within the centres, at times teaching certain topics has seemed politically fraught only to become *de rigueur* soon after… or vice versa. One time when EEC personnel had to keep their heads low was at a change in governance when climate change was definitely taken off the agenda and funding and favour fell away almost overnight. The following quote exemplifies the experience of an EEC during the change over from the Howard to Rudd era.

> Well, I mean, that was my thing that I was most proud of as an environmental education centre person. I ran three years running some climate change debates in our state parliament here and I managed to get groups from the great majority of high schools in this region. So, in the end we got about 60 odd schools in there and I equipped them to have debates around the whole issue of climate change and all the different elements of that. And they were government and opposition and they argued for and against. We did the whole political thing because I've got a strong bent in that way. I could see that the way things happen is by political means. I was skating on thin ice when I first ran this. But again, ups and downs. …John Howard was in, and he was still almost denying climate change and the region was very afraid of me going into state parliament and running a debate on it. I think they thought it would be in the news and negative for them. Within a year or two, Rudd was in and… Garnaut was producing his report and we were going to have a great and wonderful climate change policy. And we were just students doing the right thing. QA

At one stage there was significant Federal money supporting programs such as "Climate Clever" and the "School Climate Change Initiative."[12] They supported action, student-led participatory inquiry-based learning similar to the Sustainable Schools programs (Environmental Education NSW Chapter of AAEE, n.d). For some EECs, the apex was 2010 when the "Year of Sustainability" was celebrated in NSW schools. There was a principals' conference with a sustainability theme for the North Sydney Region, the tail end of the climate change project funding, and

---

[12] Climate Clever is another program piloted in around 2010. It now has an online program that it sells to schools for $8 per student (Climate Clever, n.d.). There were and are a plethora of ESE programs in schools. For instance, CarbonKids is a CSIRO initiative in partnership with the pharmaceutical company, Bayer, closely linked to AuSSI (Australian Education for Sustainability Alliance, 2014). Developments associated with the School Climate Change Initiative appear to have either faded into obscurity, are unavailable online, or have been rebadged.

significant activity within schools. Yet, for a few, some of the funded project work was viewed as unrealistic and ultimately disappointing.

> The reality was that the schools found it very, very difficult to find the time to do that. And if they didn't have support and very, very strong support from not only the school administration, the principal etc. they had to have very strong support from the school community....We got involved in some projects that there seemed to be all this support for and promises of funding and things, we'd go out to schools and then six month later there'd be a change of minister or sometimes a change of government and the thing would fall over. We've had a number of cases where things like climate change were on the agenda and there was a push for it. It was put into syllabuses and now it's been taken out again. It's very difficult to keep a focus going and especially… it's very frustrating sometimes that you put your heart and soul into something and then you get the rug pulled from under you. That Climate Change Learning Community was particularly… one that was fairly galling. WA

The ESE funding contracted in the early stages of the last decade (2010s). Additionally, with a change in government, "climate change" became a topic to be wary of teaching for fear of repercussions. Centres shifted back to their safe space—teaching fieldwork within the curriculum.

> There was a lot of fieldwork and supporting schools with sustainability but usually they were kind of the one-off activities from our end… Green Days, things like that that we were supporting. And then we started running professional learning on sustainability aspects. And there was a lot of money for it. There was a lot of push for it. And it almost fell away overnight when there was changes in government I felt… And then after that, it just… It wasn't good to have climate change in your name. There was just a change in… climate change became a bit of a word that you had to be careful using…and that was after a change in government. There is absolutely no doubt about it. And it became… sustainability became… It was a very tricky time and…, at centres we often had conversations about ensuring that we were still relevant in a way… I don't think it was a conscious move but a lot of centres… we kind of almost went back to fieldwork in a way, I felt. And supporting syllabus… there's been a trend for the centres to support curriculum and I think that was about making sure that we remained relevant. VC

To illustrate the waxing and waning of favour of ESE within NSW bureaucracies: the definitions of EE and education for sustainability (EfS) in the glossary of the NSW Department of Environment and Climate Change's guide to using research in sustainability programs (NSW Department of Environment and Climate Change, 2009) were quite progressive.

> **Education for Sustainability** Also known as EfS and sometimes referred to as "learning for sustainability", it involves people working together to: envision a sustainable future; critically think and reflect about the power, politics, structures and information flows in society that influence change; think systemically and broadly about issues; and work in cross-sectoral partnerships to achieve change.
> **Environmental Education** Any process or activity that assists the development of awareness, knowledge, attitudes and skills leading to environmentally responsible practices and behaviour and more sustainable societies. (NSW Department of Environment and Climate Change, 2009, p. 2)

In contrast, the NSW Office of Environment and Heritage and the NSW Environment Protection Authority *Sustainability Strategy 2015–2020—Sustainability Leadership: Let's Take Action Together* document does not mention education

(NSW Office of Environment and Heritage and Environment Protection Authority, 2015). It is interesting to note the absence of reports from NSW Office of Environment and Heritage website and the NSW Department of Education from time to time. For instance, in the course of my research (2010–2019), at one stage it was very difficult to locate information about the EECs and the NSW policy. Now they are easily accessible—or were (now they are again—a very streamlined and uniform presence). Additionally, there is now a sustainability section within the NSW Department of Education infrastructure section that is actioning sustainability education that may provide support. There has been a resurgence of interest in ESE since the completing of the case studies.

## 9.16 Rationalisation and Precarity in ESE/EECs

With contracting government support, the EE Unit kept diminishing, even when there was a supportive Director General like Michael Coutts-Trotter (2007–2011). As an anomaly outside the power structures of the institutionalised siloed curriculum, the EE Unit was an easy target for funding cuts. "And on education when there was any kind of review of the operations of Curriculum Directorate and accountability of Curriculum Directorate, and funding for Curriculum Directorate, then strictures were put on the Environmental Ed Unit" (XC).

Much of Butler's time was spent writing ministerial briefings and letters. Letters of complaint to the Minister relating to ESE support would land on Butler's or Caddey's desk for response. Butler retired in 2010 and Caddey took on the caretaking role of centres, yet again, in a less senior role. With the position in the EE Unit looking precarious, Caddey moved to the NSW Office of Environment and Heritage in 2014 where he supported EE within education where possible. The NSW Department of Education and Communities did not fill Caddey's position. For EECs it was the start of a few years in the wilderness.

> It was in a vacuum for a period of time and it was quite difficult to find anyone in the Department who was technically managing the policy area. Administratively they're managed by each of the directors of that local area, but no one has a policy leadership position at a Director level for the EECs and that's one of their main issues. So there is no director level person that can advocate on their behalf for these sorts of issues. VB

Centres had quite a bit of experience dealing with being within a bureaucracy amid considerable flux.

> And we've had to be very strategic in terms of promoting ourselves at times when we felt under threat. But a lot of other times you feel [the need] to keep your head down because… you can run things at your own pace, what you considered to be the important things without having to worry usually about these other things. Now that also depends upon who your SED is, your school education director… The strategic direction and the systemic support has changed so often. It is very hard to plan on where you're going when you don't know whether that unit is going to be there next year, whether they'll be funding for it… in terms of any staffing and support for EECs where do you go for it, who do you apply to? If a

centre has a really good program at the moment and a really good case for say grabbing a second or third teacher how do they do that? And what happens is that really… as I used to say at the time, "I'm sorry guys but you just have to bury your own dead." WA

Centres kept their heads down given the political climate—shifting back to fieldwork, their safe space.

To me policies change, some go in and out of favour over time and then the syllabus and all the rest changes as well. For us what we've tried to do regardless of whatever system is in place, and whatever curriculum's in place, and all the rest, is to find our niche and how we can actually interpret whatever policy and whatever syllabus exists to make it work in an outdoor setting. And I think in some cases… at the end is our core business. If we look at the syllabus and go, "No, there's nothing in there for us," there's a lot of danger there in terms of keeping us relevant and connected. I think part of the reason that we exist is because all the EECs have basically been able to maintain a really strong connection to syllabus. Because at the end we are teachers. All the environmental ed centres are actually classed as schools. And our job is to deliver a curriculum. We're just delivering it in the best possible classroom that exists. KB

It was not just the EE Unit within the Department that was contracting. EE officers within many organisations have disappeared or diminished in number over the years. The once strong Museum EE group seems to be non-existent.[13]

If we look at where the Department of Education previously had teachers in cultural institutions including the Art Gallery, the museum, all of those positions have disappeared over time and now those establishments are expected to provide their own education staff. Really the only relationship that exists with key government organisation are the Zoos—the Zoo Education Centres are really the only locations where that arrangement still exists. VB

### 9.16.1 Reflection of This Repressive Period with a National and Queensland Focus

During this period of policy disruption in the Australian ESE field, triggered by conservative governments coming into power, particularly in NSW (March 2011), Queensland (March 2012), and the Abbott national government (September 2013), a shift towards far-right neoliberalism occurred. These governments, marked by climate change denial or skepticism, instigated several consequential outcomes, as outlined by Smith and Stevenson (2017). These outcomes include the withdrawal of various policy documents from Australian government websites, AuSSI existing in name only since 2015 and being hosted on the website of an international non government organisation based in Croatia, the elimination of positions in central offices responsible for coordinating sustainability education in NSW and Queensland, and the disbandment of Queensland Sustainable Schools Initiative and Earth Smart Science programs in Queensland. Moreover, government departments were instructed not to use the term "climate change," and the state Liberal Party in

---

[13] These people may have been rescued within AAEE.

Queensland voted against teaching climate change in schools (Smith & Stevenson, 2017).

A policy brief from the UK National Commission for UNESCO in 2013 parallels this situation. It described a reduction in support for ESE after the election of a conservative government in the UK (Smith & Stevenson, 2017).

By 2013, with the adoption of the Queensland state-mandated curriculum (C2C) linked to the national curriculum and an increasing focus on high-stakes testing and workforce skills development, the impact on ESE work in Australia was profound. While sustainability remained one of three "cross-cutting priorities" within the national curriculum, its significance was overshadowed by literacy, numeracy, and subject-specific courses. The emphasis on raising student test scores and international competitiveness contributed to a significant decline in ESE efforts both in policy and practice. For example, a school in northern Queensland that was once acclaimed for its wetland and schoolyard habitat projects had, by the end of 2013, scaled back these initiatives due to pressures from an increasingly restrictive curriculum (Smith & Stevenson, 2017).[14]

### 9.16.2 Communities of Practice: EECs Aligning with Departmental Priorities

With declining systemic support and the developing Australian Curriculum feeding a cross-curricular priority into new NSW syllabi, focused learning communities or communities of practice were perceived as a way forward for EECs. Communities of practice play a significant role in addressing challenges in ESE, particularly in handling controversial topics within classrooms (Hong, 2020, as cited in Zint et al., 2024). Zint et al. (2024) highlight the importance of establishing such communities nationwide and integrating ESE into teacher education programs to provide real-world, solution-oriented learning experiences. The communities of practice concept, introduced by Lave and Wenger (1991) and expanded by Wenger (1998), suggests that educational research thrives on mutual engagement where members leverage collective competence for learning and problem-solving (Windsor & Kitooke, 2023). Wenger (1998) and Windsor and Kitooke (2023) describe communities of practice as networks where members engage in situated learning, relying on each other for support, feedback, and collaborative thinking. Such communities are crucial for effective learning transitions and understanding praxis (Kemmis & Smith, 2008; Windsor & Kitooke, 2023).

> In a proactive move, DeLandre, principal of the Illawarra EEC, secured National Partnership funding of $50,000 in about 2012 to start a leadership program and support a learning community. It was a move to establish a more cohesive and active community of practice across the Environmental and Zoo Education Centres (EZEC) Network. Michele McFarlane at

---

[14] Similar phenomena was experienced in NSW schools.

Red Hill EEC secured another $20,000 in 2015 to continue the work. DeLandre led the way in developing portfolio groups for the EZEC Network to improve performance in certain areas—aligned with the NSW Department of Education and Communities priorities. Certainly, the communities of practice are one of these: "We've never worked as cooperatively as we do now". (VC)

EZECs have often been in the vanguard of new initiatives be they pedagogies, policies, or Departmental strategic directions. They have often assisted with the rollout of policy and practice or testing of new equipment such as smartboards, Apple computers and connected classrooms. They undertake the same lessons, so often they can hone lessons faster than teachers in schools who may teach them once or at best a few times every year or two. The centres can be models of best practice when it comes to not only ESE but the active, experiential, and inquiry-based pedagogies that accompany it. They embrace many of the elements proven over the years to enhance learning (NSW Department of Education and Training Professional Learning and Leadership Development Directorate, 2008; RA; EB;—evidenced throughout many of the case study interviews).

## 9.17  UNESCO: Sustainable Development Goals

In 2015 the 70th session of the UN General Assembly adopted the *Sustainable Development Goals* (SDGs) after the Millennium Development Goals had not been experienced equally around the globe (Gibbs, 2015). The SDGs are to be achieved by 2030 (United Nations, 2019). They ambitiously include no poverty; zero hunger; good health and wellbeing; quality education; gender equity; clean water and sanitation; affordable and clean energy; decent work and economic growth; industry, innovation and infrastructure; reduced inequities; sustainable cities and communities; responsible consumption and production; climate action; life below water; life on land; peace, justice and strong institutions; and partnerships for the goals (see Fig. 9.3). However, EE and educating for an ecological sustainability seem to have been lost within an anthropocentric priority within the economic paradigm, reduced to a dot point in Target 4.7 together with a lot of other "adjectival educations" (Gough et al., 2024, p. 81).

It is noted that EE appears to be buried further and further under the rubble of the industrial neoliberal state of play (The Political Compass, 2019; UNESCO, 2019). Take Global Education: while the Global Perspectives framework connects with EE via the *Educating for a Sustainable Future: A National Environmental Education Statement for Australian Schools* (Australian Government Department of Environment and Heritage, 2005), the framework itself had "sustainable futures" as one of its five learning emphases (Australian Government: AusAID, 2011). The ecocentric connection seems a little lost and not so significant in the framing. This fading of ESE within global interests was acknowledged by Gough (2011), as was the inaccessibility of some of the important ESE documents on departmental websites from time to time. The anthropocentric dominance continues.

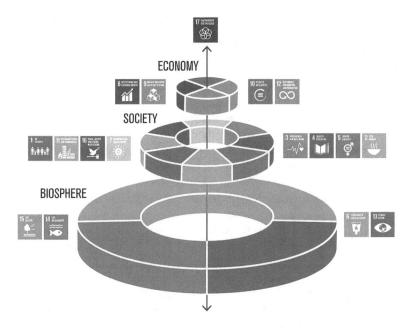

**Fig. 9.3** SDG_wedding_cake. (Attribution: Azote for Stockholm Resilience Centre, Stockholm University, CC BY 4.0. https://creativecommons.org/licenses/by/4.0, via Wikimedia Commons)

> Despite what appears to be the ever increasing diversity of WIIFM (What's in it for me?) supporters that includes some members of the more radical recreational groups of four-wheel drivers, motorcycle riders, prospectors, hunters and fishermen, they often seem to be using very similar words. We regularly hear: "We have a right to do as we please in our parks and we need to unlock these areas for all to use." It seems both state and federal governments agree with some of this rhetoric as we are witnessing the lowering of the protection standards across our park systems to accommodate some of their demands. (Lawrence, 2014, para. 5)

## 9.18 Who Cares About the Environment?

A measure of the people of NSW's environmental understanding, care for and behaviour toward their environment can be gleaned from the EPAs *Who Cares About the Environment?* triennial reports. The first report in 1994 produced a benchmark survey of the environmental knowledge, skills, attitudes and behaviours of the citizens of NSW (NSW Environmental Protection Agency, 1994). Findings were that people believed that a healthy environment and a prosperous economy were compatible, and the environment was an important issue. Unemployment was people's biggest concern but 10 years later, the environment was nominated as the biggest concern. By 2003 it was reported that the people of NSW had a more sophisticated environmental knowledge—identifying and discussing specific environmental issues in more detail. Fewer people were unsure or did not know about environmental issues (Department of Environment and Conservation [NSW], 2003).

In 2012 people continued to value their environment, making the most of outdoor spaces. They were less concerned about their environment but had "varied concerns about complex global environmental problems, influenced by the confusing nature of debate over these issues" (NSW Government: Office of Environment and Heritage, 2012, p. 2). Almost half thought there was not enough emphasis on natural habitat protection in relation to other land use needs and that mining and development environmental regulation was too lax.

The 2015 Report is the last publication to date with these reports now available as the "legacy Who Cares about the Environment survey" on the NSW Department of Planning and Environment website (NSW Government: Office of Environment and Heritage, 2019). Environmental issues disturbingly ranked sixth as a priority in 2015 and eighth as a projection for 10 years' time—transport, health, education, social issues and unemployment outranked them in 2015, and they were additionally outranked in the 10-year projection by planning and development, and the cost of living (NSW Government: Office of Environment and Heritage, 2015). A large proportion of people were concerned about environmental problems (73%) with over half of these being concerned for future generations.

## 9.19 ESE: Initiatives

One foray into EE politics is the Australian Education for Sustainability Alliance (AESA). It was established in 2012 with group members being the AAEE, the Australian Conservation Foundation, Australasian Campuses Towards Sustainability, the Australian Education Union, Australian Council of State School Organisations, the Australian Youth Climate Coalition, Catholic Earthcare Australia, the Environment Institute Australia and New Zealand, the Independent Education Union, the National Tertiary Education Union, and, the National Union of Students. AESA moved the agenda forward with research benchmarking where sustainability was within the Australian education system and providing resource support for teachers. Many of these politically active environmental and union groups see sustainability education as essential, and an alliance as a way forward to provide a powerful, safe, capacity building environment in times of austerity and a backlash against sustainability given the impact of public managerialism. With the change in Federal Government in 2013 to a decidedly, unapologetic climate change denying, pro-coal, leadership, AESA was a particularly insightful strategy.

In 2012 the Australian Conservation Foundation was contracted by the Australian Government Department of Education and Training on behalf of the AESA to "identify, verify, recommend and facilitate ways to improve the integration of ESE as a cross-curriculum priority across all subject areas under the Australian Curriculum" (AESA, 2014, p. 9). The final report, *Education for Sustainability and the Australian Curriculum Project* found that while 92% of teachers thought that sustainability was important and should be integrated into the curriculum, 80% of teachers did not comprehensively understand it. Of those that did understand it over half (54%) were not teaching it to a standard that meets ACARA guidelines (p. 14). The findings of the project included that ESE in active schools had been built on programs such as "Waterwatch" and experiences such as those of EECs and camps, and that the 25 environmental and zoo education centres provided professional learning in the form of workshops and ESE learning resources (AESSA, 2014, pp. 32 & 52). Other EECs, or similar centres around Australia, including those within the Queensland Department of Education, were also named as key providers or resources and support. Additionally: "There is also the implication that outdoor experiences, whether in the school grounds or at an EEC, need to be seen as "part of school learning"" (Skamp, 2009 cited in AESA, 2014, p. 35).

More recently, The BEATS (Biodiversity, Endangered and Threatened Species) organisation, in partnership with AAEE (NSW[15]), instigated "The State of Australian Sustainability Education" survey (The BEATS, n.d.). Although the current data set is relatively small and predominantly focused on sustainability-oriented teachers from NSW, the goal is to expand the survey's scope. Survey results from 2022 indicated a significant majority of teachers recognised the importance of teaching sustainability, yet only 32% felt they had sufficient professional learning opportunities. There was a noted gap in access to quality professional development materials and the survey highlighted that enhancing sustainability teaching practices would require stronger leadership at school, state, and federal levels. Additionally, time constraints and an overcrowded curriculum were identified as key barriers to effectively teaching sustainability (The BEATS, n.d.).

The NSW Chapter of AAEE has taken up the challenge of supporting the Sustainably Schools NSW Program and the NSW Regional Sustainability Education Networks (AAEE, 2019). In advancing communities of practice, AAEE NSW has developed a framework with significant input from international best practice and extensive stakeholder consultation. *Make the Change: A Framework for Education and Engagement for Sustainability 2014–2021* provided a "unified, coordinated and collaborative" approach to sustainability education in NSW (AAEE, 2015, p. 4). The project was in partnership with the NSW Office of Environment and Heritage.[16]

---

[15] The NSW Chapter of AAEE was rebadged as EE(NSW) in 2023.

[16] The Environment is no longer a standalone entity having merged with the Department of Planning, Industry and Environment in 2019.

## 9.20 Australian Curriculum: Further Compromise

Nationally, the release of the *Review of the Australian Curriculum* (Donnelly & Wiltshire, 2014) took place with significant consequences for the cross-curricular priorities (Hill & Dyment, 2016)—specifically for this study, the sustainability priority, although the First Nations priority is also of significance. Following the review ACARA proposed to reduce the amount of curriculum content—adding depth and reducing breadth. Additionally, and importantly for ESE, the cross-curricular priorities and general capabilities were to be simplified (Mockler, 2018). Added to this, the NSW Board of Studies Teaching Education Standards argued that the cross-curriculum perspectives and most of the general capabilities compromise subject discipline integrity: They do not approve of them as mandatory curriculum content and outcomes (Hughes, 2018).

Notably, for ESE, Donnelly and Wiltshire recommended a shift away from inquiry learning, significantly beneficial in ESE, back to explicit instruction (Stevenson et al., 2016). In addition to implementing this new curriculum and dealing with the conflicting directives and power play between state and federal governance, there were severe cutbacks to the resourcing of the Australian Curriculum transition. (Patty, 2017).

NSW and Victoria were reluctant to change their curricula in line with the Australian Curriculum as they thought their curricula were already robust (Hughes, 2018). By 2013, NSW was the only jurisdiction not in the process of implementing the Australian Curriculum. Board of Studies Teaching and Educational Standards NSW chose an "adopt and adapt" model whereby they adopted the new National Curriculum but adapted their existing curriculum with the National Curriculum if similar curricula already existed. These new syllabi were rolled out from 2014 to 2018.

In 2018, the Berejiklian State Government announced a review of the curriculum which was hailed as heralding the biggest overhaul since 1989 (Hughes, 2018). Findings suggested the curriculum was too crowded and "lock-step" in nature, with the senior years overly focused on exam preparation. A "back to basics" approach was supported by the Premier (NSW Government: Education Standards Authority, 2018; Raper, 2019). The revised curriculum aims to provide students with more hands-on outdoor experiences involving animals, habitats, and various ecosystems, alongside increased content on climate change, energy, solar systems, electricity, and food chains. However, the shift from "processes," "capabilities," and inquiry-based learning towards more explicit teaching raises concerns for ESE as such an approach undermines the importance of cross-disciplinary learning, critical thinking, diverse teaching practices, and comprehensive system-wide educational initiatives and repertoires of practice crucial to ESE (Morley et al., 2024).

On a national level, the *Alice Springs (Mparntwe) Education Declaration* (Ministerial Council on Education, 2019), one of the curriculum framing documents, has downgraded environmental and climate change references compared to its predecessor, the *Melbourne Declaration* (MCEETYA, 2008). This has resulted in a less comprehensive environmental focus (Gough et al., 2024). The latest Australian Curriculum revisions have adopted the same approach. Sustainability has been retained as a cross-curriculum priority (ACARA, 2022) yet its integration remains fragmented rather than adopting a holistic approach. The content of the learning areas does not enact the 9.0 revision's description of sustainability, key emphases on protection of the environment and ecocentric justice have been deleted, endorsements of actions have been downgraded to awareness and recognition and, in general, the revised organising ideas remain disconnected from the learning areas (Gough, 2024; Gough et al., 2024). Although the Sustainability Overview Statement theoretically supports holistic EE, the actual content and lack of teacher guidance fail to reflect this intent (ACARA, 2022; ACARA 2021 cited in Gough et al., 2024).

Maude (2022) found the revised geography curriculum could diminish the development of place attachment and limit students' understanding of their environmental interdependence and sustainability concepts. They found that the revision significantly weakens conceptual understanding and reduces essential content, with elaborations not aligning with content descriptions. Additionally, references to climate change are minimal, confined to Year 10 Science in the context of energy flow, reflecting a policy emphasis on safe knowledge that avoids creating community dissent or anxiety, and which is unlikely to be thoroughly assessed (Buchanan, 2021; Gough et al., 2024). Victoria and NSW's stance on the Australian Curriculum may offer some protection against these ESE negative changes to the curriculum yet states who adhere to the Australia Curriculum may not be so lucky.

## 9.21 Chameleons: EEC Educators Keeping Ahead of the Game

Over time EEC educators have proven to be chameleon like given their adaptation abilities. While fieldwork is emphasised as a key component of EEC operations in the NSW Department of Education's salary and conditions documentation, their role in supporting the implementation of ESE is also prominently featured.

> "Environmental Education Centre" means a teaching and learning facility operated by the Department which students attend to participate in educational programs relevant to all primary and secondary key learning areas and/or to receive specific instruction in field work, and which provides support to schools in implementing environmental education. (Industrial Relations Commission of New South Wales, 2017)

However, with the surging and diminishing of ESE/EEC support and leadership experienced throughout their existence EEC teachers-in-charge/principals have learnt to adapt—making the most of opportunities and finding and implementing survival strategies when needed, individually and collectively.

The EEC community has a niche. With the downsizing of staffed curriculum areas within departmental education regions, the centres provide the only personnel able to offer support, advice and resources to schools on ESE—and also offer professional development in other areas such as effective pedagogies that connect students to the real world.

> We're left to our own devices in a way and even to represent environment/sustainability within the Department of Education. They look to us now. ...Then they got rid of positions of curriculum areas in regions... As I said, the whole aim was to put funding back in schools but it just left a massive gap in curriculum. And ...that's meant that environmental ed centres have picked up a lot of that, I must admit. We've got coordinated approaches to HSIE and the new geography syllabus. It would be the same with science. VC

At times the curriculum had been advantageous for EECs. A good example is the NSW geography syllabus circa 2017 which was compatible with ESE.

> In terms of political policy, I get pretty disappointed with some of the politics that go on. But you need to look at things like... geography now, for me geography nearly is the embodiment of the environmental education policy because it has everything that good environmental education should have about developing future focused learners with kids that are willing to take action. And that's part of the change that's happened. Now we finally have a syllabus that is being written for us, it feels... like it's not perfect, but it's there and it's far stronger being written in syllabus then it is in a separate policy, which people would never enforce religiously at all. KB

However, this syllabus is set to change. EECs, as with schools, are always adapting to new curriculum which seems to change at the impulse or fancy of governance.

There has been a general shift back to families wanting their children to experience nature, and this has fed a resurgence in EEC visits.

> There's been a real trend back to Scouts at the moment. And so getting kids outdoors, getting kids experiencing walking on uneven surfaces. So there's a lot of developmental skills I think as well that we provide. Connecting kids with the environment. Providing those opportunities to connect. I think all those things are really, really important... that we do. VC

One strategy utilised to ensure an EEC voice when the EE Unit was disbanded was a decision agreed on in 2016. It involved the centres contributing to a fund to pay for one of them to be their EZEC representative. To this end, David Smith from Gibberagong EEC had been recruited one day per week to work on EZEC representation at all levels. The NSW Department of Education, seeing the value, contributed some funding to assist in this practice. One of the initiatives was to form strategic partnerships to drive state-wide student action programs—aligning with academic partners for action research to develop much needed evidence of practice. With new technologies, the time was right to start developing smart ways of assessing student learning rather than "numbers through the gate" and evaluative feedback of experience (which has served its purpose). Robust data on learning outcomes are now possible using various digital tools—programs that enable the assessment of digital work, for example.

One of the premises of this study is that the FSC/EECs develop and conduct EE as opposed to outdoor education, conservation education, and nature study. Critical was the inclusion of the distinctive EE qualities "concerned with values, attitudes and social action in resolving environmental problems" (Greenall, 1987, p. 12). This, however, would be disregarding the complexity of the situation. There would have been a mixture of all of these types of education across time and place, given the circumstances. Most of the FSC/EECs do primarily set out to change people's attitudes and behaviours, to motivate action for the environment, and consequential to that, sustainability. But due to occasional and sometimes frequent necessity, they have been subject to incorporation within the existing hegemony of the epistemological paradigm of traditional education for survival.

Over time, our FSC/EEC educators have become the ultimate change agents, able to disguise and survive in shifting circumstances (see Fig. 9.4 for a photo of Gibberagong's celebration of 50 years of ESE).

The understanding of what activates people to take action on environmental/sustainability problems has become more sophisticated over the years. It is thought that people change their behaviour when:

- the environmental problems are understood,
- the complicated interaction of social and political causes of environmental problems are understood, and
- the future is uncertain and thus learning needs to be fluid and open-ended, involving "reflective social learning" (Scott & Gough, 2003; Vare & Scott, 2007; NSW Department of Education and Training, 2009; Skamp, 2009, p. 39).

Curriculum that will serve our young into a global, sustainable future needs to support the facilitation of learning for active citizenship at a local, state/national and

**Fig. 9.4** Muogamarra Field Studies Centre | 50 Years of Environmental Education Celebrations, August 2022

global level (Bezzina et al., 2009). In addition to the moral, value-laden aspect of this endeavour, system-wide change, amongst other things, will need "a clear and consistently espoused moral purpose which forms the link between systems thinking and sustainability" (Fullan and Baber cited in Bezzina et al., 2009, p. 551). While the first iterations of the Australian curriculum, and thus the state curriculums, was informed by the Sustainability Curriculum Framework, it has become something of a political issue, susceptible to the whim of changing governments whose ideologies leave teachers unsure and jaded. This does not assist in moving the agenda forward. NSW's EEC educator chameleons, able to fit in with prevailing circumstances without being sacrificed thus far, provide support to teachers in navigating a curriculum, subject area and teaching methodologies that classroom teachers themselves, generally, are ill-resourced to provide.

## 9.22 Conclusion

Evident in this chronology of function and change within the NSW DE-EECs is the power of the inertia that extreme conservatism has brought to the education system in NSW, indeed, to all of our bureaucracies. It is evident that ESE seems to be a small player in a very large power play. Indeed, it is seemingly insignificant. This insignificance was to its advantage in the early days where an *ad hoc* and opportunistic spread of FSCs was possible. There were advantages in the freedoms afforded (Renshaw & Tooth, 2018). Throughout this history, public managerialism, neoliberal or neoconservative governance, has gripped the global world and is squeezing tight. The tentacles of neoliberalism have enveloped the centres, as they have the education system and the world in general, and made terrain difficult to navigate. The centres, however, are still finding ways of progressing in positive and innovative ways that can assist in advancing and leading ESE and education generally—in the time and space in which they exist. In times where politics seems to be put before the student, the centres have placed ESE and earth citizenry, and thus the wellbeing of all students, first and foremost.

## References

Affolter, C. (2018). 30 years of engagement for education and school development. In C. Affolter & A. Varga (Eds.), *Environment and school initiatives: Lessons from the ENSI network—Past, present and future* (pp. 7–9). Vienna and Eszterházy Károly University Hungarian Institute for Educational Research and Development.

ARTD Consultants. (2010). *Evaluation of operational effectiveness of the Australian Sustainable Schools Initiative (AuSSI)*. Department of the Environment, Water, Heritage and the Arts.

Australian Association for Environmental Education (AAEE). (2002). *OzEEnews, 84*, 10.

Australian Association for Environmental Education (AAEE). (2015). *Make the change: A framework for education and engagement for sustainability 2014–2021*. Australian Association

# References

for Environmental Education. https://www.aaeensw.org.au/sites/aaeensw/files/pages/files/makethechangeframework-oct2015.pdf

Australian Association of Environmental Education (AAEE). (2019). *Australian Association for Environmental Education (AAEE) NSW Chapter: Working for sustainability*. https://www.aaeensw.org.au/

Australian Curriculum Assessment and Reporting Authority (ACARA). (2022). *Understand this cross-curriculum priority: Sustainability*. Retrieved July 26, 2024, from https://v9.australiancurriculum.edu.au/teacher-resources/understand-this-cross-curriculum-priority/sustainability. Accessed 26 July 2024.

Australian Department of the Environment Water Heritage & the Arts. (2010). *Sustainability curriculum framework: A guide for curriculum developers and policy makers*. Commonwealth of Australia.

Australian Education for Sustainability Alliance (AESA). (2014). *Education for sustainability and the Australian Curriculum project: Final report for research phases 1 to 3*. AESA. https://www.ryde.nsw.gov.au/files/assets/public/environment/education-for-sustainability-and-the-australian-curriculum-project.pdf

Australian Government Department of Environment & Heritage. (2005). *Educating for a sustainable future: A national environmental education statement for Australian schools*. Curriculum Corporation. http://www.environment.gov.au/education/publications/pubs/sustainable-future.pdf

Australian Government: AusAID. (2011). *Global perspectives: A framework for global education in Australian schools*. Education Services Australia. https://www.globaleducation.edu.au/verve/_resources/GPS_web.pdf

Australian Government: Department of the Environment and Heritage. (2007). *Caring for our future: The Australian Government strategy for the United Nations Decade of Education for Sustainable Development, 2005–2014*. Australian Government: Department of the Environment and Heritage.

Bezzina, M., Starratt, R. J., & Burford, C. (2009). Pragmatics, politics and moral purpose: The quest for an authentic national curriculum. *Journal of Educational Administration, 47*(5), 545–556. https://doi.org/10.1108/09578230910981053

Buchanan, J. (2021). Environmental trust? Sustainability and renewables policy and practice in the school years. *Curriculum Perspectives, 41*(2), 163–173.

Campbell, Ian, and Brendan Nelson, Department of Environment and Heritage and Department of Education, Science and Training. (2005). Letter to the school community. In *Educating for a sustainable future: A national environmental education statement for Australian schools*. Curriculum Corporation.

Department of Environment and Conservation (NSW). (2003). *Who cares about the environment in 2003? A survey of NSW peoples' environmental knowledge attitudes and behaviors'*. Available at https://www.environment.nsw.gov.au/research-and-publications/publications-search/who-cares-about-the-environment-2003

Department of the Environment Water Heritage and the Arts. (2009). *Living sustainably: The Australian Government's national action plan for education for sustainability*. http://www.environment.gov.au/resource/livingsustainably-australian-governments-national-action-plan-education-sustainability

Donnelly, K., & Wiltshire., K. (2014). *Review of the Australian Curriculum. Final report*. Australian Government Department of Education.

Environmental Education NSW | Chapter of the Australian Association for Environmental Education. (n.d.). *Sustainable Schools NSW*. Retrieved February 28, 2025, from https://sustainableschoolsnsw.org.au/

Environment Australia. (1999). *Today shapes tomorrow—Environmental education for a sustainable future: Discussion paper*. Commonwealth of Australia.

Environmental Education Unit, Environment Australia. (2000). *Environmental education for a sustainable future: National action plan*. Environment Australia: Department of Environment and Heritage.

Ferreira, J., Ryan, L., & Tilbury, D. (2006). *Whole school approaches to sustainability: A review of models for professional development in pre-service teacher education*. Prepared by the Australian Research Institute in Education for Sustainability (ARIES) for the Australian Government Department of the Environment and Heritage. Australian Government Department of the Environment and Heritage.

Ferreira, J., Davis, J., Cavanagh, M., & Thomas, J. (2009). *Mainstreaming sustainability into pre-service teacher education in Australia*. Prepared by the Australian Research Institute in Education for Sustainability (ARIES) for the Australian Government Department of the Environment, Water, Heritage and the Arts. Edited by Jessica North. Australian Government Department of the Environment, Water, Heritage and the Arts.

Funnell, S., & Larri, L. (2005). *Evaluation: NSW sustainable schools program*. Renshaw Hitchen and Associates for the NSW Department of Education and Training and the NSW Department of Environment and Conservation.

Garg, K. (2017, February 16). Teaching sustainability in Australian schools: Who's missing out? *SBS News*. https://www.sbs.com.au/news/teaching-sustainability-in-australian-schools-who-s-missing-out

Gibbs, D. (2015, November 19). MDG failures. *The Borgen Project*. Retrieved from https://borgenproject.org/mdg-failures/#:~:text=Shortcomings%3A%20Assessing%20the%20MDG%20Failures,countries%20concerning%20the%20same%20MDGs

Gough, A. (1999). Today shapes tomorrow - What happened to yesterday? A story of environmental education policy in Australia. *Chain Reaction*, Autumn, 25–28.

Gough, A. (2011). The Australian-ness of curriculum jigsaws: Where does environmental education fit? *Australian Journal of Environmental Education, 27*(1), 1–15.

Gough, A. (2024). Changing politics for changing times: Rethinking research stakeholders and strategies for environmental education. *Australian Journal of Environmental Education, 40*(3), 417–430. https://doi.org/10.1017/aee.2024.41

Gough, A., Reid, A., & Stevenson, R. B. (2024). Environmental and sustainability education in Australia. In M. Rieckmann & R. T. Muñoz (Eds.), *World review: Environmental and sustainability education in the context of the Sustainable Development Goals* (pp. 297–317). CRC Press.

Greenall, A. (1987). A political history of environmental education in Australia: Snakes and ladders. In I. Robottom (Ed.), *Environmental education: Practice and possibility* (pp. 3–21). Deakin University Press.

Greenall Gough, A., & Robottom, I. (1993). Towards a socially critical environmental education: Water quality studies in a coastal school. *Journal of Curriculum Studies, 25*(4), 301–316. https://doi.org/10.1080/0022027930250401

Hill, A., & Dyment, J. (2016). Hopes and prospects for the sustainability cross-curriculum priority: Provocations from a state-wide case study. *The Australian Journal of Environmental Education, 32*(3), 225–242. https://doi.org/10.1017/aee.2016.20

Hughes, J. (2018). *A background paper on the history of the New South Wales curriculum since 1989: Context, cases and commentary on curriculum change*. NSW Government: Education Standards Authority. https://nswcurriculumreview.nesa.nsw.edu.au/home/siteAreaContent/58b95b7d-a7a3-465d-b0af-cf423e74259a

Industrial Relations Commission of New South Wales. (2017, May 5). Crown employees (teachers and schools and related employees) salaries and conditions award 2017. *Industrial Gazette*, 237–205.

Karena, C. (2010). Environmental education in Australian schools. *ECOS: Science for Sustainability, 155*. http://www.ecosmagazine.com/?paper=EC155p16

Kemmis, S., & Smith, T. (2008). *Enabling praxis: Challenges for education*. Brill.

Ladwig, J. G., Mockler, N., & Ross, A. M. (2010). *Schools climate change initiative [2007–2009] evaluation report: Executive summary*. NSW Department of Education and Training. https://www.cese.nsw.gov.au//images/stories/PDF/Eval_Rep/Schools/Schools_Climate_Change_Initiative_Eval_2010.pdf

Lave, J., & Wenger, E. (1991). *Situated learning: Legitimate peripheral participation*. Cambridge University Press.

Lawrence, P. (2014, March 6). National parks aren't your personal playground. *The Drum*. Retrieved from https://www.abc.net.au/news/2014-02-19/lawrence-wiifm-campaign-threatens-our-national-parks/5268552?pfmredir=sm

Learning Through Landscapes. (n.d.). *The illustrious history of how Learning through Landscapes developed*. Retrieved July 26, 2024, from https://ltl.org.uk/our-history/

Maude, A. (2022). A critique of version 9.0 of the Australian curriculum: Geography for primary schools. *Geographical Education (Online), 35*, 6–23.

Ministerial Council on Education. (2019). *The Alice Springs (Mparntwe) Education Declaration*. Retrieved July 31, 2024, from https://www.education.gov.au/alice-springs-mparntwe-education-declaration

Ministerial Council on Education Employment Training and Youth Affairs (MCEETYA). (2008). *Melbourne declaration on educational goals for young Australians*. MCEETYA. Retrieved July 31, 2024, from https://files.eric.ed.gov/fulltext/ED534449.pdf

Ministerial Council on Education Employment Training and Youth Affairs [MCEETYA]. (1999). *The Adelaide declaration on national goals for schooling in the twenty-first century*. Retrieved July 31, 2024, from www.mceecdya.edu.au/mceecdya/adelaide_declaration_1999_text,28298.html

Mockler, N. (2018). Curriculum. In A. Welch, R. Connell, N. Mockler, A. Sriprakash, H. Proctor, D. Hayes, et al. (Eds.), *Education, change and society* (4th ed., pp. 333–360). Oxford University Press.

Morley, E., & NCA Newswire (2024, July 25). NSW primary curriculum shakeup from 2027: The changes explained. *Education Review*. Brennan Education. https://www.educationreview.com.au/2024/07/nsw-primary-curriculum-shakeup-from-2027-the-changes-explained/

New South Wales Department of Education and Training Professional Learning and Leadership Development Directorate. (2008). *Quality teaching in NSW public schools: An annotated bibliography*. NSW Department of Education and Training.

NSW Council on Environmental Education. (2001a). *Environmental education in NSW: Towards a three-year plan: Working paper* (EPA, Ed.). Council on Environmental Education.

NSW Council on Environmental Education. (2001b). *Planning for environmental education in NSW: Discussion paper* (EPA, Ed.). NSW Council on Environmental Education.

NSW Council on Environmental Education. (2002). *Learning for sustainability: NSW environmental education plan 2002–05* (EPA, Ed.). NSW Council on Environmental Education.

NSW Department of Education. (2001). *Energy management in NSW schools*. NSW Department of Education and Training.

NSW Department of Education and Training. (1999). *Department of Education and Training annual report*. NSW Department of School Education.

NSW Department of Education and Training. (2001a). *Environmental education policy for schools*. Professional Support and Curriculum Directorate, NSW Department of Education and Training.

NSW Department of Education and Training. (2001b). *Implementing the environmental education policy in your school*. Professional Support and Curriculum Directorate, NSW Department of Education and Training. https://education.nsw.gov.au/policy-library/associated-documents/Id.pdf

NSW Department of Education and Training. (2003). *Department of Education and Training annual report*. NSW Department of Education and Training.

NSW Department of Education and Training. (2009). *Earth citizenship: A conceptual framework for learning for sustainability—Draft working paper*. Professional Support and Curriculum

Directorate, NSW Department of Education and Training. http://www.curriculumsupport.education.nsw.gov.au/env_ed/teaching/framework/index.htm

NSW Department of Education and Training Asset Management Directorate. (2005). *Landscape management in NSW schools*. NSW Department of Education and Training.

NSW Department of Environment & Heritage. (2014). *Sustainable schools NSW*. https://www.sustainableschoolsnsw.org.au/

NSW Department of Environment and Climate Change. (2009). *Guide to using research in sustainability programs.* https://www.environment.nsw.gov.au/-/media/OEH/Corporate-Site/Documents/Research/Our-science-and-research/guide-to-using-research-in-sustainability-programs-090093.pdf

NSW Environmental Protection Agency (EPA). (1994). *Who cares about the environment?* NSW Environmental Protection Agency.

NSW Government: Education Standards Authority. (2018). *NSW curriculum review*. https://www.nswcurriculumreview.nesa.nsw.edu.au/home/homePageContent/view

NSW Government: Office of Environment & Heritage. (2012). *Who cares about the environment in 2012? A survey of NSW peoples' environmental knowledge, attitudes and behaviours.* https://www.environment.nsw.gov.au/research-and-publications/publications-search/who-cares-about-the-environment-2012

NSW Government: Office of Environment & Heritage. (2019). *Who cares about the Environment? View full reports of the who cares about the environment social research series.* https://www.environment.nsw.gov.au/research-and-publications/our-science-and-research/our-research/social-and-economic/sustainability/who-cares-about-the-environment

NSW Office of Environment and Heritage and Environment Protection Authority. (2015). *Sustainability strategy 2015–20—Sustainability leadership: Let's take action together*. https://www.environment.nsw.gov.au/resources/about/150353-oeh-epa-sustainability.pdf

Patty, A. (2017, September 11). NSW to slash $1.7b from education funding. *The Sydney Morning Herald*. https://www.smh.com.au/national/nsw/nsw-to-slash-1-7b-from-education-funding-20120911-25ps9.html

Posch, P. (2018). A common platform for research, development and support of EE and ESD. In C. Affolter & A. Varga (Eds.), *Environment and school initiatives: Lessons from the ENSI Network—Past, present and future* (pp. 11–29). Vienna and Eszterházy Károly University Hungarian Institute for Educational Research and Development.

Prescott, D. (2016). Telling reflections: Teaching sustainably in a complex learning environment. *Australian Journal of Environmental Education, 32*(1), 80–90. https://doi.org/10.1017/aee.2016.2

Raper, A. (2019, October 22). NSW education interim report finds curriculum too focused on HSC exams. *ABC News*. Retrieved from https://www.abc.net.au/news/2019-10-22/nsw-education-report-finds-curriculum-too-focusedon-hsc/11624880

Renshaw, P., & Tooth, R. (2018). Diverse place-responsive pedagogies: Historical, professional and theoretical threads. In P. Renshaw & R. Tooth (Eds.), *Diverse pedagogies of place: Educating students in and for local and global environments* (pp. 1–21). Routledge.

Rizvi, F. (2007). Postcolonialism and globalization in education. *Cultural Studies: Critical Methodologies, 7*(3), 256–263. https://doi.org/10.1177/1532708607303606

Scott, W., & Gough, S. (2003). *Sustainable development and learning: Framing the issues*. RoutledgeFalmer.

Skamp, K. (2009). *Critical review of current practice and research of environmental education and education for sustainability for kindergarten to year 12 from 1990*. NSW Department of Education and Training.

Skamp, K., & Bergmann, I. (2001). Facilitating learnscape development, maintenance and use: Teachers' perceptions and self-reported practices. *Environmental Education Research, 7*(4), 333–358. https://doi.org/10.1080/13504620120081241

Smith, G. A., & Stevenson, B. (2017). Sustaining education for sustainability in turbulent times. *The Journal of Environmental Education, 48*(2), 79–95. https://doi.org/10.1080/00958964.2016.1264920

Steele, F. (2010). *Mainstreaming education for sustainability in pre-service teacher education in Australia: Enablers and constraints*. A report prepared by the Australian Research Institute in Education for Sustainability (ARIES) for the Australian Government Department of the Environment, Water, Heritage and the Arts. Edited by Jessica North, Department of the Environment, Water, Heritage and the Arts.

Stevenson, R., Ferreira, J., & Emery, S. (2016). Environmental and sustainability education research, past and future: Three perspectives from late, mid, and early career researchers. *Australian Journal of Environmental Education, 32*(1), 1–10. https://doi.org/10.1017/aee.2015.49

The BEATS. (n.d.). *The state of Australian sustainability education: March 2022*. Retrieved July 21, 2024, from https://thebeats.org/sustainability-survey-2021/

The Political Compass. (2019). *The Australian federal election. 2001-2019*, Retrieved December 12, 2019, from https://www.politicalcompass.org/aus2019

Tilbury, D., Coleman, V., & Garlick, D. (2005). *A national review of environmental education and its contribution to sustainability in Australia: School education*. Australian Government Department of the Environment and Heritage and Australian Research Institute in Education for Sustainability (ARIES).

Tribe, D. (1997). State delegate report: NSW. *OzEEnews, 68*, 9.

Tribe, D. (1999). State and territory reports: New South Wales report. *OzEEnews, 79*, 13.

Tyas Tungaal, H. (1999). Learnscapes: Making significant changes in Australian schoolyards. *OzEEnews, 77*, 1, 6–7, 10–11.

UNESCO. (2005). *The decade at a Glance*. https://unesdoc.unesco.org/ark:/48223/pf0000141629

UNESCO. (2019). *Global education monitoring report, 2019: Migration, displacement and education: Building bridges, not walls*. https://unesdoc.unesco.org/ark:/48223/pf0000265866

United Nations. (2019). *Report of the Secretary-General on SDG progress 2019: Special edition*. Retrieved July 26, 2023, from https://sustainabledevelopment.un.org/content/documents/24978Report_of_the_SG_on_SDG_Progress_2019.pdf

Vare, P., & Scott, W. (2007). Learning for a change: Exploring the relationship between education and sustainable development. *Journal of Education for Sustainable Development, 1*(2), 191–198. https://doi.org/10.1177/097340820700100209

Walker, K., & Sharp, H. (n.d.). *Environmental education standards for NSW schools K-10*. Australian Association for Environmental Education.

Wenger, E. (1998). *Communities of practice: Learning, meaning, and identity*. Cambridge University Press.

Windsor, S., & Kitooke, A. (2023). Practices and experiences in educational researcher training: Reflections from research students exploring the theme, living well in a world worth living in during the covid-19 pandemic. In K. E. Reimer, M. Kaukko, S. Windsor, K. Mahon, & S. Kemmis (Eds.), *Living well in a world worth living in for all: Volume 1: Current practices of social justice, sustainability and wellbeing*. Springer.

Woolmington, E. (1972). The Australian environment as a problem area. In A. Rapoport (Ed.), *Australia as human setting* (pp. 22–38). Angus and Robertson.

Zint, M., Ostrow Michel, J., Collins, S., Sloan, E., Piñeiro, M. E., Balotin, L., et al. (2024). Pathways to achieving the sustainable development goals through environmental and sustainability education in the USA. In M. Rieckmann & R. T. Muñoz (Eds.), *World review: Environmental and sustainability education in the context of the Sustainable Development Goals* (pp. 269–296). CRC Press.

# Part III
# Changing Contexts

It is worth reflecting on what worked in establishing and implementing environmental protections, Environmental and Sustainability Education (ESE), and Environmental Education Centres (EECs) at local and state bureaucratic levels through changing times. Contemplating how efforts to enact change within ESE have evolved, and understanding how the current environment for implementing change has developed, provides valuable insights. The problems are extremely intricate. Considering the context of time and location helps in identifying potential variables. It poses a question about the socialisation of each of us within our own time and place, within colonialisation, and the various institutionalisations/medias possibly affecting us and blinded us to what else could be. The outcomes are disturbing when one considers the disconnect from the environment that the exponential and consumeristic growth of the late twentieth and early twenty-first centuries have generated.

The focus now shifts to global developments and a selection of representations of EECs within other countries. Before delving into the specificities of each locale the international landscape and the overarching factors that impact countries universally, I describe some transcending distinct place-based landscapes and conditions. This entails delving into some of the intricate interplay of influences, exploring tensions and recurring themes that impact pedagogy, curriculum, and leadership across different contexts.

# Chapter 10
# Global Flourishing: Examples of EECs Manifestation

## 10.1 Introduction: A Global Context (1949–1968)

A profound transformation occurred from 1945 through the 1970s. Following World War II, the United States ascended to superpower status, ushering in the era of the Cold War, which primarily pitted the United States against the Soviet Union in a geopolitical rivalry between the Western and Eastern blocs. It didn't finish until the collapse of the Soviet Union in 1991. The United States was a central player in international diplomacy after World War II and one of the creators of the United Nations Charter. The remarkable speed and diversity of economic expansion in core Western industrialised countries during the 1950s and 1960s can largely be attributed to the process of post-war reconstruction (Vonyó, 2008). While the war wrought a great deal of human and environmental destruction, the post war economic expansion accelerated environmental depletion and exacerbated resource exploitation, leading to further degradation of natural ecosystems.

After the war many countries, particularly in Africa and Asia, gained independence from colonial rule. For example:

- India became independent from Britain in 1947
- Kenya became independent from Britain in 1963
- Namibia struggled for independence which was gained from South Africa in 1990
- Philippines became independent from the United States in 1946
- Uganda became independent from Britain in 1962
- Israel became a state in 1948 after Palestine was partitioned into an Arab and Jewish state setting the scene for ongoing Arab Israeli conflict.
- After abolishing military rule in 1949 Costa Rica focused on education and social welfare
- Hawaii became the 50th state of the United States and experienced a tourism boom followed by cultural renaissance.

This time frame saw the Civil Rights Movement, the Women's Liberation Movement, the Counterculture Movement, the Space Race and the Korean and Vietnam Wars. While these events were primarily instigated within, or concerned, the United States they also spread and influenced other nations. For many countries there was political turmoil, military coups, rapid industrialisation, economic growth and urbanisation—for example Bolivia, Brazil, Greece, Portugal, Columbia, and Ecuador. Conversely, unlike the present time, political stability and economic growth was experienced in Mexico (Encyclopedia Britannica, n.d.-a). Between the 1950 and 1970s the United States banded with Latin American armed forces to contain leftwing government and insurgent advance in the region (Guardiola-Rivera, 2007).

## 10.2 National Parks

National parks were initially adopted in countries that had experienced recent Western colonialisation: the United States (from 1872), Australia (from 1879) and Canada (from 1885). Well-established countries in Europe and Asia embraced this concept at a later stage, when the encroachment resulting from industrialisation and urbanisation became a more significant concern. Before the 1900s instruments for preservation included, common lands, private estates, conservation efforts and early conservation laws. Europe had managed and modified land for purposes such as agriculture and forestry—the concept of preserving something as wilderness was new. Yet, land ownership patterns altered with large tracts of wilderness less common—land ownership became fragmented and complex making national parks a solution. Sweden, Switzerland, Spain and Italy were some of the first European countries to establish National Parks with the founding of Abisko National Park in Sweden in (1909) [Yui, 2014]. Russia had set aside the Barguzin Valley in Siberia as a protected area in 1916 (Encyclopedia Britannica, n.d.-b). National Parks continued to be set up through-out the post-world war period with 99 established after the war (Yui, 2014).

South Africa provides a different experience for national park establishment. Like Australia's experience, the British influence of game protection was the original rationale (Carruthers, 1997). However, in southern Africa the preservation of wildlife in the industrialising Transvaal also contributed to the emergence of the necessary working class given the encloser prohibited the gaining of animals as a food source (Carruthers, 1997). The first national parks in South Africa were in Namibia in 1907 and South Africa in 1916 (Yui, 2014). Seventeen were set up by the late 1960s.

National parks are often a nexus for ecological research and environmental education (EE). Consequently, many environmental education centres (EECs) are connected to these natural sanctuaries. Other forms of EE that can evolve from national parks include interpretive signage, visitor centres providing educational material and environmental educators providing EE in situ (Day & Monroe, 2000; Lugg & Slattery, 2003).

## 10.3 Conservation Education

As an example of conservation education development around the globe, formal conservation education in Kenya commenced in 1966 with the establishment of the first education centre in Nairobi. This initiative was inspired by the Nairobi Animal Orphanage, which started operating in 1964. The orphanage's primary goal was to provide a temporary home and rehabilitation for orphaned wildlife before their release back into the wild. The education centre used animals from the orphanage for educational purposes. Prior to these developments, there was no organised system for educating the public about wildlife conservation. Indigenous knowledge, folklore, and myths were the main sources of information. Since 1966, the number of education centres has grown to 15, with plans for further expansion into national parks like Lake Nakuru, Tsavo East, Tsavo West, and Meru. Smaller information centres also exist in various national parks and reserves (Mbugua, 2012).

These education programs primarily target students, aiming to enhance their experiences during visits to the parks. The curriculum is designed to complement their school education, covering subjects like biology, ecology, geography, history, and nature conservation. Various themes are addressed, such as wetlands, climate change, energy, species, and forests. The programs follow established procedures and offer in-house and outreach activities, collaborating with teachers and community leaders to determine topics and delivery methods during visits (Mbugua, 2012).

Wildlife Clubs of Kenya is a non-profit organisation established in 1968 by Kenyan students, making it the first conservation education program of its kind in Africa. It has gained recognition for its grassroots efforts and was recognised with a place on the United Nations Environmental Program (UNEP's) Global 500 Honour Roll in 1986. Wildlife Clubs of Kenya has not only stimulated a continental wildlife club movement in Africa but also inspired the creation of similar clubs in Asia, Latin America, and other parts of the developing world (Wildlife Clubs of Kenya, n.d.).

Wildlife Clubs of Kenya actively engages in conservation advocacy, contributing to significant achievements such as the ban on hunting and wildlife trophies in Kenya, increased tree planting and soil erosion control activities, and the vigorous preservation of natural resources. Over the course of its history, the organisation has educated more than one million young Kenyans and has played a role in placing many of them in influential positions (Wildlife Clubs of Kenya, n.d.).

Apartheid in South Africa led to racial segregation and international condemnation, noticeable in the not-for-profit conservation movement. Steyn (2002) while acknowledging the artificiality of dividing time frames into distinct periods provides three categories of environmental non-government organisations in South Africa in order to better analyse their evolution. The first period, from 1972 to 1982, was marked by the dominance of conservation issues in the South African environmental non-governmental organisation sector. These concerns primarily catered to the interests and priorities of the white population and often excluded or overlooked the environmental concerns of people of colour (Steyn, 2002). Colonialist hegemony overriding Indigenous communities and knowledges was happening in most colonialised environments. Another example is in Arabia where rather than engaging Indigenous communities as collaborative partners in sustainable conservation and development efforts, conservation organisations often treated local communities as challenges to be managed, either through financial compensation or preferential employment conditions (Chatelard, 2003; Chatty, 1998).

## 10.4 Outward Bound: Embracing Adventure and Personal Growth

The Outward Bound schools, believed to stem from Germany in the 1800s (Pearson, 1978), were the precursors of the school camping experience, which plays a substantial role in the development of EE. Outward Bound, an educational concept developed by Kurt Hahn, began in the 1930s at Gordonstoun School in Scotland, emphasising physical skills, outdoor experiences, expeditions, and the development of character alongside academic achievement (Outward Bound International, n.d.). It later evolved into a program to teach survival skills to young British sailors during World War II. The program's core principles included physical fitness, challenging expeditions, self-reliant projects, and compassion through service (Outward Bound International, n.d.).

The Outward Bound process is an experiential learning approach. It involves learners demonstrating motivational readiness, followed by immersion in a unique physical and social environment, often outdoors, within a small group. Participants engage in problem-solving tasks that challenge them in various ways. The process induces adaptive dissonance, where learners must adapt to discomfort and challenges. The ultimate goal is mastery, achieved when learners are motivated, alert, supported by their group, and successfully address structured problems. Mastery leads to a reorganisation of self-awareness, self-esteem, and a sense of belonging, with the aim of fostering an "outward bound" orientation to living and learning, emphasising personal growth, teamwork, and problem-solving skills through outdoor experiences (Walsh & Golins, 1976). Outward bound development is another example of the synchronicity around the world given America, Australia, New Zealand and quite a few countries, generally western, took up the mantle of improving resilience, wellbeing, health and fitness through experiences in the outdoors. It juxtaposes and has convergences with EE throughout their histories. Experiences within outdoor and environment education centres vary greatly along the spectrum from anthropocentrism to ecocentrism across different time and spaces.

## 10.4.1 The Wegscheide Centre

The Wegscheide centre in Frankfurt is one of the largest resident centres in Europe (Pearson, 1978). Its history started from the early 1920s, when Frankfurt played a prominent role in the reform pedagogy movement, emphasising communal living and a connection with nature. August Jaspert, the head of the Frankfurt Kaufungerschule, discovered an abandoned military camp on the Wegscheideküppel near Bad Orb, which he saw as an ideal location to put his educational reform principles into practice. In 1920, Jaspert, along with his colleagues, established the Wegscheide children's village, consisting of simple barracks set in a beautiful natural environment.

Boys and girls coexisted within a community, learning in an outdoor setting. Their education focused on simple living and equal conditions for all children, regardless of their social backgrounds. Students also learned to work together for the benefit of the community.

There was great patronage and an unfortunate intervening war break before the Frankfurt mayor reclaimed the Wegscheideküppel area for Frankfurt schools in 1952, securing a leasehold agreement with the city of Bad Orb to maintain the school camp. The camp, upon its revival, welcomed not only Frankfurt students but also groups from various regions, including England, France, Spain, and Berlin (Wegscheide, n.d.).

In the 1970s the Wegscheide accommodated 1000 students and emphasised social living (Pearson, 1978). In the 1990s when the Wegscheide faced monetary challenges there was financial and curricular redirection and while improving its financial situation, it adopted a new focus on EE (Wegscheide, n.d.).

## 10.5 Charting ESE Global Governance

International and national documents supported the development of environmental and sustainability education (ESE). There has been a slow metamorphosis of formal ESE curriculum from the 1970s through to the present, with many of the earlier years influenced by science education approaches (Disinger, 1993) and many of the later by the concept of education for sustainable development (ESD). These approaches were aimed chiefly at assisting the conservation of natural resources with economic development—"without changing anything quickly or fundamentally" (Gough, 1997, p. 31). The concept of sustainability had been established in a contemporary sense through movements such as the Club of Rome's "Limits to growth" (Meadows et al., 1972). It was embedded in the subtitle for the "World Conservation Strategy: Living Resource Conservation for Sustainable Development" (International Union for the Conservation of Nature and Natural Resources (IUCN), 1980) and in 1984 it became a mission when the World Council for the Biosphere and the International Society for EE joined forces (Australian Association for

Environmental Education pers. comm., January 22, 2018). *Our Common Future*, the Brundtland Report (the World Commission on Environment and Development [WCED], 1987) provided further propagation. The "sustainable development" terminology was a technocratic call for people to live within the earth's carrying capacity without a clear understanding of what these dimensions would be (Gough, 1997).

## 10.5.1  International Conferences

Shining a light on international conference outcomes and offshoots highlight important influences and deviations crucial to EECs and this narrative. Reflectively, the increasing call for action, exasperation with the gradual, and sometimes retrograde, pace of change, and the repetition of various aspects are noted. However, there are unique dynamics that arise when conferences take place in developing countries like Rio or India. In such settings, there is a notable increase in authenticity and immediacy.

In 1987 the Second International Conference on Environmental Education and Training, convened in Moscow, Russia. Organised by the United Nations Educational, Scientific and Cultural Organisation (UNESCO), UNEP, and the State Committee for Higher Education of the Soviet Union, the conference followed up on the Tbilisi Conference in 1977. Its objectives were to assess advancements in EE, exchange knowledge, and address emerging challenges. The conference concluded with the issuance of the Moscow Declaration on Environmental Education, reaffirming the commitment to EE, and advocating increased global collaboration (UNESCO, n.d.-a).

The Rio Earth Summit (1992) produced *Agenda 21*, progressing sustainable development by providing a comprehensive blueprint of actions for governments, organisations, and individuals to achieve sustainable development in the twenty-first century (United Nations, n.d.). However sustainable development amassed a lot of criticism. In addition to the critique already levelled at sustainable development within this narrative, documents such as *Our Common Future* (WCED, 1987) and *Agenda 21* (UN, 1992), were seen to have embraced an anthropocentric and utilitarian environmental ethic rooted in mechanistic science rather than holism (Merchant, 1992 cited in Gough, 1997). They displayed a preference for Western scientific knowledge over Indigenous knowledge, the adoption of a growth-oriented industrial development model, and the reliance on Western cultural and economic perspectives. They were accused of relegating other species as resources rather than having their own intrinsic value (Merchant, 1992 cited in Gough, 1997). Other critics (Salleh, 1992; Delgado, 1993 cited in Gough, 1997) pointed to the marginalisation and suppression of alternative perspectives—particularly those of First Nations people and women in general.

However, international and thus national, state and local initiatives continued to shift toward "sustainable development" and "education for sustainability" with the

## 10.5 Charting ESE Global Governance

replacement of "environment" with "environment and development" (Gough, 1997). The technocentric world order was bolstered with EE given only a supporting role in its attainment. For example, the Australian Department of the Prime Minister and Cabinet had produced a report on Ecological Sustainable Development (1990), written in preparation for Rio and instrumental to formal ESD (Gough, 1997). Sustainability is built into *Caring for the Earth: A Strategy for Sustainable Living* produced by the IUCN in collaboration with the International EE Programme and the World Wildlife Fund (1991)—the successor document to the *World Conservation Strategy*. ESD is referenced in "Learning for a Sustainable Environment" by Maclean and Fien, 1994, a joint Australian/UNESCO regional project (Gough, 1997).

A month before the Rio UNESCO conference in 1992 The World Conference of Indigenous Peoples on Territory, Environment and Development produced an Earth Charter demanding their and natures' right to life. With 109 points the Declaration covered human rights and international law, lands and territories, biodiversity and conservation, development strategies and culture, science and intellectual property (The World Conference of Indigenous Peoples on Territory, Environment and Development, 1992). At the UNESCO Rio conference, the knowledge and perspective of indigenous peoples in relation to sustainable development are acknowledged as contributing to education and training (UNCED, 1992 cited in Gough, 1997), yet the dominant western voices override with the neoliberal western world order within.

The 1997 UNESCO International Conference, Environment and Society: Education and Public Awareness for Sustainability, in Thessaloniki, Greece, produced the Thessaloniki Declaration on Environmental Education and Sustainable Development (UNESCO, 1997). It reinforced the importance of EE. However, EE got scant mention and it was suggested that EE be referred to as education for environment and sustainability (Knapp, 2000).

The Millennium Development Goals (MDGs), supported by an international alliance for sustainable development were agreed at the Millennium Summit of the UN General Assembly in New York in September 2000. They emphasised poverty eradication, infant, maternal and sexual health, literacy, housing, water security and environmental protection.

At the World Indigenous Peoples' Conference on Education in 1999 "The Coolangatta Statement on Indigenous Peoples' Rights in Education" was revised and published. It is significance given it is specific to education. It presents a framework created by an international task force for the discussion of indigenous educational rights and self-determination (World Indigenous Peoples' Conference on Education, 1999). The struggle and longing for culture, for existence, is clear. While the environment is not specifically mentioned the embodiment and intrinsic connection of First Nations' with place is a given (Dahr, 2023).

The 2002 World Summit on Sustainable Development in Johannesburg, South Africa, approved a Political Declaration and Implementation Plan. This plan outlined actions and measures aimed at achieving environmentally respectful development, including a frame for the Decade of Education for Sustainable Development (2005–2014). The summit produced decisions on various critical issues such as water, energy, health, agriculture, biological diversity, and more (United Nations, n.d.).

## 10.5.2 The Earth Charter

The Earth Charter was created in response to unfinished business of the 1992 Rio Earth Summit (Corcoran, 2002). A civil society effort formulated the Earth Charter by engaging in a global, multicultural, and multisectoral consultation (The Earth Charter, n.d.). The Earth Charter's principles find resonance in the standards developed by social justice, peace, and EE groups, incorporating Indigenous perspectives and international declarations (Andrzejewski, 2005). While there was a growing agreement on the content and format of an Earth Charter representing universal ethical principles embraced by people across various backgrounds, governments within the United Nations expressed disagreement with the concept of a binding ethical commitment, leading to the termination of related efforts within the UN structure at the 2002 Earth Summit for Sustainable Development (Rockefeller, 2002 cited in Corcoran, 2004; Gruenewald, 2004).

The Earth Summit disappointed many, with critics labelling it the W$$D due to its perceived pro-business stance and extravagant staging on the outskirts of poverty-stricken Soweto shantytowns. Despite Kofi Annan's positive announcement of $235 million in public–private partnerships, the summit faced criticism for favouring corporate and governmental interests over grassroots initiatives. United States delegates, along with other large states and non government organisations (NGOs), exerted pressure, leading to the rejection of the Earth Charter's holistic, socialist, and non-anthropocentric educational framework. Instead, the Summit emphasised ESD as a crucial field to be integrated across disciplines and educational levels (Kahn, 2008).

Despite not receiving explicit endorsements in key declarations, the Earth Charter's values were acknowledged in the ESD Toolkit (McKeown, 2002 cited in Howard, 2019; The Earth Charter, n.d.). So, regardless of not being adopted at the Rio+10 follow-up meeting on sustainable development in Johannesburg in 2002 (Hjorth Warlenius, 2022), UNESCO embraced the Earth Charter in 2003, recognising it as a significant ethical framework for sustainable development—further solidifying its role as an ethical guide for sustainable development, encouraging member states to implement it in education (Hjorth Warlenius, 2022). The importance of considering local values and traditions is highlighted, emphasising the Earth Charter's relevance in enriching educational practices (Karrow et al., 2019).

## 10.5.3 The United Nations Decade of Education for Sustainable Development

The United Nations Decade of Education for Sustainable Development, spanning from 2005 to 2014, sought to incorporate the principles and methodologies of sustainable development throughout the entire spectrum of education and learning. Its objective was to foster shifts in knowledge, values, and attitudes, aspiring to create a world that is more sustainable and equitable (Buckler & Creech, 2014).

## 10.5.4 International Conferences Continued...

The fourth UNESCO International Conference on Environmental Education in Ahmedabad, India, in 2007 highlighted challenges in implementing experiential context-based EE. It emphasised the need for comprehensive, holistic policy approaches and discourse, signalling a new paradigm. Urgency was underscored, calling for radical changes in economics, production, and lifestyles. The Enlightenment's influence on modern education, rooted in progress and the separation of nature for human use, was discussed. The conference urged citizens to hold governments accountable for ESD policies and funding (UNESCO, 2007).

In 2009, the UNESCO World Conference on Education for Sustainable Development in Bonn, Germany, led to the Bonn Declaration. The first declaration to be specific to ESD, this pivotal document urged the integration of sustainable development principles into all education levels, emphasising the role of education in promoting sustainability. It built upon earlier UNESCO frameworks like *Agenda 21* and the Johannesburg Plan of Implementation (United Nations, 2002), and advanced ideas for a UNESCO Road Map for ESD implementation.

At Bonn, the Decade for ESD was a significant focus given 2009 was the halfway mark. In the initial 5 years of the Decade, progress had been made in implementing innovative policy frameworks across various countries. Numerous entities, including UN agencies, NGOs, and regional bodies, were actively contributing to specific aspects of ESD, supported by a global monitoring and evaluation framework. Education was recognised as a pivotal factor in improving human well-being, with a growing understanding of enhancing education systems, promoting lifelong learning, and integrating different forms of education through ESD. There was an emphasis on sharing knowledge about educational change processes. Scientific advancements were said to have provided insights into climate change, health challenges, biodiversity, and the necessity for sustainable development. The next 5-year phase was projected as involving the translation of knowledge into action, strengthening the outcomes of the Decade of Education for Sustainable Development, and ensuring long-term implementation (UNESCO, 2009).

### 10.5.5 The Future We Want and the Education We Need for the World We Want

Subsequent conferences continued to shape the narrative. The United Nations Conference on Sustainable Development, also known as Rio+20, took place in Rio de Janeiro, Brazil, in 2012. Commemorating the 20th anniversary of the Rio Earth Summit, this conference aimed to secure renewed political commitment for sustainable development. It resulted in the adoption of the outcome document, *The Future We Want* which did not explicitly endorse the intrinsic value of nature but acknowledged that many individuals hold such moral sentiments (Washington et al., 2017). At the conference, participating nations agreed to initiate a series of actions aimed at formulating a framework for Sustainable Development Goals (SDGs). This effort builds upon the achievements and failures of the Millennium Development Goals (MDGs) while aligning with the post-2015 development agenda (United Nations, n.d., 2012).

Alongside the Rio+20 Summit was the "Peoples' Summit" which released *The education we need for the world we want* (2012) which highlighted the socio-economic and environmental ramifications of financialisation within neoliberal frameworks. It addressed the global strains caused by both development and underdevelopment, which have intensified social movements seeking radical alternatives in response to these crises (Huckle & Wals, 2015). It expanded the analysis beyond the immediate context to consider the roles of power, politics, and citizenship, as well as the impacts of neoliberalism and alternative models of social and environmental interactions (Huckle & Wals, 2015). A key component of this discourse is the emphasis on critical and transformative education.

The 2014 Education for Sustainable Development Conference, organised by UNESCO, occurred in Nagoya, Japan. This conference focused on sharing experiences, best practices, and innovative approaches in ESD implementation. The *Aichi-Nagoya Declaration on Education for Sustainable Development* emphasised the importance of integrating ESD into all levels of education (UNESCO, n.d.-b).

### 10.5.6 The UNESCO Roadmap for Implementing the Global Action Program (GAP) and Education for Sustainable Development

Adopted during the 38th session of the UNESCO General Conference in 2015, the Global Action Program is a framework for advancing ESD worldwide, and the roadmap outlines strategies and actions for implementation of the goals of the program. The Road Map is closely linked to the Global Education 2030 Agenda, which is part of the broader United Nations 2030 Agenda for Sustainable Development. The SDGs, including SDG 4 on Quality Education (UNESCO, 2016), were adopted at the United Nations Sustainable Development Summit in New York in 2015. Of specific interest to ESE is goal 4.7 "Education for Sustainable Development and Global Citizenship" which is a key enabler for all the other SDGs. It states:

> By 2030, ensure that all learners acquire the knowledge and skills needed to promote sustainable development, including, among others, through education for sustainable development and sustainable lifestyles, human rights, gender equality, promotion of a culture of peace and non-violence, global citizenship and appreciation of cultural diversity and of culture's contribution to sustainable development. (UNESCO, 2020)

The five Roadmap priorities include:

- Policy: ESD must be integrated in global, regional and national and local policies related to education and sustainable development.
- Education and training settings: Attention is required to promote the whole-institution approach to ensure we learn what we live and live what we learn.
- Building capacities of educators: Focus is on empowering educators with the knowledge, skills, values and attitudes needed for the transition to sustainability.
- Youth: Young people must be recognised as key actors in addressing sustainability challenges and the associated decision-making processes
- Local level action: Emphasises the importance of actions in the communities as they are where meaningful transformative actions are most likely to occur. (UNESCO, 2020)

### 10.5.7 ESD: A Foundational Element of Education

The conferences persist, but I don't find it beneficial to delve further with the exception of the Berlin UNESCO World Conference on Education for Sustainable Development 2021 where delegates expressed their commitment to use the transformative power of education in order to address global challenges. The *Berlin Declaration on Education for Sustainable Development: Learn for our planet: Act for sustainability* (UNESCO, 2022) noted the climate emergency, widespread biodiversity loss, pollution, global health crises, severe poverty, deep-rooted inequalities and violent conflicts before reasserting the importance of EE and nature with promising statements about the urgency of action required to address the interrelated challenges the world faces.

> We believe that the urgency of these challenges, exacerbated by the Covid-19 pandemic, requires a fundamental transformation that sets us on the path of sustainable development based on more just, inclusive, caring and peaceful relationships with each other and with nature… We believe that ESD must be based on and promote respect for nature, as well as human rights, democracy, the rule of law, non-discrimination, equity and gender equality. (p. 3)

It talks of including the notion of responsible and active global citizenship—the promotion of intercultural understanding, cultural diversity, peace and a non-violent culture. And there are commitments to the recognition of Indigenous knowledges, transparency, democracy, networking, whole-institution approaches, authentic curriculum and pedagogy that recentres environment and climate action within curriculum.

> Ensure that ESD is a foundational element of our education systems at all levels, with **environmental** and **climate action** as a **core curriculum component** (p.4)

## 10.6 Reflection: Global Governance

While some may doubt the effectiveness of conference declarations, historical evidence indicates that these statements possess a degree of influence. They serve as shared foundations for discussions about potential transformations on both national and international scales (Lotz-Sisitka, 2009). It is clear from this close analysis of the New South Wales (NSW) and Australian adaptation of ESE that international influence was a catalyst and support, along with the essential local impetus, in moving ESE forward. However, it seems that over time, governance systems beholden to the neoliberal ethos have incorporated ESD rhetoric into policies without the necessary support and accountability mechanisms to ensure implementation—they speak in platitudes that lack depth and sincerity.

These ESE conferences specifically have played/play pivotal roles in shaping global EE agendas, emphasising sustainability, international collaboration, and transformative education processes. Despite progress, persistent challenges include Western-centric perspectives and potential exploitation of developing countries in global environmental initiatives. The reflection of Western conceptions of EE, seems ironic given the western broader disconnect from the environment and the prevalent penchant for consumerism—a practice largely associated with the West. Historically, western approaches to EE have been ambiguously understood, while for countries in the global south, the Western conception of EE was generally deemed irrelevant (Fensham, cited in Gough, 1997). While the inclusion of non-western perspectives have gained greater ground over the years there remains an intrinsic problem with the neoliberal agenda and dominance of western metalanguage and socialisation comfortably pervading the work of the dominant international agencies.

Refocusing on the wicked problem of western hegemony, in the early days of the UNESCO EE conferences, countries in the southern hemisphere advocated for a new international order. However, Mazower (2012) notes that the United States undermined these calls and exploited the shift towards neoliberalism to establish a new international economic order under American influence, utilising institutions such as the International Monetary Fund and implementing structural adjustments. This move had the effect of sidelining critical forms of EE and subsequent ESD. As global elites leaned towards right-wing ideologies, democracy and socially critical education became targets of attack. Consequently, the focus shifted from power, politics, and citizenship to values, behaviour, and lifestyles (Huckle & Wals, 2015).

There are many spin-offs/divergences to ESD given the often lax connection or omission of the crucial environmental component in addition to the view that ESD is operating within the neoliberal paradigm and thus impotent when it comes to critically appraising the detrimental effects that this economic structure has on the earth (Huckle, 2015). Indeed, many of the UNESCO documents read as sanitised—which can be said for much documentation which is beholden to funding/livelihood influences (Gough, 1998, 2000). Earlier documentation was more explicit in relation to the global economic political order and the need for change (Huckle & Wals, 2015).

Documentation disseminating from the Decade of Education for Sustainable Education did analyse values, behaviours and lifestyles necessary for sustainability. Yet, missing was discourse of the power, politics and citizenship and the difficulties of acquiring the desired sustainable understandings and practices within the current dominant economic and political model and any reckoning of liberal or radical views of social change that may get the critical mass on track with sustainability (Huckle, 2012; Huckle & Wals, 2015). Add to this the shift in societal trust, with people relying more on the internet than political representatives or TV experts. Governing institutions are seen as losing touch with collective public values as they prioritise capital defense (Mazower, 2012).

Selby and Kagawa (2010) argue that ESD represents the culmination of the "closing circle" of policy-driven EE. They contend that ESD is characterised by definitional vagueness, a tendency to obscure inconsistencies rather than expose them, and an unreflective association with the globalisation agenda. In this context, mainstream ESD implicitly embraces the neoliberal marketplace worldview, aligning with economic growth and endorsing an instrumentalist and managerial perspective on nature. This viewpoint emphasises the technical and tangible aspects over the axiological and intangible (Selby & Kagawa, 2010; Selby & Kagawa, 2014 cited in Huckle & Wals, 2015). However, within the global governance network, specifically for ESE, an ethics of care dimension started to evolve around the time of the Rio conference in 1992. In more recent times, UNESCO had declared that EE must be a core curriculum component by 2025 (UNESCO, 2021) and launched an initiative for greening education in classrooms (UNESCO, 2024). While ESE has a difficult time being heard within the SDGs UNESCO is actively advocating for ESE inclusion via SDG Target 4.7. Like the centres within the NSW Department of Education, EECs around the world often play a key role in ESE.

## 10.7 Emerging Field Study(ies)/Environmental/Outdoor Education Centres

There were many field studies centres (FSCs) specifically focussed on conservation and building EE emerging around Australia and the world in the 1970s. In Dorothy Pearson's (1978) global list of centres most were listed in the UK, the United States,

Canada, New Zealand and Australia. Denmark's listing of centres is worth a mention but for all other countries there were only a handful of centres and it seems that in many cases centres were just getting off the ground or informants were clutching at a centre contribution to the study. It is clear that the whole pursuit of centres was generally an Anglo/western enterprise in its infancy. In Australia there were centres staffed by education department personnel, by tertiary institutes, by private bodies or individuals and by the Department of Sports and Recreation personnel (Webb, 1980). There were also centres controlled by individual schools, both public and private—for example Para Wirra in South Australia and Bumberry in NSW (public), and Timbertop (Victoria) and Camp Knox, NSW (private). In the late 1970s in NSW, enterprising organisations and people set up private FSCs to fill the void created by the NSW Department of Education avoiding taking the lead in planning centres and refusing to take non-government school pupils (Webb, 1980). However, to be fair, Queensland, South Australia and Victoria also had private ventures, albeit not to the extent of NSW.

In the 1970s, FSCs in Australia offered a diverse array of program categories ranging from experiences that primarily engaged the senses and aesthetics in natural settings, to academic or interest-based studies focusing on biological phenomena or landscapes. There were also programs teaching environmental knowledge that fostered general awareness and concern for the environment, often aligning with the curriculum for students in years 3–4. Additionally, some programs were closely aligned with the guiding principles of EE as defined in the Belgrade Charter (Webb, 1980).

Queensland was early in establishing field study centres within the Department of Education. Before 1976 there were five—three in old schools, one a Sport and Recreation centres and one utilising an old water resource. By the end of the 1970s there were 13 (ZZ). The Queensland Department of Education were systematic in developing their field study centres and were one of the few Australian states to have a policy statement on EE, endorsed by the Director General in 1976. Centre development within the NSW Department of Education was in comparison, ad hoc. Queensland planned to establish two centres in each educational region with a mobile centre in Western region centres (see Fig. 10.1 for a photo of one of the Queensland FSC). The Queensland Department of Education seemed to have good collaborative working relationships with other departments given that some of their centres were set up within old forestry and water resources (Webb, 1980). There were three sections interested in environmental issues in schools, the Agricultural Project Club Branch, the Physical Education Branch and the Curriculum Branch so an EE standing committee was set up to coordinate activities within the Department. They were responsible to the Director General of Education. The FSCs established in natural, modified and non-natural, modified and artificial environments was in response to national and international reports categorising them as essential elements for education systems. Right from the start the centres were intended to be an integral part of EE in schools rather than a total field experience (Webb, 1980) (See Fig. 10.2 for another example of Queensland's EECs).

**Fig. 10.1** "Pullenvale Field Study Centre" (Webb, 1989, p. 19). (Attribution: Joan Webb and the National Parks and Wildlife Service (now Parks Australia))

**Fig. 10.2** Bunyaville Environmental Education Centre. (Attribution: The State of Queensland (Department of Education), CC BY 4.0. https://creativecommons.org/licenses/by/4.0, via Wikimedia Commons)

## 10.8 Global EEC Habitats: Diverse Environments Across Borders

There is a complex combination of historical, ecological and socio-economic factors that feed the present state of any country. For example, the eastern philosophies of Taoism and Confucianism from China, or Shintoism from Japan, the Happiness index from Bhutan, or the Ubuntu movement in Africa stand in contrast to the dualism that has developed within western culture (Internet Public Library, n.d.; Skirry, n.d.). It seems important to highlight some differences within countries given the influence this will have on EECs or ESE within these environments.

Countries such as Italy, Greece, Portugal and Spain have extensive histories associated with trade within the Mediterranean, Asia and Africa that predate colonialism and thus were more influenced by these relationships (Abulafia, 2003). Colonialist countries, often associated with the major colonial powers of western Europe (including Britain, France, Spain, Portugal, the Netherlands), had primarily focused their colonial activities outside of Europe, particularly in Africa, the Americas, Asia, and of course, Australia—exploration, conquest, trade, and the establishment of colonies in distant regions. However, the interactions between neighbouring European countries, and for those to the east, interaction with neighbouring Asian countries, were influential in shaping geopolitical, economic, and cultural factors. Each country's historical experiences are unique and contribute to their complex relationships with other nations and this impacts EECs and the ESE within.

## 10.8.1  Nordic Countries

Some of the factors that have influenced the Nordic countries being more closely aligned to nature include:

- a harsh environment making connection to the natural environment imperative (Universitas Gadjah Mada ASEAN Society, 2022),
- a historical reliance on farming practices—with sustenance and livelihoods reliant on farming, fishing and forestry (Hilson, 2008),
- a strong connection between humans and the natural world through way of a rich tradition of mythology, folklore, and storytelling (Gelter, 2000; Kvideland et al., 1989; Olsen, 2014),
- outdoor lifestyles part of the culture (Gelter, 2000; Jūrmalis et al., 2022), and
- a focus on the collective rather than the individual (McWhinney, 2022; Partanen, 2017).

The Scandinavian countries of Denmark, Norway and Sweden have distinctive socio-political and economic characteristics from most other western countries. They are strong welfare states with high levels of social equality, albeit historically they have less ethnic diversity comparatively, though they are becoming more multicultural due to increased immigration in recent decades. Attributes include generous social benefits, robust health and education systems and comprehensive social security programs. Cooperative relationships and consensus-based decision making are integral to the Scandinavian model of governance.

Finland, part of the broader Nordic region, has synergies with Scandinavian countries and their excellent international educational standing. Many western countries admire the quality of education in schools within these nations, where they spend time connecting to nature within each school day. Additionally, forest schools and Eco-schools originated within these countries. Interestingly Sweden and Finland are among the countries that have ESE accountability measures embedded in their education practice—there is a reporting mechanism through ESE being authentically embedded within the curriculum. This is an anomaly within Western education systems where summative assessment in literacy, numeracy and science typically drives school practice, notwithstanding the specified curriculum. Consequently, the non-academic outcomes of the curriculum are not a priority (Ladwig, 2010; Conseil supé-rieur de l'éducation, 2018; ETAG, 2015d; Robinson & Aronica, 2015 cited in Twining et al., 2021)—bearing in mind the double-edged sword the colonialised restrictive logic that measurement entails (Weber cited in Ladwig, 2010).

However, ESE within Nordic countries is not without its challenges. While Finland's highly regarded education system is often associated with factors such as teacher autonomy, decentralisation, the emphasis on play-based learning, and a flexible curriculum—qualities that support ESE implementation—Wolff et al. (2017) argue that sustainability education is still struggling. This is due to several factors, including the constraints of university teacher education which remains discipline-specific, a fragmented school curriculum, the need for deep ecoliteracy, and the fact that ESE is inherently dependent on values. Finland, and other Nordic countries, have not been immune to neoliberal infiltration (Mulinari et al., 2009; Skedsmo et al., 2021). In 2012 educational policies in Sweden promoted a shift towards a more restricted, subject-focused approach, making it increasingly challenging to effectively teach sustainable development (Dimenäs & Alexandersson, 2012). Tomren (2022) found Norwegian students involved in climate strikes wanted a more action oriented and politically focused curriculum.

Nevertheless, the emphasis on outdoor learning is seen as a factor in Finland's success in developing one of the world's best primary school systems. Denmark, Sweden, and Norway integrate outdoor teaching into their education systems with terms such as udeskole, utomhuspedagogik, and uteskole respectively, which translate roughly to school-based outdoor teaching integrated into the local environment. In Norway, it is part of the national curriculum, while in Denmark, it originated as a grassroots movement among teachers and spread widely. Outdoor learning in these countries, often interdisciplinary, occurs in natural or cultural settings and involves activities like measuring tree volumes in mathematics or writing nature-inspired poems for language classes. Australian schools are beginning to adopt similar practices, inspired by Finland's approach to outdoor education (Planet Ark, 2017).

Given their close affinity with nature and the integration of ESE into their culture and schooling systems, representations of EECs often focus on immersive experiences and ecotourism. These centres leverage the natural landscapes and cultural values of sustainability to provide hands-on, experiential learning opportunities that emphasise a deep connection with the environment and can be connected to school experiences (EcoTourism World, n.d.; Hjem, n.d.; Naturvårdsverkets, n.d.).

However, the Nordic countries are revealed to have some of the highest ecological footprints globally[1] (Jónsson et al., 2021)—see Fig. 10.3.

#### 10.8.1.1 Finnish Nature Centre Haltia, Espoo, Finland

Haltia, adjacent to the Nuuksio National Park half an hour's drive from Helsinki, is a nature and outdoor centre dedicated to promoting Finnish nature and culture. It features interactive exhibitions, guided nature trails, and educational programs on topics such as biodiversity, wilderness, and sustainable living. While it is a commercial enterprise it has a nature school that offers 95 yearly, free-of-charge nature school days to school groups that serve the municipalities of the Helsinki Metropolitan Area. While programs are nature focused their pedagogical approaches encourage learners to be active, think and act for themselves, be creative, be reflective and think for the future. Student voice is heard. Staff are very experienced with

**Fig. 10.3** Country Overshoot Days 2024. (Attribution: Global Footprint Network 2024, www.overshootday.org)

---

[1] Most of the countries studied had an Overshoot Day far exceeding what the Earth has to offer (Earth overshoot day 2024).

10.8 Global EEC Habitats: Diverse Environments Across Borders

a high standard of discipline and education qualifications. The school utilises sensory awareness and metacognitive skills in their teaching (Haukka et al., 2020). Programs combine many subjects, such as environmental studies, biology, geography, history, social studies, physical education and home economics and are connected to the latest curriculum (Haltia, n.d.). Professional development is offered to teachers and educators (Haaukka et al., 2020).

One noteworthy initiative was the NANOL project—Nurturing Affinity to Nature through Outdoor Learning in Special Places. The Nature School of Haltia aimed to support the curriculum effectively and engage learners through cooperative activities. This involved collaborating with participating children to ensure their voices and interests in the forest environment were integrated into the planning. The focus was on making learners active participants and central to the learning process, alongside fostering collaboration with both teachers and students in shaping the educational experience. Insights gained from the project were shared through trainings and a new reference guide for student-centred forest education, helping educators implement these methods. The project highlighted key practices such as involving students in planning and organising excursions, tailoring activities to student interests and abilities, promoting inclusivity, building on existing knowledge and skills, encouraging reflective practice, and facilitating active student participation (Haukka et al., 2020).

## *10.8.2 EECs in Extreme Environments*

The Arctic, Antarctic and desert regions are known for their harsh environments, which are characterised by extreme conditions. There is also significant curiosity about these extreme areas. Importantly, these regions are rich in resources, which creates a critical boundary between resource extraction and environmental degradation. This dynamic often leads to increased environmental concern and underscores the need for ESE.

In the 1970s, research stations and field centres were often scattered and strategically located. Some of these centres were situated in areas like the Arctic and Antarctic, where land and resources were contested, and there was much to learn about the environment. Some of these centres are research and tertiary education focused such as the Murmansk Marine Biological Institute, Russia, established in 1881. Others have a research and general tertiary or tourist education/experience focus, such as the not-for-profit Churchill Northern Studies Centre, Canada, established with community support in 1976 (Churchill Northern Studies Centre, n.d.; Murmansk Marine Biological Institute of the Russian Academy of Sciences, n.d.).

### 10.8.2.1 The Bamfield Marine Science Centre, British Columbia, Canada

In 1971, the Pacific Cable Board (PCB) Cable Station site in Bamfield, within the traditional territory of the Huu-ay-aht First Nations in Barkley Sound on the west coast of Vancouver Island, began its transformation into the Bamfield Marine Sciences Centre (BMSC, n.d.) (see Fig. 10.4). Positioned adjacent to the Pacific Rim National Park Reserve, BMSC offers access to a variety of environments, including coastal, marine, and rainforest habitats. It provides immersive field trips for K-12 and undergraduate students. These trips, run by graduate students and researchers, include activities like boat trips, laboratory investigations, and nature walks. They focus on socioscientific issues such as climate change and marine ecology, fostering a connection with nature and strengthening pro-environmental beliefs through experiential learning. For students unable to visit, BMSC offers Live Dive and Live Lab programs that allow students to interact with biologists in real-time as they explore underwater environments, aligning with grades 7–12 curriculum objectives and covering topics like ocean acidification, species at risk and invasive species. Post-learning materials are provided (Ewing, 2011).

A study by Mayer in 2016 highlighted the positive impacts of the environmental experience at BMSC. Participants reported strengthened pro-environmental beliefs, a heightened sense of connection with nature, and a preference for experiential and

**Fig. 10.4** Bamfield Marine Sciences Centre from Bamfield Inlet. (Attribution: David Stanley, CC BY 2.0. https://creativecommons.org/licenses/by/2.0, via Wikimedia Commons)

EE methods. The study also noted evidence of metacognitive awareness and assimilation throughout the environmental experience (Mayer, 2016).

### 10.8.3 Oases of Learning: Exploring Environmental Education in Desert Regions

Wadi Rum Protected Area, the Wadi Rum Desert, Southern Jordan, the Har HaNegev Field School, near Mitzpe Ramon, Israel, and Desert Park, Alice Springs, the Northern Territory, Australia were investigated for sites of EECs (Alice Springs Desert Park, 2024; The Society for the Protection of Nature in Israel, n.d.; UNESCO World Heritage Convention, n.d.). Each seemed to emphasise ecotourism with education experiences. Personnel associated with Wadi Rum Protected Area were developing ESE material for schools however according to Chatelard (2003) the teaching practices within these schools were alienating Bedouin children from their traditional environment.[2]

#### 10.8.3.1  Har HaNegev Field School, Mitzpe Ramon, Negev Desert, Israel

Har HaNegev Field School is one of nine schools run by the not-for-profit Society for the Protection of Nature in Israel (The Society for the Protection of Nature in Israel, n.d.). This NGO, one of Israel's largest and among the world's oldest nature conservation organisations (1953), was founded in response to growing tensions between the public's desire for environmental preservation and the state's drive for rapid development (Sagy & Tal, 2015). They concentrate on conservation, education, research, activism, eco-tourism, and promoting sustainability. They run various classroom and hands-on educational programs for all ages with a variety of educational, camping and recreational programs adapted for schools[3] (The Society for the Protection of Nature in Israel, n.d.).

#### 10.8.3.2  Alice Springs Desert Park, Northern Territory, Australia

Alice Springs Desert Park situated on 1300 hectares of land near to Alice Springs, in the Northern Territory, Australia, plays an important role in interpreting the unique desert environment through three distinct habitats—Desert Rivers, Sand Country, and Woodland—offering a glimpse into authentic desert life (see Fig. 10.5). Connected to the local Arrernte people, it honours traditional Dreaming stories like

---

[2] Once more, this is not an anomaly with a long world history of educational cultural alienation experienced by Indigenous students.
[3] Note, it was difficult to source information in English about ESE provision.

**Fig. 10.5** *Melopsittacus undulatus* (Budgerigar) Bird-Alice Springs Desert Park. (Attribution: Richard. Fisher, CC BY 2.0. https://creativecommons.org/licenses/by/2.0, via Wikimedia Commons)

the Akngwelye and Yeperenye Altyerre, blending cultural heritage with EE (Alice Springs Desert Park, 2024). It fosters a spiritual and physical connection between people and the land—more essential in the face of climate change, habitat loss, and species decline. The park undertakes desert research, conservation, and breeding programs—a proactive role in preserving Australia's desert flora and fauna. Traditional Owners offer guidance and training (Alice Springs Desert Park, 2024).

Education opportunities include guided and self-guided tour programs for local, remote and interstate students in the areas of science, flora and fauna, geography and history. Programs such as Cultural Walks introduce students to desert survival strategies, encouraging them to explore traditional First Nations' knowledge while developing critical thinking and research skills. Nocturnal tours provide an opportunity to observe rare and endangered species, offering a hands-on experience of desert biodiversity (Alice Springs Desert Park, 2024).

There was evidence of the waning of ESE growth with connection to economic and political changes in the late nineties when a restructure of the Northern Territory Department of Education saw downsizing effecting policy and advisory services. While the two positions at the Park were intact there were limited ESE services for teachers (Norman, 1999).

## 10.8.4 Nature's Rights and Resistance

Many countries do include EE within their formal sustainable development education discourse nowadays. Approximately 149 nations have recognised environmental rights and/or responsibilities within their constitutions. Those that do not recognise these rights and responsibilities within their constitution include the UK and 27 former British colonies. However eleven of 13 English-speaking nations of the Americas do not (Boyd, 2013). Ninety nations recognise a substantive right to live in a healthy environment (Boyd, 2011). More recently a further 11 nations have included a dedicated climate provision or clause in their constitution (Toral et al., 2021). With climate change education an imperative, island representation warranted attention as samples of ESE/EECs. However, investigations found many associations with ecotourism and NGO ESE initiatives with or without connection to formal school education yet not necessarily associated with a centre as such. Online organisation is effectively the hub of the activities. There are many movements around the world associated with climate change education and activism. One example is the ePop Platform, based in New Caledonia, amplifying the voices and stories of communities vulnerable to climate change around the world (ePOP Network, n.d.).

Few countries have explicitly recognised the rights of nature—or many do but the rights are based on instrumentalist rationality favouring human entitlement (Kotzé & Calzadilla, 2017).[4] Exceptions include Ecuador and Bolivia—and Columbia and New Zealand who have recognised the Atrato River and the Amazon Rainforest, and the Te Urewera Forest and the Whanganui River/Te Awa Tupua River system respectfully within their constitutions/law (Calzadilla, 2019; Calzadilla & Kotzé, 2018; Kotzé & Calzadilla, 2017). While these four countries were within my research gaze, New Zealand yielded the greatest information given the lack of a language barrier allowing the viewing of the greatest amount of documentation relating to their Māori/English bilingual practices and the Enviroschools program influence throughout New Zealand's education system.

Māori culture and language has a strong influence, and the Enviroschools program is prominent in a desktop search for EECs in New Zealand. Additionally, many site-specific EE experiences are available to the general public, such as those offered at wildlife and nature reserves, sanctuaries, and botanic gardens.

### 10.8.4.1 Zealandia Te Māra a Tāne and the Kaipatiki Project, New Zealand

Zealandia Te Māra a Tāne, outside Wellington, run by the Karori Sanctuary Trust a not-for-profit community-led organisation, offers well-structured, curriculum-aligned school ESE programs that actively involve students and teachers in

---

[4] An acknowledgement that these statistics may have altered.

conservation and biodiversity education. They have robust educational outreach programs catering to individual school needs and resources including pre and post activities (Zealandia Te Māra a Tāne, n.d.). Research has looked at ways children and young people link their experiences at Zealandia Te Māra a Tāne to their involvement with environmental, social, cultural, and political challenges facing the world today—their connection to sustainability and critical thinking—guardianship (kaitiakitanga) and connection to one's place and identity and independence within it (tūrangawaewae) (Milligan et al., 2021). The researchers proposed supporting student learning by clearly linking nature sanctuaries to complex sustainability issues, being attentive to the identities, lived experiences, and emotional reactions of children and young people, and offering opportunities for students to critically assess different perspectives and sustainable futures (Milligan et al., 2021).

The Kaipatiki Project, is an ecological restoration project in Auckland's north. Established in 1998 the hub undertakes a multitude of practices and activities connected to the environment and culture. They invite schools and the community to participate in conservation, sustainable living skills, and citizen science activities that are connected to national databases. The Kaipatiki Project EcoHub is a community initiative working for a sustainable future (Kaipatiki Project, n.d.).

## 10.8.5 South America

Many countries in South America have been resisting colonialist oppression since the late 1400s justifying many of these countries being of interest in this study. Paulo Freire's influence on education of the oppressed being based in Brazil gave EECs within Brazil recognition in this study. Likewise, Mexico was of interest being in a similar situation and near the United States. It is home to the Zapatista resistance movement who have ESE programs. Costa Rica, in Central America has recognition as a leader in ESE and is home to the Earth Charter.

### 10.8.5.1 Mexico

The 1990s witnessed a global push for EE, leading to the promotion of green schools in Mexico. These schools, ranging from primary to university levels, emphasise sustainability projects, collaborative efforts, and the exchange of teaching materials through national and international networks. Despite these efforts, formal EE in schools face challenges, including the intrinsic nature of education, the influence of marketing, financial crises, and systemic issues within the education system (González-Gaudiano et al., 2020). Attempts to displace EE with ESD have been imposed globally, inflicting a high cost on countries consolidating EE (Gonzalez-Gaudiano, 2016). Those advocating a 'transformation' approach, rooted in concerns for equality and the environment, recognise systemic issues within societal structures, echoing the perspectives of ecofeminists, ecosocialists, and the Zapatistas

(Jordan & Kristjánsson, 2016). Autonomous education, as exemplified by the Zapatistas in Chiapas, remains limited to specific regions, emphasising the need for broader implementation (Czarny, 2017). However, ESE evolving through conservation education, ecotourism and movements involved in activism are evident.

The State of Mexico Hosts Five EE and Climate Change Centres (CEACC)

Located in the municipalities of Atlacomulco, Metepec, Texcoco, San Martín de las Pirámides, and Valle de Bravo these centres are within the Ministry of Environment and Sustainability. They were established to raise public awareness about the severe impacts of climate change. They employ advanced technology to alter citizens' habits and perspectives, demonstrating how human actions can rapidly damage what nature has taken thousands of years to create. A broad range of subjects include, air pollution, present conditions and future forecasts, global warming, wildfires, flooding, hurricanes, tsunamis, overconsumption of energy, the solar system, air travel, and environmental documentaries, among other topics (Ministry of Environment and Sustainable Development Government of the State of Mexico, n.d.). However, a search on their website produces no results for school education.[5]

The Ecoguardas Environmental Education Centre in Ajusco

The Ecoguardas EEC is one of three centres operated by the Ministry of the Environment in Mexico City. The other two centres are Yautlica, located in the Santa Catarina Sierra in Iztapalapa, and Acuexcomatl, in the Chinampa area of Xochimilco. All three centres aim to raise environmental awareness and encourage habit changes through workshops, courses, training sessions, and recreational activities. These programs are accessible to the general public (López González, 2019). Due to the language barrier it is difficult to assess any formal school education, although González-Gaudiano et al. (2020) generally considered formal ESE an instrument of environmental management not having the impetus required given the planetary emergency—in this Mexico is not alone.

### 10.8.5.2 Costa Rica

Interest in Costa Rica's biodiversity began in the mid-1800s, particularly in Europe and North America. By the 1970s, concerns over environmental degradation led to significant investments in conservation, education, and tourism, benefiting the economy (Blum, 2008a). Costa Rica is a leader in ESE, using ecotourism for economic

---

[5] Understanding Spanish would have been advantageous.

growth and attracting NGOs to innovate in environmental management. Public support for EE is strong, bolstered by media coverage (Blum, 2008b).

The Corcovado Foundation, Costa Rica

The Corcovado Foundation, founded by local neighbours of Corcovado National Park, works with the Ministry of Environment to combat illegal hunting and logging while safeguarding the Osa Peninsula's natural heritage. It promotes EE, engages in regenerative agriculture and ecosystem restoration, supports local communities, and advocates for sustainable tourism (Fundacion Corcovado YouTube Channel, n.d.). Over 18 years, the Foundation has educated more than 4500 students, engaged 500 children in youth groups, and once served 22 schools weekly. Currently, it works with six schools and five youth groups, focusing on raising environmental awareness (Initiative 20x20, n.d.; The Corcovado Foundation, n.d.).

### 10.8.5.3 The Black Lion Tamarin Conservation and Guajajara Women Warriors, Brazil

The Institute for Ecological Research (IPÊ), officially founded in 1992, emerged from Claudio Pádua's decision in 1978 to leave a successful executive career and focus on the conservation of the critically endangered black lion tamarin in São Paulo's Pontal do Paranapanema. Recognising the importance of community involvement in conservation, Suzana Pádua led IPÊ's EE initiatives. Originally developed through the Mico-Leão-Preto Project, IPÊ is now one of Brazil's leading environmental NGOs, demonstrating the intrinsic link between conservation and education (IPÊ, 2017).

The Black Lion Tamarin Conservation Program (BLTCP), a cornerstone of IPÊ's work since 1984, targets the endangered Leontopithecus chrysopygus, the symbol of São Paulo. IPÊ's efforts contributed to the species' reclassification from "Critically Endangered" to "Endangered" by the IUCN in 2008 and Brazil's Red List in 2014. Key achievements include community outreach, scientific research on tamarin biology, and habitat restoration, including forest corridor reconnections and the prevention of illegal squatter invasions in the Morro do Diabo State Park (IPÊ, 2017).

IPÊ's goals for the BLTCP encompass metapopulation management, involving demographic monitoring, health and genetic assessments, and extensive habitat protection. Education programs integrate conservation themes into local school curricula, conduct community outreach, and train educators. Habitat restoration projects prioritise protected zones and community-driven efforts. IPÊ also engages in media outreach, data analysis, and fundraising to ensure the program's sustainability (IPÊ, 2017).

IPÊ's evolution from tamarin-focused research to a broader conservation model underscores the deep connection between biodiversity conservation, EE, and

## 10.8 Global EEC Habitats: Diverse Environments Across Borders

community engagement. The BLTCP exemplifies the synergy between species preservation, habitat restoration, and public awareness, highlighting education's essential role in achieving sustainable outcomes.

The Guajarjara Women Warriors

Complementing the concept of diverse cumulative impacts, and serving as a powerful example of community engagement and transformative education, the Guajajara Women Warriors from the Indigenous Guajajara community in Maranhão, Brazil, patrol and protect their ancestral rainforest territory. Through their community outreach and EE initiatives, the women warriors emphasise the significance of conserving their forests for future generations. They conduct training sessions to raise awareness about environmental issues, showcasing how traditional knowledge and cultural practices can coexist with modern conservation efforts (Loures & Sax, 2020). There is no specific indication that the Guajajara women are involved directly in ESE programs within schools, or at least not as part of formal educational curricula. However, their influence extends through public awareness and community mobilisation, promoting environmental protection, which could indirectly inspire educational activities or partnerships.

The Guajarjara Women Warriors are part of a movement aimed at protecting their land from increasing deforestation and illegal logging, which has intensified in recent years due to governmental negligence. Recognising the crucial role of gender equality in environmental movements, these women have become instrumental in diversifying strategies and fostering new alliances. Their proactive stance reflects the urgent need for inclusion in environmental conservation efforts, as their work directly contributes to the preservation of vital ecosystems that combat climate change (Loures & Sax, 2020).

The Guajajara women, organised into a collective, emerged in response to challenges faced by predominantly male patrols, actively combating illegal activities that threaten their territory. By stepping up their engagement, they have not only gained visibility but have also made significant strides in reducing logging within their area. Their approach includes collaborating with other Indigenous groups, highlighting the importance of unity in territorial protection (Loures & Sax, 2020).

### 10.8.5.4 The Rainforest Awareness Rescue Education Centre (RAREC), Iquitos, Peru

This centre plays a vital role in ESE in a region often hindered by an inflexible education system. RAREC equips communities with the knowledge and skills necessary for environmental stewardship, community coexistence, and eco-friendly employment opportunities. As highlighted by the organisation, both species and environmental conservation rely heavily on education, prompting RAREC to lead initiatives that offer educational opportunities to communities living near key species habitats.

RAREC provides EE for children of all ages, as well as sustainable development classes for local communities. Additionally, the centre offers English language courses and after-school activities in local schools, believing that ensuring access to quality education is crucial for the Amazon's long-term preservation.

These educational efforts aim to address critical issues like unemployment, poverty, wildlife poaching, and deforestation, while fostering conservation and sustainable development. RAREC underscores the importance of innovation and collaboration with local communities to shift the current course of Amazon degradation. Furthermore, RAREC promotes the adoption of eco-friendly technologies and simple practices, such as reducing litter, conserving water, and avoiding deforestation. Educating the community on sustainable practices, such as alternative protein sources, can significantly impact the region's ecological health (Rainforest Awareness Rescue Education Centre, n.d.). RAREC funding comes from organisations around the world keen to see the Amazon survive and thrive, in particular Zoos in the USA. It is difficult to gauge the degree of colonialist conservation ethics and Indigenous autonomy within ESE enactment from a desktop study.

### *10.8.6 EEC: Science/Conservation Foundation*

The research on ESE emanating from around the globe reminded me of the important work that EECs do in transforming scientific/sociological information into education/citizen science, and, opening up that inquiry into "why", for children and adults, and conversely their connectivity in support for environmental, scientific ecological, and sustainability projects. For example, Moreton Bay EEC is part of the shorebird resilience collaboration in the Moreton Bay/Brisbane area, in Queensland, Australia—one example of conservation/science programs educating and advancing science and conservation cooperatively (Bush et al., 2022). Another that started out to conserve the birdlife associated with an important wetland surrounded by urban encroachment is Rondevlei Environmental Education Centre in Cape Town, South Africa. Other examples of centres that focus on education and collaborate with science and conservation initiatives include the Save Our Seas Foundation Shark Education Centre in Cape Town, South Africa; the CPR EEC in Chennai, Southern India; the Wildlife Conservation Education Centre in Uganda; the Science Centre of Northern Norway; and as discussed, the Black Lion Tamarin Environmental Education Centre in Brazil and the Bamfield Marine Sciences Centre in British Columbia. Many of these centres have evolved from conservation or science-focused institutions into key players in ESE while others are still focused on conservation education.

### 10.8.6.1 Rondevlei Environmental Education Centre, Grassy Park, Cape Town

The Rondevlei Environmental Education Centre plays a vital role in EE within the City of Cape Town's framework, of 11 centres. Positioned within the Table Bay Nature Reserve, Rondevlei offers tailored programs on biodiversity, wetlands, flora, birds, and fish, including holiday programs, environmental days, and activity-based learning (City of Cape Town Isixeko Sasekapa Stad Kaapstad, n.d.). Schools visit the reserves and education officer guided excursions are available with concessions for certain groups.

Beyond its educational role, Rondevlei holds historical significance as a pioneer in community-based conservation during apartheid, challenging traditional conservation models. Developed by Howard Langley, this innovative approach aimed to integrate marginalised communities through controlled access, managed exploitation, and EE (van Sittert, 2019). Rondevlei's unique conditions, surrounded by urban development, served as a laboratory for post-apartheid conservation reforms, contributing to the national system's transformation (van Sittert, 2019).

Initially established to address conservation concerns on the Cape Flats, an area lacking educational facilities, Rondevlei evolved from a bird sanctuary to an EEC. Its historical journey reflects the changing strategies in response to environmental challenges (Wood & Gibbs, 1997).

Under Langley's leadership, strategies, such as the reintroduction of charismatic species like hippos and the dismantling of fences, were instrumental in the centre's success (van Sittert, 2019). His approach, blending scientific ecology and pragmatic futurism, broadened Rondevlei's mandate from elite recreation to popular education, leading to its expansion in the late 1980s (van Sittert, 2019).

Langley's reintroduction of hippos showcased that urban conservation could successfully reclaim land from urban development and engage local communities through employment and EE (van Sittert, 2019). Rondevlei's historical significance as a laboratory for new conservation strategies underscores its crucial role in shaping contemporary approaches to urban conservation in South Africa.

### 10.8.6.2 CPR Environmental Education Centre, Chennai, Southern India

The CPR Environmental Education Centre (CPREEC), established in 1989 as a Centre of Excellence in EE by the Ministry of Environment, Forests and Climate Change and the CPR Foundation in Chennai, plays a vital role in spreading awareness about environmental issues. CPREEC focuses on both formal and non-formal EE, offering innovative programs and promoting sustainable practices (CPR Environmental Education Centre, n.d.).

In formal education, CPREEC has integrated environmental studies into school curricula, developed textbooks, and conducted teacher training programs. It also provides input for national and state-level EE initiatives (CPR Environmental Education Centre, n.d.). One key project, the Green School Initiative (GSI), involves students in hands-on activities to enhance environmental responsibility, reduce resource use, and cultivate sustainable school practices (Sharma & Kanaujia, 2020). In non-formal education, CPREEC engages youth, women, and local organisations through exhibitions, workshops, and publications. Notably, its 'video-on-wheels' program travels across South India delivering EE through audio-visual presentations (CPR Environmental Education Centre, n.d.).

The Centre has led major programs like the National Environment Awareness Campaign and National Green Corps, collaborating with various organisations for workshops and festivals. International partnerships have also expanded its reach beyond India (CPR Environmental Education Centre, n.d.). CPREEC aims to increase environmental awareness, especially among teachers, children, and communities, promoting nature conservation. It also conducts research on biodiversity and ecological traditions while managing sacred groves across India (Kumar & Sahoo, 2021).

Following the Supreme Court's 2003 directive for compulsory EE, CPREEC has focused on enhancing teaching methods and practical experiences to strengthen EE across India. Non-governmental organisations like CPREEC are integral to this movement, supporting both regional and national initiatives (Roberts, 2009; Eames & Barker, 2011 cited in Gericke et al., 2020).

#### 10.8.6.3 Uganda Wildlife Conservation Education Centre, Africa

The facility known as the "Entebbe Zoo" was established in 1952 by the Colonial Government in Uganda as a reception centre for distressed wild animals. In the early 1960s, it transitioned into a traditional zoo, featuring non-native species as attractions. However, in May 1994, the Uganda Wildlife Education Centre Trust was founded, shifting the focus toward conservation education. Located on the shores of Lake Victoria, the centre offers a diverse range of plants and animals, making it an attractive place for both education and visitors (Uganda Wildlife Conservation Education Centre, 2023) [see Fig. 10.6].

### 10.8.7 Change Makers: People, Culture, and Environment in and Beyond EECs

There are so many variations of ESE support/EECs. Sifting through examples of ESE highlighted the fact that it is truly about the people within the systems—their culture, and power structures and their stance on environmental matters—the space where people sit on the ecocentric/anthropocentric binary. The Uttarakhand Environmental Education Centre, Almora, India has a long history and is an example of an EEC working with communities and ESE within the central Himalayas.

**Fig. 10.6** Sitting Grey Crowned Crane (*Balearica regulorum*) at the Uganda Wildlife Education Centre, Entebbe. (Attribution: sarahemcc, CC BY 2.0. https://creativecommons.org/licenses/by/2.0, via Wikimedia Commons)

### 10.8.7.1 Uttarakhand Environment Education Centre, India

The Uttarakhand Seva Nidhi, a public charitable trust founded in 1967, has been involved in community development in the Uttarakhand region since 1987. Initially appointed by the Ministry of Human Resource Development, the organisation implemented EE programs in schools and villages across Uttarakhand, then part of Uttar Pradesh (Uttarakhand Seva Nidhi Paryavaran Shiksha Sansthan, n.d.). Located in the fragile central Himalayas, Uttarakhand faces significant ecological challenges exacerbated by human activity, climate change, and migration. Traditionally isolated, the region is now rapidly changing due to globalisation and improved infrastructure (Uttarakhand Seva Nidhi Paryavaran Shiksha Sansthan, n.d.).

As the organisation's efforts expanded, they were consolidated under the Uttarakhand Seva Nidhi Paryavaran Shiksha Sansthan (USNPSS), also known as the Uttarakhand Environmental Education Centre (UEEC) (Uttarakhand Seva Nidhi Paryavaran Shiksha Sansthan, n.d.). The foundation of their EE initiatives stems from India's 1986 New Education Policy, which emphasised the integration of environmental awareness in education. A committee led by BD Pande, then Chairman of the Uttarakhand Seva Nidhi, developed the program with support from the government and local partners (Uttarakhand Seva Nidhi Paryavaran Shiksha Sansthan, n.d.).

Key individuals like BD Pande, Lalit Pande, and notable contributors such as Sri Madhava Ashish and Dr. MG Jackson played significant roles in developing EE materials and implementing grassroots programs. The EE course, Our Land Our Life, which focuses on village land rehabilitation and sustainable management, has been integrated into the school curriculum for classes 6–8 in Uttarakhand. Launched in 1988, the program expanded to include around 500 schools and involved 65,000 students and 1000 teachers by 2000. By 2002, the Department of Education formally adopted it as a separate subject, and today, nearly half a million students study EE in schools across the state. The course addresses real-life environmental and livelihood issues raised by women's groups and community-based organisations, with local communities contributing by sharing traditional knowledge of land, water, and forest management. Students engage in practical activities and learn about community organisations and their operations. To support the program, master trainers and teachers have been trained, workbooks and tools have been provided, and school visits conducted for guidance and progress evaluation. Orientation sessions were also held for school principals and education officials. Remarkably, this is the only known instance where an NGO-developed EE course has been fully integrated into a state's curriculum (Uttarakhand Seva Nidhi Paryavaran Shiksha Sansthan, n.d.).[6]

Educators associated with this Centre are an example of the importance of research emanating from centres with Jackson's contributions around the early twenty-first century. For instance, Jackson (2011) argued that transformative learning, particularly focused on worldviews, is crucial for addressing sustainability challenges. He called for ESD educators and policymakers to engage in transformative learning to determine how it should be integrated into education. Jackson emphasised the need for an alternative worldview, as the current model, shaped by Enlightenment ideals, impedes true cultural transformation. He outlines three phases of transformative learning; recognising cognitive dissonance, "standing outside oneself," and testing new assumptions. Furthermore, Jackson distinguished between passive and active learning, advocating for transformative approaches that reshape entire curricula to meet contemporary challenges.

### 10.8.8 *Other Searches for EECs*

A few representations of ESE within China were desired given the extreme polarisation between the dominant powers of the United States and China. However, the language barrier and possible censorship or power struggles limited the acquisition of information. This is true for the data from many countries with different languages and governance structures. This history already acknowledges United States influence within EEC development.

There are many centres and ESE forms within universities and formal government structures that would have complicated, possibly obfuscated the data collection and study, and made it too unwieldy. Some of these ESE programs most likely have links to schools but unless they demonstrated surprising ESE outcomes, they did not warrant attention. Furthermore, centres or ESE associated with businesses or with corporate responsibility were of little interest, unless of course there were surprising results that contribute further to the quick critical mass paradigm shift required. Representation of the centres within the South African National Park

---

[6] Please note it is difficult to verify the currency of this information… or much of the information retrieved.

System that had been corporatised—such as the Gold Fields EECs in South Africa, were however observed. Given the administering of many national parks around the world by governmental departments, this was potentially an interesting contrast.

#### 10.8.8.1 Goldfields Environmental Education Centres. Where Have They Gone?

Goldfields, a prominent South African mining company, engaged in EE through its Parks and Wildlife Service, establishing a centre in Pilanesberg National Park in 1984. Funded by the Goldfields Foundation and others, this centre benefited over 60,000 students, 3000 teachers, and 1000 college and university students (Holt-Biddle, 1987).

The educational programs, managed by the National Parks Board, emphasised practical field ecology to impart knowledge, foster appreciation, and establish a connection to nature. Staff, supported by the Bophuthatswana Department of Education, provided specialised modules aligning with school curricula and national policies (Holt-Biddle, 1987). In collaboration with Pilanesberg Game Reserve, the centre aimed to foster harmony between humanity and the environment, offering programs on basic ecology, population dynamics, bird identification, and practical field ecology. The Intensive Education Zone featured outdoor teaching experiences, including an aviary, soil erosion simulations, and food garden programs (Irwin, 1993 cited in Mudzunga, 2006). The centre extended its initiatives beyond Pilanesberg, establishing environmental clubs, partnering with educational institutions, and collaborating with Bophuthatswana Postal Services and the Defence Force (Mudzunga, 2006).

In Kenya, the Goldfields Centre initiated environmental clubs and provided outdoor education to address past apartheid restrictions (Irwin, 1993 cited in Mudzunga, 2006). Programs included video showings, a mobile film van, workshops for educators, and media collaborations to promote environmental messages. The centre contributed to syllabi revisions and promoted social responsibility through traditional nature-themed games (Irwin, 1993 cited in Mudzunga, 2006).

Goldfields Environmental Education Centres seem to have ceased operations or transformed into another entity, with only a few articles available online. One such centre still exists at the Kirstenbosch National Botanic Garden (South African National Biodiversity Institute, n.d.).

### *10.8.9 EECS and Religion*

ESE associated with religion was another variety of ESE that I thought wise to avoid. However, the EEC associated with the Evangelical Lutheran Church in Jordan and the Holy Land (ELCJHL), in Israel, was of interest. While this area has a diversity of population and religious affiliations the centre works with people of differing religions in promoting a holistic awareness of the environment, and stewardship in working towards reconciliation, justice, and wellbeing for the community.

### 10.8.9.1 Talitha Kumi School Campus, Beit Jala, Palestine, EEC

The ministry of what would become the EEC began as a wide-ranging educational initiative in 1986 (Evangelical Lutheran Church in Jordan & the Holy Land, n.d.). The subsequent establishment of Children for the Protection of Nature in Palestine (CPNP) in 1992 formalised the commitment to EE (Talitha Kumi School Campus Beit Jala Palestine: EEC, n.d.). In 1998, this work was formally integrated as an educational ministry within the Evangelical Lutheran Church in Jordan and the Holy Land (ELCJHL). Since then, the EEC has taken on the central mission of fostering environmental stewardship, focusing its efforts on education, direct action, and empowerment (Evangelical Lutheran Church in Jordan & the Holy Land, n.d.). The Centre operates atop a mountain in Beit Jala, Palestine, emphasising a holistic understanding of the environment and responsible stewardship. Situated in a lush area surrounded by diverse indigenous Palestinian trees and plants, the EEC's unique setting serves as a platform for international advocacy, drawing attention to environmental issues resulting from the Israeli occupation (Talitha Kumi School Campus Beit Jala Palestine: EEC, n.d.). There is a vision, "To protect the Palestinian nature and its environment and make it clean and empty of all solid, liquid, industrial remnants." The centre has evolved to include a botanical garden, a Palestinian natural history museum, an interactive environmental exhibition, and a bird migration monitoring station. With a focus on education, the EEC works on projects involving civic engagement, peace-building, and eco-justice in Palestine (Talitha Kumi School Campus Beit Jala Palestine: EEC, n.d.).

Each year, the EEC organises over 32 workshops, collaborating with about eight schools in the Bethlehem and Ramallah areas. These workshops delve into crucial environmental topics such as climate change, renewable energy, biodiversity, and waste management, all aimed at nurturing the next generation of environmentally conscious citizens. Throughout the challenges of the COVID-19 pandemic, the EEC was a beacon of support, offering vital information on safety measures and health protocols to the wider community (Evangelical Lutheran Church in Jordan & the Holy Land, n.d.).

The centre firmly believes that classroom learning is best reinforced by hands-on experience. With this in mind, it has led students in bi-annual campaigns focused on waste clean-ups, harvesting, planting, and hiking excursions. Additionally, the EEC has helped establish environmental clubs in schools, which have gone on to create composting systems, greenhouses, and lead awareness campaigns on environmental sustainability (Evangelical Lutheran Church in Jordan & the Holy Land, n.d.).

Beyond the classroom, the EEC extends its reach into the community by hosting several public events. Chief among these is the annual Olive Harvest Festival, a vibrant celebration of Palestinian culture and the labor of farmers. Partnering with the Bethlehem Municipality, the festival includes a market for farmers to sell their harvest, while students perform traditional dances, songs, and poetry honoring the significance of the olive to Palestinian heritage (Evangelical Lutheran Church in Jordan & the Holy Land, n.d.).

Internationally, the EEC is known for its annual Palestinian Environmental Conference, which draws environmentalists from across the globe. This event serves as a platform for exchanging research, building partnerships, and strategising global initiatives for better stewardship of the planet. Twice a year, the EEC also organises Bird Week, at its Talitha Kumi Bird Ringing and Monitoring Station. Bird researchers gather to present their findings, offering the public a chance to witness the variety of species that stop in Palestine during their migratory journeys between Europe and Africa (Evangelical Lutheran Church in Jordan & the Holy Land, n.d.). A joint project with the European Natural Heritage Fund resulted in an exhibition named The White Stork, highlighting migration routes and the human impact on these creatures (Talitha Kumi School Campus Beit Jala Palestine: EEC, n.d.).

At its heart, the EEC is committed to creating a community of environmental advocates—individuals who are not only knowledgeable about the intricate environmental challenges unique to Palestine but who are also ready to take meaningful action to protect it. This mission of environmental citizenship drives everything the centre does, weaving together education, cultural preservation, and activism into a holistic vision for a sustainable future (Evangelical Lutheran Church in Jordan & the Holy Land, n.d.).

## 10.8.10  Diversity in EECs

There are countless not-for-profit organisations, ranging from grassroots to international, and some with a unique grassroots-international focus. Several were given special recognition within this study. Many not-for-profit NGOs benefit from a level of independence and flexibility that is often absent in more rigid governance or business structures. With financial resources and influence to shape decision-making, these organisations can bring critical thinking, global foresight, and a commitment to exemplary ESE principles to the forefront of their work. The not-for-profits that have a focus on environmental concerns tend to have their specific cause at heart. Soetwater, Kommetjie, Cape Town is an EEC presenting itself as a classroom by the sea. They focus on outcomes-based education in accordance with the national education policy. Other centres or representations of ESE emerging from not-for-profit organisations that were investigated for possible inclusion in this history were:

- The Wildlife and Environment Society of South Africa which operates four education centres and runs programs for schools.
- AfriCat Environmental Education Centre, Namibia, Africa. And,
- World Wildlife Fund's Living Planet Centre in Surrey, UK. One of nearly 100 WWF offices operating around the world, WWF UK offers many resources for

schools including environmental leadership programs and teacher development (World Wildlife Fund (n.d.).

## 10.8.11 Africa

There does seem to be a strong focus on areas in Africa/South Africa, which coincide with general histories of colonialism and a past and present involving inequity, resource depletion, and flora and fauna diversity under threat. The journey toward independence for African nations unfolded in the aftermath of World War II, characterised by negotiations, peaceful protests, and armed struggles. This period witnessed the global surge of anti-colonialist sentiments and the gradual dismantling of European empires. Despite attaining political independence, the enduring legacy of colonialism lingers, exerting profound impacts on social structures, economies, and governance systems. These influences continue to shape Africa's development trajectory and its relationship with the broader world (Guardiola-Rivera, 2010).

The following examples in the realm of ESE in Africa are contextualised within this historical backdrop of post-colonial struggles and their enduring effects. It is important to acknowledge the evolution of conservation practices. Community-based conservation emerges as a significant departure from earlier models, such as buffer zones introduced by UNESCO's Man and the Biosphere program in 1979 and Integrated Conservation and Development Projects popularised in the late 1980s and early 1990s. Criticisms of these predecessors often revolved around their insufficient inclusion of local communities in the planning process (Steyn, 2002).

In contrast, community-based conservation represents a paradigm shift, placing the active involvement of local communities at its core. The overarching objectives extend beyond wildlife and biodiversity conservation to include providing economic incentives for local populations. Participatory, decentralised, and village-based approaches unfold through time in the context of ESE in Africa (Steyn, 2002).

### 10.8.11.1 The Okonjima Nature Reserve/AfriCat EEC, Namibia

In Namibia, then South West Africa, in the 1970s a farming family responded to witnessing the challenges faced by farmers dealing with losses from carnivores, particularly leopards, by transitioning from traditional farming and trophy hunting to managing a private nature reserve, Okonjima Nature Reserve. The goal was to restore the land to its natural state and protect cheetahs and leopards from harm. To finance their efforts and educate others, they opened their converted farmhouse to guests. This venture eventually grew into one of Namibia's premier places for observing large carnivores in the wild and learning about conservation (AfriCat Namibia, n.d.). This story continues into the 1990s where the family establishes the AfriCat Environmental Education Centre to compliment the nature reserve (see Fig. 10.7).

## 10.8 Global EEC Habitats: Diverse Environments Across Borders

**Fig. 10.7** Leopard, Okonjima, Namibia. (Attribution: Sonse, CC BY 2.0. https://creativecommons.org/licenses/by/2.0, via Wikimedia Commons)

Okonjima Nature Reserve and the AfriCat Foundation provide valuable insights into the changing landscape of conservation and ESE in Africa. As already stated, from 1972 to 1982, the environmental non-governmental organisation sector was dominated by conservation issues, primarily catering to the interests of the white population. The second period, spanning from 1982 to 1988, witnessed a notable shift. Environmental non-governmental organisation sectors began diversifying their focus to encompass environmental issues relevant to people of color, moving away from predominantly white conservation concerns. The final period, from 1988 to 1992, saw the emergence of radicalised environmental activism. Environmental non-governmental organisation sectors directed their efforts toward challenging governmental and business activities considered harmful to both the human and natural environment. This period emphasised the interconnectedness of social and environmental issues, leading to more politically charged and activist approaches within the South African environmental non-governmental organisation sector (Steyn, 2002).

Namibia, gained independence from South Africa in 1990. Many of the environmental problems experienced stem from the apartheid regime where social, resource and economic inequalities existed (Smego, 2002). Namibian Indigenous people were pushed out of the fertile lands to smaller plots. For Namibia there was no consideration given to the environmental problems that would eventuate when resource limited land is overpopulated. In northern Namibia where there is greater human population and virtually no remaining wildlife, ESE efforts are concentrated on remedying deforestation and alternate energy sources such as solar. In north central Namibia ESE is concentrated on initiatives to address conflicts between farmers and predators given this is where most of the leopard and cheetah populations live (Smego, 2002). The Okonjima Nature Reserve and the founding family's Africat Foundation established in 1993 is a major provider of ESE. The AfriCat Foundation, a non-profit organisation focuses on welfare, education, communal carnivore conservation, and research that complements the work at the Okonjima Nature Reserve—important for the long-term conservation of Namibia's large carnivores (AfriCat Namibia, n.d.). The AfriCat EE Program had its beginnings in 1998 with the opening of the World Society for the Protection of Animals/AfriCat Environmental Education Centre. In a one-to-3-day visit students get to role play surviving in the bush as an animal. It is a game emphasising the necessity of balance between populations of herbivores, carnivores and humans and is seen as particularly important given the history of large carnivores being a food source for Indigenous populations. From the late 1990s the AfriCat EEC started to visit schools to extend their work. Smego's (2002) covers familiar ground for EEC projects when it discusses the difficulty in gaining evidence of program impact. To that end, in 2002 the Centre was undertaking a Caring for the Earth Community Campaign with six schools over a 1-year period. This program showed much more transformative education potential given it was to raise awareness of current local environmental issues through student participation in campaigns designed and motivated by the students themselves. It was hoped that an evaluation of this project would yield evidence of program impact. Teacher education and funding seem to be some of the biggest hurdles for ESE which has been encompassed within the curriculum within specific subjects and also as a cross curricula component (Smego, 2002).

### 10.8.11.2 The Wildlife and Environment Society of South Africa and Their Centres

An example of an NGO that has morphed with the changing times in Africa is the Wildlife and Environment Society (WESSA) of South Africa that runs a few EECs—at Umngeni Valley Nature Reserve, Twinstreams EEC located at Mtunzini in Zululand and one at Treasure Beach near Durban. They seem to, on the whole, be changing their nomenclature, calling their centres 'education centres.' The centre at Groenkloof, located in Pretoria no longer seems associated with WESSA (WESSA, n.d.). All these centres provide environmental, ecological and nature conservation education and, hands on training for teachers, and scientific education up to tertiary level.

One innovative program provided at these centres integrates EE into the STEAM (Science, Technology, Engineering, Arts, and Mathematics) framework by adding a crucial environmental component, transforming it into eSTEAM. This innovative approach emphasises creative problem-solving and hands-on learning, where students engage with real-world environmental challenges. By identifying these issues and collaborating on solutions, learners develop critical thinking skills and are empowered to take ownership of their education, becoming proactive agents of change. Through an 8-step process, the program allows students to work together to solve specific environmental problems, while meeting academic goals across different subjects. This cross-curricular method encourages interdisciplinary learning, blending EE with core academic subjects. The eSTEAM program not only addresses pressing societal and environmental concerns but also nurtures creativity and entrepreneurial thinking. By doing so, it equips learners to contribute positively to South Africa's economy and work toward social equity. Graduates are envisioned as not just job seekers, but creators, with the potential to inspire innovation and drive societal change. Through workshops and challenges, teachers and students are given the tools to incorporate this process into their regular classroom lessons. This holistic approach fosters a new generation of learners who are capable of driving positive change in their communities and the broader world (WESSA, n.d.).

On a broader scale WESSA, with a history spanning over 90 years, collaborates extensively with schools and teachers across South Africa, enhancing school curricula with EE and promoting sustainable practices through local and international programs. Promoting environmental responsibility WESSA leads various educational initiatives, including Foundation for EE (FEE) programs the Blue Flag and Green Key program and coordinates eco-schools (since 2003) programs in South Africa. It also supports ESD in collaboration with UNESCO (Dirty Boots, n.d.; The Green Directory, n.d.; WESSA: The Wildlife and Environment Society of South Africa, n.d.). Of significance is Share-Net, a collaborative network focused on grassroots EE resource development in Southern Africa. The Umgeni Valley Project, operated by WESSA, hosts Share-Net and the Southern African Development Community Regional EE Programme (SADC REEP) (Taylor & van Rensburg, 2002; O'Donoghue & Russo, 2004).

## *10.8.12 Some European Examples of EECs*

Evidence suggests greater success when formal school ESE learning is place-based with teachers and schools having autonomy and flexibility in developing and actioning curriculum—connecting with parental interest and community involvement in ESE projects (Buckler & Creech, 2014). However, countries such as Italy and Greece, with centralised education systems, have given greater attention to ESE within the curriculum and consequently were of interest in this analysis.

### 10.8.12.1 EEC Collaboration in Italy

In Italy, an intriguing collaboration exists between the government departments of education and environment, which includes EECs. This partnership has created a network involving a teacher from each school, regional authorities, and research and innovation institutes. A parallel network encompasses EECs and EE territorial labs, focused on communicating and mediating ESE among schools. Programs emphasise additional sustainability learning at both pedagogical and socio-organisational levels, addressing non-structured issues and promoting a culture of communication and mutual respect (Buckler & Creech, 2014; Posch, 1998 cited in Mayer & Morgensen, 2005).

Italy's commitment to EE dates back to 1996, when challenges in integrating ESE into school practices prompted an agreement driven by a Movement of Educational Cooperation inspired by French reformer Celestin Freinet emphasising student autonomy (Global Education and Cultural Diversity, n.d.; Morgensen & Mayer, 2005). The networks established within the Ministries of Education and Environment aimed to foster collaborative efforts, though by 2005, the relationship was deemed stronger at local and regional levels than nationally. A notable outcome was the Charter of Principles for EE, emphasising changes in teaching roles and cross-disciplinary approaches (Buckler & Creech, 2014; Morgensen & Mayer, 2005). This national INFEA (EE, Information, and Training) program, coordinated by regional governments to promote grassroots ESD involving collaboration between the Ministry of Environment and regional authorities supports ESD activities at local levels through various entities, including NGOs, universities, schools, and environmental agencies (Buckler & Creech, 2014).

For example, in the Abruzzo region, over 30 EECs (CEA) play a crucial role in implementing sustainable development projects tailored to local contexts as their part in the INFEA program. They are recognised for their diverse activities—including educational programs and collaborations with schools, private sectors, and local authorities—their heterogeneity promotes diversity in sustainability efforts (Fedarene, n.d.; Welcome to the National Park of Abruzzo Lazio and Molise, n.d.).

In November 2019, Italy became the first country to mandate climate change education for students aged 6–19, requiring 33 h per year. Prime Minister Lorenzo Fioramonti, from the Five Star Movement, spearheaded this initiative, integrating environmental and societal considerations into core education (Bored Teacher, 2020). Influential experts, including Jeffrey D. Sachs and Jeremy Rifkin, contributed to reshaping Italy's curriculum with an emphasis on a comprehensive and interdisciplinary approach to sustainability (Bored Teacher, 2020).

Italy's initiatives are recognised as pioneering and align with the United Nations' emphasis on integrating sustainable development across education levels. UNESCO supports interdisciplinary education as a critical component of this effort (UNESCO, 2019, cited in Fioramonti et al., 2021). Fioramonti et al. (2021) explore Italy's reforms, highlighting challenges such as the impact of the COVID-19 pandemic, delays in implementation, and resource constraints. Despite these challenges, the transformative potential of integrated education and research in addressing global issues is underscored, advocating for ongoing research to assess the long-term impact of Italy's reforms and encouraging comparative analyses with other countries adopting similar strategies.

### 10.8.12.2 An ESE Perspective in Greece

Greece has a focus on teacher education within 46 centres for ESE amidst their education ministry. ESE within teacher education and teacher professional development has been difficult to establish and develop and was highlighted it the final Decade of Education for Sustainable Development report as a major priority in stakeholder findings (Buckler & Creech, 2014). For these reasons EECs with a focus on teacher education were of interest.

Greece's delayed adoption of EE projects, attributed to emerging environmental problems in the late 1970s, started taking root by 1991. Challenges such as teacher workload and limited training had hindered participation in EE programs (Spyropoulos, 1986, cited in Flogaitis & Alexopoulou, 1991; Buckler & Creech, 2014).

The aim of EECs is to raise awareness and educate students, teachers, and the local community on environmental issues. They conduct various programs, create educational materials, and collaborate with scientific institutions, focusing on themes such as local biodiversity, wildlife, and the sustainable management of energy resources (Discover Kastoria, n.d.).

The pivotal role of EECs in Greece is exemplified by the centre in Kastoria founded in 1995.

> The main objective of the establishment and operation of the CESE/EEC Kastoria is to raise awareness and educate students, teachers and the local community on issues of environmental practice, in order to develop knowledge, attitudes and behaviours that will contribute to the protection of ecological balance, quality of life and sustainable development. (Discover Kastoria, n.d.)

Kastoria CESE

Kastoria CESE, has been actively promoting EE since its staffing in 1996. Operated under an agreement between the Ministry of Education and the Municipality of Kastoria, the centre focuses on nurturing a deep understanding of environmental issues among students. Staffed by dedicated teachers from primary education, CESE is funded through a mix of European and national resources, with support from the Youth and Lifelong Learning Foundation. Its home is located within the Environmental Park by Lake Kastoria, a site recognised for its ecological significance (Discover Kastoria, n.d.).

To fulfill its mission, Kastoria CESE offers a variety of educational programs for young students (1st and 2nd grade) and informal, extracurricular EE programs for youth groups, including day-long and three-day EE initiatives. It also supports local schools by collaborating with educational authorities to enhance their environmental curricula. In addition, Kastoria CESE creates educational materials in both print and digital formats, and organises training seminars for teachers and community members (Discover Kastoria, n.d.).

The centre engages with scientific institutions nationally and internationally to share knowledge, conduct research, and develop joint educational projects and by participating in scientific conferences and publishing findings contributes to the broader discourse on EE. A key focus of Kastoria CESE's activities is the unique natural and cultural characteristics of the local area, particularly Lake Kastoria and its surrounding ecosystems, which serve as both study subjects and educational platforms. The Centre emphasises themes such as local biodiversity, sustainable resource management, and the climate crisis, while also exploring the intersection of natural and cultural heritage. Kastoria CESE leads two national School Thematic Networks of EE—"Lakes: Sources of Inspiration for Environmental Education Programs," launched in 1999, and "Biodiversity: The Laboratory of Life," established in 2003. Additionally, it acts as a coordinator for various School Networks throughout Greece, furthering its commitment to EE across the country (Discover Kastoria, n.d.).

The integration of formal and non-formal EE in Greece, specifically through Centres of EE established by the Ministry of National Education and Religious Affairs, is explored by Skanavisa and Petreniti (2016). While these centres play a vital role in sensitising youth to environmental issues, supporting local schools, and organising teacher training, challenges persist. These include inadequate infrastructure, reliance on EU funding, limited promotion of EE objectives, and non-interdisciplinary approaches.

In Greece, the aftermath of the 2007–2008 financial crisis prompted a discussion on the institutionalised, school-based approach to EE. Despite initial setbacks resulting in the closure of 40% of EECs and the abolishment of EE counsellor positions, the decentralised structure and interdisciplinary methods have fostered resilience. This recovery is supported by EU funds, local, and national government backing. However, sustaining funding diversity without compromising public control poses a challenge. The ongoing debate about integrating EE into the standard curriculum raises questions about the long-term resilience of EE in Greece (Yanniris & Garis, 2018).

### 10.8.12.3 An ESE/EEC Perspective in Spain

During the 1970s and 1980s in Spain, Paulo Freire's influence in critical popular education impacted Enrique de Castro, a working-class priest in Madrid. De Castro's pragmatic interpretation of Freire's concepts, emphasising cooperation, solidarity, and self-management, led to a unique educational approach (De Freitas Ermel & Hernández Huerta, 2022).

### Huerto Alegre Center for Educational Innovation

Huerto Alegre, as a cooperative founded in 1982, employs an interdisciplinary team of 30 people dedicated to EE and raising awareness. The team's diverse expertise enables them to face educational and professional challenges, contributing to the development of a more just, balanced, and sustainable society. The centre plays a crucial role in providing training programs, facilitating outings into the natural environment, and fostering collaborations with educational professionals and students (Huerto Alegre, n.d.).

Huerto Alegre's program, designed for children and youth, goes beyond traditional ESD practices by fostering critical thinking and connections with the natural environment through collaboration with educators. It redefines ESD within the Earth Charter (EC) framework (Martínez-Rodríguez & Fernández-Herrería, 2022).

> We educate people in order to teach them to live, to solve real problems, to be with others, in contact with reality, reflecting, studying, exploring, exchanging ideas, and getting excited about different everyday situations.
>
> Learning, therefore, is not limited to the space and timetable of the educational center. It is necessary to have experiences which put you in contact with different realities and contexts. (Huerto Alegre, n.d.)

Huerto Alegre, as a Centre for Educational Innovation, has chaired the Andalusian Network of EECs since 2007. Aligned with various networks, it holds a unique position, promoting alternative visions beyond the prevailing economic model (Martínez-Rodríguez & Fernández-Herrería, 2022).

Resisting the neoliberal co-optation of ESD Huerto Alegre stands as a dissident voice, advocating for a civic pedagogy connecting educational institutions with communities. The experience is viewed as a form of resistance, constructing new subjectivities capable of responding to socio-environmental challenges (Martínez-Rodríguez & Fernández-Herrería, 2022).

Huerto Alegre's socio-environmental practices contribute to the development of resistant subjectivities, challenging the dominant discourse and offering alternative visions within the Community of Life. The experience emphasises an ecocentric view, rooted in ethics of care and the sustenance of life, proposing structural changes in societal models. However, the absence of a systematic assessment model prompts a call for further evaluation (Martínez-Rodríguez & Fernández-Herrería, 2022).

In the realm of teacher leadership and Deep Ecology, Smith's (2020) work illustrates how teachers, through enhanced connections with and love for the environment, become examples of sustainability. This aligns with an ecocentric perspective, crucial for fostering sustainability (Martínez-Rodríguez & Fernández-Herrería, 2022).

ESE in Barcelona, Spain

Barcelona, Spain, has demonstrated a longstanding commitment to ESD, seen in initiatives like the 2002 Citizen Commitment to Sustainability, involving 800 local organisations, including EECs. It has a well-established local network involving formal and non-formal education in place-based ESE issues and education (Buckler & Creech, 2014). The Escoles + Sostenibles program (formerly known as School Agenda 21) has seen significant participation. This program offers training and resources to enhance sustainability in schools. To address challenges within the official curriculum, several educational projects have emerged, emphasising collaboration and networking between primary and secondary schools. Many schools have made environmental issues the central focus of their social and educational commitments (González-Gaudiano et al., 2020).

A few EECs can be found in the Barcelona area, for example, the Natura Angeleta Ferrer, a facility of Badalona City Council (Provincial Council of Barcelona, n.d.), but it is difficult to gauge their influence and input into such networks without further exploration. However, González-Gaudiano et al. (2020) talk of EECs being very popular for school visits after the financial crisis indicating that they play an important role in local ESE networks.

These brief case studies from Barcelona and Huerto Alegre illustrate diverse approaches to ESE, emphasising critical perspectives, community engagement, and alternative visions that challenge prevailing economic models—influenced by Paulo Freire and ecopedagogy. The transformative potential of education is highlighted as these initiatives seek to reshape subjectivities and foster a deeper connection with the environment and the sustainability needed to sustain it.

## 10.9 Conclusion

A diverse selection of EECs with a variety of historical, social, cultural, political and environmental differences—with a plurality of connections to colonialism, have been traversed throughout this chapter. This work presents a rich tapestry of EEC examples worldwide—highlighting and exploring their characteristics and evolution. Starting with the early establishment of national parks and conservation education to initiatives such as the Outward Bound movement and the Wegscheide Centre—companions along the historical progression of emerging EECs. Platforms for fostering awareness and engagement with the environment, if not with an often anthropocentric orientation.

The framework of global governance in developing ESD underscores the impact of neoliberalism and international conferences—and initiatives, such as the Earth Charter, the United Nations Decade of Education for Sustainable Development and UNESCO's ESD Roadmap. These global efforts have shaped the landscape of EECs, and ESE in general, and have prompted both the promotion of and resistance

## 10.9 Conclusion

toward addressing blind spots within this framework associated with anthropocentrism (see Fig. 10.8) and neoliberal agendas.

The chapter highlighted the diverse environmental, social, economic and political habitats in which EECs operate, from Nordic countries and marine ecosystems to extreme environments like the poles and deserts, to centres dealing with post colonialisation. Each EEC offers unique insights and approaches, demonstrating the importance of contextualising EE within local cultures and ecosystems. Ecotourism seems to play a significant role for many EECs around the world prompting questions about the environment's sustainability within this onslaught and possibly the authenticity or possibility of transformative ESE within these settings. There is an understanding of ecotourism being an essential source of income for some communities within the engulfing Western frame.

In regions such as South America, Africa, India and Australia, there is the intersection of colonialist ecological and education practices and the valuable input of Indigenous knowledges and local community involvement together with ESE practices, illustrating the role and necessity of best practice within EECs in championing biodiversity and cultural heritage. These was a colonialist conservation culture dominating the field yielding to the valuable input of local community involvement and Indigenous knowledges. There was an exploration of how EECs have addressed the complexities of identity and diversity, including intersections with religion. Some EECs adopt an overtly positivist stance, linked to ecological institutions, while others foster a more socio-cultural connection—and at times transformative. However, ecotourism and economics play a part and distinguishing between authentic ESE and coercive control (either colonialist or neoliberal) that undermines

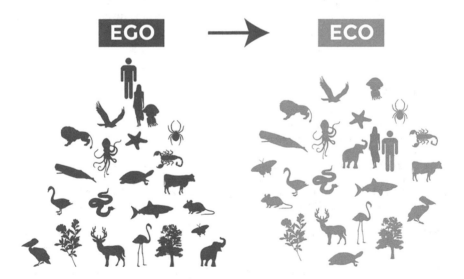

**Fig. 10.8** Anthropocentric vs ecocentric graphic. (Attribution: IDA Projekt, CC BY-SA 4.0. https://creativecommons.org/licenses/by-sa/4.0, via Wikimedia Commons. The image of a woman is an addition to the original image)

Indigenous autonomy and agency is difficult to determine within a desktop study. While EECs play a crucial role in sensitising and connecting students to the environment, as well as fostering important within ESE, and good ESE can be transformative, many countries still face the problem of having a ecological footprint far greater than the Earth's carrying capacity. Most of the countries studied had an Overshoot Day far exceeding what the Earth has to offer (*see* Fig. 10.3). The only countries within this study that lived within their capacity were Kenya, Namibia, Uganda, Jordan, Palestine and India (Earth overshoot day 2024). Mexico, Brazil, Peru and Costa Rica were at least overshooting in the last half of the year.

There are many networks of ESE which are EEC centre like but seem to operate purely through online resources and administration with no physical hub. While this may be economically essential, and in some cases environmentally beneficial, if there is no actual rather than virtual place to meet, it also diminishes the important element of the tactile and sensory nature of the environment. This may contribute to the illusion of disconnect given we are intrinsically connected to our environment—inside and outside. Anthropocentrism leads to the Illusion of separation (Naess, 1989; Seed, 2024). However some EECs can and do play an important part as hubs of such centres—utilising networking and resourcing technology to full advantage.

Reflecting on EECs as champions of change, they can serve, not only as hubs for environmental knowledge, understanding, and action but also as critical players in fostering stewardship. This stewardship can encourage individuals to embrace personal growth and develop a deeper connection to the natural world—an understanding of being connected to and an intricate part of the environment. Best practice EECs can promote and support critical thinking through a systems-oriented, future-worldview-focused approach, paving the way for a sustainable future that embodies an ecocentric sensibility, education global citizenry. In many instances EECs seem integral to the dynamic pulse of ESE networks.

# References

Abulafia, D. (2003). *The Mediterranean in history*. Getty Publications.
AfriCat Namibia. (n.d.). *Our story. AfriCat, Namibia*. Retrieved November 8, 2023, from https://africat.org/our-story/
Alice Springs Desert Park. (2024). *Education*. Retrieved July 23, 2023, from https://alicesprings-desertpark.com.au/main/education/desert-explorer-program
Andrzejewski, J. (2005). The social justice, peace, and environmental education standards project. *Multicultural Perspectives, 7*(1), 8–16. http://www.informaworld.com/10.1207/s15327892mcp0701_3
Bamfield Marine Sciences Centre. (n.d.). *Education: Hands on learning • Small class sizes • Field research opportunities*. Retrieved November 16, 2023, from https://bamfieldmsc.com/bmsc-overview
Blum, N. (2008a). Environmental education in Costa Rica: Building a framework for sustainable development? *International Journal of Educational Development, 28*, 348–358. https://doi.org/10.1016/j.ijedudev.2007.05.008

Blum, N. (2008b). Ethnography and environmental education: Understanding the relationships between schools and communities in Costa Rica. *Ethnography and Education, 3*(1), 33–48.

Bored Teachers. (2020, June 21). Italy becomes first country to mandate climate change education. *Bored Teachers.* https://www.boredteachers.com/post/climate-change-italy-education

Boyd, D. R. (2011). The implicit constitutional right to live in a healthy environment. *Review of European Community & International Environmental Law, 20*(2), 171–179. https://doi.org/10.1111/j.1467-9388.2011.00701.x

Boyd, D. R. (2013). *The status of constitutional protection for the environment in other nations: Paper 4.* David Suzuki Foundation. https://davidsuzuki.org/wp-content/uploads/2013/11/status-constitutional-protection-environment-other-nations.pdf

Buckler, C., & Creech, H. (2014). *Shaping the future we want: UN Decade of Education for Sustainable Development: Final report.* UNESCO. https://unesdoc.unesco.org/ark:/48223/pf0000230171

Bush, R. A., Coleman, J. T., Coleman, L. A., Driscoll, P. V., & Woodworth, B. K. (2022). *Growing capacity to support migratory shorebird resilience at three of Queensland's coastal Ramsar sites: A two year volunteer-led field project.* Queensland Wader Study Group A special interest group of the Queensland Ornithological Society Inc. https://waders.org.au/shorebirds/wp-content/uploads/2022/12/Growing-capacity-to-support-migratory-shorebird-resilience-at-three-of-Queensland.pdf

Calzadilla, P. V. (2019). A paradigm shift in courts' view on nature: The Atrato River and Amazon Basin cases in Colombia. *Law Environment & Development Journal, 15*, 1–11. http://www.lead-journal.org/content/19001.pdf

Calzadilla, P. V., & Kotzé, L. J. (2018). Living in harmony with nature? A critical appraisal of the rights of Mother Earth in Bolivia. *Transnational Environmental Law, 7*(3), 397–424. https://doi.org/10.1017/S2047102518000201

Carruthers, J. (1997). Nationhood and national parks comparative examples from the post-imperial experience. In T. Griffiths & L. Robin (Eds.), *Ecology and empire* (pp. 125–138). Edinburgh University Press.

Chatelard, G. (2003). Conflicts of interest over the Wadi Rum reserve: Were they avoidable? A socio-political critique. *Nomadic Peoples, 7*(1), 138–158.

Chatty, D. (1998). Enclosures and exclusions: Conserving wildlife in pastoral areas of the Middle East. *Anthropology Today, 14*(4), 2–7.

Churchill Northern Studies Centre. (n.d.). *School programs at the centre.* Retrieved Accessed August 13, 2023, from https://churchillscience.ca/school-programs/

City of Cape Town Isixeko Sasekapa Stad Kaapstad. (n.d.). *Environmental education centres.* Retrieved June 20, 2023, from https://www.capetown.gov.za/Family%20and%20home/See-all-city-facilities/Our-recreational-facilities/Environmental%20education%20centres

Corcoran, P. (2002). The values of the Earth Charter in education for sustainable development. *Australian Journal of Environmental Education, 18*, 77–80. https://doi.org/10.1017/s0814062600001154

Corcoran, P. B. (2004). What if? The educational possibilities of the Earth Charter. *Educational Studies, 36*(1), 108–117. http://search.ebscohost.com/login.aspx?direct=true&db=tfh&AN=14535858&site=ehost-live

CPR Environmental Education Centre. (n.d.). *History.* Retrieved June 12, 2023, from https://cpreec.org/

Czarny, G. (2017). Schooling processes and the indigenous peoples in urban contexts in Mexico. In W. T. Pink & G. W. Noblit (Eds.), *Second international handbook of urban education* (pp. 487–504). Springer.

Dahr, J. (2023, October 9). Holding the fire: Indigenous voices on the great unravelling ancient wisdom with Anne Poelina [Podcast]. *Resilience.* Post Carbon Institute. Retrieved December 8, 2023, from https://www.resilience.org/stories/2023-10-09/holding-the-fire-episode-2-anne-poelina/

Day, B., & Monroe, M. (Eds.). (2000). *Environmental education & communication for a sustainable world: Handbook for international practitioners*. United States Agency for International Development.

De Freitas Ermel, T., & Hernández Huerta, J. L. (2022). Brazilian influences on Popular Education in Spain. The hallmarks of Paulo Freire in Enrique de Castro's work. *Journal of New Approaches in Educational Research, 11*(2). https://doi.org/10.7821/naer.2022.7.970

Dimenäs, J., & Alexandersson, M. (2012). Crossing disciplinary borders: Perspectives on learning about sustainable development. *Journal of Teacher Education for Sustainability, 14*(1), 5. https://doi.org/10.2478/v10099-012-0001-0

Dirty Boots. (n.d.). *Wessa uMngeni Valley Nature Reserve and Education Centre—Howick, KwaZulu-Natal*. Retrieved April 20, 2024, from https://www.dirtyboots.co.za/outdoor-education/umngeni-valley-nature-reserve-and-education-centre

Discover Kastoria. (n.d.). *Environmental Education Centre (E.E.C.)*. Retrieved May 29, 2024, from https://www.discoverkastoria.gr/en/place/environmental-education-centre-e-e-c/

Disinger, J. (1993). The search for paradigms for research in environmental education. In R. Mrazek (Ed.), *Alternative paradigms in environmental education research: Monographs in environmental education and environmental studies* (Vol. VIII, pp. 19–25). North American Association for Environmental Education.

Eames, C., & Barker, M. (2011). Understanding student learning in environmental education in Aotearoa New Zealand. *Australian Journal of Environmental Education, 27*(1), 186–191. https://doi.org/10.1017/s0814062600000173

EcoTourismWorld. (n.d.). *Environmental education in Nordic countries*. Retrieved June 30, 2024, from https://ecotourism-world.com/environmental-education-in-nordic-countries/#google_vignette

Encyclopedia Britannica. (n.d.-a). *Britannica*. Retrieved December 12, 2023, from https://www.britannica.com/search?query=country+independance

Encyclopedia Britannica. (n.d.-b). *Barguzinsky Nature Reserve*. Britannica. Retrieved October 10, 2023, from https://www.britannica.com/place/Barguzinsky-Nature-Reserve

ePoP Network. (n.d.). *ePoP platform*. Retrieved July 12, 2023, from https://epop.network/en/

Evangelical Lutheran Church in Jordan & the Holy Land. (n.d.). *Environmental education centre*. Retrieved July 26, 2024, from https://elcjhl.org/eec

Ewing, N. (2011). Bamfield marine sciences centre live dives. *Green Teacher, 92*, 43.

Fedarene. (n.d.). *Abruzzo Region Network of Education Centre for Environment: A reference for education*. Retrieved May 29, 2024, from https://fedarene.org/best-practice/abruzzo-region-network-of-education-centre-for-environment-a-reference-for-education/

Fioramonti, L., Giordano, C., & Basile, F. L. (2021). Fostering academic interdisciplinarity: Italy's pioneering experiment on sustainability education in schools and universities. *Frontiers in Sustainability, 2*. https://doi.org/10.3389/frsus.2021.631610

Flogaitis, E., & Alexopoulou, I. (1991). Environmental education in Greece. *European Journal of Education, 26*(4), 339–345.

Fundacion Corcovado YouTube Channel. (n.d.). *Fundacion Corcovado*. Retrieved June 26, 2024, from https://www.youtube.com/@funcorco?app=desktop

Gelter, H. (2000). Friluftsliv: The Scandinavian philosophy of outdoor life. *Canadian Journal of Environmental Education (CJEE)*, 77–92.

Gericke, N., Manni, A., & Stagell, U. (2020). The green school movement in Sweden—Past, present and future. In A. Gough, J. Chi-Kin Lee, & E. PoKeung Tsang (Eds.), *Green schools globally: Stories of impact on education for sustainable development* (pp. 209–332). Springer.

Global Education and Cultural Diversity. (n.d.). *Celestine Freinet—The modern methodology*. Retrieved June 9, 2023, from https://globaleduca.hypotheses.org/med-the-museum-global-education-and-cultural-diversity/autonomy-pedagogy-educators-gallery/the-modern-school-movement/celestine-ferrer-the-modern-methodology

González-Gaudiano, E. J. (2016). ESD: Power, politics, and policy: "Tragic optimism" from Latin America. *Journal of Environmental Education, 47*(2), 118–127. https://doi.org/10.1080/00958964.2015.1072704

González-Gaudiano, E. J., Meira-Cartea, P. A., & Gutiérrez-Bastida, J. M. (2020). Green schools in Mexico and Spain: Trends and critical perspective. In A. Gough, J. Chi-Kin Lee, & E. PoKeungTsang (Eds.), *Green schools globally: Stories of impact on education for sustainable development* (pp. 269–288). Springer.

Gough, A. (1997). *Education and the environment: Policy, trends and the problems of marginalisation*. Australian Council for Educational Research.

Gough, A. (1998). Researching a baseline: Science in Victorian schools, better known as "the truth is out there but I can't talk about it": The S Files or stories from the garden of good and evil. In *Australian Association for Environmental Education 10th Biennial Conference*. Australian Association for Environmental Education.

Gough, A. (2000). Governmentality and the state: (of) science education research in Victoria. The FBI* vs the state: Stories of science education research. Paper presented at the *Foucault and Education SIG program at the AREA Annual Meeting*, New Orleans, USA.

Gruenewald, D. A. (2004). A Foucauldian analysis of environmental education: Toward the socio-ecological challenge of the Earth Charter. *Curriculum Inquiry, 34*(1), 71–107. https://doi.org/10.1111/j.1467-873X.2004.00281.x

Guardiola-Rivera, O. (2007). Return of the fetish: A plea for a new materialism. *Law and Critique, 18*(3), 275–307. https://doi.org/10.1007/s10978-007-9016-4

Guardiola-Rivera, O. (2010). *What if Latin America ruled the world?: How the South will take the North through the 21st century*. Bloomsbury Press.

Haltia. (n.d.). *Welcome to Haltia—The Finnish Nature Centre*. Retrieved July 1, 2024, from https://haltia.com/en/

Haukka, A., Pilke, E., & Salin, M. (2020). My Forest—Student-centred approaches for outdoor learning. In R. H. Colas (Ed.), *Nurturing affinity to nature* (pp. 42–52). Girona.

Hilson, M. (2008). *The Nordic model: Scandinavia since 1945*. Reaktion Books.

Hjem. (n.d.). *Læring i Friluft Læringsportal*. Retrieved June 30, 2024, from https://www.friluftsrad.no/laeringsportalen

Hjorth Warlenius, R. (2022). Learning for life: ESD, ecopedagogy and the new spirit of capitalism. *The Journal of Environmental Education, 53*(3), 141–153. https://doi.org/10.1080/00958964.2022.2070102

Holt-Biddle, D. (1987). Pilanesberg National Park and Gold Fields Environmental Education Centre. *Southern African Journal of Environmental Education, 6*, 27–29.

Howard, P. (2019). Re-Visioning teacher education for sustainability in Atlantic Canada. In D. Karrow & M. DiGiuseppe (Eds.), *Environmental and sustainability education in teacher education: Canadian perspectives* (pp. 179–191). Springer.

Huckle, J. (2012). Teacher education for sustainability in network society: Combining digital and sustainability literacies. *Journal of Teacher Education for Sustainability, 14*(2), 130–146. https://doi.org/10.2478/v10099-012-0013-9

Huckle, J. (2015). Putting global citizenship at the heart of global learning: A critical approach. *Geography, 100*, 76–83. https://doi.org/10.1080/00167487.2015.12093959

Huckle, J., & Wals, A. E. J. (2015). The UN Decade of Education for Sustainable Development: Business as usual in the end. *Environmental Education Research, 21*(3), 491–505. https://doi.org/10.1080/13504622.2015.1011084

Huerto Alegre. (n.d.). *Who we are*. Retrieved June 10, 2023, from https://www.huertoalegre.com/en/

Initiative 20x20. (n.d.). *Corcovado Foundation*. Retrieved June 26, 2024, from https://initiative20x20.org/partners/corcovado-foundation

International Union for Conservation of Nature (IUCN). (1980). *World conservation strategy: Living resource conservation for sustainable development*. IUCN.

Internet Public Library. (n.d.). *Confucianism and Taoism similarities| Daoism and Shinto similarities*. Retrieved September 1, 2023, from https://www.ipl.org/essay/Confucianism-And-Taoism-Similarities-F3VEPRWMUXPV#:~:text=Within%20the%20religions%20of%20Daoism,practices%20with%20openness%20and%20acceptance

IPÊ—Institute for Ecological Research. (2017). *Black Lion Tamarin Conservation*. Retrieved June 9, 2023, from https://ipe.org.br/en/projects/pontal/black-lion-tamarin-conservation/

Jackson, M. G. (2011). The real challenge of ESD. *Journal of Education for Sustainable Development, 5*(1), 27–37. https://doi.org/10.1177/097340821000500108

Jónsson, Ó. P., Guðmundsson, B., Øyehaug, A. B., & Didham, R. J. (2021). *Mapping education for sustainability in the Nordic countries*. Nordic Council of Ministers. https://www.rannis.is/media/skyrslur/SustainableyoungpeopleNordic.pdf

Jordan, K., & Kristjánsson, K. (2016). Sustainability, virtue ethics, and the virtue of harmony with nature. *Environmental Education Research, 23*(9), 1205–1229. https://doi.org/10.1080/13504622.2016.1157681

Jūrmalis, E., Lībiete, Z., & Bārdule, A. (2022). Outdoor recreation habits of people in Latvia: General trends, and changes during the COVID-19 pandemic. *Sustainability, 14*(14), 8478.

Kahn, R. (2008). From education for sustainable development to ecopedagogy: Sustaining capitalism or sustaining life? *Green Theory & Praxis: The Journal of Ecopedagogy, 4*(1), 1–14. https://doi.org/10.3903/gtp.2008.1.2

Kaipatiki Project. (n.d.). *Kaipatiki Project: Share in nature's revival*. Retrieved June 30, 2024, from https://kaipatiki.org.nz/our-work

Karrow, D., DiGiuseppe, M., & Inwood, H. (2019). Environmental and sustainability education in teacher education: Canadian perspectives. In D. Karrow & M. DiGiuseppe (Eds.), *Environmental and sustainability education in teacher education: Canadian perspectives* (pp. 1–18). Springer.

Knapp, D. (2000). The Thessaloniki Declaration: A wake-up call for environmental education? *The Journal of Environmental Education, 31*(3), 32–39. https://doi.org/10.1080/00958960009598643

Kotzé, L. J., & Villavicencio Calzadilla, P. (2017). Somewhere between rhetoric and reality: Environmental constitutionalism and the rights of nature in Ecuador. *Transnational Environmental Law, 6*(3), 401–433. https://doi.org/10.1017/S2047102517000061

Kumar, A., & Sahoo, R. H. (2021). Traditional knowledge systems for biodiversity conservation in India: An analytical review. *Kalyan Bharati, 36*(6), 229–236.

Kvideland, R., Sehmsdorf, H. K., & Simpson, E. (1989). *Nordic folklore: Recent studies*. Indiana University Press.

Ladwig, J. G. (2010). Beyond academic outcomes. *Review of Research in Education, 34*(1), 113–141. https://doi.org/10.3102/0091732x09353062

López González, B. (2019). Centro de Educación Ambiental Ecoguardas. *Ecopedagogica, 2*(3), 74–77.

Lotz-Sisitka, H. (2009). How many declarations do we need? Inside the drafting of the Bonn Declaration on education for sustainable development. *Journal of Education for Sustainable Development, 3*(2), 205–210. https://doi.org/10.1177/097340820900300217

Loures, R., & Sax, S. (2020, August 21). Amazon 'women warriors' show gender equality, forest conservation go hand in hand. *Mongabay series: Global forests*. https://news.mongabay.com/2020/08/amazon-women-warriors-show-gender-equality-forestconservation-go-hand-in-hand

Lugg, A., & Slattery, D. (2003). Use of national parks for outdoor environmental education: An Australian case study. *Journal of Adventure Education & Outdoor Learning, 3*(1), 77–92. https://doi.org/10.1080/14729670385200261

Martínez-Rodríguez, F. M., & Fernández-Herrería, A. (2022). Huerto Alegre: An ecocentric socio-educational experience as a critical practice of education for sustainable development. *Australian Journal of Environmental Education, 38*(2), 138–151. https://doi.org/10.1017/aee.2021.8

Mayer, C. (2016). *Growing closer to nature: Students' environmental attitudes and perspectives after a field trip to the Bamfield Marine Sciences Centre*. Masters, The University of British Columbia.

Mayer, M., & Mogensen, F. (2005). Evaluation in environmental education and the use of quality criteria. In F. Morgensen & M. Mayer (Eds.), *ECO-schools—Trends and divergences: A comparative study on ECO-school development processes in 13 countries* (pp. 26–41). Austrian Federal Ministry of Education, Science and Culture.

Mazower, M. (2012). *Governing the world: The history of an idea.* Allen Land/Penguin Books.

Mbugua, P. (2012). Wildlife conservation education. *The George Wright Forum, 29*(1), 59–66.

McWhinney, J. (2022). *The Nordic model: Pros and cons.* Investopedia. Retrieved September 1, 2023, from https://www.investopedia.com/articles/investing/100714/nordic-model-pros-and-cons.asp

Meadows, D., Meadows, D., Randers, J., & Behrens, W. (1972). *The limits to growth: A report for the Club of Rome's project on the predicament of mankind.* Retrieved January 6, 2023, from http://www.donellameadows.org/wp-content/userfiles/Limits-to-Growth-digital-scan-version.pdf

Milligan, A., Ritchie, J., McRae, H., & Gordon, B. (2021). Using nature sanctuaries to consider sustainable futures. *Teaching and Learning, 3*, 6–13. https://doi.org/10.18296/set.0206

Ministry of Environment and Sustainable Development. (n.d.). *Environmental education and climate change centers.* Retrieved June 24, 2024, from https://sma-edomex-gob-mx.translate.goog/ceacc?_x_tr_sl=es&_x_tr_tl=en&_x_tr_hl=en&_x_tr_pto=sc

Morgense, F., & Mayer, M. (Eds.). (2005). *Eco-schools—Trends and divergences: A comparative study on eco-school development processes in 13 countries.* Austrian Federal Ministry of Education, Science and Culture. http://www.ubu10.dk/downloadfiles/comparative2.pdf

Mudzunga, H. D. (2006). *The role of Schoemansdal Environmental Education Centre in the development of environmental awareness in its neighbouring schools.* Masters, University of South Africa. https://uir.unisa.ac.za/handle/10500/2478

Mulinari, D., Keskinen, S., Irni, S., & Tuori, S. (2009). Introduction: Postcolonialism and the Nordic models of welfare and gender. In S. Keskinen, S. Tuori, S. Irni, & D. Mulinari (Eds.), *Complying with colonialism gender, race and ethnicity in the Nordic region* (pp. 1–16). Ashgate.

Murmansk Marine Biological Institute of the Russian Academy of Sciences. (n.d.). *History.* Retrieved October 26, 2023, from https://mmbi.info/en/integration-with-universities/

Naess, A. (1989). *Ecology, community and lifestyle: Outline of an ecosophy.* Cambridge university press.

Naturvårdsverkets. (n.d.). *Naturum—Visitor centres in nature.* Retrieved June 30, 2024, from https://www.naturvardsverket.se/en/topics/protected-areas/sa-forvaltas-skyddade-omraden/naturum/

Norman, J. (1999). President's report. *OzEEnews, 79*, 3.

O'Donoghue, R., & Russo, V. (2004). Emerging patterns of abstraction in environmental education: A review of materials, methods and professional development perspectives. *Environmental Education Research, 10*(3), 331–351.

Olsen, C. (2014). More than mythology: Narratives, ritual practices and regional distribution in pre-Christian Scandinavian religions by Ed. Catharina Raudvere and Jens Peter Schjødt (review). *Scandinavian Studies, 86*(1), 105–109. https://doi.org/10.1353/scd.2014.0004

Outward Bound International. (n.d.). *Our history.* Outward Bound International. Retrieved August 13, 2023, from https://www.outwardbound.net/our-history/#:~:text=The%20Birth%20of%20 Outward%20Bound,start%20a%20school%2C%20Schloss%20Salem

Partanen, A. (2017). *The Nordic theory of everything: In search of a better life.* Prelude Books.

Pearson, D. (1978). *Fieldwork in environments out-of-doors.* University of New England.

Planet Ark 8. (2017). *Learning from trees: Life lessons for future generations.* Planet Ark. https://treeday.planetark.org/documents/doc-1537-ntd17-full-report.pdf

Provincial Council of Barcelona. (n.d.). *Angeleta Ferrer Nature School (municipal facility).* Retrieved July 26, 2024, from https://parcs.diba.cat/web/marina/detall/-/contingut/193969/escola-de-natura-angeleta-ferrer

Rainforest Awareness Rescue Education Centre. (n.d.). *Environmental education: Spearheading education programs.* Retrieved June 23, 2024, from https://rarec.org/education

Roberts, N. S. (2009). Impacts of the National Green Corps program (eco-clubs) on students in India and their participation in environmental education activities. *Environmental Education Research, 15*(4), 443–464. https://doi.org/10.1080/13504620902994127

Sagy, G., & Tal, A. (2015). Greening the curriculum: Current trends in environmental education in Israel's public schools. *Israel Studies, 20*(1), 57–85.

Seed, J. (2024, September 19). *The philosopher's zone D. Rutledge deep ecology* [Podcast]. ABC Listen: ABC Radio National.

Selby, D., & Kagawa, F. (2010). Runaway climate change as challenge to the 'closing circle' of education for sustainable development. *Journal of Education for Sustainable Development, 4*(1), 37–50. https://doi.org/10.1177/097340820900400111

Sharma, P. K., & Kanaujia, P. R. (2020). Journey of green schools in India. In A. Gough, J. Chi-Kin Lee, & E. PoKeungTsang (Eds.), *Green schools globally: Stories of impact on education for sustainable development* (pp. 203–226). Springer.

Skanavis, C., & Petreniti, V. (2016). Non-formal environmental education in formal education: Centers on environmental education in Greece. In *International conference on protection and restoration of the environment VIII, Chania, Greece*. ResearchGate. https://www.researchgate.net/profile/Constantina_Skanavis/publication/260421601_Nonformal_Environmental_Education_Centers_of_Environmental_Education_in_Greece/links/0f31753121dbcaf581000000/Nonformal-Environmental-Education-Centers-of-Environmental-Education-in-Greece.pdf

Skedsmo, G., Rönnberg, L., & Ydesen, C. (2021). National testing and accountability in the Scandinavian welfare states: Education policy translations in Norway, Denmark and Sweden. In S. Grek, C. Maroy, & A. Verger (Eds.), *World yearbook of education 2021* (pp. 113–129). Routledge. https://doi.org/10.4324/9781003014164-9

Skirry, J. (n.d.). René Descartes: The mind-body distinction. In *Internet encyclopedia of philosophy: A peer reviewed academic resource*. Retrieved July 26, 2023, from https://iep.utm.edu/rene-descartes-mind-body-distinction-dualism/#:~:text=One%20of%20the%20deepest%20and,from%20that%20of%20the%20body%20

Smego, A. A. (2002). Coming together for conservation: Environmental education in Namibia. *Green Teacher, 68*, 40–43. https://eric.ed.gov/?id=EJ651235

Smith, W. (2020). The leadership role of teachers and environment club coordinators in promoting ecocentrism in secondary schools: Teachers as exemplars of environmental education. *Australian Journal of Environmental Education, 36*(1), 63–80. https://doi.org/10.1017/aee.2020.8

South African National Biodiversity Institute. (n.d.). *Kirstenbosch NBG: Biodiversity education programme*. Retrieved April 20, 2024, from https://www.sanbi.org/community-initiatives/kirstenbosch-nbg-biodiversity-education-programme/

Steyn, P. (2002). Popular environmental struggles in South Africa, 1972-1992. *Historia, 47*(1), 125–158.

Talitha Kumi School Campus Beit jala Palestine: Environmental Education Center. (n.d.). *Environmental Education Centre*. Retrieved June 10, 2023, from https://www.eecp.org/

Taylor, J., & van Rensburg, E. J. (2002). Share-Net: Environmental education resource networking in a risk society. In D. Tilbury, R. B. Stevenson, J. Fien, & D. Schreuder (Eds.), *Education and sustainability: Responding to the global challenge* (pp. 113–124). Commission on Education and Communication, The World Conservation Union.

The Corcovado Foundation. (n.d.). *Environmental education*. Retrieved June 26, 2024, from https://corcovadofoundation.org/home-corcovado-foundation/educacion-ambiental/

The Earth Charter. (n.d.). *The Earth Charter*. Retrieved October 23, 2023, from https://earthcharter.org/read-the-earth-charter/

The Green Directory. (n.d.). *Treasure Beach Educational Centre*. Retrieved April 20, 2024, from https://www.thegreendirectory.net/listings/treasure-beach-educational-centre/

The Society for the Protection of Nature in Israel. (n.d.). *SPNI (Society for the Protection of Nature in Israel) Field Schools*. Retrieved July 23, 2023, from https://natureisrael.org/field-schools/

# References

The Wildlife and Environment Society of South Africa. (n.d.). *Overview.* Retrieved November 17, 2023, from https://www.wessa.org.za/education-centres/

Tomren, T. S. (2022). Climate strikes and curricula: Insights from Norway (Article). *Journal of Teacher Education for Sustainability, 24*(1), 105–115. https://doi.org/10.2478/jtes-2022-0008

Toral, K. M., Higham, C., Setzer, J., Ghaleigh, N. S., Welikala, A., & Arena, C. (2021). *The 11 nations heralding a new dawn of climate constitutionalism.* Retrieved from https://www.lse.ac.uk/granthaminstitute/news/the-11-nations-heralding-a-new-dawn-of-climate-constitutionalism/

Twining, P., Butler, D., Fisser, P., Leahy, M., Shelton, C., Forget-Dubois, N., & Lacasse, M. (2021). Developing a quality curriculum in a technological era. *Educational Technology Research and Development, 69*(4), 2285–2308. https://doi.org/10.1007/s11423-020-09857-3

Uganda Wildlife Conservation Education Center. (2023). *Our story.* Retrieved December 15, 2023, from https://uwec.ug/about/history/

UNESCO. (1997). *Declaration of Thessaloniki.* Retrieved December 6, 2023, from https://unesdoc.unesco.org/ark:/48223/pf0000117772

UNESCO. (2007). Moving forward from Ahmedabad… Environmental education in the 21st century: Final recommendations. In *4th international conference on environmental education.* Ahmedabad, India. Retrieved October 8, 2023, from https://unevoc.unesco.org/fileadmin/user_upload/docs/AhmedabadFinalRecommendations.pdf

UNESCO. (2009). Bonn declaration. *Journal of Education for Sustainable Development, 3*(2), 249–255. https://doi.org/10.1177/097340820900300227

UNESCO. (2020). *Education for sustainable development: A roadmap.* UNESCO. https://unesdoc.unesco.org/ark:/48223/pf0000374802

UNESCO. (2021, May 20). UNESCO declares environmental education must be a core curriculum component by 2025. *UNESCO News.* https://www.unesco.org/en/articles/unesco-declares-environmental-education-must-be-core-curriculum-component-2025

UNESCO. (2022). *Berlin Declaration on Education for Sustainable Development: Learn for our planet: Act for sustainability: ESD for 2030.* UNESCO. https://unesdoc.unesco.org/ark:/48223/

UNESCO. (2024, June 5). *UNESCO launches new initiatives for "greening education" in classrooms.* Retrieved October 28, 2024, from https://www.unesco.org/en/articles/unesco-launches-new-initiatives-greening-education-classrooms

UNESCO. (n.d.-a). *The Moscow Declaration.* UNESCO digital library. Retrieved November 23, 2023 from library http://unesdoc.unesco.org/images/0008/000805/080583eo.pdf

UNESCO. (n.d.-b). *The Aichi-Nagoya Declaration on Education for Sustainable Development.* UNESCO digital library. Retrieved November 23, 2023, from library https://unesdoc.unesco.org/search/fd6176b3-43b1-4284-814d-39adc532a51f

UNESCO World Heritage Convention. (n.d.). *Wadi Rum Protected Area.* Retrieved July 23, 2003, from https://whc.unesco.org/en/list/1377/

UNESCO: Sustainable Development Goals. (2016). *Unpacking Sustainable Development Goal 4: Education 2030—Guide Sustainable Development Goals.* United Nations Educational, Scientific and Cultural Organization. Retrieved November 11, 2023, from https://unesdoc.unesco.org/ark:/48223/pf0000246300

United Nations. (1992). *Agenda 21. United Nations conference on environment and development.* Retrieved July 26, 2023, from https://sustainabledevelopment.un.org/content/documents/Agenda21.pdf

United Nations. (2002). *Plan of implementation of the world summit on sustainable development.* Retrieved January 18, 2023, from http://www.un.org/

United Nations. (n.d.). *World Summit on Sustainable Development, 26 August-4 September 2002, Johannesburg: Background.* Retrieved December 5, 2023, from https://www.un.org/en/conferences/environment/johannesburg2002

United Nations: Sustainable development knowledge platform. (2012). *Future we want—Outcome document.* Retrieved December 12 2023, from https://sustainabledevelopment.un.org/futurewewant.html

Universitas Gadjah Mada ASEAN Society. (2022). *Scandinavian lifestyle on sustainability: Envisioning environmentally friendly lifestyle for southeast Asia*. Retrieved August 15, 2023, from https://ugmasean.medium.com/scandinavian-lifestyle-on-sustainability-envisioning-environmentally-friendly-lifestyle-for-922ffb3b7d19

Uttarakhand Seva Nidhi Paryavaran Shiksha Sansthan. (n.d.). *Uttarakhand Seva Nidhi Paryavaran Shiksha Sansthan*. Retrieved June 9, 2023, from https://www.sevanidhi.org/

van Sittert, L. (2019). Elbows over the fence: Rondevlei and the invention of community-based conservation in apartheid Cape Town. In H. Ernstson & S. Sörlin (Eds.), *Grounding urban natures: Histories and futures of urban ecologies* (pp. 277–302). The MIT Press.

Vonyó, T. (2008). Post-war reconstruction and the golden age of economic growth. *European Review of Economic History, 12*(2), 221–241.

Walsh, V., & Golins, G. (1976). *The exploration of the Outward Bound process*. Colorado Outward Bound School. Retrieved August 11, 2023, from https://eric.ed.gov/?id=ED144754

Washington, W., Taylor, B., Kopnina, H. N., Cryer, P., & Piccolo, J. J. (2017). Why ecocentrism is the key pathway to sustainability. *Ecological Citizen, 1*(1), 35–41. https://www.ecologicalcitizen.net/pdfs/v01n1-08.pdf

Webb, J. (1980). *A survey of field studies centres in Australia*. Australian National Parks and Wildlife Service.

Webb, J. (1989). *A review of field studies in Eastern Australia*. Australian National Parks and Wildlife Service.

Wegscheide. (n.d.). *Story/Geschichte*. Retrieved November 3, 2023, from https://www.schullandheim-wegscheide.de/wegscheide/geschichte/

Welcome to the National Park of Abruzzo Lazio and Molise. (n.d.). *What are the CEA (Environmental Education Centres)*. Retrieved June 9, 2024, from https://www.ecotur.org/en/environmental_education_center_%28CEA%29.xhtml

Wildlife Clubs of Kenya. (n.d.). *History*. Wildlife Clubs of Kenya. Retrieved October 8, 2023, from https://wildlifeclubsofkenya.or.ke/

Wolff, L.-A., Sjöblom, P., Hofman-Bergholm, M., & Palmberg, I. (2017). High performance education fails in sustainability?—A reflection on Finnish primary teacher education. *Education in Science, 7*(1). https://doi.org/10.3390/educsci7010032

Wood, J., & Gibbs, D. (1997). False Bay coastal park. *Veld and Flora, 83*(3), 70. https://journals.co.za/doi/pdf/10.10520/AJA00423203_3237

World Commission on Environment and Development (WCED). (1987). *Report of the 1987 World Commission on environment and development: Our common future* (p. 59). Oxford University Press. http://www.un-documents.net/wced-ocf.htm

World Conference of Indigenous Peoples. (1992). Kari-oca Declaration and Indigenous Peoples' Earth Charter. In *World conference of Indigenous peoples on territory, environment and development—Kari-oca, 25–30 May*. Retrieved August 22, 2023, from https://cendoc.docip.org/collect/cendocdo/index/assoc/HASH51e7/4adac409.dir/Kari-Oca_and_Earth_Charter_1992.pdf

World Indigenous Peoples' Conference on Education. (1999). *The Coolangatta Statement on Indigenous Peoples' rights in education*. Retrieved November 11, 2023, from Available at https://wipce.net/coolangatta/#page-content

World Wildlife Fund. (n.d.). *Our work with schools*. Retrieved September 8, 2024, from https://www.wwf.org.uk/get-involved/schools

Yanniris, C., & Garis, M. K. (2018). Crisis and recovery in environmental education: The case of Greece. In G. Reis & J. Scott (Eds.), *International perspectives on the theory and practice of environmental education: A reader* (pp. 117–129). Springer.

Yui, M. (2014). The development of national parks and protected areas around the world. *Nat Environ Coexistence Technol Association Japan, 1*, 1–20.

Zealandia Te Māra a Tāne. (n.d.). *Learning with Zealandia*. Retrieved July 1, 2024, from https://www.visitzealandia.com/Education#ECE

# Chapter 11
# Global Echoes, NSW Reflections: A Study of EECs with NSW Insights

## 11.1 Introduction

The term "echoes" suggests reverberations or reflections of ideas, practices, and impacts of environmental education (EE) across different regions. It implies that the concepts and lessons from one environmental education centre (EEC) resonate in others, highlighting shared themes or contrasting approaches globally.

Adding examples of EECs from around the world to the closer analysis of those within the New South Wales (NSW) Department of Education has been beneficial in the development of a greater conscientisation[1] of EECs and environmental and sustainability education (ESE)—and colonialism, the tentacles of neoliberalism and conversely the diaspora of ecocentric reconstruction gaining momentum. There is a nesting of EEC/ESE progress within developments on an international, national and state level. There is a chronological description of some of the contributions of these centres within their communities, within curriculum and pedagogy, and more broadly within formal schooling—in addition to an intermittent gaze on the influence of their governance structures. There is a glimpse of their histories, and functioning and the environments in which they exist—some brief, some a little more detailed. The study supports Blum's analyses emphasising that ESE is shaped by the relationships between educators and their communities and is influenced by local resources and the community's needs and viewpoints—it exposes the complex, socially embedded nature of ESE and its connection to overarching national and international policies (Blum, 2008a, 2008b). There is importance in situating analysis of ESE within a specific social, economic and political habitat in order to understand the mechanics of the ESE approach (Blum, 2009). This final chapter develops

---

[1] The process of developing a critical awareness of one's social, political, and economic environment.

© The Author(s), under exclusive license to Springer Nature Switzerland AG 2025
A. M. Ross, *The Politics of Environmental Education Centres*, International Explorations in Outdoor and Environmental Education 17,
https://doi.org/10.1007/978-3-031-82567-5_11

themes throughout this history, focusing closely on the NSW case studies given their detailed nature—weaving the voices of the NSW EEC educators into the narrative while also drawing on findings from global examples of EECs around the world.

## 11.2 Change Agents—Avant Garde

EE, with its action component was a new concept in the 1970s. While it was a natural element for EECs within a more Indigenous/ecocentric society, for centres ensconced in the Western, colonialist, consumeristic society it was seen as 'other'. NSW Department of Education EEC (DE-EEC) teachers-in-charge/principals and staff of EECs were some of the foot soldiers of the change from conservation to EE to ESE at a local level. There was significant support and contribution from local communities, EE associations and at times departmental personnel, bureaucrats and politicians. Support from other state and national departments was significant for ESE and the centres, evidenced when the NSW Department of Education generally needed to be compelled to support the centres—apparently there was generally a fair degree of coercion. Yet, for NSW and Queensland, in the end, even in times of economic efficiency and departmental competition, the Departments of Education support the work the centres are doing, in the face of the withdrawal of prior support from other departments. That the Centres can charge students to support their function in this economic environment has no doubt been a way to increase capacity yet also has been a difficult point for some EEC educators with strong views on equity in education. The Federal Department of Education ceased supporting ESE decades ago, and while most support came from the national Environment Department, that has also ceased, as has support from the NSW state Environment Department. Juxtaposed with the local/ground level support is the top-down effect of the international United Nations Educational, Scientific and Cultural Organisation (UNESCO)/International Union for the Conservation of Nature and Natural Resouces (IUCN) movement which has been substantial.

While there were many other foot soldiers over the years assisting in the shift to an ESE agenda, at times the NSW DE-EECs have been some of the only environmental educators in their jurisdiction supporting the move given the initial slow change in development followed by repeated waxing and waning of support within a dominant economic paradigm. There is an argument that ESE within the centres is technocratic, and to some extent, and by necessity at times, there is truth to this claim. However, there is evidence of action, innovation and the development of earth citizenry—connected, enquiry-based, problem solving, experiential ESE pedagogies—being developed and disseminated by these centres.

ESE has advanced around the world in many varied and diverse forms. In large part, this is an intricate history of the development of centres and ESE within a large and complex bureaucracy, the NSW Department of Education, over a period of significant economic change. It illustrates the importance of place, community, political involvement and time in the development of an individually unique range of resources contributing to a healthy, diverse, collaborative and resilient whole. Within this narrative are glimpses of how EECs contributed to evolving ESE within their communities and within curriculum and pedagogy. The enduring themes and tensions narrated throughout this history shed light on some broader contributions to curriculum and pedagogy in formal schooling, as well as how the centres and individuals within these centres managed to maintain their existence within a bureaucratic structure. This chapter teases out some of the major themes of this study drawing on the echoes, or not, from other centres around the globe.

## 11.3 Transforming Learning: Exploring Pedagogy, Curriculum, and Evaluation

Centres have made an ongoing contribution to our understanding and transformation of curriculum and pedagogy to more engaging and immersive forms—while theorists have theorised about these practices within schooling over the years, many EECs were already experiencing the effects through their EEC specific pedagogies and curriculum connected to the environment or place. Scattered throughout the interview data are anecdotes of the effect of ESE on students—improvements in both their disposition to and engagement in the learning, an element in improving curriculum learning outcomes (Lieberman & Hoody, 1998). For instance, if we unpack the elements of the NSW Quality Teaching Model we find positive connection within all the dimensions—Intellectual Quality, Quality Learning Environment and Significance (NSW Department of Education and Training Professional Learning and Leadership Development Directorate, 2008).

### *11.3.1 Teaching Practice and Impact*

Centre staff were/are always in the spotlight. Their lessons are open to observation and team teaching—something which is encouraged as best practice professional development within teaching. They teach lessons repeatedly and thus have greater opportunity to hone their craft. They have, by necessity, an excellent holistic understanding of the whole curriculum and teach within and across it. Many are across a multitude of sites and some EEC principals have stressed the importance of a background in environmental science/management as well as a strong commitment, motivation and passion to teach ESE.

Many of the principals were consistently determined about having a positive memorable impact on their students every day—particularly when there was only a window of 4 h to have an influence on long term outcomes.[2] An affective experience was often seen as essential.

> I wanted an emotional outcome because I thought if they had that then the learning would follow so my outcome for the students was first enjoyment, then the learning.... "I don't care how you're feeling or how I'm feeling; this is the only day the students get in the bush so make sure they enjoy themselves." AA

The relationships between field studies centres (FSC)/EEC teachers and their students, the valuing and understanding of the starting point of the visiting students, was seen as essential.

> You've got those kids for a small window of time. They've got to be the most important people in your mind. So that's where that relationship with teachers, the communication beforehand to find out about them, the needs of the kids, the teachers' needs, special backgrounds of the kids that we might need to know to ensure we deliver.... And then in that first 10–15 minutes of intro just working out where the kids have come from in terms of their prior learning, language that they might have that you can optimise or whether this is just a launchpad for the unit of work. And then that relationship with the kids. Get to know their names, talk to them by name. Slow things down. Make it a quality experience for the kids. It works, Anni.... It's just simple things like talking to the children by name, being calm, getting them in that moment, and putting yourself second. Just enjoying the kids being excited. RA

The positive experience was seen as what would be remembered by students in years to come, an experience that may just turn them towards an environmental ethos.

> The main thing I want to see any kid walk away with at the end of any day is... having the most positive experience they can possibly have out in nature, or based on any program. Because those really positive feelings at the end... you know in six months' time that's what they're going to remember. And that's really where you begin to have that influence on how kids value being outdoors, or how kids value being out in nature and exploring and investigating and enquiring about what's going on around them. KB

## 11.3.2 Assessment

Early on it was thought that the effect of ESE could not be measured until tested via the undertaking, or not, of environmental action later in the affected student's life (Webb, 1980). Evidence of ESE effect is dotted throughout case study interviews and can be gleaned from the social media of many centres. As noted, Jack Miller experienced one of his students branching into sustainable farming many years after the fact. Another example is one principal's relayed experience.

> He was up at National Parks and came down and said to me he was doing a PhD into the broad-headed snake, a rare and endangered snake found in the sandstone country... and I

---

[2] Often, evaluative pre and post data has been rigorously obtained over the years. There are generally consistent results yet long-term outcomes have proved elusive to measure to this point.

said, "I can't tell you anything about the broad-headed snake" and he said, "No, I'm not here to ask you about that." He said, "I'm here to tell you that you're the reason I'm doing it." AA

These stories within the context of their historical time, place and space do not, on their own, give the generalisability and reliability necessary to satisfy methodological research rigour. Indeed, one of the issues prominent in the data is the difficulty in providing evidence when there is such a complexity of causes and effects that are difficult to substantiate or separate from other learning.

> But in the longer term it's very hard to tell whether this actually bought about a new world of environmentally literate people because that is really what we were aiming to do, and these days it would be more those that carry out sustainable practices throughout their life. Did this actually happen? I'm not really sure.... So, I suppose from a cost benefit analysis, if I was going to take that hard economic line I would, you know, question the value; but deep in all our minds, our psyches, we all think this has been worthwhile. FA

Yet these accumulated ad hoc stories form a formidable body of evidence of the positive effect student-centred, hands on, experiential, inquiry based, well taught ESE within an engaging environment can have on positive student outcomes, and the elements that contribute to this.

Over the history of the FSCs/EECs, teacher and student pre and post-evaluations have been conducted on a regular basis with very positive outcomes. They show that learning had occurred and that the experience was positive. Parents have also been surveyed—garnering positive feedback. In the past, teachers-in-charge have been requested to develop performance indicators for accountability purposes. This has been a difficult ask. A thorough analysis of knowledge retained has been close to impossible given pre and post testing constraints. Post testing would require:

- teachers with specific aims to be measured—not necessarily the case with primary school,
- the time to go to schools and conduct the test which would have meant taking on fewer students in the face of numbers being an important benchmark for the Department and the great need for many students to have the experience with relatively few centres per student population,
- teacher cooperation, yet they usually moved on from the fieldwork quickly; gaining teacher cooperation for assessment was difficult, and
- distinguishing what was learnt from the centre experience from what was learnt elsewhere. Too many variables.

While the centres have been proactive and successful in developing accountability, the time taken is considerable, and this contributes to the strain that is placed on teachers within the system. Automation of assessment technology may have helped ease the burden of data collection, collation and analysis. As discussed in the previous chapter, centres were proactively studying ways and means of utilising new technologies in advancing research into student outcomes from their interaction with EECs.

The issues of evaluation and the ad hoc success stories of EECs was evident for other EECs globally (Medir et al., 2014). Additionally, student and teacher feedback tell a story. As with NSW, the Queensland Department of Education EEC executive summaries consistently highlighted the presence of high-quality teaching and learning, with visiting teachers and students regularly providing positive feedback about the outdoor and EECs (Thomas, 2018).

One emergent theme within the data was the positive effect of learning in a hands-on experiential way for students who otherwise are stereotyped as ineffective learners and/or disruptive to the learning experience. The extracts cited below illustrate this phenomenon: The positive effect of learning with animals, for example, has been observed consistently (see Fig. 11.1):

> And certainly, animals do that for all types of learners and all backgrounds. I'm very blessed and lucky to have live animals as a learning resource and we have kids meet them up close. Kids can feel them, smell them—multisensory learning—that's incredible…. And one of the best roles we play is we often rebadge naughty kids in a way which is positive….So, there's a correlation between… naughty kids and animals—there's a sweet spot there, and even naughty kids, and I know this from doing work with Juvenile Justice and doing work with DOCS, naughtier kids and reptiles, there is a direct link between those two factors which come into play. And it's a lovely opportunity for those kids, in front of their teachers, to be seen as leaders and experts in a way that really does rebadge them… I think we play

**Fig. 11.1** Desert immersive classroom, Taronga Institute of Science and Learning, Taronga Conservation Society. (Photo taken at the Environmental and Zoo Education Centre Conference July, 2022)

lots of roles, and lots of outcomes, some of them are the hard curriculum ones, but I think there's something around values and around civics—that we really do switch kids' lights on. And we talk about that nature switch, that we can get kids in a different environment to show their unique skills and their unique knowledge in a way that can often surprise themselves and surprise their teachers and surprise their peers as well. VA

Furthermore, the positive effect of centre learning experiences for students with learning difficulties such as attention deficit hyperactivity disorder (ADHD) was frequently observed:

> Because teachers will say it to you. The kid that's got ADHD, the kid that can't sit still, the kid that's naughty all the time at school, is often the kid that's just shining and having the best day ever when they're on an excursion with you. TA

Moreover, the positive learning experiences for students with physical and emotional disabilities were substantial:

> I don't know what it is but kids that had behavioural difficulties, concentration difficulties, attention difficulties, often responded, very surprisingly to their classroom teachers, not to us, in the outside environment. And the other thing, I once had a group of kids, well not once, I had a school that visited me often at Longneck who were from a special school… often for those kids it was the first time they had walked on ground which was not an even pavement or a carpeted corridor. And the excitement, and the joy, the wow experience of those things were very, very… they've stuck with me, obviously. Bad kids turn good in bush. KA

These teaching experiences point to a serious disconnect within our education system and society, highlighting the need to shift from the neoliberal education paradigm to a more connected experience (Lieberman & Louv, 2013; Robinson, 2010).

### 11.3.3 *The Lucas Framework*

The EE framework developed by Lucas (1972), "in", "about" and "for" the environment, had a strong influence in EECs, as it did in EE more broadly. The "in" the environment was covered well at FSC/EECs and in many instances this element would have been unique to them. There were many cases of students who had never encountered the natural environment before who were introduced to, and in many cases lost a fear of, the unknown—misconceptions were shattered.

> We took students into rainforest environments, and of course many of them were paranoid about leeches. So we had to kind of overcome that even though maybe a few of them were leeched in time but to say that they weren't going to hurt you, you might be a little bit itch for a day or two… We had students at Wambangalang that used to come from Newtown Public in Sydney. These students were from a broad range of culturally and linguistically diverse communities, as we call them these days, that had had no experience other than city life or life overseas. And to take them into the vastness of our rural areas, and for them to experience being in the environment, in a different environment, was quite an amazing experience for them. So the experiential side is a critical education function. ND

Furthermore, students who had little experience in the important art of socialising experienced extended periods of living, working and playing with others when attending residential FSCs.

> So these were School of the Air students that were being taught remotely so when they came to Wambangalang I remember one of the first things they had to do is to learn how to form a line. They'd never formed a line before and also to learn to live with other students in a dorm style accommodation. ND

The "about" element of the Lucas' framework was the component that was easiest for "formal education" to incorporate into their practice, but also a necessity, and one of the hooks for getting education authorities on board with FSC/EECs. Learning about the environment was already embedded within the science and geography curriculum. The changes through the Wyndham Report for extended compulsory schooling which required education to be made accessible to all rather than a few, made learning in FSCs with experienced, skilled pedagogues, in environments that encouraged enquiry, enticing—it tapped into curiosity.

> So for example, the science curriculum and the geography curriculum in secondary school, always have a requirement for fieldwork, particularly in… year 11 and 12. But even in junior secondary and also of course in primary school there's always been some part of a teaching unit which suggests some form of learning about the environment. So primary schools have had rainforest units, units about people and places, a whole range of different units that could be taught in environmental education centres… If we ran down the marketing line of environment ed many schools could opt out. But if we said we're here to do a particular HSIE activity or a particular English activity or environmental math or something like that… science and technology… that is where we had a lot more traction, that's where we built the numbers. FA

The centres tailored their curricula to the visiting teachers' requests as it was critical that learning was linked to the syllabi. Educators with strong environmental commitments staffed centres; they were aware that they had to impact many diverse student and teacher sociological lens and have empathy with and understanding of the worldviews and backgrounds of their clientele.

> You know we also had the view that we had strong, if you like, environmental philosophies and ideals whereas we have to understand that our "customers" (those students and teachers that came) didn't have those same ideals, so we had to kind of claw-back, you know. The reality that… these people, particularly going back now 40 years ago, didn't have the environmental knowledge and the skill set to be able to understand. So just to basically give them some experiences, a bit of knowledge behind that, even just a good time somewhere else, you know, was really, really important. FA

Learning was often about fieldwork data collection. For high schools the fieldwork associated with the curriculum justified the trip. With the cross-curricular nature of primary school, it was relatively easy to broaden out into the environment with the inclusion of values and ethics in the History, Society and its Environment (HSIE) key learning area (KLA). There was, and is, great success across most KLAs—across the whole K-12 spectrum. For example, Syd Smith called Foott into the office when he was the coordinator of the Higher School Certificate (HSC) Geography Program to ask him questions about what he was doing to get such good results in the HSC geography fieldwork. Foott was teaching with a program he had developed which studied a river from its source to delta—"Peats Bight Creek: A Study of a River's Ecosystem" (1983). This kind of recognition assisted in raising the profile of the work centres were doing to support the HSC.

Education "for" the environment has always been the most difficult element to enact within formal education given its value laden, affective character which often goes against the dominant hegemony—generally unconsciously so. Advocating "for" the environment requires students to critique established practices in order to understand the studied phenomenon. The expected result is citizens who understand and want change and are empowered to assist in making the change (Apple, 2000). Initially, however, teaching the concepts of how the natural environment works can support education "for" the environment and some centres embraced teaching the underlying concepts relating to it where they could. "I think there are just those basic concepts of solar energy, relationships, recycling, diversity, adaptation, change, etc. to understand and certainly with lots of interaction with the natural world" (AA).

Centres spent a lot of time mapping their activities to all the curricula in order to attract visitation from schools. The role of the teaching staff at the centres was seen to be conducting fieldwork but centre educators mission was to broadened this to include EE and eventually to support classrooms and schools ESE journey. ESE eventually became the dominant factor with fieldwork still playing a crucial role, for student education and the survival of the centres.

> The most important thing is to get children out into nature so they touch the earth, so they fall in love with the planet they live on and they're not scared of everything that wriggles and moves. Certainly be wary and respectful of it but don't be frightened of it… just get them out there touching the dirt and smelling the leaves, out doing fieldwork. AA

Learning was never didactic. It was experiential. Teaching across the large age range from K-12 required a good understanding of educational psychology in order to ensure age appropriateness. Centres challenged students, there were high expectations but conversely audiences for riskier activities such as a difficult walk, would be carefully targeted. Inquiry learning, critical thinking, and values clarification were also within centre educators' pedagogical toolkits—important in learning around controversial issues.

> a lot of stuff that we really are saying now in terms of critical thinking, and trying to empower kids to take action for the environment, and having an understanding of all the different perspectives of all the different players in the environment. I think we've got a lot of similar messages, we've just sort of retagged things and done a little bit more research over the years and refined it and the problem has obviously got worse in terms of you know the environment needing protection. But I think a lot of good stuff was there in the beginning as well and, you know, a similar sort of purpose. (PB)

The examples of global EECs revealed similar pedagogical approaches, with many emphasising immersion in the environment and experiential, action-oriented learning. However, some EECs, particularly those with ESE embedded within their standard curricula or those with an ecopedagogy focus, leaned more toward enquiry-based learning and fostering critical thinking/global citizenship. Most centres maintained strong links to the school curriculum, though a few, predominantly in countries influenced by Freirean and eco-pedagogical principles, exhibited confidence in their own curricula and pedagogies as the core of quality education—whether it was connected to the standard curriculum or not. Notably, there were perceptions of education systems being problematic, as highlighted by the Rainforest Awareness Rescue Education Centre (RAREC) (RAREC, n.d. para. 3). Some countries such as Italy and the Nordic countries have authentic ESE within their standard curriculum and thus highlight the importance of ESE leadership at all levels in addition to strong ecocentric societies.

### 11.3.4 Indigenous Knowledges/Education

A theme of Indigenous Knowledges/Education is present in EECs within countries that have experienced colonisation. There seems to be an element of autonomy and authenticity within some centres such as the RAREC and the Uttarakhand Environment Education Centre, India. However, it is difficult to gauge from a desktop study. There does seem to be an overarching western controlling conservation ethic observed but generally from older sources. But what is evident is the necessity for Indigenous knowledges and practices in moving forward to an ecocentric world becoming more normative—the need for ecojustice has been gaining strength for many years and comes with justice issues more broadly.

### 11.3.5 First Nations' Knowledges/Education

The importance of First Nations' knowledges was indicated early on at EECs within the NSW Department of Education with Muogamarra/Gibberagong, developing resources, supporting First Nations knowledges within their EEC, and supporting early development within the NSW Department of Education. There is evidence that Muogamarra/Gibberagong and Rumbalara's leadership on First Nation's knowledges may have influenced other EECs. There are references to First Nations' knowledges and connections throughout the case study data. This is understandable given EEC's connection to place. A quick look at the internet presence of EECs within the NSW and Queensland Departments of Education, as well as other EECs worldwide, shows First Nations' knowledges and practices significance for many EECs. For example, Education at Desert Park includes First Nations ESE in situ. The shift from colonialist conservation toward incorporating Indigenous knowledge, involvement, inclusion, and ownership or autonomy in EECs is evident in many of the highlighted EECs, which showcase a variety of approaches along this binary. However, at times the difference between appropriation and appreciation is difficult to decipher.

## 11.3 Transforming Learning: Exploring Pedagogy, Curriculum, and Evaluation

First Nations' knowledges are increasingly being recognised as vital in rectifying and healing society and the environment for the future—to transform and eliminate the legacy of educational inequity—equity in general (another interconnection). First Nations' ways of learning have synergies with ESE. As an example, see Fig. 11.2 which outlines the eight ways of learning identified in western NSW through research exploring First Nations' knowledge systems (Yunkaporta, 2010).

With Aboriginal and Torres Strait Islander Histories and Cultures a cross-curricula priority along with Sustainability within the Australian Curriculum, progress can be stifled with the waxing and waning of political and established education power and the neoliberal/colonialist agenda. While there seems to be a grass roots groundswell for inclusion, Cooper et al. (2024) points out a missed opportunity for the Australian Curriculum to be more culturally responsive in the latest revision (9.0). First Nations science represents knowledge that is deeply rooted in local environmental connections and adapted to specific contexts. It integrates broader scientific principles with foundational ontological and epistemological beliefs, emphasising relationality, interconnectedness, and storytelling. This highlights the harmonious coexistence of localised scientific knowledge with broader perspectives that resonate across diverse First Nations cultures. This unrealised potential that could reenergise disengaged, disenfranchised students is still relegated as "peripheral or optional" within the curriculum revision (Cooper et al., 2024, p. 8).

Anne Poelina's insights (Dahr, 2023) exemplify how First Nations across Australia, plus Indigenous populations globally, have been advocating and effecting

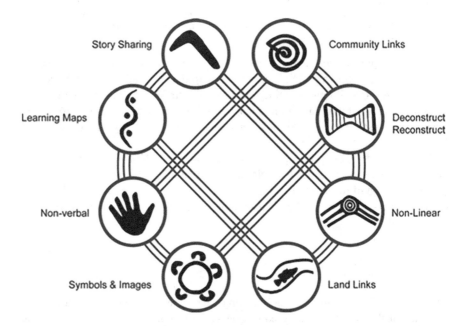

**Fig. 11.2** The Eight Ways of Learning Framework (Yunkaporta, 2010, p. 40). (Printed with permission from Sydney University Press)

change since colonialisation. These communities embed ESE in their ethos, demonstrating resilience and innovation in the face of ongoing challenges. Poelina emphasises the importance of embracing Ancient Wisdom and fostering a symbiotic relationship with the environment, particularly for Poelina, the Martuwarra River, seen as an ancestral being by the Martuwarra Fitzroy River Council. This council, composed of Senior Elders from six Nations, challenges the dominant species narrative and advocates for recognising the river's rights, highlighting its role in guiding identity, establishing the first law, and conveying moral obligations for its care (Dahr, 2023).

The need for a shift in methodology is emphasised, urging people to feel and hear the lands, Country, and rivers, incorporating Ancient Wisdom to move away from destructive energy systems. This perspective contrasts Western crisis views with Indigenous concepts of time dreaming, like bukarara, connecting past, present, and future. Poelina advocates for a pluralverse approach, integrating First Nations and Western science (Dahr, 2023).

Walungarri law, the first law, governs the land and river, promoting unity and self-regulation, contrasting Western legal failures in youth court scenarios. A fusion of philosophies, such as Wonnun law's regional governance model, emphasises reciprocity and collective wellbeing. Poelina challenges current democratic governance, advocating for a redefinition that values citizens over industry and aligns with the circular nature of time (Dahr, 2023).

> People will learn a lot about this Australia in the coming decades long after the federal Opposition decided to vote against the proposition that Aboriginal people should be recognised as the First People of the continent. It makes you cringe with embarrassment at the petty malice of this view. Many people are shortsighted but few deliberately blind themselves. (Pascoe, 2024, p. 222)

Sharing wisdom, stories, and a collective dream provides antidotes to despair. Poelina highlights the importance of hearing with the eyes and seeing with the ears, urging bravery in building a coalition of hope. She stresses the value of new economies, recognising First Nation knowledge, and the necessity of change to avoid a business-as-usual approach, aiming for a shared responsibility for a sustainable future (Dahr, 2023).

Poelina's story exemplifies just one of the many First Nations' knowledges and practices that are, to borrow a First Nations' festival title, "Rising from the Embers" (a collaboration of the Wollotuka Institute, Local Land Services and the University of Newcastle—First Nations' and sustainability networking) (see Fig. 11.3).

## 11.3.6 STEM

Currently, STEM (science, technology, engineering and mathematics) education is a dominant theme within many education systems—fitting with the technocratic, industrialised, accountability measures embedded within Western society and thus

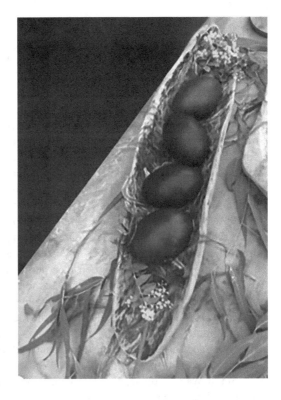

**Fig. 11.3** Emu eggs and wattle in a coolamon. (Photo taken at Craig Duncan's display at the Rising from the Embers Festival at the Park on the Hill, Newcastle University, NSW, May 2022)

education. STEM education could be improved to include critical reflection and future-oriented perspectives to ensure it aligns with sustainable economic, social, and environmental development (Smith & Watson, 2019). There is a need for the inclusion of a meaningful ecological, systems thinking approach within STEM which generally has a very industrial influence. Gough advocates for deeper integration of ecological education into the Australian curriculum (Gough, 2021). EECs can and do play a crucial role in this process.

With their roots often in science education and a colonialised past many centres are adapt at promoting systems thinking and breaking down traditional disciplinary silos, fostering deeper connections with the natural world. Many EECs have established strong links to STEM programs. Examples include institutions like Taronga Zoo and Rumbalara EEC in NSW, as well as the centres in Brisbane Urban and Moreton Bay in Queensland, in addition to the centres affiliated with the Wildlife and Environment Society of South Africa. EECs can and do act as catalysts for integrating ESE and STEM.

## 11.3.7 Comradery and Larrikinism

Impossible to detect within the desktop data was the solidarity between EEC educators. However, it was evident within the NSW DE-EEC interview data. With centres and their personnel experiencing being outsiders or "other" within the NSW Department and general society they found comradery and a healthy dose of Australian larrikinism assisted in keeping centre personnel sane and connected. Strong bonds were formed between centre educators. These bonds are still formed to this day but back when there were only six or seven educators, in an environment devoid of ESE, comradeship and professional bonds were very solid and strong—values and personality alignments were more "in sync". In saying that, there were differences in environmental ethos. One has to remember these educators started in the 1970s where "hippydom" was rife—whilst this may have been an easy fit for centres close to some urban areas, or areas with a penchant for alternative lifestyles, this image could place a teacher-in-charge as even more of an "outsider" (EE equalled hippy and was often seen in a derogatory light) in some communities. Some teachers-in-charge at rural centres embraced their alternativeness and were gradually accepted within their given community due to their commitment, good and hard work, and steady familiarity with the locals. Others decided on an approach that fitted more their personality and environmental ethos and, being more conservative, blended into the rural surrounds and culture. They made gradual changes once they had the respect of the locals. "Where we taught, which is out in Western New South Wales, you wouldn't last long in society if you took that more deep ecological line" (FA).

Throughout the history of NSW's DE-EECs, at times there have been significant differences in personality, worldviews, capacity, strengths, political stances and so on, yet generally foremost was the desire to push the envelope of EE, through excellent education, into the mainstream for the preservation of the environment. There is evidence of an altruistic focus on shifting society toward an ecocentric/sustainable paradigm where we are conscious and act knowingly, accordingly and respectfully of humans' place in the web of life and living as lightly on the earth as possible. Illustrative of their altruistic nature is their commitment to keep ESE on the agenda and to maximise its teaching. An example of Environmental and Zoo Education Centre (EZEC) Network altruism is their attempt to pay for a .2 casual for the one principal centres in order to increase capacity.

One difference in the early days of the centres was the ethic of testing one's mettle in the natural environment which had developed early in Australia's history and reached a crescendo with the bushwalking movement. It was very evident in early FSC history but now has fully dissipated. At times throughout the data, informants implied or explicitly stated that they found testing of one's mettle and the raw, original environmental ethic was absent from some of the newer breed of educators.

Synergies with other forms of being "other" are detected and can make visible the work of ecofeminism which works to uncover and change the injustice of the dominant hierarchy. However, over the years with ESE being part of the complex fabric of most western societies maybe "other" is a little more convoluted now and in need of considerable reflection. "How does eco-feminism decolonise this violent process of a war against life itself, and a war against women, and a war against the future? By removing the false assumptions of superiority and separation. Ecofeminism removes these false assumptions" (Dr Vandana Shiva, 2024).

## 11.4 Enduring Tensions and Themes

EEC principals, teachers and administration staff work in unique, isolated environments, separated from the school mainstream, working to their own brief, yet connected by the departmental policies governing education. They share a connection and they also share professional development, projects and the collaborative circumstances that their distinctive organisational structure, and vision brings. Not to be underestimated is the effect of past role model educators. Within this history many teachers engaged in EE were educated by people such as Strom, Harris and Webb. These teachers were dispersed across the state and within the Department. The importance of being connected to the environment, and understanding the environment and sustainability in order to be empowered to work towards it, or teach it, is an important element within this narrative.

ESE involves educators in a wide variety of organisations and interest groups; other Department of Education personnel; other government departmental environmental/sustainability-focused staff (when they exist); the state and federal environment departments in particular; non-profit environmental organisations, in Australia, the Australian Association for Environmental Education (AAEE) in particular; council education officers; special interest groups (e.g. plant or bird enthusiasts); and advocacy groups. All of these make up the eclectic group that constitute the movement that supports the environment and thus ESE. EECs personnel within education systems have a specialised position within this broader environmental/sustainability group. They have knowledge and skills within the education discipline, and ESE and are part of the education system—difficult terrain for anyone not within this specific bureaucratic structure.

Themes that appeared early in the establishment of the NSW Fauna Protection Panel have been evident throughout the history of NSW DE-EECs and are often reflected in global examples of EECs. The exploration of EECs across various global contexts has deepened the understanding of colonialism and our place within this history—an essential but often overlooked reality for many living in predominantly disconnected Western cultures. It also highlighted the advantages of strong leadership for ESE at all levels (e.g. Italy), fostering a culture attuned to nature (e.g. Nordic countries) and authentic ESE integration within the curriculum. This inquiry has broadened the view of the interrelatedness between the environment, society, economics, and politics on a global scale, emphasising the importance of a holistic approach and history and habitat in understanding the circumstances of each EEC. Themes running throughout include the anthropocentric domination of the ecocentric, grounded, local, community change and the global, top down effort. Collegiality, networking and collaboration—comradery is evidenced, at a local level—but also at a much wider ESE world network level. Waxing and waning of ESE political power is evident throughout and while it is difficult to read the placating of egos, the NSWDE-EEC case study evidence it occurring. There is an attempted silencing of ESE and environmental/sustainability action throughout and preservice and teacher education is still a major issue those some countries have tried to remediate this albeit at the whim of economics.

## 11.4.1 Preservice and Teacher ESE Education

Teacher education is one of the biggest impediments to the uptake of environmental and sustainability practices—along with our embeddedness within the neoliberal frame. How do pre-service teachers get the confidence to utilise their environment, natural or otherwise, as a teaching backdrop for fieldwork and experiential/inquiry learning, connecting their students to their environment and sustainability, if they are not taught? There were publicity campaigns through the Federation and Departmental publications, yet it was still primarily word-of-mouth and return visits that provided centre visitation in NSW. It came down to individual teacher priorities.

In the early days, it was common practice for centres to take on teacher practicum students. Maddock, an academic within the School of Education at the University of Newcastle, NSW, and a well-known environmental educator, utilised the Awabakal and Shortland centres. Maddock had a love of egrets and was one of the main driving forces in having the Shortland Wetlands established. One of his academic papers was on utilising wetlands in teacher education (Maddock, 1986). Centres could only accommodate a small number of practicum students, so Maddock utilised Rumbalara in addition to Awabakal and Shortland for regular student visits and practicums. "So, strong educational outcomes but also strong linkages with those teaching and those wanting to teach into the future." (ND).

Wambangalang took teacher students for practicum from Mitchell College of Advanced Education, now Charles Sturt University. Educators were paid a small stipend to be the teachers in charge of managing these students. There were strong links between Longneck Lagoon EEC and the University of Western Sydney with Dufty lecturing in Environmental Fieldwork. Many students gained fieldwork experience through their teacher practicum at Longneck Lagoon. Stuart DeLandre at the Illawarra FSC /EEC had strong ties with the University of Wollongong. He wrote and taught two courses as electives for fourth year Bachelor of Education candidates for 6 or 7 years. Illawarra FSC/EEC also hosted preservice teachers in the 1990s and early 2000s.

It became progressively harder and therefore rarer to have university students, and in particular teaching students, visit centres and gain experience. There was a distinct lack of teacher educators educating in the field. Teachers generally will not take students out of the classroom to explore and investigate the natural environment unless they have experienced it within their own teacher education and have learnt its value. Note that there are teachers, principals and schools throughout NSW who are teaching ESE efficiently and effectively—most admirably. But many schools are not.

Centre educators have at times resorted to going to the schools of education within the universities to take the field studies experience to the students. At one stage Gibberagong was visiting the University of Technology Sydney at Lindfield because internal policies stopped pre-service teaching students from visiting. Plants were taken along so that students could use their senses of sight, smell, touch and taste to experience them.

Centre teachers were actively providing professional development in how to teach EE to visiting teachers as they were teaching their students—role modelling. "We didn't see ourselves as being the be-all and end-all; we saw ourselves as being conduits for a broader movement of environmental education teachers" (FA). They encouraged teachers to become involved, guided them through the process, and supported them in learning so that they gained the confidence to teach EE. "I was hoping teachers would go back and use their playground for learning experiences" (AA).

There were many professional learning courses developed and run by centres. It was a big thing in the 1980s and 1990s and was supported by funding. This raised the profile of the centres for those who could attend, yet attendance was small in comparison with the size of the NSW school system. The "teach the teacher" practice was a professional development method at the time. This has been proven to be ineffective as the teachers who experience the professional development do not have the skills, resources nor environment to pass on the learning. Without other teachers experiencing it for themselves, the schools were often left with one "converted" teacher supporting the cause.

## *11.4.2 Networking and Advocacy*

NSW DE-EECs used a degree of political leverage to advance ESE and many teachers-in-charge/principals were involved in organisations working for the purposes of environmental efficiency. You gain an idea of the political interconnectedness through reading this history—from EE advocates connecting to politicians, or bureaucrats, to not-so-serendipitous occurrences at election time through strong political advocacy. It was/is a diverse and multidimensional network. It may be an assumption, but it seems that there were once closer connections to the machinations of power. The intransigence of bureaucracy seems greater or has economic rationalism made things much tighter and less equitable? Or both?—This idea needs further unpacking on a much broader scale.

Illustrated throughout this narrative is the influence of strong community action, as is the effect of the many global initiatives on instigating pressure for governments to change policy—both a top-down and bottom-up approach. The manifold challenges in progressing ESE are also evident within the influence of environmental advocacy groups. Examples are provided throughout this study, but some examples not previously mentioned are the Environmental and Zoo Education Centre (EZEC) Network contending for involvement in the curriculum in the NSW State Government's *Consultation on Defining Mandatory Outcomes in the K-12 Curriculum (2004) report*, and the AAEE seeking input into the national curriculum.

### 11.4.3 ESE Contestation—Bureaucracy and Politicking

The growth of ESE has been hampered often by bureaucracy and politicking. This political power play of bureaucracy is evident in ESE policy formation, with contestation from an international, to national, to state, to EEC level (Gough, 1987, 1997, 1999, 2013a, b; Stevenson, 2013) and between education and environment cohorts. One significant factor is the power play between the stronghold of traditional curriculum disciplines within education with ESE decidedly dismissed or encompassed in ineffective ways, ensuring it does not disturb the entrenched. It could be surmised that these factors may have been involved in the Federal Department of Education lack of interest in supporting ESE from the 1980s, with the Environment portfolios, both national and state, the main supports in development.

There is the intransigence of the education system in effecting change. The broader social changes of the mid twentieth century did little to change the fundamental nature of schools and teaching within those schools (Hargreaves, 2003). Rhetoric outstripped reality. Teacher-centred learning remained firmly in favour, using the age-old techniques of "question and answer" in classrooms made up of children categorised by age and assessed by the same old standard methods. There has been a historical expectation that education can provide social redemption (Popkewitz, 1986). Yet educational professionals and bureaucrats seemingly look inward to the custom and certainty of their expertise and routine rather than focusing on being at the service of students, families and communities, as they ought to be (Hargreaves, 2003). What is needed are ideas for solutions to practical, technical and social problems. We need ingenuity (Homer-Dixon quoted in Hargreaves, 2003). Indeed, Greenall's (1981) Australian Association for Research in Education paper introduction was apt in quoting Machiavelli (1513). "There is nothing more difficult to carry out, nor more doubtful of success, nor more dangerous to handle, than to initiate a new order of things." (Greenall, 1981, p. 48).

### 11.4.4 Waxing and Waning of Political and Curricula Favour

Part of this perplexing situation is the waxing and waning of political favour which is disconcerting given the pressing need for a permanent change in behaviour and attitude toward the environment and sustainability. Many of the teachers-in-charge/

principals have experienced and understand this variability and are very adept at managing the situations they are dealt. One principal pointed out wisely that change and evolution are inevitable, part of the process, part of the ebb and flow.

> And since the centres are still there, are still operating, and environmental education is going through different incarnations because the audience is changing, the children have a different starting point, the parents of those children have a different starting point of belief and knowledge and so on. I think fluctuation is a normal healthy part of society, ebbing, flowing, changing, adapting, reinventing. KA

Yet much of the change that is experienced by the centres is change due to political qualms and lobby group power—the proclivities of those in power. One trend noticed by long-term centre educators was the Department's routine of reinventing the educational wheel approximately every 5 years, usually at the whim of some politician, or an academic having influenced a politician. Then there was the effect of pressure groups adding extra to the curricula. There was the teaching of subject areas at the expense of important others, and teachers taking the easy way out by teaching the less difficult areas rather than the sciences—which they possibly did not totally understand.

> And politics comes into education all the time. In environmental education politics is even more important. You've got to keep it on the political agenda… Well, as we know, we've got more or less environment education and fieldwork within the curriculum depending on who was pushing the politicians more. AA

Some EEC educators were a little more sceptical about the changing times, not holding their breath waiting for the pendulum to swing back the other way. At times ESE is in vogue and at other times it is seen as a dangerous area to teach so field studies are reverted to as a means to keep ESE alive, rendering ESE links within the curriculum and the cross-curriculum priorities essential, as is the policy. Accountability would be an appropriate next step. Additionally, the stand-alone subjects such as the senior Earth and Environmental Science subject are necessary as prototypes for the field, given the lack of understanding within a large majority of the teaching fraternity.

Yet another example of the "swings and roundabouts" the centres and all teachers deal with is the change in curriculum. The last iteration of the geography curriculum, for example, was disconnected from fieldwork but in doing so lost popularity with the students. The current geography curriculum includes hands-on work and is close to an EE syllabus, which EEC principals find expansive and fit for ESE purpose. This was a pivotal change for the EECs in 2017, however, this curriculum is set to change once more.

## 11.4.5 Action Orientation

Consistent with action-oriented curriculum and pedagogy is an overall action orientation to FSC/EEC work. Not unlike Strom, the old guard of EEC principals, and some of the not so old guard, had a defining trait in "action"—"doing." It is integral to how they shifted the agenda for ESE and their centres. It is integral to their teaching. They get things done, as the following quote, heard on a number of occasions, portrays. "I think I probably sought forgiveness rather [than] sought permission" (HA).

Given that the NSW Department of Education, as with most bureaucracies, moves slowly and is often wary of authority and change, those who move for change can be perceived as dangerous.

> I thought about the probability of movers-and-shakers in the environment movement in general ever "getting anywhere", "in positions of power", within the Department of Education & Training, as being rather minimal, as such people are often regarded as "slightly dangerous" within bureaucracies because they might want to change things too much! (McDonald, email December 12, 2017)

The FSCs/EECs' action orientation ethos has had a significant impact in assisting the shift toward a more ecologically sustainable society. In the scheme of things, EECs have impacted on a global scale in an indirect, implicit way. For instance, the early teachers-in-charge/principals were the instigators of the NSW *EE Curriculum Statement* and they had input into the NSW school *EE Policy*. They were heavily involved in the dissemination and implementation of both of these documents. They also input into the Earth Citizen document and thus the National Curriculum Sustainability Framework.

The teachers-in-charge/principals were sought after to contribute to inquiries and advise on matters such as forestry and reserves, and to assist with specialised documentation such as the rainforest material instigated by the Wran Government. NSW DE-EEC educators have also been instrumental in curriculum change. For example, Foott was involved in the committee that developed the Stage 6 Earth and Environmental Science syllabus (2002) for NSW.[3] A search of centre teachers-in-charge/principals in Trove, the Australian online library database, highlights the many resources produced by centre staff, only a few of which have been outlined in this study. For example, in 1990, Koettig and colleagues produced a resource titled *Greening your School* which was launched simultaneously with the greening school policy (Koettig et al., 1990). The centres/zoos are very important in keeping ESE on the formal education agenda and thus have the potential to impact on a large scale. This action orientation is observed in many of the global examples of EECs.

Centres have overall always been enormously popular venues. One principal estimated their centre had taught one hundred thousand students over a 13-year period. Add to this several thousand teachers and other committee and associated people, and then multiply that by the twenty-three centres and two zoos and there is

---

[3] Note that it is suspected that these examples are the tip of the iceberg.

## 11.4 Enduring Tensions and Themes

a multiplier effect not to be denied. Zoos teach up to approximately 150,000 school students annually[4] and one interviewee estimated 10,000 students visited each EEC annually, with some exceeding this number by several thousand. Parents were often involved in the learning and teachers-in-charge/principals often gave talks at community events in addition to educating politicians—in fact, anyone in their path. "And a lot of my activism has come from really living out the education "for" the environment. You know, I think of dealing with politicians. Educating them as much as lobbying them. That's happened in my philosophy" (HA).

### 11.4.6 Fractured Connections and Eroding Resilience—Reconnection

There was an observed resurgence in NSW DE-EEC visits towards the end of the 2010s. While centres have overall always had huge visitation,[5] many are now pushing capacity. The disconnect from nature has parents keen on their children having experiences in nature. One observation within the data was that teachers and students no longer build endurance on long walks. They opt for a few kilometres and thus miss an opportunity to build resilience, and the sense of accomplishment that comes from achieving something perceived as difficult. One principal noted that six-kilometre walks are now one- or two-kilometre walks. Field trips are shorter and shorter. Gentle slopes are preferred to rigorous hills. Technology is given as one of the reasons for the decline. Some of the younger teachers had never been out in the bush. Camping has given way to holidays in resorts in many middle-class families, the class from which many teachers are drawn—there is less basic camping experience. There are students who had never seen a wood fire or used a tea towel, who grew to love the experience in a few days. Comments shifted from "You shouldn't make people do this" to, "I think everyone should have an experience like this. No one should be allowed to go through life without having this experience" (AA).

There is a huge complexity of issues at play. Yet this is part of the disconnect from nature that needs to be addressed. "You wonder if the people in high-rise will have enough contact with the natural world to actually care about the natural environment. That's the problem" (AA).

With the huge growth in population since Webb's analysis in 1989, it can be extrapolated, and it is evident in the data, that the number of centres in NSW has not grown in line with the growth of the population, and thus there is even more

---

[4] While the zoos get a shorter time with students they have been working on greater relationships with their students through, for example, their Zoomobile and Project Insitu, a longer-term program based on penguins.

[5] It is unfair to compare some of the regional centres who offer quality experiences without being immediately accessible to the majority of the population.

pressure on the centres.[6] The Blue Mountains was mentioned by some interviewees as an ideal location for a new centre given its ecosystems and proximity to the largest population in NSW. One solution already mentioned by a few principals is more staffing to enable greater capacity for some of the centres but some centres would already be running at capacity given finite sites and the need to ensure these sites are sustainable and not ravaged by overuse. Some of the NSW DE-EECs had started EEC outreach in NSWs western region (personal conversation EZEC conference 2022).

One could refer back to the NSW DE-EECs, originally envisioned as being accessible to all—much like many examples around the world. However, achieving this would require significantly more resources, as well as a higher level of coordination and cooperation between departments and other organisations. Case studies reveal that teachers-in-charge and principals often go above and beyond in networking and collaborating across sectors, and even within bureaucracies. Yet, the cumbersome bureaucratic structure has struggled to enable authentic collaboration. This stands in contrast to the partnerships seen in the 1970s when this competitive environment was just beginning to emerge. That said, some effective and efficient partnerships have developed. Looking forward, we can hope for synergistic partnerships that are enabled—rather than hindered—by bureaucracy.

## 11.5  Ch-ch-ch-changes: Turn and Face the Strange

It was envisaged that significant education for concern and connection to the environment (Curriculum Development Centre [CDC], 1978), and sustainability within the environment (including economic and social and political), would take some time but slowly there has been a dissemination throughout NSW, Australia and globally. For NSW, we have evidence of the change in the "Who Cares about the Environment" reports, as outlined in Chap. 9. Yet arguably the major inhibitors to ESE are the anthropocentric nature of our society, aided and abetted by our consumeristic culture and political intransigence rather than systemic change.

Some of the factors that distinguish ESE from other forms of education, which at times have been muddled by hegemonic interests diffusing and making evasive the terminology (for example, "sustainability" and the "greenhouse effect/climate chaos/climate change"), are now generally incorporated into education. For example, "critical and creative thinking" is a general capability in the Australian Curriculum, and is, along with student-centred, action, enquiry learning, part of the education discourse. However, these attributes are difficult to teach within the paradox of schooling where the nature and use of conflict are associated with negativity and citizens (students) with being recipients rather than creators, of "values and

---

[6] One ex-principal estimated the figure at less than five percent of the population per year visiting EECs given the 35 EEC staff.

## 11.5 Ch-ch-ch-changes: Turn and Face the Strange

institutions" (Apple, 1990, p. 86). This tacit, hidden curriculum is geared for preparing students for a market economy (Kanpol, 1999). It is fair, reasonable, and necessary to discuss what have been perceived as controversial issues.

> And the way we used to get around that in developing policy was to talk not about involvement in political actions. We'd use the word participation. We hardly ever used the word advocacy, or fighting for the environment. Participation was the thing that we were aiming for… of some sort, at the appropriate age level. HA

That is how many of the centre staff operate when able to do so—that is ESE—action research through studying natural and human knowledge systems with world, future and systems thinking in repertoires of practice. Noted throughout this history has been the difficulty of encompassing ESE within the curriculum over the last 50 years. Besides a space and support to do this, the centre staff and the supports that were gained through the Department have contributed to revealing ESE to many teachers and others. They have provided those support structures that are necessary to encompass something new—for teachers and students to look at knowledge as problematic, to take risks in being involved in change—such an issue for some, understandably, given that we are still enmeshed in the capitalist paradigm.

A theme within the interview data is concern not to be tarred with the activist brush, to be on the side of the technocrat—the scientific right, not an emotive activist. The adage of "not rocking the boat" still rings true.

Centre staff have always had an enormous freedom to innovate, while literacy, maths, and to some extent science are valued above other subject areas. This is explicit, as evidenced through the curriculum and the structure of schooling, and implicitly, through the hidden curriculum (Welch, 2018). In the last few decades, this subject matter favouritism, exacerbated by high stakes testing and the competitive nature of our times, has ensured that ESE has not taken its rightful place of importance within the schooling system which would have ensured evaluation, and thus power as a subject. Without it, however, ESE has enjoyed a freedom to develop without the intrusive gaze of the hegemonic power structures capable of dismantling and disempowering subjects not within its value structure—the intrinsic values have remained untouchable, and less vulnerable to corruption. In this environment, there is a thirst for innovative pedagogy.

However, that freedom comes with risks. A deep understanding of both the theoretical and lived experiences of ESE provides a significant advantage. Such understanding fosters an altruistic motivation to shift the agenda in favour of the environment and sustainability. In extrapolating about the form of EE, Strom (1987) noted that one needed the moral courage and perseverance to apply knowledge and see it through to the end. He understood that knowing is not enough and that often one's own vested interests can win out over the good of the environment for the whole. Strom, with all his experience, was convinced that attention and perspectives focused on the local environment was the way through. He lamented that the environment and thus our future was in the hands of bureaucracy! Strom believed it is a teacher's responsibility to be aware of these forces and how they work, and to reveal the consequences of these forces in a meaningful way. In pleading for change,

Strom concludes that our government cultivates a "syndrome" to pacify the "greenies:"

> Give them wildernesses and all is well, whilst within the urban communities are the people who will never experience the wilderness only the clutter, confusion and social conflict of the urban consolidation, a living culture that is alien to our climate and our life style. Environmental education must be about changing the syndrome. In my opinion, it starts with making the sufferers aware of what is happening to them. (Strom, 1987, p. 8)

The need and want for change gained momentum in the 1960s, but the issues that need addressing have changed and become more complex. At first it was about land clearing and development—problems associated with urbanisation and industry. Gaining momentum and coming to consciousness since then have been the accumulating issues of climate change, species extinction, biodiversity loss, land clearing, erosion, salinity, and eutrophication; water theft, population stress, excessive consumerism, excessive non-renewable energy consumption, and resource depletion (AI exponentially compounding this); air, water, and land pollution; the damage caused by many exotic plants and animals; and ozone depletion (Withgott & Laposata, 2012)—along with the social injustice these issues entail. Whilst in the 1970s the concepts of environment and sustainability were alien to many privileged in the West, now they are embedded in our collective psyche, if often in a rhetorically and superficial sense.

The following two quotes illustrate both the changes over time and the changes to which centre education has contributed. "So those types of things were the more deep ecology whereas these days it's a lot more around sustainability and to a certain extent now resilience: both economic, social and of course environmental resilience" (FA).

> Centres have played an important role in getting the environment into people's psyche at an early level and hence have also had a role in the ultimate enshrinement of environment in legislation and where it now is integrated to some extent across the board in education (curriculum perspective and policy) and in awareness of broader community including government at all levels… The challenge for EECs going forward is that they need to adapt to the fact that they are not the only bastion of environmental enlightenment anymore, however they are still a stalwart of this and as the political pendulum swings in emphasis towards and then away from environmental sustainability in our rapidly evolving world, they (in my view) need to better adapt to this and focus on this in the now broader environmental framework, but to do so they need to be aware of this wider perspective and position they hold. PA

However, there was also an understanding of the unravelling and contestation of some of the wins. "… they started to pretty much dismantle a lot of the things that we fought for in environmental ed centres and within schools." (FA).

There is evidence within this research that EECs are indeed adapting to the rapidly changing conditions.

There was an intention within this study to give voice where possible to the marginalised, the indigenous folk, and women—those suffering from the injustices of colonisation. In writing the case studies, narrative, voice has been given to people using privilege in an altruistic fashion. There is the issue of the technocratic, yet important, "about" education being given a voice. Many researchers say that understanding and awareness is not enough as it masks environmental problems and excludes alternatives. Thus, maintaining technocratic environmentalism—addressing but not solving the problems (Apple, 2000; Carr & Kemmis, 1986; Greenall, 1987; Gough, 1987; Robottom, 1983; Stevenson, 1987). These power dynamics are recognised within the interview data as the following quote exemplifies. ESE is seen as transformative education.

> If a person is an educator most of the time the discipline within which they operate is a reflection of the status quo. If you are taking environmental education seriously then by definition your role as an educator is educating for change. GA

In many respects "about" EE has been a vehicle for moving ESE forward within the dominant hegemony. Where possible the "in" and "about" has enabled the "for" of ESE and at times "for" the environment has been the focus. However, the extent to which the "for" EE was enabled is in question. ESE is the marginalised within this narrative. These case studies gave voice to ESE and some of the people who have shifted the agenda within the NSW Department of Education. Like Annette Gough (1997, p. 170), this narrative endorses and yet questions the dominant discourse. There are no claims of certainty and methodological orthodoxy within this narrative (Gough, 1997).

Lucas' construct of "in," "about," and "for," the environment has been used within this narrative due to its dominant theme within both the primary and secondary data collection. Nevertheless, as noted previously, even the author found it overly and inappropriately used. To shift the ESE agenda forward, further exploration is necessary. Vare and Scott (2007) in addition to the "about," "in," and "for," ("what," and "how,") include a "why". In some respects, the "why" within this study is addressed in analysis of past political influences and economic priorities. However, generally environmental advocacy, apart from a few brief vignettes, has been implicit within the narrative. Yet, the "why" is what fuels the EEC educator's passion and drive. "The ultimate goal of EE is for people to develop an awareness of their environment that will lead to a personal sense of involvement and eventually to the shaping of an environmental ethic to guide each person's behaviour" (IA). Past and present FSC/EEC educators' love of the environment is palpable within every interview—their desire to effect positive change in a world skewed toward destruction is admirable.

Vare and Scott (2007) concluded that in order to address the "why," the complementary approaches of Education for Sustainable Development 1 (ESD1) (informed, skilled behaviours and ways of thinking, useful in the short-term) and ESD2 (building critical thinking capacity and developing enquiring minds inherent in sustainable living) need to be addressed. Strategies for doing so include:

- promoting learning as an outcome, as well as a means to an end,
- balancing the employment of information and communication on one hand with facilitation of learning through mediation,
- trusting the unplanned direction learners may take, and
- evaluations that go beyond the "what has been learned?" outcomes to the "how do we know" as an additional source of learning. (Vare & Scott, 2007)

Research data indicates that the first three strategies are well developed within EEC pedagogies with the fourth developing as a practitioner action-research project in 2017 when the last interview was undertaken.

Centres provide hands-on experiences "in" the environment, allowing students to connect with a world from which they are often disconnected, often a detachment from the environment aided and abetted by a consumerist society. In the natural environment, they provide a connection that is intrinsic to wellbeing (Louv, 2005). These hands-on experiences provide the best form of pedagogy—doing—connected to the environment, enquiry-based, experiential, problem solving and empowering learning. Their teaching of the curriculum material is memorable and effective (Lieberman & Hoody, 1998; Renshaw & Tooth, 2018; Tooth & Renshaw, 2009). Centres have the "in" and "about" of ESE comprehensively covered. Furthermore, in relation to the intrinsically personal nature of learning (Apple, 2000), there is potential for innately personal knowledge acquisition through these thought provoking, connected, enquiry-based, experiential, action-based learning experiences. There is difficulty evaluating curriculum knowledge acquisition from EECs. Yet, anecdotally on multiple occasions, and at times through rigorous research, there is veracity that student experiences encompass essential learning.

Centres provide experiences in leadership, peer support, well-being, connection to the environment and recreational activities. They provide specific sustainability and curriculum-based programs that enhance those taught within mainstream schools. Centre staff have specific training in these areas. They expose the environmental, sustainability issues, and their possible remediation through connecting students to the environment with experiential, enquiry-based, problem solving learning: "Finding ways for students to become empowered, and working with them in the empowerment process, rather than empowering them" (Gough, 1997, p. 163).

They also provide role modelling for students. "Do as I say, not as I do" does not provide the authenticity required. In developing and surviving over time in an increasingly rationalised public managerialistic environment, centres have proved themselves the ultimate chameleons, able to change and adapt to bureaucratic policy, utilise it to their advantage and assist the NSW Department of Education, in developing best practice.

The desire to 'reveal more compelling possibilities for addressing sustainability issues and the challenges of learning to live more sustainably' (Stevenson, 2013, p. 516) may or may not have been fulfilled, depending on whether the ideas in this study present new perspectives to the reader. The conundrum found with the case studies is that the centres, and the personnel within the centres, are generally controlled by the dominating technocratic paradigm in which the NSW Department exists—a problem for education in general. Until there is a significant shift away from our consumerist economics to a more ecocentric way of living, there will always be a need for teacher and student support in the ESE field. Furthermore, it seems logical, and empirically valid, that the environments alone, and connecting to these environments, are essential elements for ESE and schooling. In an environment that cannot afford political disempowerment, intransigence and politicisation, without assistance, it will be generally difficult for many teachers and students to visualise alternatives outside of this existence.

## 11.6 EECs and ESE Within the Normative Paradigm

ESE has always been about questioning the status quo, challenging socio-political and economic structures that contribute to environmental degradation. Pioneers like Allen Strom and Thistle Harris criticised the sanitised version of history taught in schools, advocating for an authentic education that piqued student curiosity inspiring intrinsic empowerment for students to take action against environmental inequities. The social, political and economic dimensions were always included in EE—they just were not understood or were marginalised or sidelined within the system. The silencing of ESE is tied to its inherently political nature, which threatens vested interests entrenched in neoliberal ideologies.

For some time, we have needed to move towards an education for cultural transformation in light of the need for radical change and uniformity in the understanding of "development" and the ambiguity of "sustainability" (Jackson, 2011). With the action oriented/change agent aspects of ESE not well embedded within school education, and teacher education, and the hegemony within curriculum, EECs play an important role in allowing a safe, active learning space. This learning sanctuary is needed given the widening cognitive dissonance gap produced within the contexts of learning handed down passively through informal and formal education culture (Jackson, 2011).

The case studies provided evidence that EEC educators had experienced transformative experiences, and further, that they endeavoured to facilitate and mediate transformative experiences for their students, indeed there is some rich evidence to support this claim. However, it is within the habitus of centre time and place. The initial closed analysis of the case studies was useful in revealing the politics, people, power and pedagogies of the centres within the NSW Department of Education. However, comparison of ESE entities using the chosen heuristic frame and a focus on language has allowed further exploration of the relevance and significance of findings to the wider construct of centres throughout the world. It has made visible Australia's involvement/immersion in a colonialised/globalised ESE setting. Science, technology, industrialisation and its sociology is heavily embedded within Western civilisation and Australia's centres within it.

## 11.6.1 The Silencing of EECs Within Established Bureaucracies

EECs often find themselves navigating a delicate balance within larger, entrenched bureaucracies and non-governmental organisations (NGOs) that are influenced by neoliberal agendas. While EECs have long been advocates for ESE, they face systemic challenges that stifle their transformative potential. This silencing arises from the need for survival within systems that value conformity to the normative structures of society, making it difficult for them to act as radical, or rational, agents of change.

Historically, and currently, organisations such as the AAEE, AEE (NSW) and the Gould League of NSW fought to elevate EE. However, their efforts were often met with limited support from mainstream environmental movements, which were focused on more immediate environmental crises like pollution and climate change. At the same time, ESE within or associated with bureaucracies has sought to distance itself from the perception of politicised environmentalism, positioning itself as educational and positivistically objective rather than activist—often encouraged to focus on individual rather than collective change. This divide, as Whelan (2005) observes in the context of non-formal education (though it could also apply to formal education, given the tendency to focus on learning "about" rather than "for" change), highlights a disconnect between environmental educators and activists. Educators were often seen as focusing on raising awareness or as constrained by bureaucratic, disciplinary, or societal boundaries (Elshof, 2010; Hodson, 2010; Roth, 2010), while activists push for direct action, emphasising ESE's political nature. ESE of course, involves much more than awareness, with understanding aiming to support a deep and connected "knowing" of the how and why of phenomena (Pritchard, 2014) in order to foster engagement with environmental behaviors. However, the critical political element of ESE is often missing—and as discussed in Chap. 9, Australian Curriculum iterations are weakening ESE from "understanding" to "awareness".

The division between activism and ESE reflects the broader neoliberal paradigm in which EECs operates. The bureaucratic structures that fund and oversee these centres often have vested interests in preserving existing systems, viewing the political aspects of ESE as a threat to economic development and industrial priorities. Consequently, EECs encounter significant barriers when trying to implement transformative education, restricting their capacity to challenge prevailing ideological frameworks.

## 11.6.2 Conforming to Normative Society for Survival

Many EECs, whether within government departments or NGOs, are bound by the funding and constraints of neoliberal systems. These centres often find themselves/ or are confined to normative societal expectations within this paradigm, unable to push the boundaries of the critical and transformative education needed—consciously or unconsciously. This alignment with the status quo can limit their ability to address the social, economic, and political dimensions of sustainability and environmental justice—particularly the political dimensions.

It seems that EECs within privileged societies will always be on the fringe pushing the boundaries given the intransigence of normative conditions to change. It brings to the fore the imperative of critical thinking, global citizenship and the democratisation of society in the face of neoliberalism. The importance of transformation or conscientisation. In Freire's (1970) view, conscientisation is possible because consciousness, though shaped by external conditions, can critically recognise its own conditioning. This awareness enables individuals to set transformative goals and act upon the world accordingly. Freire argues that conscientisation is a collective process, where individuals engage in reflection and action together to understand and change their reality. It is not merely about overcoming "false consciousness" but involves a deeper, critical engagement with a demystified world.

Waxing and waning of political favour for ESE can be surmised as being similar in many countries. ESE in countries where the education system is aligned in a better position for ESE also experienced a waxing and waning of support for ESE cultivation. Jónsson et al. (2021) for instance discusses shifts towards a more restricted, subject-focused curriculum impacting ESE. Seemingly in other locations, efforts towards ESE appear to be ad hoc, lacking methodical organisation, and predominantly occur on a small scale compared to subjects with measurable academic outcomes in formal educational systems—or the urgency with which it is required.

In Greece EECs seem to remain largely peripheral to daily school life, with only a few programs implemented in each prefecture. Programs lacked consistency and continuity and there was no substantial evaluation so impact of sustainability at both personal and community levels remained unclear (Pitoska & Trikka, 2012; Pitoska & Lazarides, 2013). However, the significance of these centres for students, communities, and lifelong learning was highlighted. Such programs helped children connect with their local natural and economic environments, as well as their parents' professions. Most importantly, these initiatives informed children about environmental issues, potentially shaping them into future sustainability advocates (Pitoksa & Lazarides, 2013).

González-Gaudiano et al.'s (2020) stated that governments and public administrations often praise themselves for signing international treaties in support of ESE, claiming a commitment to sustainability. However, these pledges rarely translate into tangible commitments with actual budgets. In fact, in many cases agreements become barriers to progress. As seen in countries like Mexico and Spain over recent decades, shifts in government often lead to new objectives, laws, and curricula. This inconsistency means that efforts made by one government to support EE are often undone by the next. Findings from the case studies support these claims and glimpses of this phenomena can be surmised from the desktop study.

Scandinavian countries have a strong EE ethic. Yet sustainability can be superficial at an aim or subject level—even though it is mentioned on numerous occasions within curricula (Jónsson et al., 2021). "Political rhetoric rather than educational reality" (p. 64)—often seen from an EE perspective in these countries… they are talking about sustainability only being rhetoric (Jónsson et al., 2021) Scandinavian countries are often regarded as leaders in ESE given their strong policy frameworks, ecosystem based learning and their involvement with global initiatives created by the Foundation for Environmental Education (FEE) [e.g. Blue Flag, Eco-Schools, Green Key] as well as having a strong tradition of quality education (Andreou & Tramarin, 2016; Ball, 2005; Eco-Schools, n.d.; Sahlberg, 2011). However, as mentioned, some indicators reveal that these nations rank among the least sustainable in terms of their ecological footprints, largely due to high consumption levels and resource use—as discussed most countries within this study do overshoot their biocapacity.

In some EEC instances the root cause of environmental and societal destruction, colonialism, industrialisation, neoliberalism, seems hidden within conservation, EE "about" and "in" and sustainability education that places the need for change squarely and earnestly on individuals and communities. However, this is probably more indicative of earlier ESE efforts. Areas that seem to have ESE embedded within their schooling system, relatively consistently and authentically often touch on transformational ESE. While some of these efforts seem inspirational, particularly those that have been are on the front line of environmental and societal destruction, others seem to be just touching the edges.

While there is greater knowledge and awareness, lack of political action on environmental and sustainability issues exacerbates disquiet and worry (Ravnbøl & Neergaard, 2019; Who Cares about the Environment Reports, 2012, 2015). And EECs play an important part in mediating this divide by fostering environmental citizenship and critical thinking. Through their flexible and adaptive approaches, many centres manage to weave sustainability into broader educational goals, emphasising personal and social capabilities, ethical understanding, and active citizenship. Yet, without a transformation of the underlying normative conditions, ESE remains on the fringe, continually waxing and waning depending on political, social, and economic climates.

## 11.7 Inspiration from Movements Working Outside the Normative

Despite these challenges, there are examples of movements and initiatives that operate outside normative structures and succeed in shifting societal values. The Green Belt Movement in Kenya, founded by Wangari Maathai, exemplifies how grassroots environmental movements can foster environmental conservation, climate resilience, and democratic spaces, particularly empowering women (Schell, 2013; The Green Belt Movement, n.d.). Similarly, the Chipko Movement in India helped prevent deforestation through ecofeminism and community action, offering an inspiring model of resistance to destructive environmental policies (Bandyopadhy, 1999; Gaur, 2023).

These movements illustrate that achieving transformation hinges on stepping outside the constraints of neoliberal agendas. They show that real change is possible when communities and individuals are empowered to act, usually under duress, challenging the normative structures that dominate EE today.

Another example is the Hunter Community Environment Centre, for me, a local place-based citizen science not-for-profit organisation working on ecocentric systemic change. Founded in 2004 the Centre aims to promote and support environmental and social justice advocacy and education in the Hunter region of NSW, Australia. Their dedication lies in collaborating with community to preserve local diversity and unique locations. There is active involvement in various campaigns covering topics such as biodiversity, climate change, community well-being, air and water quality, and social justice. Additionally, the Centre serves as a resource hub for both groups and individuals who are working toward environmental and social justice causes. The Centre offers space, expertise, and training to facilitate networking and cooperation among groups, thereby contributing to the improvement of the region's overall quality of life (Hunter Community Environment Centre, n.d.). An example of citizen science is fieldwork in the monitoring of water quality and species in Lake Macquarie around the Vale's Point Power Station and its pollution impacts. Another example is squirrel glider habitat relief around the Newcastle area. While the Hunter Community Environment Centre offers citizen science experience, it is clear there is transformative ESE in action.

Another localised example is Rising Tide, an influential Australian grassroots climate group which operated actively from 2005 to 2012, engaging in impactful endeavors such as blockades and legal challenges related to coal's climate impacts (Rising Tide, n.d.). Recognised for its community campaigning and nonviolent direct actions, Rising Tide has been reactivated in the last few years to address the pressing demand for targeted and inclusive climate action (Rising Tide, n.d.). Grassroots activism, exemplified by groups like Rising Tide Australia, challenges the coal industry's narrative and plays a pivotal role in disrupting the coal industry's social license (Connor et al., 2009) (see Fig. 11.4).

Australia's role as a major coal and gas exporter raises environmental concerns, with Rising Tide's activism against the Port of Newcastle underscoring the urgency

**Fig. 11.4** The Peoples' Blockade of the world's biggest coal port, Rising Tide, November, 2023. (Printed with permission from Rising Tide)

for climate action. The critical role of legal challenges, grassroots activism, and global cooperation is highlighted in addressing the multifaceted challenges posed by climate change and environmental degradation. The IPCC has faced critical examinations concerning its origins, norms, and governance, emphasising the localised and situated nature of climate change knowledge (Hulme & Mahony, 2010). While governments may sign treaties or adopt the Earth Charter, the commitment to these agreements hinges on civil society's vigilance and pressure. Gadotti (2008) argues that for meaningful change, societal constructs must undergo transformation collectively, fostering the belief in the possibility of an alternative world and globalisation. The interconnectedness of global challenges demands collaborative efforts, emphasising the need for joint action (Gadotti, 2008).[7]

---

[7] I have noted a local movement and centre within my sphere of the world, but point out that these entities tend to be everywhere—fitting into local habitats as needed and society wills. There is importance of place-based connection.

## 11.8 Effecting Change

The clash between institutionalised compliance and transformative education underscores the significance of leadership in driving meaningful change. EECs play a crucial role in connecting people to their environment and in fostering ecocitizenship within the silencing that weaves its way through the fabric of this story. While the EECs seem to have played a part in the ESE diaspora that has been experienced in the last 50 years, for the greater effect needed, a paradigm shift is required—one that moves beyond normative constraints and embraces significant change involving stepping outside our comfort zone. We can draw inspiration from movements like the Green Belt and Chipko, climate change and community ESE centres and movements that work independently, we can envision a future where ESE and EECs transcend constraining limitations and becomes a powerful, unified and systemic force for transformation in society—some of the global EEC examples give insight into how this is possible. It is worth reflecting or imagining where Australia would be if the strong ESE incentives set up at the start of the millennium had been stable and more of a priority—less susceptible to the influences of political and economic ideology. This includes the productive ESE responsibility of regional directors in the NSW Department of Education. For example, constructive action on climate change would be much more advanced.[8]

ESE and EECs plays a crucial role in fostering the competences necessary for social and ecological action at both individual and collective levels. However, this requires the development of collective infrastructures that enable/allow ESE/EECs to express its political dimension. Political competence integrates essential learning elements such as knowledge of socio-political structures, including laws, regulations, and the dynamics of power and actors, alongside practical skills in analysis, debate, and strategy formulation. It also emphasises the importance of personal power, citizenship, and a readiness for individual and collective involvement. Ultimately, political competence is the ability to act effectively in specific contexts—denouncing, resisting, proposing, and creating. Political identity is shaped through the recognition of one's own power in relation to situations, other people, and institutions (Sauve, 2015).

## 11.9 Leadership

Leadership has played and continues to play a crucial role in the effective functioning of EECs and the development of ESE, as well as in shaping their ethos of educating for the future. The holistic approach of many centres, including those in NSW and Queensland, is evident in their offerings, which provide experiences in leadership, peer support, well-being, and connection to the environment.

---

[8] Maybe an EEC with mandatory ESE at all parliaments would be beneficial.

> We don't just do science and geography. We're not just here to help you teach a bit of your program. We're here to allow your kids to experience, to develop greater understandings, to develop leadership skills. We're here to help you become better teachers. So the impact of the EECs is also about opening up opportunities for the environmental education centre staff to take on a greater leadership role in the Department. VB
>
> we did a lot around supporting student leadership sustainability activities (VC)

This multifaceted focus underscores the importance of creating supportive environments that foster leadership among students and educators alike.

The Guajarjara Women Warriors exemplify how local leadership can drive change, while the Uttarakhand Environment Education Centre emphasises the need for connection to community leaders. The Nairobi Animal Orphanage Education Centre points out that many students have grown into positions of advocacy, showcasing the potential for EECs to cultivate future leaders. Similarly, the World Wildlife Fund's Living Planet Centre in Surrey, UK, contributes to this initiative by offering resources for schools, including environmental leadership programs and teacher development, highlighting how leadership in managing these centres can influence broader educational outcomes.

Smith's (2020) work on teacher leadership and Deep Ecology illustrates how educators, through enhanced connections with and love for the environment, become exemplars of sustainability. Arnold et al. (2009) found that structured outdoor nature experiences were pivotal in developing environmental and sustainability leadership skills, particularly where nature play is absent in people's lives. This indicates the essential role of EECs in fostering these skills amidst an increasing disconnect with nature. The role of EECs in nurturing this love for the environment and supporting educators, and students, in ESE praxis is crucial. EECs provide immersive, hands-on experiences that not only deepen teachers' and students' understanding of ecological principles but also inspire them to incorporate these principles into their teaching and living practices. By offering professional development programs, resources, and collaborative opportunities, EECs empower teachers to cultivate their passion for the environment and translate it into effective pedagogical strategies.

Reflecting on the history of EECs, an early group of individuals appointed as Teacher-in-Charge of the first dozen FSCs across NSW provided valuable leadership for the growing network. "this core group provided the leadership for those that followed for many years. This created a really valuable continuity across the EECs in NSW." (EB). This idea resonates with evidence that leadership in centres like Muogamarra/Gibberagong and Rumbalara has influenced other EECs in embracing and working with First Nations knowledges. This continuity in leadership and networking has been instrumental in supporting ESE in the centres and their environments and sustainability initiatives in schools. This illustrates the multifaceted impact of EECs on both student and teacher leadership.

The interconnection between leadership and governance is woven throughout various case studies, emphasising how the lack of government and governance ESE leadership—or the ebb and flow of it—affects centres, schools, and communities alike.

## 11.9 Leadership

*And then in more recent years* [not so recent now] *see how destructive it can be when we have a leadership that wants to, not only deny, but just wants to throw science and that out the door. You know, what Abbott did there three or four years ago we're not going to get over that… denial about climate change and then all of a sudden, at all levels, all of a sudden you had pet bureaucrats making decisions…* [saying things like] *"why have we got this whole layer in the Department of Education doing environmental education. No we don't need that. We can consume that with something else until it disappears."* RA

The tension between leadership for environmental sustainability and compliance with traditional educational mandates is evident in the observation that "having it addressed as a real priority…is getting people to sit up and take notice" (DB). This sentiment emphasises the necessity for leadership that can effectively advocate for ESE at high levels within existing educational and governance frameworks that desperately need change.

### 11.9.1 Shaping the Future: Environmental Educators—A Critical Role

In discussing EECs and leadership the importance of EEC staffing comes to the fore. Case study informants talked of the importance of EEC teachers-in-charge/ principals having environmental management and education knowledge and skills in addition to excellent networking and leadership skills. Passion for the environment was a given.

> if you haven't got the technical environmental management skills with the teaching ability… you've got to have those I think, at a high-level…
> 
> So I chaired the National Parks and Wildlife Service Advisory Committee. These were all voluntary activities. Both of us were on Catchment Management Committees. And we saw that we have a role in the community but also we'd learn from the community and from these activities ourselves. So, you know, to me that's another accountability for looking at that… so the point is that you really should have had a strong background in environmental management. FA
> 
> And the important freedom yet responsibility to invest in the EEC teaching experience wisely:
> 
> That's one of the big things about the role, is that the role, if you are a single teacher in an environmental education centre then the role is only limited by your imagination. And you can fit in anywhere if you decide to… and that's hugely distracting because, you know, who are you serving. But professionally it's the key because professionally you can do new stuff every week, you're not stuck with the syllabus… you know, you tune into the syllabi but you're not stuck with one and so there is this huge, I believe, a huge flexibility to apply those resources in really unusual ways and in ways that have great outcome FA

The effectiveness of EECs hinges on strong, transformative leadership that can navigate the complexities of environmental and educational issues. The role of leaders in these centres is vital—not only in advocating for ESE but in empowering students and teachers to enact meaningful change and become collaborative leaders in change. Effective leadership extends beyond managing educational programs; it fosters a culture of sustainability, advocacy, and resilience within communities.

The tensions between departments of environment and education has often left ESE leadership fragmented. History, in Australia, tells us that it is generally the environment department that has taken the lead. A problem arising, not only in Australia, from this institutional connection is that education is seen primarily as a tool for environmental management. As a result, instead of having its own intrinsic goals, the role of education is shaped to focus on supporting ecological conservation and enhancing environmental quality, among other objectives—considered a clash with established education ethos (González-Gaudiano et al., 2020). The inconsistency within education sectors, governance, and the value systems they engage and enact reflects the challenges faced in establishing stable and supportive ESE networks. The case study narratives also highlight the leadership within and outside the NSW Department of Education that steered and steer these EECs and ESE through unsupported times.

### 11.9.2 Leadership for Transformational Change

On a societal level, the movement for change in sustainability requires a shift in how we understand leadership—a shift that is happening. As noted by Ferreira et al. (2022), eco-psychology offers valuable perspectives on tackling the mental health and well-being effects of climate change—important to take account of in leadership. For instance, there is Solastalgia, the emotional distress caused by negative environmental changes, helping clarify the connection between human emotions and the state of both the natural and built environments (Albrecht, 2005). To counteract the grief and anxiety brought on by solastalgia, Albrecht (2020) developed the concept of the symbiocene to represent an era where positive emotions, rooted in a harmonious relationship with the Earth, counter the negative emotions associated with environmental degradation. The idea is that the destructive forces of the Anthropocene, which have fuelled solastalgia and other negative Earth emotions, will be challenged by a new generation—Generation Symbiocene—whose positive Earth emotions will guide the way forward (Albrecht, 2020). There is importance in incorporating psychological insights into the training and development of sustainability leaders.

Leadership in education is one of the enablers of effective formal ESE—that and teachers with an interest in the area. Further, the accentuated need for transformative environmental and sustainability practices highlights the need for education systems capable of nurturing leaders with the capacity to challenge hegemonic systems impeding transformative change (Ferreira et al., 2022). Furman and Gruenewald (2004) explored the potential of critical leadership of place in advancing socio-ecological justice within schools. In developing the concept, they suggested initial steps serving as entry points for addressing socio-ecological justice in educational settings. Their analysis contributed to the discourse on leadership for social justice in schools by highlighting the interconnectedness of ecological justice, social justice, and pedagogy. For instance, the authors caution against pursuing social justice through policies that reinforce narrow definitions of achievement and accountability, ultimately restricting the possibilities for teaching, learning, and educational leadership (Furman & Gruenewald, 2004). Here we can see where ESE leadership clashes with compliance. However, throughout the literature, project evaluation reports, case studies and EEC insights, we find empires and lighthouses of ESE leadership and practice within schools (Affolter & Varga, 2018; Gough et al., 2020; Liebermann & Louv, 2013, these case studies and EEC insights).

Furman and Gruenewald (2004) acknowledged the challenges of applying specific leadership practices to pursue moral objectives like socio-ecological justice in schools. They cautioned against the potential pitfalls of idealistic generalisations and reducing complex concepts to measurable outcomes. Their approach, grounded in socio-ecological justice and a critical pedagogy of place, emphasises the interconnectedness of biological and cultural diversity, the links between social and environmental domination, and the importance of sustainability. This perspective advocates for a leadership model that is moral, transformative, and communal, calling for a commitment to socio-ecological values and actions.

To foster socio-ecological justice in schools, Furman and Gruenewald recommend that leaders at all levels engage in educative processes, develop socio-ecological analyses, and embrace transformative leadership practices. Key strategies include shaping the cultural politics of the school, addressing ideological dissonance, collaborating with the community, securing resources, and prioritising professional development for educators and community members. Modern leadership involves collaboration—it is empathetic and adaptable emphasising empowerment, open communication, and inclusivity.

ESE plays a crucial role in developing leaders capable of promoting collective social transformation. It also seeks to challenge the conservative tendencies of educational systems and recognises that systemic change must occur simultaneously at multiple levels to be effective. A primary objective of ESE is to disrupt unsustainable practices and ideologies by cultivating leaders who can critically evaluate existing assumptions and implement transformative strategies for sustainability (Ferreira et al., 2022).

Empowering learners to take action and lead social change is central. Key strategies involve leadership training, community building, and using critical thinking to challenge traditional beliefs. This educational framework draws from Marxist and Freirean principles, emphasising liberation and social transformation. Techniques commonly employed include political literacy, engagement with real-world issues, reflective practices, and community involvement in social and environmental initiatives (Ferreira et al., 2022).

Despite the emphasis on transformative sustainability within ESE, the actual implementation of these principles often falls short in practice, particularly as discussions around the Anthropocene increase the demand for robust transformative educational systems that foster leaders who can effectively challenge the status quo (Ferreira et al., 2022). EECs can and do serve as some of the entry points and supports for environmental and sustainable leadership.

Skills in evoking inclusivity and democracy, the ability to catalyse the empowerment of others while being adaptable to navigate dynamic and unpredictable situations are leadership attributes for sustainability. These are antithetical to traditional forms of leadership (Ferreira et al. 2022) that often, with adult leadership, are about influence or position (Bass & Bass, 2008; Northouse, 2012 cited in Armstrong & Gough, 2019). Leadership for sustainability amongst adolescence works collaboratively for sustainable outcomes in addition to educating and influencing others (Armstrong & Gough, 2019). An example of youth leadership can be found in the organisation of the School Strike for Climate movement.

### 11.9.3  *Learning Leadership: School Strike for Climate (SS4C)*

The process by which individuals become community leaders within social movements challenges the notion of fixed leadership concepts (Tattersall et al., 2022). An examination of the School Strike for Climate (SS4C) revealed dynamic processes, illustrating how leaders evolve over time to address encountered challenges (Harmon, 1990, cited in Tattersall et al., 2022). Amid declining participation in traditional civic entities and escalating crises in the.

economy, climate, and healthcare, it becomes crucial to comprehend how to establish robust participatory movements characterised by distributed leadership. The School Strike for Climate (SS4C) movement exemplifies such a model, implementing three distinct strategies—mobilising strikes (see Fig. 11.5), organising through training, and engaging in political lobbying. Each strategy plays a unique role in fostering leadership skills among young participants, combining cognitive, emotional, and practical experiences. Despite strategy-specific strengths and limitations, SS4C's success lies in integrating various approaches to people power, offering a holistic platform for leadership development in youth climate movements and social movements globally.

## 11.10  Conclusion

Over this 50-year time period a shift along the binary of a moralistic to a critical thinking future, world, systems thinking paradigm can be detected. This is important given the challenges faced cannot be addressed with a reductionist approach (González-Gaudiano et al., 2020).

Medir et al. (2014) noted that EECs play a crucial role in non-formal education, formal education, and lifelong learning (Ballantyne & Packer, 2006; Murga-Menoyo, 2009; Romi & Schmida, 2009; UNESCO, 2009). EECs are more adaptable than formal education institutions, allowing them to respond to evolving educational challenges (Romi & Schmida, 2009). Gough et al. (2024) acknowledge the contributions EECs in NSW and Queensland have made and make to ESE for

## 11.10 Conclusion

**Fig. 11.5** 2019-03_Fridays_For_Future_Dresden_(45). (Attribution: Ralf Lotys (Sicherlich), CC BY 4.0. https://creativecommons.org/licenses/by/4.0, via Wikimedia Commons)

students and informal professional development for teachers. Over the 50-year history of NSW DE-EECs, and in the glimpses of EEC practice globally it is evident that these centres play an important role in connecting students and people in general to their environment and environmental and sustainability knowledges and practices—individually and collectively. In addition, they are often an important, and sometimes essential, instigator and collaborator in ESE initiatives.

This chapter has illuminated some of the intricacies in the history of pedagogy, curriculum, and the politics, tension and themes that have shaped the establishment and development of EECs and ESE within the NSW Department of Education and centres globally—including, First Nations ESE and STEM education. The broadening of this study to global iterations of EECs draws attention to the need for conscientisation of the history of the post-colonialisation of the globe and where we fit within. There is a highlighting of examples of the impact of ESE leadership, or not, across all levels of governance and within EECs—within schools and society in general. A desktop study of centres within countries such as Italy, the Nordic Countries and Spain emphasise the importance of having a curriculum that is authentically aligned with ESE practices—missing from many countries where rigidly focused accountability measures are practiced. There is an exploration of some centres and movements working outside conventional EEC/ESE practices.

Stevenson's advice for educator practitioners is important when charting the course forward. He advises educators to stay/be involved in constructing the discourse, to have input in its historical, pedagogical and political positioning, and to be involved in the research process as part of the transformation. Ferreira also stresses the need to be involved in writing the future (2022). In addition, Stevenson (2006) recommends "learning forward" in order to stay nimble in our unpredictable future (Stevenson, 2006).

# References

@maturegirl7. (2024, May 21). *Eco-feminism, Dr Vandana Shiva* [Instagram post]. Retrieved October 1, 2024, from https://www.instagram.com/maturedgirl7/reel/C7MW9VhyoZu/

Affolter, C., & Varga, A. (Eds.). (2018). *Environment and school initiatives: Lessons from the ENSI network—Past, present and future*. Vienna and Eszterházy Károly University Hungarian Institute for Educational Research and Development.

Albrecht, G. (2005). 'Solastalgia'. A new concept in health and identity. *PAN: Philosophy Activism Nature, 3*, 41–55.

Albrecht, G. A. (2020). Negating solastalgia: An emotional revolution from the Anthropocene to the Symbiocene. *The American Imago, 77*(1), 9–30.

Andreou, N., & Tramarin, A. (Eds.). (2016). *Foundation for environmental education: A story*. Foundation for Environmental Education (FEE).

Apple, M. (1990). *Ideology and curriculum* (2nd ed.). Taylor & Francis.

Apple, M. (2000). *Official knowledge: Democratic education in a conservative age* (2nd ed.). Routledge.

Armstrong, P., & Gough, A. (2019). Developing and motivating young leaders for sustainability. In D. B. Zandvliet (Ed.), *Culture and environment: Weaving new connections* (pp. 163–187). Brill | Sense. https://doi.org/10.1163/9789004396685_010

Arnold, H. E., Cohen, F. G., & Warner, A. (2009). Youth and environmental action: Perspectives of young environmental leaders on their formative influences. *The Journal of Environmental Education, 40*(3), 27. https://doi.org/10.3200/Joee.40.3.27-36

Ball, S. (2005). Education reform as social Barberism: Economism and the end of authenticity. *Scottish Educational Review, 37*(1), 4–16.

Ballantyne, R., & Packer, J. (2006). Promoting learning for sustainability: Principals' perceptions of the role of outdoor and environmental education centres. *Australian Journal of Environmental Education, 22*(1), 15–29.

Bandyopadhy, J. (1999). Chipko Movement: Of floated myths and realities. *Economic and Political Weekly, 34*(15), 880–882. https://www.jstor.org/stable/4407841

Bass, B. M., & Bass, R. (2008). *The bass handbook of leadership: Theory, research & managerial applications* (4th ed.). Free Press.

Blum, N. (2008a). Environmental education in Costa Rica: Building a framework for sustainable development? *International Journal of Educational Development, 28*, 348–358. https://doi.org/10.1016/j.ijedudev.2007.05.008

Blum, N. (2008b). Ethnography and environmental education: Understanding the relationships between schools and communities in Costa Rica. *Ethnography and Education, 3*(1), 33–48.

Blum, N. (2009). Teaching science or cultivating values? Conservation NGOs and environmental education in Costa Rica. *Environmental Education Research, 15*(6), 715–729. https://doi.org/10.1080/13504620903420064

Carr, W., & Kemmis, S. (1986). *Becoming critical: Education, knowledge and action research*. Deakin University.

Connor, L., Freeman, S., & Higginbotham, N. (2009). Not just a coalmine: Shifting grounds of community opposition to coal mining in Southeastern Australia. *Ethnos, 74*(4), 490–513. https://doi.org/10.1080/00141840903202132

Cooper, G., Fricker, A., & Gough, A. (2024). Promoting First Nations science capital: Reimagining a more inclusive curriculum. *International Journal of Science Education. International Journal of Science Education*, 1–14. https://doi.org/10.1080/09500693.2024.2354077

Curriculum Development Centre (CDC). (1978). *Report of the Curriculum Development Centre study group on environmental education*. Curriculum Development Centre.

Dahr, J. (2023, October 9). Holding the fire: Indigenous voices on the great unravelling Ancient Wisdom with Anne Poelina. *Resilience* [Podcast]. Post Carbon Institute. https://www.resilience.org/stories/2023-10-09/holding-the-fire-episode-2-anne-poelina/

Eco-Schools. (n.d.). *Eco-Schools history*. Retrieved October 30, 2024, from https://www.eco-schools.global/ourhistory

Elshof, L. (2010). Transcending the age of stupid: Learning to imagine ourselves differently. *Canadian Journal of Science, Mathematics and Technology Education, 10*(3), 232–243. https://doi.org/10.1080/14926156.2010.504483

Ferreira, J., Ryan, L., & Davis, J. (2022). A deep dive into sustainability leadership through education for sustainability. In F. English (Ed.), *The Palgrave handbook of educational leadership and management discourse* (pp. 829–849). Springer.

Foott, B. (1983). *Peat's Bight Creek: A study of a river's ecosystem*. Muogamarra Field Studies Centre/NSW Department of Education.

Freire, P. (1970). Cultural action and conscientization. *Harvard Educational Review, 68*(4), 499.

Furman, G. C., & Gruenewald, D. A. (2004). Expanding the landscape of social justice: A critical ecological analysis. *Educational Administration Quarterly, 40*(1), 49–78. https://doi.org/10.1177/0013161x03259142

Gadotti, M. (2008). What we need to learn to save the planet. *Journal of Education for Sustainable Development, 2*(1), 21–30. https://doi.org/10.1177/097340820800200108

Gaur, M. (2023, August 10). *Chipko Movement in India 1973, leader, state, comprehensive study*. Retrieved November 2, 2023, from https://pwonlyias.com/chipko-movement/

González-Gaudiano, E. J., Meira-Cartea, P. A., & Gutiérrez-Bastida, J. M. (2020). Green schools in Mexico and Spain: Trends and critical perspective. In A. Gough, J. Chi-Kin Lee, & E. PoKeungTsang (Eds.), *Green schools globally: Stories of impact on education for sustainable development* (pp. 269–288). Springer.

Gough, N. (1987). Learning with environments: Toward an ecological paradigm for education. In I. Robottom (Ed.), *Environmental education: Practice and possibility* (pp. 49–68). Deakin University Press.

Gough, A. (1997). *Education and the environment: Policy, trends and the problems of marginalisation*. Australian Council for Educational Research.

Gough, A. (1999). Today shapes tomorrow—What happened to yesterday? A story of environmental education policy in Australia. *Chain Reaction, Autumn*, 25–28.

Gough, A. (2013a). The emergence of environmental education research: A "history" of the field. In R. Stevenson, M. Brody, J. Dillon, & A. Wals (Eds.), *International handbook of research on environmental education* (pp. 13–22). Routledge for the American Educational Research Association.

Gough, A. (2013b). History, contextual, and theoretical orientations that have shaped environmental education research. In R. Stevenson, M. Brody, J. Dillon, & A. Wals (Eds.), *International handbook of research on environmental education* (pp. 9–12). Routledge for the American Educational Research Association.

Gough, A. (2021). All STEM-ed up: Gaps and silences around ecological education in Australia. *Sustainability, 13*, 3801. https://doi.org/10.3390/su13073801

Gough, A., Chi-Kin Lee, J., & PoKeungTsang, E. (Eds.). (2020). *Green schools globally: Stories of impact on education for sustainable development*. Springer.

Gough, A., Reid, A., & Stevenson, R. B. (2024). Environmental and sustainability education in Australia. In M. Rieckmann & R. T. Muñoz (Eds.), *World review: Environmental and sustainability education in the context of the Sustainable Development Goals* (pp. 297–317). CRC Press.

Greenall, A. (1981). *Environmental education in Australia: Phenomenon of the seventies: A case study in national curriculum development*. Curriculum Development Centre.

Greenall, A. (1987). A political history of environmental education in Australia: Snakes and ladders. In I. Robottom (Ed.), *Environmental education: Practice and possibility* (pp. 3–21). Deakin University Press.

Hargreaves, A. (2003). *Teaching in the knowledge society: Education in the age of insecurity*. Teachers College Press.

Hodson, D. (2010). Science education as a call to action. *Canadian Journal of Science, Mathematics and Technology Education, 10*(3), 197–206. https://doi.org/10.1080/14926156.2010.504478

Hulme, M., & Mahony, M. (2010). Climate change: What do we know about the IPCC? *Progress in Physical Geography, 34*(5), 705–718. https://doi.org/10.1177/0309133310373719

Hunter Community Environment Centre. (n.d.). *A resource hub for environmentally conscious citizens since 2004: About the HCEC*. Retrieved October 8, 2023, from https://www.hcec.org.au/about

Jackson, M. G. (2011). The real challenge of ESD. *Journal of Education for Sustainable Development, 5*(1), 27–37. https://doi.org/10.1177/097340821000500108

Jónsson, Ó. P., Guðmundsson, B., Øyehaug, A. B., & Didham, R. J. (2021). *Mapping education for sustainability in the Nordic countries*. Nordic Council of Ministers.

Kanpol, B. (1999). *Critical pedagogy: An introduction* (2nd ed.). Garvey.

Koettig, C., Cooper, K., Eggins, A., & Gleeson, W. (1990). *Greening your school*. NSW Department of School Education, Metropolitan North Region.

Lieberman, G., & Hoody, L. (1998). Closing the achievement gap: Using the environment as an integrating context. *State Education and Environment Roundtable*. Retrieved January 10, 2010, from http://www.seer.org/extras/execsum.pdf

Lieberman, G. A., & Louv, R. (2013). *Education and the environment: Creating standards-based programs in schools and districts*. Harvard Education Press.

Louv, R. (2005). *Last child in the woods: Saving our children from nature deficit disorder*. Algonquin Books.

Lucas, A. M. (1972). *Environment and environmental education: Conceptual issues and curriculum implementation*. Doctoral dissertation. Retrieved April 24, 2016, from http://files.eric.ed.gov/fulltext/ED068371.pdf

Maddock, M. (1986). Teacher training using wetlands. *Australian Journal of Environmental Education, 2*, 31–34. https://doi.org/10.1017/s0814062600004390

Medir, R. M., Heras, R., & Geli, A. M. (2014). Guiding documents for environmental education centres: An analysis in the Spanish context. *Environmental Education Research, 20*(5), 680–694.

Murga-Menoyo, M. A. (2009). Educating for local development and global sustainability: An overview in Spain. *Sustainability, 1*(3), 479–493. https://doi.org/10.3390/su1030479

New South Wales Department of Education and Training Professional Learning and Leadership Development Directorate. (2008). *Quality teaching in NSW public schools: An annotated bibliography*. NSW Department of Education and Training.

NSW Government: Office of Environment & Heritage. (2012). *Who cares about the environment in 2012? A survey of NSW peoples' environmental knowledge, attitudes and behaviours*. https://www.environment.nsw.gov.au/research-and-publications/publications-search/who-cares-about-the-environment-2012

NSW Government: Office of Environment & Heritage. (2015). *Who cares about the environment? A survey of the environmental knowledge, attitudes and behaviours of people in New South Wales in 2015*. https://www.environment.nsw.gov.au/research-and-publications/publications-search/who-cares-about-the-environment-2015

Pascoe, B. with Harwood, L. (2024). *Black duck*. Thames & Hudson Australia.

Pitoska, E., & Lazarides, T. (2013). Environmental education centers and local communities: A case study. *Procedia Technology, 8*, 215–221.

# References

Pitoska, E., & Trikka, M. (2012). Environmental education centers and local community: The case of the Environmental Education Center in Meliti. In *52nd Congress of the European Regional Science Association: "Regions in Motion -Breaking the Path"*, 21–25 August 2012, Bratislava, Slovakia. http://hdl.handle.net/10419/120511

Popkewitz, T. (1986). Educational reform and its millennial quality: The 1980s. *Journal of Curriculum Studies, 18*(3), 267–283.

Pritchard, D. (2014). Knowledge and understanding. In A. Fairweather (Ed.), *Virtue epistemology naturalized: Bridges between virtue epistemology and philosophy of science* (pp. 315–327). Springer. https://doi.org/10.1007/978-3-319-04672-3_18

Rainforest Awareness Rescue Education Centre (RAREC). (n.d.). *Environmental education: Spearheading education programs*. Retrieved June 23, 2024, from https://rarec.org/education

Ravnbøl, K., & Neergaard, I. (2019). Nordic youth as sustainable changemakers. In F. Rehula (Ed.), *The transition to sustainable consumption and production*. Nordic Council of Ministers.

Renshaw, P., & Tooth, R. (Eds.). (2018). *Diverse pedagogies of place: Educating students in and for local and global environments*. Routledge.

Rising Tide. (n.d.). *About Rising Tide*. Retrieved November 20, 2023, from https://www.risingtide.org.au/

Robinson, K. (2010, October 14). *Changing education paradigms*. RSA ANIMATE. [YouTube]. Retrieved July 6, 2023, from https://www.youtube.com/watch?v=zDZFcDGpL4U

Robottom, I. (1983). Science: A limited vehicle for environmental education. *The Australian Science Teachers' Journal, 29*(1), 27–31.

Romi, S., & Schmida, M. (2009). Non-formal education: A major educational force in the postmodern era. *Cambridge Journal of Education, 39*(2), 257–273. https://doi.org/10.1080/03057640902904472

Roth, W.-M. (2010). Activism: A category for theorizing learning. *Canadian Journal of Science, Mathematics and Technology Education, 10*(3), 278–291. https://doi.org/10.1080/14926156.2010.50449

Sahlberg, P. (2011). *Finnish lessons: What can the world learn from educational change in Finland*. Teachers College Press.

Sauvé, L. (2015). The political dimension of environmental education: Edge and vertigo. In D. Selby & F. Kagawa (Eds.), *Sustainability frontiers: Critical and transformative voices from the borderlands of sustainability education* (pp. 103–116). Barbara Budrich Publishers.

Schell, E. E. (2013). Transnational environmental justice rhetorics and the Green Belt Movement: Wangari Muta Maathai's ecological rhetorics and literacies. *Journal of Advanced Composition, 33*(3/4), 585–613.

Smith, W. (2020). The leadership role of teachers and environment club coordinators in promoting ecocentrism in secondary schools: Teachers as exemplars of environmental education. *Australian Journal of Environmental Education, 36*(1), 63–80. https://doi.org/10.1017/aee.2020.8

Smith, C., & Watson, J. (2019). Does the rise of STEM education mean the demise of sustainability education? *Australian Journal of Environmental Education, 35*(1), 1–11. https://doi.org/10.1017/aee.2018.51

Stevenson, R. (1987). Schooling and environmental education: Contradiction in purpose and practice. In I. Robottom (Ed.), *Environmental education: Practice and possibility* (pp. 69–82). Deakin University Press.

Stevenson, R. (2006). Tensions and transitions in policy discourse: Recontextualizing a decontextualized EE/ESD debate. *Environmental Education Research, 12*(3), 277–290. http://www.informaworld.com/10.1080/13504620600799026

Stevenson, R. (2013). Researching tensions and pretensions in environmental/sustainability education policies. In R. Stevenson, M. Brody, J. Dillon, & A. Wals (Eds.), *International handbook of research on environmental education* (pp. 147–155). Routledge for the American Educational Research Association.

Strom, A. (1987). *A background to environmental education: Some memoirs of Allen A. Strom, A.M. Occasional Publication*. Association for Environmental Education (NSW).

Tattersall, A., Hinchliffe, J., & Yajman, V. (2022). School strike for climate are leading the way: How their people power strategies are generating distinctive pathways for leadership development. *Australian Journal of Environmental Education, 38*(1), 40–56. https://doi.org/10.1017/aee.2021.23

The Green Belt Movement. (n.d.). *Our history*. Retrieved November 10, 2023, from https://www.greenbeltmovement.org/who-we-are/our-history

Thomas, G. J. (2018). Pedagogical frameworks in outdoor and environmental education. *Journal of Outdoor and Environmental Education, 21*(2), 173–185. https://doi.org/10.1007/s42322-018-0014-9

Tooth, R., & Renshaw, P. (2009). Reflections on pedagogy and place: A journey into learning for sustainability through environmental narrative and deep attentive reflection. *Australian Journal of Environmental Education, 25*, 95–104. https://doi.org/10.1017/S0814062600000434

UNESCO. (2009). *United Nations Decade of Education for Sustainable Development (DESD) (2005-2014). Review of contexts and structures for education for sustainable development*. UNESCO.

Vare, P., & Scott, W. (2007). Learning for a change: Exploring the relationship between education and sustainable development. *Journal of Education for Sustainable Development, 1*(2), 191–198. https://doi.org/10.1177/097340820700100209

Webb, J. (1980). *A survey of field studies centres in Australia*. Australian National Parks and Wildlife Service.

Welch, A. (2018). Cultural difference and identity. In A. Welch, R. Connell, N. Mockler, A. Sriprakash, H. Proctor, D. Hayes, et al. (Eds.), *Education, change and society* (pp. 139–188). Oxford University Press.

Whelan, J. (2005). Popular education for the environment: Building interest in the educational dimension of social action. *Australian Journal of Environmental Education, 21*, 117–128. http://search.informit.com.au/documentSummary;dn=660010828930991;res=IELHSS

Withgott, J., & Laposata, M. (2012). *Essential environment: The science behind the stories* (4th ed.). Pearson.

Yunkaporta, T. K. (2010). Our ways of learning in Aboriginal languages. In J. Hobson, K. Lowe, S. Poetsch, & M. Walsh (Eds.), *Re-awakening languages: Theory and practice in the revitalisation of Australia's Indigenous languages* (pp. 37–49). Sydney University Press.

# Chapter 12
# Conclusion: Challenging Times| Changing Tides—Meeting a Critical Juncture

## 12.1 Conclusion

One of the old guard sums up environmental education centres (EECs) succinctly and knowingly:

> I think EECs are at the centre of traditional education systems' attempt at environmental education. They're the place where students actually do environmental education and where teachers can be in-serviced on what sustainability means. You've got to have somewhere outside the classroom where fieldwork in environmental education can take place. As things change EECs can change to accommodate and include new environmental concepts. In saying that we've tried to infuse environmental education into other curriculum areas with varying success but certainly not with the rigor that well, the early teachers and myself in the centres wanted. Not to the point of bias but just to be even handed because the powers to be, the modern paradigm, is leaning so far to the right anybody that speaks anything near the middle is a left-wing radical now. It's very difficult to push an environmental bent within education without being seen as some sort of radical, that you're not, you're actually teaching very conservative views of the planet. You say, "Let's stop and think about what we're doing." You're not actually saying, "Get out there and chop everything down, dig it up and sell it for what you want" but that's what everybody's doing. So if you go against it you're some sort of radical and a Luddite and holding back the future. AA

This historical account has opened a wide frame of many threads of history woven through a relatively large expanse of time,[1] space and place—global to local—the 1970s to 2017 with a desktop update (to 2024) and earlier historical context setup from the founding of colonial Australia—early colonialisation. Given the time covered, this analysis leaves plenty of spaces for people to continue the investigation and documentation, to right the wrongs, extend the field—fill in the blank and blind spots. This is important given the significance of history, place and time in any particular habitat. One suggestion for further study would be in-depth case studies of

---

[1] In written historical account terms.

individual centres such as those showcased in *Diverse Pedagogies of Place: Educating Students in and for Local and Global Environments* (Renshaw & Tooth, 2018). As outlined in the preface, these studies detail EECs within the Queensland Department of Education system, theorising both the contexts of influence and the distinct pedagogical approaches to ESE in-depth. Each EEC has unique characteristics depending on its topography, history, sociological lenses and place within the post-colonialised, neoliberal globe. This study, while giving voice to one iteration of centres, has only touched the edges of EECs globally. However, using a Weberian analysis of bureaucratic reasoning it has shed light on phenomena influencing the current state of NSW Department of Education EECs while giving insight into broader structural and organisational dynamics. While not all findings may apply universally, it seems likely that certain aspects resonate with other EECs.

In understanding history, we can start to understand our present. It may make visible things that can be seen over a long period but are difficult to conceive in a shorter scenario. History can also give us a perspective on change or the lack of change—the dominant culture and power structures within which we live, and how or if they have shifted over time. Good history can provide solutions or supports for today. Through the history of the establishment and development of EECs in the NSW Department of Education and other examples around the globe, the importance of participation in society, as well as collaboration and understanding of ESE at all levels, becomes evident. There is an opportunity for perception, and acquisition of empathy, for different times and places and the enactments that occurred. The dominance and intransience of the power structures in which we live are apparent. These structures control the reproduction of society through, for instance the curriculum. They both silence and enable entities that threaten the dominant paradigm's existence. Yet, we can also observe the paradigm shift and the possibilities and budding of the reconstruction of a more ecocentric paradigm. Within this environment, there is an understanding of the importance of courage to take risks—to work outside the square that is bureaucracy, while finding ways and means of working inside, and changing, this structure. The value and power of comradery and humour in collaboration seems emancipatory. Additionally, observable is the fundamental importance of place and time, the uniqueness of specific places, in the establishment and development of a diverse range of entities that together form a dynamic network that can survive, thrive, and push an agenda that is antithetical to the dominant culture—but essential.

An action-oriented ethos, and enablers within and outside the NSW Department of Education, has facilitated the centres' significant contribution in shifting the agenda toward a more sustainable future. Centres globally have unique situations—enablers, inhibitors and ethos—yet often there are similarities and global networking facilitates connection (see Fig. 12.1).

Importantly, centres connect students to the environment, specific places that are essential in our globalised context. Descriptive analysis reveals centres with an ecocentric rather than the anthropocentric skew dominated by a world heavily influenced by our consumeristic society. EEC educators have fashioned themselves to

## 12.1 Conclusion

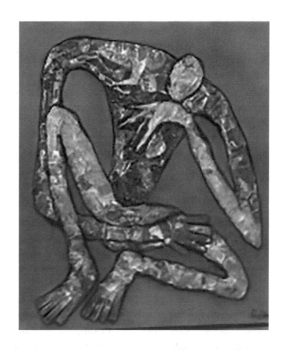

**Fig. 12.1** What I interpret as existential angst! An artwork created with lolly wrappers.—artist unknown or difficult to identify. Displayed at the Waste as Art exhibition, The World Environmental Education Congress, Marrakech 2013

fit. Moreover, ESE must fit for a worthwhile future, or indeed any future involving humans. The anthropocentric bribe.

The validity of comparing Environmental Education Centres (EECs) based on varying data sources is understandably open to question. On one hand, over 35 in-depth interviews and extensive document analysis provide rich insights; on the other, a review of desktop evidence regarding EEC examples worldwide is only as good as the information available in the public faces of the centres. A key issue lies in the reduced transparency of critique, as centres increasingly rely on external funding and bureaucratic structures, making them less inclined to disclose information—a situation detrimental to both research and Environmental and Sustainability Education (ESE) praxis. Additionally, reduced funding and restricted access to critical evaluations contributes to the decline in publicly available assessments of EECs. We are once more reminded of the interconnectedness of all—political, environmental, sociological and economic, at a local and global level.

The unpacking of a detailed study of EECs within one bureaucracy provides insights for comparison. It is important to note that the case study data was collected specifically within the context of a history. Many of the interviewees were foundational educators, asked to reflect on the historical development of these centres. However, there remain significant gaps in the narrative, particularly when considering that this data was generated in 2017 and written up in 2020—and I'm now writing into 2024. The past 7 years are largely characterised by desktop research, personal observations, and minimal interactions with centres. As such, the reflections presented here are an attempt to build upon case study findings, while also acknowledging the uncertainties involved in drawing parallels between these distinct data sets and global examples—making any conclusions speculative at best. However, it has highlighted some interesting insights that may be useful in understanding the EEC/ESE agenda. At the very least it provides an accessible history of EECs and the environments in which they operate and the politics that have got them where they are, indeed we are, today. Hopefully it provides useful insights to accelerate understanding for newcomers or those curious but uncertain or confused about the field.

In this exploration of EECs and their role within ESE networks, we have traversed a complex landscape of formal and non-formal education. The case studies and discussions throughout have demonstrated that EECs are more than just physical spaces connecting people to their environment—they can be catalysts for transformation, fostering critical thinking, and enabling communities to flourish in the face of environmental challenges. It is easy to generalise, and thus important to point out that there is a wide binary from conservation education, within a colonialist frame, to transformative ESE. However, it is difficult to be connected to the environment and not be concerned for the pollution and depletion that is occurring at an increasingly rapid rate.

The growth and sustainability of EECs depend on the creation of the right conditions—community involvement—First Nations' and Indigenous knowledge and practices—government or NGO support—ideally all of these. As outlined in earlier chapters, the establishment of robust support structures and a clear vision for environmental education (EE) are key to ensuring that these centres not only endure but flourish. The evolution of EECs, has shown that effective ESE must be grounded in local knowledge while embracing supportive global initiatives. Local initiatives are key as are continual learning and connection to change.

The discussion on colonialism and environmental justice reminds us that the fight for sustainability is intertwined with social equity. The lessons highlight how EECs can empower communities to address not only environmental degradation but also the social structures that perpetuate it and inequality.

EECs play a crucial role in navigating the ever-changing tides of ESE—often an essential cog in the wheel. ESE is important in ensuring people have a profound and integrated comprehension of the underlying causes and mechanisms of our environment and our effect on it and in fostering active participation in environmentally responsible behaviours. EECs are a vital component in the broader network of ESE, adapting and responding to the dynamic needs of societies facing the dual pressures of climate change and social transformation. These centres often contribute to envisioning a future where education serves as a tool for sustainability, resilience, and collective flourishing.

As we move forward, it is important to stay mindful of how policies impact ESE and EECs and similar entities, the environment and the environmental movement in general—to question frameworks that limit their potential. We need to be unafraid to question the neoliberal frameworks that often shape environmental policies and our place within this given ESE and EECs are necessary Western constructs counteracting Western destruction. Listening to, appreciating and supporting First Nations knowledges and practices, as many EECs do, seems like a logical way forward. Listening to, appreciating and supporting ESE and post-colonialist, post neoliberal diaspora seems logical.

In the face of daunting challenges, Tim Winton reminds us that hope is a powerful force. "If I can measure a certain level of progress in my grandchild's lifetime, we'll have managed to pick some tentacles off," (Cain, 2024) he notes, reflecting the collective desire to break free from the constraints of a system that prioritises corporate interests over human well-being. As Vandana Shiva articulates, the mechanistic thought and alienated economic structures that have shaped our Western reality are reaching their maturity, prompting critical reflection (Vandana Shiva via @**wise.wild**.feminine). "We discount the power of our determination, but I think that's what will save us. We won't be saved by our scientific genius. The only thing that's likely to save us as a species is solidarity." (Winton cited by Cain, 2024).

While a multitude and diversity of collectives are engaged in this transformative journey, many EEC educators have the specialised knowledge and skills, and environment, to support and collaborate with individuals in cultivating and embracing an ecocentric worldview— a future that honours the interrelatedness of all life.

## References

Cain, S. (2024, October 3). Tim Winton: 'I lived in the worst possible space for seven years. It knocks some paint off you, I can tell you'. *The Guardian*. https://www.theguardian.com/books/2024/oct/03/tim-winton-juice-book-interview

Renshaw, P., & Tooth, R. (2018). Diverse place-responsive pedagogies: Historical, professional and theoretical threads. In P. Renshaw & R. Tooth (Eds.), *Diverse pedagogies of place: Educating students in and for local and global environments*. Routledge.

# Author Index

**A**
Abulafia, D., 308
Affolter, C., 252, 383
Agyekum, B., 2
Albrecht, G., 382
Alexandersson, M., 309
Alexopoulou, I., 333
Andrzejewski, J., 300
Annear, R., 83
Apple, M., 51, 276, 355, 369, 371, 372
Armstrong, K., 146, 147
Armstrong, P., 384
Arnold, H.E., 380

**B**
Bacon, F., 51
Baker Proudfoot, H., 20–24
Balderstone, S., 26
Ballantyne, R., 384
Bandyopadhy, J., 377
Barcan, A., 26, 46, 103, 127–129
Barker, M., 322
Benjamin, K.A., 1
Bergmann, I., 258
Berryman, T., 7
Bertrand, K.A., 2
Bessant, B., 26, 27, 83
Bezzina, M., 284
Bird, C., 53
Blum, N., 317, 347
Bonyhady, T., 24, 25, 27, 81, 82, 117
Boom, K., 29, 31, 33, 34
Boyd, D.R., 315

Bridger, G., 149
Bristow, W., 51
Bruyninckx, H., 13
Buchanan, J., 281
Buckler, C., 301, 331–333, 336
Bullard, R.D., 6
Bullen, A., 13
Burford, C., 284
Bush, R.A., 320

**C**
Cain, S., 395
Calzadilla, P.V., 315
Carron, L.T., 37
Carruthers, J., 294
Carson, R., 54, 63
Chatelard, G., 296, 313
Chatty, D., 296
Cohen, B., 213
Coleman, C., 141, 142
Collins, C., 203
Collins, J., 151
Connell, R., 70
Connor, L., 377
Connors, L., 21, 23–29, 31–37, 40, 41, 81, 88, 103, 104, 106
Conrad, S., 71
Cooper, G., 357
Corcoran, P., 300
Cornell, J., 162, 191
Creech, H., 301, 331–333, 336
Croft, D., 33

Curtis, W., 21
Czarny, G., 317

**D**
Dahr, J., 8, 299, 357, 358
Day, B., 294
De Freitas Ermel, T., 334
Deleuze, G., 62
Dennis, D., 50, 51, 62
Descartes, R., 51
Dewey, J., 36, 51, 62
Dimenäs, J., 309
Dingle, T., 80
Disinger, J., xv
Dittmar, H., 1
Dobson, A., 13
Dowd, P., 213
Dryzek, J., 7, 14, 68
Dufty, N., 110, 133, 155, 214
Dunlap, R., 20
Dyment, J., 268, 280

**E**
Eames, C., 322
Edelstein, D., 51
Ewing, N., 312

**F**
Fawns, R., 50
Fensham, P., 119, 123, 124, 126, 230, 304
Fernández-Herrería, A., 355
Ferreira, J., 280, 382–384, 386
Ferreira, J.G., 10
Fioramonti, L., 332
Flannery, T.F., 80, 81
Flogaitis, E., 333
Foott, B., 164, 189, 192
Foreman, B., 126
Fox, A., 1, 25, 27, 33, 44–46, 63, 87, 88, 90–96, 98–109, 117, 119, 121, 130, 132, 133, 137–140, 143, 144, 146, 148–150, 155, 156, 159, 160, 162, 186, 187, 193, 210, 211, 241
Fox, J., 1
Freire, P., 13, 61, 316, 334, 336, 375
Frew, B., 216
Funnell, S., 258, 263
Furman, G.C., 382, 383

**G**
Gadotti, M., 378
Gammage, B., 21, 23, 24, 80, 81
Garis, M.K., 334
Gaudelli, W., 13
Gaur, M., 377
Gelter, H., 308
Gericke, N., xvi, 322
Gibbs, D., 276, 321
Gifford, R., 65, 66
Gilbert, R., 13, 203
Gilligan, B., 132, 133, 154, 155, 198, 199
Godfrey, K., 226, 230
González-Gaudiano, E.J., 316, 317, 375
Gough, N., 1, 5, 53, 69, 119, 120, 123, 202, 203, 209, 230, 231, 252–254, 260, 267–269, 276, 281, 283, 297–299, 304, 305, 359, 364, 371, 372, 382, 384
Gould, S.J., 20
Gowers, R., 39, 143
Greenall, A., 7, 118–120, 123–126, 203, 282, 364, 371
Griffiths, A., 83
Gruenewald, D.A., 300, 382, 383
Guardiola-Rivera, O., 52, 70–72, 294
Guattari, F., 62

**H**
Haddon, F., 148, 149, 162, 163, 166, 177, 180, 188, 190, 191, 206, 207
Hamblin, J.D, 54
Hamilton, B., 144–146, 163, 199
Harari, Y., 71
Hardy, T., 28
Hargreaves, A., 364
Harris, C., 216
Harris, T., 42, 139, 141, 373
Hartley-Brewer, E., 159
Harvey, D., 181
Haukka, A., 311
Heck, D., 241
Heilman, E., 13
Held, D., 14
Helmers, H., 51
Henry, J., 1, 25, 64, 131, 163
Hernández Huerta, J.L., 334
Hill, 24, 25, 185, 191, 199, 200, 209, 213–215, 224–225, 276, 359
Hill, S., 20, 21, 27, 38, 39, 268, 280
Hilson, M., 308

Hjorth Warlenius, R., 300
Hodson, D., 374
Hollander, R., 31, 32
Holt-Biddle, D., 325
Hoody, L., 128, 349, 372
Hopwood, B., 14
Huckle, J., 2, 12–14, 65, 67, 68, 232, 302, 304, 305
Hughes, J., 26, 117, 118, 127–129, 138, 216, 220, 230, 232, 253, 260, 280
Hulme, H., 378
Hutton, D., 21, 23–29, 31–37, 40, 48, 81, 88, 103, 104, 106
Huxley, T., 21

# I
Idin, S., 52

# J
Jackson, M.G., 70, 323, 324, 373
James, P., 49
Jeffes, E., 81
Jenkins, E., 47
Jickling, B., 13
Johnston, C., 130, 148, 149, 162, 188, 191
Jónsson, O.P., 376
Jordan, 67, 313, 325–327, 338
Jordan, K., 317
Jorgenson, A., 20
Jūrmalis, E., 308

# K
Kagawa, F., 305
Kahn, K., 300
Kanaujia, P.R., 322
Karena, C., 253, 254
Kass, D., 42, 45–47
Kasser, T., 1
Kaukko, M., 65
Kemmis, S., 275, 371
Kitooke, A., 275
Klein, N., 1
Knapp, D., 50, 51, 62, 299
Koettig, C., 189, 200, 220, 366
Kohlstedt, S., 47
Koole, B., 159
Kotzé, L.J., 315
Kristjánsson, K., 317
Künzler, D., 71
Kvideland, R., 308

# L
Ladwig, J.G., 263, 265, 266, 270, 309
Laposata, M., 6, 370
Larri, M., 258, 263
Lave, J., 275
Lawn, J., 68
Lazarides, T., 375
Lengieza, M.L., 229
Lever, C., 22
Lewis, W., 26, 103–105
Li, Y., 1
Lieberman, G., 128, 349, 353, 372
Lines, W., 81, 82
Lingard, B., 61, 62, 69
Linke, R., 63, 118–120, 122, 123, 129
Locke, J., 51
Lockhart, J., 70
López González, B., 317
Lotz-Sisitka, H., 304
Loures, R., 9, 319
Louv, R., 353, 372, 383
Lucas, A.M., 69, 119, 353–356
Lucas, J., 29
Lucas, R., 98
Lugg, A., 294
Luypaert, T., 6
Lyons, M., 26, 29

# M
MacPherson, R., 148, 207, 220, 225, 232, 233
Maddock, M., 199, 214, 362
Magni, G., 72
Mahony, M., 378
Margaret Senior, xx, 89, 97, 100, 102
Marsh, G.P., 36
Marshall, A.J., 24, 81, 83, 117
Martens, C., 25
Martínez-Rodríguez, F.M., 335
Maude, A., 281
Mayer, C., 313
Mazower, M., 304, 305
Mbugua, P., 295
McDonald, K., 28, 109–111, 119, 132, 133, 153, 155, 199, 201, 206, 210, 366
McGrew, A.G., 14
McKern, G., 93
McLean, S., 1
McLeod, K., 1
McLoughlin, L.C., 24
McQuade, J., 71, 79
McWhinney, J., 308
Meadows, D., 54, 297

Medir, R.M., 352, 384
Mellor, M., 14
Menton, M., 2
Merchant, C., 19, 298
Middelman, R., 22
Milkis, S., 36
Miller, J., 149, 350
Milligan, A., 316
Mills, C., 71
Milton, V., 193
Mockler, N., 202, 260, 265, 266, 280
Monroe, M., 294
Morgense, F., 332
Morris, D., 22, 35
Morrison, C., 49–50, 95
Mudzunga, H.D., 325
Mulinari, D., 309
Mulligan, M., 20, 21, 27, 38, 39
Munck, T., 51
Murga-Menoyo, M.A., 384

**N**
Naess, A., 338
Neergaard, I., 376
Nietzsche, F., 64
Nilsson, A., 65, 66
Norman, J., 314
Nthuku, J.S., 9

**O**
O'Brien, G., 14
O'Connell, J., 23
O'Donoghue, R., 331
OECD, 62, 252
Olsen, C., 308
Otto, S.L., 1

**P**
Packer, J., 384
Paddle, R., 35, 80
Palmer, J.A., 20
Parker, C., 1
Partanen, A., 308
Pascoe, B., 20, 23, 72, 80, 81, 358
Pearson, D., 9, 129, 192, 200, 296, 297, 305
Perkins, R., 73, 81
Perry, T., 21
Petreniti, V., 334
Pettigrew, C., 26, 29, 230

Pitoska, E., 375
Pizzey, G., 46, 49, 50, 63
Poelina, A., 8, 357, 358
Popkewitz, T., 364
Posch, P., 252, 332
Pratley, J., 48
Prentice, C., 68
Prescott, D., 268
Pritchard, D., 374
Pusey, M., 185

**R**
Ravnbøl, K., 376
Reid, A., 202
Renshaw, J., 211
Renshaw, P., 192, 284, 372, 392
Reucassel, C., 64
Richmond M., 27
Riordan, G., 220
Rizvi, F., viii, 61–63, 69, 252
Roberts, B., 153
Roberts, J.E., 146
Roberts, N.S., 322
Roberts, T., 25
Robin, L., 54, 111, 112, 117, 118
Robottom, I., 69, 180, 252, 371
Rolls, E., 80, 81
Romi, S., 384
Roth, W.-M., 374
Rowell, L., 48
Russo, V., 331

**S**
Sagy, G., 313
Sauvé, L., 7
Sax, S., 9, 319
Schaefer, K., 110
Schell, E., 9
Schell, E.E., 377
Schliesser, C., 66, 67
Schmida, M., 384
Schwartz S.B., 70
Scott, W., 8, 23, 48, 66, 69, 216, 283, 371
Selby, D., 305
Sharma, P.K., 322
Shongwe, E., 10
Short, J., 33
Shultz, L., 13
Silencing, 374

Simard, S., 52, 53
Simpson, E., 223
Sinwell, L., 61
Skamp, K., 258, 264, 266, 279, 283
Skanavis, C., 334
Skedsmo, G., 309
Skilbeck, M., 28
Slattery, D., 294
Smego, A.A., 329
Smith, A., 9, 71
Smith, C., 359
Smith, K., 226, 235
Smith, S., 133, 235, 240, 242
Smith, T., 275
Smith, W., 335, 380
Smout, R., 21
Sokoloff, S., 154
Stapp, B., 119, 121, 162, 190, 229
Stapp, W., 119, 190
Starratt, R.J., 283
Steeves, K.A., 53
Steffensen, V., 72
Sterling, S., 65, 70
Stevenson, R., 8, 61, 69, 274, 275, 280, 364, 371, 372, 385
Steyn, P., 328
Strom, A., 33, 38, 39, 41, 43–48, 50, 54, 63, 87, 88, 90–109, 114, 117, 120, 121, 127, 130–132, 137–150, 161–163, 176, 180, 193, 211, 214, 241, 361, 366, 369, 370, 373
Sullivan, S., 71
Swinnerton, B., 47

**T**
Tal, A., 313
Tattersall, T., 384
Taylor, G., 48
Taylor, J., 331
Thomas, A., 215
Thomas, G.J., 352
Thomas, R., 44
Tilbury, D., 229
Tompkins, P., 53
Tomren, T.S., 309
Tooth, R., ix, xv, 192, 284, 372
Toral, K.M., 315
Tribe, D., 109, 130–133, 148, 149, 161–163, 166, 176, 188, 190–192, 201, 207, 221, 225–227, 230, 232, 233, 235, 239–242, 254, 258
Trikka, M., 375
Tuana, N., 71

Tudge, C., 53
Twining, P., 309

**V**
Vandenabeele, J., 13
Van Matre, 228
Van Poeck, K., 13
van Rensburg, E.J., 331
van Sittert, L., 321
Vare, P., 69, 283, 371
Varga, A., 383
Vijaykumar, S., 1
Vilaysack K., 9
Vonyó, T., 293

**W**
Wals, A.E.J., 12–15, 68, 302, 305
Walsh, G., 42
Walsh, V., 296
Warner, D., 224
Washington, W., 302
Watson, D., 27
Watson, I., 80
Watson, J., 359
Webb, J., xx, 132, 147, 151, 152, 154, 156, 163, 167, 177, 178, 307
Webb, L., 158
Weber, M., 66, 309
Welch, A., 149, 369
Weller, S., 220
Wenger, E., 275
Wheeler, K., 19, 20, 36, 119, 120
Whelan, J., 374
White, M., 80, 216, 327
Whitehead, M., 13
Williams, L., 163, 180
Williams, M., 83
Wilson, E., 28
Wilson, J., 119, 168
Wilson, K., 23
Wilson, V., 31
Windsor, S., 166, 275
Withgott, J., 6, 370
Wohlleben, P., 53
Wolff, L.-A., 309
Womersley, J., 27, 123, 124, 126
Wood, J., 321
Woolley, D., 144, 146, 163
Woolmington, E., 252
Wright, S., 210, 228, 229
Wyndham, H., 44, 47, 108, 127–129, 138, 144, 149, 185, 216, 354

## Y

Yanniris, C., 334
Yates, L., 203
Young, 261, 303
Young, Geoff, 133, 201, 206, 207, 220, 221, 254, 257
Young, Gordon, 44
Yue, J., 1

Yui, M., 294
Yunkaporta, T.K., 357

## Z

Ziltener, P., 71
Zint, M., 275
Zittoun, T., 159

# Subject Index

**A**

Acclimatisation Societies, 22–23
Action-learning, 175
Action orientation, 366–367
Action oriented, 309, 338, 373
Administration, 169
The *Adelaide Declaration*, 265
Advocacy, 28–46, 104–105, 166, 198–201, 231–241, 363–364
Africa, 70, 73, 79, 80, 293–295, 299, 307, 308, 320, 321, 325, 327–331, 337, 359
Agenda 21, 298
Alice Springs Desert Park, Northern Territory, Australia, 313–314
The *Alice Springs (Mparntwe) Education Declaration*, 261, 280
Allan Fox, 94, 109
Allen Strom, 43–44, 88, 101, 109, 147, 161, 373
Alternate forms of social and environmental relations, 12
Anthropocentric, 40, 67, 265
Anthropocentric *vs.* ecocentric, 37
Archetype of rationalism, 66
ARTD Consultants, 258
Artists, 23–26
Assemblages, 62
Assessment, 36, 48, 93, 170, 208, 232, 266, 268, 282, 309, 335, 351
Association for EE (NSW), 132–133, 240–241
Australian Association for Environmental Education, 251
Australian Association for the Advancement of Science, 26, 36

Australian Curriculum, ix, 12, 120, 203, 251, 260, 261, 264, 266–268, 275, 278, 280–281, 357, 368, 374
Australian Curriculum Assessment and Reporting Authority (ACARA), 260
Australian Education for Sustainability Alliance (AESA), 278
Australian Federation, 26–27, 31, 36, 41–43, 104, 145, 157, 180, 181, 185, 189, 196, 227, 228, 362
Australian Government Department of Environment and Heritage, 259, 276
The Australian Museum, 88, 180
Australian Sustainable Schools Initiative (AuSSI), 257
Awabakal Field Studies Centre, 153–155

**B**

The Bamfield Marine Science Centre, British Columbia, Canada, 312–313
The Belgrade Charter, 123
Beyond EECs, 322–324
Biology, vii–ix, 6
Bird, 29–33, 41, 42, 99, 130, 139, 198, 314, 327
Bird and Animal Protection Legislation, 29–32
Botany Bay Field Studies Centre, 214
Bottom-up, 110, 114, 245, 363
Bournda Field Studies Centre, 151–153, 193, 194
Brewongle Field Studies Centre, 167–168
Bureaucracies, 127–129, 364, 374
Bushwalkers, 39–44, 88, 104

## C

The Caloola Club, 45
Camden Park Education Centre, 222
Camden Park EEC, 222
Capacity, 199–200
Capacity Building, 216–218
Capitalism, 5, 9, 66–68
Cascade Field Studies Centre, 211
Centre collaboration, 160–161
Change Agents, 348–349
The Chipko Movement in India, 377
Citizen science, 377
Citizenship, vii, 11–14, 68, 72, 127, 264, 265, 283, 302–305, 327, 356, 375, 376, 379
Clerical and General Assistance, 173
Climate change, 6
Club of Rome, 54
Collectors, 23–26
Colonialisation, 79–84
Complexity, xiii, xiv, 2, 7, 10, 52, 232, 282, 351, 367
Comradery, 360–361
Conservation, xx, 5, 10, 28, 29, 31–33, 35, 36, 39, 41–43, 45–50, 54, 87, 88, 90, 93–96, 98–102, 104–114, 117–122, 127, 130–132, 137–143, 146, 151, 152, 156, 162, 175, 177, 186, 191, 193, 195, 196, 208, 209, 212, 221, 223, 225, 226, 252, 258, 266, 278, 282, 294–297, 299, 305, 313, 314, 316–322, 328–330, 336, 337, 348, 352, 356, 376, 377, 382, 394
Consumerism, 6
Controversial issues, 197–198, 208
The Coolangatta Statement on Indigenous Peoples' Rights in Education, 299
The Corcovado Foundation, Costa Rica, 318
Cornucopian, 63
Cornucopian mindset, 27
Costa Rica, 72, 293, 316–318, 338
Country Overshoot Days 2024, 310
CPR Environmental Education Centre, Chennai, Southern India, 321–322
Critical thinking, 2, 8, 50, 64, 68, 69, 120, 187, 280, 314, 316, 327, 330, 335, 338, 355, 356, 371, 375, 376, 383, 384, 394
Crosbie Morrison, 49–50, 95
Cross-curricular, 11, 44, 129, 174, 191, 208, 220, 235, 261, 267, 268, 270, 275, 280, 331, 354

Cross-curriculum, viii, 203, 268, 280, 281, 365
Curriculum, vii–ix, xi, xii, 7, 8, 11–13, 45, 46, 49–51, 69, 98, 99, 103, 114, 118–120, 123, 124, 126–129, 132, 141, 151, 156, 161–163, 167, 168, 172, 174, 176, 180, 181, 188, 189, 191, 194, 198, 201–204, 206–209, 215–217, 221, 223, 225, 226, 230, 232–237, 242, 243, 245, 251, 254–256, 258, 261, 264–268, 272–275, 278–282, 284, 291, 295, 297, 304–306, 309, 311, 312, 315, 323, 330–332, 334, 336, 347, 349, 353, 354, 356, 357, 359, 361, 364–366, 369, 370, 372, 373, 375, 385, 391, 392
Curriculum Development Centre (CDC), 118, 123–126

## D

David Tribe, 131, 161, 162, 176, 190, 226
Day field trip, vii
Declaration, 202, 203, 221, 253, 298, 299, 301–303
Desert Regions, 313–314
Development, 11, 12, 67–68, 93, 95–97, 111, 117, 118, 122–126, 152, 162, 191, 209, 228–230, 236, 252, 260, 276–277, 297, 299, 300, 302, 303, 317, 323, 328, 331, 349, 368
Disconnecting from the environment, 5
Dorroughby Field Studies Centre, 157–158, 217

## E

Earth Charter, 14, 299, 300, 316, 335, 336, 378
Earth Education, 225, 228–230, 252
Ecocentric, xx, 2, 8, 37, 51, 65, 67, 68, 110, 114, 130, 231, 265, 276, 281, 322, 335, 337, 338, 347, 348, 356, 360, 362, 372, 377, 392, 395
Ecofeminism, 360, 377
The Ecoguardas Environmental Education Centre in Ajusco, 317
Ecology, xv, 6, 7, 20, 38, 45, 72, 81, 95, 100, 120, 122, 139, 178, 204, 215, 295, 312, 321, 325, 370
Economic rationalism, 219
Ecopedagogy, 13, 336, 355

Index 405

Education for sustainable development (ESD), xvi, 8, 11, 13, 67, 68, 231, 260, 265, 269, 297, 299, 301–303, 333, 336, 371
Education for sustainability (EfS), viii, 8
Education policy, 62
Educational policy, 61, 62
Educational Reform, 216–219
*The Education We Need for the World We Want*, 12, 302
EEC collaboration in Italy, 331–332
EEC Policy Statement, 242–243
EECs in Extreme Environments, 311–313
Embargo, 109, 175, 177, 185, 187, 199–200
Enquiry learning, 368
Enviornmental education centres
    capacity, 171
Environmental and sustainability education (ESE), xi–xvi, 1, 2, 5–15, 32, 50, 51, 53, 55, 61–65, 68, 79, 120, 126, 133, 160, 176, 187, 192, 202, 205, 209, 210, 220, 227, 231, 233, 235, 239–243, 245, 251–261, 263–267, 269–276, 278–284, 291, 297–305, 308, 309, 311, 313–317, 319, 320, 322, 324, 325, 327–329, 331–338, 347–351, 355–366, 368, 369, 371–377, 379–385, 392–394
Environmental and Zoo Education Network (EZEC), xix, 234, 263, 275, 282, 360, 364, 368
Environmental awareness, 2, 5, 19, 20, 28, 46, 53, 55, 79, 87, 88, 118, 162, 191, 245, 252, 317, 318, 322, 323
Environmental education (EE), viii, xi, xvi, xix, xx, 2, 5–15, 19, 61–73, 87–114, 119–123, 125, 126, 132–133, 137, 145, 155, 162–171, 185, 187, 188, 190, 191, 198, 203, 205, 206, 208–209, 212, 220–227, 231–239, 241–244, 251–260, 262–264, 266, 271, 272, 276, 281, 283, 291, 294, 298, 299, 301, 307, 313–314, 317, 320–323, 325, 327, 328, 330, 334, 347, 361, 370, 376, 393, 394
Environmental education centres (EECs), vii, ix, xi, 2, 5, 19, 88, 132, 161, 188, 204, 251, 256, 291, 294, 354, 391, 393
    embargo, 175–176
    working conditions, 188–190
The Environmental Education Curriculum Statement, 208, 242

Environmental Education Policy for Schools, 255–257
The Environmental Education Unit, 226–227
Environmental impacts, 117
Environmentalism, 1, 54, 110, 113, 114, 117, 118, 121, 126, 149, 160, 175, 371, 374
Environmental management, 35
ESE in Barcelona, Spain, 336
An ESE/EEC perspective in Spain, 334–336
An ESE perspective in Greece, 333–334
Evaluation, 12, 123, 124, 163, 208, 263, 269, 301, 324, 330, 335, 352, 369, 375, 383
Explorers, 20–22

**F**
Fauna, 21, 23, 28, 41, 46, 49, 54, 79, 87, 88, 90, 93–96, 98, 99, 101, 142, 166, 314, 328
Faunal protection societies, 101
Fauna Protection Panel (FPP), 19, 87–102, 139
    capacity, 48, 93–94
    demise, 19, 87, 89, 92–93, 97, 98, 100, 102–109, 139, 361
    education, 98–101
Field of Mars Field Studies Centre, 200–201
Field Studies Centre Educator Conferences, 160–161
Field Studies Centres (FSCs), 121
    *See also* Environmental Education Centres (EECs)
Field trips, 100
    residential, 173
    day visit, 169
Fieldwork, 9
Finnish Nature Centre Haltia, Espoo, Finland, 310–311
First Nations', 8
    history, viii, 81, 111
    knowledges, 15, 356–358
Flora, 198–200, 223
Forestry, ix, 35, 36, 41, 53, 111, 158, 186, 193, 194, 294, 306, 308, 366
FSC Policy, 208–209
Funding Opportunities, 216–219
The Future we Want, 302

**G**
Generational equity, 79
Geography, ix, xii, 6

Georges River Education Centre, 222–224
Georges River EEC, 223–224
Gibberagong FSC, 210
Global Education 2030 Agenda, 302
Global Governance, 297–305
Globalization, xiii, xv, 14, 61, 65, 69, 71, 127, 305, 323, 378
Goal 4.7, 303
Gould League Advisory Service, 130–132, 141–148
Gould League of NSW, 130–133, 146, 148, 162, 166, 178, 180, 181, 188, 191, 213, 240–241, 243, 245, 374
  the Gould League of Bird Lovers, 32, 130
The Gould Leaguer, 131, 191
The Green Belt Movement in Kenya, 377
Greenwashing, 1, 2
Growing Demand, 147–148
Guajajara Women Warriors, Brazil, 318–319, 380

**H**
Hands-on, 20, 119, 128, 131, 145, 147, 164, 243, 280, 309, 313, 314, 322, 326, 330, 352, 365, 372, 380
Har HaNegev Field School, Mitzpe Ramon, Negev Desert, Israel, 313
Heuristic Frame, 69–70
History, 6
Huerto Alegre Center for Educational Innovation, 335
Hunter Community Environment Centre, 9, 377

**I**
Impact, 118, 220–225, 349–350
Indigenous knowledges, 5, 10, 303, 337, 356
Indigenous knowledges/education, 356
Indigenous populations, 72–73
The Industrial Relations Commission Hearing (1994), 227–228
Institute for Ecological Research (IPÊ), 318
Institutionalisation, 185–245
International conferences, 298–301
International Union for the Conservation of Nature and Natural Resources (IUCN), 119, 297
Interrelationships, 10, 15, 49

**K**
The Kaipatiki Project, New Zealand, 315–316
Kamay Botany Bay EEC, 214
Kastoria CESE, 333–334

**L**
Leadership, 9, 233, 269, 270, 272, 273, 275, 276, 278, 279, 281, 291, 321, 328, 335, 349, 356, 361, 372, 379–385
Learnscapes, 8, 225, 258, 259
Limits to growth, 297
Little Desert dispute, 110–113
Longneck Lagoon Field Studies Centre, 166–167
The Lucas Framework, 353–356

**M**
Managing risk, 159–160
Margaret Senior, xx, 89, 97, 100, 102
The *Melbourne Declaration*, 261, 264, 265, 280
Mexico, 73, 294, 316–317, 338, 375
Millennium Development Goals (MDGs), 302
Mt. Kembla/Illawarra Field Studies Centre, 215
Muogamarra Field Studies Centre, 143–146, 163–165, 210, 262, 283

**N**
National Curriculum, 202, 260–261
  *See also* Australian Curriculum
National Environmental Education Council and Network, 252–253
The National Fitness Camps, 44–45
National Parks, xx, 29, 31, 33, 38, 41, 47, 48, 54, 88, 89, 94, 96, 97, 100–102, 104–109, 111, 139, 140, 147, 150–152, 154, 156, 167, 186, 191, 193, 201, 205, 210, 294, 307, 325, 350, 381
Native flora, 38
Naturalists, 20–22, 25, 32, 42, 93, 111
Nature Conservation Council of NSW, 96
Nature play, 20, 192, 380
Nature's Rights and Resistance, 315–316
Nature study, 20, 41–47, 49–51, 98, 120, 282
Neoliberal, 2, 7–9, 13, 14, 68, 69, 181, 220, 251, 276, 284, 299, 302, 304, 305, 309, 335, 337, 353, 357, 362, 373–375, 377, 392, 394

Neoliberalism, xiii, xiv, 12, 14, 68, 114, 251, 274, 284, 302, 304, 336, 347, 375, 376
Networking, xx, 10, 26, 41–42, 90, 110, 114, 132, 157, 181, 206, 252, 262, 304, 336, 338, 358, 362–364, 368, 377, 380, 381, 392
Non government organisations (NGOs), 15
Non-Viable Primary Schools, 148–158
Nordic countries, 308–311, 385
Normative paradigm, 373–376
NSW Department of Education, viii, xiv, 10–12, 19, 45, 49, 51, 55, 84, 87, 96, 110, 114, 127, 128, 130–133, 141, 143, 144, 146–152, 154, 157, 161–163, 166, 168–170, 173–175, 178, 180, 181, 185, 187–191, 193, 195, 197, 199–201, 204–207, 210–213, 215–217, 219, 222–224, 227, 228, 232, 234–239, 241–245, 251, 252, 254–259, 261, 263–265, 270, 273, 276, 281–283, 305, 306, 348, 349, 356, 366, 371–373, 379, 382, 385, 392
NSW Department of Education and Training, *see* NSW Department of Education
NSW Department of Education Environmental Education Centres (NSW DE-EECs)
  teaching capacity, 243
  Wirrimbirra, viii, 141–143, 146–148, 150, 160, 161, 169, 170, 180, 199, 222, 223, 227, 238, 239, 244
NSW Education reform, 103
NSW Environmental Protection Authority, 127, 226, 233, 254
NSW National Parks and Wildlife Service, 54, 89, 97, 100–102, 139, 191, 210
The NSW EE Council, 254–255

## O
Observatory Hill Field Studies Centre, 213
The Okonjima Nature Reserve/AfriCat EEC, Namibia, 328–330
*Our Common Future*, the Brundtland Report, 298
Outdoor Education, 178, 305–307
Outward Bound, 296–297, 336
*OzEEnew*, 126

## P
Parks and Playgrounds Movement, 42, 43, 104
Paul Vare and Bill Scott's (2007) addition of "why", 69
Pedagogy, xv, 8, 13, 69, 141, 147, 152, 161, 176, 180, 192, 202, 266, 291, 297, 304, 335, 347, 349, 366, 369, 372, 382, 383, 385
Place-based, xv, 7, 9, 10, 150, 252, 256, 291, 331, 336, 377, 378
Planet Ark, 309
Politics, 175
Power, xi, xiii, xv, 1, 8, 11, 12, 14, 36, 52, 53, 66, 67, 69–72, 81, 82, 104, 105, 111, 113, 117, 127, 149, 176, 177, 202, 206, 207, 216, 225, 232, 233, 240, 245, 272–274, 280, 284, 302–305, 322, 324, 357, 362–366, 369, 371, 373, 379, 384, 392, 395
Preservice Teacher Education, 45–46
Pro environmental behaviour, 65–66
Problem-based learning, ix
Progressive education, 128–129
Progressivism, 36–37

## Q
Queensland Department of Education, xv, 279, 306, 352, 392

## R
The Rainforest Awareness Rescue Education Centre (RAREC), Iquitos, Peru, 319–320
Rangers
  the Rise of Ranger Leagues, 38–39
Rationalization, 185–245, 273–276
Red Hill Field Studies Centre, 224–225
Reflection, xiii, 46, 109–110, 120, 186, 274–275, 304–305, 359, 361, 371, 375, 395
Relationships, 8, 51, 53, 63, 80, 155, 157, 168, 181, 195, 197, 212, 264, 303, 306, 308, 347, 350, 355, 367
Religion, 66–67
Research, viii, ix, xi, xiv, xv, xix, xx, 5, 44, 50, 52, 69, 87, 88, 101, 103, 105, 118, 121, 122, 126, 130, 133, 142, 144, 146, 163, 177, 190, 195, 203–205, 221, 229, 231, 252, 253, 266, 272, 273, 275, 278, 282, 294, 311,

313–315, 318, 320, 322, 324, 327, 330–332, 334, 351, 355, 357, 369, 370, 372, 386, 393
Residential, vii, 45, 146, 155, 158, 169, 173, 178, 211, 227, 354
Resistance, 13, 47, 73, 202, 316, 335, 336, 377
Resource depletion, 6
Rio Earth Summit, 298, 300, 302
Rio+20, 302
Rising Tide, 9, 377, 378
Riverina Field Studies Centre, 212
Rondevlei Environmental Education Centre, Grassy Park, Cape Town, 321
Royal National Park, 29, 48, 104, 148, 164–166, 180, 190, 191, 214
Royal National Park Field Studies Centre, 164–166
Rumbalara Field Studies Centre, 213–214

**S**
School Strike for Climate (SS4C), 384
Science, vii, ix, xv, 1, 9, 10, 15, 35, 44, 46, 47, 50–53, 66, 67, 72, 81, 110, 111, 117, 121, 128, 130, 138, 146, 151, 154, 155, 157, 164, 176, 191, 193, 207, 210, 211, 223, 229, 235, 236, 260, 264, 267, 268, 282, 297–299, 309, 314, 316, 320, 349, 354, 357–359, 369, 377, 380, 381
  scientific activity, 28
Science/Conservation Foundation, 320–322
Scientists, 8, 20–22
SDG 4, 302
Sensory, 162, 190, 311, 338
Shortland Wetlands EEC, 185, 198–199, 205, 239, 244, 362
Silence, 392
Silencing, 374
Sloganism, 8, 69
Social justice, 5, 14, 300, 377, 382
Social reconstruction, 65
Social reproduction, 65
Solastalgia, 382
Some European Examples of EECs, 331–336
South America, 70, 79, 316–320, 337
Species destruction, 33–35
The State of Mexico hosts five EE and Climate Change Centres (CEACC), 317
The State of Queensland (Department of Education), 307
STEM, 52, 53, 358–359, 385

Stevenson (2006) discusses the abstraction of ESD, 8
Sustainability Curriculum Framework, 12, 231, 266, 267
Sustainable Development Goals (SDGs), 11, 67, 276, 302, 305
Sustainable Schools NSW, 257
Symbiocene, 382
Systems thinking, 7, 12, 53, 62, 257, 266, 284, 359, 369, 384

**T**
Talitha Kumi School Campus, Beit Jala, Palestine, EEC, 326–327
Taronga Park Zoo, 191, 206, 234–235
Teacher ESE Education, 362–363
Teaching Practice, 349–350
Thalgarrah Field Studies Centre, 150–151
Tbilisi UNESCO-UNEP Intergovernmental Conference on Environmental Education, 123
Top-down, 61, 110, 114, 202, 348, 363
Transformative ESE, 337, 377
Transformational Change, 382–384
Transformative education, 371

**U**
Uganda Wildlife Conservation Education Centre, Africa, 322
UNESCO, 11, 50, 68, 119, 120, 123, 124, 179, 203, 209, 260, 275–277, 298–305, 313, 328, 331, 332, 336, 348, 384
The 1997 UNESCO International Conference, Environment and Society: Education and Public Awareness for Sustainability, in Thessaloniki, Greece, 299
The UNESCO Roadmap for Implementing the Global Action Program, 302–303
The UNESCO-UNEP international program, 123
United Nations, 11, 12, 50, 68, 119, 123, 203, 259–260, 276, 293, 295, 298, 300–302, 332, 336, 348
Urban reformists, 39–43
Uttarakhand Environment Education Centre, India, 323–324, 356

**V**
Visitation cost, 218–219

## W

Wambangalang Field Studies Centre, 155–157
Warrumbungles Field Studies Centre, 211–212
Waxing and Waning, 271–273, 364–365
Wedderburn Outdoor Resource Centre, 223
The Wegscheide centre, 297
Well-being, 301, 372, 377, 379, 382, 395
Western Plains Zoo, 234–235
Wetlands Campus of the Awabakal EEC, 198–199
Who Cares About the Environment, 277–278
Whole school, 129, 175, 208, 258, 259, 270
The Wildlife and Environment Society of South Africa and their centres, 330–331
The Wildlife Preservation Society of Australia, 32, 42, 43, 88, 104, 109, 141, 143
World Commission on Environment and Development (WCED), 298
World Indigenous Peoples' Conference on Education in 1999, 299
Writers, 23–26

## Z

Zealandia Te Māra a Tāne, 315–316